FINANCIAL INSTITUTIONS

Financial
Institutions

By ERWIN W. BOEHMLER, M.B.A., J.D.

(EDITOR)

Professorial Lecturer in Finance

ROLAND I. ROBINSON, Ph.D.

Professor of Banking

FRANK H. CANE, Ph.D.

Associate Professor of Business Finance

AND

LORING C. FARWELL, M.B.A.

Lecturer in Finance

ALL OF NORTHWESTERN UNIVERSITY

1953

R I C H A R D   D .   I R W I N ,   I N C .

HOMEWOOD, ILLINOIS

First Printing, May, 1951
Second Printing, February, 1952
Third Printing, October, 1953

TO

PAUL LESLIE MORRISON

WHO ENVISIONED A BREAK WITH TRADITION IN
THE APPROACH TO FINANCE AND ENCOURAGED
THE EXPLORATION THAT FINDS REFLECTION IN
THIS VOLUME

PREFACE

THIS volume has been prepared to provide suitable text material for an institutional approach to finance. It is designed to introduce the reader to the whole field of finance and reflects a departure from the traditional approach under which concentrated attention is given to a very limited number of highly specialized phases. At many colleges and universities, money and banking and corporation finance are the basic finance courses and emphasize, respectively, historical and theoretical aspects of commercial banking and the financing of corporations through stock and bond issues. Other financial institutions and phases of finance receive scant treatment, although, admittedly, in some of the more recently published texts in economics and money and banking the institutional approach is coming to the fore.

A broad survey course emphasizing institutions more appropriately meets the needs of the student who will take no further work in finance. On the other hand, the student who plans advance study gains an understanding of the functions and interrelationships that should be exceedingly helpful as he embarks on specialized study. Rather than displacing a course in money and banking, such a survey course prepares the student for a more sophisticated and penetrating course in money and banking.

Although written primarily as a college textbook to provide either a terminal course of study or a foundation for advanced work, *Financial Institutions* is, in the opinion of the authors, appropriate for other applications as well. In its several preliminary editions *Financial Institutions* has been used to supplement money and banking courses in graduate divisions as well as in undergraduate schools and has been used for finance courses based on a money and banking prerequisite. Furthermore, at least two segments of the financial community—investment banking and the savings and loan field—have used the preliminary editions for in-service training to provide a comprehensive background for trainees. This volume should likewise prove suitable for the general reader.

More specifically, *Financial Institutions* has been developed for the basic course in new sequences that are being developed by members of the Finance Department at the Northwestern University School of Commerce. Shortly prior to World War II, members of the Department, under the leadership of Paul L. Morrison, then Chairman, initiated a reorganization of the departmental offerings. The program contemplated in part the expansion of the two traditional introductory courses—money and banking and corporation finance—into four courses through the addition of (1) a course to provide a survey of the whole field of finance offered without prerequisite but itself a prerequisite for all sequences of the Department and (2) a course in business finance to emphasize the internal and budgetary aspects of finance, including the financing of small business.

The war interrupted the projected revision; but in the years since, with the expansion of the Department and the return of staff members from the service, reorganization has been resumed. Pertinent text materials have now been developed—the instant volume for a broad survey course in institutions and another volume that presents an introduction to business finance.

This pioneering effort to introduce financial institutions at an elementary level presented a problem of organization. Where should the circle be cut? Because the course is offered without prerequisite, a quick survey of those basic economic concepts most pertinent to finance provided a logical starting point. It was resolved to present the nonmonetary institutions first (institutions with which the reader would be somewhat familiar), and thus furnish a good point of transition, and to defer the consideration of the more complex monetary institutions and governmental phases for the later portions of the course. It is pedagogically sound to start with the familiar, and this treatment has been found to work satisfactorily through several years of classroom trial. Under this approach the discussion of day-to-day happenings of monetary implication are deferred until the later phases of the course.

All four authors teach the course in Financial Institutions at Northwestern University and co-operated in its development. To achieve the highest possible degree of integration in the face of multiple authorship, the manuscript for various chapters was prepared first by one of the authors and then by another through the several preliminary editions. Furthermore, throughout the preparatory stages and in the development and preparation of this volume a policy of cross-reading was adopted. The individual differences that were bound to occur were submerged in the interest of the whole.

The authors regard this presentation of an institutional approach to finance as still in the developmental stage and recognize that there is room for improvement. To this end they welcome reports on the experiences of others in using the text and the suggestions and comments of their students.

Evanston, Illinois
April, 1951

Erwin W. Boehmler
Roland I. Robinson
Frank H. Gane
Loring C. Farwell

ACKNOWLEDGMENTS

THE authors gratefully acknowledge the counsel of their colleagues, members of the departmental Curriculum Committee, in delimiting the scope of the text so that it might fit appropriately into the over-all course offerings of the Department: Harold W. Torgerson, Chairman of the Department; Harry G. Guthmann, Chairman of the departmental Curriculum Committee; and R. Miller Upton. The authors also gratefully acknowledge contributions to the 1948 preliminary edition on the topics indicated by the following, all of whom were members of the Department at the time: Charles M. Bliss, Assistant Cashier, Harris Trust and Savings Bank, Chicago—direct placement and term loans; Francis J. Calkins, Marquette University—investment banking and regulatory bodies; Paul L. Howell, New York University—securities dealers and organized exchanges; Norman Strunk, Executive Vice-President, United States Savings and Loan League—urban real estate finance; Kenneth R. Wells, Vice-President, National Bank and Trust Company, Chicago—consumer credit. Their co-operation speeded the completion of the preliminary edition, and much of the material they prepared has been included in the present edition.

Instructors in various parts of the country who used the preliminary editions of *Financial Institutions* in their classrooms were most helpful in their comments and suggestions; and in this respect the authors are particularly indebted to the following instructors at Northwestern University: E. P. Crossen, James R. Gormley, Bion B. Howard, Henry I. Kester, Thomas J. McNichols, Ralph G. Ringgenberg, and Donald Wales; and to Burton A. Kolb, University of Washington; James S. Early, University of Wisconsin; and George W. Woodworth, Dartmouth College.

Constructive criticisms on the preliminary editions were provided by John W. Chapman, Columbia University; F. W. Mueller, Jr., DePaul University; Eli Shapiro, University of Chicago; Nathan L. Silverstein, Indiana University; Audley H. F. Stephan, Rutgers University; Kenneth L. Trefftzs, University of Southern California; and John M. Van Arsdell, University of Illinois. The authors are indebted to Harry C. Sauvain, Indiana University, and Donald M. Halley,

Tulane University, for helpful critical reviews of the manuscript for this edition.

Appreciation is expressed for the secretarial and other preparatory assistance of Mrs. Mildred Johnson, Frances Fenn, Martha Ravlin, Mrs. Jack F. Lewis, Marion Ludwig, Walter G. Silver, Mrs. J. Guillory, and John F. Chetlain. Specialists of many financial institutions, financial trade associations, and organized exchanges were helpful in checking the descriptions and interpretations of their respective operations.

In gratefully acknowledging the assistance received from these many sources the authors nevertheless accept full responsibility for the content of their respective chapters.

TABLE OF CONTENTS

PART I: INTRODUCTION

CHAPTER

OUR MATERIAL WELFARE. CHARACTERISTIC FEATURES OF OUR ECONOMY: Division of Labor and Specialization. Exchange. Capitalism. Capital Formation. FINANCE AND FINANCIAL INSTITUTIONS: Divisions of Finance. Functions of Finance. Financial Institutions. SCOPE AND IMPORT OF THIS VOLUME. SUPPLEMENT: MAJOR FINANCIAL INSTITUTIONS CLASSIFIED ACCORDING TO PRIMARY SERVICES PERFORMED.

PART II: FINANCIAL INSTITUTIONS AND FUNCTIONS (NONMONETARY)

CREDIT: The Nature of Credit. Credit Defined. The Function of Credit. The Flow of Credit. Social Basis of Credit. The Bases of Credit in a Specific Situation. Credit and Wealth. Classification of Credit. Benefits of Credit. Dangers in Inept Use of Credit. Magnitude of Credit Volume. CREDIT INSTRUMENTS: Uniform Negotiable Instruments Act. Endorsement. Promises to Pay. Significance of Negotiability. Orders to Pay. Auxiliary Documents. SUPPLEMENT: COMMERCIAL CREDIT INSTRUMENTS AND AUXILIARY DOCUMENTS

PART A: INTRODUCTION; CHARTER AND ORGANIZATION; OPERATIONS; SOURCES AND USES OF FUNDS

AN INTRODUCTION TO COMMERCIAL BANKING: Origin and Development of Banking. Rise of Goldsmith Banking in England. Banking Development in the United States. Commercial Banking Functions. "Department-Store" Banking. BANK CHARTER AND ORGANIZATION. BANK OPERATION— THE BALANCE SHEET APPROACH: Banking Transactions. Summary of Transactions. Transactions—Continued. Additional Transactions. SOURCES AND USES OF COMMERCIAL BANK FUNDS: How Commercial Banks Obtain Funds. How Commercial Banks Use Their Funds.

PART B: BANK CREDIT AND THE BANKING PROCESS

COMMERCIAL BANK DEPOSITS. COMMERCIAL BANK LOANS: Credit Analysis. The "Line of Credit." Classes of Loans. Secured Loans. Term Loans. Consumer Installment Loans. BANK INVESTMENTS. EARNINGS

xiii

PART IV: INTERNATIONAL FINANCIAL INSTITUTIONS

INDEX

LIST OF EXHIBITS

LIST OF TABLES

PART I

●

INTRODUCTION

Chapter • *1*

THE ROLE OF FINANCE

The chief activities of Finance are the manufacture and provision of currency and credit, the handling and distribution of the capital that is saved by the community and put into the equipment of industry, and the collection and spending of the revenue of the nations, and the raising of debts for any purposes that they choose to pay for by this means. The work of Finance is thus divided between private enterprise and public control.—HARTLEY WITHERS.[1]

THE people of the United States enjoy the highest standard of living ever attained by any nation. The necessities of life—food, clothing, and shelter—are available in abundance. In addition, the typical citizen has more of conveniences, creature comforts, and luxuries than the kings and emperors of old.

At Schoenbrunn, the Hapsburgs had a world-renowned menagerie and arboretum and could summon from the stablehouse an elaborate equipage for any occasion; but they lacked central heating, automatic refrigeration, modern sanitary facilities, and a host of commodities and services that enrich life today. In contrast, the family car, whether Cadillac or jalopy, is now commonplace in our country, and the same can be said of the tub and shower and a great variety of electrical and mechanical servants. Back-breaking labor has, for the most part, been eliminated, and leisure time has been steadily increased for all. Hours of entertainment, or at least pastime, can be had in the home by the flick of a finger and the turn of a dial. Room temperature and humidity are controlled in many public buildings, and air conditioning is rapidly spreading to homes. Air express makes it possible to enjoy fresh sea food and fruits a thousand miles or more from their source.

---

[1]Hartley Withers, *The Business of Finance* (London: John Murray, 1920), p. 12.

OUR MATERIAL WELFARE

Much of our economic growth and progress reflects man's inven-tiveness in an effort to improve his lot. However, there are many other contributing factors, including geographic location, favorable climate, and a fairly rich endowment of natural resources. Skilled workers and enterprising management operate under stimulating incentives to increase output. Organized research in factory and laboratory multiply applications of existing materials and develop myriads of entirely new materials and new products. One of the most significant factors is the extent to which the machine and sources of power are employed to supplement man's manual efforts in the productive process, with a resultant manifold increase in output.

The level of material welfare that has been achieved reflects the industry and initiative encouraged by the high degree of political and economic freedom that prevails. An unusual opportunity is pro-vided for personal development and individual well-being. The legal framework within which business and industry operate is established through representative government. The individual may own, not only property, but the tools of production as well, in contrast to limitations in many other countries. He may engage in any type of work anywhere he pleases; or may go into a business of his own— to reap the reward of profit or suffer the penalty of loss. The prospect of personal gain in serving society is a strong driving force that stimulates industry, enterprise, and resourcefulness.

There are more than 60 million workers in the United States, ap-proximately 4 million businesses, and various units of government— federal, state, and local. The industrial organization of our country is the greatest ever created. It not only supplied the domestic civilian requirements and the needs of our own armed forces during World War II, but helped feed, clothe, and arm some ally nations. In the postwar years, extensive help is being provided for the rehabilitation of many nations in various parts of the world.

These millions of workers have been classified into more than 20,000 vocational groupings. A large number are engaged in direct physical production, and the end products of their labor are readily apparent. The art of the cabinetmaker is on display in quality shops throughout the country. Mass-produced furniture is sold in large and small stores in cities throughout the land, including the shop of the rural undertaker that "doubles" in furniture. The efforts of the farmer, supplemented by the work of the creamery and dairy employee, grace our tables at breakfast.

Workers in the extractive industries—farming, mining, and fishing—are engaged in direct physical production. Other workers make up a large second group, those employed in manufacturing and construction. They change the form of and process raw material and prepare it for market. There are many other industries not so directly related to physical production; and their contribution, while essential, is not so obvious in the final product. These industries include transportation, wholesale and retail distribution, and finance. Still other workers provide a variety of personal and physical services and perform governmental functions.

Finance, as just noted, is an essential field of economic activity and operates through financial institutions, which are the subject matter of this text. Finance is a complex concept and cannot readily be defined in a single simple statement. For the time being, it will serve our purpose to say that finance deals with the pecuniary or money aspects of society and that it is frequently termed the "science of money." Finance has to do with obtaining money, with saving and spending, with borrowing and investing. It facilitates the transfer of goods and services and channels savings into productive use by business and government.

The large number and great variety of institutions engaged in the work of finance in our country have evolved with our business and industrial development. They parallel the magnitude and complexity of our economy. Financial institutions are an integral part of modern civilization and perform functions indispensable to present-day economic life.

To gain a more precise understanding of the role of finance and the nature of the various financial institutions, it will be helpful to review briefly certain characteristic features of the United States economy, those attributes that are most pertinent to financial operations and financial institutions.

CHARACTERISTIC FEATURES OF OUR ECONOMY

Much is being written and said about the "American way of life," "political and economic freedom," "individual enterprise," "competitive capitalism," and similar expressions and concepts for the purpose of contrasting our tradition with communism, socialism, and other ideologies. It is not the purpose here to discuss relative advantages and disadvantages of the various forms of economic and political organization. Rather, the existing order, the prevailing delegation of power and responsibility, is accepted as fact; and it is our aim to sketch briefly the environment in which finance and financial institutions operate. The following features of our economic system will be discussed in turn: division of labor and specialization; the process of exchanging the products and the services of specialists; capitalistic production, the use of tremendous amounts of machinery and power; and capital formation.

Division of Labor and Specialization

The individual in a primitive culture has few requirements, exerts himself just enough to take care of his needs each day, and may be completely self-sustaining. He will fish and hunt for food and raiment and provide crude shelter. At a later stage of evolution the individual may find that he excels in hunting, and he may specialize in such activity and occasionally trade (barter) a pelt or meat for part of the catch of another individual who concentrates on fishing. In this way, both the hunter and the fisherman may become more adept in their respective fields. Thereby they may reduce the effort required to make a living, or they may improve their standards of living by trading with still other specialists in production. The worker who concentrates on a limited task tends to become expert through repetition, and his output will tend to increase in volume and improve in quality.

The same principle is applicable in modern-day society. Businesses concentrate on one or a limited number of products, processes, or services. This tends to be true no matter what legal form the business takes—whether an individually owned and operated business, a partnership, or a corporation. As a general rule, the larger the business and the more complex the operation, the greater is the division of labor and specialization likely to be within the business itself. The manufacture of a given product may be divided into a number of separate steps performed in sequence, each step completed by workers that are expert in that particular part of the process.

Division of labor and specialization makes for greater efficiency and is a significant factor in making possible mass production and a large volume of output and, as a consequence, a higher standard of living. There is the further advantage of a standardized product and interchangeable parts, but also the disadvantage that the individual worker may not have the satisfaction of turning out a finished product and may have difficulty in identifying his contribution to the end result.

Exchange

BARTER.   In a simple society the individual who produces all he consumes has no occasion to exchange the products of his labor with others; but in a slightly more advanced society, where there is some measure of specialization, the hunter and the fisherman can barter their products directly one for the other and can barter with still other specialists. But barter has limitations, for it requires what the economist calls "double coincidence of demand." If the fisherman wants pelts, he must have fish to trade, and this at the same time that the hunter has pelts and wants fish. There is also the problem that the string of fish may not be considered adequate in exchange for the skins. How settle the difference?

Notwithstanding the cumbersomeness of trading commodity for commodity and service for service, barter is still in limited use today. It has been used in recent periods between nations. For instance, a predominantly industrial country and an agrarian country have exchanged offsetting quantities of precision equipment and slaughter-house products, respectively.

MONEY.   Early in his economic development, man resolved the problem of double coincidence by adopting some commodity, readily and widely acceptable in exchange for goods and services, as a medium of exchange. The commodity used varied with the culture and with the location, whether on the water or inland, whether in tropical or temperate climates. This medium of exchange was generally some object prized in the community either as an ornament or because it was useful as a tool, food, or clothing. If there was no occasion to use the medium of exchange for effecting a trade, it had an alternate application as an adornment or as a utensil. Thus a wide variety of objects (see Exhibit 1) could be used and actually were used, including

Grain	Beads	Ivories
Spices	Brick tea	Human hair
Rock salt	Animal claws	Shark teeth
Skins	Banana seeds	Plummage
Shells	Fishhooks	Stone discs

and many others. The precious metals, gold and silver, and various base metals were fashioned into a variety of shapes to serve as media.

Exhibit 1

COMMODITY MONEY

Courtesy: The Chase National Bank Collection of Moneys of the World

(1) Cocao Beans (Mexico and Central America until fifty years ago). (2) Hard Candy (Eskimos). (3) Grain (one of the earliest media of exchange). (4) Cheese (northern China, 1850–70). (5) Salt (Dongola Province, Africa; weight, 14½ ounces). (6) Nails (handmade nails used in Scotland and Colonial New England). (7) Cigarettes (World Wars I and II in many parts of Europe and in Asia). (8) Tobacco (South Sea Islands; about 50 per cent licorice). (9) Cartridge Shell (Ethiopia up to modern times). (10) Tea (tea bricks used in Siberia and China). (11) Pepper Corns (spices used along the Baltic Coast). (12) Leather Token (Mexican hacienda token about 1800); stamped with brand mark on thick leather 1½ × 2 inches).

Exhibit 1—Continued

ODD AND CURIOUS COINS

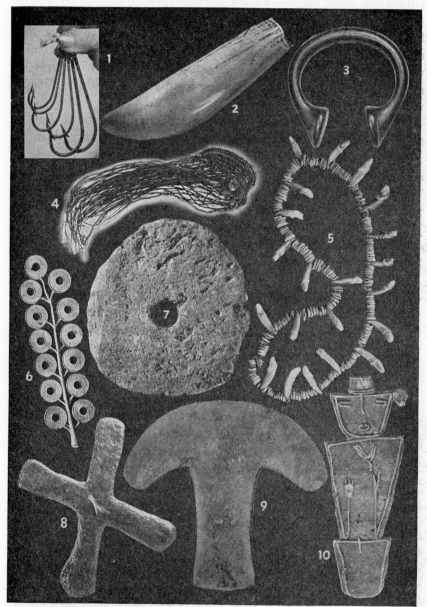

Courtesy: The Chase National Bank Collection of Moneys of the World

(1) Fishook Money (Alaska). (2) Whale's Tooth (Fiji Islands). (3) Money Ring (West Coast of Africa; popular for over a hundred years; made in England). (4) Elephant Tail Bristles (Portuguese West Africa). (5) Canine Tooth (Solomon Islands; trading value about 6 pence each). (6) Tree Money (tin coins, Malay Peninsula; called "pitis"; cast 8¾ inches long, but broken apart for use). (7) Stone Money (Yap; one 30-inch stone valued at 10,000 cocoanuts or a wife). (8) Copper Cross (Belgian Congo, Baluba tribe; 8 × 8½ inches; used as special money for buying a wife). (9) Aztec Money (equivalent to 8,000 cocao beans). (10) Aztec Gold (these curious wrought-gold images used by Aztecs of Mexico to settle debts).

Ultimately some of the metals were shaped into uniform pieces (coins) distinctly imprinted by the government to certify weight and fineness and to simplify identification. In the early days in our country, wampum, furs, tobacco, cotton, whiskey, and iron nails were used. More recently the cigarette has functioned effectively as a medium of exchange, as those who served abroad in World War II will remember.

The availability of a medium of exchange simplifies and facilitates trade. If rock salt is the exchange medium in a community, then the individual with a possession or service to trade may accept the salt and then may use it to acquire whatever he wants when he wants it. There is no need to ferret out one of a few individuals interested in making a direct exchange (swap). The need for two demands in juxtaposition is obviated.

As the division of labor is extended and specialization increases, the production process becomes more and more complex and the individuals become increasingly interdependent. In our country today, very few people are self-sufficient enough to produce all their requirements. Nearly everyone depends on others in the community to supply at least some, if not a major portion, of his needs and wants. Providing goods and services for 150 million people in the United States, who have an aggregate annual income of more than $200 billion, presents complicated problems of organization, production, and exchange. The enormity of the exchange problem is suggested by the more than 100,000 items carried in the catalogue of just one mail-order house, Sears, Roebuck & Company, and the many thousands of articles sold at retail under one roof by Marshall Field & Company, a large Chicago department store. Each of the articles represents many production steps and a long sequence of exchanges —from the raw-material stage through the production process, transportation, wholesaling, and final placement in the hands of the ultimate consumer by the retailing agency. At each point in the exchange sequence, payment must be made. Obviously, an economy of such size and complexity would be impossible under barter. Nor would the bulkier commodities that have served as exchange media in earlier days be practicable. A suitable and convenient medium of exchange is indispensable.

Money is the medium of exchange that serves this purpose in the United States and in all modern economies. The evolution of money from earliest times is a long and frequently told story found in practically every introductory text on money and banking and in

many other places as well; and so with the history of money in our
country. It is not our intention to cover in detail either of these
developments in this volume, although a later chapter treats th
monetary system of the United States and makes reference to suc
historical aspects as seem necessary for the purpose.

For the time being, we can define "money" as that which is g
erally accepted as a means of payment for goods, services, and del
To many, money may be merely that which does money's work;
there may be no recognition of distinctions. Money may, howe
be classified in various ways, including classifications with res
to the source from which it emanates and according to its phy
forms (see Exhibit 2).

Exhibit 2

MONEY CLASSIFIED

SOURCE	PHYSICAL FORM
United States Treasury	*Coins*
Silver coins	Silver
Dollar	Dollar
Half dollar	Half dollar
Quarter	Quarter
Dime	Dime
Minor coins	Minor
Nickel	Nickel
Penny	Penny
Paper money	*Paper*
United States notes	Federal Reserve
Silver certificates	United States no
Federal Reserve System	Silver certificate
Federal Reserve notes (issued	*Checkbook Money*
through the commercial	Bank deposits
banks)	
Commercial Banks	
Bank deposits	

NOTE: In addition to the paper moneys listed, there are als
fications of notes outstanding, but they are of dwindling impo
serve bank notes issued by the Federal Reserve banks from tim
emergency use; national bank notes, formerly issued by the
gold certificates which have been called for redemption.

Thus it can be said that there are three source
Treasury of the United States, the Federal Reserv
commercial banks; and that there are three forms
paper money, and commercial bank demand d
transferable by bank check. Why there are so ma

of money is explained by historical and political considerations that need not concern us at the moment.

All writers are agreed that coins and paper money, together constituting *currency*, are money; but all do not regard bank deposits as money. The reason for this difference is found in the fact that coins and paper money are accepted without reference to the offerer, whereas the check used to transfer bank deposits does not pass from hand to hand with equal facility. A check is generally not accepted without reference to the bearer but depends upon identification and endorsement. However, most payments in our country (probably nine tenths or more) are made by a transfer of bank deposits. From a practical standpoint, demand deposits are part of the money supply and will be so regarded in this volume. If, then, money is defined in this way, by far the greater part of the total money supply consists of bank deposits, which are also called "deposit currency" or "checkbook money." In Chapters 3, 17, and 18 we will learn more about deposit currency and how it comes into being.

Not only does money provide a medium of exchange, but it serves a second primary function—it is a standard or measure of value. For instance, the owner of a once elegant automobile, say a Cadillac or a Lincoln, but now of ancient vintage, might be able to trade his car for a sparkling new Plymouth or Studebaker Champion on an even basis, without any money passing hand. This would almost constitute a barter transaction. But undoubtedly both parties to the deal would calculate the worth of the respective automobiles in dollars. In such an instance the dollar would serve not as a medium of exchange but as a measure of value.

Money also has two secondary functions: *It is a store of value;* the recipient need not spend it upon receipt but may save it for use at some future time. It also serves as *a standard of deferred payment,* in that loans and payments to be made and agreements to pay in the future are invariably stated in terms of money.

In addition to the four economic functions of money just considered, the businessman finds money a very useful and convenient device in other respects. It provides him with a unit in which he may express the results of his operations, whether at a profit or at a loss; he calculates the wisdom of plant expansion in terms of money; and expresses the value of his enterprise in money. In short, money is to him a common denominator of value.

While we may have many forms of coin and paper money in the United States, the distinctions are without a practical difference.

Since 1933 all coins and paper money of the United States have been made full legal tender for paying all debts, public and private. This is equivalent to saying that an individual owing a debt may offer coins and paper money in any amount in settlement of an obligation; and if payment is refused, interest on the obligation no longer accrues. Prior to 1933, all coins and currency did not have such full legal tender.

In summary, money is a medium of exchange that provides a convenient means of payment and related services without which our complex industry and business structure could not function at its present level of effectiveness.

CREDIT. As already noted, our economy is characterized by a continuous flow of goods and services and a counterflow of payments. With respect to any given commodity there are a great many transactions from the raw-material stage through to the delivery of the final product into the hands of the consumer. Most of these transactions are on a credit basis; that is, the buyer receives the goods in the present in exchange for his promise to pay in the future. A manufacturer may obtain raw materials now on the strength of his promise to pay later; he may then sell the finished product to a wholesaler on credit, on the strength of the wholesaler's promise to pay at a subsequent time. In each instance the promise to pay—manufacturer to supplier and wholesaler to manufacturer—is invariably expressed in money. The manufacturer expects to use the money that will ultimately be paid to him by the wholesaler as an offset against the amount he is obliged to pay the raw-material supplier. Most credit transactions are part of a long chain of similar relationships. Rather than utilize trade credit, the manufacturer may borrow from a bank and obtain money immediately with which to pay the supplier, in which case the manufacturer promises to pay the bank at a later date.

In much the same way, a business may borrow money for the erection of a new plant or the addition of equipment in order to increase production facilities. Individuals utilize credit to obtain money to meet emergencies or to buy home appliances and other rather durable objects. Governments use credit, borrow money by selling bonds, in order to balance their budgets if tax collections and other income are not sufficient to meet all obligations.

Through credit the savings of society are channeled into productive use by industry and government. Because a great majority of the dollar volume of transactions is on a credit basis, our economy is called a "credit economy"; and credit is frequently called the "lifeblood of business." If the promise to pay is in writing, this written promise is called a "credit instrument." There are many forms of credit instruments, and together with money they constitute the chief stock in trade of financial institutions.

Credit and credit instruments are the subject matter of the next chapter, and credit instruments are also discussed in Chapter 7.

Capitalism

The material possessions, the economic goods, of a society are called "wealth"; and wealth is generally divided into two classifications: those things in the hands of consumers that are being used up to yield satisfactions and which are called "consumer goods," and those things used in further production, called "producer goods" or "capital goods." Capital goods include factory buildings, machinery, equipment, power plants, rolling stock of railroads, goods in process, and even finished goods up to the time they come into the hands of the consumer.[2]

---

[2] There are a number of words and concepts frequently met in finance with which the reader should be familiar. For the most part, these terms and phrases will be clarified in the text. A few of them are defined now to obviate later explanation.

Capital. In this chapter, several terms incorporating either the word "capital" or a derivative are used and defined: "capital goods," "capitalistic production," "circulating capital," and "capitalism." The use of the word "capital" alone has, up to this point, been sedulously avoided. "Capital" is one of the most troublesome words in public discussions because it has so many different connotations. Writers in economics, money and banking, and finance use it to mean:

1. Wealth used in further production, the tools of production, physical things; as synonymous with capital goods.
2. The money value of capital goods, of physical things. Thus a drill press is capital goods; it represents an invested capital of, say, $2,000.
3. A sum of money, savings, available for investment, available for capital formation.
4. A fund of value. In this concept the $2,000 in money would be capital, and so would the drill press purchased with the $2,000. The money is liquid capital; the machine, $2,000 worth of capital goods; but both are capital. Capital, a sum of money, is not lost through investment but merely changes its form. This "fund of value" concept is equivalent to points 2 and 3 above.

There are other meanings that reflect the views of businessmen, lawyers, and accountants, respectively:

5. Total assets. This is often the concept of the businessman who has not had accounting training. It includes all assets—physical assets and such intangible assets as goodwill and patents. In other words, all the assets used in the business.
6. Capital stock. This is the legal concept. Lawyers tend to use the contraction "capital" to refer to "capital stock." For example, a lawyer might say "the corporation will have a capital of $1,000,000" when he is referring to a company that is to have outstanding 100,000 shares of capital stock with a par value of $10 a share.
7. Net worth: capital stock and surplus. This is the accounting concept. The accountant also speaks of "net working capital," the amount by which current assets (circulating capital) exceed current liabilities.

Because there are so many meanings and there is no general agreement, the reader must be careful to determine the meaning intended from the context. In this book the

Even the aborigines recognized that tools permit more effective use of time and energy. They fashioned a variety of implements, including spears, fishhooks, tomahawks, and bows and arrows; and they hollowed out logs for water transportation. The extent to which tools of production are used in modern nations is common knowledge and is one of the chief reasons for the high rate of productive capacity and resultant high standard of living. If man relied on his hands alone, his output would be a small fraction of the goods produced when capital goods are used.

Any country that utilizes vast amounts of capital goods is said to engage in capitalistic production and, therefore, is a capitalistic economy. Capital goods are used in production to a greater extent in the United States than in any other nation, but socialist England and communist Russia are also capitalistic. There is this difference, however: Most of the tools of production in the United States are privately owned, whereas all of the tools of production in Russia and the socialized industries in England are owned and operated by government.

The private ownership of capital goods is, then, one of the distinguishing features of the United States economy. There are other significant characteristics. The individual here is free to work for others or to engage in any economic activity he may elect. He may establish his own business or join with others in forming a partnership or in organizing a corporation and then give employment to others. The owners and managers of a business are relatively free to elect what, how much, and when to produce; and there is a minimum of government directives. Both consumers and producers are guided in their activities by the prices in the market place, so that in

---

"fund of value" concept of capital will usually be employed; "capital goods" will be used to indicate the physical tools of production; "capital stock" will be used to indicate certificates of ownership; and "net worth" will be used to indicate the ownership interest which consists of capital stock plus surplus.

There are three other words, closely related to the concept of capital and frequently found in literature dealing with finance and used in this volume, with which the reader should be familiar: "cash," "financing," and "funds."

Cash is synonymous with money, which has been defined to include coins, paper money, and bank deposits. Most businesses consider checks in the till as part of their cash, and similarly most businesses include bank deposits in the balance sheet item "cash on hand or in banks." An individual paying for a purchase in a shop by check considers that he has bought for cash. Actually a check is a claim to cash and is usually convertible into cash within twenty-four hours. All writers, however, do not regard checks or bank deposits as part of cash.

Financing provides the money (funds) needed for the operation of a business.

Funds refers to cash and securities that are readily convertible into cash; i.e., immediate purchasing power.

the final analysis consumers largely guide production. (This is in contrast to government regulation and control in a totalitarian society such as the Russian.)

The hope of reward in the form of profit stimulates the enterprisers who risk their property in business ventures; if they are not successful, there is the penalty of failure and loss. They are motivated by the prospect of gain.

In general, business in the United States is competitive. Producers tend to vie with one another in introducing new products and processes and in their attempt to make a better product and at a lower cost and thus attract the consumer. Not only is there competition within individual industries, but each industry competes with other industries—television versus home freezers, for instance. Competition encourages efficient operation and stimulates innovation.

Capitalistic production as conducted in the United States has become known as "capitalism," a term that derives from the characteristic of private ownership of capital goods. From the foregoing brief description of capitalism it is easy to see why our system of organizing for production is also known as a "free economy," a "private enterprise system," and "competitive capitalism."

In organizing for production and distribution in our country we have not achieved perfection. For instance, our economic history has been marked by alternating periods of prosperity and depression; competition and the direction of production through prices are not fully effective; some may question the emphasis on self-seeking; and others may question whether the output of our industrial organization is equitably distributed. These are questions outside the scope of our inquiry; they are in the domain of the social scientist and are adequately discussed in the many treatises on economics. It is probably a fair generalization to say that we have no absolute measure of the relative advantages of capitalism. However, it probably is also a fair generalization to state that most people in the United States believe that capitalism, despite any shortcomings, nevertheless represents a way of organizing the nation for production that is superior to any other method known or tried. Capitalism provides the environment within which finance and our financial institutions function.

Capital Formation

There must be saving if capital goods are to be accumulated; consumption must be held below production and the difference must find reflection in added tools of production. Thus, if a primitive fisherman were to catch enough fish on one day to meet requirements for that day and one day more, then on the second day he might devote his time to making a spear or hollowing out a boat so that his future efforts might be more productive. He would be providing capital goods and would be engaged in the process of capital formation. He would be saving and investing directly. Similarly, if a farmer spends some time in erecting a fence or building a corncrib, living in the meantime on food previously produced and stored, he, too, would be forming capital goods. In both instances the effort would be spent not to provide goods for immediate consumption but rather to make capital goods so that future consumption might be increased.

Capital formation is obviously of utmost importance to modern capitalistic production in view of the vast quantity and variety of capital goods that are required. In totalitarian Russia the government controls all production through the ownership of the tools of production and determines what portion of the product is to be diverted to capital formation. The flow of goods into consumption has been restricted; and the citizens collectively have been forced to save to permit a more rapid creation of modern industrial equipment, with the explanation that ultimate improvement of living standards is the goal.

In contrast to such forced saving in a controlled economy, saving is largely voluntary under capitalism in the United States. Individuals themselves decide how much of their income will be set aside. Such savings may be used in establishing or expanding the saver's own business; or they can be channeled into productive use by others through one or more of a variety of financial institutions, as will be noted presently. Corporations save by paying out only a part of the profits in dividends and by retaining the balance for use in the business, for expansion or modernization; or such savings may be made available to others, much as in the case of individual savers. Capital formation also occurs when a government uses tax income or borrows for the purpose of erecting a schoolhouse or for building highways.

Capital formation is not usually as direct in our country as in the instances of the fisherman and farmer cited above, but occurs for the most part in two separate steps—saving in the first place and then investing. It is not enough that there be saving, that there be refraining from consumption; but the savings must be invested, must be placed in the form of capital goods. Financial institutions serve an important function as intermediaries between the saver and the user of savings—i.e., in translating savings into capital goods.

Savers who use their accumulations in a business of their own expect to receive a return in the form of profits if the venture is successful. More frequently, savings are either loaned to other individuals, to corporations, or to governments or are used to purchase stock (ownership) of a corporation. Savers receive income, called "interest," for savings that are loaned to others. The borrower agrees to pay back at some future date the amount advanced, and in the meantime to pay interest periodically.

The rate of interest is generally agreed upon in a contract between lender and borrower and does not vary with the success of the enterprise. It depends upon a number of factors; but relative certainty of interest and ultimate principal repayment, i.e., the risk entailed, are of primary importance. In recent years the interest received on the bonds of the United States government has been around 2½ per cent; the bonds of well-established companies about whose ability to pay there is little question have sold to yield about 3 per cent; companies not in an equally strong position have found it necessary to pay from 3½ to 5 per cent on their obligations; and money loaned on real estate mortgages has received about 4 to 5 per cent.

Instead of lending his money, the saver may buy stock and become a part owner of a corporation and share in its profits through dividend payments. Corporations, as a rule, pay out only a portion of their profits and retain the balance in the business; and this tends to make the ownership interest more valuable. The amount of the dividend payments tends to vary with the earnings of the corporation. The common stocks of financially sound companies with demonstrated earning power have sold in recent periods to afford a return of from 4 to 6 per cent on market prices. The common stocks of companies in a more speculative position have sold to return 6 per cent and up to 10 or 12 per cent or more.

Rather than making their savings available to industry for capital formation through the direct purchase of bonds and stocks, many savers place their savings with any one of a number of different financial institutions that serve as investment specialists and direct the savings into use. The saver then receives either interest or dividends from the intermediary institution.

In a later chapter, consideration will be given to reasons why individuals and corporations save. Certainly one of the factors encouraging saving is the expectation of a return, in the form of profits, interest, or dividends; but there are others.

In connection with capital formation it should be noted that modern capitalistic production is specialized and roundabout production. The individual worker or the particular business does not generally work on the entire production process from raw material to finished goods, including the building of the machines used in production. The worker and the company engaged in making automatic screw machines represent an early stage in the production of the final consumer product, passenger cars. When the metal fabricator started in business, he probably bought screw machines from the inventory of the machinery manufacturer. The screw machine had to be acquired before fabrication of screws could begin. When screw manufacture got under way, the fabricator built up an inventory consisting of a variety of screws to be delivered to the automobile parts manufacturer. The parts manufacturer, in turn, had to acquire plant and machinery to start his business; and then he, too, built up an inventory of parts to supply the automobile manufacturer. This oversimplification suggests how extensive business interrelations are and also that businesses require savings to provide not only machinery and similar fixed assets but also to provide *current assets* or circulating capital to assist them in carrying goods in process, finished goods, accounts receivable, and similar items.

FINANCE AND FINANCIAL INSTITUTIONS

Divisions of Finance

Finance, as already stated, deals with the pecuniary or money affairs of society. The term was originally used to denote only the management of government receipts and expenditures, equivalent to what is now called "public finance." In this book the term "finance" is used in a much broader sense to include:

Money and banking	—the work of the monetary financial institutions—provision of currency and the operation of the commercial banking system
Private or business finance	—the money and credit aspects of commerce and industry
Individual or personal finance	—the money affairs of the private citizen
International finance	—the money transactions between nations
Public finance	—the management of government receipts and expenditures

Here we will touch on public finance only to the extent that the discussion of the other phases of finance may require.

Functions of Finance

The brief review of certain pertinent characteristics of the United States economy in the preceding section should facilitate an explanation of the role of finance and the work of financial institutions and their essentiality to present-day life. On the basis of our broad concept, finance encompasses three primary functions:

1. The provision of a satisfactory medium of exchange and a measure or common denominator of value—money—which is so essential to the facilitation of exchange in an economy characterized by a high degree of division of labor and specialization.
2. The transfer of savings from the saver (who does not use the savings for capital formation himself) to the user of savings to permit creation of the capital goods required in capitalistic production and to provide the financial requirements of government.
3. The provision of a market for the transfer from hand to hand of such claims to wealth as written promises to pay (credit instruments) and ownership instruments (shares of corporation stock), and for the conversion of such instruments into money.

Numerous subordinate and incidental services are performed by finance in addition to these primary functions, and they will be considered later as our inquiry proceeds.

Financial Institutions

Finance operates through financial institutions—organizations, agencies, enterprises—that relate to, create, or deal in money and promises to pay money (credit instruments) and in evidences of ownership (stocks). These institutions have transactions with individuals, private businesses, governments, and with each other. The financial structure of the United States is made up of a large number and an intricate system of specialized institutions, which, in the aggregate, provide numerous ancillary services as well as the three primary functions already enumerated in the preceding section. These institutions range from the small post office in the outskirts of a metropolis or in a little village where the individual may purchase a United States savings stamp for twenty-five cents, to a metropolitan bank such as the Chase National, with total assets of over $5,000,-000,000, or a life insurance company such as the Metropolitan Life Insurance Company, with total assets of more than $10 billion.

Many writers consider the creation and provision of money as a subject apart from, and not a part of, finance. However, money and promises to pay money constitute the stock in trade of the institutions

through which finance operates. A large portion of our money supply
—Federal Reserve notes and bank deposits—is supplied by the
commercial banks in collaboration with the Federal Reserve banks.
The commercial banking system is essentially the heart of our financial structure. Most individuals and practically all businesses and
government units have dealings with the banks. Accordingly, in this
book the services of monetary financial institutions are included as
a part of finance as just defined.

Many of the financial institutions operate in a narrow field and
offer a highly specialized service, whereas others perform a multiplicity of services and participate in many fields. Accordingly, there
is considerable overlapping. It has been said that, in finance, specialization is extensive rather than intensive and that the correlation
of institutions and functions is not readily apparent to the beginner.
It is the over-all aim of this volume to assist the reader in gaining a
comprehension of the various types of financial institutions and the
particular work they do. In the meantime, in view of the complexity
of the financial structure, it would serve little purpose to attempt even
a brief description of *all* component institutions and their functions.
It may be helpful, however, by way of introduction, to consider (in
the next section) some of the more important institutions that have
dealings with individuals and with which the reader is therefore likely
to be somewhat familiar.

Thus far, the term "financial institution" has been used in a
"brick-and-mortar" sense to refer to an establishment, a business
organization, or a government agency, including the personnel and
the place of business—for example, a commercial bank, a savings
and loan association, the Reconstruction Finance Corporation, an
investment banking house. The term "financial institution" may also
refer to an established practice, law, custom, or usage having to do
with finance—for example, the use of money in paying for goods
and services; the practice of buying on account, i.e., obtaining goods
immediately on the strength of a promise to pay for them in the
future. We will deal with financial institutions in both senses of the
term—including business organizations and government agencies, on
the one hand, and practices and customs, on the other. Whether the
one meaning or the other, or both, is intended will appear from the
context.

INSTITUTIONS THROUGH WHICH INDIVIDUALS SUPPLY SAVINGS.
Most individuals have an income of some sort. They receive money
in payment for services performed, or as shares of the income from

a business or other property, or as interest on funds loaned to others. A part of this income may be used for day-to-day living expenses; and the balance may be set aside for future spending, or it may be accumulated for ultimate investment in stocks or bonds, the purchase of a home or other property, or perhaps for the purchase of a business in which the saver would apply not only his savings but his mental and physical effort as well.

Most persons, under ordinary circumstances, seek a safe place for their savings and place them in one or more of a number of savings or thrift institutions. There are, of course, exceptions: the miser who likes to keep his hoard about him for periodic fingering; persons who lose confidence in the financial structure in times of stress; and those who, for one reason or another, prefer the fullest possible secrecy with respect to their money affairs. Except for necessary pocket money, cash that is not immediately needed, but also not planned for a longer-term investment, is generally deposited in a checking account in a commercial bank, from which account funds can be conveniently withdrawn by writing a check (discussed in Chapter 3).

If savings are not intended for early spending but are being set aside indefinitely, perhaps toward the methodical accumulation of a large sum for a definite goal, then the saver has the choice of a variety of savings and thrift institutions. These include: several types of savings banks—mutual, stock, United States postal, the savings division of a commercial bank; United States savings bonds; credit unions; savings and loan associations; and the contracts issued by life insurance companies, most of which contracts include an element of savings along with the insurance feature (see Chapters 11 and 12). Some individuals who do not have checking accounts may use a savings bank for the periodic deposit and withdrawal of funds as needed from day to day; but this is not the function of a savings bank, and such practices are discouraged by the banks.

The institutions just enumerated, the commercial banks, the savings banks, and the other thrift institutions, all provide custody for funds, accumulate the funds of many individuals, and make these funds available for loan to those who may have need for them. Users of such funds include commerce, industry, agriculture, individuals, and government. In placing their funds with these institutions, the individual savers pool their accumulations and indirectly, through the institutions as intermediaries, make the savings available for productive use.

An individual may make his savings directly available to business through the purchase of corporation bonds, which represent a loan to the particular enterprise, or through the purchase of stocks, which represent an ownership interest in the issuing company. If the securities (stocks and bonds) are newly issued, they will probably be bought through an investment banker who serves as a middleman between the supplier of funds and the user of funds. If the securities have been issued some time ago, and are already in the hands of the public, and if the securities are listed on a stock exchange, such as the New York Stock Exchange, then they may be purchased through a member (broker) of that exchange. Or, if not listed, the securities may be bought through a securities dealer in the over-the-counter market. Brokers act as middlemen and receive a fee for bringing buyer and seller together; dealers buy and sell for their own account and make either a profit or a loss on individual transactions (see Chapters 8 and 9).

Persons who recognize that they have neither the training, aptitude, nor inclination to assume responsibility for managing a direct investment in a diversified portfolio of stocks and bonds may turn for help to such agencies as an investment company, investment counsel, or a trust institution (see Chapters 10, 13, and 14). Through the investment company a large number of individuals pool their funds for investment in a diversified list of stocks and bonds under the specialized supervision of the management of the investment company. Investment counselors serve purely as financial advisers on a fee basis, counsel their individual clients with respect to the purchase, sale, or retention of stocks and bonds, but do not, as a rule, physically handle the funds or the securities of their clients.

Trust institutions—either separate companies or, often, the division of a commercial bank—provide a service similar to that of the investment counselor but, in addition, render a variety of other services to both individuals and corporations. Services rendered to individuals include: executor, administrator, or trustee under a will; guardian for minors; conservator for the estates of incompetents; and safekeeping and general management of property (see Chapter 14).

INSTITUTIONS THROUGH WHICH INDIVIDUALS BORROW. We have now considered how some of the financial institutions serve the individual in his role as a supplier of funds. These same institutions, and still others as well, serve the individuals as a user, or borrower, of money.

Individuals are substantial users of funds for a short period through consumer credit, which takes three main forms: the charge accounts of the retailer or the professional man; the installment or deferred-payment purchases of such durable consumer goods as automobiles, television sets, and household appliances; and installment cash credit or small loans. The retail charge account is common knowledge, offers many conveniences, and is the largest source of consumer retail credit (see Chapters 2, 5, and 6).

Installment sales credit makes it possible for many persons to enjoy immediately relatively high-cost goods and services, the enjoyment of which might otherwise have to be deferred. Funds to finance these purchases are provided by commercial banks and a variety of specialized institutions generally identified with serving the businessman and the ends of distribution. Such institutions buy the installment paper (notes signed by the consumer) from the retail dealer.

Small loans make it possible for the individual without collateral (stocks or bonds that might be pledged) to obtain cash funds to meet an emergency, albeit at a cost above the so-called "legal rate of interest." Because a necessitous borrower is in a weak bargaining position, and to protect him against loan sharks, many states have adopted legislation to license various types of consumer lending agencies which are permitted to charge a rate of interest above the legal commercial or bank rate. Thus there is legislation authorizing small loan companies, pawnbrokers, industrial loan companies, and credit unions. These institutions are permitted to charge a higher rate of interest to compensate them for the extra risk involved in making loans to marginal borrowers and for the extra administrative effort in checking the credit of the borrower and in collecting the principal and interest in installments.

The individual may also obtain a cash loan from the small-loan division of a commercial bank; by borrowing on the cash surrender value of his life insurance contract; and from a number of other agencies, including credit unions, which in the aggregate are not of great consequence from the standpoint of the volume of business done.

There may also be a need for borrowing funds for a long period of years. A family may be desirous of buying or building a home but may not have the full purchase price. The difference may then be borrowed through any one of several agencies: savings banks, commercial banks, insurance companies, savings and loan associations, and mortgage dealers (see Chapters 3 and 15).

We have considered a variety of financial institutions with which the individual may have dealings either as a supplier of funds or as a borrower of funds. There are still other functions of a primarily service nature performed by any one of a number of the financial institutions mentioned, including the transference of funds, payment and collection both here and abroad, and the issuance of travelers' checks and money orders, as well as other methods for the transfer of money. Arrangements can also be made for the complete detailed administration and operation of a business or other property, no matter what its character (see Chapter 14).

SCOPE AND IMPORT OF THIS VOLUME

This brief description of some of the financial institutions that serve the individual and the summary statement of the work they do should make it clear not only that the field of finance represents a division of labor and specialization within the economy but that within the field there is again a further specialization accompanied by some overlapping of the services performed.

Every reader of this page is familiar with money and undoubtedly with credit. Certainly he uses money and probably he has used credit, at least to a limited extent. But there is a less common understanding of how money and credit originate and how the quantity, quality, and regulation of money and credit affect the everyday lives of all citizens. An understanding of the origin and operations of the various financial institutions and their co-ordination into a working whole will serve to throw some light on such problems.

Most of the institutions briefly considered thus far serve the business community and the corporation as well as the individual. All of the financial institutions that serve the individual, business, and government make up an interrelated web. No attempt will be made to describe additional institutions or functions at this point. As we proceed, each institution will be taken up in turn—those we have already briefly surveyed, plus some others. We will trace the evolution of these manifold institutions, outline their functions and operational relationships, and consider their social and economic justification.

In the Supplement at the end of this chapter there is a list of financial institutions classified according to primary services performed.

It should be noted that government is playing an increasingly important role in the field of finance. Not only do the various private financial institutions operate under either state or federal laws, subject to the supervision of regulatory bodies, but the federal government itself has set up a large number of credit institutions through which funds are made available to business and agriculture. Furthermore, whether the federal government is operating under a balanced budget or is operating at either a surplus or a deficit has profound effect not only on the value of money but on the economy generally.

Financial institutions are not only a factor of influence in stimulating or retarding business activity but are themselves seriously affected by business change. As we proceed with our study, it will be our aim to get an understanding of the force and significance of private and government efforts in shaping our national destiny. We will find that the fiscal policy of the government—management of the debt in recent years—is one of the most potent forces for influencing the economic trends of the nation. We will also find that it is a matter of controversy as to how far the government should go in the direction of attempting to moderate fluctuations in business activity. How this problem is finally resolved will profoundly affect every one of us and, therefore, constitutes an important field for study.

The credit concept is essential to an understanding of the work of financial institutions, and this fundamental importance of credit is reflected in the fact that many of these institutions are frequently also called "credit institutions." For this reason we will discuss credit and credit instruments in some detail in Chapter 2 before embarking on an examination of the various organizations that make up our financial structure.

—ERWIN W. BOEHMLER

SUPPLEMENT

MAJOR FINANCIAL INSTITUTIONS CLASSIFIED ACCORDING TO
PRIMARY SERVICES PERFORMED

I. PROVISION OF CURRENCY
   United States Treasury
   Federal Reserve banks
   Commercial banks

II. COMMERCIAL CREDIT (short-term, temporary capital)
   (Mercantile credit)
   Commercial banks
   Federal Deposit Insurance Corporation
   Nonbanking
      Commercial paper houses
      Factors
      Finance companies

CONSUMER CREDIT
    Retail credit
    Small-loan divisions of commercial banks
    Industrial loan banks
    Small loan companies
    Credit unions — *MUTUAL SAVINGS BANKS*

CAPITAL FUNDS (long-term, permanent capital, largely provided through bonds
      and stocks)
    Investment bankers
    Over-the-counter securities market
    Organized securities exchanges

FINANCIAL MANAGEMENT (supervision of securities holdings and property
      generally and various related services to individuals and corporations)
    Investment counsel
    Corporate trustees

SAVINGS AND THRIFT
    Savings institutions
      Mutual savings banks
      Savings divisions of commercial banks
      Stock savings banks
      United States savings bonds
      Credit unions
    Savings and loan associations
    Insurance companies
    Pension plans

INVESTMENT INTERMEDIARIES (*see also* Savings and Thrift)
    Investment companies

URBAN REAL ESTATE AND FARM CREDIT
    Urban real estate
      Commercial banks
      Savings and loan associations
      Insurance companies
      Mortgage houses
      National Housing Agency (United States government)
        Federal home loan banks
        Federal Savings and Loan Insurance Corporation
        Federal Housing Administration
        Federal Public Housing Authority
        Home Owners Loan Corporation (in liquidation)
    Farm credit
      Trade credit
      Commercial banks   *table 13-1*
      Mortgage companies   *13-2*
      Farm Credit Administration (United States government)
        Federal Farm Mortgage Corporation
        Federal land banks
        Federal intermediate credit banks

Central Bank for Cooperatives
Production Credit Corporation

IX. GOVERNMENT CREDIT AGENCIES
National Housing Agency
Farm Credit Administration } *see* Urban Real Estate and Farm Credit
Reconstruction Finance Corporation
Commodity Credit Corporation (primarily a price-support agency)

X. INTERNATIONAL FINANCE
United States Treasury
Federal Reserve banks
Commercial banks
Foreign departments
Foreign branches
Export-Import Bank
International Monetary Fund
International Bank for Reconstruction and Development

The foregoing list is by no means complete. There are a large number of additional institutions, both private and government, that make up the over-all financial structure of the country. This tabulation is designed to provide a guide for classification so that other institutions may be fitted into their appropriate niches as they are discussed. Such regulatory agencies as the Comptroller of the Currency, the Securities and Exchange Commission, and the National Association of Securities Dealers are obviously omitted.

QUESTIONS AND PROBLEMS

1. What is encompassed by the term "financial institutions" in its broadest sense?
2. What are some of the principal factors that have contributed to the economic growth and progress and the high standard of material welfare achieved in the United States?
3. Of what significance are division of labor and specialization in our business life today?
4. Discuss the feasibility of a return to a completely barter system in the United States at this time.
5. What do you understand money to be? Describe its functions.
6. Classify United States money from the standpoint of physical form; source of issue.
7. Explain why deposit currency may appropriately be considered a part of the money supply.
8. What might be meant by the phrase "circularity of credit"?
9. The nature and functions of credit are to be discussed in detail in the next chapter. In the meantime, what is your understanding of credit and its importance in our society?
10. "Capital" is a confusing term because it is used to denote various concepts. List and explain those concepts with which you are familiar.

11. Is totalitarian Russia capitalistic? Socialist England? United States?

12. Distinguish: wealth; capital goods; money; cash; funds.

13. What is your view of capitalism as a way for organizing production?

14. May there be capital formation without the benefit of financial institutions?

15. In what forms is the saver rewarded for making his savings available to society?

16. What constitutes the "stock in trade" of financial institutions?

17. Into which divisions may the subject of finance be classified?

18. What are the functions of finance in broad terms?

19. List the financial institutions ("brick-and-mortar" sense) *with which you are familiar*, through which individuals supply funds to the economy. Classify the items into some sort of logical grouping.

20. Is finance productive?

BIBLIOGRAPHY

Chapter 1 has provided but the briefest examination of the characteristic features of the United States economy which establish the environment in which financial institutions operate. Readers wishing to pursue this subject further may consult any one of a host of recently published textbooks in introductory economics. One such volume that provides a lucid and analytical presentation, including a discussion of free enterprise versus other forms of economy, is the work by Shorey Peterson, *Economics* (New York: Henry Holt & Co., 1949), which deals in a practical way with the current scene and is written as a terminal text rather than as a theoretical base for more advanced study. It has a good discussion of capital formation and finance.

Similarly, there are a large number of elementary texts on money and banking that develop the nature and functions of money, monetary history, problems of exchange, etc. Increasingly, money and banking texts are introducing more institutional material. This is true of C. L. Prather's *Money and Banking* (4th ed.; Chicago: Richard D. Irwin, Inc., 1949), chaps. xxvii–xxxii, and of C. R. Whittlesey's *Principles and Practices of Money and Banking* (New York: Macmillan Co., 1948), chap. iv, on the structure of the financial system. Probably the pioneer volume based on an institutional approach to finance is H. G. Moulton's *Financial Organization and the Economic System* (New York: McGraw-Hill Book Co., 1938), which, while not current, still has much of value, though it is perhaps too weighted with history and theory for the reader just starting his study. A recent volume by the same author, H. G. Moulton, *Controlling Factors in Economic Development* (Washington, D.C.: The Brookings Institution, 1949), includes a chapter (vi), "Alternative Types of Economic Organization," which was also printed separately as a booklet likewise published by the Brookings Institution under the title *Economic Systems—Free Enterprise, Communism, Socialism, Hybrids; Regulations Compatible with Private Enterprise*. This is a concise explanation and comparison, clearly presented.

Because very little is said about capitalism in this chapter and the free enterprise system is taken for granted as providing the setting in which financial institutions operate, the reader may be interested in additional literature on this topic: D. M. Keezer and Associates, *Making Capitalism Work* (New York: McGraw-Hill Book Co., Inc., 1950), and S. H. Slichter, *The American Economy—Its Problems and Prospects* (New York: Alfred A. Knopf, 1950), both of which recognize weaknesses but champion capitalism and indicate paths toward improvement. Not quite so recent a volume, that by Carl Snyder, *Capitalism the Creator* (New York: Macmillan Co., 1940), summarizes the thesis suggested by the title in capsule form in a twenty-page eight-point statement (pp. 401–21).

Almost the entire issue of *Fortune*, February, 1951, was devoted to the theme "U.S.A.—Permanent Revolution," which was presented in fourteen articles, divided into three groups as follows: the American way of life, its origin and political principles; the transformation of American capitalism; and the problems of the future.

PART II

•

FINANCIAL INSTITUTIONS AND FUNCTIONS
(Nonmonetary)

Chapter • 2

CREDIT AND CREDIT INSTRUMENTS

CREDIT

UNDOUBTEDLY every reader of this page has been a party to a credit transaction; certainly he has handled credit instruments and has dealt with, or is at least aware of, some of the financial institutions that deal in credit and credit instruments. Anyone who has written or cashed a bank check, or who has bought a United States savings bond, has handled a credit instrument; anyone who has opened a savings account or who has taken out an insurance contract has had dealings with a financial institution.

The place of financial institutions in modern economic society was outlined in the preceding chapter. Before proceeding with an examination of the evolution, function, and operational relationships of the individual units that constitute the financial fabric of the nation, it is desirable to have an understanding of the nature of both credit and credit instruments. It is the purpose of this chapter to discuss what credit is and how it serves the economy and to present an introduction to the use of credit instruments—the written promises and orders to pay, which are used in short-term credit transactions. Capital instruments (stocks and bonds), used to provide the long-term capital requirements of business, are discussed in Chapter 7, "The Corporation and Finance," which deals with the legal forms of organization and with the financing of business enterprise.

The Nature of Credit

Notwithstanding the extensive use of credit and its essentiality to our present-day economy, writers in the field have not been able to agree on a definition of credit. It will be helpful to gain an understanding of credit and related terms through discussion and by way of illustration, rather than seek to compress the meaning of the term in a single simple definition.

The word "credit" is derived from a Latin word (*creditus*, past participle of *credere*), meaning "to believe" or "to trust." Credit is inherent in every transaction that has to do with the transfer of goods or money in exchange for a promise to return an equivalent amount in the future. Two simple and familiar transactions that are typical will serve to illustrate: (1) purchase and sale, and (2) borrowing and lending.

PURCHASE AND SALE. Assume that a hatless collegian enters the local haberdashery and selects a hat. Instead of paying for it, he tells the shopkeeper to "Charge it." The merchant (seller) agrees, and the young man (buyer) wears the hat out of the store. By implication the buyer says: "I promise to pay for the hat by the tenth of the following month." He *offers* credit by giving a promise to pay, in exchange for the immediate use of the hat. The seller, on the other hand, *accepts* the buyer's promise—accepts his credit. This language differs from everyday practice. In common parlance: the buyer receives or is granted credit; the merchant gives or extends credit. Actually the seller cannot give or extend credit. He merely recognizes the existence of credit by accepting the offer of the buyer to pay in the future. The buyer does not receive credit—he receives the present use of the hat. He does, however, offer credit—he promises to pay in the future. The extent to which the seller will accept the offer of the buyer depends upon the seller's appraisal of the "credit standing" of the buyer. Business jargon is, however, well rooted, and we cannot quarrel with tradition. *Accordingly, it is convenient to accept, and even to use, the expressions "the buyer receives credit" and "the seller gives or extends credit."*

BORROWING AND LENDING. Assume that a young man plans to enter business but needs money in addition to his savings. He therefore seeks to borrow the money. A friend of the family learns of his plan and lends him $2,000 in cash. In this example the young man offers his credit, his promise to pay in the future, and receives cash. The friend of the family accepts the credit (promise) of the young man and gives him the money.

With respect to a borrowing-lending transaction, the borrower may elect to receive, in lieu of immediate cash payment, a deposit credit or claim to future payment in cash. Assume that a businessman requires additional money to meet the peak seasonal requirements of his business—say the Easter season. He calls on the neighboring banker, explains his requirements, and asks for a loan of $5,000. If the credit standing of the businessman justifies trust, the banker may accept the offer of credit (the promise of the businessman to pay in the future), open up an account for the businessman, and make $5,000 available to him in a checking account. The businessman may then write checks against the agreed amount, and the banker will honor the checks. In this instance there is essentially a promise for a promise. The businessman promises to pay the bank at some future time; the bank promises to pay immediately on demand up to the stipulated amount. There is an element of trust on both sides.

Credit Defined

Whenever a borrower or a buyer offers credit, promises to pay in the future, and the offer is accepted, the borrower incurs a debt. He receives a commodity, cash, or a promise to pay cash; he engages to pay the equivalent at some future time.

On the basis of the discussion thus far, a twofold definition of credit, from the standpoint of the buyer or borrower and from the standpoint of the seller or lender, seems tenable:

1. *Credit from the standpoint of the borrower* is the ability to obtain goods, services, money, or the promise of money, in return for a promise to pay an equivalent amount in the future.
2. *Credit from the standpoint of the lender* is the confidence felt in the integrity and solvency of a prospective borrower which enables such borrower to obtain goods, services, and money in the present on the strength of his promise to pay an equivalent amount in the future.

From a narrower (legal) viewpoint, it is often said that credit is the obverse or counterpart of debt, and "a credit" is then defined as "the right of the lender to receive future payment from the borrower." With respect to any given transaction in which credit is offered and accepted, the borrower obviously incurs debt to the extent of his promise. However, it should be noted that credit is a potential ability, so far as the prospective borrower is concerned. Only to the extent that the borrower has used his credit can there be claims to future payments on the part of lenders, and therefore only to that extent has debt been incurred. The prospective borrower may have credit, yet have no debt. In the sense of our twofold definition of credit, credit and debt are not absolute counterparts.

RELATED TERMINOLOGY. There are several terms related to credit to which brief attention should be given:

"Credit standing," along with such modifiers as "good," "satisfactory," or "poor," is often used to denote the ability to obtain credit. Similarly, "line of credit" is often used by a lender to express the maximum extent to which the lender is disposed to trust the borrower.

"Credit transaction" refers to any business deal in which there is a promise to pay in the future—a promise that is given in exchange for goods, services, or money.

If the promise to pay is in writing, rather than oral, the written promise is known as a "credit instrument." Credit instruments serve various purposes and take many forms, and these will be considered briefly later in this chapter and in the Supplement following this chapter.

"Credit system" encompasses the whole sphere of the lending-borrowing process and the facilitating agencies and institutions: credit, credit transactions, credit instruments, credit markets, financial institutions (which are essentially dealers in credit instruments), and the traditions and the common and statutory laws which govern such transactions.

It is interesting to note the derivation of the related accounting terminology: "credit" and "creditor"; and "debit" and "debtor." Early in the days of bookkeeping, records were kept for only two classes of accounts: the amounts that borrowers or debtors owed, and the amounts that were due to lenders or creditors. The amount that a debtor owed was known as a "debit" (from the Latin, meaning "he owes"); the amount that was due to a creditor was known as a "credit" (from the Latin, meaning "he trusts"). The debits were recorded on the left-hand side of a page, and the credits on the right-hand side. With the further evolution of bookkeeping the use of the terms "debit" and "credit" was extended to other accounts as well, and not applied merely to the accounts with debtors and creditors.

The Function of Credit

Credit provides a highly convenient device for the transfer of the use of wealth, and in this way gives high fluidity to the savings of society. In the preceding chapter we have already referred to credit as the lifeblood of business. It stimulates the production of wealth, facilitates exchange, and increases consumption—all of which spells a higher standard of living.

Through the use of credit the savings of the economy can be more effectively mobilized. Persons who have had an income in excess of their expenses and who have no immediate need for their savings may make their accumulations available to others who see an opportunity and have the ability to employ the funds profitably. For example, a businessman may borrow money to acquire raw material and to employ labor in order to fill a given contract. When the finished goods are delivered, the sale price is expected to yield enough to meet the costs of production, to pay off the loan with interest, and to leave a profit for the enterpriser. Without the loan, the borrowing businessman might not have been able to accept the contract; with the loan, he was enabled to accept the opportunity and make a profit and at the same time serve the community by adding to the stock of wealth.

The lender of the money either may have been disinclined to use his savings directly in a business of his own or may have recognized his inability to use the savings to advantage. Accordingly, he was pleased to forego using his savings immediately, or was willing to place his savings in less liquid form, and to lend his accumulations to another on the prospect of receiving not only the principal but also interest for the use of the money at the end of the loan period.

The foregoing example represents a short-term loan, or commercial credit running for several months. The facts would be much the same, except for the element of time, in a long-term loan or capital credit running for a period of years.

A business operating its plant at capacity determines, on the basis of a survey, that it could substantially increase its sales volume and profits if production could be increased. The business does not have sufficient funds to erect an additional plant but arranges to borrow the needed sum for a period of ten years. Through the expanded production facilities the company is able to increase its sales volume, pay interest on the loan, earn a larger profit, and set aside a sum each year sufficient to retire the obligation at maturity in ten years. The business is willing to pay for the use of the loan on the expectation of adding to its income; the lender is willing to advance the funds in return for the periodic interest payments and the ultimate repayment of the principal.

Both of the above illustrations are examples of business credit. The consumer may also make use of credit. In order to have the convenience of laborsaving equipment in the home immediately, a family may be willing to pay, in addition to the cost of the equipment, interest on the purchase price and then pay off the loan out of future income.

Credit thus makes funds available in the present in exchange for a promise to repay the loan with interest in the future. Through credit the use of the savings of the community can be transferred from those who have no immediate use for the funds into the hands of those in a position to apply the funds in furtherance of production, distribution, and consumption. The lender receives interest for deferring the use of his savings. The borrower pays interest to have the immediate use of the savings and borrows on the expectation of using the loan to realize a profit or other benefit in the present.

The Flow of Credit

Credit permeates our entire economy, and most business is done on a credit basis. Credit makes possible large aggregates of producer goods that permit economical mass production. Roundabout production and the minute division of labor entail a long-time interval between the creation of the producer goods and the early stages of production and through to the finished goods ready for consumption on the shelves of merchants. Credit finances production throughout these various steps and finances distribution and even consumption.

While many credit transactions may stand alone and terminate at the end of the loan period, most credit transactions are part of a continuing chain of transactions. The manufacturer may buy his equipment, as well as raw materials, on credit; and to this extent he is a borrower. On the other hand, he may sell his output to a wholesaler on credit, and then he becomes a creditor. He expects to offset his claim for payment from the wholesaler against his own obligation to the supplier of raw material. If he does not want to wait for payment from the wholesaler, he may sell his claim to a bank or other lending agency.

Similarly, the wholesaler may buy on credit and sell on credit; and he, too, plans to offset his claim on the buyer against the claim that the manufacturer holds on him. It is apparent, therefore, that except for an occasional credit transaction, which stands independently and terminates when the terms are met, most credit is part of a whole chain of interrelated transactions. The businessman is continuously buying his requirements on credit and selling his product or service on credit. Various specialized financial institutions assist in this flow and give liquidity to the claims through the use of credit instruments.

Social Basis of Credit

A credit transaction involves a promise to pay in the future and usually a promise to pay in money. The one who accepts such a promise to pay incurs risks: the debtor may not be disposed to pay at maturity; the money in which payment is to be made may not be stable in purchasing power; and society may not have provided adequate safeguards to protect the creditor in his claim. Therefore, the creditor is likely to accept a promise to pay in the future only to the extent that he has confidence that the payment will be made with reasonable promptness and that the payment will be reasonably equitable.

To provide the basis for such confidence three elements are essential:

1. A high code of business ethics; a disposition on the part of members of the business community to meet obligations—to do the right thing.
2. A standard of deferred payment, money, that is reasonably stable in purchasing power.
3. A well-developed legal system and enforcing machinery to protect property rights.

To the extent that these elements are present in a society, the development of a credit system will be encouraged; without the assurance of these elements, business on a credit basis would be stifled.

The Bases of Credit in a Specific Situation

Assume that the essential social elements are present. Then, whether a creditor will accept the promise of a debtor depends upon the creditor's estimate of the debtor's ability to pay and also upon his willingness to pay. Stated another way: Is the amount due likely to be paid promptly at maturity?

In reaching a decision as to whether credit should be granted, and on what terms, the creditor will usually raise a number of questions, which can be conveniently classified under the following four main headings:

Reputation of the Prospective Borrower.   Does the business seeking credit have a reputation for honesty and fair dealing and for meeting obligations promptly? Do the principals possess those personal qualities that would entitle them to be considered good moral risks? There is little sense in extending credit if there is a likelihood that payment will not be reasonably prompt and that expensive collection procedures may become necessary.

Financial Position of the Borrower.   Is the financial and economic position of the borrower such that in the ordinary course of events operations of the business will make it possible to meet the obligation? Does the business have sound management? Is the amount and the maturity of the credit sought reasonable in the light of business itself and in the light of practices in the trade? Is the borrower a leader in the field or a marginal unit? Is the borrower vulnerable to competition from new products or new processes? Most lenders use a questionnaire form with a carefully developed list of points to be considered in credit granting, including financial ratios that are applied to the balance sheet and operating statement of the prospective borrower. (See Chapter 3, Supplement B.) The lender may require the prospective borrower to provide a budget, a statement of estimated cash income and outgo, to demonstrate the ability to meet the obligation if credit is granted.

General Business Conditions.   Are business conditions in the industry and in the economy as a whole favorable? What is the trend of volume, prices, costs, and profits? Under favorable general business and industry conditions, credit risks are reduced, and business on a credit basis is encouraged. On the contrary, when the outlook for business is adverse, risks increase and credit transactions will be more carefully scrutinized.

Hedge against the Unexpected.   The lender may wish to protect himself against unforeseen contingencies and may insist on certain conditions to strengthen his position. Rather than extend credit on an open-book account, the lender may require written evidence of the debt, a credit instrument, which may facilitate the establishment of his claim should that become necessary in the event of disagreement or default. A document generally provides stronger evidence to support a claim in court than does a ledger account. The lender may require the pledge of an asset so that, if the debtor defaults, the lender may have the pledged property sold and be reimbursed from the proceeds in satisfaction of his claim. The lender may require the borrower to give a written promise to pay in a form that is readily transferable (negotiable) in order that the lender may be in a position to sell the instrument and realize cash should the funds be needed prior to maturity of the debt. (Negotiability is briefly considered later in this chapter.)

Persons professionally engaged in passing on the credit standing of prospective borrowers often refer to the "three C's" as the bases of credit: character—record for honesty and fair dealing; capacity —business ability for managing wisely; and capital—present means of payment.[1]

---

[1] T. N. Beckman, in his *Credit and Collections in Theory and Practice* (4th ed.; New York: McGraw-Hill Book Co., Inc., 1939), p. 146, expresses the "three C's" in an equation from which he has developed nine gradations of credit standing. To continue the alliterative presentation of the bases of credit, writers have in recent years introduced additional "C's" to supplement the trinity: collateral—a pledge to secure a debt, and if the collateral

Credit and Wealth

Credit is not wealth. It is not a physical thing. Credit does, however, provide an easy means for the transfer of wealth and in this way makes possible the creation of additional wealth. A person of means may have money or physical property that he himself does not wish to use in production. However, he may accept the credit of another and make the money or capital goods available to this second person for use in the creation of wealth. In this way, credit makes possible the productive use of capital and adds to the total wealth of the nation. Similarly, credit may enhance the standard of living by facilitating exchange and thereby expediting the flow of goods from producer to consumer.

Through the use of credit an individual with little or no capital may be able to establish a business; and if he is successful, he may not only serve the community but at the same time build an estate for himself.

The fact that credit is not wealth, that it does not in itself create anything but is merely an agency for transferring wealth, is often demonstrated by using the accountant's approach:

Assume that a man has been in the trucking business and has decided to retire. He owns a motor truck that has a fair market value of $2,000. A young man, son of the former trucker's good friend, wishes to start in business and has $1,000 in savings. The respective situations of the ex-trucker and the young man can then be expressed as follows:

Ex-trucker		*Young Man*	
Asset—truck	$2,000	Asset—cash	$1,000
Liability	0	Liability	0
Ownership	$2,000	Ownership	$1,000

The ex-trucker and the young man make a deal. The young man is to receive title to the truck in return for an immediate payment of $500 and a note (promise to pay in the future) for $1,500. The situations of the two men would then be as follows:

Ex-trucker			*Young Man*		
Total assets		$2,000	Total assets		$2,500
Note	$1,500		Truck	$2,000	
Cash	500		Cash	500	
Total liability		0	Total liability—Note		1,500
Ownership		$2,000	Ownership		$1,000

is adequate, collateral transcends character and capital as a criterion of ultimate payment; coverage—adequacy of insurance protection carried by the debtor; and conditions—status of the particular company, the industry, and the economy generally.

Prior to this transaction the two men had a total combined wealth of $3,000—a truck worth $2,000 and cash of $1,000. After the transaction the total wealth remains the same, but the title to the truck has changed hands and part of the cash has changed hands.

Although the wealth in the community has not been increased through this credit transaction, the potentialities for the creation of additional wealth have been increased. Three parties have benefited: the ex-trucker through transferring his truck has received immediate purchasing power and an income in the form of interest on the promissory note given by the buyer of the truck; the young man has been enabled to establish a business and thus serve society and accumulate wealth; and society has the advantage of a continued trucking service.

Without credit, the truck might have remained idle in the hands of the retired trucker; the young man might not have been able to start a business, at least not as trucker; and the community might have had to forego a much needed service. (This illustration is, of course, an oversimplification. The truck might have been sold to someone with adequate capital, or the retired trucker might have rented the truck to another operator. In either event, the owner of the truck and society might have fared just as well. But the young man, without credit, would have been limited in his choices.)

Classification of Credit

Credit finds use in many forms through a great variety of lenders and borrowers. For this reason, credit can be classified in a variety of ways. Some of the more evident and practical classifications are on the basis of the following: legal character of the parties, nature of the transaction, purpose, time of payment or maturity, security, location of the borrower or debtor, and the type of credit instrument that evidences the credit. Possible ways of classifying credit and the pertinent subclassifications are summarized in Exhibit 3.

Most of these classifications necessitate little elaboration. The classification on the basis of use or purpose is, however, fundamental to an understanding of credit and credit instruments and, accordingly, merits some attention.

PRODUCTIVE CREDIT. Most businesses, whatever their legal form or their type of economic activity, generally require two types of assets and utilize credit for the two related purposes: fixed assets, representing mainly land, buildings, and equipment; and current assets, the circulating funds used in the day-to-day operation of the business and represented by cash, accounts receivable, inventory, and other items that are likely to be converted into cash within a short time.

Investment Credit. Credit transactions related to the fixed assets of a business, related to the relatively permanent capital, are termed

Exhibit 3
WAYS OF CLASSIFYING CREDIT
(This enumeration is suggestive, not exhaustive)

Legal Character of a Party or the Parties
   Public......................Federal, state, and local government
   Private......................Personal; business (including single pro-
                                       prietorship, partnership, and corporate)
Nature of the Transaction
   Retail
   Mercantile
   Bank or commercial
   Open market (commercial
     paper)
   Government
   Personal or small loan
   Industrial
   Farm or agricultural
   Investment
Purpose or Use
   Productive..................Investment and commercial
   Consumptive..................Sale and loan
   Speculative
Time of Payment or Maturity
   Short term..................Payment within one year
   Intermediate..................Payment within one to five (or ten) years
   Long term..................Payment after five (or ten) years
Collateral or Security
   Endorsed..................Without collateral, but endorsed
   Guaranteed..................Without collateral; but guaranteed
   Secured..................Protected by the pledge of collateral
   Unsecured..................Without the deposit of collateral
Type of Instrument
   Open book..................No document, but mere ledger entries
   Acceptance..................Evidenced by a special form of draft
   Promissory note..............May be secured or unsecured
Location of a Party or the Parties
   Domestic
   Foreign

"investment credit transactions" and usually give rise to investment credit instruments (mainly bonds). Investment credit is used to provide plant and equipment, as well as working capital, for establishing or enlarging a business. The borrowed funds are intended to be retained in the business indefinitely as permanent capital, and the date of repayment is usually remote. Operations of the business are expected to provide periodic interest payments on the sum borrowed and are expected to provide funds for the gradual or ultimate repayment of the loan.

Commercial Credit. In contrast, credit transactions related to the temporary money requirements of a business are termed "commercial credit transactions" and generally give rise to commercial credit instruments (unless they are book credits, mere ledger entries). "Commercial credit" is short term. It is expected that the transaction that gave rise to the credit will at an early date provide the funds for repayment. For example, a merchant may borrow money to enable him to acquire and carry a seasonal inventory—say straw hats. These hats, bought weeks or months before the season, should be sold at a profit well before the end of the short season, and the funds should be available to liquidate the loan at maturity.

In this connection it is interesting to note the significance of the two-to-one ratio of current assets to current liabilities, a ratio that is usually considered to be the minimum tolerable ratio by creditors. If the current assets are twice the current liabilities, it generally means that the owners of the business are providing an amount of working capital equal to the amount of short-term capital provided by creditors. Creditors are reluctant to accept further credit if the ratio falls below two to one, because the creditors would then be providing a major portion of the working assets, and this they regard as an inequitable distribution of the risk.

Both investment credit and commercial credit are productive. They facilitate manufacture and exchange—the steady flow of goods from the raw-material state through distribution channels until ready for consumption.

Consumptive Credit. In contrast to investment and commercial credit, consumptive credit does not generate its own repayment, it is not self-liquidating. If a consumer purchases, on a deferred-payment basis, a television set for use in his home, such use will not provide the funds to meet the installment payments. If the consumer is to make the payments as they fall due, he must do so either out of previously accumulated funds or out of some source of income.

Although the distinction between productive and consumptive credit is generally made, it should not be assumed that all consumer credit is necessarily used for immediate consumption purposes. Consumer credit may serve to supply basic wants of the consumer and promote individual well-being, but it also has productivity implications. For instance, consumer credit may make it possible for a worker to obtain much needed medical or surgical attention and hospitalization through which he may be restored to gainful employment. Or a college student may borrow to see himself through the current semester, with the intention of making repayment the following summer, and through the additional training thus made possible, he may become a more useful and productive member of society. The whole subject of consumer credit is examined in more detail in Chapter 6.

SPECULATIVE CREDIT. A person who seeks to use credit solely to take advantage of a prospective change in market price, by buying stocks or commodities, is making speculative use of credit. Such transactions are likely to be short term, as in the case of commercial credit transactions, but are not similarly productive.

Speculation is too often regarded as having a derogatory connotation. Actually the speculator performs an essential economic function. This is best illustrated by the professional speculator in those commodities that come onto the market seasonally. The stock of wheat, for instance, is greatest after harvest, and the large supply would tend to depress prices and encourage consumption at a rate greater than can be maintained until the next crop comes in. Toward the end of the crop year, wheat would become scarcer and the price rise. However, through such organized exchanges as the Chicago Board of Trade, all those that grow wheat, process it into flour, and distribute the flour, as well as the wheat speculator, may express their opinion on the supply-and-demand situation and establish a price somewhat in line with expected conditions throughout the crop year. If the informed speculator believes prices are too low, he will buy future wheat (take a long position) with the expectation, not of accepting delivery of the wheat, but of selling it later at a higher price. If his judgment is correct, he will make a profit. In the event he thinks the price is too high, he will sell future wheat (i.e., sell short, sell something he does not then possess) with the expectation of buying wheat later at a lower price in order to make delivery. Again, if his judgment is correct he will make a profit.

Through the market action of informed speculators and all others that grow and deal in the grain and process and sell the flour, prices for wheat are adjusted to conditions. Such a market permits the miller to hedge and protect himself against a price change in wheat between the time of purchase of the grain and the milling and sale of the flour. At the time that the miller buys wheat for immediate delivery to be milled into flour, he may sell future wheat. This is known as a "hedging operation." If the price of wheat declines between the purchase of the grain and the sale of the flour, the selling price of flour will tend to drop in proportion, and the miller will suffer a loss on his milling operation. However, he will realize an offsetting gain on his futures contract because he will be able to buy wheat at a lower price than at the time he sold wheat for future delivery. The loss on the purchase of physical wheat will be approximately balanced by the gain on the future transactions. The miller minimizes or eliminates the risk of change in market price. Without an active speculative market, he would not be able to shift the risk through hedging; with such a market, he can concentrate his attention on milling wheat and making a processor's profit protected against adverse price movements. Through hedging he of course also gives up the opportunity of making a speculative profit, in addition to the milling profit, in the event of a rise in the price of wheat.

The experienced professional speculator bases his actions on specialized knowledge, familiarity with the market, information on supply and demand, and a forecast based on an analysis of ascertainable facts. When an uninformed amateur speculates, he engages essentially in gambling, blindly hoping that eventualities will bring him gain; he is virtually creating a risk much as any participant in a game of chance. The true speculator, on the other hand, assumes a risk that exists and which would need to be borne by someone; and by specializing in such risk-taking the speculator relieves the business of some of the more hazardous risks attending business operation. All business—and, of course, life itself—involves risks, and risk cannot be completely avoided or shifted.

Benefits of Credit

In the discussion of credit thus far, a number of the advantages of credit have already been touched upon. These advantages and others can now be enumerated in summary fashion. The full implication of the several benefits will be more apparent as the development of the whole subject of financial institutions progresses.

The advantages of credit can be grouped on the basis of benefits primarily to the saver or lender, benefits primarily to the borrower, and benefits to society in general. Obviously, as a general rule, every benefit to a saver, lender, or borrower is, in the long run, a benefit to the community as a whole.

Benefits to the Saver and Lender:

1. Credit gives mobility, or liquidity, to savings; it enables thrifty persons with small accumulations of capital to pool their resources

and give employment to their savings by making these savings available to others who wish to use the funds productively. The lender can thereby derive an income in the form of interest.

2. Credit aids the individual in accumulating funds for meeting emergencies and for providing for old age and retirement.

Benefits to the Borrower:

3. Credit enables the man of energy and enterprise, but with inadequate resources, to obtain the requisite funds for the establishment of a business.

4. Credit enables the businessman to effect a happy adjustment of the funds employed to the asset requirements of his business; he is able to supplement his own capital with short-term borrowing to meet seasonal peak requirements.

Benefits to Society as a Whole:

5. Credit provides a convenient medium of exchange; it obviates the need for having large sums of money at hand; permits low-cost transfer of funds for great distances; and supplements media of exchange of general acceptability.

6. Credit facilitates production, distribution, and consumption.

7. Credit makes possible large-scale enterprise and specialized production for which substantial sums of money are needed.

8. Credit encourages a high sense of business ethics; a businessman must maintain a good credit standing to preserve his competitive position.

9. Credit provides government a means of raising funds.

All of these advantages stimulate the more effective use of the manpower and natural resources of a nation and thus make possible a higher standard of living for all citizens than would otherwise be possible. On the other hand, the ill-advised use of credit invariably breeds serious problems for the individual and for the community as a whole.

Dangers in Inept Use of Credit

The extent to which the credit system has been developed in our country is undoubtedly responsible for much of the progress that has been made in all phases of the economy—production, exchange, distribution, and consumption—and for the resultant high standard of our general well-being.

There is danger both to the individual and society generally, however, in the overextension of credit. If credit is too easily granted, it may encourage recklessness, or at least the assumption of greater obligations on the part of individuals and businesses than circumstances may warrant. Or, an overoptimistic appraisal of the credit standing of persons offering credit may likewise lead to excesses. Widespread liberality or misjudgment in extending credit will usually lead to price inflation, overexpansion of business, extravagance, and general lack of prudence. Periods of boom are usually followed by a reaction—by a reduced volume of business activity that may be only a recession or may be, if the need for correction is more serious, a depression.

It is in such periods of adjustment that penalties must be paid for the injudicious use of credit. Individuals and businesses face embarrassment. If a debtor has credit in excess of the debts already incurred, it may be sound and advantageous for him to make further use of his credit and incur still more debt. However, if debt exceeds true credit—the actual ability to pay—trouble invariably ensues.

Classic and rather clear-cut instances illustrating the dangers in the unwise use or overextension of credit are found in the commodity markets following World War I and in the Florida real estate boom of the 1920's. In 1935–37 there was a business boom in the United States which culminated in 1937 in the most precipitous decline of business activity in our history. Numerous political and economic influences are generally named as causative elements in that boom-bust episode, including credit factors. At the present time, there is great concern about the inflationary potentialities inherent in the greatly expanded federal debt which is the result of deficit financing before World War II as well as during the war. Various proposals are being made by Federal Reserve authorities, bankers, and others to minimize the effect of this vast volume of government credit on the economy.

It should be noted that the unwise or excessive extension of credit is not necessarily the only possible cause of business shrinkage and the collapse of the credit structure. A general feeling of uncertainty about business prospects, a loss of confidence in the outlook, may generate a downward spiral of economic activity, accompanied by less favorable credit conditions and even actual stringency.

Those who exercise control over credit have an important responsibility. If they are too cautious, they tend to retard business expansion, stifle initiative, and thwart the general welfare by denying credit to deserving members of the community. If the granters of credit are not sufficiently selective and extend credit too generously to weak risks, they are inviting business failures and perhaps a sweeping economic disaster that may have repercussions throughout the land. A neat balance of courage and caution tempered by good judgment is essential.

Magnitude of Credit Volume

Credit permeates our entire economy and is a fundamental financial institution. In fact, our capitalistic society is often termed a "credit economy." Although there are no precise figures available, it is generally accepted that upward of 90 per cent of the business in this country is done on a credit basis.

As early as 1910 a study made for the National Monetary Commission indicated that 95 per cent of the wholesale business was then on a credit basis and that about 60 per cent of retail payments were made by check. Assigning appropriate weights to wholesale and retail business, it was estimated that 86 per cent of the total retail and and wholesale business was then done by checks and other credit instruments.

Many changes have taken place since that time to increase, on net balance, the use of credit. The following have been sources of increase: installment credit on consumer durable goods; retail stores offering convenient weekly payment plans; retail store charge accounts, with payments made increasingly by check; various federal credit agencies; pay-as-you-go checking accounts; and the relatively higher average income of the lower income groups, resulting in greater use of charge accounts, checking accounts, and money orders. Sources of decrease: the supermarts and other cash-and-carry retail establishments; and wholesale distributors operating on a cash basis.

There has been a similarly broadening interest in investment credit. The financing of the two world wars did much to familarize a great number of people with investment securities. The investment companies, discussed in Chapter 13, appealed to many persons of modest means. The public relations policies of corporations, including the "humanizing" of financial reports, are also a factor.

CREDIT INSTRUMENTS

Most business in the United States is done on a credit basis. When the obligation to pay is expressed in writing, the written evidence is a credit instrument, and these instruments are the stock in trade of financial institutions. Various credit instruments have been developed to meet the many needs of business; and their form depends upon trade convenience and practices, social custom, legal requirements, and the nature of the transaction.

Two major classes of credit instruments are used in business: *commercial credit instruments*, which are used to provide funds on a short-term, temporary basis to finance the day-to-day needs of commerce and industry; and *investment credit instruments*, which are used to provide long-term, permanent requirements.

In passing, it should be noted that business obtains long-term funds for current working needs and for the purchase of land, buildings, and machinery from two sources: persons who invest their money to become *owners* of the business through the purchase of stock, and persons who lend their money to the business through the purchase of bonds or notes and thus become *creditors* of the business. These two classes of investment instruments—stocks, on the one hand, and bonds and notes, on the other—are discussed in Chapter 7.

The balance of this chapter is devoted to a discussion of commercial credit instruments, promises to pay, and orders to pay.

Uniform Negotiable Instruments Act

More than 2,000 years ago the ancients used legal documents, baked in clay, comparable to certain of our modern commercial credit instruments. The law governing commercial instruments, however, can be traced to the English common law in this way: Originally under the common law the English courts did not hear business cases. The businessmen therefore established their own courts to settle disputes, and the decisions developed into the *law merchant,* which ultimately became a part of the English common law. In 1882 Parliament passed the Bills of Exchange Act; and in this country the Uniform Negotiable Instruments Act, which was largely patterned after the English act, was adopted by a number of states in 1897, and since then by all other states.

Under the Negotiable Instruments Act a promise to pay, exemplified by the promissory note, and an order to pay, exemplified by a bill of exchange, are defined as follows:

Promise to Pay (Promissory Note)	*Order to Pay* (Bill of Exchange)
An unconditional *promise* in writing made by one person to another	An unconditional *order* in writing addressed by one person to another
Signed by the maker	Signed by the person giving it

Promise to Pay—Continued	*Order to Pay—Continued*
Engaging to pay on demand or at a fixed or determinable future time	*Requiring* the person to whom it is addressed to pay on demand or at a fixed or determinable future time
A sum certain in *money*	A sum certain in *money*
To order or to bearer	To order or to bearer

If a commercial credit instrument meets the above requirements, it is a negotiable instrument, which is equivalent to saying that it passes from one person to another very much like money. Such instrument contrasts with ordinary contracts, which are not negotiable, in the same sense, and this is significant from a legal standpoint. A commercial credit instrument that does not meet all of the requirements is nonnegotiable, as defined by the act, and is governed by the ordinary law of written contracts. (See "Significance of Negotiability," later in this chapter.)

Endorsement

Title to a negotiable commercial credit instrument may be transferred by the holder by his endorsement, i.e., his signature, generally placed on the back of the document, to indicate the transfer of title. There is an exception, however, in that an instrument "payable to bearer" may be transferred by mere delivery without endorsement.

There are five kinds of endorsement:

1. *Blank,* which is a mere signing of the holder's name. This makes the document bearer paper.
2. *Special,* which names the person to whom the paper is being transferred. Example: "Pay to James Smith or order." Generally when an instrument has been endorsed in this way (specially), it cannot be negotiated again until endorsed by the person named.
3. *Restrictive,* which prevents further transfer. Examples: "Pay to John Jones, only"; "For collection."
4. *Conditional,* which stipulates a condition that is to be fulfilled. Example: "Pay to John Jones upon delivery of my dress suit."
5. *Qualified,* which is designed to limit the liability of the endorser by including the words "without recourse."

Endorsement may also be used to lend the endorser's credit as an accommodation endorser, in which case the endorser assumes a contingent liability to pay if the person primarily liable fails to pay. An endorsed promissory note is an example of two-name paper: it bears the signature of the person making the promise and the signature of the endorser. The holder of the endorsed instrument may look to both parties for payment.

The person who endorses qualifiedly (without recourse) says to the endorsee, in effect, that he, the endorser, does not intend to pay if the person primarily liable fails or refuses to pay. But he does transfer title and does say that, in so far as he knows, the instrument is valid and the party primarily liable is solvent.

In contrast, the person who endorses unqualifiedly (in blank or special), in addition to transferring title to the instrument, agrees to pay the endorsee in the event that the person primarily responsible fails, for any reason, to pay. He agrees to make such payment, however, only if the instrument has been promptly and properly presented for payment to the party primarily liable and if upon default the holder has given prompt and proper notice of default to the endorser.

Both the qualified and unqualified endorsers say by their endorsement (a) that the instrument is genuine and valid, (b) that the prior parties were competent to contract, and (c) that the endorser has good title.

The law of negotiable instruments is highly complex, and nothing beyond the most cursory treatment is here attempted. It is aimed merely to point out the liability assumed by an endorser and to distinguish a little more fully the difference between qualified and unqualified endorsements.

Promises to Pay

There are two common types of commercial promises to pay: the open, or book, account; and the promissory note.

BOOK ACCOUNT. The open-book account is the simplest form of commercial credit and arises when a buyer says to a merchant, "Charge it." It is really not a credit instrument at all, but merely a record in the ledger of the creditor, whether a merchant, manufacturer, or retailer. It is a convenience to both debtor and creditor because it saves time, and it may encourage additional buying. Book credit is a tribute to the debtor because the creditor receives no tangible evidence of his claim to facilitate collection. It is more difficult, or at least more costly, for the creditor to discount (sell for the principal amount less an allowance for interest) such an account receivable than a credit instrument.

PROMISSORY NOTES. Promissory notes are one of the more commonly used credit instruments and have certain advantages over the open account: they provide tangible evidence of the debt; constitute

Exhibit 4
PROMISSORY NOTE (BLANK FORM; TIME)

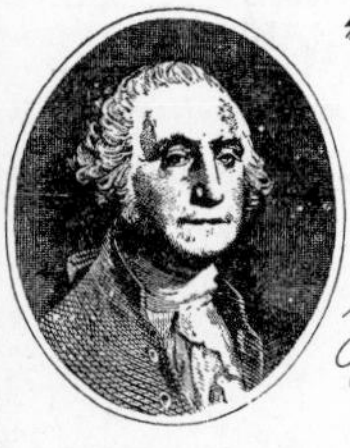

better collateral, a better pledge for a loan; facilitate collection; establish the time and the amount of payment; and minimize disputes with respect to the obligation. However, only in relatively few industries is the promissory note used in preference to the open account —those businesses in which the credit terms are generous—or in retail trade for high-cost consumer durable goods. But the promissory note is the instrument most widely used in borrowing from banks.

Promissory notes are also used to convert overdue open accounts into writing and in granting credit to a buyer with a not too satisfactory credit standing.

There are two primary parties to a promissory note: the *maker*, the one who promises and signs the note; and the *payee*, the one to whom payment is promised. In addition, there may be secondary parties: the *endorser*, the person who, by placing his signature on the instrument, transfers his interest in it; and the *endorsee*, the person

Exhibit 5
PROMISSORY NOTE (UNSECURED; TIME; TWO MAKERS)

Exhibit 6

PROMISSORY NOTE (UNSECURED; DEMAND; ONE MAKER)

No. 4890   SPECIMEN $ 6,000.00
                                          Chicago, Ill.,   June 21, 1951

On demand, for value received, undersigned promises to pay to the order of City National Bank and Trust Company of Chicago at its office in Chicago,
Six thousand and no/100 - Dollars,
with interest at the rate of ....5..... per cent. per annum after date until paid, and attorney's fees and costs of collection.
Said Bank or the legal holder of this note may, at any time hereafter, appropriate and apply thereon any monies and other property due or owing from said Bank or legal holder to, or held for, the undersigned, or any or either of the undersigned (if more than one) or to any endorser or guarantor upon this note, without protest, or demand upon, or notice of any kind to anyone, and may make such appropriation and application as and in such proportion as said Bank or legal holder may deem best. Demand, presentment, notice of dishonor, protest and notice of protest are hereby severally waived by all endorsers and all guarantors. If this note be signed by more than one person, every obligation and authorization of the undersigned shall be joint and several.

Rate   Approval   *John Doe*

NEW   RENEWAL   BUSINESS ADDRESS: 15 E. Wacker Drive, Chicago, Ill.
P-36

to whom the ownership of the instrument is transferred by endorsement.

Notes may be due on demand, on a given date, or at the expiration of a given number of days or months. They may be negotiable or not; may be interest bearing or not; and may be secured or unsecured. They may be one-name paper (as in the case of the notes sold through a commercial paper dealer, which are signed and endorsed by the maker) or two-name paper. The place of payment may or may not be designated. (See Exhibits 4, 5, and 6.)

Significance of Negotiability

It should be noted that whether an instrument complies with the Uniform Negotiable Instruments Act, and is therefore negotiable, or whether it fails to comply, and is therefore nonnegotiable, is of little importance with respect to the original parties to the instrument. A promissory note may in either event constitute a valid and enforceable contract so far as the original parties are concerned. However, if the instrument passes into the hands of others, the presence or lack of negotiability becomes very important. A third party who receives a negotiable promissory note from the payee, for instance, may obtain a better claim than that of the original payee, whose title may have been defective. While the maker may set out a certain defect as reason for not paying the original payee, he may not, under the law of negotiable instruments, use such defect as a defense against a third party. On the other hand, if the instrument is nonnegotiable, the third party has no better title than the original payee.

For example: Assume that Brown purchases a machine from Smith and signs a simple contract that is nonnegotiable, agreeing to pay

Smith $500 in thirty days, and Smith in turn assigns the contract to Mason. (The promise may not have constituted a negotiable instrument, may not have met the requirements of the Uniform of the Negotiable Instruments Act, for any one of a number of reasons. For instance, the promise may not have included words of negotiability such as "Pay to the order of bearer" or equivalent phraseology to indicate that negotiability was intended; the promise may not have been unconditional because provision may have been made for payment out of a specified fund rather than a promise to pay absolutely; the promise may have included an option for the maker to pay in money or in services rather than in money only.) At the end of thirty days Mason demands payment, but Brown refuses to pay on the ground that the machine proved defective and did not perform as Smith warranted it would. Because the contract is nonnegotiable, Brown may properly set up the defense of breach of contract against the third party, Mason. It would be otherwise if Brown had instead given Smith a promissory note that met all the requirements of the Uniform Negotiable Instruments Act. If such a note had been bought from Smith by Mason, in good faith, Mason could recover in full from Brown. Brown may, in the instance of the negotiable note, use breach of contract as a defense against Smith but not against a third party, in this case Mason, who had acquired it in good faith.

It is this feature of negotiability derived from the law merchant that is the distinguishing characteristic of negotiable instruments and is responsible for the wide use of negotiable instruments as a substitute for money.

It has already been noted that the law of negotiable instruments presents a highly complicated and technical field; and persons handling such credit documents, whether promises to pay or orders to pay, should be thoroughly familiar with the Uniform Negotiable Instruments Act, including the procedures closely related to negotiability: presentment and demand for payment or acceptance; notice of dishonor if payment is refused; waiver of presentment and waiver of notice; and protest, which is a notarized record of dishonor. Detailed consideration of such law and procedures is obviously beyond the scope of this treatise. For such information the reader is referred to textbooks on business law.

Orders to Pay

Credit instruments that are orders to pay take many forms, but they are all essentially bills of exchange (also called "drafts"). There are three parties to a draft: the *drawer*, who signs the order; the *drawee*, to whom the order is addressed and who is therefore ordered to pay; and the *payee*, to whom payment is to be made. Frequently the drawer and the payee are the same person. As in the case of the promissory note, there may also be secondary parties, endorsers, and endorsees.

BANK CHECKS. Not only is the personal bank check the most familiar of all of the orders to pay, but it is one of the most important

Exhibit 7

BANK CHECK (Blank Form)

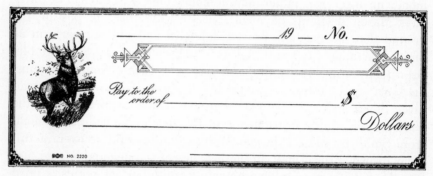

in view of its wide use. The check is an order addressed by a bank depositor to the bank in which he has a demand deposit or checking account, ordering the bank to pay to a third party (or to himself). Checks are payable on demand and provide a most convenient means of transferring funds. Because a check is payable on sight, some writers hold that the check is not a credit instrument because there is no deferred payment. However, it seems tenable to maintain that there is enough of an element of futurity and of risk in accepting a check to warrant considering it a credit instrument.

In addition to the simple personal bank check just described, bank checks may take special forms: if a check is drawn by one bank upon another, the instrument is a *bank draft;* a check drawn by the cashier of a bank on the bank itself is a *cashier's check;* and a personal check drawn in the usual way but presented to the bank for certification (a stamping across the face of the instrument of the word "Certified" and accompanied by the signature of an appropriate bank official) is a *certified check,* and the process indicates that funds have been set aside for making payment. These several forms are discussed and illustrated in the Supplement to this chapter.

OTHER ORDERS TO PAY. Although the bank check in its various

forms is the most frequently used order to pay, there are a number of other orders to pay, each serving a particular purpose, including: *trade draft; commercial draft; trade acceptance; bankers' bill* or *acceptance; commercial letter of credit; travelers'* or *circular letter of credit; postal* and *express money orders;* and *cable* or *telegraphic transfers.* These orders to pay are likewise discussed and illustrated in the Supplement to this chapter and in some instances in the body of the text of other chapters.

Orders to pay may be classified in various ways. If used in domestic trade, they are generally called "drafts"; and if used in foreign trade, they are called "bills of exchange." They may be classified on the basis of the drawee—those drawn on banks (bank bills or drafts) and those drawn on persons, businesses, and institutions other than banks (the latter being called "trade bills"). They may be sight drafts, payable immediately, or time drafts, payable at some stated future time. They may be three-party drafts, bearing the signatures of the drawer, the payee, and an endorsee, in which case any subsequent endorsee may look to any one of the three parties for payment; or if the drawer and payee are identical, two-party drafts.

Auxiliary Documents

There are several kinds of documents of title that are used in certain credit transactions and which support credit instruments but are not in themselves credit instruments: *bills of lading, warehouse receipts,* and *trust receipts.* These documents are illustrated and their use explained in the Supplement. These instruments are evidences of ownership of specific goods and, as such, may be used to supplement credit instruments by providing security.

In this chapter we have discussed: credit; the simplest form of promise to pay—the promissory note; the simplest form of order to pay—the bank check; and reference has been made to auxiliary documents. In the Supplement that follows, additional commercial credit instruments and auxiliary documents are illustrated and discussed.

We have already noted that financial institutions deal primarily in money, credit, and credit instruments. The commercial credit instruments considered in this chapter are used by practically all financial institutions but are particularly important in the work of commercial banks and to the nonbanking institutions that provide short-term funds to business. The next two chapters (3 and 4) are devoted to commercial banking; and Chapter 5 is devoted to specialized forms of commercial credit and the nonbanking institutions that operate in the area of specialized commercial credit, an area that is served by the commercial banks as well.

—ERWIN W. BOEHMLER

SUPPLEMENT
COMMERCIAL CREDIT INSTRUMENTS AND AUXILIARY DOCUMENTS
COMMERCIAL CREDIT INSTRUMENTS

Bank Draft

A bank draft is a check drawn by one bank upon another (second) bank in which it has a deposit. Such a check (see Exhibit 8) is preferred to a personal check because both the drawee and the drawer are banks. If John

Exhibit 8
BANK DRAFT OR CHECK

Brown, living in Chicago, wishes to send a remittance to a merchant in New York City, he may of course send his personal check. But the merchant may not forward the goods ordered by Mr. Brown until the check has cleared. However, if Mr. Brown will send a draft on a New York bank, purchased from his Chicago bank, there is no question on the part of the merchant as to whether the check is good; and in any event, immediate collection can be made.

In purchasing this draft Mr. Brown should have it made payable to himself and then endorse the draft to the New York merchant. In this way there will be no doubt as to where the draft came from, in the event that the accompanying supporting papers have become separated.

Cashier's Check

A cashier's check (see Exhibit 9) is a check drawn by the cashier of a bank on the bank itself. Such a check may be used by a bank for its own account in making a purchase or a payment. It may also be sold to a customer of the bank to use in much the same way as the bank draft described above. In this instance, again, the purchaser of the check should make himself the payee and endorse the check to the third party.

Exhibit 9

CASHIER'S CHECK

Certified Check

A certified check (Exhibit 10) is one that has been drawn in the usual way but which has been presented to the bank for certification—a stamping across the face of the instrument of the word "Certified," accompanied by the signature of an appropriate bank official. Certification indicates that the drawer has sufficient funds in the bank and that these funds are being set aside to make payment upon presentation of the check. Certification makes the check more acceptable because the credit of the bank has been substituted for the credit of the drawer.

Exhibit 10

CERTIFIED CHECK

Either the drawer or the payee may have a check certified. The payee would do so because he does not want cash immediately. However, the payee does not eliminate all risks by having a check certified. Should the certifying bank fail before the check is cashed, the obligation of the drawer would be discharged because the payee might have had cash at the time of certification.

The cashier's check and the certified check serve much the same purpose. A customer with a checking account in a bank may use either; a nondepositor is not in a position to draw a check and have it certified but may purchase a cashier's check.

Commercial Draft

A commercial or trade draft (see Exhibit 11) serves much the same purpose as a promissory note. There is this difference: the debtor takes the initiative in the case of a note, as a rule, and promises to pay. On the other hand, the creditor takes the initiative in the case of a draft; he in effect demands payment.

The seller or creditor addresses to the buyer or debtor an order to pay, usually naming himself as payee. If the drawee is agreeable (and arrangements are usually made in advance), he writes across the face of the bill "Accepted," signs and dates the document, and indicates the bank at which it will be payable. The draft is then returned to the drawer, and in his hands it is much like a promissory note. Until the draft is accepted, it has no value. After it is accepted, the draft can be held by the drawer until maturity, or he may discount it at his bank.

Exhibit 11
DRAFT OR BILL OF EXCHANGE (Blank Form)

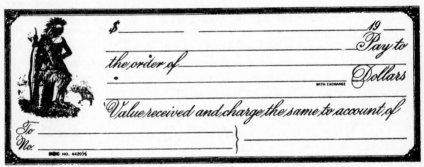

The sight draft may be used, in collecting an overdue account, to bring pressure to bear on the debtor, who may find his credit standing impaired through refusal to accept. The sight draft may also be used to assure cash payment prior to giving physical possession of merchandise to a purchaser. This is accomplished by obtaining an order bill of lading from the carrier, attaching it to a sight draft, and sending the sight draft to a banker in the city of the purchaser. The purchaser is not able to get the shipment of goods without the order bill of lading and may not have the order bill of lading without paying the draft.

In much the same way, a time draft may be used with an order bill of lading attached. (See "Bill of Lading" under "Auxiliary Documents" later in this supplement.) The bill of lading is surrendered upon acceptance, which gives the seller a written promise to pay.

Again, the time draft may be used to convert a past-due book account into a credit instrument, an accepted draft, which is equivalent to a written promise to pay.

Trade Acceptance

A trade acceptance differs from the ordinary commercial time draft in that it has printed on its face the following statement or its equivalent (see Exhibit

Exhibit 15

COMMERCIAL LETTER OF CREDIT

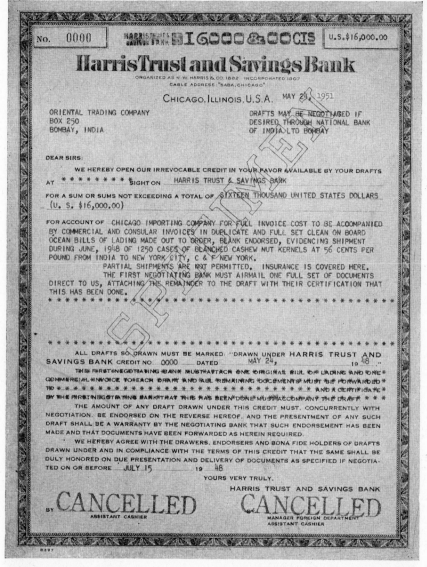

authorize bills to be drawn at sight or on time; they may be stated in domestic or foreign currency; and there are many additional possible features. See Exhibit 15 for an example of an import commercial letter of credit.

Traveler's Letter of Credit

A traveler's letter of credit (circular letter of credit; see Exhibit 16) is a formal letter addressed by a bank to its correspondent banks in the various

Exhibit 16

CIRCULAR LETTER OF CREDIT

CIRCULAR LETTER OF CREDIT

No. 0000

$3,000.00

Harris Trust and Savings Bank

ORGANIZED AS N. W. HARRIS & CO. 1882   INCORPORATED 1907

Chicago, Illinois, U.S.A, FEBRUARY 2, 1951

To Messieurs the Banks and Bankers named in our Letter of Indication

Gentlemen: *This letter will be presented to you by*

MR. R. A. JONES *

in whose favor we have opened a credit of THREE THOUSAND * * * * * * * * *
* *Dollars, up to the aggregate
of which amount* HE IS *authorized to draw demand drafts on*

**HARRIS TRUST AND SAVINGS BANK, CHICAGO, OR
THE CHASE NATIONAL BANK OF THE CITY OF NEW YORK, N.Y.**

*We engage that such drafts shall meet with due honor on presenta-
tion, if drawn on or before* JUNE 2, 1951 *, and we request you
to purchase them at the current rate for demand drafts on Chicago or
New York, as the case may be.*

*All drafts must be plainly marked "drawn under Harris Trust
and Savings Bank's Dollar Letter of Credit No* 0000 *." The amount
of each payment must be endorsed in the space provided for that purpose
on the back hereof, and this Letter, properly cancelled, must be attached
to the draft which exhausts the credit.*

For purposes of identification, the signature × of
MR. R. A. JONES *
*will be found in a separate Letter of Indication of like number and
date issued in conjunction with this Letter of Credit.*

Thanking you for your attention to these matters, we are,
Dear Sirs,

Very respectfully yours,
HARRIS TRUST AND SAVINGS BANK,

By

By

parts of the world that the bank customer expects to visit. It authorizes the individual named in the letter to draw clean (undocumented) drafts on the bank that issued the letter of credit. This provides immediate funds for a traveler at any of the banks shown on the list that is given to the traveler along with a letter of introduction and identification that contains the traveler's signature. In contrast, a "specially advised" letter of credit permits the bearer (who expects to remain in one city) to draw drafts on only a single designated bank.

Postal and Express Money Orders

Money orders are a means of transmitting funds to someone at a distance, and they serve much the same purpose as checks or bank drafts. However, they have these advantages: they do not have to be returned to the place of purchase for final payment, and they provide a convenient method for a person without a checking account to transfer money.

There are three parties to a money order: the payer, the one who remits the money; the payee, the person to whom the money is being sent; and the drawee. Postal money orders (see Exhibit 17) permit but one transfer by

Exhibit 17

POSTAL MONEY ORDER

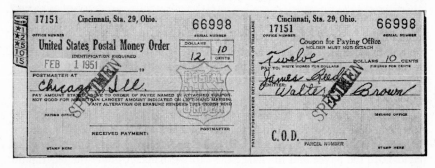

Exhibit 18

EXPRESS MONEY ORDER

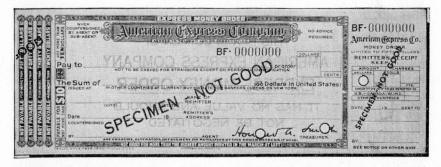

endorsement; express company money orders (Exhibit 18) may pass from hand to hand by continuous endorsement. Some large banks also sell money orders, and there are international money orders available.

Traveler's Check

For the traveler who feels that he may need more money on his travels than he wishes to carry in cash, the travelers' checks (see Exhibit 19) issued by

Exhibit 19

TRAVELER'S CHECK

some of the larger commercial banks or by the American Express Company are a convenience. They are essentially drafts which are purchased from one of the agencies noted. They may be used in this country or abroad.

Cable or Telegraphic Transfers

A cable transfer is a means of remitting funds abroad immediately. An American desiring to make an immediate payment abroad will pay his banker the requisite sum, and the banker will cable its foreign correspondent to make payment to the payee and to charge the cabling bank. A domestic telegraphic money transfer is similar but does not involve foreign exchange rates.

AUXILIARY DOCUMENTS

There are several kinds of documents of title that are used in certain credit transactions and which support credit instruments but are not in themselves credit instruments. One of these, the order bill of lading, has already been mentioned. There are two other documents of this sort that are relatively important: warehouse receipts and trust receipts. They are used as collateral to secure loans on commodities.

Bills of Lading

A bill of lading is issued by a common carrier or transportation company to a shipper to indicate the receipt of goods for shipment under required conditions, and it serves as a contract to transport and as a document of title. There are two kinds (see Exhibit 20) : a straight bill of lading, which is non-negotiable and which conveys title to the consignee; and an order bill of lading, which is negotiable and without which the consignee is not able to obtain shipment because title remains (generally) in the shipper. Under an order bill of lading the carrier will not deliver the shipment unless the order bill of lading, properly endorsed, is presented. The order bill of lading is good collateral to a bank. The straight bill of lading, on the other hand, is not

Exhibit 20

STRAIGHT AND ORDER BILLS OF LADING

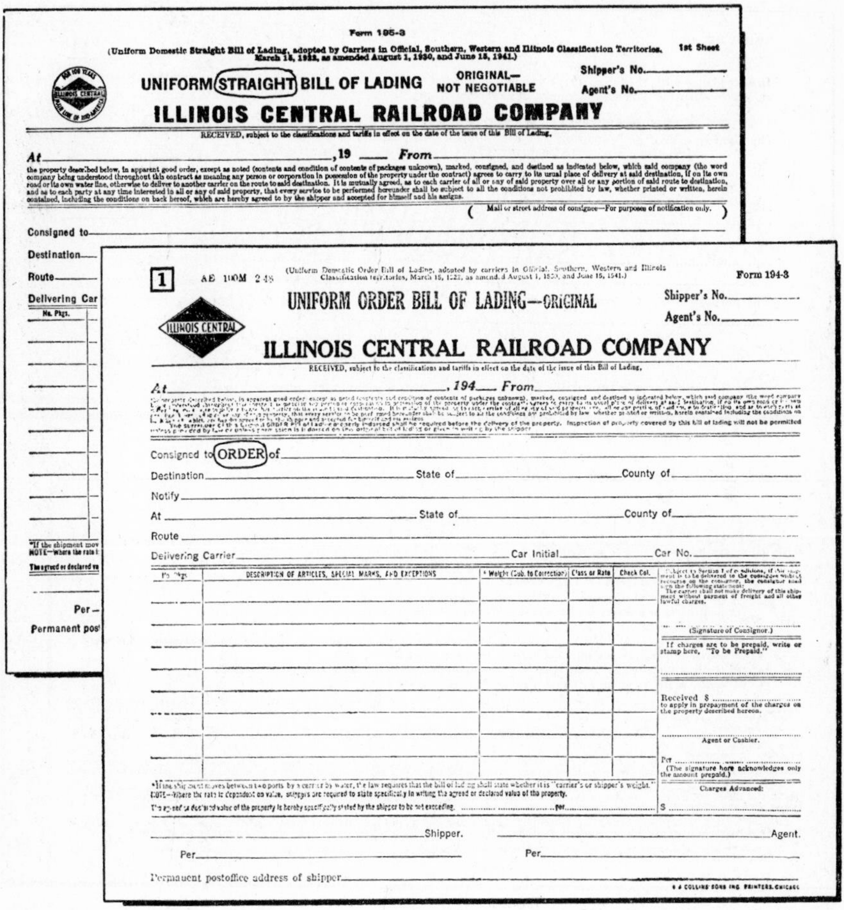
Form 195-3

(Uniform Domestic Straight Bill of Lading, adopted by Carriers in Official, Southern, Western and Illinois Classification Territories, March 15, 1922, as amended August 1, 1930, and June 15, 1941.) 1st Sheet

UNIFORM STRAIGHT BILL OF LADING ORIGINAL— NOT NEGOTIABLE Shipper's No. Agent's No.

ILLINOIS CENTRAL RAILROAD COMPANY

RECEIVED, subject to the classifications and tariffs in effect on the date of the issue of this Bill of Lading,

At ..., 19 ... From ...

(Mail or street address of consignee—For purposes of notification only.)

Consigned to

Destination

Route

Delivering Car

No. Pkgs.

Per—

Permanent pos

1 AE 100M 2-48 (Uniform Domestic Order Bill of Lading, adopted by carriers in Official, Southern, Western and Illinois Classification territories, March 15, 1922, as amended August 1, 1930, and June 15, 1941.) Form 194-3

UNIFORM ORDER BILL OF LADING—ORIGINAL Shipper's No. Agent's No.

ILLINOIS CENTRAL RAILROAD COMPANY

RECEIVED, subject to the classifications and tariffs in effect on the date of the issue of this Bill of Lading,

At ..., 194... From ...

Consigned to ORDER of

Destination ... State of ... County of

Notify

At ... State of ... County of

Route

Delivering Carrier ... Car Initial ... Car No.

No. Pkgs. | DESCRIPTION OF ARTICLES, SPECIAL MARKS, AND EXCEPTIONS | *Weight (Sub. to Correction) | Class or Rate | Check Col.

(Signature of Consignor.)

If charges are to be prepaid, write or stamp here, "To be Prepaid."

Received $ ... to apply in prepayment of the charges on the property described hereon.

Agent or Cashier.

Per ... (The signature here acknowledges only the amount prepaid.)

Charges Advanced: $

...Shipper. ...Agent.

Per ... Per ...

Permanent postoffice address of shipper

satisfactory collateral because the consignee may obtain possession of the shipment without actually having the bill of lading in his possession.

Warehouse Receipts

It is sometimes found desirable to place goods in a warehouse and receive in return a warehouse receipt for the goods. The receipt may be nonnegotiable, and the goods will then be surrendered only to parties specifically named in the receipt. If the receipt is negotiable in form, then goods may be delivered to bearer on order.

Trust Receipts

If a bank or other creditor holds a warehouse receipt on certain goods, as collateral for a loan, it may agree to release the warehouse receipt to the debtor so that he may get the goods for processing or resale, if the debtor will

Exhibit 21

TRUST RECEIPT

TRUST RECEIPT

Chicago, Illinois, ___June 21_____ _19_ _51_

In accordance with the terms of the agreement printed on the reverse side hereof, the undersigned (hereinafter called the "trustee") hereby acknowledges receipt from

CITY NATIONAL BANK AND TRUST COMPANY OF CHICAGO

(hereinafter called the "entruster") of the following instruments or documents, or both:

100 shs. Socony-Vacuum Oil Company--common stock

$1,000.00 U.S. Treasury 2 1/4% Bonds due 9/15/67/72

250 shs. No-Par Corporation 4% Pfd. Stock

SPECIMEN

The purpose of this transaction is as follows : ___Sale thereof.___

Richard Roe

NO.

Note: The purpose must be substantially equivalent to one of those specified in the agreement.
P-3

(Front)

AGREEMENT

The trustee hereby acknowledges receipt of value from the entruster and that the entruster has a security interest hereunder in each and all of the foregoing instruments or documents, or instruments and documents.

It is hereby agreed that the purpose of this transaction is substantially equivalent to one or more of the following:

1. The sale or exchange of said documents or instruments, or both.
2. The procuring of the sale or exchange of said documents or instruments, or both.
3. The manufacturing or processing of goods covered by the documents with the purpose of
   (a) ultimate sale; or
   (b) loading, unloading, storing, shipping, transshipping, or otherwise dealing with such goods in a manner preliminary or necessary to their sale.
4. The delivery of instruments to a principal under whom the trustee may hold them.
5. The delivery of instruments for the consummation of some transaction involving delivery to a depositary or registrar.
6. The delivery of said instruments for their presentation, collection or renewal.

The entruster shall be entitled to, and the trustee hereby agrees to give the entruster immediate possession of said instruments or documents, or both, upon the happening of any one or more of the following events: (1) any default by the trustee in the payment of any obligation or obligations to the entruster which are secured hereby; (2) any acceleration for any reason of the maturity date or dates of such obligation or obligations; (3) demand by the entruster upon the trustee for such possession; (4) the accomplishment of the purpose or purposes of this transaction; (5) or in any event upon the expiration of the period ending thirty days from the date hereof. In the event the sale, exchange, renewal, or collection of any instruments or documents, or both, is included in the purposes specified above, the entruster shall be immediately entitled to the proceeds (including any debt thereby owing to the trustee and any security therefor) of such sale, exchange, renewal, or collection, and the trustee agrees hereby forthwith to account for and turn over such proceeds to the entruster. If the trustee illegally or improperly sells, renews, exchanges, or collects any instruments or documents, or both, the entruster, in addition to all its other rights and remedies, shall be immediately entitled to the proceeds (including any debt thereby owing to the trustee and any security therefor) of such, sale, renewal, exchange or collection.

The trustee hereby agrees to comply with each and all of the terms and provisions of this trust receipt and of the Uniform Trust Receipts Act now in force in the State of Illinois. In the event said Act, or any part thereof, shall be held invalid, all the express terms and provisions of this trust receipt shall remain fully binding upon and enforceable against the trustee. Reference is hereby made to said Act for definitions of the terms "instruments" and "documents."

Nothing herein or in said Act contained shall limit, impair, affect, or prejudice the rights, powers, or remedies which the entruster may have under the law or by virtue of the provisions of any bills or notes, or both, drawn, accepted, made, indorsed, or guaranteed by the trustee and held by the entruster.

The term "trustee" as used herein shall be taken to include one or more persons, corporations, or partnerships, or any combination thereof.

(Reverse)

execute a trust receipt in favor of the bank. Under this arrangement the bank retains title to the goods, and the creditor gets physical possession as a trustee. As the goods are processed and sold, the proceeds must then be turned over to the creditor by the debtor. The trust receipt may serve other functions as well, as is indicated on the reverse side of the trust agreement shown in Exhibit 21.

QUESTIONS AND PROBLEMS

1. What is credit? Is is synonymous with debt? Discuss.

2. What economic function does credit perform?

3. What are the bases of credit from the social standpoint? From the standpoint of the individual borrower?

4. What might a writer mean who speaks of "circularity of credit"?

5. Discuss the relationship of credit and wealth.

6. Indicate the ways in which credit may be classified, and develop one of these classifications.

7. May consumptive credit be considered as having production attributes?

8. Is credit employed for speculative purposes wasteful?

9. What is meant by the "unwise use of credit"? Why may it be socially and individually harmful?

10. Draw up the form for a promise to pay; fill in the parties, dollar amounts, dates, etc., and identify the parties.

11. Draw up the form for a specimen order to pay; fill in the parties, dollar amounts, dates, etc., and identify the parties.

12. What does endorsement accomplish? Is there more than one kind of endorsement?

13. Does it make any difference to the holder of a commercial credit instrument whether the instrument complies with the Uniform Negotiable Instruments Act?

14. What is meant by "credit system," "line of credit," "credit standing"?

15. Classify:

Bank check	Banker's acceptance
Letter of credit	Traveler's check
Trade acceptance	Book account
Order bill of lading	Certified check
Promissory note	Commercial bill
Money order	Trust receipt

16. What is the difference between a commercial draft and a trade acceptance?

17. In purchasing a bank draft is there any advantage in having the purchaser named as payee?

BIBLIOGRAPHY

Extended discussions of the nature and classification of credit and of credit instruments will be found in the following texts on credit and collections:

Chapin, A. F. *Credit and Collection Principles and Practice.* 5th ed. New York: McGraw-Hill Book Co., Inc., 1947.

Beckman, T. N. *Credit and Collections in Theory and Practice.* 4th ed. New York: McGraw-Hill Book Co., Inc., 1939.

Ettinger, R. R., and Golieb, D. E. *Credits and Collections.* 3d ed. New York: Prentice-Hall, Inc., 1949.

Schultz, W. J. *Credit and Collection Management.* New York: Prentice-Hall, Inc., 1947.

And most general textbooks on money and banking deal with the same subject matter in varying degrees.

The nature, functions, and bases of credit are discussed in chapter viii, and credit instruments, with emphasis on negotiability, in chapter ix of H. G.

Moulton, *Financial Organization and the Economic System* (New York: Mc-Graw-Hill Book Co., Inc., 1938) ; and a comprehensive comment on the various points of view in defining credit is found in chapter v of W. H. Steiner, *Money and Banking* (New York: Henry Holt & Co., 1933).

Treatises on business or commercial law include a consideration of commercial credit instruments, negotiability, and the related topics: presentment, notice of dishonor, waiver of presentment and notice, and protest. A clear presentation, including case illustrations, will be found in Part IX of H. F. Lusk, *Business Law: Principles and Cases* (4th ed.; Chicago: Richard D. Irwin, Inc., 1951).

The economic function of speculation is discussed in most introductory texts in economics, and a fairly full statement with particular reference to the commodity exchanges appears as chapter iii in J. B. Baer and O. G. Saxon, *Commodity Exchanges and Futures Trading* (New York: Harper & Bros., 1949).

Chapter • 3

COMMERCIAL BANKING

PART A: INTRODUCTION; CHARTER AND ORGANIZATION;
OPERATIONS; SOURCES AND USES OF FUNDS

IN THE opening chapter it was pointed out that our productive system
depends upon the accumulation and maintenance of adequate supplies of funds. The more far-reaching the division of labor and the
larger the scale of operations in an economy, the greater the demands
for both temporary and permanent funds. Circulating capital flows
endlessly through the productive processes from the purchase of raw
material to the sale of finished goods; investment capital is tied up
for years in plant and equipment. In both instances, financial operations are carried on in terms of money and credit.

AN INTRODUCTION TO COMMERCIAL BANKING

A great number and a large variety of financial institutions perform one or more functions in the funneling of funds from savers and
into productive use, whether in the form of temporary or permanent
capital. Some of these institutions are classified as engaged in banking activity and are, in turn, subdivided into three subgroups: savings
banking, investment banking, and commercial banking. Our immediate interest in this chapter is commercial banking, but it is important first to distinguish this type of banking from the other two types.

Savings banking is carried on by institutions that accept deposits
technically subject to withdrawal only after notice. These "time deposits" are expected to remain with the bank for long periods. They
represent funds put aside by individuals for use on the proverbial
"rainy day" or for other future needs. The savings banker considers
these funds as available to him for placement in long-term investments, such as real estate mortgages and high-grade bonds. The interest earned on investments is practically the only source of income

to the bank; from it the bank defrays its expenses and makes interest payments to depositors. Savings banking will be treated in Chapter 11.

Investment banking is concerned mainly with the application of savings to financing long-term capital requirements. Investment bankers assist corporations in providing long-term capital through the sale of stocks and bonds. They may agree to purchase, for resale, an entire issue of securities for a sum which they guarantee to turn over to the issuing corporation at a definite date. Or they may agree to exert their best effort to sell an issue at the highest price possible. The profits of investment bankers are obtained from the "spread" between purchase and sale price, or from commissions received from the issuing corporation. Details of the operations of investment banking will be explained in Chapter 8.

Commercial banking functions include, not only the receipt of deposits and the lending of surplus balances to individuals and business enterprises, but also the creation of deposits through the granting of loans and discounts. Some funds are accumulated in banks as temporary deposits; their owners will soon spend them. The bank cannot put such deposits to work for long periods of time. Other deposits are not so restricted but are available for long-term use wherever attractive investment opportunities arise. Banks thus act as intermediaries between the savers and users of capital and must apportion the funds to productive use with due regard for the deposits of the suppliers and the needs of the users. A successful banking system is one that is able to satisfy both groups of customers—the savers with funds on deposit, and the borrowers who make use of such funds.

The function that places commercial banks at the heart of the entire credit structure is not, however, the mere redistribution of surplus funds among a variety of borrowers. Of the greatest significance is the fact that these institutions are empowered, in co-operation with the Federal Reserve banks, to add to the money supply and thus create net additions to the effective purchasing power of the nation. This unique function is accomplished by exchanging deposit credit for the promissory notes or securities of borrowers. How this is done will be discussed in Chapters 18 and 20.

Commercial banks are the most familiar of financial institutions. They accept our deposits and permit us to write checks against them. They issue letters of credit; accept and pay drafts; and rent safety boxes to customers for the storage of important papers, cash, jewels, and other valuable possessions. They lend money directly through advances to local borrowers and indirectly through the purchase of corporation bonds. They aid in financing governmental units by pu[r]chasing federal and municipal bonds or notes and by assisting the issuing agencies in the payment of interest and in the final redemption of the obligations.

Commercial banking is big business. Approximately 14,140 banks of this type were in operation in the United States in June 1950. Their loans and investments totaled more than $121 billion, cash assets over $33 billion, total deposits more than $132 billion, and capital accounts (owners' interest) approximately $11.4 billion. Commercial banks and commercial banking constitute the subject matter of this and the following chapter.

Origin and Development of Banking

Although the exact origin of banking is hidden in antiquity, there is evidence to show that the practices of safekeeping and savings banking flourished in the temples of Babylon as early as 2000 B.C. Clay tablets discovered in the ruins of Babylonia indicate that credit instruments in the form of promises and orders to pay gold and silver coins were used in the ninth century B.C., much as promissory notes and bank checks are used today. Loans made on the security of real estate mortgages and silver coins were recorded as early as the sixth century B.C.

For several centuries before the development of private banking, the priests of the Greek temples carried on a thriving business. Operations at first were confined to the safekeeping of valuables in the sacred vaults, but later were expanded to include lending. Even after the rise of private banking enterprise, the priests continued to receive a large volume of savings and continued lending operations. Private bankers, however, became more than mere "money changers" by lending their own accumulated profits in addition to some of the precious metal deposited with them for safekeeping.

Many practices common to present-day banking flourished in the Roman Empire at the zenith of its power. Bankers accepted deposits, purchased drafts drawn on banks and on traders in foreign and domestic cities, made commercial loans, sold mortgages, and issued letters of credit. Deposits in the banks were classified on the basis of their maturity dates, and interest was paid on time accounts.

The art of banking fell with the Empire, reappearing only with the Renaissance, when trade and commerce began to flourish in Venice and Florence. A public bank established in Venice (1587) became a pattern for public banks established in Amsterdam (1609) and Ham-

...nd ultimately influenced the growth of banking in

...ith Banking in England

British merchants and tradesmen made deposits for
...the Tower of London; but in that year King Charles I
seized £130,000 for his own uses. These funds were finally restored to
their rightful owners, but in the meantime merchants had begun placing their money in bullion in the vaults of local goldsmiths who were
not only artisans in precious metals but also served as money changers.

Although the owners of precious metals, jewels, and other items
of wealth originally made deposits to obtain safety for their valuables,
they soon recognized an additional advantage—the convenience of
making payment by transferring the goldsmith's receipt, or by writing
a draft on their deposit ordering the smith to transfer a designated
portion of the account to the bearer of the order. Later, instead of
giving a personalized receipt for money or bullion received, the goldsmith issued a formal promissory note which served as a medium of
exchange upon endorsement. When notes payable to bearer, requiring
no endorsement, were issued by the smith, the prototype of the modern
bank note was created. Thus, ownership of deposited wealth was
transferred from hand to hand, and exchanges of goods and settlements of debt were effected while the valuable assets remained as a
reserve in the vaults of the goldsmith.

The convenience of the new method of payment, coupled with confidence in the integrity of the goldsmith, served to hold down demands
for coin and paper money to a volume much smaller than the funds
on deposit. It was practicable, therefore, for the goldsmith to use some
of the deposited gold in his own craft or to lend his notes to others.
When first introduced, the lending operations were not publicized.
Rather, they were carried on in strictest secrecy. Depositors at that
time expected later to obtain the identical object or items of wealth
left with the goldsmith and would have considered his loan of their
property a breach of trust. In making a loan the smith obtained a
promise from the borrower to repay the funds in kind on demand or
at the end of a short, definitely determinable period. The borrower
agreed to repay not only the full amount borrowed but an amount in
addition to compensate the smith for his service as lender and risk
taker.

It was at this point in his evolution that the goldsmith became a
commercial banker in the modern sense. By lending, sometimes gold

and sometimes bearer-notes payable in cash on demand, the smith had created obligations in excess of his liquid assets. He had, therefore, taken possession of the promissory note of a borrower and created a net addition to the volume of purchasing power in the form of an acceptable medium of exchange.[1] The risks incurred required the smith to invest his own funds in the banking operation, to borrow from others, and to take the chances of going bankrupt. The fee paid by each borrower included some compensation for assuming these risks. The community as a whole was served by the increase in the amount of money made available by the lending process.

Banking Development in the United States

Pre-revolutionary banks in America operated under charters granted by British or colonial authority. They were few in number and confined their operations largely to lending their own note issues. Deposit banking was slow to develop in pioneer regions, where people were poor and transportation and communication were difficult.

After the Revolutionary War and the release of American colonies from British law, the need for a satisfactory means of payment became increasingly apparent, and banks were chartered under authority of state governments in Philadelphia, Boston, New York, and Baltimore in the years 1781, 1784, and 1791, respectively.

Congress authorized the establishment of two federal institutions that operated with twenty-year charters: the First Bank of the United States, from 1791 to 1811, and the Second Bank of the United States, from 1816 to 1836. Although both these banks operated branches in various sections of the country, neither was a central bank in the sense that the term was applied to the Bank of England at that time, or as the Federal Reserve banks are in our country today. The two Banks of the United States did not have a monopoly on the issuance of bank notes; neither of them held liquid assets as reserves for commercial banks; nor was it possible for individual banks to acquire funds from them for use in emergencies.

State banking in America spread rapidly after 1811. Many of the new institutions were the fly-by-night type or "wildcat" banks opened by unscrupulous promoters who flooded the country with worthless

---

[1] The exchange of bank notes or deposit credit for the promissory notes of borrowers is now known as "monetization of debt." Notes are evidence of the borrowers' indebtedness to the bank. By exchanging these notes for its own promise to pay, or by establishing a deposit account permitting the borrower to draw checks on it, the bank has increased the volume of money available for general use as a circulating medium. Monetization of government debt occurs in similar fashion when obligations of the public treasury are left with banks in exchange for creation of government deposits. Chapters 17, 18, 20, and 21 contain references to monetization of government debt.

ıcked by few or no assets of value. On the other hand,
ble exceptions of banks being founded upon sound
later became integral parts of commercial banking
es. Among these was the Suffolk Bank of Boston
ıy the use of an ingenious collection system, forced
˳anks to redeem their notes in specie at face value. Another was the "safety-fund" plan applied to certain banks organized
in New York after 1829. Banks chartered under this statute contributed to a state-administered fund that was used to pay creditors
(i.e., noteholders and depositors) of banks that failed. This was the
earliest American forerunner of the plan of deposit insurance now
in effect in this country under the administration of the Federal Deposit Insurance Corporation. A third outstanding attempt to attain
higher standards of bank practice and greater safety for holders of
bank notes was found in the "free-banking" plan adopted by New
York in 1839. Provisions were made to grant charters to newly incorporated banks through a state board rather than by special action
of the state legislature. The latter practice had resulted in graft and
bribery that permitted unprincipled promoters to start banks which
"fleeced" the general public. "Free-banking" law also made it necessary for a bank to deposit high-grade bonds with a state banking
official in an amount equal to the total note issue of the bank. In the
event of bank failure the state official sold bonds and distributed cash
to reimburse the noteholders. Both aspects of this law were incorporated into the national banking law in 1863.

In 1842 the State Legislature of Louisiana enacted a sweeping reform of its banking law and included a requirement that each bank
should maintain a cash reserve equal to one third of all its liabilities
to the public. The other two thirds of its liabilities were to be represented on the asset side of the balance sheet by short-term commercial
paper having maturities of ninety days or less. The specie-reserve
principle of this act also became part of federal law in 1863. Federal
chartering of banks was reintroduced during the Civil War by passage of the National Bank Act (1863). This act, as amended, is still
in effect. In contrast to its actions in connection with the First and
Second Banks of the United States, the government, under the new
legislation, did not subscribe to shares of stock or occupy a position
as administrator of local bank operation. Although individual banks
receive a charter and operate under the administration of a federal
bureau (Office of Comptroller of the Currency), national banks are
privately owned institutions. They operate in all states of the Union

alongside similar banks chartered and administered under laws rulings formulated by state governments.

In 1913 the Federal Reserve System was established. This is the American version of a central bank. Unlike most foreign central banks, consisting of a parent and several branches, the Federal Reserve System is composed of twelve regional banks that have a measure of local autonomy under the general oversight of one Board of Governors. The twelve regional banks and their branches are owned by commercial bank "members," including all national banks and state banks who wish to belong to the system. Federal Reserve banks now have a monopoly on bank-note issue, hold liquid reserves for their member banks, act as agents in the clearing and collecting of checks drawn on commercial banks, provide funds for members by lending to them or purchasing assets from them, and have regulatory power with respect to credit extension to business by member banks. (Chapter 20 is devoted to a detailed discussion of the Federal Reserve System.)

Commercial Banking Functions

The processes of present-day commercial banking which distinguish it from other types of banking are all illustrated in the operations of the seventeenth-century goldsmith. They are: the acceptance of deposits for safekeeping and convenience in making payments by check; the granting of loans or advances of funds to meet the needs of individuals or business firms; and, in this process, the creation of net additions to the effective supply of money. Although a savings institution may accept deposits and make loans, the right to transfer funds by the use of checks is found only in commercial banks; and in no other type of bank is there the opportunity to create additional new purchasing power by establishing a deposit account for a borrowing customer.

"Department-Store" Banking

Large metropolitan banks perform additional services that fall naturally into the hands of institutions dealing with the purchase and sale of credit instruments and the administration of savings and trust funds. An examination of Exhibit 22, adapted from an advertisement of the Continental Illinois National Bank and Trust Company of Chicago, clearly indicates that the modern big city bank is a veritable "department store" of banking services. This chapter and the next are devoted primarily to operations of the "commercial department" and

Exhibit 22

BANKING SERVICES

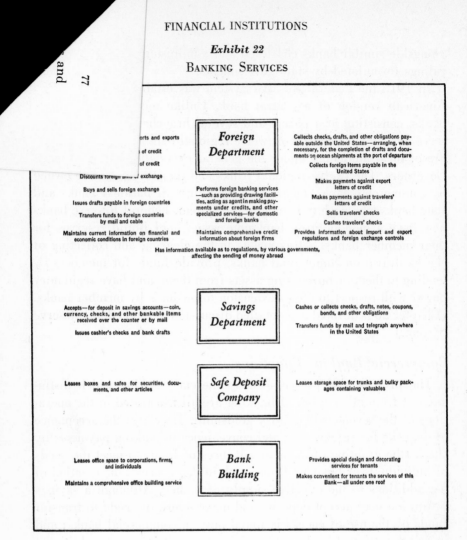

orts and exports

of credit

of credit

Discounts foreign bills of exchange

Buys and sells foreign exchange

Issues drafts payable in foreign countries

Transfers funds to foreign countries by mail and cable

Maintains current information on financial and economic conditions in foreign countries

Foreign Department

Performs foreign banking services —such as providing drawing facilities, acting as agent in making payments under credits, and other specialized services—for domestic and foreign banks

Maintains comprehensive credit information about foreign firms

Has information available as to regulations, by various governments, affecting the sending of money abroad

Collects checks, drafts, and other obligations payable outside the United States—arranging, when necessary, for the completion of drafts and documents on ocean shipments at the port of departure

Collects foreign items payable in the United States

Makes payments against export letters of credit

Makes payments against travelers' letters of credit

Sells travelers' checks

Cashes travelers' checks

Provides information about import and export regulations and foreign exchange controls

Accepts—for deposit in savings accounts—coin, currency, checks, and other bankable items received over the counter or by mail

Issues cashier's checks and bank drafts

Savings Department

Cashes or collects checks, drafts, notes, coupons, bonds, and other obligations

Transfers funds by mail and telegraph anywhere in the United States

Leases boxes and safes for securities, documents, and other articles

Safe Deposit Company

Leases storage space for trunks and bulky packages containing valuables

Leases office space to corporations, firms, and individuals

Maintains a comprehensive office building service

Bank Building

Provides special design and decorating services for tenants

Makes convenient for tenants the services of this Bank—all under one roof

to the interrelationships of the departments which weld banks into a system. Later chapters will present more detailed views of other functions, such as savings and trust services.

BANK CHARTER AND ORGANIZATION

Although banks are private enterprises organized for the profit of shareholders under federal or state "free-banking" statutes, they are not easily started. Laws and administrative regulations are designed to safeguard the public interest by preventing the incorporation of undesirable banking ventures not likely to succeed. Applicants for bank charters must demonstrate, to the satisfaction of state bank-

Exhibit 22—Continued

BANKING SERVICES

Commercial Department

Performs all the duties of "correspondent" for banks—giving specialized deposit, safekeeping, credit, and other services

Arranges for the collection of money due on contracts, mortgages, warrants, and other obligations

Maintains special facilities for accepting and supplying coin and currency

Accepts deposits of coin, currency, checks, and other bankable items received over the counter or by mail

Cashes and certifies checks

Collects checks payable at other Chicago banks

Collects—by messenger—drafts, notes, and other obligations payable in Chicago and suburbs

Collects—through correspondent and Federal Reserve banks—checks, drafts, notes, coupons, bonds, and other securities payable anywhere outside the Chicago area

Issues cashier's checks and bank drafts

Maintains records of all customer transactions and submits advices and statements covering the transactions

Grants lines of commercial credit

Makes secured and unsecured loans

Maintains comprehensive credit and financial information

Buys and sells, for customers, securities of the United States Government and its instrumentalities, and securities of States, counties, cities, and other municipal bodies

Purchases commercial paper for customers

Places customers' orders, with brokers, for the purchase and sale of securities

Acts as cashier for brokers

Transfers funds by mail and telegraph anywhere in the United States

Arranges for the shipment, transfer of ownership, and exchange of denomination of securities, also for delivery of securities against payment, and a variety of other such services

Trust Department

Acts as executor, or co-executor, of estates—seeing to the probate of the wills and the collection, conservation, and distribution of the assets

Performs all the services of trustee under will, managing and distributing the assets in accordance with the provisions of the will

Acts as administrator, under court appointment—collecting, managing, and distributing the assets of estates

Serves as conservator of estates of incompetent persons and as guardian of estates of minors, managing the assets until distributed

Relieves individual administrators, executors, conservators, and guardians of detailed work, by providing various depositary arrangements

Acts as trustee under agreements entered into by individuals for specific purposes—managing and distributing the assets in accordance with the trust agreements

Performs the duties of insurance trustee—under a special form of trust under agreement—when the proceeds of insurance policies comprise all or part of the assets of a trust

Relieves individuals of the details of caring for their securities, by acting as depositary for safekeeping or as agent, with or without investment assistance

Serves individuals as escrow agent, by holding property or documents in accordance with the terms of the escrow agreement

Performs—for corporations—all duties as trustee under indentures controlling bonds, notes, debentures, and equipment trust certificates

Pays—as agent—maturing bonds and coupons for corporations and for governmental units and agencies

Performs—as transfer agent for corporations—all work incident to the transfer of stock from one owner to another

Provides—as registrar—an independent control over the amount of corporate stock issued and transferred

Relieves corporations of the work involved in paying dividends, by acting as dividend disbursing agent

Acts as depositary for securities in corporate reorganizations

Relieves banks, corporations, associations, societies, and institutions of the details of caring for their securities, by acting as depositary for safekeeping or as agent, with or without investment assistance

Serves corporations and other organizations as escrow agent, by holding property or documents in accordance with the terms of the escrow agreement

Acts—for corporations—as trustee under agreements covering retirement and profit-sharing systems and other arrangements

ing authorities, or the Comptroller of the Currency in Washington, D.C., not only that the community needs additional banking capital and services but also that the applicants are able to supply these needs. When the requirements of formal application have been satisfied, the public authority grants a charter of indeterminate length (i.e., of unlimited life) and a certificate to begin operations.

BANK OPERATION—THE BALANCE SHEET APPROACH

The general nature of commercial bank functions and operations have been indicated in the preceding pages. The great variety and number of transactions involve a complex system of record keeping that is almost beyond the comprehension of anyone not employed in the bookkeeping department of a bank. Fortunately, however, each bank must publish its balance sheet several times yearly to provide the information needed by its customers to keep them aware of the condition of their institution. Students of banking require little knowledge of the detailed manner in which records are kept, but should be introduced to illustrations showing how daily transactions affect quarterly published reports.[2]

Banking Transactions

1. *Sale of Capital Stock.* The first transaction reflected on the balance sheet is the sale of capital stock at a premium, i.e., at a price above its par value. From this sale the bank acquires an asset in the form of cash in exchange for stock certificates indicating the evidence of the ownership interest of the corporation to its shareholders. The premium is noted in bank records, and later will appear in the published report as a paid-in surplus or capital surplus. Thus, if we assume distribution of 2,000 shares of stock of $100 par value sold at a premium of 20 per cent, the balance sheet will show:

Assets		Liabilities	
Cash	$240,000	Common Stock	$200,000
		Paid-in Surplus	40,000

Increases and decreases in the value of assets and liabilities from this point forward will be indicated by plus ($+$) and minus ($-$) signs, respectively, placed to the left of the item which is affected. No attempt will be made at this time to cumulate the effect of individual transactions. That is, we are not at this point interested in building a statement on the foundation laid in the first transaction.

2. *Purchase of Stock in Federal Reserve Bank.* If the new institution is chartered as a national bank, or is a state bank joining the Federal Reserve System, it must spend an amount equal to 3 per cent of its capital and surplus for Federal Reserve bank stock:

$+$ Federal Reserve Bank Stock . . $7,200
$-$ Cash 7,200

3. *Purchase of Banking House.* The bank must acquire fixed assets either by purchase or lease. The dollar value of this entry is of

---

[2] Readers having no previous experience with bookkeeping will find Supplement A at the end of this chapter helpful in understanding material presented on the pages that follow.

little consequence to us; but, assuming $40,000 in cash is expended to purchase a banking house, the statement change is:

+ Building and Equipment.... $40,000
− Cash.................... 40,000

4. *Checks Deposited.* The bank is now ready to open its doors to the public and will become active in the solicitation of new business. Local shareholders will immediately transfer deposits from other banks into their own institution. Other local individuals will open new accounts by depositing their salary checks, and business firms will bring in daily receipts of checks and cash. Of the checks deposited, some will be drawn on banks outside the city and others on local institutions. For purposes of illustration they will all be shown as "Items for Collection." It is assumed that the sum of $540,000 is placed in checking accounts as demand deposits and $60,000 in savings or time deposits. These transactions are recorded as follows:

+ Items for Collection..... $600,000   + Demand Deposits....... $540,000
                                             + Time Deposits.......... 60,000

5. *Cash Deposited.* The bank will also receive cash deposits, especially from local tradesmen who collect coins and paper money from retail sales. If cash deposits of $80,000 are received and credited to checking accounts the following change occurs in the bank statement:

+ Cash.................. $80,000   + Demand Deposits....... $80,000

6. *Check Collections and Due from Federal.* The "items in process of collection" are checks drawn on other banks; they are in the process of collection because the institution in which they are deposited sends them forward for collection from the drawee banks. As shown later, there are several routes by which they may be collected or cleared; but at this point it is assumed that all collections are made through the Federal Reserve System with instructions that the proceeds shall be left on deposit at the Federal Reserve bank of the district:

− Items in Process of Collection... $600,000
+ Due from Federal Reserve Bank. 600,000

Commercial banks having membership in the Federal Reserve System are required to keep a deposit in the Federal Reserve Bank of their district. The deposit is called a "legal minimum-reserve balance" and must be equal to a stipulated percentage of demand deposits and a smaller, but stipulated, percentage of time deposits.

Assuming that the legal minimum-reserve requirements were 20 per cent of demand deposits and 5 per cent of time accounts, this bank would be forced to have a deposit balance at the district Federal Reserve bank of at least $127,000. Of this amount, $124,000 would serve as the 20 per cent reserve for $620,000 in demand deposits and $3,000 would provide a 5 per cent backing for $60,000 in time deposits. Since this bank has $600,000 on deposit at the Federal Reserve bank (resulting from the collection of checks), it has substantially more than the required minimum. In fact, it has "excess reserves" of $473,000. In a sense, the deposit of a commercial bank at the Federal Reserve bank is much like the account of a businessman at his commercial bank.

7. *Due from Banks.* For convenience in operations, most banks maintain deposit balances with a few big banks in large cities—their "city correspondents." In the next chapter we shall consider the origin of the correspondent relationship and the part it plays in banking. For the moment, we shall simply assume that our bank establishes such an account by transferring $100,000 from its Federal Reserve balance to a "Due from Other Banks" account.

— Due from Federal Reserve Bank.$100,000
+ Due from Other Banks......... 100,000

Summary of Transactions

Now we are in a position to summarize the transactions that we have so far considered separately, setting up a balance sheet as follows:

Assets		*Liabilities*	
Cash......................	$272,800	Capital Stock............	$200,000
Due from Federal Reserve		Paid-in Surplus...........	40,000
Bank.................	500,000	Demand Deposits..........	620,000
Due from Other Banks.....	100,000	Time Deposits.............	60,000
Federal Reserve Stock......	7,200		
Building and Equipment....	40,000		
	$920,000		$920,000

Thus far in its operation the bank has been acquiring funds from owners and depositors, making expenditures for fixtures and meeting legal requirements. With the exception of purchasing Federal Reserve stock, which pays a 6 per cent dividend, nothing has been done that will yield an income. The institution is now ready, however, to accept loan applications or to take the initiative in purchasing investments that yield interest.

Transactions—Continued

8. *Loans to Customers.* Assume that a local merchant now wishes to purchase more inventory than he can buy with his cash resources, or more than he can acquire on open account from his trade creditors. He may approach the new bank—to which he has already transferred his deposit account—and request a six-month loan of $20,000. When the loan officer of the bank has satisfied himself that the merchant can be expected to repay the loan at maturity with interest, the borrower will be asked to make out a promissory note to the bank and the advance of funds will be made. Ordinarily, borrowed funds are not paid out immediately in the form of currency or other cash; rather, the borrower's demand deposit account is increased, and the borrower then writes checks against his account as funds are needed. The bank has acquired an earning asset by receiving the written promise of the merchant to pay the face value of the note, with interest, six months hence. This transaction is recorded and is reflected in the balance sheet of the bank in this form:

+ Loans and Discounts......$20,000   + Demand Deposits........$20,000

9. *Loan Repaid.* Six months later the merchant will "take up his note" at the bank by drawing a check for $20,600 on his deposit account in favor of the bank. The $20,000 is in repayment of the principal of the loan, and $600 is for interest at 6 per cent for six months. In return the borrower receives his canceled promissory note to file in his own records. The bank has earned $600, which will be shown on its balance sheet as an addition to the stockholders' ownership interest. The transaction requires the following entries to maintain a balance in the bank statement:

− Loans and Discounts......$20,000   − Demand Deposits........$20,600
                                      + Undivided Profits........   600

Interest received on loans and investments is usually shown on published bank statements, after it has been earned, as "undivided profit" —that is, profit the disposition of which has not yet been decided. It may later be paid out as a cash dividend or retained by being placed in an earned surplus account.

10. *Loans on a Discount Basis.* It will be noted that a bank does not make use of the term "notes receivable" when it obtains a promissory note from a borrower. Its loans are, for purposes of these illustrative transactions, however, assumed always to be made only upon receipt of such instruments.

Banks may lend on an interest or on a discount basis. The term "discount" when used in this sense means an advance to a borrower in which the interest charge is deducted at the time the transaction originates rather than when the note falls due. For example, if in transaction No. 8, above, the bank has discounted the note of the merchant, the entry on the original date (assuming that discount rate is 6 per cent) would have been:

+ Loans and Discounts.....$20,000	+ Demand Deposits........$19,400
	+ Interest Collected but Un- earned.................. 600

Although the bank "collected" interest on the date the advance was granted to the borrower, the interest was not yet earned and the undivided profit account was not built up at once. Periodically, a part of this interest is considered earned and is transferred to undivided profit. At the date of maturity of the loan, the $600 discount will all have been transferred from "interest collected but unearned" to undivided profits.

In this instance the borrower has the use of only $19,400 for six months; yet he pays $600 for its use. The actual rate of interest is somewhat higher than the nominal rate of 6 per cent [($600 ÷ $19,-400) × 2 = 6.18 per cent].

Banks are unable to lend unless there are borrowers. Generally speaking, most banks in recent years have not had adequate loan demand to absorb the available funds. In order to maintain income they have had to assume the initiative. Many banks have organized "new business" departments to seek out desirable borrowers. They have also gone into the market and purchased earning assets in the form of government and corporate bonds.

11. *Investments.* Good bank-management policies may dictate maintenance of a large bond account even when the demand for commercial and industrial loans is great. In order to diversify its assets to reduce the risks of "placing too many eggs in too few baskets," a bank may prefer to spread its advances by purchasing some assets that are unrelated to its own geographical area, and unrelated to the seasonal pattern of local industry and trade. By so doing, the bank can also space the maturities of its bondholdings so that a flow of cash from bond redemptions or repayments will correspond closely to the anticipated withdrawals of cash by local depositors.

Purchase of Government Bonds. Detailed statements of condition usually list as bank investments the bonds of United States government, municipalities, railroads, and public utilities. When the investment asset is purchased, the bank may employ cash or pay for it from a deposit held in the Federal Reserve bank or a correspondent bank. Assuming that the first alternative is used in buying bonds worth $40,000, the statement change is:

+ Bonds.................... $40,000
− Cash.................... $40,000

During World War II, banks assisted the federal government by granting deposit credit directly in exchange for government bonds. On these "war-loan accounts," as in the case of business loans, funds were not immediately paid out but a deposit account was established for the United States government. Bank-statement changes at the time bonds were acquired were:

+ United States Securities... $40,000   + United States Deposits.... $40,000

When interest is received on bonds owned by the bank, cash and earned surplus or undivided profit are increased:

+ Cash.................... $1,000   + Undivided Profits......... $1,000

Additional Transactions

12. *Letters of Credit.* The foreign department of a commercial bank assists in the movement of merchandise between nations by substituting its credit for that of a merchant whose financial position is not known in foreign circles. This is accomplished when a bank issues a commercial letter of credit and accepts drafts drawn against itself under the terms stated in the letter. The transaction shows up on both sides of the published report of the bank. An asset item called "Customer's Liability, Account Letters of Credit and Acceptances" appears on the statement; the same amount is shown as a liability, "Letters of Credit and Acceptances Outstanding." The usual pattern for the transaction is as follows:

An American importer desiring to obtain foreign goods several weeks or months before paying for them may ask his bank to forward to the foreign exporter a commercial letter of credit authorizing the foreign shipper to draw a time draft on the American bank. The bank agrees to pay drafts drawn under circumstances clearly set forth in the letter. On the date of shipment the exporter will draw on the American bank, attach the ocean bill of lading, consular invoice, insurance policy, and other documents necessary to get the cargo out of his nation and into a United States port. The draft will then be discounted or purchased by a bank in the exporter's country. The exporter has disposed of his goods and been paid. The foreign bank will then forward the time draft and attached documents to the American bank for acceptance and ultimate payment. The American importer, on his part, has agreed to reimburse the local bank before the latter is required to pay the holder of the draft at maturity. By accepting the draft, the bank has promised to meet the obligation and will insist that its domestic customer live up to his bargain by paying the bank on or before the date of maturity of the instrument. The transaction is reflected by the following entries on the published statement:

+ Customers' Liability, Account Letters of Credit and Acceptances.......$18,000

+ Letters of Credit and Acceptances Outstanding.. $18,000

If the importer's hopes are realized, he will have sold the foreign product in the time intervening between receipt of shipment and date of maturity of the draft. The bank, by permitting substitution of its well-known name, as drawee on the draft, for the name of its relatively unknown customer, has assisted in financing a short-term, self-liquidating commercial transaction. For its services the bank will collect from the local merchant a service charge of possibly one fourth of 1 per cent of the face amount of the authorization in the letter of credit. If the item on the left side of the statement ("Customers' Liability") shows a somewhat lower amount than the corresponding item on the right side (Letters of Credit," etc.), the explanation is that some customers may have taken up their obligations at the bank a day or two ahead of the date on which the acceptances are paid by the bank.

13. *Payment of Outside Checks.* When a depositor draws checks against his commercial account and forwards them to payees outside his immediate locality, the local bank loses funds. Checks are usually routed back to the drawee bank through the district Federal Reserve bank and must be paid. Since the Reserve bank acts as a depository for commercial banks, it is a simple bookkeeping operation for it to reduce the drawee bank's balance and transfer funds to the credit of payee banks in its own or other Federal Reserve districts. In any case, the transaction will be shown on the balance sheet as a reduction in demand deposits and a corresponding decrease in the asset item "Due from Federal Reserve Bank." If $130,000 in checks are drawn and sent back for collection, the changes are recorded in this manner:

− Due from Federal Reserve Bank................$130,000

− Demand Deposits.......$130,000

14. *Borrowing by the Bank.* Commercial banks are sometimes forced to borrow. They may get advances that will permit them to

grant more loans, or they may borrow to replenish dwindling reserves. The source of their funds may be other commercial banks or the district Federal Reserve bank. In either case, the funds will probably be used to swell the borrowing bank's deposit in the Federal Reserve bank and will be offset in the published statement by an increase in notes payable or rediscounts. A $50,000 transaction of this nature would change the statement as shown below:

+ Due from Federal Reserve Bank...............$50,000	+ Bills Payable and Rediscounts...............$50,000

In recent years commercial banks have usually sold government obligations to obtain funds and have remained almost entirely out of debt to Federal Reserve banks; the liability item shown above is now seldom present on published bank reports.

Various Services. The list of operations noted in connection with "department-store banking" is evidence that many other transactions might be examined and their effect upon the balance sheet explained. Among these would be certification of a personal check by either drawer or payee to assure the recipient that funds available for encashment are on deposit in the drawee bank; issuance of a cashier's check by a bank officer in exchange for a check drawn by an individual on his own balance; and crediting a depositor's account for interest received on bonds when the bank has forwarded the coupon to the issuer for collection. These and other transactions are commonplace practices of commercial banks but are subordinate to the more significant functions of accepting deposits and making loans.

Capital Account. After a period of successful operation the income received in the form of service charges on deposits, fees, and interest on loans and investments is carried from temporary accounts into "Undivided Profits" or "Earned Surplus" and shown on the balance sheet. These items are part of the bank's capital account; they represent ownership interest of holders of bank shares. During periods when bank earnings are regular and adequate in size, the board of directors of the bank votes a cash dividend. After being voted, but before being paid, dividends declared appear as a liability on the statement under the caption "Reserve for Dividend." An entirely different type of account is set up as a "Reserve for Taxes," which represents funds needed later to discharge the property and income-tax obligations of the banking corporation.

Now that the reader has an understanding of the usual items contained in the statement of condition or balance sheet of a commercial bank, he may wish to examine the accompanying statement (see Ex-

Exhibit 23

THE NORTHERN TRUST COMPANY*

Statement of Condition, June 30, 1950

RESOURCES

Loans and Discounts..........	$102,232,888.06

This is the amount loaned to customers.

U.S. Government Securities†....	266,859,176.11

This amount is invested in obligations of the United States Government, such as bonds, notes, certificates and treasury bills.

Other Bonds and Securities.....	146,776,974.45

This amount is invested in state, municipal and other high-grade bonds.

Federal Reserve Bank Stock....	510,000.00

As a member of the Federal Reserve System, we are required to own this stock of the Federal Reserve Bank of Chicago.

Bank Premises...............	1,400,000.00

This represents the book value of real estate and the main bank building used in carrying on our business.

Customers' Liability Account Letters of Credit and Acceptances..................	1,028,527.21

This is our customers' liability for drafts accepted, the payment of which is guaranteed by the bank.

Other Resources..............	150,440.00

This represents miscellaneous items, not appropriately classified above.

Cash and Due from Banks......	151,904,352.58

This represents cash held in our vaults, on deposit as our reserve at the Federal Reserve Bank, or due to us from correspondent banks.

Total......................	$670,862,358.41

* Member Federal Deposit Insurance Corporation.
† United States Government securities carried in the above statement at $22,648,351.56 are pledged to secure public and other monies, as required by law; and United States Government and other securities carried at $581,955.48 are deposited with the State Authorities under the Trust Act.

LIABILITIES

Capital Stock . . . . $ 3,000,000.00

The bank is owned by 594 stock-holders, who hold the 30,000 shares of its common stock with a par value of $100.00 per share.

Surplus 14,000,000.00

This is the amount allocated by the Directors as a surplus fund, originating in part from contributions by stockholders and in part by transfers from Undivided Profits or Reserves.

Undivided Profits 4,963,950.38

This amount represents accumulated earnings belonging to the stockholders but not yet distributed as dividends or transferred to surplus or reserves.

Reserve for Taxes, Interest, etc. .   14,914,134.45

This is the amount set aside for accrued taxes, interest not yet due and as a reserve for contingencies.

Dividend Payable July 1, 1950 . .   135,000.00

Represents dividend declared but not yet paid to stockholders.

Letters of Credit and Acceptances Outstanding 1,028,527.21

Represents the bank's liability on its guaranty of the payment of foreign or domestic drafts drawn on behalf of our customers.

Other Liabilities 295,081.74

This amount represents miscellaneous items not classified above.

Deposits:

Demand	$439,999,092.30	
Time	172,840,789.63	632,525,664.63
U.S. Government .	19,685,782.70	

Total $670,862,358.41

hibit 23) of a large metropolitan institution, viz., the Northern Trust
Company of Chicago.

SOURCES AND USES OF COMMERCIAL BANK FUNDS

A review of the transactions discussed in the foregoing section of
the chapter will serve to highlight certain significant aspects of commercial banking. These are primarily considerations of the sources
and uses of bank funds.

How Commercial Banks Obtain Funds

Funds available for the use of a bank in performing its lending
and investing functions are acquired from three sources: from the
sale of capital stock, from reinvestment of earnings, and from depositors.

SALE OF CAPITAL STOCK. Cash derived from the sale of bank
stock varies with the size of the community in which the bank operates. Federal and state law stipulates minimum capital requirements.
For example, national banks, chartered under federal statute, may
organize with capital of only $50,000 if 6,000 or fewer inhabitants
live in the town where the bank is located. In towns having between
6,000 and 50,000 residents, minimum capital is $100,000; and in
cities over 50,000, at least $200,000 is required. In each case the
stock of a national bank is sold at a premium of at least 20 per cent
to provide funds for absorbing some of the early operating costs.

REINVESTMENT OF EARNINGS. Earnings from current operations
are seldom all paid as dividends to stockholders but are often "plowed
back" and added to the undivided profits account or to surplus. In
many well-established banks such accumulations are several times as
large as the capital obtained from sale of stock. Note, for example,
the amounts shown as "Capital Stock, Surplus Fund and Undivided
Profits" of the Northern Trust Company of Chicago. Data published
by the Federal Deposit Insurance Corporation show that 13,423 operating insured commercial banks in the United States and possessions had capital accounts aggregating $10,454 million on June 30,
1949. Of this amount, $3,368 million were classified as capital,
$4,552 million as surplus, and $2,534 million as undivided profits
and reserves.[3]

---

[3] Federal Deposit Insurance Corporation, Report No. 31, *Assets and Liabilities of Operating Insured Commercial and Mutual Savings Banks, June 30, 1949.*

DEPOSITS. Deposits, however, are by far the most important source of banking funds. In individual bank balance sheets, gross deposits sometimes are from ten to twenty times as large as the so-called "capital funds" obtained from sale of stock and reinvestment of earnings. In the aggregate data cited by the Federal Deposit Insurance Corporation as of June 30, 1949, total deposits were over $135 billions, or approximately thirteen times aggregate capital accounts. Another way of stating the relationship of outside funds to owners' equity in the banking field is to say that, for every dollar controlled by bank management, only about 8 cents were contributed or owned by stockholders while the remaining 92 cents represent the claims of creditors or depositors.

Two classes of deposits are found in commercial banks: *demand* deposits and *time* deposits. Demand deposits are subject to withdrawal by check, or payable to the depositor without previous notice to the bank. All other deposits fall within the broad classification of time deposits and are not subject to transfer or withdrawal by check. A large portion of time deposits are placed in banks by wealthy individuals or business corporations. Although they may be withdrawn as needed, their velocity of turnover is very slow. They are classified as time deposits in order that owners may collect interest on them. The remaining portion of time deposits, called "savings accounts," consists of funds accumulated by individuals or nonbusiness associations and remain in the bank for relatively long periods of time. Depositors receive interest on them. They may be required to give the bank notice prior to withdrawal. Notice ranges from 30 days in some states and under the federal law, to 90 days in other states, but the provision is usually waived.

Deposits may be also classified as *primary* and *derivative*. The former arise when the bank receives cash or claims, such as checks and drafts, that enable it to collect cash. Such deposits always increase the bank's ratio of liquid reserves to deposit obligations. "Derivative deposits," on the other hand, are created when banks make loans to borrowers who leave the funds temporarily as deposits in the bank. An expansion of derivative deposits reduces the ratio of reserves to deposits. Needless to say, time or savings deposits are not created; they are not derivative.

The foregoing classification of deposits indicates that only primary deposits are a source of funds to any bank. Our discussion of the process of creating derivative demand deposits or "checkbook money" is deferred to Chapter 18.

How Commercial Banks Use Their Funds

Banks are business enterprises organized to provide an income for the shareholders. The principal income derived is in the form of interest received on investments and on direct loans to business concerns. It might be assumed that every available penny would be put to work in order to maximize profits; but we must remember that many depositors have left funds with the bank on a temporary basis and, without notice, may either call upon the bank and request cash or order the bank to transfer cash or credit to someone else. If all resources were invested, the bank would be unable to meet sudden or unexpected demands for cash. Hence, it must have cash or ready access to cash.

RESERVES. A reserve of cash or its equivalent is regarded by the individual bank as a fund that will insure its liquidity. Banking statutes of state and federal governments require the maintenance of minimum reserves against deposits, but the banker will keep a somewhat larger amount which custom and experience have shown to be necessary. Reserves are nonearning assets held in the form of cash in a bank's own vault or as deposits in other banks. Legal minimum reserves of banks that are members of the Federal Reserve System must be maintained as deposit balances in the Federal Reserve banks. Nonmembers hold the bulk of their reserves as deposits in other commercial banks, known as "correspondents."

Several factors influence a bank to increase or decrease the proportion of deposits maintained as a liquid reserve. For example, if demand deposits are converted into time or savings accounts, demand obligations will decline and a smaller liquid reserve is needed; and vice versa. If a larger number of its customers have seasonal needs for cash, the bank must increase its reserves shortly before these demands occur. If the institution has a few large depositors whose accounts exhibit erratic variation, the bank will be forced to maintain larger reserves than if it has many depositors whose deposits and withdrawals offset each other or whose withdrawals can be more accurately anticipated. Two other factors are significant. One is the liquidity of the bank's loans and investments. That is, the ease or rapidity with which its earning assets can be converted into cash or reserve balances in other banks. If a large portion of noncash assets can be converted speedily with little or no shrinkage in value, the bank can safely maintain a relatively small liquid reserve. The other factor relates to the organization of the banking system. If there is a central bank in which commercial bank reserves are mobilized, the central bank may advance funds to needy members by making direct loans or rediscounting commercial paper presented by the members. If a central bank performs a clearing and collection service, as described in the next chapter, such service enables commercial banks to operate with lower reserves than would otherwise be possible.

From time to time it is noted that proportionate reserves tend to rise or fall for the system as a whole. This is not a result of localized or isolated bank policy. It is due to widespread developments, such as a general increase or decrease in lending activity, long-continued imports or exports of gold, changes in the confidence of depositors in the banking system, or perhaps to changes in rulings or statutes governing bank policy and operation.

Some degree of conscious control over reserves is maintained by the local bank management. The foregoing paragraphs have indicated that an increase in reserves will result from the sale of assets and from borrowing or rediscounting at a central bank. Moreover, a commercial bank may request customers to pay up their loans at once and in this way add to its reserve. But there are times, as we shall see in Chapter 20, when a commercial bank's control over its reserve position is considerably reduced by the actions of central banks.

EARNING ASSETS. A second major class of bank assets is that portion of total resources through which credit is advanced for personal or business uses. Two large subgroups, to be considered in more detail later, are: (1) securities or investments and (2) loans and discounts. Some items of each of the latter groups are called "secondary reserves." Although they yield an income to the bank in the form of interest payments, the real reason for the presence of secondary reserves among bank assets is the fact that they may readily be liquidated with little or no shrinkage in value. They are a second line of defense maintained behind primary or liquid reserves for conversion into cash to meet unexpected demands for funds by depositors. Items found here include United States Treasury bills which may be sold to Federal Reserve banks at a fixed price, open-market loans payable by borrowers on demand or call, bankers' acceptances or bills of exchange for which a good market exists, other Treasury obligations that fall due within three years and are readily marketed, and items that can be used as security for a loan from a Federal Reserve bank or may be rediscounted at a Reserve bank. It is evident, also, that all securities or loans fall into this category as they approach maturity and are about to be paid.

Earning assets not included in the secondary reserve are often termed "the investment account" and, as would be supposed, consist mainly of long-term bonds of the federal or local governments, railroads, public utilities, or industrial companies and some long-term loans made to finance real estate transactions. Federal Reserve bank stock owned by members of the Federal Reserve System is also included, for it must be held as long as the bank retains membership in the System. The rate of interest earned on assets in this group tends to be higher than the rate on secondary reserves because of long-deferred maturities and consequent greater risks.

OTHER ASSETS. The few items not included among reserves and earning assets are of minor significance. Chief among them are the bank premises, furniture and fixtures, and miscellaneous operating assets. These are necessary requisites of bank operation, however, and would be liquidated only if the institution were to dissolve.

Table 1, a summary statement covering all commercial banks insured by the Federal Deposit Insurance Corporation, shows major sources and uses of commercial bank funds in dollar amounts, with each class of items stated as a percentage of total resources. This statement shows a primary reserve of almost 23 per cent of total assets; earning assets, composed of loans and discounts and securities,

TABLE 1

SUMMARY OF ASSETS AND LIABILITIES OF OPERATING INSURED COMMERCIAL BANKS, JUNE 30, 1949, UNITED STATES AND POSSESSIONS
(DATA FOR 13,423 BANKS)
(Amounts in Thousands of Dollars; Percentages of Total Assets)

Assets, Liability, or Capital Account Item	Amounts	Percentages
Assets		
Cash, balances with other banks, and cash items in process of collection—total........	33,731,946	22.8
Securities—total.........................	71,243,147	48.3
Loans and discounts, net—total.............	40,535,377	27.8
Bank premises, etc........................	1,117,896	0.7
Miscellaneous assets......................	588,001	0.4
Total Assets.........................	147,216,367	100.0
Liabilities		
Deposits:		
Total demand.........................	99,286,051	67.5
Total time...........................	36,130.301	24.5
Miscellaneous liabilities..................	1,345,851	1.0
Capital accounts—total..................	10,454,164	7.0
Total Liabilities and Capital Accounts....	147,216,367	100.0

Source: Federal Deposit Insurance Corporation, Report No. 31, p. 5.

are over 76 per cent. Holdings of securities constitute almost one half of total resources; loans and discounts are more than one fourth the total. Earning assets aggregate almost $112 billions, or 83 per cent of total deposits. The ratio of liquid reserves to total deposits is slightly less than 25 per cent. Stockholders' equity represented by the capital accounts are 7.1 per cent of total resources, and creditors' claims in the form of total deposits are over 91 per cent of total liabilities and net worth.

Exhibit 24

PERCENTAGE COMPOSITION OF ASSETS OF INSURED COMMERCIAL
BANKS DECEMBER 31, 1935, 1940, 1945, AND JUNE 30, 1949

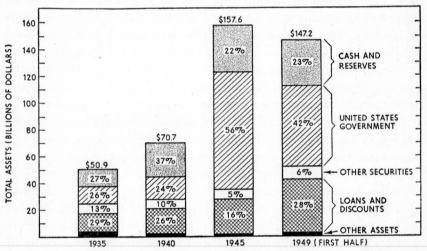

Source: Federal Deposit Insurance Corporation, Report No. 31, p. 39.

Percentage relationships change with variations in business conditions, regulations by banking authorities, decisions of bank management, and conditions imposed as the nation shifts from a peacetime into a wartime economy, or vice versa. An indication of such changes, as well as the shifts in total value of the assets of insured commercial banks, is found in Exhibit 24.

PART B: BANK CREDIT AND THE BANKING PROCESS

THE fundamental processes of commercial banking are too significant in our economy to be dismissed by a consideration of bank balance sheets alone. Published reports convey some idea of the nature of operations and the relative importance of each in quantitative terms. But the true character or qualities of commercial banking are not disclosed in a discussion of the formalized mechanics of operation. A knowledge of essential realities grows from the study and discussion of the nature of bank loans, investments, and deposits. For that reason we now devote a few pages to the amplification of these topics. Our discussion will indicate, more clearly than it has to this point, the relationship of banks to the business and economic structure as a whole.

COMMERCIAL BANK DEPOSITS

We have already noted that deposits in commercial banks result from the lodgment of cash or collection items and from the common practice of crediting a borrower's deposit account with the proceeds of his loan. The fact that an individual or business firm has placed coin or currency in a bank does not mean, however, that coin or currency is on deposit. The word "deposit" merely indicates that the depositor has an amount due him on the books of the bank. It represents the depositor's right to demand an equivalent sum of coin or currency from the bank. Until the depositor exercises his claim, the bank may use the funds left with it for any legitimate purpose—i.e., as reserve, for lending, for investing, or for safekeeping.

We have also noted that some deposits, called "time deposits" or "savings accounts," are not subject to check but may be withdrawn only after due notice has been given to the bank. In contrast, demand deposits are maintained as a working liquid balance by depositors wishing to draw checks presently and frequently in the conduct of business operations.

Payment by check, for a number of reasons, is a favorite mode of making purchases or settling debts. Checks may be drawn for a specified amount and mailed to a distant creditor without the bother of a return of "change." Checks are safer than cash because they are negotiable only by the payee. It is no more expensive to write a large than a small check, and the canceled voucher received from the bank at the month end is a legal receipt of payment. From the standpoint of the economy as a whole, checks are convenient and cheap in that they are rapidly cleared with but little use of cash; most payees prefer to have their deposit balance credited rather than to handle coin or currency.

Checks, by which deposit credit is transferred are valid only when drawn against an existing balance, and circulate only by endorsement. The great majority of checks change hands only once, but a large turnover does occur in the deposit accounts on which they are drawn. For these reasons it may be concluded that an individual check is not properly called "a medium of exchange," but the deposit account that is transferred is truly the medium. In the United States at the end of 1949, adjusted demand deposits were $85.7 billion. Total payments made with checks drawn on demand accounts for the year were approximately $1\frac{1}{5}$ trillion dollars. This was equivalent to an average turnover of demand deposits for the nation as a whole of over fourteen times a year. In 1949 the velocity of demand deposit turnover in New York City averaged 28.2, and in other leading cities 18.7. These figures are more impressive than words. American methods of doing business on a check-deposit basis convince everyone of the significance of commercial banking in our financial system.

COMMERCIAL BANK LOANS

A close relationship exists between the depositing and the lending functions of banks. Through lending and investing operations, banks put to work funds entrusted to their care. By making short-term advances, they enable borrowers to acquire funds for temporary use in business undertakings. By purchasing securities with longer-term maturity, banks supply funds that enable borrowers to gain control over equipment that has years of productive life.

Many kinds of wealth owned by individuals and business units are not in liquid form and obviously do not pass currently from hand to hand as money. Yet these may often be used as security for a bank loan that provides purchasing power in the form of deposit credit.

Economies in the use of wealth are not the only advantages growing out of the lending process. The bank distributes its advances in a discriminating manner among its customers by directing funds into the hands of producers best able to use them. In this way the use of credit definitely fosters the effective utilization of productive equipment and the maximum expansion of consumer goods.

Through the banking system, purchasing power is shifted from one user to another as a sort of revolving fund. Many loans are made to assist business concerns in meeting temporary and seasonal demands for funds. As one such loan matures and is paid off, the bank diverts the proceeds to a borrower in a different line of business whose peak season lags behind that of the prior borrower. If it were not possible for enterprises to borrow to cover irregular seasonal needs, their permanent investment would necessarily be larger or the seasonal volume of business would have to be less. As integration and inter-bank relationships are fostered within the banking system, the shift of funds from business to business and from one geographical area to another is made with a minimum of disturbance to the capital markets and to the activities of producers.

Credit Analysis

Loans and discounts are made by lending officers or by a loan committee to whom that function is delegated by the bank directorate. But before making a loan the bank attempts to obtain assurance that it will be repaid. This ordinarily means that the financial standing, worth, and character of the prospective borrower will be investigated.

In small banks, credit analysis may be the function of an individual, perhaps the president or cashier. But in large metropolitan institutions, a credit department is usually entrusted with the job. Regardless of whether analysis is by a large or a small bank, the methods used are similar and the type of information sought is fairly well standardized. In fact, most banks "spread" or enter the information provided by the applicant on forms especially designed and approved by the Bank Management Commission of the American Bankers Association. For examples of these forms see Supplement B at the end of this chapter.

All forms for use in credit analysis are similar in nature. If the applicant wishes a business loan, he must submit a balance sheet of assets and liabilities and a profit and loss statement. He is requested to declare: any contracts or commitments outstanding; the amount of insurance carried on merchandise inventory, on machinery and fixtures, and on buildings; the amount of credit insurance on notes receivable; use and occupancy insurance; and life insurance.

Additional information relative to the quality and nature of borrowers is to be listed on the last two pages of the forms approved by the American Bankers Association. These forms are designed to show the methods used in the operation of the business, with reasons for same.

From this information, and from that received from mercantile agencies such as Dun & Bradstreet, local credit bureaus, trade journals, other banks, and from personal interview with a representative of the applicant, the credit department attempts to determine the ability of the debtor to pay, based on a consideration of reputation, business competence, assets employed, and possible collateral that might be pledged.

All information gathered from the sources mentioned is placed in a file maintained in the credit department. If the applicant is granted a loan, he is required to keep the file up to date by reporting changes in assets, liabilities, sales volume, income and expenses, profits, or other information that might modify his ability to repay the loan.

The "Line of Credit"

Bank loans are usually made as the result of a direct application by the borrower, who very often is also a depositing customer of the bank. In the event that the customer wishes to borrow at intervals during the year, the bank may agree to establish a "line of credit." This is merely an expression of the bank's willingness to lend, on an unsecured basis, up to a certain amount if the customer's credit standing is maintained. After the line is established, the borrower may obtain credit to the maximum amount without further negotiation whenever funds are needed. Ordinarily, the agreement is subject to review and extension on an annual basis. When the borrower needs funds, he forwards his promissory note to the bank and receives a credit of equal amount to his deposit account. The bank may request the borrower always to maintain a certain percentage, say 20 per cent, of his line as a deposit balance. It probably will also insist that the customer agree to "clean up" or repay all loans at least once a year.

Banks also lend indirectly to nondepositing customers through the purchase of notes in the open market, commonly through the medium of commercial paper houses, which will be discussed in Chapter 5. Notes acquired in this manner are paid for by check or draft, and in this way increase individual or business deposits of the banking system, although deposits of the lending bank are not usually affected. When such "open-market paper" matures, the bank collects the face of the note and interest just as when direct loans are repaid.

Classes of Loans

Traditionally, commercial banks were supposed to make only short-term extensions of credit for the purpose of giving temporary assistance to commercial borrowers. This tradition, even in the early years of commercial banking, was probably more of an ideal than a reality. Surely today in the United States many loans are not short-term, not commercial, and not self-liquidating. The wide variety of loans may be classified for purpose of discussion on the basis of (1) purpose, (2) security, and (3) maturity. Published loan reports of federal and state banking authorities are sometimes confusing because the bases of classification are not uniform and at times appear to overlap.

The classification of loans by insured banks reporting to the Federal Deposit Insurance Corporation is shown in Table 2. The loans listed are classified primarily on the basis of purpose or the occupa-

TABLE 2

LOANS AND DISCOUNTS OF OPERATING, INSURED COMMERCIAL BANKS,
JUNE 30, 1949
(Amounts in Thousands of Dollars)

Loans and discounts, net—total	40,535,377
Commercial and industrial loans (including open-market paper)	16,295,925
Loans to farmers directly guaranteed by the Commodity Credit Corporation	532,666
Other loans to farmers (excluding loans on real estate)	2,201,037
Loans to brokers and dealers in securities	1,971,913
Other loans for the purpose of purchasing or carrying securities	900,863
Real estate loans:	
On farm land	878,476
On residential properties	8,059,651
On other properties	1,954,647
Other loans to individuals:	
Retail automobile installment paper	1,669,839
Other retail installment paper	840,999
Repair and modernization installment loans	788,039
Installment cash loans	1,140,499
Single-payment loans	2,733,004
Loans to banks:	99,151
All other loans (including overdrafts)	922,598

Source: Federal Deposit Insurance Corporation, Report No. 31, p. 10.

tion of the borrower. Some are secured; some are to be repaid in a lump sum and others in installments. Nothing definite about the maturity of any loans is indicated. The most important classes of loans in terms of dollar volume of credit advanced are commercial and industrial loans (including open-market paper), real estate loans on residential properties, single-payment loans to individuals, and loans to farmers (excluding loans on real estate). These four groups aggregate over $29 billion, or approximately 72 per cent of net total loans outstanding.

Secured Loans

In an attempt to gain protection against losses that may arise from failure of borrowers to repay loans, banks often insist, when advances are made, that title to specific assets be left in their possession. The collateral pledged may consist of stocks and bonds; merchandise or inventory covered by warehouse receipts, trust receipts, or bills of lading; mortgages on real estate or personal property; discounted notes receivable or assigned accounts receivable; life insurance; and other assets. When collateral is left with the bank, it is accompanied by a power of attorney authorizing the bank to obtain title to the security and to liquidate it if that is necessary for the protection of the bank against loss.

A survey made by the research division of the Federal Reserve System in November, 1946, revealed that almost two thirds of the number of all business loans made by members banks were either secured or endorsed. However, because loans to large companies are less often secured than are advances to moderate- or small-sized borrowers, only about 44 per cent of the dollar volume of the business loans outstanding were secured. The four types of assets most commonly pledged by borrowers in 1946 were (by percentage distribution): inventories, 20.6 per cent; stocks and bonds, 18:5 per cent; plant and other real estate, 16.3; and equipment, 12.2 per cent. In other words, the four types of assets enumerated provided security for two thirds of the secured loans to business.[4]

In addition to the safeguard for loans provided by the types of security mentioned above, commercial banks have received protection in recent years through guaranty provisions of federal laws. For example, the Federal Housing Administration (FHA) has, since 1934, insured commercial banks and other lending agencies against loss on loans made to private borrowers for the acquisition and maintenance of residential property. Other instances of federal guaranty are: loans granted for the purpose of producing munitions of war; termination loans made to aid producers operating under government contracts to revert or reconvert to their peacetime pursuits; and loans under the GI Bill of Rights to eligible veterans for use in acquiring homes, farm equipment, or other assets required to set the borrower up in business.

Term Loans

Notable among the exceptions to credit advances of short maturity traditionally made by commercial banks are "term loans," which are granted for periods running from one year to ten years. Data released by Federal Reserve authorities indicate $4,558 million outstanding

---

[4] Board of Governors of the Federal Reserve System, *Business Loans of Member Banks* (Washington, D.C., 1947), Table 16, p. 45.

through all member banks in November, 1946. This was about 34.5 per cent of all business loans of member banks.[5]

The development of these loans to finance intermediate- and long-term capital needs of business has been one of the most significant banking developments of recent years. Almost three fourths of all member banks, large and small alike, had term loans outstanding on the date the survey was made.

Term loans are said to be "tailor made" in that details of the agreement are fixed only after a careful analysis of the borrowers' financial needs and his ability to repay has been made. Their most common feature is a serial plan of installment repayment under a schedule that is arranged when the analysis has been completed. Small loans are commonly secured, often by the equipment or facilities acquired by the borrower when he spends the proceeds of the loan. Large loans are frequently unsecured. Although term advances have not been confined exclusively to small- or moderate-sized borrowers, approximately 90 per cent have been made to firms with assets below $250,-000.

Consumer Installment Loans

Another class of noncommercial loans of growing importance to commercial banks is being made by the "personal-loan department." Banks in rural communities have always made small consumer loans in considerable volume. Beginning in the late 1920's, metropolitan banks began establishing distinct departments to process personal-loan applications. The development became nation-wide during the depression of the 1930's, when declining earnings encouraged many of the banks to enter this field.

Personal loans of commercial banks are typically small, are usually repaid on an installment plan, and are made for a variety of purposes—chiefly consumption. Average maturities appear to be about twelve months, although some are known to have exceeded eighteen. Regulation W, established by the Federal Reserve Board of Governors and in effect during the years 1941–46, tended to standardize maturities of installment loans at twelve months and single payment consumption loans at ninety days. It is possible to obtain some information about loans of this type from Table 2 (above, p. 100). Five such items are shown under the title "Other loans to individuals." They are: retail automobile installment paper; other re-

---

[5] *Ibid.*, p. 12. The majority of these matured within five years and only 2 per cent ran for as long as ten years.

tail installment paper; repair and modernization loans;[6] installment cash loans; and single payment loans. The volume of consumer installment loans made by commercial banks is reported monthly and published in tables of consumer credit statistics in the *Federal Reserve Bulletin*. Growth in the totals was from $43 million outstanding December 31, 1929, to $784 million at year-end 1941. Wartime restrictions imposed through Regulation W and the system of wartime rationing and priorities caused a reduction to $316 million in 1943. Thereafter as credit stringency was relaxed, as prices increased, and as consumer goods again became available for private use, the volume expanded rapidly, reaching $956 million on December 31, 1946, and $1,951 million by the end of 1949.[7]

BANK INVESTMENTS

Attention has already been directed to the fact that the principal earning assets of banks are: (1) loans and discounts and (2) investments. These usually differ in several respects. Lending normally includes only extensions of funds to regular customers who maintain deposit balances at the bank. These customers come to the bank for loans. In its investing operations, however, the bank takes the initiative. As a lender, the bank has a personal relationship with the borrower and usually is the only creditor in the transaction. As an investor, the bank often deals as one of several creditors and does so on an impersonal basis. In a loan, the credit instrument is usually a simple promissory note; in an investment, it is more than likely a complex technical instrument in the form of a bond.

The average maturity of a loan is generally much shorter than in the case of an investment, and the purpose of the loan is usually to provide circulating or working capital rather than fixed capital. But in a more fundamental respect, investments and loans are alike. Each represents a channeling of funds into the hands of those requiring purchasing power in the conduct of their personal or business affairs. By using discrimination in making both types of advance, the banker is playing his part in maximizing the productive power of the country and elevating its standard of living.

The reasons why a commercial bank extends credit by purchasing

---

[6] Repair and modernization loans, called "FHA Title I loans," are considered later, in Chapter 15, "Urban Real Estate Finance."

[7] *Federal Reserve Bulletin*, May, 1950, p. 580. Data includes cash loans, retail automobile direct loans, and a small amount of miscellaneous retail direct loans.

bonds may be that: it desires to reduce the risks of loss by diversi-
fying its assets; it wishes to space its maturities so that the inflow of
cash will correspond to the expected withdrawals by depositors; it
wishes to have high-grade marketable securities to liquidate if its
primary reserves become inadequate; it may be forced to investment
because the demand for loans has decreased or is not sufficient to
absorb its excess reserves; and a final reason may be that in periods
of national emergency the bank wishes to aid the government in providing a market for federal securities.

None of the above reasons requires elaboration here; but any one
who examines bank statements and statistics may wonder at the
changing relative size of investments, as compared to loans, in recent
years. Among national banks in 1913, loans were about 75 per cent
of all earning assets; investments were 25 per cent. Gradually, and
almost steadily, loans declined relatively and investments grew until,
in 1939, loans were slightly over 40 per cent and investments almost
60 per cent. Moreover, during these years real estate loans, which are
similar to bond investments with respect to maturity, increased from
1.2 per cent of all loans to over 21 per cent. An examination of banking data after the end of World War II (December 31, 1945) for all
insured commercial banks shows that the trend away from loans and
toward investments was accelerated after 1939. Total loans and investments in 1945 were $121,809 million; of this total, loans were
$25,765 million, or only 21 per cent, and investments were $96,043
millions, or 79 per cent of earning assets.

In the years immediately following World War II, a reversal of
this trend set in. By the middle of 1949, total earning assets had
dropped to about $119 billion, of which loans were more than 36 per
cent and investments approximately 64 per cent. The shift from investments to loans as related to total bank assets may be observed in Exhibit 24 on page 95, above. From 1940 to 1945 loans decreased
from 26 per cent to 16 per cent, while investments were rising from 34
per cent to 61 per cent of total assets. During this period, loans were
increasing slightly in absolute amounts, but banks were being flooded
with government securities. The tide turned after the war; and between December 31, 1945, and June 30, 1949, loans increased from
16 per cent to 28 per cent of total assets, while securities dropped to
48 per cent.

The postwar reversal may or may not be temporary. Nevertheless,
the reasons why loans of commercial banks grew relatively less important in the thirty years preceding World War II are of great

importance. The sensational shift in the positions occupied by bonds and loans in the earning-asset portfolio of banks is based upon several factors. One factor seems to be the growth of time deposits. Bankers have long held the belief that the structure of their deposit accounts should be a partial determinant of the structure of their assets. Therefore, an increase in the volume percentage of savings deposits, having a slow velocity of turnover, dictated an increase in the volume and percentage of assets the banker could tie up in long-term investments.

Another factor was the expanded volume of government bonds purchased by commercial banks in financing World War I. The same thing occurred in an exaggerated fashion again in 1940–45. Meantime, in the period 1921–29, although loans and investments both expanded absolutely, the relative growth of bank-held investments was much greater. Funds for corporate needs were cheaply obtained by the issuance of securities during this period when public interest in the stock and bond markets was of growing intensity. As crisis and depression struck our economy during the 1930's, the demand for loans practically disappeared. Increased expenditure by the government in its effort to prime the business pump and reduce the ravages of depression contributed to the growth of excess reserves. After devaluation of the dollar in 1934, large imports of gold added to the volume of loanable funds and were instrumental in driving interest rates to lower and lower levels. In such circumstances the interest income of financial institutions declined. Banks acquired a large volume of investment securities to buttress earnings.

The failure of bank loans to expand, as might have been expected, during World War II was due to the program of direct financing of military requirements adopted by the government. Advances to industries providing military equipment and supplies came through governmental agencies such as the Reconstruction Finance Corporation, Smaller War Plant Corporation, and others, rather than through commercial banks. But the volume of federal securities acquired by banks far exceeded any movement of this sort ever seen in the nation before. From the end of 1941 to December 31, 1945, total assets of all banks in the United States and possessions increased from $91 billion to $178 billion; more than 88 per cent of this rise was accounted for by increased bank holdings of federal debt. The expansion was from $25 billion, on December 31, 1941, to $102 billion four years later.[8]

[8] *Annual Report of the Federal Deposit Insurance Corporation for the Year Ended December 31, 1945*, Table 18, p. 40.

Government spending and lending declined immediately after 1945, while private enterprise expanded. The postwar boom created excessive demands for business and consumer loans that continued into the third quarter of 1950. And the position of loans and investments in bank portfolios tended to reverse itself. The outbreak of armed conflict in Korea in the summer of 1950 hastened this movement; but in view of the imposition of wartime controls and restrictions and the increased volume of federal securities issued thereafter, it is not unlikely that the trend of the years 1915–45 will reassert itself.

EARNINGS OF COMMERCIAL BANKS

Current operating earnings received by insured commercial banks in 1949 were $3,607 million. Interest and discount on loans was $1,734 million, or 48 per cent of the total. Income on government obligations was $1,014 million; and from other securities, $202 million. Income on securities was thus about one third of the total earnings. The average rate of yield on loans was 4.2 per cent and on securities was 1.68 per cent for the year. Earnings from other sources, including $194 million in service charges on deposit accounts and $160 million for trust services, comprised less than 10 per cent of earnings for the year.[9]

INTEREST RATES ON LOANS

The income received by banks from loans has a double significance. Not only is it one of the largest sources of revenue out of which current operating expenses of banks are paid; but when viewed from another angle, it is the amount paid for the use of commercial bank loan credit.

The classification of loans noted earlier has reflected the fact that bank income on loans and discounts is received from thousands of borrowers using bank credit for many purposes. Rates paid are often different for various classes of loans and are often not the same to separate borrowers on identical types of grants. Variations are commonly due to differences in the elements of risk, time, and size. Relatively low rates are charged when the risk of loss is low,

---

[9] *Annual Report of the Federal Deposit Insurance Corporation for the Year Ended December 31, 1949*, pp. 41–42, and Table 111, "Earnings, Expenses, and Dividends of Insured Commercial Banks, 1941–1949," p. 160.

when the loan is for a very short time, and when the loan is for a large amount. Short-loan rates are low because the maturity date will fall in the near-term or "foreseeable" future and the entrance of unexpected risk factors is, therefore, at a minimum. Rates on large loans may be low because the character of the borrower is unquestioned and the costs of making a credit survey and administering the loan are relatively less than for a smaller borrower on whom adequate data may not be readily available.

Rates also vary from one geographical area to another at the same time and on the same classes of paper. In southern and western cities

TABLE 3

OPEN-MARKET MONEY RATES IN NEW YORK

(Per Cent per Annum)

YEAR, MONTH, OR WEEK	PRIME COMMERCIAL PAPER, (4- TO 6-MONTH)	PRIME BANKERS' ACCEPTANCES (90-DAYS)*	STOCK EXCHANGE CALL-LOAN RENEWALS†	U.S. GOVERNMENT SECURITY YIELDS		
				3-Month Bills‡	9- to 12-Month Certificates of Indebtedness	3- to 5-Year Taxable Issues
1947 average....	1.03	0.87	1.38	0.604	0.88	1.32
1948 average....	1.44	1.11	1.55	1.043	1.14	1.62
1949 average....	1.48	1.12	1.63	1.104	1.14	1.43
1950 January....	1.31	1.06	1.63	1.100	1.12	1.39
February...	1.31	1.06	1.63	1.130	1.15	1.44
March.....	1.31	1.06	1.63	1.140	1.16	1.45
April......	1.31	1.06	1.63	1.164	1.17	1.45

* Monthly figures are averages of weekly prevailing rates.
† The average rate on 90-day Stock Exchange time loans was 1.50 per cent, August 2, 1946–August 16, 1948; and 1.63 per cent beginning August 17, 1948.
‡ Rate on new issues offered within period.
Source: *Federal Reserve Bulletin*, May, 1950, p. 554.

of the United States, interest charges are higher than in northern and eastern cities; lower rates prevail in New York City than elsewhere. Discrepancies are apparently due to the drift of idle funds from rural area of the South and West to centers of financial activity where the large supply of loanable funds in commercial banks tends to depress interest rates.

Several of the factors influencing rates are noticeable in Tables 3 and 4, which have been adapted from tables published monthly in the *Federal Reserve Bulletin*. For example, in Table 3 rates on commercial paper maturing in four to six months are slightly higher than on bankers' acceptances, which may be slightly less risky and are of shorter maturity. Also, the rate on three-month government bills is lower than on bankers' acceptances of the same maturity. The difference may be attributed to a slight difference in risk. In Table 4 it can

TABLE 4

BANK RATES ON BUSINESS LOANS: AVERAGE OF RATES CHARGED ON SHORT-TERM LOANS
TO BUSINESSES BY BANKS IN SELECTED CITIES
(Per Cent per Annum)

AREA AND PERIOD	ALL LOANS	SIZE OF LOAN			
		$1,000–$10,000	$10,000–$100,000	$100,000–$200,000	$200,000 and Over
Annual averages:					
19 cities:					
1947	2.1	4.2	3.1	2.5	1.8
1948	2.5	4.4	3.5	2.8	2.2
1949	2.7	4.6	3.7	3.0	2.4
Quarterly:					
19 cities:					
1949—June	2.74	4.63	3.70	3.04	2.44
September	2.63	4.62	3.64	2.98	2.31
December	2.65	4.53	3.61	2.98	2.35
1950—March	2.00	4.45	3.54	2.94	2.31
New York City:					
1949—June	2.35	4.22	3.43	2.78	2.17
September	2.32	4.23	3.41	2.74	2.13
December	2.38	4.14	3.35	2.73	2.21
1950—March	2.29	3.85	3.22	2.64	2.13
7 northern and eastern cities:					
1949—June	2.86	4.67	3.64	2.98	2.66
September	2.64	4.71	3.63	2.93	2.39
December	2.67	4.63	3.65	3.00	2.41
1950—March	2.55	4.04	3.60	2.91	2.28
11 southern and western cities:					
1949—June	3.17	4.80	3.89	3.26	2.69
September	3.07	4.74	3.79	3.18	2.58
December	3.03	4.66	3.74	3.12	2.56
1950—March	3.12	4.64	3.71	3.15	2.74

Source: *Federal Reserve Bulletin*, May, 1950, p. 554.

be seen that rates fall as the size of loans increases. In December, 1949, an average rate of 4.53 per cent was charged on loans in the $1,000–$10,000 classification. At the same time, 2.35 per cent was charged on large loans of $200,000 and over. Moreover, the New York City rate on loans of $10,000 or less was 4.14 per cent, but the average in seven northeastern and eastern cities was 4.63 per cent and in eleven southern and western cities was 4.66. It is also evident in Table 4 that the differential grows between New York City rates and those of the South and West as the size of loans increases.

Interest charges on term loans by banks are usually on a flat annual rate, although sometimes they are graduated for long-term, large-sized advances. If this is done, low rates are placed on the shorter installments. In 1946, term-loan rates ranged from 2.0 per cent per annum on amounts of $1 million and over to 9.1 per cent on amounts less than $500. An average rate of 6 per cent prevailed on loans between $1,000 and $5,000; the average rate on all term loans covered in the survey by Federal Reserve authorities was 2.8 per cent per annum.[10]

Some loans payable in monthly installments over a period of fifteen to thirty months may properly be classed as term loans and also as personal-consumption loans. Rates on these are usually quoted at 5 or 6 per cent on an annual basis but may be accompanied

TABLE 5
AVERAGE INTEREST RATES OF BUSINESS LOANS OF MEMBER
BANKS, NOVEMBER 20, 1946, BY PRINCIPAL TYPES
OF SECURITY
(Estimates of Outstanding Loans)

Type of Security	Per Cent
Unsecured.	2.5
Secured:	
Endorsed and co-maker.	3.7
Inventories.	3.1
Equipment.	4.4
Plant and other real estate.	4.3
Stocks and bonds.	2.7
Accounts receivable.	4.5
Life insurance.	3.4
Government participation or guarantee.	4.0

Source: Board of Governors of the Federal Reserve System, *Business Loans of Member Banks*, (Washington, D.C., 1947), Table 7, p. 38.

by an investigation charge that brings the actual rate up to 10 per cent or more. Assessment of such fees is becoming less common than formerly, and quoted rates are often the actual charge.

Usually interest rates charged on unsecured loans are less than on secured advances. This may appear strange because the security is designed to reduce risk of loss to the bank. The principal explanation is that only borrowers of the highest credit standing are able to borrow without security. It should be noted, also, that secured loans are relatively small, that they are made to small borrowers, and that handling collateral introduces elements of cost that are passed on to the borrower in the form of higher interest charges.

Rates on secured business loans bear less relation to the nature of the security, or type of collateral, than to size of borrower and size of the loan. Almost without exception, rates are lower on large loans

[10] Board of Governors of the Federal Reserve System, *Business Loans of Member Banks* (Washington, D.C., 1947), pp. 22–23.

to large borrowers than on small loans to small borrowers. Average rates on secured loans held by member banks in November, 1946, are shown in Table 5 (p. 109).

YIELDS ON INVESTMENT SECURITIES

It was mentioned that in 1949 the average rate received by banks on loans and discounts was 4.2 per cent and on securities was 1.68 per cent. The differential is so great that, when an opportunity to make direct loans arises, banks are inclined to liquidate low-yield securities in order to expand loans. The shift from bonds into loans in the years following World War II put the market under pressure and had its effect in reducing bond prices.

Average rates on short-term obligations of the federal government have ranged from 0.375 per cent per year on three-month bills in 1946 to 1.104 per cent in 1949. Yields on taxable United States seven- to nine-year bonds ranged upward from 1.45 per cent in 1946 to 2.00 per cent in 1948 but fell back to 1.71 per cent in 1949. On longer-term bonds with maturities of fifteen years or more, yields on governments averaged 2.19 per cent in 1946, 2.44 per cent in 1948, and 2.31 per cent in 1949. High-grade municipal bonds were quoted to yield 1.64 per cent on the average in 1946, 2.40 per cent in 1948, and 2.21 per cent in 1949. The pattern of interest rates on corporate bonds of high quality has followed that of the federal government and municipal issues since World War II but on a slightly higher plane. In 1946, rates averaged 2.74 per cent, rose to 2.81 per cent in 1948, and eased back to 2.65 per cent in 1949. Bonds of somewhat lower quality, yet still eligible for investment by commercial banks, averaged higher yields, but variations in rates were similar to those already described. Rates on all investments in 1950 were slightly higher than at year-end, 1949.[11]

The variety of bonds eligible for ownership by banks, and the differential in their yields, places a distinct burden of management upon bankers. The bank desires to earn all it can, commensurate with safety to its creditors and soundness for society. But it may not put all investment funds into long-term obligations having relatively high yields. It is forced to space its maturities so that funds from maturing issues flow into the bank to meet drains imposed by depositors and the payment of taxes and cash dividends.

---

[11] Data from *Federal Reserve Bulletin*, December, 1949, p. 1478; May, 1950, p. 554; and November, 1950, p. 1506.

In addition, security holdings must be diversified to reduce the risk of loss. It would be indiscreet—not to say unlawful—for a bank to purchase bonds of only one company, or of companies in the same industry, in the same geographical area, or with the same maturity date. Diversification on all these bases must be observed if a balanced portfolio of investments is to be maintained and the success of the bank is to be complete.

—FRANK H. GANE

SUPPLEMENT A

THE ACCOUNTING EQUATION

Although the nature of the operations of any business may be described in words common to all forms of descriptive writing, a more effective approach utilizes the descriptive and specialized terms of the accountant. Accounting provides a record of business transactions in financial terms. It makes use of a careful and systematic recording of all assets and liabilities and of the changes that take place in the volume and value of each.

Large business units require a complex system of record keeping and accounting; but no less significant is the simple set of books, or even the vest-pocket notes, kept by almost every individual, whether business proprietor or merely an employee.

Each of us has the ever-recurring desire to know just where we stand financially. We make a list of our assets, including items of value we now possess plus whatever is owed to us by others. But from total value thus obtained we deduct the sum of our debts to others. The resulting figure shows our net worth or the excess value of assets over liabilities.

To illustrate: Assume that a grade-school boy asks his father: "Daddy, just what are we worth?" The parent may begin to make a list of valuable items, at the top of which he places *residence* valued at $22,000 but with only $16,000 paid, the balance due on a mortgage note. Then he lists *household* goods, all clear of debt, $3,400. Next the new *automobile*, cost $2,100 but with six monthly installments of $80 each remaining to be paid. The father lists his *deposit* in the local bank, $380; an *insurance* policy having a cash surrender value of $950; five shares of *corporate stock* quoted at $70 per share; and some *government savings bonds* now worth $840. He estimates personal property in the form of family clothing, watches, jewelry, silverware, canned and frozen foods, and a few miscellaneous items as worth $400. A business acquaintance owes him $100. But he owes the public service company, the drugstore, two department stores, and a local hardware dealer a total of $170.

For convenience the assets are grouped together and their total value recorded. Liabilities or debts are grouped separately, and their value summarized. The resulting two columns appear in the form shown in Table 6. It is apparent, even to the son, that the real worth of this family is the difference between $30,520 and $6,650, or $23,870.

An accountant, or a bookkeeper, would insert an item called "Net worth, $23,870" below the notes payable figure on the liability side of the statement so the two sides of the account would equalize. Such a report of assets and liabilities would then be called a "balance sheet."

In a similar manner, business units, including banks and other financial institutions, evaluate all their possessions, and all claims against them, to determine the extent of ownership interest or the net worth of the business concern.

The fundamental balance sheet equation is: *Assets = Liabilities + Net worth* or *proprietorship*. It shows the equality of balance between property and rights to property and the claims of creditors against the property. It may be stated in the account form shown in Table 6 or in report form in which liabilities are subtracted from assets to give the residual net worth. Any item may be transposed, as in any algebraic equation; for example, *Assets − Liabilities = Net worth.*

TABLE 6

Assets		Liabilities	
Residence	$22,000	Mortgage note payable	$6,000
Household goods	3,400	Due on car	480
Automobile	2,100	Accounts payable (total)	170
Bank deposit	380		
Insurance policy	950		
Corporation stock	350		
Savings bonds	840		
Personal property	400		
Note receivable	100		
Total Assets	$30,520	Total Liabilities	$6,650

The reader will recognize that a balance sheet presents the condition of a business as of a given moment in its history. But the condition of the institution changes from moment to moment as business is carried on. The first summary will soon not reflect the current condition, and a second summary statement will be required to give a true picture of the new position. The second summary could be obtained in the same manner as the first—by listing and evaluating all possessions, debts, and the owner's claims. This is a costly process, in practice, and not too satisfactory even in theory. A better way to keep a reasonable record of the changing condition of the firm is to record transactions as they occur.

Each individual or business firm must select a method, or establish a system, for recording transactions. The details of the method selected are of no significance here, but we do wish to demonstrate a simple and convenient method to show how each transaction finds reflection in balance sheet changes. In an arithmetic illustration the data growing out of each transaction is shown on what is called an accounting "T-form." The "T" represents the business concern.

Value of things owned (*Assets*)	Value of things owed (*Liabilities*) Net ownership interest (*Net Worth*)

On this "T," the possessions owned by the firm are recorded under the left arm, and the debts and owners' claim are recorded at the right. In a commercial bank the items for which values will be found are indicated below:

(Owns)	BANK	(Owes)
Cash on hand...........$1,000	Deposits...............$5,200
Loans.................. 2,000	Owners' claim or net worth 1,325
Investments............ 3,000	
Building............... 500	
Miscellaneous.......... 25	
$6,525	$6,525

As daily operations are performed, the values recorded above change. Some transactions have no effect upon the totals because they are merely a trade of one asset for another or an exchange of one liability for another (transactions Nos. 1 and 2, below, are of this type). In other cases, the aggregate figures are increased or reduced. Additions are indicated with a plus sign ($+$) and subtractions by a minus sign ($-$). Examples follow:

1. The bank spends cash to acquire equipment such as filing cases.

+ Equipment	
− Cash	

2. A depositor purchases stock in the bank and pays for it by writing a check on the bank. The depositor reduces his claim as a creditor and transfers it into a claim of ownership.

	+ Capital
	− Deposits

3. A customer brings currency to the bank for deposit.

+ Cash	+ Deposits

4. Stockholders are paid a cash dividend out of earnings that have accumulated in the bank. This reduces the amount of claims of owners against the bank.

− Cash	− Surplus

Since the two sides of the balance sheet must equalize, it can be observed that only four general types of transaction occur. They balance out in the manner shown in Table 7.

TABLE 7

Assets	*Liabilities and Net Worth*
Plus	Plus
Minus	Minus
Plus Minus	
	Plus Minus

By keeping an accurate record of daily transactions as they occur, it becomes a relatively simple matter to add or subtract values from the proper accounts to arrive at a current statement of assets, liabilities, and net worth.

SUPPLEMENT B

FORMS FOR USE IN CREDIT ANALYSIS DESIGNED AND APPROVED BY THE BANK MANAGEMENT COMMISSION OF THE AMERICAN BANKERS ASSOCIATION

Revised Form No. 3—CORPORATION—Revised, 10-27.

FORM DESIGNED AND APPROVED BY THE CLEARINGHOUSE SECTION, AMERICAN BANKERS ASSOCIATION.

FINANCIAL STATEMENT

CORPORATE NAME..

BUSINESS... ADDRESS..

STATEMENT FOR...

CONDITION AT CLOSE OF BUSINESS.., 19.......... .

ASSETS	LIABILITIES
Cash—On Hand, $..............; In Bank, $................; $	Notes payable for merchandise.................$
Notes receivable of customers—Due within 90 days..	Trade acceptances—Payable....................
Notes receivable of customers—Due beyond 90 days..	Notes payable to banks.......................
Trade acceptances of customers...................	Bankers acceptances—Made for our account......
Accounts receivable of customers—Not due.......	Notes payable for paper sold..................
Accounts receivable of customers—Past due......	Notes and accounts payable to officers, directors and stockholders..................................
Mdse.—Finished (How valued................).....	Notes payable to others......................
Mdse.—In process (How valued ....)...	Accounts payable—Not due....................
Mdse.—Raw (How valued.................).........	Accounts payable—Past due...................
U. S. Government obligations...................	Deposits of money with this company...........
Other quick assets (itemize on page 3)..........	Provision for Federal taxes....................
	Accrued interest, other taxes, etc...............
Total Quick Assets....................$	Chattel mortgages..........................
Due from controlled or subsidiary concerns:	Portion of funded debt maturing................
For merchandise.......................	Any other quick liabilities (itemize on page 4).....
For advances........................	Total Quick Liabilities.................$
Stocks, bonds and investments (itemize on page 3)..	Mortgages or liens on real estate................$
Land...............	Bonded debt.............................
Buildings............ See per contra	Any other liabilities (itemize)..... ; ....
Machinery, equipment for depreciation	Reserves (itemize).........................
and fixtures...... reserve	Capital Stock—Preferred outstanding...........
Notes and accounts receivable—Due from officers, stockholders and employees.	Capital Stock—Common outstanding (Par value, $.................)...
Goodwill, patents and trade marks..............	Capital Stock—Common (no par value)..........
Prepaid expenses......................	Number of shares...........
Other assets (itemize)......................	Undivided profits (see below)...................
Total....................$	Total....................$

CONTINGENT LIABILITIES—Upon trade acceptances and/or notes receivable discounted or sold....... ....Upon trade acceptances and/or notes receivable assigned or pledged............. ....Upon customers' accounts sold, assigned or pledged ....Upon accommodation paper or endorsements or upon notes exchanged with others. ....As guarantor for others on notes, accounts or contracts...................For bonds or unfinished contracts....................Any other contingent liability..........

TOTAL CONTINGENT LIABILITIES...................

RECONCILEMENT OF SURPLUS

Surplus and undivided profits at close of previous fiscal year...............			$			
Items not applicable to current year, viz.:...........................$						
Net addition or deduction...........................			$			
Balance..... (						
Net profit or loss as per statement following..........................					$	
Less dividends { Preferred (.......... per cent.)..			$			
{ Common (.......... per cent.).......................						
Undivided Surplus (see above)...........					$	

Names of all banks and brokers where accounts are maintained. State credit line as well as amount owed to each on date of statement.

....

....

FOR SALE BY M. B. BROWN PRINTING & BINDING CO.
NEW YORK, N. Y.

CONDENSED INCOME OR PROFIT AND LOSS STATEMENT FOR THE PERIOD BEGINNING...................19......AND ENDING.................19........

GROSS SALES...$........
    Less: Returns and allowances...............$.................Other $.................$........

NET SALES...$........
Cost of goods sold..$........
    Total inventories at beginning of period..$........
    Add: Purchases..$........

For   Direct labor...$........
Manufacturers Depreciation..$........
Only   Other factory overhead..$........

        Total..$........
    Deduct: Total inventories at close of period..$........

GROSS PROFIT..$........
Selling expenses..$........
General and administrative expenses...$........

OPERATING PROFIT...$........
Add: Other income from investments...................$........
    Discounts..........$................Other $........
Deduct: Interest........$...............Discount $..............Other $..............$........

NET PROFIT OR LOSS...$........

    Provision for Federal taxes for current period..$........
    Or: Federal taxes actually paid during current period............................$........

NET TO SURPLUS...$........

    State total amounts included in above figures for—
    Salaries, commissions and bonuses paid to officers and directors...........$........
    Depreciation..$........
    Reserve or charge-off for bad accounts or notes...............................$........
    Advertising..$........

COMMITMENTS—State outstanding contracts for construction or for purchase of materials or otherwise: ....
....
....

Are any of your assets pledged or assigned?...If so, state amount, $..............
Chattel mortgages payable. When due?..
R. E. mortgages payable. When due?..
Bonds payable. When due?..
    Sinking fund requirements?..
    Amount to be retired during coming fiscal year?..

INSURANCE—Fire insurance carried: On merchandise, $....................; on machinery, equipment and fixtures, $..............
on buildings, $.................... Is the insurance carried by Old Line or by Mutual Companies?................... Liability ins., $..............
Credit insurance on notes and accounts receivable, $................. Use and occupancy insurance, $................ Life ins. carried, $..............
On what officers?.. Is there a disability clause?..............

OFFICERS (Name in Full)	Number of Shares Held		Residence Address
	Preferred	Common	
President, ...			
Vice-President, ...			
Secretary, ...			
Treasurer, ...			
Name officers who are authorized to sign notes of the corporation...........			

(Form of declaration or contract)

For the purpose of procuring and maintaining credit from time to time in any form whatsoever with the above named bank for claims and demands against the undersigned, the undersigned submits the above which is guaranteed to be a true and accurate statement of..............financial condition on the date of signing hereof; and agree—that if any change occurs that materially reduces the means or ability of the undersigned to pay all claims or demands against..................or materially weakens the financial condition as shown in this statement, the undersigned will at once notify the bank of such change whether application for further credit is made or not. In the absence of such notice it is expressly agreed that the bank in granting or continuing credit may continue to rely on this statement as a true and accurate statement of the financial condition of the undersigned to have the same force and effect as if delivered as an original statement of financial condition at the time additional credit is requested or existing credit continued unless another statement in writing shall be substituted for this or this statement is recalled.

CORPORATE NAME ....

Date signed............................., 19..........   By ....
                                                  (Officer's title must be given)

ADDITIONAL INFORMATION RELATIVE TO STATEMENT DATED...

Details Relative to Assets.
(Fill in Replies to All Details Following, Using the Words "Yes," "No" or "None" When They Apply)

NOTES RECEIVABLE OF CUSTOMERS—What amount does not represent mdse. sales?...

Amount that is probably uncollectible...Amount past due?..

ACCOUNTS RECEIVABLE OF CUSTOMERS—What amount does not represent mdse. sales?..

Amount that is probably uncollectible?..What are your usual terms of sales?....................................

Give names of concerns to which you sell in large quantities..

....

....

MERCHANDISE—Average amount carried?............................Last inventory taken by whom?.........................Date?.....................

Amount included in your assets for which the invoices have not yet been entered as liabilities?.........................Amount pledged?................

Amount in outside warehouses?.....................Held under trust receipt?.................Under consignment?.................Terms of sale?...........

OTHER QUICK ASSETS—Itemize..

....

....

DUE FROM CONTROLLED OR SUBSIDIARY CONCERNS:

Name of Concern	Location	For Advances	When Due	For Merchandise	Terms
		$		$	
		$		$	
		$		$	

STOCKS, BONDS AND INVESTMENTS—Give description and values.

....

....

....

LAND AND BUILDINGS:

Description and Location	Title in Whose Name	Assessed Value	Appraised Value	Mortgages	Name of Mortgagees	Insurance

If book value has decreased or increased during the year, account for same..

....

MACHINERY, EQUIPMENT AND FIXTURES—Assessed value $.......................What amount has been charged to depreciation during

the last year on this item?.....................What amount is owing for machinery, equipment, etc.?.................................

NOTES AND ACCOUNTS RECEIVABLE DUE FROM OFFICERS, STOCKHOLDERS AND EMPLOYEES:

Name	Amount	Date	Date Due	Is It Secured?	How?	Represents What?

DETAILS RELATIVE TO LIABILITIES

NOTES PAYABLE

State maximum amount borrowed from all sources at any one time during fiscal year $ .... Date ....

State minimum amount borrowed from all sources at any one time during fiscal year $ .... Date ....

Do your branches or subsidiary concerns borrow locally? .... Where? ....

....

Are any of your notes endorsed or guaranteed? .... By whom? ....

State net worth of each endorser—outside of interest in this business ....

Amount of your notes payable secured by collateral $ .... Describe the collateral ....

ACCOUNTS PAYABLE—What are your average terms of purchase? ....

.... Do you discount? ....

Give names and addresses of concerns from which you buy:

Name	Street Address	City and State

DEPOSITS OF MONEY WITH THIS COMPANY—By whom? ....

On time or demand? .... Amount secured by collateral $ ....

OTHER QUICK LIABILITIES—Itemize ....

....

BONDED DEBT—Interest rate? .... On what assets a lien? ....

Amount authorized $ .... Amount issued $ .... Who is trustee? ....

Chattel mortgages—to whom? .... On what assets a lien? ....

LEASES—Duration? .... Rental per annum $ ....

Location of property ....

MISCELLANEOUS

CORPORATION ORGANIZED—When? .... Under laws of what state? ....

CAPITAL—How paid in? .... Cash $ .... Other property and how valued? ....

Preferred authorized $ .... Par value? .... Common authorized ....

Par value .... Are preferred stock dividends cumulative? .... Dividend rate? ....

Present unpaid accumulation $ ....

Time of year receivables generally maximum .... Minimum ....

Time of year merchandise generally maximum .... Minimum ....

State net sales for the past three years .... , 19 ... $ .... , 19 ... $ .... , 19 ... $ ....

Where is your principal sales territory? ....

If your books have been audited by a certified public accountant, give name of accountant and date of audit ....

Are there any judgments unsatisfied or suits pending against your corporation, and for what amount? ....

Give date you regularly take inventory and close your books ....

For what years have your Federal Income Tax returns been subjected to field audit examination? ....

....

(Form of Declaration or Contract)

For the purpose of procuring and maintaining credit from time to time in any form whatsoever with the above named bank for claims and demands against the undersigned, the undersigned submits the above which is guaranteed to be a true and accurate statement of .... financial condition on the date of signing hereof; and agree—that if any change occurs that materially reduces the means or ability of the under-signed to pay all claims or demands against .... or materially weakens the financial condition as shown in this statement, the undersigned will at once notify the bank of such change whether application for further credit is made or not. In the absence of such notice it is expressly agreed that the bank in granting or continuing credit may continue to rely on this statement as a true and accurate statement of the financial condition of the undersigned to have the same force and effect as if delivered as an original statement of financial condition at the time additional credit is requested or existing credit continued unless another statement in writing shall be substituted for this or this statement is recalled.

CORPORATE NAME ....

By ....

(Officer's title must be given)

Date signed ....

Revised Form No. 2—INDIVIDUAL—Manufacturing or Mercantile.   9-36

FINANCIAL STATEMENT

NAME..

BUSINESS...ADDRESS...

STATEMENT FOR..

CONDITION AT CLOSE OF BUSINESS...,19...........

ASSETS				LIABILITIES			
Cash—On Hand, $..................; In Bank, $............$				Notes payable for merchandise...................$			$........
Notes receivable of customers—Due within 90 days..				Trade acceptances—Payable.......................			
Notes receivable of customers—Due beyond 90 days..				Notes payable to banks..........................			
Trade acceptances of customers....................				Bankers acceptances—Made for my account.......			
Accounts receivable of customers—Not due.......				Notes payable for paper sold.....................			
Accounts receivable of customers—Past due.......				Notes payable to others.........................			
Mdse.—Finished (How valued..................).....				Accounts payable—Not due.......................			
Mdse.—In process (How valued..................).....				Accounts payable—Past due.......................			
Mdse.—Raw (How valued..................)...........				Deposits of money with me.......................			
U. S. Government obligations.....................				Provision for Federal taxes......................			
Other quick assets (itemize)....................				Accrued interest, other taxes, etc.................			
				Chattel mortgages.............................			
				Other quick liabilities (itemize).................			
Total Quick Assets......................$				Total Quick Liabilities...................$			
Due from controlled or subsidiary concerns:				Mortgages or liens on real estate............... $			
For merchandise...........................$				Other liabilities (itemize)......................			
For advances......................							
Stocks, bonds and investments (itemize on separate sheet)..							
Land...............				Reserves (itemize).............................			
Buildings............} See per contra reserve for							
Machinery, equipment depreciation and fixtures......}							
Goodwill, patents and trade marks................							
Prepaid expenses........................							
Other assets (itemize).....................				Net worth (see below).........................			
Total.......................$				Total.......................$			

CONTINGENT LIABILITIES—Upon trade acceptances and/or notes receivable discounted or sold...................Upon trade acceptances and/or notes receivable assigned or pledged....................Upon customers' accounts sold, assigned or pledged....................Upon accommodation paper or endorsements or upon notes exchanged with others....................As guarantor for others on notes, accounts or contracts....................For bonds or unfinished contracts....................Any other contingent liability....................

TOTAL CONTINGENT LIABILITIES...........$.......................

RECONCILEMENT OF NET WORTH

Net worth at close of previous fiscal year...........						$	
Items not applicable to current year, viz:...........				$....................			
				....			
				....			
Net addition or deduction........................				....	$....................		
Balance....................				....			
Net profit or loss as per statement following.........				....		$	
Less withdrawals (other than salary)...............				....			
Net worth (see above)...........................							

Names of all banks and brokers where accounts are maintained.   State credit line with each and amount owing each on statement date.

....

....

....

CONDENSED INCOME OR PROFIT AND LOSS STATEMENT FOR THE PERIOD BEGINNING................19......AND ENDING.............19......

GROSS SALES.......
    Less: Returns and allowances............$..............Other $..............

NET SALES........
Cost of goods sold:
    Total inventories at beginning of period.............$
    Add: Purchases........$

For   { Direct labor........$
Manufacturers Depreciation........$
Only   Other factory overhead........$

        Total.......$
    Deduct: Total inventories at close of period.......$

GROSS PROFIT........$
Selling expenses........$
General and administrative expenses.......$

OPERATING PROFIT........$
Add: Other income from investments............$
         Discounts..........$............Other $............
Deduct: Interest......$............Discount $............ Other $............

NET PROFIT OR LOSS........$
    Provision for Federal taxes for current period............$
    Or: Federal taxes actually paid during current period............$

NET TO SURPLUS........$
    State total amounts included in above figures for—
      Salaries, commission and bonuses withdrawn............$
      Depreciation........$
      Reserve or charge-off for bad accounts or notes........$
      Advertising........$

COMMITMENTS—State outstanding contracts for construction or for purchase of materials:
....
....

Are any of your assets pledged or assigned?.....................................If so, state amount, $..........
Chattel Mortgages payable. When due?...
R. E. mortgages payable. When due?...
Are you a partner in any firm?..
Is there any other person interested in your business either as special or limited partner?................
Have you any individual assets not included in this statement?..
Have you any individual debts not included in this statement?...

INSURANCE. Fire insurance carried: On merchandise, $..............; on machinery, equipment and fixtures, $..............
on buildings, $.............. Is the insurance carried by Old Line or by Mutual Companies?.......... Liability ins., $..........
Credit insurance on notes and accounts receivable, $.......... Use and occupancy insurance, $.......... Life ins. carried, $..........
To whom payable?.................................. Does life insurance include disability clause?..........

(Form of declaration or contract)

    For the purpose of procuring and maintaining credit from time to time in any form whatsoever with the above named bank for claims and demands against the undersigned, the undersigned submits the above which is guaranteed to be a true and accurate statement of..............financial condition on the date of signing hereof; and agree—that if any change occurs that materially reduces the means or ability of the undersigned to pay all claims or demands against..................or materially weakens the financial condition as shown in this statement, the undersigned will at once notify the bank of such change whether application for further credit is made or not. In the absence of such notice it is expressly agreed that the bank in granting or continuing credit may continue to rely on this statement as a true and accurate statement of the financial condition of the undersigned to have the same force and effect as if delivered as an original statement of financial condition at the time additional credit is requested or existing credit continued unless another statement in writing shall be substituted for this or this statement is recalled.

Date signed.................................., 19.......... ....

ADDITIONAL INFORMATION RELATIVE TO STATEMENT DATED ....

Details Relative to Assets
(Fill in Replies to All Details Following, Using the Words "Yes," "No" or "None" When They Apply)

NOTES RECEIVABLE OF CUSTOMERS—What amount does not represent mdse. sales?..
Amount that is probably uncollectible..Amount past due?..
ACCOUNTS RECEIVABLE OF CUSTOMERS—What amount does not represent mdse. sales?..................................
Amount that is probably uncollectible?...What are your usual terms of sales?..............................
Give names of concerns to which you sell in large quantities..
....
....

MERCHANDISE—Average amount carried?...........................Last inventory taken by whom?.........................Date?........................
Amount included in your assets for which the invoices have not yet been entered as liabilities?...........................Amount pledged?...................
Amount in outside warehouses?.......................Held under trust receipt ?.......................Under consignment?.......................Terms of sale?...........
OTHER QUICK ASSETS—Itemized..
....
....
....

DUE FROM CONTROLLED OR SUBSIDIARY CONCERNS:

Name of Concern	Location	For Advances	When Due	For Merchandise	Terms
		$..........		$..........	
		$..........		$..........	
		$..........		$..........	
		$..........		$..........	

STOCKS, BONDS AND INVESTMENTS—Give description and values.
....
....
....

LAND AND BUILDINGS:

Description and Location	Title in Whose Name	Assessed Value	Appraised Value	Mortgages	Name of Mortgages	Insurance

If book value has decreased during the year, account for same..
....

MACHINERY, EQUIPMENT AND FIXTURES—Assessed value $...........................What amount has been charged to depreciation during
the last year on this item?...........................What amount is owing for machinery, equipment, etc.?...........................

DETAILS RELATIVE TO LIABILITIES

NOTES PAYABLE

State maximum amount borrowed from all sources at any one time during fiscal year $...............................Date..................

State minimum amount borrowed from all sources at any one time during fiscal year $...............................Date..................

Do your branches or subsidiary concerns borrow locally?.................Where..

Are any of your notes endorsed or guaranteed?....................By whom?..

State net worth of each endorser—outside of interest in this business...

Amount of your notes payable secured by collateral $.........................Describe the collateral..

ACCOUNTS PAYABLE—What are your average terms of purchase?..

....Do you discount?..........................

Give names and addresses of those from whom you buy:

Name	Street Address	City and State

DEPOSITS OF MONEY WITH ME. By whom?...

On time or demand?..Amount secured by collateral $..........................

OTHER QUICK LIABILITIES—Itemize..

MORTGAGES OR LIENS ON REAL ESTATE..

Interest rate?......................................On what assets a lien?......................................

Who is mortgagee?..

CHATTEL MORTGAGES—To whom?..On what assets a lien?...............

LEASES—Duration...Rental per annum $...............

Location of property...

MISCELLANEOUS

How long engaged in present business?...

What amount of capital did you start with and of what did it consist?..

What amount of capital have you contributed since?...

Time of year receivables generally maximum..Minimum.....................

Time of year merchandise generally maximum...Minimum.....................

State net sales for the past three years...............19.....$.....................19.....$..................19.....$.........

Where is your principal sales territory?...

If your books have been audited by a certified public accountant give name of accountant and date of audit............

Are there any judgments unsatisfied or suits pending against you and for what amount?...............................

Give date you regularly take inventory and close your books...

For what years have your Federal Income Tax returns been subjected to field audit examination?.....................

(Form of Declaration or Contract)

For the purpose of procuring and maintaining credit from time to time in any form whatsoever with the above named bank for claims and demands against the undersigned, the undersigned submits the above which is guaranteed to be a true and accurate statement of..............
financial condition on the date of signing hereof; and agree—that if any change occurs that materially reduces the means or ability of the under-signed to pay all claims or demands against....................or materially weakens the financial condition as shown in this statement, the undersigned will at once notify the bank of such change whether application for further credit is made or not. In the absence of such notice it is expressly agreed that the bank in granting or continuing credit may continue to rely on this statement as a true and accurate statement of the financial condition of the undersigned to have the same force and effect as if delivered as an original statement of financial condition at the time additional credit is requested or existing credit continued unless another statement in writing shall be substituted for this or this statement is recalled.

Date signed.......................................19.......   ....

Form FH-1
(Rev. 6-50)

FHA TITLE I CREDIT APPLICATION
(PROPERTY IMPROVEMENT LOAN)

Form approved.
Budget Bureau No. 63-R037.4.

To: .... DATE ...., 19........

This application is submitted to obtain credit under the terms of Title I of the National Housing Act.

NET AMOUNT
CREDIT REQUIRED $................ NUMBER MONTHS .... Have you any other application pending at this time for an FHA Improvement loan?.........Yes ☐ or No ☐

Name of applicant .... How long at present address? .... years.

Address .... Telephone ....
 (Street)   (City)   (P. O. Zone)   (State)

Year of birth .... Single ☐ Married ☐ Name of wife (or husband) .... Number of other dependents ....
                                                                                                (Age)

Name and address of nearest
relative not living with you ....
                                   (Name)   (Street)   (City)   (State)

EMPLOYMENT OR BUSINESS

Employed by ☐ or business if self-employed ☐ .... For past .... years.

Address .... Kind of business ....
        (Street)   (City)   (State)

Present salary or net
income from business, $............. per month ☐ per year ☐ Your position .... Business telephone ....

Other income (net), $............. per month ☐ per year ☐ Source of other income ....

Previous employer .... For .... years
                        (Name)   (Street)   (City)   (State)

REFERENCES
GIVE NAME AND ADDRESS OF BANKS, FINANCE COMPANIES, OR STORES WHICH HAVE EXTENDED YOU CREDIT

1. .... 3. ....

2. .... 4. ....

DEBTS

List fixed obligations, installment accounts, mortgages, FHA LOANS and debts to banks, finance companies and Government agencies.

To Whom Indebted (Name)	Describe Debts	Date Incurred	Present Balance	Monthly Payments	Amount Past Due	Is Debt an FHA Mortgage or Repair Loan? (State which)
....	....	....	$..........	$..........	$..........	....
....	....	....				....
....	....	....				....

PROPERTY TO BE IMPROVED

Address .... Type ....
        (Street)   (City)   (County)   (State)   (House, apartment, store, farm, etc.)

FILL IN ONE

Is owned by.. Date purchased .... Price paid, $......
              (Name of titleholder)

OR

Is being bought on contract by .... Contract dated .... Price paid $..........
                          (Name of purchaser)

OR

Is leased to .... Lease expires ....
                 (Name of leaseholder)   (Month) (Day) (Year)

.... Rent per month, $................
   (Landlord's name)   (Address)

PROCEEDS OF THIS LOAN WILL BE USED ON ABOVE PROPERTY AS DESCRIBED BELOW

DESCRIBE EACH IMPROVEMENT PLANNED	ESTIMATED COST	NAME AND ADDRESS OF CONTRACTOR/DEALER
1.	$..........	....
2.	$..........	....
3.	$..........	....

APPLICANT—IMPORTANT—READ BEFORE SIGNING

The selection of a contractor or dealer, acceptance of materials used, and work performed is YOUR responsibility. Neither the FHA nor the financial institution guarantees the material or workmanship or inspects the work performed.

I (we) certify that the above statements are true and that no unfavorable information known to me (us) or called for herein has been omitted. This application shall remain the property of the lending institution to which submitted.

WARNING

Name .... (L. S.)

Name .... (L. S.)

NOTE TO FINANCIAL INSTITUTION.—If proceeds will be disbursed to
dealer the person selling the above-described improvements must sign here .... (L. S.)

If applicant is self-employed, a business enterprise, a partnership, or a corporation, fill in Exhibits A and B on reverse side. 16—8222-9

If applicant is self-employed, a business enterprise, a partnership, or a corporation the following information should be given in as complete a manner as possible.

Exhibits A and B are designed primarily for the self-employed, a business enterprise, a partnership, or a corporation. Applicants may find it necessary to submit their own financial statements, making them a part of this application; therefore, applicants may attach a recent balance sheet and profit and loss statement, preferably certified to by an independent accountant, provided that such statements present detailed information substantially in accord with the following:

EXHIBIT A—Balance Sheet as of ...., 19......

ASSETS		LIABILITIES	
Cash..................	$.............	Notes payable...............................	$.............
Notes and accounts receivable............	....	Accounts payable............................	....
Merchandise............................	....	Mortgages on real estate................	....
Stocks and bonds.......................	....	Other liabilities.........................	....
Land and buildings.....................	....	Net worth................................	....
Machinery, equipment, and fixtures.......	....		
Other assets...........................	....		
TOTAL............	$.............	TOTAL........	$.............

EXHIBIT B—Profit and loss statement for year ending ...., 19......

Sales, net....................	$.............	Gross profit.................	$.............
Inventory—beginning.......... $.............		Operating and general expense $.............	
Purchases, net...............	....	Officers' salaries.................	....
Inventory—end...............	....	Taxes............................	....
Cost of sales................	....	Income from other sources....	....
Gross profit.................	$.............	Net profit or loss............	$.............

Title I Plan—GROSS CHARGE TABLE

For use of insured institutions which add the finance charge to the amount to be financed

Based on a discount of $5 on a 1-year note payable in equal monthly installments

When amount to finance is	12 MONTHS		18 MONTHS		24 MONTHS		30 MONTHS		36 MONTHS	
	Amount of note	Monthly payment	Amount of note	Monthly payment	Amount of note	Monthly payment	Amount of note	Monthly payment	Amount of note	Monthly payment
$1.........	$1. 05	$0. 09	$1. 08	$0. 06	$1. 10	$0. 05	$1. 13	$0. 04	$1. 15	$0. 04
$2.........	2. 11	. 18	2. 15	. 12	2. 20	. 10	2. 25	. 08	2. 30	. 07
$3.........	3. 16	. 27	3. 23	. 18	3. 30	. 14	3. 38	. 12	3. 45	. 10
$4.........	4. 21	. 36	4. 31	. 24	4. 40	. 19	4. 50	. 15	4. 60	13
$5.........	5. 26	. 44	5. 38	. 30	5. 51	. 23	5. 63	. 19	5. 75	. 16
$6.........	6. 32	. 53	6. 46	. 36	6. 61	. 28	6. 75	. 23	6. 90	. 20
$7.........	7. 37	. 62	7. 54	. 42	7. 71	. 33	7. 88	. 27	8. 05	. 23
$8.........	8. 42	71	8. 62	48	8. 81	37	9. 00	. 30	9. 20	26
$9.........	9. 47	79	9. 69	54	9. 91	. 42	10. 13	. 34	10. 35	. 29
$10.........	10. 53	. 88	10. 77	. 60	11. 01	46	11 26	. 38	11. 50	. 32
$20.........	21. 05	1. 76	21. 54	1. 20	22 02	. 92	22. 51	. 76	23. 00	. 64
$30.........	31. 58	2. 64	32. 31	1. 80	33. 04	1. 38	33. 77	1. 13	34. 49	. 96
$40.........	42. 11	3. 51	43. 08	2. 40	44. 05	1. 84	45. 02	1. 51	45. 99	1. 28
$50.........	52. 63	4. 39	53. 85	3. 00	55. 06	2. 30	56. 28	1. 88	57 49	1. 60
$60.........	63. 16	5. 27	64. 62	3. 59	66. 07	2. 76	67 53	2. 26	68. 99	1. 92
$70.........	73. 68	6. 14	75. 38	4. 19	77. 09	3. 22	78. 79	2. 63	80. 49	2. 24
$80.........	84. 21	7. 02	86. 15	4. 79	88. 10	3. 68	90. 04	3. 01	91. 98	2. 56
$90.........	94. 74	7 90	96. 92	5. 39	99. 11	4. 15	101 30	3. 38	103. 48	2. 88
$100.........	105. 26	8. 78	107 69	5. 99	110. 12	4. 59	112. 55	3. 76	114. 98	3. 20
$200.........	210. 53	17. 55	215. 38	11. 97	220. 24	9. 18	225. 10	7 51	229. 96	6. 39
$300.........	315. 79	26. 32	323. 08	17. 95	330. 36	13. 77	337 65	11. 26	344. 94	9. 59
$400.........	421. 05	35. 09	430. 77	23. 94	440. 49	18. 36	450. 20	15. 01	459. 92	12. 78
$500.........	526. 32	43. 86	538. 46	29. 92	550. 61	22 95	562. 75	18. 76	574. 90	15. 97
$600.........	631. 58	52. 64	646. 15	35. 90	660. 73	27. 54	675. 30	22. 52	689. 88	19. 17
$700.........	736. 84	61. 41	753. 85	41. 89	770. 85	32. 12	787. 85	26. 27	804. 86	22. 36
$800.........	842. 11	70. 18	861. 54	47. 87	880. 97	36. 71	900. 40	30. 02	919. 84	25. 56
$900.........	947. 37	78. 95	969. 23	53. 85	991. 09	41. 30	1, 012. 96	33. 77	1, 034. 82	28. 75
$1,000.........	1, 052. 63	87. 72	1, 076. 92	59. 83	1, 101. 22	45. 89	1, 125. 51	37. 52	1, 149. 80	31 94
$2,000.........	2, 105. 26	175. 44	2, 153. 84	119. 66	2, 202. 43	91. 77	2, 251. 01	75. 04	2, 299. 59	63. 88
$2,500.........	2, 631. 58	219. 30	2, 692. 31	149. 58	2, 753. 04	114. 71	2, 813. 77	93. 80	2, 874. 50	79. 85

Monthly installment payments have been set at the next full cent nearest the fractional result. *An adjustment should be made in final payment to have the total payments equal the face amount of the note.*

U. S. GOVERNMENT PRINTING OFFICE   16—8222—5

QUESTIONS AND PROBLEMS

1. What are the essential differences between savings banking, investment banking, and commercial banking?

2. What is the "monetary" function of commercial banks?

3. What early American banking practices became crystallized into federal statute in 1863?

4. How may a large bank be "departmentalized"? Point out the main functions of each department.

5. From what sources do commercial banks acquire funds?

6. What elements compose "proprietorship equity"? How important are they as sources of bank funds?

7. Differentiate "loans and discounts" and "investments." How may each account be subdivided?

8. What is the difference between "customers' loans" and "open-market loans"? Between "discounts" and "straight loans"?

9. What is the nature of a "self-liquidating loan"?

10. What is a "secured loan"? What kinds of assets were most used to secure loans to business in 1946?

11. Why do bankers favor stock-exchange collateral as loan security?

12. Why are term loans said to be "tailor made"?

13. For what reasons are rates of interest on short- and long-term loans often not the same?

14. In what respect are real estate loans similar to bank investments?

15. In your community, what is the average yield on bank loans? On investments?

16. Do banks in your community require borrowers to keep a deposit balance in the bank? If so, what percentage of the loan must be maintained?

17. What proportion of all commercial bank earnings are from loans and discounts, and what proportion from investments?

18. What important changes took place in the combined statements of commercial banks as they assisted in financing the war, 1940–45?

19. What is the "secondary reserve" of a bank? Why is it maintained, and what specific items does it usually contain?

20. Do the terms "self-liquidating" and "shiftable" mean the same thing when applied to bank assets? Explain.

21. Could the banking system as a whole ever be highly liquid?

BIBLIOGRAPHY

(Bibliographical material for Chapters 3 and 4 is grouped at the end of Chapter 4.)

Chapter • 4

BANKING STRUCTURE, SUPERVISION, AND INTERRELATIONS

THUS FAR we have discussed the functional aspects of banking—what the banking system does. Now we shall examine how the banking system is organized to perform its functions; the manner in which the units co-operate with one another; and some of the limitations imposed by banking laws and regulations.

The structure of the banking system of the United States has many unique features. It is vastly different than that of Canada or Mexico, that of England and the European nations—or, for that matter, any other country. Differences are, for the most part, explainable in terms of our historical development. For example, most of our banks are "unit" operations—a system in which one corporation maintains only one office or place of business. This is in distinct contrast to the practice in other nations, which have a wide extension of the multiple-office branch banking system. Why? The reason is largely due to traditional American independence and a competitive spirit combined with apprehension with respect to the possible development of a "money trust." It is due in part also to the fact that our central government is one of delegated powers; states have always had the right to organize banks within their own borders and to grant charters of incorporation to individuals desiring to begin a banking business. The power to organize is accompanied with power to regulate. As a consequence, banking law and regulation in America have reflected local conditions, with a resulting diversity of detail. The system has been compared to the "crazy quilts" made by our grandmothers from scraps of material of many colors, shapes, and sizes.

The discussion of banking structure will be limited to several major points: the dual system of bank charter; unit banking and its modifications in the form of branch, group, and chain systems; the multiple system of supervision and regulation; and voluntary bank co-operation through correspondents and clearinghouse associations.

STRUCTURE OF THE BANKING SYSTEM

The preceding chapter has made it reasonably clear that commercial banks may be chartered by the federal government or by the individual states. This "dual" chartering practice is found in no other country; it is a feature of banking structure carried over directly from our political system, which is characterized by a constitutionally divided sovereignty. Many other phases of American economic life are marked by this division of authority.

Dual System of Bank Charter

A group of businessmen wishing to start a bank under federal charter make application to the Comptroller of the Currency in Washington, D.C. Application for a permit to incorporate under state law is made to a banking commission, auditor of public accounts, or other duly constituted state authority.

The structural result has been that both state and federal authorities have sought to "attract" banks into their supervisory domains; consequently, banking regulation has often been modified in the interest of not driving banks into the other camp. This sort of competitive laxity was one of the reasons that capital and other requirements for bank organization were minimized in the early part of the present century. Many banking authorities believe that the low requirements then in force were an important cause of the difficulties that subsequently prevailed—the thousands of bank failures that shook our system during the 1920's and early 1930's. This phase of competition has passed, but our dual system remains.

The data of Table 8 point to the fact that state-chartered institutions are of a smaller average size than national banks. This is true with respect to deposits, earning assets, and capital accounts. Only about 35 per cent of all banks operate under national charter, but their deposits (the most commonly used measure of the size of banks) are 57 per cent of all deposits.

Although national banks may be of larger average size, it is not difficult to find reasons for the continued existence of large numbers of state-chartered institutions. State regulations, in general, permit more freedom in the use of funds and an enhanced earning position when compared with national regulation. The ratio of required reserves to deposits in state banks may be smaller than in national banks. In most states, cash on hand and balances with other banks are accepted as reserves. Some states accept securities as reserves, which permits a bank to hold a part of the legal reserves in the form of earning assets. Limitations on the dollar amount of loans to single individuals and on the types of bonds allowed for investment tend to be less restrictive. The amount of capital required to organize a state bank may be less.

In addition, state bankers can take advantage of membership in the Federal Reserve System if they wish to comply with Federal Reserve regulations. In effect, however, by joining the System, they

TABLE 8

STATE AND NATIONAL BANKS IN THE UNITED STATES,
DECEMBER 31, 1949

	National	State	Total
Number................	4,975	9,184	14,159
Loans*................	23,853	19,117	42,970
Investments*...........	44,090	33,154	77,244
Deposits*..............	83,113	62,077	145,190
Capital accounts*........	5,920	5,048	10,968

* Millions of dollars.
Source: *Federal Reserve Bulletin*, June, 1950, p. 699.

yield many of the advantages of their state charters. As state banks, they need not: agree to pay checks at par or face amount when presented by mail but may deduct an exchange charge; meet the higher national bank standards for capital accounts; submit certain operating policies to Federal Reserve review; or maintain part of their funds at the Federal Reserve Bank to meet legal requirements. State banks outside the Federal Reserve System are not subject to Comptroller of the Currency examination. Exchange charges or deductions made from the face value of checks by the drawee bank may be made by nonmember state banks that remain outside the Federal Reserve clearing system. Although these charges add to operating income, they are relatively unpopular except among small banks of the South and West. For example, on December 31, 1949, the Federal Reserve "par list" of banks that pay the face value of checks included 6,887 member banks and 5,291 nonmember state banks. Only 1,873 nonmember state banks were not on the par list and were able, therefore, to collect the exchange fee.

Nonmember state banks can take full advantage of state regulations permitting branch banking, while national banks and members of the Federal Reserve System are restricted somewhat by federal regulations. At the end of 1949 there were 328 national and 216 state member banks—a total of 544—having more than one office. Six hundred and eighty-two nonmembers maintained one or more branches. However, branches of member banks were more numerous than those of state nonmember institutions.

American Unit Banking System

Most of the commercial banking offices in the United States are "independent" and individual units, each representing a separate business corporation. This situation contrasts with that of many other countries, where there are few banking corporations but many banking offices that are branches of a main corporation. In Canada there are 10 banks, but these banks operate over 2,800 branch offices. In England there are 5 leading banks and less than a dozen other smaller and fairly specialized banks. The "big five" operate branches throughout England. In contrast, over 90 per cent of our banking offices are independent, and in nine states branch banking is prohibited.

The prevalence of unit banking is at least in part attributable to a fear of monopoly in finance—sometimes called "money trusts." During a large part of our history, while state banking laws were being crystallized, there was greater demand for credit than could be met with existing facilities. Many citizens feared that local branches would collect funds and would then "ship them to the head office" for relending. It was the constant fear of a money and credit shortage, as well as local pride, that made the early frontier states prohibit branch banking. This fear was probably unfounded; Canadian branches in frontier areas lend *more* than their deposits, rather than less. Well founded or not, this attitude left a permanent mark on our banking structure by retarding the development of branch and group organizations.

Modifications of the Unit Banking Principle

Not all banks in the United States are independent units, however. Almost 10 per cent of them are a part of one of the so-called "multiple-office" banking systems in states which allow an organization to conduct its business in more than one location. Multiple banking includes branch banking, group or holding-company systems, and bank chains. Although there is only moderate discussion of the controversy currently, the debate over merits of multiple and unit banking has not been settled. It will be continued sporadically for years to come and is most likely to be revived if the banking system feels the pressure of financial panic or industrial depression.

BRANCH BANKING. "Branch banking" means that one corporate organization carries on its banking operations at more than one office. In that respect the corporation is similar to any chain-store organization that sells groceries, drugs, or shoes. There is one corporation, one charter, one board of directors, one group of stockholders, but two or more places of business.

Nothing was mentioned in the National Banking Act of 1863 about branch banking, although some states permitted this form of organization at that time. However, as an increasing number of states legalized branch banking, the national law was modified (McFadden-Pepper Act of 1927) to permit national banks to operate branches within the *city* of the parent organization if state laws permitted state banks to have such branches. Pressure for adotpion of nation-wide branch banking developed after 1927 but eased when the Banking Act of 1933 permitted national banks to establish state-wide branches within those states where state banks operate branches. National banks in such states are bound by the laws that govern operation of branches by state banks. If state law permits only city-wide branches, national banks may maintain multiple offices only within the city; if state law permits state-wide operation, national banks have that privilege also. National banks must have a minimum capitalization of $100,000 in order to establish branches regardless of the minimum capital provisions of competing state banks. A state-bank member of the Federal Reserve System must receive approval of Federal Reserve authorities before establishing branches outside its home city. Eighteen states and the District of Columbia have legalized state-wide branch banking, while seventeen others permit it on a more restricted basis. Nine states have statutory or constitutional prohibitions against any form of branches except those located at military reservations; the remaining state laws are silent on the issue, but silence is usually construed as a prohibition. States in which no branch banking is practiced are: Illinois, Missouri, Kansas, Oklahoma, Texas, West Virginia, Montana, Wyoming, and Colorado.

On December 31, 1949, there were 328 national banks that operated 2,085 branch offices, and 898 state banks maintained 2,494 branches. Branches of 216 state-bank members of the Federal Reserve System numbered 1,302. For the commercial banking system as a whole, the number of branch operations has changed but little in recent years. In 1945, Federal Reserve authorities reported 3,947 branches and four years later, 4,579. More than 40 per cent of the branch offices are located in the same city as the parent organization, and approximately 70 per cent are in the head-office city and county. Only about 17 per cent spread out over the state in counties not contiguous to the county in which the parent operates. Thus, in few states do we have anything closely resembling state-wide branch bank operation.

Four states contained almost 50 per cent of all branch banks operating in 1949. California, home of the vast Bank of America system, led with 949, closely followed by New York with 850; and Michigan and Ohio were next in that order.

Advantages Claimed for Branch Banking.   Branch banking is said to provide the safety that results from wide diversification in the type of bank assets. It is contended that loans made at the several offices would automatically provide a reduction in risk of loss which might accompany the practice of a single-office bank in "placing too many eggs in one basket." This argument loses much of its force when the restricted nature of branch banking in the United States is considered. As we have just noted, most branches now being operated are in the city of the parent bank and are subject to about the same commercial and industrial conditions. Thus, a recession in business that impaired the credit worth of one borrower would probably exert a similar influence upon many borrowers in that city or county. The argument would have more weight if we had, or contemplated having, nation-wide branch banking of the type existing in England and Canada.

A second claim favoring branch banking has somewhat more validity. Interoffice relations within a branch system make the transfer of funds quick and easy and promote mobility of banking resources. This flexibility has been of significance in Canada, where an office of a large bank may be set up in a frontier mining region or oil field and makes large sums of bank credit immediately available to an area whose population would hardly justify the existences of a unit bank. Moreover, if the economic resources in such a location should be rapidly depleted, a local unit bank might fail, but a branch can carry on. The branch system may merely discontinue its office or have a representative on the site on a part-time basis. Reduction of the local service would entail no loss of banking capital. This argument is also most effective when branch banking is envisaged on a nation-wide scale.

The greater concentration of capital provided by branch banking and the relative lack of competition from numerous unit banks may make certain economies possible. Fewer spacious and grandiose buildings are used, and less fixed capital is thus required. Management may be more highly paid and more capable at top levels, making for a more efficient organization. The large number of minor positions widens the choice of management for personnel to fill administrative positions in the home office. The branch system is said to facilitate the training of officers.

Objections to Branch Banking. Always a prominent argument against branch banking is that it fosters monopoly. There may be an element of truth in this, but there would still appear to be plenty of latitude for competition. In fact, the competition between rival branch organizations of large size might be more effective in providing good banking services than would competition among a large number of smaller unit banks.

Also in the forefront of objections to branch banking is the feeling that loans made to local borrowers will be administered by bankers not especially interested in local welfare or keenly aware of local credit needs. Representatives of branch organizations are said to operate on a much less personal basis than managers in unit banks. Doubtless there are many examples to illustrate these objections; yet it should be kept in mind that the long-run success of any banking system is dependent upon the prosperity of local communities. Moreover, perhaps more objectivity and less sentimental interest in promoting an individual local enterprise, irrespective of merit, should be encouraged. The waves of unit bank failures experienced in the United States during 1920–33 may be charged in part to improper lending techniques in areas where personal requests for credit by the borrower might better have been denied when application for a loan was received.

When a large branch banking system is not competently managed and fails, the ensuing disaster is likely to be widespread. In fact, the failure of a large branch banking system may imperil the banking structure of a nation. This appears to have been true of the situation in Detroit that brought on the Michigan moratorium and the national banking holiday in 1933—an incident that lends support to a widely held objection to branch banking.

One further objection remains—that of the difficulty of adequate examination by supervisory authorities. This has always been a troublesome problem; and as state systems grow and include additional offices, the difficulty mounts. What seems to be a satisfactory plan has been adopted in California, where state examiners audit a random sample of the branch offices simultaneously.

If we were to sum up the arguments regarding branch banking, we would conclude that it has definite advantages, although these may often be exaggerated if the area over which the offices may spread is restricted to one city, one state, or one geographical region. On the other hand, early adoption of nation-wide branch banking in the United States might have resulted in substantial social saving if the failure of thousands of our small rural banks could have been avoided.

GROUP BANKING.   Group banking is an arrangement that brings two or more separately incorporated banks into the control of a holding company. The holding company usually exercises voting control by virtue of ownership of sufficient capital of the shares of each bank to dominate the individual institution. The banks within the structure may be unit banks or may be branch systems. Holding companies are always incorporated where laws permit banks to own the stock of other banks. Banks themselves sometimes act as the holding company.

The statutes of a majority of our states make no direct mention of group banking, but thirty-three states limit the acquisition by commercial banks of the stock of other banks. About a dozen states retard the development of group banking by fixing a maximum limit on the proportion of a bank's capital shares that may be owned by one nonbanking corporation, trust, or other association. Mississippi is the only state specifically prohibiting group banking. Under federal law a holding-company affiliate (which may be a bank owning the stock of other banks or may be a nonbanking corporation owning bank stock) is required to obtain permission from Federal Reserve authorities before voting the stock of member banks within its control. Federal law, since 1935, also prohibits the purchase of bank stock by banks which are members of the Federal Reserve System.

Although group banking exists primarily in areas where branches are prohibited, the large size achieved by a few groups in states permitting branches renders any generalization quite inconclusive. It is, however, well known that group banking, for the nation as a whole, is of declining importance. For example, the Federal Reserve authorities reported that fifty-five groups disappeared in the years 1932–36, inclusive, leaving fifty-two groups operating 479 banks and 1,326 offices. This was 3.2 per cent of all commercial banks, and they held 14 per cent of all deposits. At the end of 1945 the number of groups had declined to thirty-three, with only 387 banking offices.

Deposits of $18,142 millions in group banks were about 12 per cent of the aggregate deposits for the entire system; the number of banks was approximately 2 per cent of all existing commercial banks. The decline in the number of groups was more rapid than the decline in deposits in the period surveyed, which would seem to indicate that the smaller groups are being eliminated and that the larger ones are surviving. However, aside from the Bank of America and the Transamerica Corporation, whose size dominate the data, this is not necessarily true.

The largest and best-known group system is the famous Giannini banking empire, operating mainly in California. The group is headed by the Transamerica Corporation, a holding company established by the late A. P. Giannini in 1928. Transamerica owns over 11 per cent of the stock of the Bank of America Trust and Savings Association, the largest private bank in the world. In addition, Transamerica holds large stock interests in 47 other banks operating over 130 branches in five western states. The corporation has a substantial proportion of the banking facilities in California, Nevada, and Oregon and lesser interests in Arizona and Washington. In 1945 the Bank of America system was composed of twenty-one groups, including 5 branch banks operating 504 offices in California; 380 of these were in counties not contiguous to the head-office city. On December 31, 1949, the California offices numbered 525.

Other important group systems include the First Bank Stock Corporation and the Northwest Bancorporation, both of Minneapolis. Each is composed of approximately 70 active banks and trust companies, with offices in Minnesota, the Dakotas, Montana, Nebraska, Iowa, and Wisconsin.

CHAIN BANKING. A third modification of the unit bank principle found in the United States is chain banking. It is very similar to group banking except that control of multiple offices is held by one individual or group of individuals or through interlocking directorates, i.e., the same men sitting on several boards of directors.

Chain banking has been predominantly a development in agricultural areas and has achieved greatest significance in a few Middle Western states where branch banking is prohibited. In only five states have chains accounted for as much as 10 per cent of all banking offices. On December 31, 1945, 115 chains with 522 offices were in operation. Of these offices, 205 were national banks and 50 were state member banks. Forty-five chains were branch banks, operating

74 offices. Total deposits held were $4.6 billions, or 3.1 per cent of all bank deposits reported on that date. Minnesota reported 14 chains in 1945; and Texas was a close second, with 12. The West North Central group of states accounted for 46 of the 115 chains reporting. The operating banks are generally located in towns of fewer than 5,000 inhabitants—towns which seem to be losing significance as a result of improved transportation and communication. In contrast to the stability of branch banking, chains seem to have passed far beyond their zenith and are likely to become of even less significance.

Currency Exchanges

In some areas where branch banking is not permitted or where independent banks cannot readily be organized because of high capital requirements, there have developed agencies which are not banks but which perform certain limited functions normally provided by banks. The best illustration is the currency exchanges which sprang up in the 1930's as an outgrowth of bank failures in the depression. Instead of being localized in the heart of the financial district of a city, these agencies tend to concentrate near outlying factories, where large wage bills are paid by checks. They cash checks for a fee, sell money orders and travelers' checks, and may provide safekeeping facilities. Although currency exchanges do not hold deposits and do not make loans, they will accept funds for transmittal to banks and thus become part of our banking and financial structure.

BANK SUPERVISION

In every phase of its existence, from the date of original incorporation until final liquidation, a commercial bank is closely supervised and regulated. In few countries are bank operations as carefully scrutinized by public authorities as in the United States. This may be due to the dual system of chartering and adherence to the principle of free banking that has resulted in a large number of unit banks. It may partially be a remedial outgrowth of the many severe financial crises that have harassed the nation periodically.

Strangely enough, in spite of the inherent dislike and general opposition of Americans to supervision, the regulation of banking activities has created little adverse comment. Perhaps the lack of criticism is due to the quasi-public nature of banking, to an awareness of the vulnerability of loss to millions of small deposit holders, and to the recognition that special privileges had been granted to banks, such as the power to create money in the form of bank notes and deposit credit.

Banking supervision begins with the granting of charters and extends through regulations governing voluntary or involuntary liquidation. During the intervening life span of an institution, supervisory authorities maintain control by requiring periodic reports, by making unannounced examinations, and by forcing banks to take the steps necessary to correct abuses or inefficiencies of management and particularly to maintain their liquidity and solvency.

Fifty-one agencies are actively engaged in the regular supervision of commercial banks. Forty-eight of these have responsibility for the supervision of banks in the respective states; several of them antedate federal supervision by many years. The three agencies directly responsible for bank supervision on a national scale are: the Office of Comptroller of the Currency (established 1863), the Federal Reserve System (1913), and the Federal Deposit Insurance Corporation (FDIC) (1933). For purposes of supervision our commercial banks are divided into four classes: national, state member, nonmember insured and nonmember uninsured. The words "national" and "state" refer to the chartering authority; "member" means membership in the Federal Reserve System, and "insured" refers to participation in the Federal Deposit Insurance Corporation. At year-end 1949 there were 14,159 commercial banks in the United States; 4,975 were national, 1,917 were state member insured, 6,540 nonmember state banks insured, and the remaining 727 were state nonmember noninsured.

Examinations

Even though many banks are subject to regulation by more than one authority, there is virtually no duplication of bank examination in practice. Despite the fact that all national banks are members of the Federal Reserve System and are insured, they are examined by neither Federal Reserve authorities nor the Federal Deposit Insurance Corporation. National banks are examined by the staff of the Comptroller of the Currency, and the reports are accepted by the Federal Reserve Board and the FDIC. The Federal Reserve examines all state member banks but frequently conducts concurrent examinations with the state authority. The FDIC may examine national banks only after obtaining written permission of the Comptroller of the Currency, and state member banks with consent of the Board of

Exhibit 25

Principal Bank Supervisory Relationships

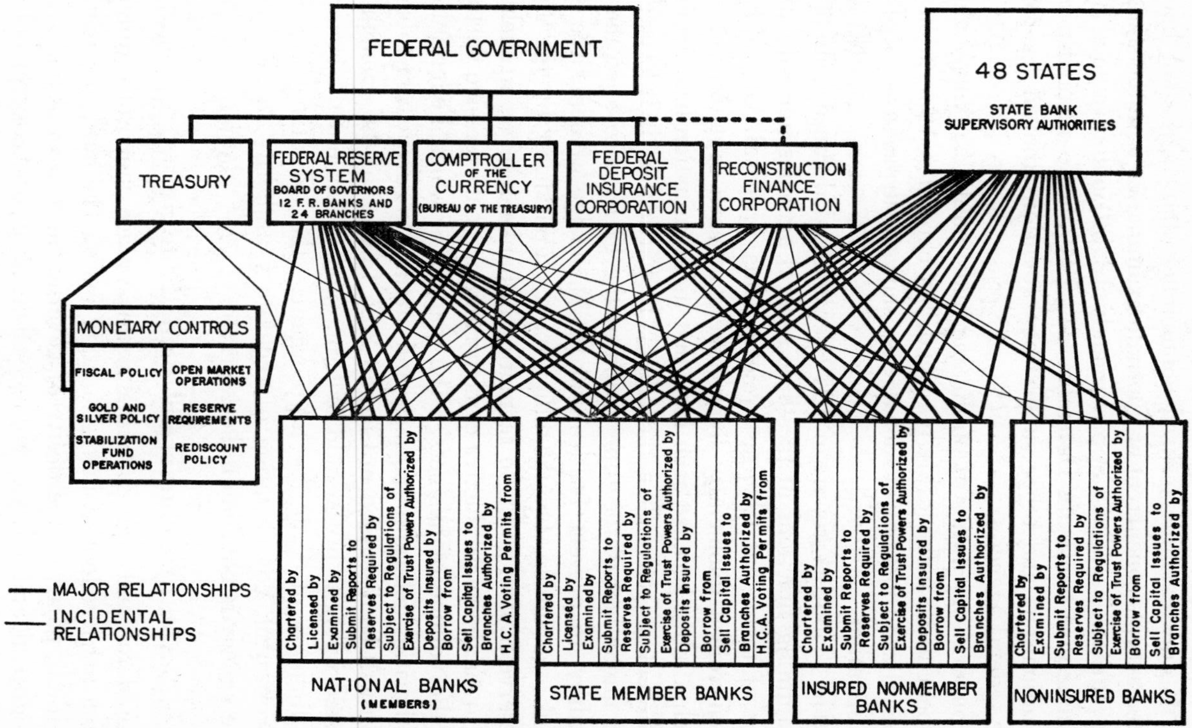

FEDERAL GOVERNMENT

48 STATES
STATE BANK SUPERVISORY AUTHORITIES

TREASURY

FEDERAL RESERVE SYSTEM
BOARD OF GOVERNORS
12 F.R. BANKS AND 24 BRANCHES

COMPTROLLER OF THE CURRENCY
(BUREAU OF THE TREASURY)

FEDERAL DEPOSIT INSURANCE CORPORATION

RECONSTRUCTION FINANCE CORPORATION

MONETARY CONTROLS

FISCAL POLICY
GOLD AND SILVER POLICY
STABILIZATION FUND OPERATIONS
OPEN MARKET OPERATIONS
RESERVE REQUIREMENTS
REDISCOUNT POLICY

NATIONAL BANKS (MEMBERS)
Chartered by
Licensed by
Examined by
Submit Reports to
Reserves Required by
Subject to Regulations of
Exercise of Trust Powers Authorized by
Deposits Insured by
Borrow from
Sell Capital Issues to
Branches Authorized by
H.C.A. Voting Permits from

STATE MEMBER BANKS
Chartered by
Licensed by
Examined by
Submit Reports to
Reserves Required by
Subject to Regulations of
Exercise of Trust Powers Authorized by
Deposits Insured by
Borrow from
Sell Capital Issues to
Branches Authorized by
H.C.A. Voting Permits from

INSURED NONMEMBER BANKS
Chartered by
Examined by
Submit Reports to
Reserve Required by
Subject to Regulations of
Exercise of Trust Powers Authorized by
Deposits Insured by
Borrow from
Sell Capital Issues to
Branches Authorized by

NONINSURED BANKS
Chartered by
Examined by
Submit Reports to
Reserves Required by
Subject to Regulations of
Exercise of Trust Powers Authorized by
Borrow from
Sell Capital Issues to
Branches Authorized by

——— MAJOR RELATIONSHIPS
——— INCIDENTAL RELATIONSHIPS

Source: *Annual Report of the Governors of the Federal Reserve System, 1938* (Washington, D.C.).

Governors of the Federal Reserve System. This it seldom does. Instead, it accepts reports prepared by the other two agencies. The FDIC does examine insured nonmember state banks but here also often accepts concurrent or alternate examination with the state banking authorities. Thus, approximately 13,430 out of a total 14,159 commercial banks on December 31, 1949, were receiving regular examinations and other supervisory attention from at least one of the federal agencies.

Supervisory duties of public and quasi-public banking authorities appear to be inextricably entwined, but careful consideration of the specialized functions of each agency shows a surprising lack of actual duplication.

The "Hoover" report of 1949 recommended concentration of the examining functions of the three federal agencies into the hands of one of them, but Congress rejected this proposal. Opposition has been voiced unofficially by members of each organization against such a move because each feels that its examination has a somewhat different objective than the others. In particular, it is avowed that the major fact of the supervision of the FDIC is to keep the banks healthy, to prevent failure and the shrinkage of deposit credit as banks go under. On the other hand, supervision by the Federal Reserve System points to regulation of banks' reserves in such a way as to maximize productive capacity and prevent excessive fluctuations in the volume of business. (The manner in which Federal Reserve authorities determine policies and attempt to carry them to completion will be discussed in Chapter 20.) In view of the strength of the vested interests in the field of bank supervision and the general unwillingness of Congress to reorganize the executive branches of government, concentration of regulatory authority in the hands of one agency is not soon to be expected.

Regulation of Commercial Bank Lending

Federal and state banking statutes place numerous restrictions upon the freedom of banks to grant loans. The basis for regulation is found partly in the desire of government to protect the clients of every bank and partly to promote efficiency of operation of individual banks and the structure as a whole. Present also, as we shall see later, is the desire to exercise control over the volume of purchasing power existing in the form of bank deposits derived from loans. This control bears most directly upon the amount of liquid reserve required behind deposits as it serves to limit the total volume of loans and investments the banks may make. Chapter 18 is devoted to detailed consideration of the manner in which this limitation affects the expansion of deposits and bank loans.

Although the pattern of loan limitations is similar for all banks, uniformity does not exist because of the separate jurisdictions of forty-eight states and the federal government. The most important restrictions force diversification of earning assets. A national bank may make unsecured loans to one borrower in an amount not greater than 10 per cent of its unimpaired capital and surplus. If the borrower's note is adequately secured, the bank may lend as much as 25 per cent of its capital. No limits are placed on extensions based on the security of (1) drafts drawn against actually existing values, (2) commercial paper of a third party owned by the borrower and endorsed over to the lending bank, (3) bankers' acceptances, (4) bills of lading on commodities in transit, and (5) government obligations.

Real estate loans by national banks were prohibited before adoption of the Federal Reserve Act in 1913. This act and more recent amendments have placed national and state banks more nearly on the same competitive level in this field of lending. A national bank may now extend real estate loans in an amount equal to 100 per cent of its total capital and surplus or to 60 per cent of its time deposits, whichever is the greater amount. The philosophy that limits loans in relation to savings deposits or the invested capital of the bank is that these items are relatively stable, thus permitting a bank to extend a portion of such funds to borrowers on long-term notes. This limitation was made before the Federal National Mortgage Association (FNMA) was established to provide a market where long-term mortgage notes can be liquidated quickly without loss to the lending bank.

Individual loans on real estate are limited to 50 per cent of the value of improved property if the note has five years or less to run; or up to 60 per cent if the note matures in ten years, provided no less than 40 per cent of the loan will be paid in installments during that period. In all cases the note is secured by a first mortgage on the property. Exceptions to these provisions may be made when the loans are insured by the Federal Housing Administration (FHA) or by the Veterans' Administration (VA).

Other miscellaneous restrictions forbid a national bank to make loans to its own officers unless the loan is approved by the board of directors of the lending institution. If approved, the loan may be for no more than $2,500. Nor can a bank lend to an officer of another bank until the board of the employing institution has received a detailed report of the amount, purpose, collateral security, and date of the loan. No loan may be made on a note secured by stock of the lending bank. Examiners of national banks may not borrow from national banks, nor may state bank examiners borrow from the banks they examine. Maximum interest rates on loans are also stipulated in federal law. Rates may be as high as the legal or usury rate of the state in which the bank is located. In the event that the state has no legal maximum, 7 per cent may be charged by the lending institution. Fees that increase total income earned above the legal maximum are allowed where the bank performs valuable and costly services related to credit investigation, title search, collections, and other operations closely associated with its lending activities. All lending regulations listed here are enforced by bank examiners.

Government Regulation of Bank Investments

Government regulation of the investments of commercial banks also lacks uniformity from state to state, although everywhere the idea of protecting the bank depositor by this means is accepted. National law on the subject changes from time to time. For example, in the year 1863 banks were forced to invest a certain percentage of their capital in federal bonds to be used as security for bank-note issues. Real estate loans were prohibited in the same statute; and, by implication, other long-term loans and bonds held for investment purposes were excluded. The provision regarding bonds was relaxed by subsequent ruling of the Comptroller of the Currency. The Federal Reserve Act of 1913 and the McFadden-Pepper Act, 1927, amended the law to permit national banks to grant real estate loans and to invest in "bonds, notes, or debentures commonly known as investment securities." The latter act also authorized the Comptroller to prescribe the nature of "investment securities." His ruling was that banks might purchase securities that were "marketable" or those having "such a market as to render sales at intrinsic values readily possible." No suggestion was made of a method to determine intrinsic values.

In the ten years after World War I, commercial banks not only expanded the volume of bonds held for their own account but became deeply involved in investment banking by establishing underwriting affiliates for the marketing of securities. The Banking Act of 1933 curtailed this activity. In fact, commercial banks are now forbidden to underwrite any issue of corporate investment securities. They are permitted, however, to underwrite state and local government issues and to deal in United States government bonds.

Diversification of the bond accounts of banks is promoted by the requirement (1935) that member banks cannot purchase securities of one obligor in an amount in excess of 10 per cent of the bank's capital and surplus. Government obligations are exempt from this provision. Purchase of bonds convertible into stocks or low-grade bonds in which speculative, rather than investment, characteristics predominate is prohibited.

Because the experience of banks with investment securities during the depression of 1929–33 was often disastrous, the quality of bank investments for all members of the Federal Reserve System was made subject to supervision of the Comptroller of the Currency. The regulation, first issued in 1936, was revised in 1938 and jointly adopted by the Comptroller of the Currency, the Federal Reserve, and the FDIC. It is enforced by examiners of each of these supervisory agencies. The revision became effective only after extensive consultation among federal officials and state banking departments, and in practice is now applied to virtually all banks.

The chief effect of the ruling is to prohibit purchases by banks of bonds not included in the four upper classes of securities as determined by investment rating services such as Moody's, Fitch, and Standard and Poor's. It has the further objective of penalizing banks for the continued holding of securities which have slipped down and out of the first four ratings. In short, the regulation provides that banks should purchase and hold only marketable bonds. Unfortunately, no very definite criterion of marketability is established.

In addition to corporate bonds, the investments eligible for ownership by commercial banks include, as noted in Chapter 3, federal government, state, and municipal issues, obligations of Federal Home Loan banks, Federal Farm Mortgage Corporation, federal land banks, and other agencies of the Farm Credit Administration, foreign bonds, and those of the newly created World Bank (discussed in Chapter 22) if they meet the standards of quality established by the Comptroller of the Currency. Bank ownership of stocks is severely restricted, however. Only issues of the district Federal Reserve bank, the Import-Export Bank, safe deposit box subsidiaries, and a few other issuers specifically mentioned in the law may be held by national banks and state bank members of the Federal Reserve System.

Deposit Insurance

Beginning in 1909 a few Middle Western states adopted deposit insurance or guaranty as an additional safeguard to depositors. Without exception, these systems fell into the discard during the 1920's, when agricultural depression swamped thousands of small banks. The depression served as the incentive for adoption of a nation-wide plan for insuring bank deposits. This was originally provided in the Banking Act of 1933 and later became an integral part of the Federal Reserve Act. The law has been in operation since January 1, 1934. As administered from 1934 to 1950, the law provided insurance for each deposit account of Federal Reserve members and qualifying nonmember banks up to $5,000. In September, 1950, the insurance coverage was raised to $10,000 per account. Insurance is made available through the FDIC.

When the plan was initiated, funds for reimbursement of depositors of failed banks became available from three sources: (1) a Treasury subscription of $150,000,000 in capital stock of the FDIC, (2) sale of stock to each Federal Reserve bank equal to one half its surplus account, amounting in total to about $139,300,000,[1] and (3) from semiannual collections of premium assessments on insured banks equal in total to one twelfth of 1 per cent of average deposits.

The amount of funds collected, and not required to settle claims of depositors or to meet current expenses of the Corporation, must be invested in securities issued or guaranteed as to principal and interest by the federal government. Temporarily, however, such funds may be placed on deposit in the United States Treasury or in Federal Reserve banks. Since the beginning of its operations in 1934, the FDIC has been able to meet all insurance losses and operating expenses from earnings on its security holdings. Interest received on investments and other income becomes a more important source of current revenue as the security reserve is enlarged. In 1948, receipts from this account were $27.6 millions, or approximately 23 per cent as much as was collected from assessments and almost five times as large as total expenses of the Corporation for the year. Annual premium receipts have been credited to the surplus account, which reached a total of more than $1.1 billion at the end of 1948.

The FDIC is administered by a three-man board of directors consisting of the Comptroller of the Currency and two other presidential appointees. It is empowered to conduct examinations of all insured nonmember state banks and may examine national and state members as noted above. It has other supervisory functions also, notably to prohibit payment of interest by banks on demand deposits and to

---

[1] In the autumn of 1947 the FDIC began installment retirement of stock held by the United States Treasury and the Federal Reserve banks. Final settlement was made in September, 1948.

limit interest paid on time and savings deposits of insured nonmember banks. The purpose of these provisions is to enhance earnings of insured banks to enable them to build up capital accounts and minimize the chance of failure. An indirect effect is to place almost all state-chartered commercial banks under federal supervision. The Corporation is appointed receiver of all failed national banks and accepts appointment as receiver of failed insured state banks if such receivership is tendered by state banking authorities.

When operating in the capacity of receiver, the FDIC liquidates assets taken over from failed banks as the opportunity for orderly conversion into cash presents itself. Insured accounts are made available to depositors as soon as possible. This is done either by transfer of the insured deposit to another insured bank in the same community, by depositing it in a new national bank organized by the Corporation for this purpose, or by giving checks in payment to depositors. In the period 1934 through 1944, 336 banks with $145 million of deposits suspended. Of these, 247 banks with over $100 million of deposits were insured. Depositors in the insured institutions had about one half their funds protected under the $5,000 maximum limit per account then in effect.

In recent years the plan of operation of the FDIC has been to preserve banks rather than to permit failure, after which it would act only as a receiver. By organizing a new national bank, administered by an appointee of the Corporation, to assume the insured deposits of a closed bank, or by transferring the business of the closed bank to an active insured bank in the same community, the FDIC has effectively insured or guaranteed payment of all deposit accounts in full, and not merely to the extent of the insurance coverage. From an economic or social point of view, the Corporation's procedure in preserving the banking institutions in a community is far superior to any action it might take as merely a liquidating agent for an insolvent bank. In a reorganization, not only are all deposits fully protected, but business in the community is not interrupted; nor are there any undesirable repercussions on neighboring banks. Moreover, the costs to the FDIC of meeting depositor losses are kept to a minimum. In more than thirteen full years of operation (1934–47), 245 banks were placed in receivership—a large percentage of them prior to 1944—and 159 were merged with active banks with financial aid from the FDIC. Losses to the Corporation were about $26 million; losses to depositors were less than $2 million.[2]

---

[2] *Federal Reserve Bulletin*, February, 1950, p. 155.

At the end of September, 1949, 87,796,000 deposit accounts in 13,440 commercial banks amounted to less than $5,000 and, therefore, were fully insured. This was 96 per cent of all deposit accounts. Insured deposits of $62.4 billions were, however, only 45 per cent of the $139.2 billions of deposits held in insured banks.[3]

The federal guaranty of bank deposits seems now to be generally accepted; in the minds of many individuals this is a firmly established institution occupying a permanent place in our banking structure. To many, the assumption of this responsibility by the federal government is considered only just. For years, bank notes have been guaranteed by the government, and extension of the same protection to depositors is not revolutionary in principle. Moreover, as long as the nation is committed to a dual system of free banking with thousands of unit banks in which the risk of loss has been relatively great, public safeguards may be necessary to preservation of the system.

Opponents of the plan have advanced several arguments against deposit insurance. One is that it will encourage "bad banking" and inefficient administration of local institutions by removing the necessity for each bank to preserve itself through "good" management. Another, that the present plan of assessment places an unfair burden upon large metropolitan banks. That is, their likelihood of failure is less than that of smaller, less diversified rural banks, and so their contribution to the fund should be relatively less. Also, that a much smaller percentage of large city bank deposits was covered by the $5,000 limit, and the amount of the guarantee was insignificant to depositors with large balances. Although sentiment has recently developed among some bankers for reduction of the premium or distribution of a "dividend" from the reserve already established, it is said in other quarters that the assessment is too small to provide a reserve adequate to meet the losses that would be incurred in a serious banking crisis.[4] The counterargument is that, if the plan creates confidence among depositors, they will not run on banks and panic will be averted. Also, if the reserves should prove inadequate in settling claims of depositors of failed banks, the FDIC may use a $3-billion drawing fund available from the federal Treasury. It is interesting to note that the reserve of the corporation in 1948 was $1.1 billions, or almost as great as the losses suffered by depositors

---

[3] *Ibid.*, p. 141.

[4] In 1950 Congress recognized the desire of many banks for a reduction in the cost of insurance by establishing a plan to rebate part of the premium, or to apply it as a credit on the next assessment, if collections proved greater than necessary. See *Federal Reserve Bulletin*, October, 1950, pp. 1325–26.

of over 9,000 commercial banks that failed in the thirty-nine-month period, January, 1930, to March 4, 1933.[5]

There has been no opportunity to test the strength of the program in the few years that federal guaranty has been in force. No one is able to determine at this time the validity of the contentions of either adherents or antagonists. We are safe in saying, however, that the FDIC has given our commercial banking structure a greater coherence and unity than it formerly possessed and, without doubt, has added stability to the system by increasing public confidence in the safety of deposits.

INTERBANK RELATIONS

In a country such as the United States, where nation-wide branch banking is prohibited and the independent unit bank is still typical of the system, separate unit banks are forced to co-operate in providing the services demanded of them. Co-operation and joint action may be the result of legal compulsion, as previously observed in the requirement that all national banks must belong to the Federal Reserve System and that all members of that system must participate in the federal program of deposit insurance. But long before the advent of central banking and deposit guaranty, commercial banks had found voluntary co-operation both valuable and necessary. These interbank contacts are exemplified in the nation-wide network of correspondent banking relationships, in local clearinghouse associations, and such organizations as the American Bankers Association.

Correspondent Banking

Early in the history of American banking, small banks in rural areas found it necessary to carry balances with other banks in the larger centers of trade. In no other way could banks finance shipment of goods into the local community and accommodate their customers in making payments at a distance. Small banks did not have adequate facilities for dealing in investment securities—either for their own portfolios or for the benefit of customers. They were often unable to transmit funds to remote places for financing foreign exchange transactions. They were at a competitive disadvantage, as compared to small banks in a branch system, in the clearing and collection of

---

[5] Board of Governors of the Federal Reserve System, *Banking and Monetary Statistics* (Washington, D.C., 1943), Section 7, "Bank Suspensions," Table No. 66, "Commercial Bank Suspensions," p. 283.

checks. As a consequence, long before the twentieth century there had developed a system of voluntary co-operation, known as "correspondent relationships," to fill these gaps.

A country bank usually chose a bank in each of a number of larger cities as its "depository" or correspondent. The latter bank held a deposit account (interbank balance) for the smaller institution and usually, until the practice was outlawed by the Federal Reserve Act, paid what was then a relatively low rate of interest—frequently 2 per cent—on the net balance. Correspondent balances were counted within limits as legal reserves against depositors claims until the Federal Reserve banks became depositories of legal minimum-reserve requirements of member banks. Upon occasion the large city correspondent would lend to its country cousin and was constantly of assistance in check clearing and collecting.

It was expected, by some, that when the Federal Reserve banks established a nation-wide system of check collection and provided rediscount facilities, thus minimizing the need for interbank borrowing, the correspondent banking system would be doomed. But this has not been the case. Correspondent relations seem destined to continue as long as our unit banking system exists.

City correspondents now commonly advise their smaller bank clients on investment operations, provide foreign exchange facilities, act as depository for liquid balances and securities, transfer funds, and extend credit information, in addition to assisting in the collection process. Correspondents also may increase an individual bank's legal reserve by selling it federal funds—that is, by transferring part of its deposit in a Federal Reserve bank to the account of the smaller individual bank. In so far as deposit balances in a correspondent are legal reserves for state nonmember banks, an individual bank may increase its legal reserve by an interbank loan from a correspondent. Working reserves of either member or nonmember banks can likewise be increased by loans from a correspondent.

Although correspondent banks make available new reserves for their customer banks on an individual basis, they are unable to add to the aggregate volume of legal reserves of the entire banking system to the extent that Federal Reserve banks have this ability. The number and severity of bank crises or "panics" that occurred before we had the Federal Reserve System attests to the fact that the correspondent system was unable to prevent the freezing of bank assets when trouble developed. The significance of the Federal Reserve banks' ability to create additional reserves will be seen in Chapter 19,

"Business Fluctuations," and Chapter 20, "The Federal Reserve System."

The country clients or correspondents repay the city banks for their services, other than direct lending operations, by keeping sizable deposit accounts with them. On December 31, 1949, interbank balances totaled $12.7 billions for the country as a whole. Of this amount, $4.6 billions were held in banks in the state of New York and $1.3 in Illinois, indicating the importance of New York City and Chicago banks as correspondents.[6]

Clearinghouse Associations

Just as the correspondent relationship provides the vehicle for co-operation within the banking system among banks in various parts of the country, the clearinghouse furnishes the means of co-operation for banks within a certain community. As the name indicates, the clearinghouse was originally an agency for the clearing of checks between banks in the same locality. But in time it has come to be much more.

Clearinghouse associations conduct bank examinations supplementary to those made by legally authorized agencies. Some have assisted distressed member banks by arranging loans or temporary clearinghouse certificates in lieu of transfers of money in settlement of the claims cleared during periods of distress. They have become, in a sense, trade associations and, as such, exert pressure upon member institutions to prevent unfair practices, untruthful advertising, or unwise competitive methods. They provide for the interchange of credit information and aid the development of uniform methods or practices where standardization is of benefit to all concerned.

THE CLEARING PROCESS. The checks a bank receives on deposit are those that are: drawn on itself, drawn on nearby banks, or drawn on banks some distance away.

The first kind of transaction is settled easily within the bank by adding to the depositing customer's balance and subtracting the same amount from the balance of the customer who drew the check. The second class of checks may be collected by messenger or through the clearinghouse. The third kind will be collected either through a city correspondent or through the Federal Reserve System. We shall discuss each of the check collection channels in order.

COLLECTION BY MESSENGER. Collection by messenger is a cum-

---

[6] *Federal Reserve Bulletin*, June, 1950, p. 701.

bersome, costly, and even risky arrangement, for, if widely used, it would place a large number of bank clerks on the streets at one time and expose banks to the risk of loss. If collections were being made in this fashion, each institution would send a different messenger to each one of the other banks to deliver the bundle of checks to be collected. The messengers would then return to their own banks with the cash they had collected. In a city having 20 banks, 380 messengers would be on the streets just before the hour of clearing.

COLLECTION OF LOCAL CHECKS THROUGH A CLEARINGHOUSE.   If a clearinghouse association is substituted for a plan of clearing by messengers, as was done in New York City in 1853, the advantages of speed, economy, and reduced risk are realized. There are variations in the details of operation, but a simple plan will illustrate the merits of any clearinghouse system.

For example, early each day Bank A will make up a bundle of checks drawn on each of the other banks of the city. The total amount represented by the checks in each bundle is noted, and at a certain time the messenger is dispatched to the clearinghouse. There he meets messengers from the other banks carrying bundles of checks received the previous day by their respective institutions. The bundles are then exchanged and calculations made to show how much Bank A should receive from each other bank. Also, it is necessary to compute the amounts owed by Bank A to the other banks who had received checks drawn by depositors of Bank A. It may be assumed that checks totaling $360,000 drawn against Bank A are presented by Banks B and C, whereas checks brought by Bank A drawn on Banks B and C total $385,000. In this case, Bank A has a favorable balance and is owed $25,000 more than it owes. But the amount due to Bank A must be owed by Banks B and C together. Those two institutions will have adverse balances totaling $25,000 due to Bank A. In the settling process, no funds are paid directly to a bank, nor are funds received directly from a bank. The respective debit and credit claims are offset on the books of the clearinghouse, and all receipts and payments are made by the manager of the association.

The accompanying diagram (see Exhibit 26) may add clarity to our illustration. Let us assume that Bank A receives during the day claims of $175,000 against Bank B and of $210,000 against Bank C; that Bank B receives claims of $115,000 on Bank A and of $150,000 on Bank C; and that Bank C claims $245,000 from Bank A and $105,000 from Bank B. The total of these claims, $1,000,000, can be settled by a transfer of $15,000 from Bank B and $10,000 from

Bank C, or a total of $25,000 to Bank A. The data are summarized in the diagram.

When the calculations of amounts due and owed have been completed at the clearinghouse, the messengers return to their respective banks with the bundles of checks received from the other banks.

Exhibit 26

ILLUSTRATION OF A CLEARING OPERATION
(Thousands of Dollars)

DRAWN ON \ BROUGHT BY	BANK A	BANK B	BANK C	TOTAL
BANK A		115	245	360
BANK B	175		105	280
BANK C	210	150		360
TOTAL	385	265	350	1,000

	Bank A	Bank B	Bank C	Total
Total claims on other banks.....	$385	$265	$350	$1,000
Total claims presented by others.	360	280	360	1,000
Difference—amount due........	$ 25	$...	$...	$ 25
—amount owed......	...	15	10	25

Following that, bookkeepers in each institution deduct the proper amounts from the accounts of depositors who drew the checks. Canceled checks are then filed to be returned to the drawer at month-end or whenever the books are balanced.

COLLECTION OF OUT-OF-TOWN ITEMS.   As already indicated, the collection of out-of-town checks is, in practice, effected either through a city correspondent or through the Federal Reserve. Since in both cases the process is very similar, we shall limit ourselves to a description of the general process and then add a few notes about the special problems of Federal Reserve collections.

Use of Correspondent Bank in Collecting Checks. Operation of the clearing process through the correspondent plan can be illustrated very simply. Small rural banks usually keep a correspondent balance in banks of several metropolitan centers with whom its customers have business. For a bank in a typical down-state town of Illinois, this may mean that deposits are maintained at Chicago, St. Louis, and Nashville. The total of these balances may be from 5 to 20 per cent of the bank's deposit obligations.

Large metropolitan banks, such as the well-known "Loop" banks of Chicago, may have from 100 to 1,000 correspondents in rural areas. In turn, these city banks have balances on deposit in New York and other large cities.

When a small bank in rural Illinois receives a check drawn on a country bank in Tennessee, it may forward the item to its Nashville correspondent for collection. If the Nashville bank also holds a deposit of the drawee bank in Tennessee, it may collect the check, after advice of acceptance, by merely adjusting the balances it holds for the two rural institutions. In the event that a check originates at a greater distance from Illinois, such as Oswego, New York, the check will be forwarded by the small Illinois bank to its Chicago correspondent for collection. The latter will send the item to a New York correspondent, who will collect through correspondent relations with a bank in Oswego.

Regardless of the distance between the point of origin and the bank in which the item is deposited, the network of correspondent relationships covering the nations makes collection relatively cheap and convenient. The system furnishes cohesion within the banking structure and introduces some of the natural advantages that would be found in a nation-wide branch system. Needless to say, if the unit banking system is ever displaced by nation-wide branch operation, check collection through correspondents is likely to wither and ultimately to die.

In some areas of the South and West, drawee banks do not honor at par checks presented by mail, but make a small deduction called an "exchange charge." These are "non-par banks." The practice is usually confined to small banks in thinly settled areas. Before the Federal Reserve System was established, exchange charges were commonly made by national, as well as state, banks. Checks being returned to the drawee bank were routed home via a correspondent which would remit to the payee bank at par. The correspondent would bear the loss of non-par remittance by the drawee bank unless it, in turn, was able to collect via one of its correspondents. The resulting system of indirect routing enlarged the volume of checks in the process of collection, called the "float," and greatly increased the over-all costs of the collection process. The Federal Reserve once tried to bring about universal par clearance. It failed, but by persuasion it has managed to reduce the "non-par" fringe to a small number of remote banks.

Check Collection through a Federal Reserve Bank.   The process of check collection through the Federal Reserve is much the same as through a correspondent bank. The chief difference is that the Federal Reserve is somewhat more exacting about the way in which it insists that collection items be forwarded; on the other hand, since member banks must keep a reserve balance with the Federal Reserve bank whether or not they use its collection facilities, they can, sometimes, keep down the amount of idle cash by using these Federal Reserve facilities, thereby avoiding the need for a large correspondent account. Since all member banks are required to maintain deposits at the regional Federal Reserve bank, the balances can be used as a clearing account for members located in the same district. Checks drawn against Bank A and deposited in Bank Z, when sent to the Reserve bank for collection, are settled as follows: the reserve balance of Bank Z is increased and that of Bank A is reduced.

This system covers the entire nation; it works between Federal Reserve districts as well as within a single district. Each Federal Reserve bank maintains a balance in the Inter-district Settlement Fund in Washington, D.C. Here daily computations are made on the basis of telegraphic reports received from each Federal Reserve bank, indicating the amount of checks received during the day that involve collections in each of the other eleven districts. Net amounts due or to be received are computed, and the accounts of some district banks are reduced while an equal amount is added to the other district accounts.

Thus, when Middle Western businessmen make large payments to their creditors along the Atlantic seaboard, not only are deposits of member banks and Federal Reserve banks in the Middle West reduced, but the deposits of Federal Reserve banks of the Middle West held in the Inter-district Settlement Fund in Washington also decline. In contrary fashion, deposits of eastern commercial and Federal Reserve banks expand, as will balances in the Inter-district Settlement Fund held for the account of the eastern Federal Reserve banks. In short, settlements through this fund are correlated with member bank deposits and reserve balances.

A few commercial banks that are not full-fledged members of the Federal Reserve System avail themselves of clearing privileges by maintaining a deposit, or clearing balance, with the regional Federal Reserve bank. Many others place themselves on the "par" list by agreeing to remit the face value of any legitimate check or draft on which they are the designated drawee.

SUMMARY

Despite the fact that nation-wide branch banking is prohibited and that there are a larger number of competing unit-plan institutions than in any other nation, the United States has a fairly well-knit commercial banking system. The unity of policy and action found in the system rests upon a large body of statutory law and administrative regulations and on the high degree of co-operation found to exist among regulatory bodies and voluntary banking organizations and associations.

Without doubt, the system is now stronger than ever before. It is manned by a body of officials and private bankers who enjoy the full confidence of bank depositors because of their acceptance of the obligations imposed by their position as trustees of the public welfare.

Although minor modifications are being made constantly to reduce frictions that exist in such a vast machine, the successful operation of banks in recent years precludes the likelihood that significant changes in the structure will occur in the near future.

—FRANK H. GANE

QUESTIONS AND PROBLEMS

1. Name some of the unique features of the banking structure of the United States.

2. Distinguish between (a) national and state banks, (b) insured and non-insured banks, and (c) member and nonmember banks. Under whose supervision are the above-named banks administered?

3. Compare federal laws and the banking statutes of your state on these points: (a) minimum capital requirements, (b) minimum deposit reserves, (c) restrictions on real estate loans, and (d) limitations on investments.

4. What provisions regarding branch banking are found in the laws of your state? Does local sentiment favor the continuance of these provisions?

5. What do you consider the most significant advantages that would be realized from (a) state-wide branch banking and (b) nation-wide branch banking?

6. Describe the organization of a group banking system. What changes have occurred recently in the number of offices operated by the three groups discussed in the text?

7. How are bank examination functions divided among federal and state regulatory agencies?

8. Guaranty of bank deposits by state banking administrators was a failure. Why is there reason to believe that guaranty will succeed when administered on a national scale?

9. Describe the system of correspondent bank relationships of the United States. Why do these relationships persist along side the co-operation provided by the Federal Reserve System?

10. Trace steps in collection of a check drawn on Planters State Bank, Salina, Kansas, and deposited in State Bank and Trust Co., Evanston, Ill. Both are member banks.

11. Why, in the absence of state or national regulation, did clearing associations fix uniform rates of interest to be paid on time deposits held by members of the association? Would local regulation not be as effective as the imposition of uniform rates administered by federal authority?

12. If 380 messengers would be required to clear the checks of 20 local banks, how many would be needed if 50 banks participated? How does a clearinghouse operate?

BIBLIOGRAPHY

Interesting accounts of the origins and development of banking are found in the following:

Conant, Charles A. *A History of Modern Banks of Issue.* 6th ed. Rev. by Marcus Nadler. New York: G. P. Putnams' Sons, 1927.

Dunbar, C. F. *The Theory and History of Banking.* 4th ed. New York: G. P. Putnams' Sons, 1922.

Hoggson, N. F. *Banking through the Ages.* New York: Dodd, Mead & Co., 1926.

The historical development of American banking is emphasized in:

Members of the Staff, Board of Governors of the Federal Reserve System. *Banking Studies.* Washington, D.C.: Board of Governors of the Federal Reserve System, 1941.

Miller, H. E. *Banking Theories in the United States before 1860.* Cambridge, Mass.: Harvard University Press, 1927.

White, Horace. Money and Banking. 5th ed. Boston: Ginn & Co., 1914.

The administration and operation of banks is well treated in the following texts:

Harr, Luther, and Harris, W. C. *Banking Theory and Practice.* 2d ed. New York: McGraw-Hill Book Co., Inc., 1936.

Robinson, R. I. *The Administration of Bank Funds.* New York: McGraw-Hill Book Co., Inc., 1951.

Rodkey, Robert G. *Sound Policies for Bank Management.* New York: Ronald Press Co., 1944.

Rodkey, Robert G. *The Banking Process.* New York: Macmillan Co., 1928.

The nature and functions of commercial banking are discussed to some extent in standard college texts on money and banking. These include:

Bradford, F. A. *Money and Banking.* 5th ed. New York: Longmans, Green Co., Inc., 1941.

Foster, Major B., and Rodgers, Raymond (eds.). *Money and Banking.* 3d ed. New York: Prentice-Hall, Inc., 1947.

Kent, Raymond P. *Money and Banking.* New York: Rinehart & Co., Inc., 1947.

Prather, Charles L. *Money and Banking.* 4th ed. Chicago: Richard D. Irwin, Inc., 1949.

Thomas, Rollin G. *Our Modern Banking and Monetary System.* 2d ed. New York: Prentice-Hall, Inc., 1950.

Westerfield, Roy B. *Money, Credit and Banking.* Rev. ed. New York: Ronald Press Co., 1947.

Woodworth, George Walter. *The Monetary and Banking System.* New York: McGraw-Hill Book Co., Inc., 1950.

Current developments of a statistical nature may be found in monthly issues of the *Federal Reserve Bulletin* and in annual reports issued by the Comptroller of Currency, Federal Deposit Insurance Corporation, and the Board of Governors of the Federal Reserve System.

Chapter • 5

SPECIALIZED SHORT-TERM FINANCING

IN ALMOST any field of business there are specialists who handle particular problems beyond the scope of the major producers of the field. In the field of finance, specialization has long played a part because a specialist can seek out and arrange financing which the major producers, the commercial banks, are unable or unwilling to handle and because some problems are better solved by special methods of financing than by the unsecured short-term lending characteristic of bank operation. As a result, bank credit otherwise unavailable is extended through specialized agencies to some borrowers, and funds from other sources are also made available.

Throughout the history of the United States, but more particularly in past decades than in the present, commercial banks have operated under restrictions, imposed by law and by tradition, which limited the scope of their lending. During the 1800's the effects of banking law tended to make difficult the transfer of funds from one section of the country to another and prevented local banks from supplying enough funds to meet all of the demands which might be made on them by local business. This meant that some borrowers found it necessary to arrange for loans in areas distant from their home office, and a specialized device for handling this problem—the commercial paper market—came into being. Bankers have always been willing to lend money against the security of staple goods in the hands of responsible warehousemen, but many businesses were unable to meet the requirements for an inventory loan until "field" warehousing was developed as a specialized method of meeting these requirements. The difficulties inherent in controlling and collecting loans based on a heterogeneous collection of accounts receivable were first overcome by "commercial receivables companies" which specialized in making such loans. Furthermore, not all financing prob-

155

lems are solved most efficiently by *borrowing;* they may be solved in many cases by obtaining goods but deferring payment for them (e.g., using trade credit), or in other cases by selling assets not directly necessary to the operation of the business (e.g., factoring[1]). Traditional reluctance of bankers to make loans to consumers—that is, nonproductive, noncommercial loans—opened the way for the development of consumer finance companies and the allied commercial process called "wholesale" or "floor-plan" financing. For reasons such as these, specialized financing agencies and specialized financing methods have been and continue to be important in the short-term field. Some specialized practices have been developed to a high degree of efficiency. Indeed, some of these practices are continually being adopted by the commercial bankers, and specialists continue to develop new methods.

In many instances, individual businessmen look to persons related to the business—its employees, officers, customers, co-owners—for special forms of short-term financing. In other instances, agencies established by public or private groups supply funds to businesses which would not be able to obtain them elsewhere. In this chapter the discussion is related to five commonplace, although specialized, short-term financing methods referred to above: trade credit, commercial paper, loans secured by current assets, factoring, and wholesale or floor-plan financing.

TRADE CREDIT

The most familiar way in which a businessman can obtain the use of goods without immediately paying for them is for him to utilize what is known as "trade credit." In the everyday life of individuals it is to be recognized as the agreement reached when a customer says "Charge it." The buyer obtains possession of the goods, not by paying for them, but by agreeing to make payment in the future in accordance with the specific terms of the trade.

The Credit Process

The acceptance by the seller of the buyer's offer of credit is evidenced by delivery of the goods to him. When the buyer receives title—that is, when ownership of the goods passes to him—he becomes obliged to make payment according to the credit terms. The obligation of the buyer is recorded on the books of the seller as an

---

[1] For a discussion of "factoring," see p. 171.

"account receivable." It is probably also recorded on the books of the buyer as an "account payable." In most trade-credit agreements, the exchange of goods for credit is on "open account"; that is, there is no formal written evidence of the agreement, such as a promissory note or a draft. In a few industries, however, it is customary to use promissory notes or drafts, and creditors may be expected to ask customers who are not strong financially to provide a note or draft as evidence of the agreement.

CREDIT STANDARDS TEND TO BE LOW. The acceptance of a customer's credit as a step in the sale of goods is an important part of the process of exchange. The terms on which trade credits are accepted are influenced to a greater extent by the dual seller-creditor functions of the supplier than are terms in other forms of short-term finance. Unless a customer's credit is accepted and the terms customarily used in the trade are granted, a seller may lose the business to other merchants who will accept the credit on customary terms. Sellers, of course, must investigate the creditworthiness of their customers. A credit sale to an individual obviously unable or unwilling to make payment according to the terms of agreement would be foolish. However, there are two factors which tend to make the seller willing to accept credit when other types of creditors might refuse to do so. Sellers seek to gain new customers and to continue trading with old customers. By taking risks on some buyers, the trader can distinguish between those buyers who are in fact poor risks and those who, despite apparent financial weakness, continue to purchase and manage to pay for goods consistently. The poor risks can be eliminated after events have proved them poor; the others continue as profitable customers. Thus, by taking some losses, the seller is able to establish profitable customer relationships which more than offset any losses incurred in the long run. Furthermore, the seller is in a position to stand losses better than other short-term financing agencies. The gross profit margin on credit sales is greater than the gross profit margin on credit extension alone. At any one time, the credit seller is able to absorb a larger proportion of losses without endangering his ability to earn a profit or, at least, without incurring the risk of "technical" insolvency. ("Technical" insolvency is the inability to make payment immediately. A firm may have more than enough assets to extinguish all debt, if given time to turn them into cash in an orderly fashion, and yet be unable to supply immediately the cash needed to pay maturing debt. Such a firm would be not "actually" but "technically" insolvent.)

TRADITION HAS ESTABLISHED TERMS.   Sellers usually are obliged to accept credit on terms dictated by custom. Terms vary with the conditions in different industries and with the function of the seller within an industry. Historically, producers and distributors in or adjacent to financial centers have been in a more advantageous position to obtain the funds needed to carry accounts receivable. Outlying retailers and other distributors more remote from the financial centers have not been equally favored. This has tended to be reflected in credit terms; maturity dates are placed far enough ahead (thirty, sixty, ninety days) to permit the outlying sellers to collect from their customers before paying their own debts. Cash from the ultimate sale of goods tends to flow back along the lines of distribution and, as it is passed from hand to hand, extinguishes the series of credits which were created to facilitate the distribution process. It is customary to allow discounts for prompt payment at each of the points at which credit sales are made. These discounts for prompt payment—usually called "cash discounts"—originated during the Civil War at a time when prices were rising rapidly. It was to the advantage of sellers to encourage customers to pay promptly; the more quickly the seller (creditor) received payment for goods he had sold, the less was his loss of ability to pay the rising costs of the goods which he himself needed to purchase. Today, the cash discount, if allowed, serves largely as a collection device. It is an inducement to those who can pay promptly to do so, and thus is a means of separating "weaker" from the stronger accounts for closer supervision.

COMPETITION AFFECTS TERMS AND STANDARDS.   The acceptance of credit on customary terms is necessary in many industries if sellers are to maintain' customer good will. Buyers expect to purchase on established terms and are displeased by any suggestion on the part of the seller that the terms be different. On the other hand, credit terms provide one device by which sellers may offer discriminatory prices in an effort to obtain the business of important buyers. Buyers themselves may abuse the credit arrangement by seeking to take cash discounts after the discount period has elapsed or by deferring payment even beyond the agreed maturity date. The weakness of the open account receivable as a legal instrument and the cost of collecting accounts encourage such abuse. Furthermore, competitive pressures often militate against action through refusal to accept additional credit or insistence upon written evidence of indebtedness which might limit abuse.

Extent of Use of Trade Credit

With the general development of credit institutions and facilities for transfer of funds, trade credit has become relatively less important as a short-term financing device than it was a century ago. Nevertheless, trade credit remains the largest single source of short-term credit for business.[2] A study published by the National Bureau of Economic Research indicates that trade credit accounted for 44 per cent of current liabilities on the books of nonfinancial corporations in the United States in 1939.[3] It will be noted in Chapter 7, however, that the number of corporations is small, compared to the total number of businesses in the United States, and that most businesses which are not corporations are small in size. Since it is probable that smaller businesses use trade credit more than larger businesses, the proportion of trade credit on the balance sheets of all business would probably be greater than the figure given in the National Bureau of Economic Research study. In other words, it would appear that at any given time the amount of trade credit on the books of American businesses is probably between two fifths and one half of the amount of all short-term liabilities.

Function Performed

Credit permits goods to move without *simultaneous* countermovement of cash. The problems of physical production and distribution

---

[2] It is not, however, the largest source of short-term financing for all businesses. Owing to the high rates of taxation of the income of incorporated businesses and the fact that the payment of taxes is deferred from the date when income is earned until payment dates in the following year, an important—and in many cases, the most important—source of short-term credit today is the federal government. This is indicated by the following data showing the current liabilities of all manufacturing concerns in the United States for the four quarters of the year 1949:

	(DATA IN MILLIONS OF DOLLARS)			
	1st Quar.	2d Quar.	3d Quar.	4th Quar.
Bank loans payable within one year.....	2,826	2,196	2,258	2,233
Other notes and accounts payable*......	7,239	6,906	6,988	7,145
Federal income taxes accrued..........	7,342	6,870	6,624	6,190
Other current liabilities...............	4,286	4,359	4,272	4,105
Total current liabilities............	21,693	20,331	20,142	19,673

* Trade credits are probably the largest part of the group of credits called "other notes and accounts payable."

Source: Federal Trade Commission and Securities and Exchange Commission, *Quarterly Industrial Financial Report Series*, Fourth Quarter, 1949 (May 14, 1950).

[3] Neil H. Jacoby and R. J. Saulnier, *Business Finance and Banking* (New York, 1947), Table 3, p. 41.

and the problems of payment differ. Credit facilitates exchange by permitting the traders to solve these different problems separately. Trade credit is particularly important as the *immediate* device by which many problems of selling and of payment are separated.

Nature of the Debtors

The use of trade credit as an immediate means of exchange is universal. In this respect it is unlike other financing devices which are customarily used by some industries and not by others, or by some companies within an industry and not by others. For this reason, there is little opportunity to generalize significantly about the nature of the debtors. It is probably true that firms which depend on deferred payment beyond the cash discount period are financially weak. The cost of trade credit is high, as will be explained in the following paragraphs; and businesses which can use other, less expensive financing devices might be expected to do so. Smaller firms may depend more on trade credit, despite its expense, simply because it is convenient and because several of the sources of funds available to larger businesses are not available to smaller firms. On the whole, however, it should be recognized that the choice which confronts any business is not so much *whether to use* as *how much to use* its trade credit.

Cost to the Debtor

The terms of a trade-credit agreement usually refer to two periods: a brief period, most frequently ten days, during which the debtor may take a discount on the face amount of the billing as a consideration for prompt payment; and a second, longer period, by the end of which the full amount of the bill is expected to be paid if the cash discount was not taken. Typical terms are: 2/10, n/30 (2 per cent discount for payment within ten days, face amount due in any event in thirty days); or 2/10, n/60. Other familiar terms are: 10 E.O.M. (full amount due ten days after the end of the month in which the transaction took place—the usual terms of agreement on personal charge accounts at retail stores); and C.O.D. (cash on delivery).

Under the latter terms, 10 E.O.M. or C.O.D., there is no explicit measure of the cost of credit to the buyer. Terms such as 2/10, n/30, however, clearly imply a cost to those debtors who do not take the cash discount. If an invoice is not paid by the tenth day, the buyer must pay 2 per cent for the privilege of deferring a payment of 98 per cent of the amount of the invoice until he does pay. He is expected to pay the bill, in any event, within the next twenty days—i.e., on or before the thirtieth day. This payment of 2 per cent for deferment is a definite cost. On an invoice for $100 which remains unpaid until the end of the agreed period, the cost is $2. The time and payment relationship may be converted into an annual rate of charge as follows: $2 × 360/20 equals $36—i.e., payment of $2 for the use of money for 20/360ths of a year is equivalent to payment of $36 for the use of the same amount of money for a full year. Since the amount of money which was left available by the privilege of deferred payment was $98 rather than $100, the annual rate of charge is slightly greater than 36 per cent. Similarly, the annual rate of charge for deferring payment to the sixtieth day under terms of 2/10, n/60 would be approximately 14½ per cent.[4] Under these conditions it is apparent that the rate of charge for acceptance of trade credit may be high relative to the rates of charge which are ordinarily associated, for example, with bank borrowing. The business which uses its trade credit beyond the cash discount period usually pays a high price for the privilege.

Sources of Creditor Funds

In those fields where trade credit is customary, sellers necessarily invest in receivables. In order to sell goods and make profits, they must accept customer credit. When they do so, they supply goods without receiving cash in return; instead, they record an account receivable. If the investment in receivables is not made, the business is not selling. For many businesses, some minimum investment is necessary if they are to prosper. As one customer pays his account, a sale to another customer gives rise to another receivable. At all times, this minimum portion of the funds of the business are tied up in customer accounts. If the amount falls below the minimum, the firm is not selling at a profitable rate. Because a minimum investment in receivables is essential and represents a continuing use of funds, these funds should be obtained from sources which will provide them on a long-term basis. Additional investments in receivables which occur during periods of temporarily increased selling, such as the Christmas season at department stores, can be financed by obtaining funds for a short-term period, and this includes the use of trade

---

[4] Note that the longer the period which elapses between the end of the discount period and the date of payment, the smaller is the effective annual rate of charge. It is in this sense that a debtor who defers payment beyond the customary maturity dates of trade credit obtains an advantage over competitors who pay their bills when due. This underlies the abuse already referred to in the paragraph on "Competition Affects Terms and Standards."

credit. On the whole, therefore, trade creditors obtain a large proportion of the funds invested in receivables from permanent sources
—that is, from owners, or from creditors who lend on a long-term
basis.

COMMERCIAL PAPER

Bank loans, which were discussed in Chapter 3, provide the most
important form of short-term loan credit to business. In Chapter 3,
however, there is also reference to "open-market paper." The notes
and acceptances of business concerns, purchased by bankers on the
open market, provide a useful type of earning asset for the banking
system. In the paragraphs below, we will discuss the characteristics of
the process by which commercial paper becomes available on the
open market.

The Lending Process

Commercial paper, in the sense relevant here, consists of promissory notes and acceptances of short maturity which are sold on the
open market by commercial paper houses. The marketing process
enables the debtor to borrow at the lowest available rate of interest.
Nearly all commercial paper is purchased by banks. In the end, therefore, the process is one by which the borrower is enabled to find the
bank or banks which will lend to him on the most advantageous terms.

A borrower who desires to sell notes or acceptances in the open
market executes a number of these instruments in amounts ranging
from $2,500 to $5,000, or $10,000, or more. The most common loan
periods are from four to six months. The instruments are made payable to the borrower himself and then endorsed by him without quali-
fication. In this fashion, the notes or acceptances become bearer instruments. They can pass from hand to hand without further endorsement and are payable at maturity to the bearer upon presentation to
the debtor for payment. The borrower will sell these instruments to
a dealer. The dealer's salesmen contact the customers on their lists
to find those interested in buying this issue. The dealer, since it is
unnecessary to endorse the instruments, incurs no direct risk in selling
the paper except, possibly, during the short time that he has the instruments and is seeking a buyer for them. Indirectly, as one might suppose, the dealer must assume some responsibility for investigating the
creditworthiness of borrowers. He risks the loss of customer good will
if some paper he has sold proves to be of poor quality. At the end of

the loan period, the notes or acceptances are returned to the debtor for payment.

Extent of Use of Commercial Paper

The amount of commercial paper outstanding declined from a peak in 1920 to the lowest point in 1933. Although there has been some increase in the amount outstanding since then, as the data in Exhibit 27 indicate, there has not been a return to levels of earlier years.

Exhibit 27

AMOUNT OF COMMERCIAL PAPER OUTSTANDING IN THE UNITED STATES, DECEMBER 31, 1918–49

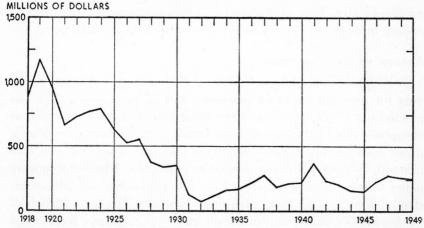

MILLIONS OF DOLLARS

Source: 1918–34, inclusive: *Banking and Monetary Statistics* (Federal Reserve Board, 1943), pp. 465–67; 1935–48, inclusive: *Survey of Current Business*, 1949 Supplement, p. 80; 1949: *Survey of Current Business*, March, 1950, p. S-15.

The decline from the peak outstandings of 1920 is explained by three factors: Passage of the Federal Reserve Act in 1913 served to reduce the usefulness of the open-market type of operation for short-term financing because local banks were placed in a better position to make short-term loans to business. During the 1920's many businesses took advantage of favorable conditions and raised substantial amounts of long-term funds. At about the same time, improvements in manufacturing and distributive processes enabled businesses to get along with smaller investments in inventories and thereby reduced the need for current assets. In short, the need for investment in current assets was reduced; a greater part of the need was met by raising long-term funds; and local banks were better prepared to handle the remaining requirements.

Functions Performed

The need for an open market was most pronounced during the period before the Federal Reserve Act became effective. The restrictive effect of reserve requirements and other limitations on local bank lending led many borrowers to seek funds in areas other than their immediate locality. Before the Civil War, commercial paper houses acted as brokers. They brought borrower and lender together, for a commission. After the Civil War, these houses acted as dealers, buying paper from the borrower and holding it until sold to the ultimate lenders. In either case, commercial paper houses served to link borrowers and lenders who were, in most instances, widely separated geographically. They also served as a medium to assist borrowers in finding those lenders who would advance funds at the least cost.

Nature of the Borrowers

In the discussion of bank lending, the necessity for rigorous standards for granting credit on two-name and on unsecured paper was pointed out. Such standards have tended to restrict the number of businesses eligible to borrow from banks. But, the banker making a direct loan has the distinct advantage inherent in his personal contact with the borrowing concern and its personnel. A lender acquiring paper through the open market loses this advantage and adjusts his standards by making them even more rigorous. The investigation of the borrower's ability to "throw off cash"—i.e., to pay loans when they fall due—is more intensive; the strength displayed on the balance sheet must be greater; the historical record of the borrower's operating results and promptness in paying debts must be better than that required for a direct loan. In general, borrowers have been in industries producing staple goods—textiles, lumber, drug and chemicals, metals, food wholesaling—and, even in these industries, usually only the larger concerns borrow on the open market.

Cost to the Borrowers

An open-market borrower can expect to obtain funds at the lowest available short-term rate of interest. In addition, he gains the advantage of favorable public relations. Financial strength is associated with a reputation as an open-market borrower. The borrower could command the lowest rate available on direct loans from banks. Actually, because the impersonal form of the transaction makes it easier for the banker to demand repayment of notes at maturity and avoid the problem of renewal—at least, the banker is spared the job of facing the borrower with a refusal of further loans—the rate paid on prime commercial paper is usually less than the lowest direct bank rates. In recent years the interest rate on 4- to 6-month prime commercial paper has ranged from ¾ to 1½ per cent, whereas the rate on direct bank loans to stronger borrowers has ranged from 2 to 2⅔ per cent. Because the commission charged by commercial paper dealers is ⅛ to ¼ per cent of the dollar amounts of paper handled, this cost, on an annual basis, would add from ¼ to ¾ per cent to the interest rate in the borrower's computation of his cost. On this basis, it is clear that open-market borrowing does not cost more than direct borrowing and may cost less.

Sources of Dealer Funds

Banks are, with few exceptions, the ultimate buyers of commercial paper. The bank's sources of funds have been discussed in preceding chapters. The description here is related to the financing of the intermediary, the commercial paper house.

As a broker, the commercial paper house had small asset requirements. Most of the needed funds were supplied by the owners. As a dealer, the need is greater. The dealer usually buys notes from borrowers, although he may occasionally take paper on a consignment basis—that is, agree to sell it but make no payment until he has completed a sale. When the dealer buys notes, he may advance part of the funds—say, 90 per cent of the face amount of the notes acquired—and pay the balance, less discount (interest payment collected in advance) and commission, when the notes are sold. Usually, however, the face amount less discount and commission is advanced immediately. In either case, the dealer must have funds with which to pay the borrower. The immediate need may be avoided by agreeing to pay the borrower at the end of a short period, which, however, would allow enough time for the dealer to place the notes in the hands of ultimate holders. Then the flow of funds is from creditor to borrower through the dealer. But if the dealer pays the borrower before he places the notes, he must have funds available from some other source. The high quality of the notes will permit him to use them as security for a loan from a bank to himself; but even in this case, the dealer must be prepared to put up a margin between the loan obtained and the amount paid out to the borrower. This combination, borrowing on inventory and provision of a margin of long-term funds by the owners, is the customary way in which commercial paper houses are financed.

LOANS SECURED BY CURRENT ASSETS[5]

In addition to unsecured loans to business, many banks make loans secured by the pledge of assets owned by their borrowers. These assets may take many forms, but accounts receivable and inventories are those most frequently used. Receivables loans are also made by a number of specialized credit agencies, called "commercial receivables companies." The paragraphs below are a description of the processes by which these loans secured by the pledge of current assets are made.

The Lending Process

Although many aspects of lending against pledged accounts receivables and inventories are similar, the distinctions are also of considerable importance. Therefore, in this description of the lending process, each type of loan is discussed separately.

PLEDGES OF ACCOUNTS RECEIVABLE. The details of the methods and contracts used in making loans secured by accounts receivable vary, but the essential elements are fairly well standardized. The borrower permits a thorough audit of his business, with special attention given to the receivables on his books, including verification with the customers themselves. An agreement is drawn shifting the right of collection from the borrowing concern to the lending agency. This agreement may specify the acceptance of all accounts or only of those accounts which meet certain stated credit standards. The face amount of the collateral pledged will exceed the amount of the loan by some margin. That margin will be sufficiently large to protect the lender against losses on bad debts or shrinkage resulting from returns and allowances, and to preclude the loan being essentially a prepayment of the borrower's gross profit on sales. Between two thirds and

---

[5] The author is indebted for much of the data and descriptive material used in preparation of this section on "Loans Secured by Current Assets" and the next section on "Factoring" to the authors of three recent studies: R. J. Saulnier and Neil H. Jacoby, *Accounts Receivable Financing* (New York: National Bureau of Economic Research, Inc., 1943); R. J. Saulnier and Neil H. Jacoby, *Financing Inventory on Field Warehouse Receipts* (New York: National Bureau of Economic Research, Inc., 1944); and Tynan Smith, "Security Pledged on Member Bank Loans to Business," *Federal Reserve Bulletin,* June, 1947, pp. 664–80.

four fifths of the face amount is usually advanced. As the receivables are paid, the payment is forwarded by the debtor to the lender (often in the form in which it is received—e.g., the customer's check). The funds obtained are applied to the reduction of the loan balance, or, if a continuing agreement is in force, the funds are made available to the borrower, as he supplies new receivables to replace those that have been paid. The duration of loan agreements is not standard. One report suggests that agreements have an average life of from 3½ to 4 years; a second suggests that when banks lend on accounts receivable the loan is payable either within ninety days or, for some agreements, on demand.

PLEDGES OF INVENTORIES. Receipts for goods stored in bonded, field, or other warehouses, and certain other forms of title to inventory, may be used as security for loans. For simplicity, and because the field-warehouse development has recently become important, the description here refers directly to the process of borrowing through the use of field-warehouse receipts. A field warehouse is one established by an independent warehouseman on the borrower's own premises. The same description with a few changes of terminology is applicable to other methods by which inventory may be pledged. It also applies to lending against the pledge of oil runs, stocks and bonds, savings deposits, life insurance policies, or equipment.

Where field warehousing is used, the warehouseman usually rents from the borrower the facilities necessary for the storage and adequate care of the goods, places a bonded custodian in charge, and, having obtained complete control over the inventory, issues a receipt for the stored goods. The lender advances funds against the value of the inventory, but usually not more than from two thirds to five sixths of the full value. The margin is expected to cover losses arising from price declines or deterioration. As inventory is withdrawn from the warehouse by the borrower, it must be replaced by satisfactory substitute goods or its value must be offset by a reduction of the loan balance.

In some instances, the lender will permit the withdrawal of goods on a trust receipt. This receipt places the goods in the hands of the borrower as a trustee for the lender. An example of this type of agreement is shown in the Supplement to Chapter 2. The borrower may process and sell the goods, but they are held in trust for the lender as long as they remain in the borrower's hands. Funds obtained from any sale are also held in trust for the lender until applied against the loan. The duration of lending agreements varies: bank loans are

usually for less than six months; borrowers report agreements run
ning as long as fifteen years, with an average of about four years.
Because more than nine tenths of the loans against the pledge of
inventory are made by banks, these data can be reconciled only on
the assumption that borrowers negotiate new loans as quickly as the
old mature.

Extent of Use of Loans against Current Assets

It is estimated that the volume of credit extended in 1941 on the
pledge of accounts receivable amounted to $1,488 million, and on
inventory, $150 million. The Federal Reserve Board data for the
loans of member banks alone indicate that the volume of loans outstanding on November 20, 1946, were: on accounts receivable, $180
million; on inventories $1,195 million; and other current assets (in-
cluding equipment), $2,304 million. If the relationships between
bank and other credit agency lending reflected in 1941 data prevailed
in 1946, the total volume of credit then outstanding against the pledge
of current assets would approximate $4 billion.

Functions Performed

Many borrowers who are unable to meet standards for credit on the
basis of unsecured promises to pay are able to obtain funds by pledging current assets. Other borrowers, as noted in the next paragraphs,
have found that a loan against certain current assets may be better
adapted to the needs of the business and that such borrowing may reduce interest expense.

Nature of the Borrowers

By their very nature, certain industries must carry large amounts
of inventories or receivables, or both, and therefore may find it advantageous to turn to secured loans as a means of obtaining funds.
The amounts obtained may exceed the lines of credit granted on open
account by commercial banks. Such industries as wine, lumber, food,
furniture, and machinery tend to borrow on secured notes.

Other industries, characterized by seasonal peaks, require greatly
increased investments in inventory or receivables for short periods.
The proportion of the increased investment which can be obtained by
borrowing may be greater if inventories or receivables are pledged.
Industries such as canning, seeds, and clothing fall in this category.

Still other businesses use secured notes because their financial
condition does not warrant the extension of credit on any other basis.

Such concerns are usually spoken of as "weak"; but, without in any sense denying that businesses do become weak financially and fail of recovery, two illustrations may serve to demonstrate that financial reports may well be something less than perfect reflections of a company's general condition as a going concern. First, many businesses become stronger and stronger financially as a depression proceeds. Receivables are collected; and since business sales are falling off, few new receivables are created. Inventory is sold and not replaced. Assets are depreciated and not replaced. Expenses are reduced. What little cash is generated by sales is largely retained. Thus, at the bottom of the depression, a company may show greater financial strength, by the usual tests, than at any other time. Second, many businesses tend to become financially weak as they expand. To sell, goods usually must be transferred to customers on credit. To transfer goods, inventories must be acquired. The investments in fixed assets and the expenses of operation may, and usually do, increase before the increase of receipts from sales begins. In the interim, especially if the production process is long and payments by customers are slow, the expanding concern tends to reach the point of technical insolvency— i.e., the point at which it has insufficient cash with which to pay maturing obligations. In this case, the company is "weak" and may be unable to borrow on an unsecured basis. The company may find it advantageous to turn to a lender who will advance funds on the security of the temporarily excessive inventory or receivables, or both.

The Borrowers' Cost

To estimate the cost of obtaining funds from any source is difficult. Direct payments for the use of funds can be distinguished in most agreements; but the borrower may be required to make indirect expenditures, or he may receive services other than, and in addition to, the use of money for the stated period. Those who borrow by pledging accounts receivable may be required to purchase credit insurance. The premium may well be included as part of the cost. Those who borrow by pledging inventory may be required to insulate themselves against price decline through the purchase of future contracts (hedging) on commodity markets. This may be considered a cost of borrowing. On the other hand, the borrower may obtain real service from the lending agency in the form of credit information, market analyses, financial management, or production advice. Some part of the apparent costs of borrowing as stated in the loan agreement should be allocated to these services and not charged entirely to the cost of obtaining money. The necessary allowances for costs in addition to stated costs, and for services obtained in addition to the actual loan, are not easy to make. It is perhaps not unreasonable to measure "cost" in terms of nominal payments for the use of funds, under the assumption that the indirect costs and the incidental services are approximate offsets.

ACCOUNTS RECEIVABLE LOANS. Many loan agreements require a payment at a specified rate per day on the total amount of the receivables pledged. Typical rates appear to be in the range of from one twenty-fifth to one fiftieth of 1 per cent per day, with the most frequently employed rate being one fortieth of 1 per cent per day. These rates are applicable to the full amount of receivables pledged, but the borrower obtains the use of funds equal to only two thirds to four fifths of this amount. If the advance were 70 per cent of the full amount of receivables and the rate were one fortieth of 1 per cent per day, the rate of interest on money borrowed would be $360 \times \frac{1}{40}$ (or 9) $\div 0.70$, which equals 13 per cent per year. The higher the proportionate advance, the lower the rate of interest; the lower the rate per day, the lower the rate of interest.

Other loan agreements state the payments in terms of an annual rate of interest. It is common practice for these loan agreements also to require that, as the receivables are collected, the money received shall be deposited in a special bank deposit, and, from time to time, the funds in that deposit are to be applied to reduce the loan balance. This "cash-collateral" deposit has the effect of changing the effective rate of interest. If the pledged receivables were paid up uniformly over the period of the loan, the average amount of money in the deposit account would be roughly 50 per cent of the amount loaned. If applied immediately, the receipts would reduce the amount on which the borrower paid interest by about one half. The effective rate of interest is therefore greater when, although the cash as collected is made available to the lender, the size of the loan is not reduced: the effective rate is approximately two times the nominal rate. In practice, because the flow of payments of the receivables is not uniform, the effective rate probably lies within the extremes of one to two times the nominal rate; thus, if the stated (nominal) rate were 6 per cent per year, the effective rate would probably be more than 6, but not more than 12, per cent per year.

INVENTORY LOANS. The borrower who desires to pledge inventory must pay the cost of warehousing. The cost of borrowing includes not only the interest paid on the money obtained but also the price paid for warehousing and obtaining the receipt which serves as security for the loan. The charges for warehousing vary widely. The charges on field warehousing are from $350 to $600 for installation of the facilities plus a percentage of the value of goods stored or a percentage of the amount of loan obtained. The warehousing cost probably represents a rate of 1½ to 2 per cent per year on most loans. In addition to the cost of warehousing, the borrower incurs a cost of 2½ to 6 per cent on the funds borrowed.

FACTORING

The outright sale of accounts receivable—i.e., factoring—is a device by which short-term financial requirements are covered through sale of current assets rather than by borrowing or using trade credit. The relationships between the client concern, the factor, and the concerns to which the client sells are different from those which would exist if a form of receivables loan were made. The description below indicates not only how the factoring process operates but also how it differs from the lending processes described in the previous section of this chapter.

The Financing Process

Because factoring is the outright purchase of the receivables of a business, the factor does not have recourse to his client on bad debts. The customers to whom the client of the factor sells on credit are notified that payments should be made to the factor and not to the company that sold the goods. When a sale is made, the client forwards invoices to both the factor and the customer. Before the sale, the client must know through agreement that the factor will accept the receivable. The factor pays from 90 to 95 per cent of the amount of the billing immediately, and the remainder less his commission when the bill is paid. The margin withheld during the period in which the receivable is outstanding is required to cover the possibilities that customers will take cash discounts or return some of the goods—i.e., to cover items other than the credit risks.

Utilization of Factoring

Factoring developed with the textile industries, and only in recent years has it been used as a financing device by concerns in other industries. In 1948 about $2½ billion of sales were factored. This implies average outstanding credit of about $350 million, since the turnover of factored receivables is approximately seven times a year.

Function Performed

Factoring provides a way to pass the collection, as well as the credit function of business, to a specialist. In a limited sense, it puts the client on a cash basis; i.e., under the usual contract, he may collect on his sales ten days after the end of the cash discount period. More importantly, however, investigation of the credit standing of customers and the bad-debt risk are shifted to the factor for a predetermined fixed fee.

Nature of the Borrowers

Early in the history of this country, textile manufacturing operations were performed by a large number of small mills producing similar, if not identical, products. The mills were located at sources of water power in New England. Their products were sold in the financial and commercial centers, particularly New York. The domestic producers were in competition with firms located in other countries, and these foreign firms were likewise at a distance from the commercial and financial centers of this country. It became common practice for both foreign and domestic producers to sell through agents; and these agents, because they were favorably located, assumed the credit investigation and risk-bearing functions for clients. In more recent years the selling operation has been divorced from financing. At the same time, the services of factors have been adopted by a wider variety of industries—e.g., lumber, paper, shoe, clothing, fur, electrical appliance, fuel, oil, furniture, glassware, and china. The factors' clients are in all size classes, but there seems to be a tendency for the amount of sales factored per client and for the amount of individual receivables to be somewhat larger than in the case of receivables loans.

Cost to the Client

There is a twofold charge for factoring: a rate of discount (usually about 6 per cent per year) of the full amount of each receivable, applied from the date of acceptance of the receivable by the factor to the agreed date of payment by the factor to his customer; and a commission (1 to 2 per cent of the amount of each receivable handled) for the services rendered. The rate of interest yielded for the services of factoring receivables would, therefore, be 15 to 22 per cent on receivables which are outstanding 50 days on the average.

Reserve-Plan Discounting

A form of discounting that deserves special mention is reserve-plan discounting, a compromise between the receivables loan and the factoring process. It includes the discounting of receivables much after the fashion of a factoring agreement. The receivables are sold to the financing agency. The client is under no recourse obligation. On the other hand, the lender does not assume all credit risk; he carries only the unusual or extreme risks. The client is required to maintain a deposit with the lender of about 8 to 15 per cent of the amount of receivables discounted. As receivables are paid, the client may draw against this reserve provided that it does not fall below the amount specified in relation to receivables still outstanding. Any bad debts or returns are charged against the deposit. Thus, credit losses are taken by the client unless they should be great enough to absorb all of the deposit. If they do absorb the deposit and are of even greater amount, these excessive losses are taken by the discount agency. The cost of the client tends to be at an annual rate of approximately 5 to 10 per cent.

WHOLESALE, OR "FLOOR-PLAN," FINANCING

In the distribution of high-priced consumer durable goods and of producer goods, two forms of receivables financing have assumed importance. One is that performed by the installment finance companies in buying the installment contracts of retailers. This function, however, is more relevant to the discussion of consumer financing and is described in Chapter 6. The other is wholesale, or "floor-plan," financing. The latter service solves the receivables problem of the manufacturer and the inventory problem of the dealer.

The Discounting Process

When goods are shipped from a manufacturer to a dealer, under the common procedure for floor planning, ownership of the goods shipped passes to a third party, a finance company (bank or other financial institution). The dealer possesses the goods. He may show them, sell them, and otherwise generally treat them as though he had bought them outright. But, in fact, at the time of shipment he gave the finance company notes equal to the cost of the goods. He possesses the goods as trustee for the finance company. The proceeds of any sale belong to the financing agency; and the dealer, as trustee for this agency, is expected to hold the proceeds and to turn them over to the agency in due course. Proceeds turned over will be applied against the principal and interest owed by the dealer on his notes.

Function Performed

This process of floor planning or wholesale financing has a dual effect. The manufacturer is relieved of much of a potential inventory problem. As fast as he makes goods, he can ship them to dealers and receive payment. The manufacturer, therefore, has the funds which would otherwise be tied up in inventory available for carrying on his manufacturing operations.

The dealers, on the other hand, would have to invest relatively large sums of their money in goods which, if they are shipped according to the manufacturer's production schedule rather than the dealer's selling schedule, might at times be greatly in excess of immediate requirements. Such an investment in inventory might prove embarrassing.

The finance company relieves the manufacturer by immediate payment for goods shipped and relieves the dealer by deferring payment until the goods are sold.

Nature of the Borrowers

This financing process is commonplace in the distribution of automobiles and home appliances, such as refrigerators, stoves, furnaces, and other relatively high-priced goods. It is interesting to note that this process depends, at least in part, on the fact that the dealer is sufficiently impressed by the benefits of selling the manufacturer's goods to be willing to bear the cost of inventory financing. Therefore, this process is restricted largely to situations in which the market of the dealer is protected through a franchise or license to sell the products of a well-known manufacturer.

The Borrowers' Cost

The borrower executes a note and a trust receipt. In recent years the rate of discount on the notes has run between 2 and 10 per cent per year. The maturity of notes would ordinarily be from one to six months but, of course, is determined largely by the time which will elapse between shipment of goods from the manufacturer and sale by the dealer.

THE FINANCING AGENCIES

The sources of funds of trade creditors and commercial paper houses have already been treated. The nature of the lending agencies that loan on the pledge of current assets and that factor or discount receivables has not been covered because no single type of agency can be considered characteristic. Some small firms specialize in one or another of these forms of financing; others combine two or more of the forms. The very large finance companies and some commercial banks (through special departments) may perform all of these services. The diversification of lending process of a large agency is illustrated in Table 9 with data from the balance sheets of the CIT Financial Corporation and the Commercial Credit Company (CCC), the two largest finance companies in the United States.

TABLE 9

Selected Data from the Balance Sheets of CIT Financial Corporation and the Commercial Credit Company, December 31, 1949*

(Millions of Dollars)

	CIT	CCC
Loans on Receivables and Factoring	$ 76	$ 47
Wholesale or Floor-Plan Financing	139	86
Total Commercial Financing	$215	$133
Consumer Loans and Installment Financing	620	417
Total	$835	$550

* Actual data have been rearranged to reflect classification used in the text discussion. Similar data from the reports of other finance companies would generally reveal corresponding diversification. The data for some—e.g., Walter E. Heller and Company—would show inventory loans, which do not appear in the CIT or CCC figures.

Finance companies transfer funds obtained from various sources to the borrowers whom they are specially qualified to serve. Unlike the commercial banks, finance companies do not "manufacture" money; that is, their obligations to their creditors are not accepted by the public as money. About one half to two thirds of the funds used by these companies are obtained by borrowing from banks or by discounting the receivables of their customers at the banks. Approximately a quarter to a third of the funds are obtained by issue of long-term credit obligations, such as debentures.[5] A quarter to a half

---

[5] Long-term credit obligations are described in Chapter 7.

of the funds are supplied by the owners. The rapid turnover of the loan inventory of these agencies and the rapidity with which they are able to convert their assets to cash in an emergency accounts for the very large proportion of bank borrowing. In a sense, the specialized nonbanking commercial credit agencies are arms or branches of the commercial banking system which carry bank credit to fields which the banks themselves may not be equipped to serve.

—LORING C. FARWELL

QUESTIONS AND PROBLEMS

1. Differentiate trade credit from other forms of short-term financing.
2. What conditions might lead a merchant to accept trade credit even though the customer might be unable to borrow readily from cash loan agencies?
3. A businessman finds that there is no difference in the cost to him of obtaining funds by borrowing from his commercial bank or by selling his notes on the open market. What conditions might guide him to decision as to the source on which to draw?
4. Describe and differentiate between "lending on accounts receivable" and "factoring."
5. In what respects is "wholesale" or "floor-plan" financing equivalent to factoring?
6. In what respects is "wholesale" or "floor-plan" financing equivalent to lending on the security of inventory?
7. Where do the finance companies obtain the funds which they use in lending on receivables and inventories and in factoring?
8. Why do specialized finance companies exist at a time when the commercial banking system is so fully developed?
9. What are the comparative costs to a given business of unsecured, accounts receivable, and inventory loans? What reasons would lead a business to choose one device rather than another?
10. Distinguish between: borrowing by pledging accounts receivable; factoring; reserve-plan discounting.

BIBLIOGRAPHY

Information about specialized short-term financing is scattered through articles and monographs. In recent years the work of the National Bureau of Economic Research in the monographs of its Business Finance Series has provided excellent material. Two monographs to which reference has already been made in this chapter are those by R. J. Saulnier and Neil H. Jacoby, *Accounts Receivable Financing* (New York: National Bureau of Economic Research, Inc., 1943), and *Financing Inventory on Field Warehouse Receipts* (New York: National Bureau of Economic Research, Inc., 1944). These works are important sources of detailed information on their subjects.

A book written by Walter S. Seidman (a member of one of the large factoring houses), entitled *Finance Companies and Factors* (New York: National Conference of Commercial Receivable Companies, Inc., 26 Broadway, 1949), is designed for use as a text and contains a great deal of information concerning technical aspects of both lending and factoring processes.

In November, 1946, the Federal Reserve Board conducted a survey of lending practices of commercial banks. The data resulting from the survey were published in a series of articles; and one of these, by Tynan Smith, "Security Pledged on Member Bank Loans to Business," *Federal Reserve Bulletin*, June, 1947, pp. 664–80, has already been referred to in this chapter. An older but very useful discussion of commercial paper markets is that by Roy A. Foulke, *The Commercial Paper Market* (New York: Bankers Publishing Co., 1931).

Chapter • 6

CONSUMER CREDIT

Commercial credit was the central theme of the preceding three chapters. They explained how and through which institutions business obtains the use of short-term funds and also how the commercial credit-granting institutions operate. We turn now to consumer credit.

NATURE OF CONSUMER CREDIT

Consumer credit is just what the name implies: it is credit granted to consumers for consumption purposes. When a "consumer" of automobiles buys a new car "on time," that is a consumer-credit transaction. When a family head borrows some cash from a small-loan company or a bank, it is a consumer-credit transaction. The charge accounts a family runs at department stores or elsewhere are another kind of consumer credit. Credit for the buying of homes may be thought of as consumer credit, but its character is so specialized that many persons consider it a separate type. In this text, residential-housing credit will be treated separately in Chapter 15. But the credit for repair and modernization of houses is included here. While repair and modernization credit is related to real estate credit in many respects, it is generally classed as consumer credit. Most funds for this purpose are advanced by commercial banks and sales-finance companies. For purposes of having a definition, we may say that "consumer credit" is "debt with a maturity of less than five years owed by consumers, as consumers, for consumption purposes."

Even though many individual consumer-credit transactions are for trivial amounts, the aggregate amount is large. In December, 1950, it was estimated by the Federal Reserve to be $20.1 billion. Including everyone—rich or poor, young or old—this amounted to more than one month's income. The indebtedness of many individual consumers, of course, amounts to several months' income.

In medieval times the church banned the charging of interest or "usury"; our modern interest-limiting laws are known as "usury laws." The practice of lending for consumption purposes was thought to be exploitative. But consumer credit is now a respected institution; the concerns that grant the credit occupy a recognized position in the financial community; individuals borrow or become indebted openly and without shame.

In medieval times and until late in the nineteenth century, most consumers could borrow only from "loan sharks." Such lending was not wholly legal, but it was practiced with little concealment. The persons borrowing were usually ashamed of doing so and conspired in the secrecy, which was the protection of the loan shark. The history of the loan shark comes straight through to modern times. The need for financial aid is so common and often so urgent that legal prohibition of lending at usury has never been very effective. In very recent times loan sharks have been known to operate more or less openly in the courthouses where their fellow practitioners were being prosecuted. The modern philosophy has not been to prohibit consumer credit granting but to recognize the need for consumer loans, bring the lenders into the open, and make them abide by rules and regulations which protect both borrower and lender.

The great recent growth of consumer credit is related to another modern development: the widespread purchase of automobiles and many durable household appliances. The use of consumer credit for reasons of desperation has been displaced by its use for purposes of pleasure and comfort. Modern incomes are spent more and more for the big-unit purchases which many people cannot pay for in one lump sum. The big-unit purchase has opened the way for vast consumer-credit promotion.

WHO USES CONSUMER CREDIT?

Because consumer credit has achieved respectability rather recently, it is often assumed that such credit is used largely by the lower-income groups. Research studies on this point have only recently become available. They show that consumer installment credit is not used so much by persons in the low-income class as by persons in the middle-income class. The poor do not have the standing to qualify for installment credit, and the wealthy do not need it.

The results of a survey conducted by the Federal Reserve are summarized in Exhibit 28, which shows that the users of consumer installment credit cluster around the middle of the income distribution. And it shows, surprisingly enough, that the users of credit go a considerable distance up the income scale; the fairly well-to-do use credit to a considerable extent.

Within the consumer-finance industry it has long been recognized that the factors which make applicants creditworthy are relative

Exhibit 28

USE OF INSTALLMENT CREDIT: PERCENTAGE DISTRIBUTION OF
SPENDING UNITS BY INCOME CLASSES

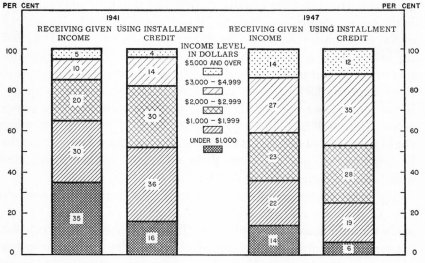

Source: Board of Governors of the Federal Reserve System.

stability of income and employment rather than size of income. Schoolteachers, for example, have long been considered prime outlets for consumer credit even though their incomes, until fairly recently (and even now, to some extent), have been on the slender side.

CLASSIFICATION OF CONSUMER CREDIT

Forms of consumer credit are so diverse that there are several ways of classifying these debts. One of the commonest is the division between *sale* credit and *loan* credit. "Sale credit" refers to a transaction in which the consumer gets a product (an automobile, furniture, or the like) or a service (electricity or gas, or medical attention) and promises to pay later. "Loan credit" refers to a transaction in which the consumer gets cash and undertakes an obligation to repay cash at some later date.

Another classification can be made: *installment* and *noninstallment*. An installment credit is one in which the amount owed is repaid in periodic (weekly, monthly) and usually equal amounts. Noninstallment transactions are those which are due in one lump sum, such as charge accounts or a note at a bank. Noninstallment forms of consumer credit are not always repaid in lump sums but often in driblets, in much the way some "slow" charge accounts are settled.

Exhibit 29

Classification of Consumer Credit

FORM	PURPOSE	
	Sale Credit	Loan Credit
Installment Credit	Buying an auto, furniture, or a refrigerator "on time" from a dealer in these goods	Borrowing cash from a small-loan company, a credit union, a commercial or industrial bank, with monthly or weekly repayment
Noninstallment Credit	"Charging" purchases at a department, grocery, or clothing store; accounts with a telephone or light company and with doctors and dentists	Borrowing cash from a commercial bank, a pawnshop, or a loan shark and promising to repay in one lump sum

There are overlaps between these two ways of classifying consumer credit. Exhibit 29 illustrates this overlapping. It should be understood that the transactions shown in this diagram are merely for illustration; many others are left out.

A third way of classifying consumer credit is by purpose. Here we meet with almost insuperable obstacles in getting figures or facts to illustrate our distinction. A consumer cash loan may be for the same purpose as a sale credit. For example: a consumer borrows from a bank in order to pay cash for an automobile rather than arranging the terms for installment payment with the auto dealer. Sometimes the purpose of consumer credit is said to be "remedial." This means that the purpose is urgent: medical or hospital needs, or consolidation of outstanding and pressing debts that break down the consumer-debtor's morale. This is an ambiguous basis of classification at best. In general the purposes of consumer credit are as broad as consumption itself; the way in which the consumer gets credit may be more a matter of convenience than an indication of real purpose. A consumer might let his charge accounts run in order to make medical outlays from current income, but the figures would show that he was borrowing to finance purchases on credit.

As a practical matter, the classification of consumer credit has been statistically possible only on rather general grounds. The figures in Table 10 were originated by the National Bureau of Economic Research and are now compiled by the Federal Reserve.

TABLE 10

CONSUMER CREDIT IN THE UNITED STATES, SEPTEMBER 30, 1950*

	Billions of Dollars		*Per Cent*
Consumer Credit—Total................		$19.3	100
Installment...........................		13.3	69
Automobile sale.....................	$4.2		22
Other sale..........................	3.6		19
Installment loan....................	5.5		28
Noninstallment.......................		6.0	31
Single-payment loans*...............	1.2		6
Charge accounts....................	3.7		19
Service credit.....................	1.0		5

*These figures incorporate a substantial revision of single-payment loan figures announced by the Federal Reserve in the fall of 1950. The charts in this chapter, drawn before this announcement, do not reflect this revision.

THE CONSUMER-CREDIT TRANSACTION AND ITS TERMS

It is not possible to generalize about the character and terms of consumer credit because the transactions assume so many forms. For this reason, the major types of consumer credit are examined separately in the following sections. The terms under which each type is usually extended and the implicit or explicit cost of the credit will be discussed. The field will be classified as in Exhibit 29.

Installment-Sale Credit

Automobile purchases, more than any other consumer expenditure, have been the basis for the extension of consumer credit. Consumer credit appears most frequently when the unit size of transaction is large relative to the income of those undertaking the transaction. The automobile is one of the largest unit expenditures ever made by families. It was the growth of the automobile and its financing that led consumer credit from the fringe to the center of respectability.

In the prewar period about 50 to 60 per cent of all new-car transactions were financed by consumer credit; it has been estimated that as much as three fourths of the deals in used cars (except junkers) were on a credit basis.

Sewing machines were one of the very first articles sold on an installment basis; more recently the electric type of household appliance—television, for example—has come to be of relatively greater importance and is the basis for much consumer credit. Exhibit 30 shows the principal kinds of installment-sale credit and their variations over the last twenty years.

Exhibit 30

COMPOSITION OF CONSUMER INSTALLMENT-SALE CREDIT OUTSTANDING

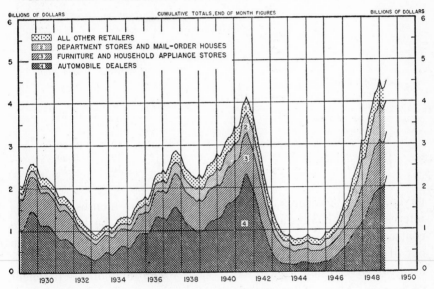

Source: Board of Governors of the Federal Reserve System.

The terms of a typical installment-sale transaction include three elements: the down-payment, the monthly payment, and the carrying or interest charge.

Down-payments assume a special importance in most installment-sale transactions because the security for the credit is the article purchased. The larger the down-payment, the larger the buyer's equity in his purchase, and the lower the ratio of credit to market value. Down-payments vary considerably among various classes of merchandise, depending in part on the custom in the trade. Table 11 shows some typical down-payments.

In some installment-sale transactions—on an automobile, for instance—the down-payment is very often made by the "trade-in" of an older car. Where this is true, the expected down-payment is customarily fairly high (partly because an overvaluation of the trade-in means that the real cost of the automobile purchased was not so great as it appeared). In some lines, such as furniture, trade-ins are much less common and down-payments are correspondingly lower.

The *maturity* of an installment credit determines the size of the monthly (or periodic) payment. If a one-third down-payment is required on an $1,800 car and the balance is to be paid off in a year, this means monthly payments of $100 plus interest and other charges; if the credit can be spread out over fifteen months, the monthly payments are only $80 plus interest; if carried to eighteen months, the

TABLE 11

TYPICAL DOWN-PAYMENTS
(Per Cent)

	Prewar	Mid-1950
Automobiles:		
New	25	
Used:		
Late models	25	10–33⅓
Older cars	33⅓	
Major household appliances	10	10–20
Radios and television sets	10	0–20
Furniture	10	0–15

payments are $67 plus interest; for twenty-four months, $50 plus interest. Many buyers are not much impressed by the length of the contract, but they may be concerned about how much they must take out of income each month. The student may have noted how often used-car advertisements will say: "Can be had for monthly payment of $———." No mention is made of total price or other factors.

The maturity of consumer installment-sale contracts is of considerable importance in another respect. As we shall find out, the amount of business done on the installment basis varies a great deal. It is high in some periods, low in others. The longer the maturity of installment-debt contracts, the longer they overhang the financial affairs of the indebted persons.

The *cost* of installment credit is often difficult to determine. The cost of credit may be expressed as an explicit interest charge, or it may be concealed in higher prices. For example, let us assume that a buyer is considering the purchase of a bedroom suite. One store offers it for $200, stating that no charge is made for twelve months' credit. Another store sells an identical set for $190 but makes a charge of $6 per $100 per year for the credit privilege. Each store requires a cash down-payment of $30, so that in the first instance there is a balance of $170 to be repaid in twelve equal payments and in the second case the balance is $160 plus the credit charge of $9.60 ($0.06 \times \$160$), which makes the total obligation $169.60. In other words, although the first store advertises that it makes no charge for credit, the buyer actually pays more than he does in the store which charges for the credit privilege!

But we must use our illustration carefully. Note that the charge was $6 per $100 of credit, which sounds like 6 per cent. Since the credit is gradually reduced, the average amount outstanding is not the full amount initially advanced but slightly more than half this amount. On a true interest basis, the interest cost is not 6 per cent but rather between 11 and 12 per cent. In the Supplement to this chapter we shall examine a formula for computing this figure.

This example shows that the true cost of sale credit is in many cases difficult to ascertain, since there are several ways in which the cost of sale credit may be passed on to the debtor, including any one of the following:

a) The cost of credit may be included in the price of the merchandise
b) Part of the cost of the credit may be included in the price of the merchandise and there may be a nominal additional charge
c) The full cost of the credit may be assessed as an additional charge to the purchaser

The dealer may hold the credit instrument; or he may elect to sell it to, or discount it with, one of the specialized financial agencies discussed in the preceding chapter. More specifically, the dealer may keep the contract and collect the payments directly from the consumer, or he may "discount" the contract with a financing agency. The financing agency may or may not require the dealer to guarantee the consumer's payments. The charges made by the dealer for the credit may be the exact amount which the financing agency in turn charges for its services, or it may be greater or less than that amount. The usual procedure is for the financing agency to furnish the seller with a chart of specified charges for definite maturities, so that in the preparation of the contract, the exact amount to be charged by the credit agency may be added to the contract as part of the total price.

It is obvious that, if the merchant has sufficient capital to carry his own paper, he not only makes the profit on the sale of the merchandise but derives additional income from the finance charges. In addition, some stores prefer to have the customer make the payment to them, in the hope that he will buy additional merchandise which is on display at the time he visits the store to make his periodic payment. In the field of automobiles and, to some extent, appliances, it is customary for the dealer to sell his installment paper to a finance company. In the furniture field, it is more common for the merchant to handle his own paper. But there are variations within fields. For example, the two leading mail-order houses follow opposite policies: Sears, Roebuck and Company discounts the installment paper it receives from sales; Montgomery Ward and Company keeps its installment paper. The financing agencies that discount installment paper are, for the most part, sales-finance companies and commercial banks.

Installment-sale credit depends to a considerable extent on the value of the article which was sold and which is security for the credit. It follows that the normal recourse of the creditor when a credit is defaulted is to "repossess" the article and resell it. Credit grantors do this when necessary, but they are very reluctant to take this step. They dislike the ill will such incidents create, and the amount recovered is often not great enough to cover the unpaid balance.

The Installment Loan

The important agencies granting direct installment loans are shown in Exhibit 31. We will subsequently consider the characteristics and history of these various lenders. Since the installment loan is a direct disbursement of cash from lender to borrower, there is no down-payment. The two most important loan terms are "maturity" and "interest."

As with sale credit, the question of maturity is largely the "carrying" capacity of the borrower. The longer the terms the lender will grant, the larger the debt burden that the borrower may assume. The institutions extending loan credit have not been as variable in their policies as have installment sellers; the maturity terms have been more nearly constant from good times to bad times.

The cost of loan credit is more readily determinable than the cost of sale credit. In transactions involving a loan of money the borrower knows how much money he receives; when the transaction is completed, he knows how much he has repaid in interest in addition to the principal. Thus it is possible easily to compute the equivalent rate of interest which was charged for the loan, although the borrower may not always know in advance what his total cost will be. Since

Exhibit 31

COMPOSITION OF CONSUMER INSTALLMENT-LOAN CREDIT OUTSTANDING

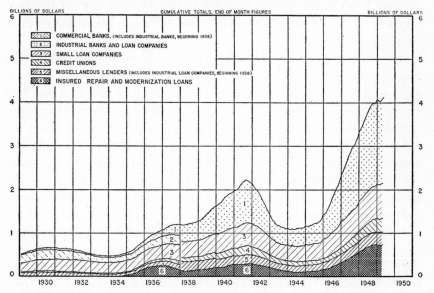

Source: Board of Governors of the Federal Reserve System.

the Supplement to this chapter presents a formula for approximation of this cost, it will be discussed only in general terms here.

On installment-loan transactions there are two commonly accepted methods for stating charges: the *discount basis* and the *per-cent-per-month basis*. On the discount basis, a flat sum in dollars or a flat percentage is charged for the loan. Service and insurance charges are also sometimes added. The dollar amount of the charge is then deducted in advance. On the per-cent-per-month basis, a monthly rate of interest is quoted, which rate is applied to the declining unpaid principal each month that the loan is outstanding.

Almost all installment-sale credit plus a large share of the loan credit is handled on the discount basis. The per-cent-per-month plan is usual for small-loan companies and credit unions. Under the discount plan, the borrower knows the dollar cost of his loan, but it is difficult for him to determine the equivalent annual rate of interest that he is paying for the money borrowed; whereas if the loan is on the per-cent-per-month basis, the borrower may readily determine the annual rate by multiplying the monthly rate by twelve. It is less easy, however, to compute in advance the total dollar cost of the loan.

In some cases, where a flat charge is made for a fixed period of time, there may be additional charges assessed against the borrower in the event that the obligation is not paid according to its terms. If the interest is on a monthly percentage basis, the total cost of the loan increases automatically if payments are not made according to their original terms.

The security for installment loans varies from case to case. In the past it was common practice to require one or two additional signatures on installment loans. Sometimes cash lenders take a chattel lien on the borrower's personal possessions, such as furniture or an automobile (although the transaction is not sale credit, since it is not for the purpose of purchasing these objects). Wage assignments are sometimes obtained. The modern tendency is for lenders to rely more on the creditworthiness of the individual and less on more specific forms of security. It is now widely recognized that consumer loans are generally repaid; the losses on them are very low. Some of the more extreme safeguards of the past have been found unnecessary.

The "Straight" or Noninstallment Loan

For many years, persons of means have been getting loans from banks for consumption purposes but in a form not materially different from business loans. Because banks prefer short-term loans, the ordinary or "single-payment" loan is very common. A businessman or a doctor or some other responsible person might, although temporarily short of cash, want to buy a car. He might have been shocked at the idea of borrowing "on time" (consumer credit has been, and continues to be, considered not quite respectable by many persons), but borrowing from a bank on this basis was considered respectable. What is more, if the bank, as a matter of accommodation, charged its ordinary business-loan rate, the cost of the credit would be materially less than the installment-loan rate.

While many of these short-term loans are retired rather promptly, many are often renewed and become, in fact, rather long-term credits. The frequently renewed single-payment loan has come to be viewed rather unfavorably by the banking community and seems to be on the way out.

These single-payment consumer loans are often secured just as any other bank loan. The persons of property who are considered satisfactory credit risks for this type of credit by banks often are the owners of securities that make very acceptable and easily manageable collateral.

In September, 1950, the amount of credit in this form was estimated by the Federal Reserve to be $1.2 billion.

The pawnshop loan is another, but vastly different, form of non-installment type of consumer credit. It is secured by the pledge of personal chattels, usually small and fairly high-value objects with a ready resale value. This type of credit has had a long and not always respectable history, but it is of small and shrinking importance. Other agencies are, more and more, displacing the pawnshop.

Still another type of noninstallment credit is the "loan-shark" pay-day loan. Those who have been in the Army will recognize the "four-for-five" or the "nine-for-ten" loan: you borrow $4 now and repay $5 on payday, or you borrow $9 now and repay $10.

The Uniform Small Loan Law and the small-loan companies, which will be discussed later, were devised to meet the social need for credit that the loan shark disclosed. Loan sharks now operate mainly in states where there are no regulated small-loan companies.

Although often pictured as a vicious and degraded character, the loan shark has sometimes deserved a better reputation. Under circumstances that encouraged competition and in closely knit communities, such as foreign-language groups, where social approval or disapproval conditioned his policies, the traditional loan shark appears often to have been a fairly useful citizen who performed many of the functions now performed by the regulated small-loan company.

Life insurance companies are required to lend their policyholders amounts which are equal to, or a large percentage of, policy reserves. (For an explanation of policy reserves, refer to Chapter 12.) These loans are not included in the statistics of consumer credit shown above, nor have they been elsewhere considered. But these loans can be looked upon as a form of consumer credit. For many families they are the best and cheapest source of such credit. Where families have control of their finances so that they can borrow on their insurance without jeopardizing the insurance protection, there are many great advantages to the use of this source of funds.

The record of insurance-policy loans shows them more likely to be "remedial" in their use than the so-called "remedial loans." Unlike the consumer loans, which increase in good times (when remedial needs are presumably least) and decrease in bad times (when remedial needs are presumably the most), insurance-policy loans do the reverse. They hit their peak of $3.8 billion in 1932. This was more than 18 per cent of total policy reserves. In relation to total insurance reserves, loans have recently been at a very low level of about $2 billion, or only about 4 per cent of policy reserves.

The Noninstallment-Sale Credit

The commonest form of noninstallment sale credit is the familiar charge account at the department, grocery, or clothing store. Other and closely related forms are the credit extended by public utilities —telephone, electric-light and power, and gas companies—and also the credit extended by doctors and dentists. There is even some credit of this type extended by such nonprofit institutions as colleges and hospitals.

A great deal of short-term sale credit is extended for the mutual convenience of the creditor and the debtor. For example, a monthly charge account at a department store eliminates the necessity of paying for individual purchases in cash and permits settlement of the entire month's business by one payment when the bill is rendered. Another typical example would be a dentist extending credit to a patient until the dental work is completed. It is more convenient for both to have one settlement rather than to attempt to compute the charge for each visit and to settle it separately.

Although much of this credit is for convenience, it often involves a very real anticipation of income. Only slightly more than half of the charge accounts in city department stores are paid the first time the customer is billed; almost half wait for the second or subsequent billing. The average period outstanding is about sixty days. In rural areas of the country the collection of charge accounts is even slower; and in some cases, such as the sharecropper credits of the South, the consumer is carried for substantial periods on charge-account credit.

There are also some kinds of charge-account credit that lie in the twilight zone between charge and installment credit. Some stores advertise: "Charge your spring clothing purchases and pay your bill in three installments."

The dollar figure of noninstallment-sale credit is sizable; at the fall of 1950 there was almost $5 billion outstanding.

INSTITUTIONS THAT ADVANCE CONSUMER CREDIT

The institutions that make cash loans to consumers usually carry these loans themselves. But those who sell goods or services, and use credit as a supplement to their main business of selling, often dispose of the credits they originate; they transfer them to specialists in that business. The major institutions that either discount or lend on consumer credit receivables are the sales-finance companies (described in Chapter 5) and the commercial banks.

Sales-Finance Operations

Some sales-finance companies were operating prior to World War I, but their real growth did not take place until after 1915. During the years 1915–29 these companies expanded with the automobile industry. The major ones were, indeed, subsidiaries of the automobile manufacturers. The only major one still so connected is the General Motors Acceptance Corporation. Automobile paper still represents the largest portion of the business handled by sales-finance companies. There are both large and small sales-finance concerns. There are a few national companies with hundreds of branch offices, a number of regional companies with branches, and many individual companies with single offices. It should be remembered that sales-finance companies do not lend money but instead discount (buy) paper acquired by merchants and dealers.

By purchasing this paper from the merchants, sales-finance companies are not ordinarily affected by usury laws. Their discount charge, reduced to a true interest-rate basis, is usually in excess of the maximum legal rate of interest.

It is customary for the sales-finance company to furnish its dealer-customers with conditional-sale contract forms and rate charts, and also to procure insurance in connection with the financing of installment sales. The merchant makes his contract with the purchaser and then offers the "deal" to the finance company. If the deal is satisfactory to the finance company, it purchases the contract from the merchant.

This discounting may be on a recourse basis, whereby the merchant assumes the risk of bad-debt losses and takes back from the credit agency any delinquent paper; or it may be on a nonrecourse basis, whereby the merchant has no liability and the credit agency assumes any bad-debt losses. A third plan is a combination of these two: the merchant and the credit agency may share the credit losses, with a limit being placed for one or the other. As an inducement to the merchant to discount the obligation with a particular financing agency, it is a common practice for the financing agency to rebate to the merchant a portion of the original amount charged to the buyer of the merchandise for the credit accommodation.

Most retail-sales financing operations are combined with a closely related function: the financing of the dealer. For example, the sales-finance concerns that buy installment paper from automobile dealers will also finance the dealer's inventory of cars. There are various plans of "wholesale financing" or "floor planning." Usually these credits are secured by the automobiles or other merchandise financed, and the dealer obtains custody through a trust receipt.

The field of sales finance is not dominated by a single leader. Because these concerns do not deal so directly with the public, their names are not as well known as some other names in finance. The General Motors Acceptance Corporation, affiliated with General Motors, is an almost pure sales-financing operation. The Commercial Credit Company (CCC) and the CIT Financial Corporation (CIT) are largely sales-finance concerns, but they also engage in other financing operations.

Sales-financing operations have not been regulated for as long as direct consumer lending. They are still not regulated in many states, but regulation is becoming more common. The usual form of regulation is to require full disclosure of all charges, and sometimes the circumstances in which collateral security may be repossessed is subject to control.

The sales-finance "pack" which was often met in earlier years is now much less common. The "pack" was an amount added by the seller to the ordinary financing charges and retained by him so that the seller might make a larger amount on a credit sale than on a cash sale. In this way, there was an incentive to "sell" credit wherever possible—that is, induce the buyer to take merchandise "on time" rather than pay cash for it.

Commercial Banks

It was mentioned earlier that commercial banks were rather slow in entering the field of consumer installment credit. However, since 1934 their activities have expanded rapidly, and it is estimated that today nearly 90 per cent of the commercial banks have some stake in installment credit. Some commercial banks extend installment-sale credit by virtue of discounting dealer paper, but many commercial banks also make direct installment cash loans. Banks were attracted to this field for two principal reasons: first, to provide income when commercial loans were at a low point; and second, as a means of improving their public relations. The banks have found that by meeting the credit needs of the average individual they build good will in the community.

Once the banks became active in the field, they grew faster than the other lenders. This is natural because of the large number of banks and their wide dispersion. The fixed charges of banking can be spread over their entire business, and commercial banks sought out the larger and safer consumer loans. As a result, the rates quoted by banks for installment loans tend to be somewhat lower than those quoted by other credit agencies. The range of discount charged by banks is from $4 to $6 per $100 per year. Many commercial banks have established separate consumer-credit departments to make direct loans.

Commercial banks are also active in the sales-finance field. They operate in much the same way as sales-finance companies through the discounting of paper in the hands of merchants. Since 1934 they have acquired a steadily increasing portion of the business, and in general they operate at rates slightly lower than those charged by the finance companies.

Small-Loan Companies

The small-loan company was an almost direct outgrowth of the effort to curb and regulate the loan shark. Since the efforts at prohibition of extortionate lending practices usually failed, the alternative was to bring the business into the open and regulate it. These regulations were aimed at allowing rates which covered the cost of this business but which outlawed the exorbitant charges loan sharks had sometimes charged. New York State, Massachusetts, and New Jersey all played a role in development of this type of experimental legislation. The Massachusetts law was one of the first to be considered "workable" by the professional lending companies. This plan for making small loans was soon copied, with variations, by several other states. The Russell Sage Foundation, established in 1907, sponsored studies and issued a report which led to the drafting of the first Uniform Small Loan Law. This law, with modifications, has been enacted by thirty-one states. The original New York law required interest to be quoted on a per-cent-per-month basis. This feature has been retained in all the revisions of the small-loan law recommended by the Russell Sage Foundation. The original act recommended a rate of 3½ per cent per month (42 per cent a year) on unpaid balances. The small-loan limit of $300 prevailed for many years, but with higher price levels this limit has been raised in a number of states.

The rate of interest has been the subject of much legislative action in the various states. It has been learned that, if the rate is set too low, lenders are not attracted to the business; a rate between 2 per cent and 3 per cent per month is now common. Some states set a rate of 3 per cent a month on small loans of $100 or less, with 2 or 2½ per cent on the portion of the loan over that amount. The interest charge is calculated on the unpaid balance. If the borrower pays his loan in advance, he reduces the amount of interest paid proportionately. On a loan of $100 in Illinois, repayable in twelve months, the amount of interest collected at the legal rate of 3 per cent per month, with even monthly payments, is $20.56. Small-loan companies are not allowed to make any additional charges in the way of delinquency fees, fines, or other handling charges.

Recently there have been upward revisions of the $300 loan limit, some states permitting as high as $1,500. In most states where such high limits are permitted, the legislation provides for a lower interest rate on the larger portion of all loans.

Small-loan companies make secured and unsecured loans. The unsecured loans are based on the borrower's character and ability to repay. The secured loans are usually made on a chattel-mortgage basis against furniture or automobiles.

It is necessary under the small-loan laws for companies to obtain a license for each office they intend to operate. Usually some state officer supervises the activities of the various licensed offices. State regulation of small-loan offices usually has the primary goal of curbing practices which exploit borrowers. Many offices are controlled by a single company. In fact, two leading small-loan companies control several hundred offices throughout the country. The bulk of the capital for small-loan companies is supplied by the owners. Some companies have debenture bond issues outstanding, and many borrow from commercial banks.

Small-loan companies are mass marketing operations; to succeed they must attract business from many persons. For this reason they use the advertising vehicles appropriate for mass merchandising. They have spot commercials on the radio: "Need money? Call the Blank Loan Company, Farmers 6–6666, for prompt service. No endorsers required; if you have a steady job you can have up to twenty four months to repay. Remember, Farmers 6–6666 for prompt loan service." They also use classified advertisements, streetcar poster advertisements, and neon-lighted flashing signs.

There are many small-loan companies, but the biggest and best known is the Household Finance Corporation. This concern and its subsidiaries operate over 520 offices in twenty nine states and Canada. At the end of 1950 it had over $238 million in more than one million outstanding installment loans. The Beneficial Loan Corporation is another large "small-loan" company.

Industrial Banks and Industrial-Loan Companies

In 1910 Arthur Morris of Virginia organized the first industrial bank. The "Morris Plan" spread to other cities under local ownership. Fundamentally, the Morris Plan provides that the maximum legal rate of interest will be charged for the term of the loan. Certain additional fees for credit investigation or for recording of necessary documents are often added. By the terms of the agreement the borrower is obligated to make uniform deposits at regular intervals in a savings account so that, at the maturity date of the loan, there will be on deposit an amount sufficient to pay the loan.

This plan, with modifications, is the basic one used by all industrial banking companies. It worked so well that many commercial banks adopted it. In some states special legislation was passed to permit the operation of industrial banks, although ordinarily they operate under the regular statutory interest limit. The courts have usually found that the deposit contract which results in a higher effective rate does not violate the usury limit. Originally, industrial banks made the bulk of their loans on a co-maker basis and confined their operation within the limits of the Morris Plan. The industrial-loan companies and banks used to be a distinct type of institution. Many of them included the name of the founder of this system—"Morris Plan"— in their corporate title. But this practice has dwindled. Some have changed their name and dropped the old title. Through the years their activities have broadened, and many have become commercial banks specializing in the consumer-credit field, while others have become, for all practical purposes, either sales-finance companies or small-loan companies.

Charges for loans quoted by industrial banks and industrial-loan companies are usually on an annual discount basis, the rates ranging from 5 to 9 per cent. In addition, there is usually a handling or investigation fee of 2 per cent for each loan. Unsecured single-name loans usually carry the highest rate, with co-maker and secured loans being given more favorable rates. A typical transaction would be a loan of $100 for twelve months at an interest cost of $6 plus a $2 investigation fee, making the total cost $8. The borrower signs a note for $108 in such a case but receives $100 in cash. Since the $108 is repaid in equal monthly installments, the borrower has an average indebtedness of about $54 over the entire year. Thus the interest cost is not 6 per cent but somewhere between 14 and 15 per cent. Additional fees may be collected from the borrower if he is delinquent; these fees may range up to 5 per cent of the amount of the delinquent payment.

Industrial banking companies usually are banks of deposit, so that a large part of their funds represent the savings or checking accounts of their customers, who in some cases may also be borrowers. The industrial-loan companies may, in some states, sell certificates of deposit; and, in effect, they are somewhat similar to savings banks in this regard. However, they usually cannot extend checking-account privileges, and supervision is not so detailed as it is in the case of savings and commercial banks.

Credit Unions

Credit unions originated in Europe and were introduced to this country around 1909. They first expanded on a substantial basis in Massachusetts. Credit unions are now authorized by special legislation in forty-four states. There are about 9,000 credit unions with assets of over half a billion dollars, including consumer loans of almost a third of a billion dollars.

Credit unions are in some ways similar to savings and loan associations in that they have savings share accounts; and they are similar to small loan companies in that they are allowed to charge rates for loans usually in excess of the normal legal rate. They are "mutual"-type organizations and may be organized under either federal or state charter. The first credit union in the United States was chartered under state authority (New Hampshire). During the next twenty five years the movement spread slowly, with more and more states enacting permissive or charter legislation. Edward A. Filene, the philanthropic Boston merchant, was deeply interested in the movement and helped it in many ways. But the most rapid period of expansion came after 1934, when legislation for the federal chartering of credit unions was adopted.

Participating or shareholding members of credit unions receive dividends. Credit unions often vary their dividends considerably from year to year, depending on earnings. In this they are more like industrial corporations, in which dividends vary, than like savings and loan associations or mutual savings banks, in which efforts are made to keep dividend rates steady, to change them only infrequently.

The most fertile ground for the organization of credit unions has been among those working for the same employer. While a church or neighborhood or trade union is often the basis for organization, the plant or place of business is the commonest unit.

The affiliated organization (such as the employer or labor union) often provides the credit union with operating facilities and assumes many of the routine expenses, so that credit unions normally have a relatively low cost of doing business. One basic weakness of any credit union organized within one industry, more particularly when limited to employees of one concern, is the lack of diversification of risk. Ordinarily, nearly all of the members will have excess funds when the industry or concern is prosperous, and nearly all may need funds when the industry suffers or when the plant closes down. Credit unions charge various rates on loans, but most use a rate of 1 per cent per month on unpaid principal balances.

THE PRO AND CON OF CONSUMER CREDIT

Installment credit has been the target of much criticism. The main argument of the critics used to be that installment credit is "a mortgage on the future" of families with limited means. But families are faced with economic emergencies from time to time which require the borrowing of money. Lending agencies should be available to meet this need at a reasonable cost. If legitimate lenders are not accessible, history has proved that people will borrow money when they need it, wherever it may be available, and will pay any rate necessary to get it. It is from such experiences that we get the term "loan shark." Emergency credit extended for the liquidation of existing indebtedness or for purposes such as hospital and medical expenses (and other items of similar nature) is generally considered to be "remedial" credit and is usually regarded as a necessary type of borrowing.

Many families find it difficult to accumulate large amounts of cash with which to make major purchases, whereas they will meet obligations incurred as the result of purchasing a major item, such as an automobile or a refrigerator; and, in addition, they have the benefit of the use of the article while they are paying for it. In other words, installment purchasing is, in effect, a form of forced saving into which people willingly enter to acquire eventually ownership of furniture, automobiles, appliances, and other household goods. Although installment credit does not include residential real eastate credit, most families purchase their home on the installment basis; they also acquire a life-insurance estate through making monthly or annual payments on a policy. It is easy to see the effectiveness of a periodic payment program when we realize that most people receive their income on a weekly or monthly basis.

It has been argued that the cost of the credit extended reduces the purchasing power of the family and that, as a result, the members of the family do not obtain as many goods as they would if they had accumulated the money and paid cash. However, without installment selling the total production of many of these articles would be lower and the price higher. Installment sales create a wide market and may lower the cost of production. Although there is a charge made for the credit, the actual cost of the article purchased may be lower as a result of the savings made possible through economies of increased production.

Another major criticism of consumer credit is that it is excessively costly. The per-month rates of small-loan companies, put on an annual basis, shock many who have become accustomed to dealing with the rates typical of business credits and investment returns. But these rates are not comparable.

The making of loans involves fixed charges; each loan, no matter how small, costs some minimum amount. If an interviewer sees the applicant for half an hour; if a credit investigator spends an hour checking the application; and if a bookkeeper puts in no more than a few minutes setting up the account, the minimum first cost for a loan is likely to be at least $5. This amount would be only a small fraction of a sizable loan; but it amounts to almost 10 per cent of the average loan balance of a loan, which starts out at $100 and is paid off in equal installments in one year.

The above factors should be kept in mind when consumer credit rates are compared with rates for other types of loans. It is a fact that because of these factors the net return to the lender on funds invested in consumer credit loans is generally not excessively higher than the net return on commercial-loan transactions even though there is a wide difference in the quoted rates of interest for the two classes of business.

With respect to installment-sale credit, the seller may quote a comparatively low rate for the credit privilege as a means of attracting customers. However, since he cannot escape the basic cost of handling installment-credit transactions, the remainder is usually concealed in a higher price for the merchandise.

But the many important advantages of consumer credit must be balanced against its undeniable disadvantages. The modern devices of promotion and advertising work so effectively that many persons are persuaded to become more indebted than may be prudent. Improvidence is as old as frail human nature. But the relative ease of getting into debt may aggravate this situation. The concerns that grant credit cannot be particularly blamed for this; to call them "merchants of debt," as some do, exaggerates their responsibility. They cannot be expected to be the financial guardians of their clients. The consumer credit system as a whole, however, must bear the responsibility of keeping the use of credit within reasonable bounds.

Economic Stability and Consumer Credit

Perhaps the most important, but a much disputed, charge made against consumer credit is that it contributes to economic instability. All credit permits the borrower to make purchases which he might not be able to make at that time without credit. If credit is extended freely during good times and then the credit grantors curtail the terms and press collection of outstanding credit during bad times,

Exhibit 32

INSTALLMENT AND NONINSTALLMENT CONSUMER CREDIT OUTSTANDING

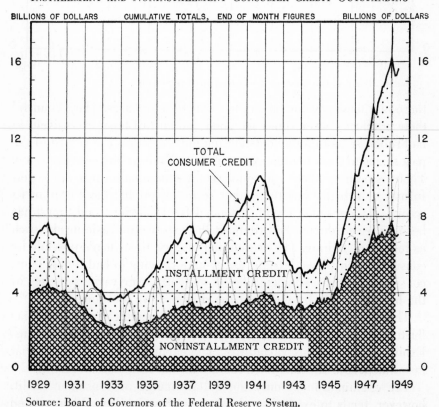

Source: Board of Governors of the Federal Reserve System.

Exhibit 33

RELATION OF INSTALLMENT CREDIT TO PERSONAL INCOME

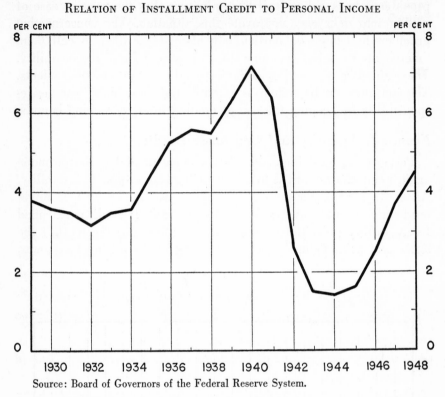

Source: Board of Governors of the Federal Reserve System.

there is a tendency for buyers to "bunch" purchases. They "bunch" their purchases when times are good and curtail them excessively in bad times, so as to repay outstanding indebtedness. The record of the past seems to show that many forms of credit have this characteristic. There is nothing about consumer credit which makes it a worse performer or a better one than other forms of credit; the test is in its record. But consumer credit, extended freely during good times, has been collected during bad times at the expense of basic needs, such as food and clothing. The overbuying of good times made possible by consumer credit must be paid for by underbuying in bad times. Thus, consumer purchases fluctuate more violently over various phases of the business cycle by virtue of the existence of consumer credit.

There is no doubt that the volume of consumer credit itself has fluctuated widely and corresponds to other economic fluctuations. Exhibit 32 shows this variability. The earlier charts also show that installment-sale has fluctuated more than installment-loan credit.

The examination of only the dollar figures of consumer credit, however, tends to exaggerate the degree of variability. When viewed as a proportion of personal income, consumer installment credit has varied less, as shown in Exhibit 33. But this lower rate is still a very high one. Not including the war period, this chart shows a range from 3 to 7 per cent in the ratio of credit to income.

Regulation W

During World War II, consumer credit was subject to special control as a means of fighting inflation. With the supply of consumer goods scarce, the administration elected to limit the use of credit to buyers so as to take some pressure off prices. The credit terms were particularly curbed for those types of goods in short supply, but all credit was curbed to some extent by down-payment minimum requirements and maturity maximum requirements.

In the postwar period the control of credit was continued until November, 1947, but it was then allowed to lapse according to congressional mandate. But less than one year later—August, 1948—in the special session of Congress devoted to inflation, the control of consumer credit was reinstated on a temporary basis. This provision was permitted to lapse without renewal on June 30, 1949.

The Federal Reserve has recommended that its general credit powers be supplemented by direct controls over consumer credit. This request for power has been strongly opposed by most of the companies that grant consumer credit. The recommendation was initially based on the premise that economic stabilization required some curb to the excessive growth of consumer credit during boom times. This recommendation did not stir much congressional enthusiasm on long-term grounds. When the Korean war crisis developed, however, Congress immediately showed itself willing to reinstate the control of consumer credit. This was done, and the Federal Reserve made the new regulation effective on September 18, 1950.

The experience so far suggests that the opinion of legislators and the temper of the public is to tolerate such a regulation primarily during wartimes or in periods of grave inflationary threat. But in those periods the principle of economic regulation of consumer credit is accepted rather generally.

—ROLAND I. ROBINSON

SUPPLEMENT

COMPUTATION OF CONSUMER-CREDIT INTEREST RATES AND CHARGES

The precise calculation of consumer-credit interest charges and monthly payments involves more complex techniques than can be introduced here.

The mathematics of annuities provides the most precise way of solving these problems but it requires special tables and techniques beyond the scope of this book. Satisfactory results, however, can be obtained by simple methods. A single approximation formula, in two forms, is adequate for the calculation of almost all consumer-credit interest problems. The formula in both forms is:

$$R = \frac{2 \times m \times I}{P(n+1)} \text{ or, transposed, } I = \frac{R \times P(n+1)}{2 \times m},$$

where

R = annual simple interest rate (in decimal form),
I = dollar cost of the credit (interest),
m = Number of payment periods in a year (twelve if monthly, fifty-two if weekly),
n = number of payments scheduled, and
P = net amount of credit advanced (principal).

Application of the formula may be illustrated as follows:

EXAMPLE 1. Suppose you should apply to a bank or an industrial-loan company for a loan of $100 to be repaid over a period of one year. You are told that the discount charge is $6 and that a service fee of $2 is also required. This makes a total cost of $8. The problem: Find the rate of interest. The solution is obtained by using the first of the forms shown above.

$I = \$8,$
$m = 12$ (twelve monthly payments in a year),
$n = 12$ (number of payments on this loan),
$P = \$100,$
$R = \dfrac{2 \times 12 \times 8}{100 \times (12+1)} = 0.14769 = 14.769 \text{ per cent.}$

Since the rate calculated on an annuity basis is 14.45 per cent, the error introduced by this approximation formula is not very great.

EXAMPLE 2. The interest rate at a credit union is 1 per cent of the unpaid balance. You wish to find the dollar cost of borrowing $100 for one year. For this purpose use the second form of the formula.

$P \qquad = \$100,$
$m \text{ and } n = 12,$
$R \qquad = 12 \text{ per cent (1 per cent a month),}$
$I \qquad = \dfrac{0.12 \times \$100\,(12+1)}{24} = \$6.50.$

EXAMPLE 3. You note from an advertising poster in a streetcar that a small-loan company will lend you $100 for one year for a monthly payment of $9.96. You want to find out the rate of interest. The formula to be used is the first of the two forms shown above. But first some preparatory calculations must be made. A monthly payment of $9.96 multiplied by 12 means that the annual payments are $119.52. The interest cost is, therefore, $19.52 (since you subtract the $100 from the total annual payments). Since $19.52 is I, you can compute the rate:

$$R = \frac{2 \times 12 \times \$19.52}{\$100(12 + 1)} = 0.360359, \text{ or } 36.04 \text{ per cent (rate on an annuity basis is 36 per cent, or 3 per cent per month).}$$

EXAMPLE 4. You are dickering for a new car. Your present car is considered a satisfactory down-payment. You are trying to determine the interest-rate cost of "buying on time." The cash payment you have to make would be $1,500 in addition to the car you turn in. You are offered the privilege of paying for the car over eighteen months at the rate of $100 a month. The monthly payments would also include the cost of the insurance ($180 for eighteen months). The first form of the formula shown above will supply the answer, but certain preparatory computations must be made. The eighteen monthly payments ($1,800) less the cost of the insurance leaves a "time-payment" total cost of $1,620. This is $120 more than the cash cost. This amount is I. The other parts of the formula are as follows:

$$m = 12,$$
$$n = 18,$$
$$P = \$1,500,$$
$$R = \frac{2 \times 12 \times \$120}{\$1,500(18 + 1)} = 0.10105, \text{ or } 10.1 \text{ per cent.}$$

QUESTIONS AND PROBLEMS

1. Clip advertisements from a current newspaper illustrating as many kinds of consumer credit as you can find. Identify each type according to the plan of classification used in Chapter 6.

2. Why is it hard to prosecute loan sharks?

3. Why did the growth of automobile sales and usage depend on the availability of consumer credit of an appropriate kind in adequate amounts?

4. What is the security back of most installment-sale credits?

5. What is the security back of most installment loans?

6. Rate the various sources of consumer credit with reference to the average cost of credit.

7. How free is installment-sale credit even though there may be "no carrying charge"?

8. Do you favor the peacetime regulation of consumer credit to reduce business fluctuation? Why?

9. A credit jeweler advertises a watch for $50 with "no down-payment, no carrying charge, and only $1 a week." The same watch can be purchased for $45 in a department store. What is the implicit interest rate per annum involved in buying the watch from the credit jeweler?

10. A $200 loan from a small-loan company at 3 per cent per month is to be repaid in equal installments over a fifteen-month period. Approximately what are the monthly installments?

11. In buying a car a $1,000 balance needs to be financed. The dealer offers to finance this for $50 monthly payments over the next two years. The dealer also declares that the finance charge is $6 per year per $100. Is there "pack" in this deal? If so, how much approximately?

12. An industrial bank charges a discount of $4 per year per $100, and also a service fee of $2 regardless of the maturity of the loan. What is the approximate true rate of interest for a one-year loan? For a two-year loan?

BIBLIOGRAPHY

The most complete institutional study of consumer credit is that made by the National Bureau of Economic Research and sponsored by the Association of Reserve City Bankers. The studies which were a part of this project, all published by the National Bureau, are as follows:

Bernstein, Blanche. *The Pattern of Consumer Debt, 1935–36.* 1940.

Chapman, John M., and Associates. *Commercial Banks and Consumer Instalment Credit.* 1940.

Coppack, J. D. *Government Agencies of Consumer Instalment Credit.* 1940.

Dauer, Ernst A. *Comparative Operating Experience of Consumer Instalment Financing Agencies and Commercial Banks, 1929–41.* 1944.

Durand, David. *Risk Elements in Consumer Instalment Financing.* 1941.

Haberler, Gottfried. *Consumer Instalment Credit and Economic Fluctuations.* 1942.

Holthausen, Duncan McC., in collaboration with Merriam, Malcolm L., and Nugent, Rolf. *The Volume of Consumer Instalment Credit, 1929–38.* 1940.

Plummer, Wilbur C., and Young, Ralph A. *Sales Finance Companies and Their Credit Practices.* 1940.

Saulnier, R. J. *Industrial Banking Companies and Their Credit Practices.* 1940.

Young, Ralph A., and Associates. *Personal Finance Companies and Their Credit Practices.* 1940.

Except for the Haberler study listed above, these works are primarily descriptive, rather than controversial, as to the cyclical influence of consumer credit. The more important treatises discussing this controversy include:

Cox, Revis. *The Economics of Consumer Credit.* New York: Ronald Press Co., 1949.

Nugent, Rolf. *Consumer Credit and Economic Stability.* New York: Russell Sage Foundation, 1939.

Parry, Carl E. "Selective Instruments of National Credit Policy," *Federal Reserve Policy.* Postwar Economic Studies, No. 8. 1947.

"Selective Methods of Regulation," chap. iv, pp. 38–48, of *The Federal Reserve System, Its Purposes and Functions.* 2d ed. Washington, D.C.: Board of Governors of the Federal Reserve System, 1947.

Articles on various current aspects of consumer credit appear fairly regularly in the following:

Federal Reserve Bulletin. (The regular monthly statistics of consumer credit are released to the press near the end of the month for the preceding month and are published about three weeks later in the *Bulletin.*)

Journal of Marketing, published by American Marketing Association.

Time-Sales Financing, published by the American Finance Conference.

Chapter • 7

THE CORPORATION AND FINANCE

MOST of our attention has, up to this point, been given to the commercial credit institutions that provide the short-term or temporary capital requirements of business and to the consumer credit institutions through which individuals borrow. With respect to both of these classes of institutions the commercial credit instruments discussed in Chapter 2 are important. We will next direct our attention to the institutions that are engaged primarily in providing the long-term permanent capital requirements of business. In view of the dominance of the corporation in our economy, and because no satisfactory or adequate institutional channels have been developed for supplying permanent capital for small business, whatever the legal form, our discussion will center largely around the corporation.

It will be our principal objective in this chapter to examine the characteristics of the capital instruments (stocks and bonds) through which the long-term or permanent capital requirements of the corporation are provided. These instruments constitute the principal stock-in-trade of the various institutions that operate in the long-term capital market, institutions that constitute the subject matter of the seven chapters that follow.

We will also discuss here only limited phases of the corporation—those aspects that are essential to an understanding of the work of financial institutions that operate in the long-term capital markets and deal in stocks and bonds. Incidentally, many financial institutions are organized as corporations and, through their very creation, give rise to stock and bond issues.

THE DOMINANCE OF THE CORPORATION

To many persons "corporation" and "business" are almost synonymous terms, and it is easy to understand why this might be so. Corporations produce most of the units of goods and services, account for a substantial majority of the annual sales volume of the nation, hire most of the gainfully employed workers, and utilize most of the funds made available to business.

While there are a large number of small and medium-sized businesses organized under the corporate form, most of them are either single proprietorships or general partnerships; and a much smaller number utilize one of the less common legal forms of organization: special forms of partnership, including limited partnership, limited partnership association, joint venture, and mining partnership; joint-stock company; Massachusetts (common law or business) trust; and co-operative.

In 1945, for example, federal income-tax returns were filed by 4,638,887 individual proprietorships, 627,049 partnerships, and 421,125 active corporations. These figures include many one-man or one-family stores and shops that barely provide a salary equivalent for the operators, despite a work week oftentimes much longer than the forty-hour standard today. On the other hand, the figures also include many corporations which are multi-billion-dollar enterprises.

The three major forms of business organization—single proprietorship, general partnership, and corporation—account for most of the business done in the United States, and the other forms are of negligible importance. Furthermore, of the three major forms, the corporation is by far the dominant type in terms of business volume. Later in this chapter we will consider why this is true, although, in passing, it can be noted that the corporation form is particularly advantageous —if not indispensable—where substantial sums of capital are required. For this reason, "corporation" and "bigness" are often associated.

How important the corporation is in our economy is reflected in figures published by the United States Department of Commerce in the July, 1950, *Survey of Current Business*. In 1949, total income originated by all business amounted to $189,579 million, derived as follows: corporations, $117,558 million; sole proprietorships and partnerships, $58,534 million; and all other business forms, $11,116 million. Compensation of employees in the same year amounted to $87,791 million for corporations and $23,827 million for single proprietorships and partnerships. Thus, corporations in the aggregate account for about two thirds of business income originated in the country and for about three fourths of the compensation to employees.

In each of seven classifications of industries which, in the aggregate, were responsible in 1937 for almost two thirds of the national income, corporations did from 58 to 100 per cent of the volume in the respective industries. (See Table 12.)

Because manufacturing represents the most important industrial classification from the standpoint of contribution to the national income, additional detail seems appropriate. According to the Census of Manufacturers, there were 184,230 establishments engaged in manufacturing in 1939, including 95,187 corporations, or 51.7 per cent of the total. These corporations accounted for 89.4 per cent of

TABLE 12
IMPORTANCE OF CORPORATE ACTIVITY BY BRANCHES OF INDUSTRY, 1937

Industry	Percentage of National Income	Percentage of Business Done by Corporations in Each Industry
Electric light and power and manufactured gas.	1.6	100
Communication.	1.3	100
Mining.	2.1	96
Manufacturing.	24.0	92
Transportation.	7.3	89
Finance.	9.3	84
Trade.	12.5	58
Government, including work-relief wages.	13.5	58*
Contract construction.	2.1	36
Miscellaneous.	4.2	33
Service.	11.9	30
Agriculture.	8.9	7

* Includes cities and local governments as well as federal government agencies operating under corporate form.

Source: Bureau of Foreign and Domestic Commerce; published in *Economic Concentration and World War II: Report of the Smaller War Plants Corporation to the Special Committee to Study Problems of American Small Business*, U.S. Senate (79th Cong., 2d sess.), Document No. 206 (Washington, D.C; U.S. Government Printing Office, 1946), p. 6.

the wage earners and 92.6 per cent of the value of products for the industry.

What accounts for this dominance of the corporate form of enterprise? A cursory description of the individual proprietorship and the general partnership and a comparison with the corporation will provide the explanation.[1] Here we will delineate the relative status of the corporation, explain how it raises permanent capital, and point out

---

[1] An exhaustive presentation of the legal characteristics and the advantages and disadvantages of the several forms of business organization will be found in most textbooks on business organization and particularly in texts on business finance or corporation finance. For a comprehensive presentation, see H. G. Guthmann and H. E. Dougall. *Corporate Financial Policy* (New York: Prentice-Hall, Inc., 1948), chaps. ii and iii.

some of the social and economic problems that grow out of the wide use of the corporate form of organization.

Characteristics of Major Business Forms

The individual proprietorships and the general partnerships are in many ways comparable. This is certainly true in that they both have very little in common with the corporation other than the fact that they are one of the three major business forms, albeit definitely of secondary importance in terms of aggregate income originated and compensation of employees. There are four commonly understood differences: ease of starting the business; evidence of ownership; the liability of the owners for the obligations of the business; and limited-life versus perpetual existence. Of these four differences, the liabilty feature transcends all others in significance.

INCEPTION. There is little, if any, formality in connection with the establishment of either the single proprietorship or the general partnership (unless articles of agreement are drawn up in connection with the latter). The organizer, or organizers, need merely start in business without obtaining sanction from anyone. Capital is usually self-provided or obtained from family, friends, or acquaintances. There is usually little, if any, attempt made to obtain permanent capital from the general public. Until the business is established as a going and profitable enterprise, there is little likelihood of getting capital from outsiders unless the organizers have means outside of the business to give them adequate credit standing.

In organizing a corporation, on the other hand, certain formalities must be observed, and the process is more expensive. The organizers (incorporators) must apply to the state for a charter by filing a certificate of incorporation, the contents of which must meet the requirements of the corporation statute. After the appropriate state official has approved the charter (the articles of incorporation), the bylaws are adopted. The latter supplement the charter in outlining the working regulations of the corporation.

EVIDENCE OF OWNERSHIP. In neither the single proprietorship nor the general partnership is there any formal evidence of ownership. In the proprietorship, the owner takes all the risk, owns all the assets, and is responsible for all obligations of the business. In the general partnership, ownership interest in the business and the right to the profits depend upon the arrangement between the partners, an arrangement that need not be in writing, although self-interest would dictate that it should be.

Ownership in the corporation, however, is represented by shares as provided in the charter and is evidenced by stock certificates. These certificates may be for one share or for hundreds of shares. A stockholder has an interest in the corporation assets and earnings in direct proportion to the number of shares he owns. A corporation may have but one class of stock (common stock); or it may have, in addition, one or more issues of preferred stock, which is stock that is preferred as to assets or as to earnings, or both.

If the corporation has a long-term debt, this is usually in the form of a bond issue on which interest must be paid before distributing any profits in the form of dividends on the stock. In the event of liquidation of the business, the bonds have a claim prior to that of the preferred stock; and the preferred stock has a claim prior to that of the common stock, the common having the residual claim.

Thus, in obtaining their permanent capital, corporations may utilize investment credit instruments (bonds) and must use common stock, at least, and sometimes preferred stock as well. Because of the very nature of the individual proprietorship and the general partnership, stocks and bonds are not applicable.

LIABILITY OF OWNERS. Obviously, the individual proprietor is responsible for all of his business debts, and he risks his entire estate, including assets not used in the business. If the business is liquidated and the assets are not sufficient to pay off all the obligations, any property that the individual holds is subject to levy.

Every general partner is likewise subject to unlimited liability for any of the partnership debts. His liability is not limited to his proportionate share or to the amount of his investment. Partners are jointly and severally liable for all the debts of the partnership. For example: assume that a millionaire invests $10,000 for a one-tenth interest in a general partnership and that the partnership ultimately fails, with net obligations of $100,000. Creditors of the partnership must sue all the partners but may collect the entire amount from any one, who, in this instance, might be the millionaire. He may, in turn, recover from the other partners if they have any assets.

In contrast, the liability of the corporation stockholder is limited to the amount of his investment. This is one of the most important distinguishing features of the corporation and is mainly responsible for the popularity of the corporate form of organization. It should be noted that it is possible in most states to limit the liability of partners through formation of a limited partnership; but even here, there must be at least one partner who has unlimited liability.

Advantages of the Corporate Form

There are a number of advantages other than limited liability that help to explain the predominance of the corporate form of enterprise.

LEGAL ENTITY. The corporation is a person in the eyes of the law; has a separate identity apart from that of the owners. Legal action is brought against the corporation and not the stockholders. In a partnership, however, legal action is brought in the name of the partnership and in the name of the individual partners.

The stockholder has little management responsibility beyond electing directors and voting on policy at an occasional stockholders' meeting, whereas general partners are usually the operating heads of the business.

PERMANENCE. Unless the business fails or the stockholders vote to dissolve, the corporation may go on without interruption for the term indicated in the charter—either a period of years subject to renewal or in perpetuity. An individual proprietorship ends at the will of the owner or with his decease. A partnership is dissolved by the withdrawal of a partner or by his legal disability, bankruptcy, or death.

TRANSFERABILITY. A stockholder may transfer his stock to others at will; and in the case of well-known listed stocks, such transfer may take no longer than the time required to telephone a sell order to the stock broker. The life of the corporation is not affected by the death, incompetence, or bankruptcy of a stockholder.

A partner may transfer his interest only with the consent of the other partners (*delectus personae*), and even then the old partnership must be dissolved.

ADMINISTRATIVE EFFICIENCY. Responsibilities in the corporation are fairly definitely established. The enabling legislation and the charter delimit the nature of the business and its activities; the stockholders elect the directors; the directors elect the officers; the officers define the duties of intermediate management; and so on down to the lowliest employee. There is a flow of authority from top to bottom, comparable to the line-and-staff organization of the military.

The individual proprietor is master of his business, and his success depends upon his effectiveness as an administrator. But this form of organization is generally limited as to the capital it is able to command.

In the partnership, each general partner is a general agent and can bind the partnership to a contract. Unless there is complete understanding and harmonious co-operation, confusion may easily arise and ultimately lead to dissolution.

EASE OF RAISING CAPITAL. All of the following characteristics facilitate the raising of capital for the corporation: limited liability; divisibility of ownership into small units; legal entity; permanence; transferability; and administrative efficiency. As already noted, limited liability is of paramount importance. It makes possible the raising of large sums of capital that would be impossible under the unlimited liability of the partnership. The divisibility of ownership into many small units enlarges the source of capital to include persons of moderate means and also facilitates diversification of investment by investors.

The variety of corporate capital issues appeals to persons of widely different temperaments, from the daring speculator in high-risk common stocks of new enterprises to the buyer of highest-grade investment bonds of established industries.

Disadvantages of the Corporate Form

There are certain weaknesses or disadvantages inherent in the corporate form of business; but obviously, in view of the large number of corporations that have been established and the large volume of business they do, these handicaps have not been seriously preclusive.

It is more troublesome and costly to organize a corporation. Being a creature of the state, the corporation is subject to a greater amount of regulation and is recognized only in the state of incorporation unless steps are taken to qualify in other states. The corporation is more likely to be subjected to investigation and is required to make periodic and special reports to public agencies. Likewise, because of their very magnitude, large corporations are more vulnerable from the standpoint of political attack.

The corporation is less flexible than the individual proprietorship and the partnership, in that certain time-consuming formalities must be observed in seeking to effect fundamental changes, and there are generally a larger number of parties that have an interest and whose consent must be won.

The corporation has more limited credit, in that creditors may look only to the assets of the corporation, whereas the creditors of the individual proprietor and of the partnership have the additional protection of the individual assets of the owners of the business.

Whether the corporate form is a tax handicap or benefit cannot be answered in a generalization but depends upon the circumstances of the business and the circumstances of the owners as well as the tax provisions at the time. Large-scale businesses have but little choice; they are almost always corporations. Small businesses, however, either may be organized as corporations or may adopt one of the other forms, and the relative tax advantage may be an important factor in making the decision. Under such circumstances the prospective tax would be calculated both ways, making due allowance for the individual tax status of each of the owners. The income-tax law may, of course, be changed from time to time, so that the partnership form may have the advantage at one time and the corporate form at another.

INSTRUMENTS OF CORPORATE FINANCE

Corporations provide their long-term, permanent capital funds (1) through the sale of shares of stock to persons who then become the owners of the business and have an equity interest to the extent of

Exhibit 34

INSTRUMENTS OF CORPORATE FINANCE

DEBTOR-CREDITOR RELATIONSHIP: *Secured Bonds:*
Represent a claim against specific pledged assets of the corporation

Unsecured Bonds (Debentures)
Represent a claim against the general credit of the corporation

OWNERSHIP: *Preferred Stock*
Represents ownership and is generally preferred as to assets or dividends, or both

Common Stock
Represents ownership—the residual interest in the assets and earnings of the corporation

the number of shares purchased; and (2) through the sale of bonds to lenders or creditors. (See Exhibit 34.) Money obtained in this way is used mainly to acquire fixed assets, such as land, buildings, and equipment, and also to provide minimum working-capital needs for the purchase of inventories and carrying accounts receivable and other current requirements. Such a provision of long-term funds contrasts with the use of commercial credit instruments, already discussed, to provide short-term, temporary funds.

Corporate Stock

The corporation charter, issued by the appropriate official in the state of incorporation, indicates the number of shares and the classes of stock that the corporation is authorized to sell in order to raise ownership capital. In the simplest situation, there would be but one class of capital stock. For example, the charter may authorize the corporation to sell 1,000 shares of stock at $100 a share to provide $100,000. An individual investor may then buy one share, ten shares, or many more shares and will receive a stock certificate (engraved, in the case of larger corporations and particularly if the stock is listed on an organized exchange) that indicates the extent of the investor's ownership in the business. If the individual purchases 100 shares, he will receive a single certificate for the 100 shares and will then be a one-tenth owner of the corporation because he will be in possession of 100 out of the total 1,000 shares authorized and outstanding.

It should be noted that the corporation is an entity apart from the owners or shareholders in the corporation, in contrast to the sole proprietorship and the partnership, in which the business assets are owned by the proprietors and the business units are not entities apart from the owners. The corporation holds ownership of the business assets, and the shareholders in turn own the corporation and are entitled only to a pro rata interest in the aggregate assets and income of the corporation.

RIGHTS OF STOCKHOLDERS. The stock certificate is essentially a contract between the corporation and the stockholders, and the terms of the contract are stated in the stock certificate and in the charter of the corporation. Some of the principal rights of the individual stockholder can be briefly summarized as follows:

1. The right to have a certificate evidencing the ownership of shares of stock
2. The right to transfer the stock certificate at will
3. The right to receive notice of and attend stockholder meetings and to vote the stock standing in his name (usually one vote per share)
4. The right to buy additional shares of stock issued by the corporation in proportion to his present holdings
5. The right to share in the assets in proportion to stock held in the event of dissolution of the corporation

6. The right to share pro rata in the profits of the corporation that are distributed as dividends

7. The right to examine the books of the corporation under certain circumstances

8. The right to seek redress through court action in the event of malfeasance on the part of officers, directors, etc.

Collectively the stockholders: elect the directors, who are responsible for shaping the policies of the corporation, and elect and supervise the work of the officers; may amend the charter and bylaws; may vote to dissolve the corporation; and may vote on matters fundamental to corporate welfare, such as the sale or mortgaging of important assets.

STOCK CERTIFICATE.   The stock certificate shows on its face the name of the issuing corporation, the number of shares it represents, and the name of the owner of the certificate. The name of the owner is kept on the stock record book of the corporation; and he is the "holder of record" who is entitled to vote the shares, receive dividends, and exercise the other rights of stock ownership. The owner may transfer his shares by completing the assignment form on the reverse side of the certificate. The old certificate will then be canceled, and a new certificate will be issued to the new owner whose name will be recorded in the stock record book. Such transfer is often effected through the services of a transfer agent and a registrar, as will be discussed in Chapter 14, "Trustee Services."

PREFERRED STOCK.   Up to this point we have been discussing one class of capital stock, common stock, which represents the residual ownership claim to earnings and assets of a corporation. Every corporation has common stock outstanding in effect if not in name. (One of the rare exceptions is the Great Northern Railway Company, which has a $6 noncumulative preferred stock as a residual issue, a common stock never having been issued.) Some corporations have a preferred-stock issue outstanding in addition to common stock; and, as the name implies, preferred stock has some degree of preference over the common stock. This preference may be a prior claim to dividends or to assets or to both dividends and assets. Because shares of stock do not grow out of a debtor-creditor relationship, a stock certificate is not a credit instrument but rather a capital or ownership instrument. This is true of preferred, as well as common, stock. A specimen of a common-stock certificate is reproduced in Exhibit 35, on pages 216–17.

A preferred-stock issue is usually offered in order to give the buyers a claim to earnings and dividends prior to that of the common stock; and this is, as a rule, the outstanding characteristic of preferred stock. Preferred stock is generally entitled to receive a stated dividend payment, limited in amount, before anything may be paid to the common stock. On the other hand, common stock is entitled to all earnings of the corporation remaining after the payment of interest on bonds and the dividend on the preferred issue. With respect to both preferred and common stocks, however, no dividend is payable until declared by the directors; and once the dividend is declared, the dividend becomes a current liability of the corporation.

Assume that a corporation has outstanding 1,000 shares of preferred stock which are entitled to a quarterly dividend of $1.25 or $5 a year and that there are also 1,000 shares of common outstanding. If the income (after taxes) available for dividends amounted to $20,000 in a given year, the preferred stock in the aggregate would be entitled during the year to receive $5,000, and there would then remain $15,000 out of which the directors might declare dividends on the common stock. If the income available for dividends in another year amounted to but $6,000, there would be only $1,000 left for the common-stock dividend after the preferred dividend of $5,000. Obviously, the earnings available for distribution to the common stock fluctuate widely with the fortunes of the corporation. They are low or even absent in poor years and high in good years. In contrast, no matter how prosperous the corporation and how large the earnings, the preferred stock receives only the stipulated amount, but to this extent it does have a claim prior to the common. If in the judgment of the directors the continuing welfare of the corporation precludes dividend payments on either or both the preferred stock and the common stock, such payments may be omitted entirely. It is otherwise with interest on bonds, as we will note later in this chapter.

Cumulative Preferred. Preferred stocks have a wide variety of provisions, and a corporation may have more than just one class of preferred outstanding, with some preferreds having priorities over others. There are a number of important preferred-stocks provisions in addition to the prior claims to earnings and assets. Preferred stocks may be cumulative, in which instance any unpaid preferred dividends accumulate, and the total accumulated dividends must then be paid before any payments may be made on the common stock. If the $5 dividend on a cumulative preferred share is passed for three years, the accumulations would amount to $15. If the preferred is noncumulative, a dividend not paid in a given year is lost forever.

Exhibit 35

Common Stock Certificate

(Front)

Exhibit 35—Continued

COMMON STOCK CERTIFICATE

REQUIREMENTS: THE SIGNATURE OF THE STOCKHOLDER TO THE ASSIGNMENT MUST CORRESPOND WITH THE NAME AS WRITTEN UPON THE FACE OF THE CERTIFICATE IN EVERY PARTICULAR WITHOUT ALTERATION OR ENLARGEMENT OR ANY CHANGE WHATEVER.

THE SIGNATURE SHOULD BE GUARANTEED BY AN INCORPORATED BANK OR TRUST COMPANY, OR BY A NEW YORK, BOSTON, PHILADELPHIA, CHICAGO OR WASHINGTON STOCK EXCHANGE MEMBER OR FIRM, WHOSE SIGNATURE IS KNOWN TO THE TRANSFER OFFICE, OR WITNESSED BY A RESPONSIBLE PERSON WHOSE SIGNATURE IS SO KNOWN. IF IT IS IMPRACTICABLE TO SECURE SUCH GUARANTEE OR WITNESS, THE SIGNATURE SHOULD BE ACKNOWLEDGED FORMALLY BEFORE A NOTARY PUBLIC, WHO MUST CERTIFY UNDER HIS SEAL WITH RESPECT THAT THE PERSON SIGNING IS KNOWN TO HIM TO BE THE PERSON NAMED ON THE FACE OF THE CERTIFICATE.

For Value received, _____ hereby sell, assign and transfer unto

_____

_____ Shares

of the Capital Stock represented by the within Certificate, and do hereby irrevocably constitute and appoint

_____ Attorney

to transfer the said Stock on the books of the within named Company with full power of substitution in the premises.

Dated, _____ 19____

IMPORTANT { BEFORE SIGNING, READ AND COMPLY CAREFULLY WITH REQUIREMENTS PRINTED ABOVE.

In Presence of

_____

(Reverse)

Participation. Some preferred issues are participating, share dividends with the common, and receive payments in excess of the preference amount. For instance, a preferred stock may be entitled to a preferred annual payment of $5 a share and may also be entitled to share in any dividend paid on the common, perhaps equally, share for share, or perhaps only to a limited extent. Participating plans take many forms. If a preferred is restricted to only the stated preference payment, it is called "nonparticipating."

Convertible. Oftentimes preferred shares are convertible, usually into common. For instance, the preferred holder may have the right to exchange his preferred share for one or more shares of common stock. This feature may have been an inducement to encourage original purchase of the preferred because conversion may have offered the promise of possible gain through the exchange. If the particular company should ultimately prosper and enjoy large per-share earnings on the common, the common stock may become much more attractive, and exchanging the preferred share for the common might yield a substantial profit. There are also other possible factors that might make conversion advisable if not attractive.[2]

Voting Power. Preferred stock may either share voting power with the common or be nonvoting. If nonvoting, it shares ownership of the corporation but does not participate in control of the corporation.

Call and Maturity. Sometimes preferred stocks are made callable at the option of the company and, if called, are redeemed, and the investor must then find a new outlet for his funds. Some preferred stocks have a maturity date; but others, like common stock, are issued in perpetuity, although they may be subject to call for redemption.

Typical Provisions. There are obviously many kinds of preferred-stock provisions, making possible a myriad of combinations; but there is no standard grouping of provisions. It is interesting to note, however, that the typical preferred stock is cumulative, nonvoting, nonparticipating, callable, without maturity, and preferred as to assets as well as dividends.[3]

PAR VALUE AND NO-PAR. Either class of stock, common or preferred, may have a par value (a dollar amount stated on the face of the certificate) or may be without par value (no-par), in which case there is no dollar amount stated on the face of the certificate, and each share represents a pro rata fractional ownership in the business. "Par

---

[2] Investment Bankers Association of America, *Fundamentals of Investment Banking* (Chicago, 1947), pp. 28–29.

[3] Guthmann and Dougall, *op. cit.*, pp. 81–91.

value" is misleading; it usually coincides with the book value of the stock, or with the market value, only at the time of issue, assuming that the stock is sold for the par amount.

If the preferred stock is of par value, the face of the certificate will generally show the dividend preference of the stock, if any, in terms of percentage of par. If the preferred is without par value, the dividend preference will be stated in a dollar amount. In contrast to the interest charge on bonds, which is fixed, the dividend on preferred stock is a contingent payment and is payable only if declared by the directors of the corporation.

POSITION OF PREFERRED STOCK. Bonds have the first claim on the assets and earnings, but the amount of income is limited to the coupon rate. Common stocks, on the other hand, have the residual claim on assets and earnings, but the possible income return is without limit and depends only on the success of the enterprise. Accordingly, bonds have a limited appreciation potential, whereas common stocks have virtually unlimited growth possibilities.

It is apparent, therefore, that preferred stocks are, in a sense, a cross between bonds and common stocks. They have the limited-income and appreciation possibilities of the bond but are often without the benefit of an equivalent asset protection. Their asset position is just above that of the residual common stock, but they do not share with the common in the prosperity of the corporation. Thus, in periods of adversity, preferreds are in a weaker position than bonds; in times of prosperity, they fail to share in the good fortunes of the common stock.

This characterization of preferred stocks is, of course, a broad generalization and should not be interpreted to mean that a preferred stock may not be a sound investment. Quite the contrary is true. If a financially sound and prosperous company has no funded debt outstanding prior to its preferred-stock issue, and if the preferred issue is outstanding in relatively small amount in relation to the common-stock equity, then the senior stock issue might well be of high-investment caliber. That would certainly be true of a company that is adequately financed and has a comfortable cash and working capital position, earnings that cover dividend requirements by a good margin, a favorable long-term outlook, and net assets equal to many times the amount of preferred outstanding. It is not the legal description of an investment item that determines its quality, but rather its economic position. For example, the common stock of the American Telephone and Telegraph Company has received a regular quarterly

Exhibit 36

SUBSCRIPTION WARRANT

AMERICAN TELEPHONE AND TELEGRAPH COMPANY
Warrant for subscription to Convertible Debentures dated March 19, 1951

000-000
of Debenture

VALUELESS IF NOT USED ON OR BEFORE MARCH 19, 1951
SEE DIRECTIONS AS TO USE — ACTION ON YOUR PART IS REQUIRED

the number of Rights
needed to subscribe for

SPECIMEN

which is

This is to
Certify that

Subscription
Warrant for

Transfer Clerk

Telephone and Telegraph Company, at 195 Broadway, New York 7, New York, is entitled to the subscription rights set forth above, upon the terms and conditions specified in the Prospectus relating to the Debentures.

or subject, upon surrender of this warrant to the Treasurer of American

Treasurer

JANUARY 29, 1951

DIRECTIONS AS TO USE

1. To Subscribe: Fill in and sign Form 1 and send Warrant together with the necessary payment for the Debentures to the Company in the return envelope sent to you with the Warrant. Be sure that it reaches the Company by March 19, 1951.

If you do not have exactly the number of rights required for your subscription, any additional rights needed should be purchased or any excess rights sold. By signing Form 1 you authorize this to be done through Bankers Trust Company. If you wish to make other arrangements for the purchase of additional rights or the sale of excess rights, you should do so before entering your subscription.

2. To Sell All of these Rights Through Bankers Trust Company: Sign Form 2 and send Warrant to the Company in the return envelope sent to you with the Warrant. Be sure that it reaches the Company by March 19, 1951.

3. To Sell Rights Through Your Bank or Banker: Sign Form 3 on back of Warrant and deliver to your bank or broker in ample time so that rights sold can be used by March 19, 1951.

4. To Transfer Rights or Divide Warrant: Fill in and sign Form 3 on back of Warrant. Warrant should reach the Company in ample time so that rights can be used by March 19, 1951.

DO NOT DETACH

000-000

FORM 1

AMERICAN TELEPHONE AND TELEGRAPH COMPANY
195 Broadway, New York 7, N.Y.

Date

I wish to subscribe as stated below for Convertible Debentures dated March 19, 1951, upon the terms and conditions specified in the Prospectus relating to the Debentures, receipt of a copy of which is hereby acknowledged.

Amount of Debentures subscribed for .... $

(Payment of this amount is required with subscription)

Total Rights required for this subscription (7 Rights for each $100 of subscription) ———— Rights

Total Rights represented by this and any other warrants submitted herewith ———— Rights

Please request Bankers Trust Company to purchase for me any additional rights required to complete my subscription or to sell any rights in excess of the number required for my subscription.

Subscriber's Signature

Address
for Delivery
if Other
than Above

A bill will be sent to you for any rights purchased at a check, and a check will be sent to you for any excess rights sold.

DO NOT DETACH

FORM 2

AMERICAN TELEPHONE AND TELEGRAPH COMPANY
195 Broadway, New York 7, N.Y.

Please request Bankers Trust Company to sell all of the rights represented by this warrant and send me a check.

000-000

Payment of this amount must accompany subscription. A check or money order, payable to American Telephone and Telegraph Company is acceptable. Make payment in United States dollars, drawn on a bank located in continental United States.

Telephone No. at which subscriber can be reached

Date

SPECIMEN
Owner's Signature

(Front)

Exhibit 36—continued

SUBSCRIPTION WARRANT

FORM 3

AMERICAN TELEPHONE AND TELEGRAPH COMPANY
195 Broadway, New York 7, N. Y.

For value received, the rights represented by this Warrant, together with all right, title, and interest therein, are hereby assigned to:

Name and Address (Please Print)	No. of Rights

Signature of
registered owner _____

Witness: _____

The signature of registered owner in the above assignment must correspond with the name as written upon the face of this Warrant in every particular, without alteration or enlargement or any change whatever. When executed by Administrators, Executors, Trustees, Guardians, Attorneys, etc., the Company must be satisfied that the person signing has authority to act.

The signature of registered owner to the above assignment should be guaranteed by an incorporated bank or trust company, or by a New York, Boston, Philadelphia, Chicago, Washington, or San Francisco Stock Exchange member or firm, whose signature is known to the transfer office of the Company, or a signature guarantee without signature is in no known. If it is impractical to secure such guarantee of signature, the signature should be acknowledged formally before a Notary public, who must certify under his seal that the person signing is known to him to be the the person named on the face of this Warrant.

(Reverse)

Warrant for Subscription To

AMERICAN TELEPHONE AND TELEGRAPH COMPANY

Convertible Debentures Dated March 19, 1951

7 rights are needed for each $100 of Debentures subscribed for.

Rights required to complete subscription may be purchased. Excess rights may be sold.

Subscription payment in full is required with subscription.

If it is desired to transfer the rights represented by this Warrant to some one else or to divide this Warrant, the assignment form at the left should be filled in and signed.

If this Warrant is sent in for transfer or division for the purpose of subscribing for Debentures in a different name or names, then to complete the transaction the following should be furnished to the Company when the Warrant is sent in:

1 — Name and address of each subscriber.
2 — Amount of each subscription.
3 — Payment for the total amount of all subscriptions involved.

The Company will deliver new Warrant(s) only on receipt of instructions, which should be given in the spaces below.

This Warrant will be valueless if not used on or before March 19, 1951. It represents rights which can be used for:

1 — Subscription for Debentures,
2 — Sale,
3 — Transfer to another.

Instructions as to subscription, sale of rights, or transfer of the rights to another should be given in the spaces provided for that purpose.

(See other side)

DO NOT DETACH

dividend of $2.25 for many years and is undoubtedly a better investment than the first mortgage bond of an industrial company that is in a weak financial position, that has lost money steadily over the years, and is likely to become insolvent at any moment.

OTHER FORMS OF STOCK.   In addition to common and preferred stocks, there are several[4] other kinds of stock, which are, however, found much less frequently. Two kinds will be briefly characterized. Some corporations classify their common stock into *Class A* and *Class B* shares, somewhat akin to the traditional separation into preferred and common, although oftentimes the A and B shares are identical in all respects except that the A may not have voting power. It has ownership denuded of control. Still another kind of stock is the *guaranteed stock,* which arises when one corporation guarantees the dividends on the stock of another company.

STOCKHOLDERS INARTICULATE.   A very large proportion of stockholders are inarticulate as owners. They do not seek to have a voice in management, do not attend stockholder meetings, and often do not trouble to send in a written authorization (called a "proxy") delegating some other person to vote the stock for them at the meeting. Their motivation is undoubtedly found in the hope of income and appreciation in value rather than in managerial ambitions. In effect, the great mass of stockholders conduct themselves more nearly like creditors than owners. In fact, this is but a manifestation of the separation of ownership and control (management) that has so frequently been noted as characteristic of our time. For this reason some writers have called stocks "investment *credit* instruments." The true nature of stocks should, however, be clearly understood—they represent ownership, not credit.

RIGHTS AND WARRANTS.   Under certain conditions, corporations may give their present stockholders the privilege of buying additional stock in the company in proportion to their present holdings. Stockholders then receive a transferable certificate called a "subscription warrant," evidencing a certain number of "rights" to buy additional shares. "Rights" are issued in connection with current financing, as against "warrants," which evidence a similar privilege to buy additional shares but which are an option that is generally part of a long-term financing program and are likely to be exercised only in the more remote future. (A specimen subscription warrant is reproduced in Exhibit 36, on pages 220–21.)

---

[4] *Ibid.,* pp. 92–94.

Corporate Bonds

Bonds are credit instruments used in raising long-term funds. They represent a borrowing-lending relationship. There are two principal kinds: *secured bonds,* secured by a mortgage on tangible property or secured by collateral; and *debentures,* or unsecured bonds, which are a claim against the general assets of the corporation and rank with other unsecured creditors, including trade creditors.

Many descriptive designations are given to bonds to indicate their nature, and one author in a "Catalogue Description of the More Important Bonds" lists more than one hundred and sixty.[5] Such an array is obviously confusing to the uninitiated. A simple classification can be made on the following bases:

Nature of the issuer—government; municipal; corporate; railroad; industrial; special revenue; etc.

Nature of security—mortgage collateral trust; debenture; assumed; guaranteed; income; etc.

Maturity—long-term; short-term; perpetual; etc.

Termination (payment and redemption)—convertible; redeemable; serial; sinking-fund; etc.

Form of instrument—coupon; registered.

Purpose—refunding; construction; development; equipment; improvement; purchase money; unifying; etc.

Bonds, whether secured or unsecured, may also be classified with respect to the payment of principal and interest, as follows:

Coupon bonds have interest coupons attached. Principal is payable to the bearer, and interest is payable upon surrender of the coupons. Because title passes without endorsement, these bonds are also called "bearer bonds."

Registered bonds have the name of the owner on the face of the instrument and cannot be transferred without endorsement. Interest checks are mailed to the holder of record.

Registered coupon bonds are registered as to principal only, and the attached coupons are payable to the bearer.

A specimen registered bond and a specimen coupon bond are reproduced in Exhibits 37 and 38.

DENOMINATION; INTEREST. Bonds are usually for a principal amount of $1,000; and unless there is a specific indication to the contrary, the term "bond" is assumed to refer to an instrument of that denomination. The rate of interest is shown on the face of the bond;

---

[5] W. E. Lagerquist, *Investment Analysis* (New York: Macmillan Co., 1922), Appendix A.

Exhibit 37

REGISTERED BOND

(Front)

Exhibit 37—Continued

REGISTERED BOND

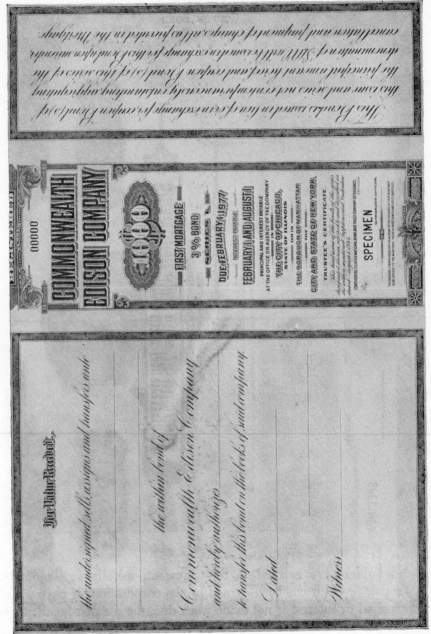

(Reverse)

Exhibit 38

COUPON BOND

(*Front*)

and holders are entitled to this payment, usually semiannually, whether or not it has been earned by the corporation. If payment of principal or interest is not made when due, the secured bondholders have the right to foreclose; debenture holders may sue and get a judgment. Bonds are often referred to as "funded debt," and the interest thereon as a "fixed charge."

CORPORATION NOTE. The corporation note is a promissory note often less formal than a bond but more formal than a commercial

Exhibit 38—Continued

COUPON BOND

(Reverse)

promissory note. It has a maturity from one to ten years and may
be secured or unsecured. Except for the shorter maturity, it is much
like a corporation bond. In contrast, the commercial promissory note
(described in Chapter 2) usually has a maturity of thirty days to six
months and is customarily used in connection with short-term borrowing from a bank.

CORPORATE MORTGAGE.   The corporate mortgage is a legal document used to pledge real property to secure a loan. It is a much more

complex instrument than the mortgage given by the home buyer, which will be discussed in Chapter 16. A detailed consideration of the corporate mortgage is beyond the scope of our immediate interest, but a brief treatment appears appropriate here.

The borrower who pledges the property remains in possession. The lender either holds title to the property by virtue of the mortgage or has a lien against the property until the loan is repaid, depending upon the law of the state in which the property is situated (this is primarily a legal and not a financial distinction). The mortgage describes the pledged property in detail and recites the obligations assumed by the borrower, such as the payment of interest and principal, maintenance of the property, payment of taxes, insuring the property, etc. When all interest and principal payments have been met, the title is restored to the borrower or the encumbrance is removed. On the other hand, if there is a default on the mortgage, the lender may start foreclosure proceedings and have the property sold under court order. If the proceeds from the judicial sale are in excess of the loan and expenses, the excess is paid to the borrower. However, if the proceeds are not adequate to meet the claims under the mortgage, the lender receives the sum realized and a deficiency judgment for the balance.

TRUSTEE AND THE TRUST AGREEMENT.   Corporation bond issues, whether secured or unsecured, are generally issued to raise substantial sums of money, running into many millions of dollars. Bonds of a given issue are usually sold to a large number of investors living in various parts of the country; these investors are not acquainted with one another and would find it difficult to take collective action. For this reason, it is expedient to appoint some third person as trustee to act for the bondholders and look after their interests because it would be impractical for individual bondholders to act independently. Such a third person is usually a corporate trustee (see Chapter 14).

The borrowing corporation enters into an agreement with the trustee, called a "trust agreement" or "indenture," at the time the bonds are being issued. This agreement outlines the obligations of the trustee: authenticate the bonds that are issued to preclude overissue; hold the mortgage or the collateral pledged to secure the loan; enforce the provisions of the indenture; submit periodic reports; notify bondholders of any default; bring suit in case of default; and generally represent the bondholders.

In the case of mortgage bonds, the indenture includes the mortgage; in the case of bonds secured by collateral, such personal property as stocks or bonds, the securities are deposited with the trustee or may be pledged by means of a chattel mortgage, as distinguished from a real estate mortgage, which is applicable only to real property.

RETIREMENT OF BONDS. Corporate bonds may be retired through *conversion*, exchanging a new security, usually a preferred or common stock, for the outstanding issue; through *redemption*, or payment of cash; or through *refunding*, replacing the outstanding bonds with another issue of later maturity, with perhaps some alteration in the provisions and rate of interest.

There are two common redemption plans designed to retire the bonds gradually over the life of the loan rather than have the full amount of the original obligation come due all at one time upon maturity. The borrowing corporation may include a *sinking-fund* provision in the indenture, stipulating that a certain sum is to be set aside each year out of earnings, the appropriation to be used either to retire outstanding bonds immediately or to be invested and used to retire the bonds at maturity. A second method is the issuance of a *serial* bond issue under which a portion of the bonds mature each year so that a substantial portion, if not all, of the bonds may be retired by the end of the loan period.

DETERMINANTS OF CORPORATE CAPITAL STRUCTURE

Corporations, as we have noted, provide their long-term capital requirements through the sale of common and preferred stocks and by borrowing through the use of one or more bond issues; but they may also add to their capital by the retention of earnings. The outstanding stocks and bonds of a corporation together with surplus make up the capital structure, and the nature of this structure depends upon a great variety of factors, both internal and external.[6]

It will be recognized that a company that utilizes bond financing assumes a fixed charge for interest and the obligation to pay the principal. In times of depression and adversity such obligations might prove burdensome, if not embarrassing. It is otherwise in the case of stock financing, because dividends are but a contingent obligation. Accordingly, only those corporations with a well-established and fairly stable level of earnings are likely to resort to bond financing. Furthermore, corporations with substantial fixed-asset requirements

---

[6] A fairly detailed consideration of capital structure will be found in Guthmann and Dougall, *op. cit.*, chap. ix.

are more likely to use bonds than companies with low fixed-asset needs. This is true because bond buyers seek the protection of a good margin of asset coverage as well as sustained earning power. Public service companies provide a good example of an industry that meets these conditions, and the utilities provide much of their capital through bonds.

Industrial companies, on the other hand, operate under competitive conditions rather than under franchise, as do the utilities. Their earnings tend to fluctuate widely and therefore do not provide as good a base for bond financing. Thus the earning and asset positions of companies vary from industry to industry, and these factors influence or condition the capital structure for the companies in any given industry.

Forces in the securities markets are an important factor in determining the type of financing that is to be employed. At a given time is the investing public receptive to bonds, to convertible issues, or to preferred or common stocks? There tend to be fashions in securities just as in other areas. The trends in corporate earnings, in interest rates, and in the price trends of stock and bonds are all elements of influence.

The judgment and policy of management and the extent to which management may wish to increase or decrease debt or increase or minimize stockholder interest also have some weight in determining capital structure, whether the company will have simply common stock or a pyramided structure consisting not only of common stock but of preferred stocks and perhaps several classes of bonds as well.

EVOLUTION OF THE CORPORATE FORM

Although the corporation as we know it today is largely a development of the nineteenth and twentieth centuries, scholars find evidence of a comparable type of organization as early as the Roman Empire, when the state recognized as legal entities associations formed for public-related purposes. The Roman law did not create such associations, but, once formed through the initiation of the associates, the state licensed them as a means of control. These associations were later established as business enterprises as well.

The corporate concept also was used in medieval England, where it is believed to have been developed independently without any relation to the Roman experience. Religious organizations and business enterprises, boroughs, and guilds used the corporate form; and a body of corporation law (not the prototype of our current corporation law) evolved. The rulers did not create the corporations but recognized them.

It is generally agreed that the corporate concept as we understand it today was first promulgated by Lord Coke about 1600; and his declaration that the corporation is an entity, an artificial person created by the sovereign, found expression by Chief Justice John Marshall in the famous Dartmouth College case (*Dartmouth College* v. *Woodward*, 4 Wheat. (U.S.) 518 (1819)). There is still, however, controversy whether the corporation is an entity created by the law or whether it is merely a group of persons bound together by a contractual relationship.

Probably the first important businesses using the corporate form were the Hudson Bay Company and the East India Company, which received charters from the crown to engage as monopolies in foreign trade and colonization, thus giving them a dual function, business and political. Later Parliament was empowered to grant charters to business groups that met the stated requirements. In the United States we followed a similar practice, and the legislatures of the several states have adopted business corporation acts under which businesses may obtain charters to operate as corporations. The first statute of this kind was adopted by the State of New York in 1811.

Although the corporate device was used in the early days of our history by the canal and turnpike companies, it was the railroad era, beginning about 1830, that greatly increased the formation of corporations. Since the last quarter of the nineteenth century the corporate form has had wide application throughout the economy. Accordingly, the history of the corporation is largely the history of the last seventy-five years. Large sums of capital were needed successively by the canal, turnpike, and railroad companies. With the establishment of a national transportation network, large-scale industry became feasible and advantageous, and this again required massive enterprises with huge fund requirements. As we have noted, the corporation is particularly appropriate for the assembly of the great sums called for by our mass-production industries of national scope.

SOCIAL IMPLICATIONS OF CORPORATE DOMINANCE

Theoretically the corporation is an ideal social instrument for organizing the economic efforts in a private enterprise society, but in actual practice the growth in the number and particularly in the size of corporations has created problems. Only through such an agency as the corporation, with its legal entity and limited liability, could we have attained within the framework of a free society the peaks of production in war and in peace that have given us the highest standard of living ever enjoyed by any nation. The case for the corporation has been admirably stated as follows:

> The corporation has proved a flexible and valuable instrument. Through it are joined the venturesome and the cautious, the wealthy and the penniless, the capable and the unskillful, and the energetic young and the retiring old into a system of contractual relationships which make it possible for each to take his most fitting part in those gigantic business enterprises which stretch across continents and over seas.[7]

The corporation provides a work opportunity for every capability from that of the freshman office boy to that of the elder-statesman chairman of the board of directors of a five- to ten-million-dollar enterprise. Whether one has great wealth or little, it is possible, either directly or indirectly, to acquire an ownership interest in any one or more of a multiplicity of businesses without assuming operational responsibility. One may purchase the well-seasoned stock of an old established company or take a "long-shot" flier in an entirely new and revolutionary venture. On the other hand, accumulated funds may be loaned to any one of thousands of corporations through the purchase of their bonds, low and medium grade, to afford relatively high return, or, if it is desired to eschew risk, then investment bonds of highest caliber. Because wide diversification is possible, even with relatively small sums, the corporation provides an ultimate opportunity for the socialization of industry in a sense quite contrary to the socialization being practiced in European laboratories—and with the retention of the existing order, including the incentive to achieve.

But what are the problems that stem from the corporation? They are largely a reflection of the size of corporations and corporate groups and the resultant possibility of monopoly; there are, however, other considerations as well. The criticism leveled at the corporation, it would seem, is in the main the result of abuse of the corporate form rather than the form itself; and it is here that public authority is at least contributorily responsible in not effecting a cure.

A hundred years ago, more or less, persons who were frugal and accumulated wealth generally invested their savings locally in some project with which they were familiar and over which they could exercise some surveillance. The money might be used to buy a farm

---

[7] *Ibid.*, p. 3.

or to start a self-owned business; might be loaned to a farmer for the acquisition of additional land, or to a homebuilder on a mortgage; or it might be loaned to a businessman with whose operations the investor was familiar. The investor would take a managerial interest; ownership and management were combined. Today accumulations are, to a large extent, made available to impersonal businesses managed by a special group of professional managers who themselves may have very little, if anything, at stake in the business they are operating. Thus ownership and control tend to be separated, and this separation is emphasized by the fact that many stockholders are inarticulate and fail to exercise their right to vote their stock. There is good reason for this—it may seem futile and not feasible to attend a stockholder meeting at a distant point and at great expense to vote ten shares of stock. So a new function has been created—that of the professional managers, who may at times be guided more by self-interest than by the welfare of the actual owners, for whom they are stewards. Just to cite one instance: stockholders are becoming apprehensive with respect to the generous pension plans that some managements are seeking to establish for themselves and sometimes for their wives. This is not necessarily an accompaniment of "bigness."

This separation of ownership and control, coupled with the disinterestedness or inarticulateness of many scattered small stockholders, gives rise to a situation that makes it possible for a small management group, or an ownership group, with little investment, to take effective control of a business.

In addition to minority control of this sort, various devices have been used in the past to control a business or even to seek control of an industry. These have been treated at length in a study *The Modern Corporation and Private Property*[8] and can be briefly summarized as (1) the holding company, (2) stock with weighted voting power, and (3) voting trust.

Holding Company. Through majority stock ownership in the stock of one company, which in turn has majority control in a second company, and that company in a third, and so on, it is possible for those in control of the first unit to control the entire series of companies with but a relatively small investment, measured against the total assets involved. This abuse of the corporate form was particularly flagrant in the utility industry (Insull Empire; Associated Gas and Electric) and led to the Public Utility Holding Company Act of 1935, which prohibited such pyramiding.

---

[8] A. A. Berle, Jr., and Gardner C. Means (New York: Commerce Clearing House, 1932).

Stock with Weighted Voting Power. By giving excessive voting power to one class of stock which represents but a small investment as against a much less potent voting power to another class of stock representing a very much greater investment, a small ownership interest may be given control. This device was likewise used in the utility industry (Cities Service Company; Standard Gas and Electric Company).

Voting Trust. If the stock of a company is placed in trust and the trustees are given the voting power, while the owners of the shares hold only voting trust certificates, control is placed in the trustees, who may have no investment in the enterprise of any sort. This is a device that may be used to perpetuate management or policies. (See Chapter 14, "Trustee Services.")

Berle and Means estimated that 200 nonbanking corporations controlled 49.2 per cent of all nonbanking corporate wealth, while the remainder was held by the more than 300,000 smaller companies; and the 200 largest corporations received 43.2 per cent of the income of all nonbanking corporations. Furthermore, they contend that about 2,000 men were in a position to control these large corporations. The implication is obvious: a small number of men influence to a substantial degree the economic life of the country. While this is a condition that cannot be ignored, it should, at the same time, be noted that these men were responsible to their respective boards of directors and that the particular companies did have to meet the competition of the thousands of other enterprises, or, in the case of utilities, were subject to regulation. Incidentally, the Berle and Means conclusions were influenced by the inclusion of railroads and utilities, both natural monopolies; and reference has already been made to the holding company legislation of 1935.

Whether "bigness" is achieved through majority or minority control, through a legal device, or through natural growth, the question may well be asked: Has an enterprise become too large to be efficient; has it reached the point of diminishing returns; and would several smaller entities be more effective? Then, too, size may carry the threat of monopoly. Years ago, in the case of the United States Steel Corporation, it was held that mere size in and of itself is not necessarily detrimental to the public interest. But the question continues to be raised, and only recently the government instituted suit against the duPont interests for the purpose of breaking down the relationship of duPont with General Motors Corporation and with United States Rubber Company.

In few industries do we find monopoly through the dominance of a single corporation. Rather, the top three, four, or five companies in an industry may give rise to monopolistic conditions if they account for a large part of the total market and there is no outside unit powerful enough to offer serious competition. Under the antitrust laws the United States is now more aggressively seeking to curb monopolistic practices after a wartime relaxation of enforcement. Both the bigness and the monopoly problem will undoubtedly be handled by eliminating the restraints on competition. It is inconceivable that our economy might seek to break up the large corporations that unquestionably have contributed so much to our progress. Certain industries characteristically need large aggregates of capital to operate effectively, and any attempt to accomplish the same goal through many smaller productive units would be wasteful and lead to a lower standard of living. The job is one of better policing, one of adapting the corporation and its bigness to serving the welfare of society as a whole in the most effective way possible.

Labor and management relations has been a topic of paramount importance in recent decades and particularly during the war and since. Undoubtedly the development of many large corporations doing a nation-wide business, with plants scattered throughout the country and employing thousands of men, hastened the development of national unions so that labor through big unions could cope with management and big business in establishing wages, working conditions, and various fringe conditions of employment.

New problems in business finance are being raised for many corporation managements as a result of the impetus that was given to industrial pensions by the Steel Industry Fact Finding Board in the fall of 1949. Where labor demands, or management offers, a pension program, and the idea is mutually accepted in principle, a specific plan must be evolved and administered and the accumulated funds must be invested. Corporations that put pension plans into effect assume a social responsibility to provide for at least a part of the retirement needs of their workers. (See Chapter 12.) The investment of the sizable funds that will accumulate in these pension funds may seriously affect the capital markets, and perhaps the very financing of corporations themselves.

—ERWIN W. BOEHMLER

QUESTIONS AND PROBLEMS

1. Distinguish the three major legal forms of business organization from the following viewpoints: ease of starting a business; evidence of ownership; and the financial responsibility of the owners.

2. What advantages does the corporation have that are not shared in equal degree by the other two forms of business organization named in the answer to Question 1?

3. How important is the corporation in the American economy in terms of the number of business units, the dollar volume of business, and the employment opportunities provided?

4. Comment on the following: A corporation has more limited credit than a similarly situated partnership with the same amount of capital.

5. Classify the instruments of corporate finance. Name at least two major classifications and two subclassifications under each.

6. Distinguish: coupon bond; registered bond.

7. Is a common stock certificate a credit instrument?

8. Briefly sketch the evolution of the corporate form.

9. What is the relative position of a preferred stock in a capital structure? From the standpoint of dividends? Claim to assets?

10. Indicate some of the implications of corporate dominance.

11. What are some of the abuses of the corporate form?

12. Why may it be said that the corporation is theoretically the ideal instrument for organizing the efforts of a free society?

13. Does the Government share in any way responsibility for the abuses of the corporate form?

14. Discuss: Stockholders are inarticulate.

15. Distinguish the following terms as applied to bonds: sinking fund; serial.

16. What are some of the factors that might explain why one company may have a simple capital structure with only common stock outstanding while another company may have in addition to common stock one or more issues of preferred stock and one or more issues of bonds?

17. What are the typical preferred stock provisions with respect to: dividends, claim to assets; voting; participation; callability; and maturity?

18. What are some of the more important rights of stockholders?

19. Explain what is meant by "the separation of ownership and control" with reference to the corporation.

BIBLIOGRAPHY

It is the primary purpose of Chapter 7 to introduce the capital instruments of corporate finance—the various classes of stocks and bonds and their characteristics—and, incidentally, to consider the corporation as a form of business organization and to point to some of the problems growing out of the dominance of the corporation in our economy.

The forms of business organization are treated in considerable detail in most standard textbooks in business organization, business finance, and corporate finance and usually in introductory texts in economics. The nature and the advantages of the various legal forms of organization are generally discussed at length.

Textbooks in corporate finance are the best source for a full discussion of the attributes of the various kinds of stocks and bonds and also for an explanation of why corporate capital structures tend to vary with the industry.

In recent years much attention has been given to the problems of "bigness" in business; and one phase of this problem, concentration, is considered in a recent report by E. W. Stocking and M. W. Watkins, on *Monopoly and Free Enterprise* (New York: Twentieth Century Fund, 1951), which argues against an arbitrary attack on size per se. A distinction between the size of the *individual plant* and the size of the *unit of ownership* or *financial control* is made in chapter ix of John Ise, *Economics* (rev. ed.; New York: Harper & Bros., 1950), and the two preceding chapters deal with business organization and the advantages and disadvantages of the corporation, respectively.

Chapter • 8

LONG-TERM FUNDS FOR BUSINESS

THUS FAR we have discussed in detail two principal classes of financial institutions: those that serve the short-term financing needs of business and those that provide credit for consumers. We have also considered legal forms of organization for business, giving particular attention to the corporation. The next subject for consideration is the supply of long-term funds for business.

In Chapter 1 the term "capital formation" was used to identify one of the important features of our contemporary society: there must be saving, and savings must be put to use maintaining and increasing the productive facilities of the country. In the postwar years, 1946–49, the new and going concerns of the United States used over $100 billion to acquire additional assets and maintain existing facilities. The way in which these funds were obtained can be judged from the generalized data of Table 13.

The great importance of the savings of the owners of businesses and of closely related individuals is emphatically indicated. Two thirds of the funds used by going concerns came from revenues retained in the business rather than distributed to the owners. Three quarters of the funds invested in the two million new concerns were supplied from the personal savings of owners and their friends.

The use of short-term credit supplied by trade creditors and banks has been a further important source. This short-term credit together with the funds obtained from owners and friends provided substantially all of the funds for new business.

Going concerns have obtained funds from distribution of new securities to a much greater extent than have new firms. Although the percentages shown in Table 13 are not large, the dollar amount of new funds represented by these percentages is over $18 billion. An outstanding example of the importance of securities distribution is found in the postwar financing of the American Telephone and Telegraph system. As a public utility, the revenues of this organization are affected by the rigidity of the rates charged for service. The demands of expansion, combined with rising costs, could not be met by the retention of earnings from operations, as is the case in many other businesses. In the postwar period, 1945–49, A. T. & T. obtained over $3½ billion through securities distributions.

In this chapter we will consider the distribution of securities

TABLE 13

APPROXIMATE PERCENTAGE DISTRIBUTION OF SOURCES OF FUNDS FOR BUSINESS

SOURCES	GOING CONCERNS (CORPORATIONS ONLY) (1946–49)	NEW FIRMS	
		Trade (1945–47)	Manufacturing (1946–48)
Owners and friends*	67	74	75
Trade credit	6	12	10
Bank loans (excluding mortgage loans)	6	13	5
Mortgage loans	3	1	7
Sales of bonds†	13	..	2
Sales of stock†	5	..	..
Total	100	100	100

* For going concerns: funds retained from revenues obtained from operations of these firms, including funds retained for payment of taxes and other current but unpaid expenses. For new concerns: funds loaned or invested in equity by owners and directors; by friends, relatives, or other personal creditors; and by (parent) companies exercising control of policies of the new firms.
† For new firms: excluding securities sold to individuals and companies referred to in preceding footnote.
Adapted from the following: For going concerns: *Survey of Current Business*, February, 1950, Table 16, p. 27; for new trade firms: Lawrence Bridge, "Capital Requirements of New Trade Firms," *ibid.*, December, 1948, esp. Table 4, p. 23; and for new manufacturing firms: Lawrence Bridge and Lois E. Holmes, "Capital Requirements of New Manufacturing Firms," *ibid.*, April, 1950, esp. Table 4, p. 17.

through investment banking firms to the public and also the private placement of securities directly with institutional investors, such as life insurance companies, banks, and investment companies. The operations of special agencies for long-term financing of business and some special problems of small business will also be discussed.

INVESTMENT BANKING

The best-known intermediaries for providing long-term funds are the investment banking houses. They purchase securities issued by corporations and public bodies and sell these securities to their customers, the nation's investors. Investment bankers derive their income from the difference between the price paid to the issuers and the price received from investors. (spread).

Early in the history of the United States, business was financed largely through the private subscriptions of wealthy individuals and through the sale of securities abroad. The need for raising a substantial volume of funds to finance the Civil War led to the development of agencies that specialized in the rapid distribution of government securities over a broad area—the prototype of the modern investment banking firm. In later years the great size of many issues necessitated the use of "syndicating," a device for pooling risks between several banking firms, and the syndicate form of organization gained prominence. Today, through syndicating and modern methods of communication, investment bankers are able to distribute very large blocks of securities widely and rapidly and can guarantee successful distribution to the issuing entities. Without such organizations and their services, many of our present-day corporations could not have obtained sizable amounts of funds necessary for their present scale of operation.

INVESTMENT BANKING FUNCTIONS. The investment banking industry provides a variety of services to investors and to corporations and governmental units seeking funds. The typical investment banker serves in the following capacities:

Originator. Advises the issuer seeking new capital in the preparation of an issue of stocks or bonds for underwriting.

Underwriter. Buys outright an entire stock or bond issue or at times agrees to buy any portion of an issue not otherwise subscribed.

Distributor. Purchases new or already outstanding stocks or bonds for sale to investors. In originating, underwriting, and distributing, the investment banker may act alone or, particularly in the case of large national issues, in participation with other investment banking houses.

Dealer. Buys and sells securities in which he has an interest. He will usually have an inventory of such securities and will buy and sell as principal. He will deal in such securities either because he was the underwriter or distributor of the issue or because he regards the issue as otherwise attractive for his investor customers.

Broker. He will act as the agent for investors and will buy or sell securities for them, whether the securities are listed on an organized exchange or traded over the counter.

Financial Adviser. In addition to advising issuers of securities, the investment banker serves in other financial counseling capacities as well. He will advise businesses on problems of a financial nature, including assistance in effecting consolidations or in the acquisition or sale of capital assets; and he will furnish information and investment advice and assistance when requested and will aid individual and institutional investors in determining the value of securities for which there may not be an adequate public market.

Origination, underwriting, and distribution are considered in this chapter. The dealer and broker functions are treated in Chapter 9.

One writer[1] has classified investment banker operations in a somewhat different way, which can be summarized as follows:

1. The investment banker plays a role in the capital formation process; he gathers surplus funds from many millions of persons directly and through financial institutions, and makes these funds available to business enterprises and to public bodies for productive use; he serves as a middleman.

2. The investment banker effects the transfer of ownership of existing wealth—outstanding securities; whole businesses; and the transfer of securities from a holding company to individuals when required by law.

3. Through security substitution the investment banker makes available as a substitute for outstanding securities a different security. Examples: investment company shares; holding company shares; refunding operations.

4. Security and portfolio management service is provided.

INVESTMENT BANKING INDUSTRY. Some measure of the scope of the investment banking industry and securities business structure is provided by the membership of the Investment Bankers Association of America (I.B.A.) and the membership of the National Association of Securities Dealers. There are roughly 750 members of the Investment Bankers Association, who maintain about 1,000 branch offices in addition to the main offices, or a total of about 1,750 places of business. Members of this Association are primarily originators and underwriters of securities with a national market and houses that participate in the distribution of such securities as well as local securities. Included among these 750 I.B.A. members are about 50 houses that deal exclusively in municipal bonds and about 90 of the larger commercial banks. (Commercial banks may deal in municipal and federal government bonds; they are precluded from dealing in corporate securities.)

---

[1] Jules I. Bogen in Section One, Part I, Investment Bankers Association of America *Fundamentals of Investment Banking* (Chicago 1947), pp. 5–9.

With the exception of the municipal houses and the commercial banks, practically all I.B.A. members also belong to the National Association of Securities Dealers, which has a total membership of about 2,800, including many smaller houses that do largely a local business. The nature of the National Association of Securities Dealers is discussed more fully later in this chapter and also in Chapter 9.

Preliminary Steps

The first step in the issuance of new securities may be taken by an officer of a corporation who seeks the assistance of an investment banking house, or by a banking firm which contacts the businessman to suggest an issue. After the initial interview with the representatives of the business, the investment banker will make a thorough study of the particular business and the industry of which it is a part, to determine the feasibility and advisability of contracting to handle the financing. Specialists such as accountants, lawyers, engineers, and industry and management consultants will be called in to assist in the investigation. This study will include a careful review of the history of the company, its operations, financial record, managerial policies, position in the industry, the competition that the enterprise must meet, and any other factors that may aid in appraising the soundness of the operation and the ability of management.

If the decision is reached that the company requires financing and that fundamental conditions, internal and external, justify the raising of additional funds, an agreement will be made by the investment banker and the issuer. The choice of the form of security will depend on the needs and wishes of the management and the temper of the market, i.e., what type of security will appeal to investors at the particular time. Agreement must be reached on: the price at which the security should be sold and, if a bond or preferred stock, the interest rate or the dividend; whether the issue should be designed to appeal to institutional investors or to individuals; and whether the responsibility for the distribution of the securities will be shared with other investment bankers who might then join in signing the agreement.

Underwriting

One decision emerging from such investigation is whether or not the investment bankers will "underwrite" the issue. Investment bankers are often called "underwriters," although this is a term which is usually associated with insurance. The marine insurer agrees to compensate the owner of goods placed on a ship if the ship fails to make port; the accident insurer agrees to pay costs resulting from accidents. In much the same way, the underwriter of a securities distribution assures the company seeking funds that the funds will be available regardless of the success of public distribution. This assurance is provided by agreement that the underwriters will pay for the securities issued whether or not the investment bankers are able to sell the issue to their customers. On a date set in the underwriting or purchase contract, each member of the underwriting syndicate will deliver to the managing house a certified check for its share of the issue. The managing house thereupon delivers the funds to the corporation or a designated agent. Under these conditions the issuing firm is insured against failure of the distribution process. It can depend upon receiving the funds it needs at the time needed.

There are two forms of underwriting contract which are common: (1) a firm contract and (2) a stand-by agreement.

A *firm contract* is one by which the bankers bind themselves to pay the corporation as indicated above. This contract may be cancelable: up to a certain date the bankers may withdraw from the agreement. On or after that date, however, they are bound by the contract.

A *stand-by agreement* is one by which the bankers bind themselves to purchase all of the securities which the issuing corporation may be unable to sell through some other distribution channel. For example, the corporation may offer a new issue to its present security holders. Under a stand-by agreement, the bankers underwrite the success of the issue by standing ready to purchase any securities which the present security holders do not buy. Regardless of whether or not the old security holders give the new issue enthusiastic reception, the corporation will receive the needed funds. The banker assumes the problem of marketing the unsold securities.

"BEST-EFFORT" DISTRIBUTION. The facilities of banking firms are sometimes employed only for distribution, and the bankers do not underwrite the issue. They contract simply to employ their "best efforts" to obtain purchasers for the new securities. The bankers receive a commission for their efforts; they do not commit themselves to purchase or distribute the entire issue; they do not depend for income upon the sale of the new issue in total to the public. If any part of the issue remains unsold at the end of the contract period, the issuer has little alternative except to withdraw the remaining portion.

The issuer loses to the extent that it fails to obtain the amount of funds which it desired. Best-effort contracts are requested by issuers whose investment appeal is so great that the need for insurance (underwriting) is negligible, and such contracts are preferred by bankers if they undertake distribution of issues which are so difficult to sell that underwriting does not seem feasible. Thus best-effort contracts are used for very strong and very weak issues. It is not unusual to observe that stock issues, especially of new firms, are offered on a best-effort basis.

RISKS OF UNDERWRITING. Examples of losses to underwriters are numerous. Although earlier and perhaps more spectacular cases might be cited, a number of "sticky" or slow-moving issues appeared in 1946. In October of that year, owing to an unexpected fall in securities prices, a syndicate of 46 investment bankers found themselves unable to sell at their offering price the 125,000 shares of Willys-Overland Motors, Inc., $4.50 preferred stock, which they had purchased at $100 a share in June for resale at $102.75 a share. They finally disposed of these shares at $53 to $68 a share. The huge offering of 1,445,000 shares of Cincinnati Gas and Electric Company common stock purchased by 156 investment banking firms at $26 a share was finally distributed at prices as low as $21.75. In 1950, about two thirds of an issue of Potomac Electric Power Company bonds for which underwriters had paid $100.80¼ were sold at prices of approximately $100.50. The risks of marketing are not, of course, confined to issues sold under firm contract or stand-by agreement. In 1939, Shell Union Oil Corporation completed the sale of bonds on a best-effort basis at 96 rather than the desired 100. On the other hand, many issues "go out the window" and are sold within a few minutes because they are priced attractively for the market at the moment of offering.

PURCHASE SYNDICATE. The distribution of an issue of securities usually occurs in two steps: wholesale and retail. After an initial contact has been made between the issuing corporation and investment bankers, one or several firms make an agreement to purchase the issue from the corporation. In times past, these firms formed a joint venture, a kind of partnership created for the definite limited purpose of purchasing the specific issue. The joint venture, in turn, sold the issue to other bankers at the retail level or direct to investors. The full advantage of gain or the full weight of loss fell on the venture and was distributed according to the agreement between the members. In more recent years, it is usual for each member of a syndicate to sign a separate contract with the corporation and assume responsibility for only a specific amount of the issue. In a divided account of this kind, losses fall directly on the firms which fail to market their particular allotment successfully. Another advantage of this separation of liability lies in the unknown potential loss arising under the federal law regulating the issue of securities, the Securities Act of 1933. Under the terms of this act, any individual responsible for a misstatement or omission of a material fact in information concerning a new issue might be asked to pay damages sustained by purchasers. In a joint venture, any one firm might be asked to pay damages as great as the full amount of the issue; with separate contracts, the damages for which a firm may become liable probably would not exceed the amount of that part of the whole issue which the firm contracted to distribute.

The number of members of a purchase syndicate and the constituency of the group are separately determined for each issue. There is, therefore, a great deal of flexibility in arranging a syndicate operation.

Most syndicates have one member acting as manager. This firm is usually the "originating house," the one which made the initial contact with the issuer and which, in any event, as syndicate manager, assumes certain responsibilities for the venture as a whole. It may handle all business dealings between the syndicate and issuer, among syndicate members, and between the syndicate and the retail group. Occasionally two or more houses co-operate in performing the management function.

SELLING GROUP.   The purchase syndicate usually contracts with a second group of banking houses to provide for retail distribution —i.e., sale to individual investors. Some or all of the purchase syndicate members will also engage in the retail distribution. Utilization of additional firms at the retail level increases the number of investors who can be reached quickly. The retail organization may take a syndicate form but usually assumes a less formal selling-group arrangement. The number of houses in the selling group varies with the issue, and many smaller dealers may be included. The selling group may be made up of dealers in all parts of the nation, and this tends to broaden distribution. Selling-group members purchase outright a participation in a new issue at an established discount from the public offering price, and their risk is limited to the extent of their participation. In the event that a dealer is not able to place the entire allotment, the manager of the underwriting syndicate may, in his discretion, repurchase all or part of the allotment without penalty to the dealer. Such repurchase generally occurs only when the syndicate is short of the issue.

MARKET SUPPORT. The prices of securities on public markets are subject to sudden and marked change. Fluctuations may occur for temporary and rather insubstantial reasons. As a new issue of securities is sold to investors by the selling group, the salesmen seek to place the securities in the hands of individuals who will retain ownership for some time—i.e., in "firm hands." Some buyers, however, will turn about and offer the new securities in the public markets. If a fairly large number of the securities are thus offered in a short period of time, the market price might well decline. This in turn would have an adverse effect on the continued sale of the new issue. If securities offered on the public market can be reacquired by the bankers and redistributed—this time into firm hands—the price is less likely to drop. For this reason, the purchase syndicate may agree to maintain a trading account. The manager will maintain a bid to purchase all securities offered at a certain price. This price is usually slightly below that at which the new issue is being sold to investors. Any securities repurchased are then distributed again to members of the syndicate for sale to the public.

The procedure of price support is known as "stabilization" and has been a center of controversy as a possible socially undesirable practice. However, the Securities and Exchange Commission, the federal agency regulating securities-market practices, ruled in 1939 that price stabilization was an essential part of securities distribution if proper disclosure of the fact is made public, for it prevents early buyers of a "slow" issue from being penalized, and conversely prevents underwriters from "holding back" for a better price on issues which are readily marketable.

Secondary Distributions and Special Offerings

Owners of large blocks of securities often find that sale of their holdings cannot easily be accomplished through the usual channels for securities marketing. A secondary distribution is a sale of such a large block of securities outside of the organized exchanges. A syndicate is formed to underwrite the distribution to the public, and it purchases the block at a given price. It then sells at a fixed price, which is usually established by the latest available market quotation for the issue just prior to the sale and to the public offering. The spread between purchase and sale price is similar in amount to that for a primary public distribution of a new securities issue. The British government used this procedure in 1940–41 to sell the holdings of its citizens; the Mellon and Rockefeller interests have also used this method to reduce their holdings in some companies.

In 1942 the New York Stock Exchange established a procedure for "special offerings" of securities ordinarily sold on the Exchange. The minimum quantity is 1,000 shares of stock or $25,000 market value, whichever is greater, or $15,000 principal amount of bonds with aggregate market value exceeding $10,000. The block is offered at a fixed price, and efforts are made to place securities in much the same way as for a secondary distribution.

Types of Clients

The investment banker serves medium- and large-sized corporate businesses and state or local governments primarily. It is essentially breadth and magnitude of securities distribution which the investment banking firms are prepared to achieve which gives them their specialized place. Sole proprietors and partnerships do not have securities to offer. On the other hand, certain forms of securities—e.g., United States government bonds, which receive wide distribution—are marketed through other channels, such as the commercial banking system or special selling organizations. In 1949, investment bankers distributed approximately three quarters of the $4 billion of new issues for the following broad industry groups: extractive, $27 million; manufacturing, $622 million; financial and investment, $850 million; merchandising, $2 million; transportation and communications, $646 million; electric, gas, and water, $1,752 million; and other groups, $118 million.

Cost to Clients

The cost of obtaining funds is reflected in the bankers' spread and the expenses paid by the client himself. The bankers' spread—commissions and discounts received—cover charges for underwriting and distribution. In the aggregate, the spread tends to be small relative to the amount of money received by the issuer. Securities and Exchange Commission estimates of costs to issuers per $100 received during the years 1945–47, inclusive, are shown in Table 14. These data are only indicative of the costs which a particular issuer might be expected to pay. There are several weaknesses in these aggregates. The data cover issues which were underwritten, as well as issues sold on a best-effort basis. The amount of commissions and discounts per

$100 tends to be greater in the latter form of distribution. A greater proportion of the common stock was probably distributed in this way. Some costs are fixed or nearly fixed. They must be covered for any issue, whether large or small; but they tend to increase the comparative cost of small issues over that of large. The common and preferred stock issues were, on the whole, smaller than the bond issues. Some of the apparently higher cost of issue for these classes of securities is really a measure of the difference in cost between

TABLE 14

COSTS TO ISSUERS PER $100 RECEIVED FROM NEW SECURITIES ISSUES, 1945–47

Type of Security	Total Cost	Commission and Discount	Other Expense
Bonds................	$ 1.33	$0.84	$0.49
Preferred stock........	4.16	3.39	0.77
Common stock........	10.03	8.83	1.20

Source: Securities and Exchange Commission, "Survey of American Listed Corporations: Cost of Flotation, 1945–1947," *Survey Series*, Release No. 147, March 24, 1949.

small and large issues rather than between classes of instruments. However, on the whole, common stocks, and also some preferreds, may require considerable selling effort, whereas many bonds readily "go out the window."

The distinction between cost of underwriting and cost of distribution is much less easily ascertainable. Relative amounts of the total spread which are allocated for underwriting and for selling are indi-

TABLE 15

PERCENTAGE OF SELLING PRICE PAID FOR UNDERWRITING AND SELLING IN NINE SECURITIES ISSUES, 1946–49

COMPANY	TYPE OF SECURITY	PERCENTAGE OF SELLING PRICE	
		Underwriting	Selling
New York Telephone Company..	Mortgage bond	0.45	0.12
West Penn Power Company.....	Mortgage bond	0.34	0.12
Armour and Company..........	Debenture	1.25	1.25
Black, Sivalls & Bryson, Inc.....	Preferred stock	1.00	2.50
R. G. LeTourneau, Inc.........	Preferred stock	1.34	0.96
Commonwealth Loan Company..	Preferred stock	2.00	2.50
Associated Spring Corporation...	Common stock	1.83	2.33
H. J. Heinz Company..........	Common stock	2.93	2.44
Timely Clothes, Inc...........	Common stock	3.94	4.54

cated in Table 15, compiled from data from prospectuses for issues offered to the public in 1946–49. There is a suggestion that the cost of underwriting tends to be less than one half, and the cost of selling more than one half, of the cost to the issuer for investment banking services.

The "other expense," which ranges from $0.49 to $1.20, as shown in Table 14, is a measure of the expense per $100 received which the issuing corporation must usually pay directly. It refers to the costs of printing and engraving, registration and recording, taxes, legal, accounting, and engineering costs, and the costs of listing the issue on an organized exchange—to the extent that these expenditures are required for any particular issue.

Long-Term Relationships with Clients

The investment banker cannot afford to dispose of his merchandise and then forget about its existence. As long as the securities he sells are outstanding in the hands of the public, the reputation of the banker is linked to the success or failure of the enterprises he helps to finance. Because of this relation of the investment banker to the investor, on the one hand, and to the issuer, on the other, he must maintain a close connection with both, and more particularly with the issuer. Often the investment banker serves on the board of directors of firms he helps to finance. Many firms use the same underwriters year after year as needed, a natural result of the intimate relationship of the banker and of the banker's acquaintance with the affairs of the corporation. If the investment banker were to act imprudently or fail to serve effectively, the corporation would replace him with a competitor eager to serve in a more efficient manner. Similarly, when an investment banker is dissatisfied with the management of a firm which he has helped to finance, he may voluntarily relinquish his underwriting position.

Sources of Bankers' Funds

A successful distribution of a security issue results in a flow of funds from investors to the issuer. The investment banker provides the channel through which these funds flow, and diverts a small amount, his spread, to himself in payment for his services. In any event, excepting best-effort distributions, whether or not the public buys the entire issue, payment of the principal amount to the issuer will be made by the banker at the time set in the contract, and this is usually before the investors have paid the banker for securities they have purchased.

If the banker is to pay the issuer before funds are obtained from investors, he must supply them from his own assets or borrow. In general, the greater proportion will be obtained by borrowing from commercial banks. Here we can observe how the capacity of the commercial banking system to supply money for short-term use facilitates the consummation of a long-term activity. The commercial bank can lend against the investment banker's note—probably secured by the deposit of the issue in question as collateral—for the length of time necessary for the collection of funds from a multitude of individual investors. This loan bridges the time gap between issue and sale in a successful distribution. The investment banker need commit only so much of his own funds to an issue as the commercial banker requires for a margin of protection on the loan.

An attempt at distribution which fails places the investment banker under financial strain. The loan at the commercial bank may be continued as long as there is adequate collateral to support it, but an inventory of unsold securities held by the investment house not only ties up the investment banker's own funds but limits his capacity to borrow more to carry other issues. It blocks the continued turnover which is fundamental to his business. Therefore, in many cases, such as those given on page 244, the investment banker will lower the price at which the issue is offered to the investing public to a point at which he can sell all of the securities, take the loss, clear the loan, and seek to free funds so that he may engage in future distribution.

Under a best-effort agreement, the investment banker advances nothing. The banker is acting simply as an agent on a commission basis and does not supply any funds of his own for the operation. He channels money from investors to the issuer and does not underwrite success.

Investment banking firms may engage in the distribution of many millions of dollars of securities in a given period—say, a year—and yet have relatively small amounts of owner investment in the business. And, only in rare instances do investment bankers seek funds for their own use in the market they serve.

Regulation

The nature of the business which the investment banker conducts has led to a certain amount of regulation of securities distribution and of the activities of persons engaged in this distribution. Investment securities are intangible. A bond or stock is merely a bundle of rights on which it is very difficult to place a precise value at any time. The strengths or weaknesses of these rights may not be apparent for years. Even the elements of strength or weakness which appear to be obvious at one moment may prove to be otherwise at some future period, owing to changes in the economy generally and of the securities markets in particular. In a dynamic world, the forecast of the future implied in the pricing of a security is, at best, an informed estimate. Since few persons are in the position to make an intelligent appraisal, they may be acting under a considerable misconception when they acquire securities. Public interest has dictated that willful exploitation of this possible weakness in the investor's ability to understand the nature of a security shall not be condoned. Regulation is directed at restraint of practices which magnify the risk of ownership through misunderstandings between purchaser and seller of securities. In a sense, a useful analogy might be drawn with the regulation of the practices of sellers of foods and drugs.

Governmental attempts to control the sale of new securities issues are based upon existence of a public offering. Statutory definitions of "public sale" are usually omitted; but by construction, a public offering may be defined as one made to the public generally. Thus, sale of an issue to one person is a public sale, if the offer might have been accepted by any individual or group. In practice, sale to fewer than twenty-five persons has been presumed a "private," rather than public, sale. These definitions are important because all laws on securities sales, of outstanding as well as of new issues, as noted, are based upon a public offering. The laws are designed to protect the *public* against fraud or deceit.

Restrictions on marketing of new securities follow the familiar pattern of much other regulation: initiated by the states; state laws found ineffective to control interstate transactions; and subsequent federal legislation.

STATE REGULATION.   The various "blue-sky laws" were the first attempts at state regulation of the marketing of security issues. Their title has been attributed to an early court decision which commented upon "speculative schemes that have no more basis than so many feet of blue sky." The first state act was adopted in Kansas in 1911, and other states followed. Such blue-sky statutes afforded some protection to the investor against outright fraud; but because of

variations in type and enforcement, the state laws are not uniformly
effective and are applicable only intrastate. Nevertheless, blue-sky
laws are now in effect in all states except Nevada.

The blue-sky laws may be classed into three types: fraud laws,
licensing laws, and registration laws. Only Delaware, New Jersey,
New York, and Maryland have fraud laws in their true sense. They
do little more than provide for penalties and for enjoining those who
are guilty of fraud in the sale of securities. These laws apply equally
to the sale of new securities and the exchange or trading of outstanding issues. Licensing laws, of the type found in Maine, place emphasis
on the dealer rather than on the securities sold. This type of law,
requiring licensing of all securities dealers, may be combined with a
required registration of securities, as in Illinois, Indiana, Ohio, and
Wisconsin. In many states such registration of dealers has become a
rather perfunctory detail with little scrutiny of the character and
ability of applicants. The registration laws, as in Massachusetts and
Ohio, resemble the federal Securities Act of 1933, being intended
to prevent deceit and fraud before it occurs, rather than, as is the
case under the fraud laws, to punish after an act has been committed.
Under such a type of law, for instance, Wisconsin has often prohibited the sale of securities where bonuses to promoters or underwriters, in the form of rights, have appeared excessive; and Ohio has
prevented the sale of a second large original offering of Kaiser-Frazer
Corporation stock because of a legal technicality precluding a second
offering before operations had actually begun and before routine
financial statements reflecting operations were available for scrutiny.

While state securities laws are reasonably good, their enforcement
is difficult, owing to weak administration at times and always to lack
of control over interstate transactions. A promoter in one state might
sell stock to residents of another state and be able to avoid, or at
least delay, his prosecution under the law of that second state for a
considerable period of time.

SECURITIES ACT OF 1933.   The two principal federal acts regulating securities distribution and markets are the Securities Act of
1933 and the Securities Exchange Act of 1934. The latter is discussed in the next chapter, since it is directed primarily to regulation
of practices in markets for outstanding securities. The Securities Act
of 1933 is concerned primarily with public offerings of new securities
issues. It provides for full disclosure, in a registration statement, of
all pertinent information regarding a proposed issue and penalties

for violations of the act, assuming that, with access to all relevant information and to digests thereof by investment services, prospective investors would be able to appraise the security more effectively. It thus does not directly attempt to prevent sale of speculative (or perhaps even worthless) issues. It does not guarantee the investment merit of registered securities. It does require full and truthful disclosure of all pertinent information. It is not a "let-the-seller-beware" statute, but a full disclosure or "truth-in-securities-offering" law.

Specifically exempt from the provisions of the act are: (1) issues of the federal government, municipalities, government corporations, and banks; (2) commercial paper with maturity of not more than nine months; (3) issues of nonprofit organizations and co-operatives; (4) railroad securities; (5) receivers' certificates; (6) insurance and annuity contracts; and (7) new securities issued pursuant to reorganization.

Other exemptions from registration apply to small enterprises which (a) sell issues not exceeding $300,000 aggregate and thus have only limited public offering, (b) sell issues wholly within a single state, or (c) sell a complete issue of securities to a limited public. This last exemption applies particularly to the private placement of an issue with institutional investment agencies.

It is significant to note that the last-mentioned exemptions from registration do not constitute exemption from civil and criminal liability in case of actual fraud in the public sale of securities of any corporation, municipality, state, or the federal government, regardless of the size of the issue. The promoter of a small enterprise who offers to sell a security to more than a limited number of persons, therefore, can protect himself against subsequent claims of fraud only by filing with the Securities and Exchange Commission an informational statement about the issue.

Registration. The registration statement, under the Securities Act of 1933, must be signed by the principal officers of the corporation and a majority of the board of directors and filed at least twenty days before any public offering is to be made. The Securities and Exchange Commission (SEC) may shorten this waiting period (accelerate the registration date) for a particular issue under certain conditions if warranted. But most issues are actually in registration for more than twenty days. A registration fee based on the aggregate proceeds of the offering must be paid. The written consent of all experts who prepared parts of the statement, such as accountants, engineers, and lawyers, must also be filed. In the form must appear a full disclosure of the name, location, and state of incorporation of the issuer and purpose of the issue, and the names and addresses and amount of securities owned by and remuneration paid to directors, officers, promoters, underwriters, and all who own more than 10 per cent of any class of stock of the issuer.

Detailed information on the new security must be given, including the underwriting agreement, estimated proceeds, net offering price, underwriting spread, and costs. Additional information on the relation of the company to the promoters and principal stockholders must be submitted, together with certified financial statements in a prescribed form for the preceding three fiscal years. The SEC has the power to ask for additional information, if necessary, to give a complete public disclosure of all material facts on the company and the security issue.

The SEC is empowered to refuse to permit a registration statement to become effective if it believes the statement is inaccurate or incomplete in any material respect. If a registration which has become effective is later found to be false, misleading, or incomplete, the SEC may issue a stop order suspending the effectiveness of the registration statement. These steps were taken, for example, in the case of the Tucker Corporation, an automobile manufacturing company which did not actually reach the production stage before attempted reorganization.

Registration is required also of all "secondary distributions" in which outstanding stock is being sold by a principal stockholder or stockholders through an underwriter, with proceeds exceeding $300,000.

Prospectus. The actual sale or delivery of securities to a banker's customer may not be made unless a prospectus conforming to the act precedes or accompanies the sale or delivery. The prospectus is in reality an abridged form of the registration statement but usually is, nevertheless, a lengthy document.

COMPETITIVE BIDDING. In order to assure "arms-length bargaining" between the managements of railroad and public utility corporations issuing new securities and the investment banking firms which undertake the marketing, both the Interstate Commerce Commission (ICC) and the SEC have adopted the device of compulsory competitive bidding. Under such regulation, a corporation is required to obtain bids from a number of individuals or purchase syndicates. The securities are then sold to the bidder making the most favorable bid.

The use of the competitive bidding device has been traditional in the marketing of municipal bonds. In 1926 the ICC made this a requirement in the issue of railroad-equipment trust certificates, special issues sold to provide funds to purchase rolling stock for the railroads. The SEC ruled in 1941 that securities of public utility companies under their jurisdiction were to be offered by competitive bidding. In 1944 the ICC extended its ruling to cover all railroad bond issues amounting to $1 million or more. Approximately 40 per cent of all corporate securities and over half of all securities (exclusive of federal-government issues) offered for sale in 1948 and 1949 were subject to competitive bidding rules.

The principal argument in favor of competitive bidding is that the issuer receives a better price for a given issue than would be received otherwise. It is probably also true that the decisions of management are less influenced by the interests of investment banking firms. On the other hand, the number of bids placed for quite small or quite large issues tends to be very small, and this lack of bids suggests that the competitive feature of the device is not strong in such cases. Some evidence suggests that on other issues where competition is a factor, the bankers' spread is too narrow to permit the careful investigation by the bankers which would provide a safeguard on the quality of securities marketed to the public. In practice the SEC has found it necessary to exempt issues from its own ruling at times when it was fairly clear that an issue could not be marketed successfully under competitive bidding. Industrial corporations have shown no tendency to adopt the device voluntarily for their own use. The mere fact, however, that competitive bidding has been invoked by rules of these two federal agencies suggests that it probably will be continued in use within their jurisdictions.

OTHER REGULATORY AGENCIES. Two other agencies play a part in the control of practices in the sale of securities: the National Association of Securities Dealers (N.A.S.D.) and Better Business Bureaus. The N.A.S.D. is a trade association for persons in the securities business, and it performs a number of functions, including self-regulation of trade practices. The Association has established rules of conduct which are said to be of assistance to the industry in following paths of useful service. Not all securities dealers are in agreement as to the value of N.A.S.D., however: many are strongly critical; others are staunch supporters. The organization and operation of this association will be discussed further in the next chapter.

Better Business Bureaus play a part in restricting the activities of fly-by-night or itinerant sellers who might enter a territory to offer securities for sale by other than the regular channels.

DIRECT PLACEMENTS AND TERM LOANS

Public sale involves the creation of marketable securities—bonds or stocks. The actual sale is usually handled through normal investment banking channels and results in a rather widespread distribution of securities into the hands of many individual and institutional investors. With few exceptions, this marketing operation must comply with registration requirements of the SEC. Through subsequent trading activity (listed securities on an organized securities exchange or unlisted securities in the over-the-counter market) these securities enjoy marketability; that is, under normal market conditions one investor may sell his securities to another investor with a minimum of difficulty and at a price in line with prevailing quotations on the particular security. This pattern of public sale has been the traditional method of raising long-term funds for medium- and large-sized corporations. It is not, however, the only method of financing.

The Nature of Private Sales

An important alternative method of obtaining long-term funds is through private sale or direct placement of securities issues. As these terms imply, this method involves negotiations between a corporation and one or a small number of investors. In most cases, assistance is given the corporation, and sometimes the investor, by an agent middleman. The corporation creates a security issue which, because of the small number of purchasers, may have only limited marketability. The securities are sold directly to investors who are willing to hold investments that are not readily marketable but who usually receive a somewhat higher rate of return than they would receive on a publicly marketed issue. At the same time, because expenses of issue are reduced, the issuer may incur less cost for the amount of funds obtained than he would incur on a marketable issue.

Direct or private placement eliminates many investment banking functions: although an investment banking house may act as the agent middleman, it does not assume any underwriting risk; there is no necessity for retail distribution; there is seldom trading in the issue after initial sale. Because these features of a public sale are eliminated, the private sale is exempt from much of the federal and state security regulation which was designed to protect the mass of investors.

In a private sale the investor must be willing to forego ready marketability and must, at the same time, be capable of appraising the soundness of the corporation and its financing program. Occasionally individuals of considerable wealth may meet these requirements, but institutional investors are more likely to provide funds in private sales. Banks, insurance companies, investment companies, and various funds controlled by universities, foundations, and others are typical sources. Whenever such institutions have excess idle funds, they actively seek investment outlets. If the volume of publicly sold securities is slight or the rate of return is low, the direct purchase of investments may be attractive. On the other hand, these investors maintain certain standards for investment which limit the number of corporations able to qualify and arrange for direct placement. Generally speaking, investment is made only in established businesses which have demonstrated reasonable profits in past years and which are of sufficient size to provide adequate financial strength. These limitations rule out new ventures, very small enterprises, and historically unprofitable concerns. To those corporations which can meet these general limitations, private sale may prove cheaper and easier and may better meet the needs of a particular financing problem.

Private sales do not represent a new financing method. Short-term credit needs have traditionally been met largely by commercial bank loans, especially after the virtual disappearance of an active commercial paper market in the 1930's. These short-term loans represent funds advanced as a result of direct negotiation between borrower and lender. Long-term funds for some businesses have always been obtained by private arrangement. The limited volume of public financing in the 1930's, coupled with drastic declines in the rate of return on new issues, however, gave impetus to more general use of the direct-placement method. The extraordinary increase in the amounts of investment by life insurance companies has been a significant factor. An idea of the extent to which this method has been used in recent years is suggested in Table 16.

Advantages and Disadvantages

By entering into a direct placement, institutional investors can obtain large amounts of one issue without difficulty. The resources of many institutional investors are so great that even the purchase of an entire issue would not violate principles of investment diversification, and by large-scale purchases the cost of investing funds is reduced.

The major disadvantage to the investor is the lack of ready marketability. In some institutions, such as commercial banks, this is a serious drawback, and accordingly bank participations in private sales are limited in amount and to short maturities. Life insurance companies and some casualty companies do not have the liquidity problem of banks and so can afford to invest more heavily in less

TABLE 16

ESTIMATED PROCEEDS OF TOTAL CORPORATE BONDS OFFERED
AND AMOUNTS OFFERED PRIVATELY, 1937–49

	Total (000,000 Omitted)	Amount Privately Offered (000,000 Omitted)	Percentage Privately Offered
1937.........	$1,618	$ 335	20.7
1938.........	2,044	692	33.9
1939.........	1,979	790	40.0
1940.........	2,386	774	32.4
1941.........	2,390	824	34.5
1942.........	917	422	46.0
1943.........	990	372	37.6
1944.........	2,669	792	29.3
1945.........	4,855	1,022	21.1
1946.........	4,882	1,918	39.3
1947.........	5,036	2,256	44.5
1948.........	6,008	3,272	54.4
1949.........	4,890	2,526	51.7

Source: Securities and Exchange Commission, *Statistical Bulletin*, May, 1950, and earlier issues.

liquid assets and to accept long maturities. To some extent the lack of marketability is partially offset by the greater influence a single investor can wield in case the corporation gets into financial difficulty. However, since all investors require some degree of marketability, there is a limit to the volume of direct placements which any one investor will accept.

Corporate officials have utilized direct placement of securities either because of necessity or desirability. Major factors affecting the use of a private sale will be outlined below.

LIMITATIONS TO PUBLIC SALE. During certain periods of the business cycle it is not feasible to raise funds by the sale of securities to the general investing public because of the lack of investor interest in purchasing new securities. When the outlook for corporate earnings appears poor, new flotations of securities are not salable to the public except perhaps at substantial sacrifice to the corporation. That is, the price at which corporate securities may be sold is so low, relative to the returns to be expected over the life of the issue, that prudent financial management cannot justify the cost of the funds. This general investor disinterest may or may not be rational, but it creates a market "climate" in which it is very difficult to distribute corporate securities through public sale.

The size of the corporation, the nature of its business, and the amount of the issue are limiting factors. First, a large, well-known corporation can probably market its securities by public sale more easily than a small, less-well-known business. Secondly, certain industries provide a romantic appeal at particular times. For example, the automobile and radio industries had tremendous popular appeal in the 1920's, while the liquor and chemical industries caught the public fancy in the 1930's. On the other hand, the poor records of both the coal-mining and the railroad industries during the depression years caused their securities to be viewed with disfavor. This "sales appeal" of various groups can prove to be a major factor in the ability of a corporation to market securities publicly. In the third place, the cost to the corporation of selling new securities issues is higher for small than for large issues. Corporate officials are likely to investigate alternative methods of financing rather than pay the costs of distributing a small security issue to the public.

These factors limiting public sale also influence investment decisions of institutional buyers. However, such buyers have research staffs capable of appraising the strong qualities and particular problems of any one company. Thus, many of the psychological market factors which affect public sales need not interfere with institutional purchases where satisfactory financial strength is evident and the rate of return is satisfactory. A corporation which finds it difficult and expensive to raise funds through public sale may convince a small group of institutional investors of the soundness of its credit and obtain funds with less difficulty and at a lower cost.

One advantage of a public sale over a private sale is the opportunity of placing the corporation's name before the investing public. It is usually more difficult to sell the security issue of a concern unknown to investors than of a concern which already has outstanding publicly traded issues. Therefore, many corporations would prefer to establish themselves by a public sale despite any immediate advantages of private sale.

COST CONSIDERATIONS. Some items of expense involved in the public sale of securities are eliminated or reduced by private sale.

In the former case, investment bankers assume and charge for the risk of underwriting and the costs of distribution. Compensation for these services is not applicable to private sale, although there may be a charge for services of an agent middleman. Such a fee, however, seldom exceeds 1 per cent, and in numerous cases there is no fee.

If the corporation is selling a preferred-stock issue, the banker's spread is generally greater than on a debt issue because the risk of underwriting an equity issue is greater and more work is involved in selling. The agent-middleman's fee for a privately placed preferred is not likely to differ much from that charged for a debt placement. Accordingly, distribution costs on a privately sold preferred offer even greater savings than on a privately sold debt issue.

The exemption of private sales from SEC registration is perhaps the most important source of savings. The major items of expense involved in registering an issue with the SEC are: printing and engraving costs for the prospectus and securities; and legal, accounting, and engineering fees for the expert opinions set forth in the registration statement. The actual registration fee and the costs of meeting the blue-sky laws of states are rather nominal in comparison with the total expense. The total, however, can easily amount to $30,000, and in some instances exceed $100,000. Because there is little relationship between the size of the issue and these charges, there is a heavy unit cost in selling a small issue of securities. In many cases the saving on these expenses is sufficient to reduce the over-all cost of obtaining long-term funds by one half or more.

Certain other expenses can also be eliminated. At present the federal transfer tax on securities sales is not applicable to private sales. The elimination of a corporate trustee can also effect savings. Even if a trustee is desired, private sales do not require qualifying the issue under the Trust Indenture Act, one of the federal regulatory statutes administered by the SEC. Because a qualified issue requires much additional work by the trustee, the fees for an unqualified issue are substantially lower.

Lack of trading with respect to privately placed securities is a disadvantage. Many corporations have retired substantial amounts of preferred stock in periods of depressed markets when their securities were selling at a discount. By utilizing funds to buy its own securities in the market at a price below par, the corporation increases its stockholder surplus. That is, if a $100 par preferred stock may be purchased at $75, the corporation extinguishes a $100 claim senior to the common; and the aggregate book value of the common stock is increased $25 for each share so bought. The two issues cited below were brought out under excellent marketing conditions in 1946. Owing to subsequent changes in market prices, these companies have been placed in a position to benefit from repurchases of their securities. Great Northern Railway, First Mortgage Bonds, Series "P," 2¾ per cent, due 1982, were offered at 101.14 on March 20, 1946. In July, 1950, the price was approximately 91, and it had been as low as 83 in 1948. General Shoe Corporation, $3.50 Cumulative Preferred Stock, no par, was offered at 102.25 on June 12, 1946. The market price in early 1950 was about 80. The likelihood of this opportunity arising depends on current market rates for debt and preferred stock. Corporate securities originally sold on a low-interest or dividend rate are more likely to experience subsequent depreciation in market value.

EASE OF ISSUANCE.   The corporation will find it much easier to fit a given financing program to its needs when negotiating directly with one lender or a small group of investors. The particular terms of the issue can be adjusted to meet unusual corporate problems. More important, the corporation will find legal agreement more flexible. A small group of institutional investors in a privately placed deal is more likely to permit a change in the agreement than is the large group of investors in a publicly sold issue. It may even be true that the investor institutions will have a sufficient interest in the company to be available for counsel.

A second way in which private sale simplifies financing is elimination of SEC registration. The twenty-day waiting period necessary for the registration to become effective subjects the underwriting to the risk of sudden market changes. In private sales there need be only a short lapse of time between agreement on terms and delivery of the securities. This, in addition to the fact that such sales are consummated without primary regard being given to current market conditions, effectively insulates direct placement arrangements against sudden market changes.

A third factor which eliminates steps in private sales is the ability to dispense with a corporate trustee. This effects a reduction, not only in expense, but also in the amount of time the corporation must devote at the initial sale and during the life of the issue to filing reports and other data.

Types of Private Sales

Private-sale transactions can be classified into debt and equity financing. Debt obligations are attractive to institutional purchasers because they are a contractual promise to pay interest and principal.

The management of the borrowing corporation does not have the power to withhold these payments at its discretion without creating a default under the terms of the debt agreement. Because such a default could lead to bankruptcy proceedings, it is not likely to occur except in times of severe business depression or otherwise troublesome circumstances. Accordingly, the risk of not receiving payment on debt obligations is generally less than in the case of equity securities. Then, too, certain classes of institutional investors are limited in their ability to purchase equities, and so there are more funds available for the purchase of debt. Commercial banks, for instance, are prohibited from buying equities, and life insurance companies are greatly restricted.

Preferred stocks represent ownership and lack the advantage of a credit obligation. Payment of dividends and principal are made at the corporation's discretion. However, these stocks do carry a fixed dividend rate, and there are usually provisions for retiring the principal amount over a given number of years. Despite the contingent nature of dividends and provisions for retirement, there are incentives for the management of a corporation to keep these payments current. The typical preferred-stock agreement prohibits common-stock dividends and gives the preferred stock voting rights if preferred dividends are not paid. These protective features, in addition to the higher rate of return available, have made the private purchase of preferreds attractive to investors who are empowered to purchase equities.

Common stocks have no provision for a fixed dividend rate or for retirement. Moreover, one of the attractive features of common-stock investment is the possibility of appreciation in market value. But, an issue of common stock held privately does not have a public market in which investors may realize profit from appreciation by selling their holdings. Lack of opportunity to gain by appreciation, coupled with uncertain income and no provision for retirement, generally eliminates common stock from consideration for private sale. Occasionally large blocks of a publicly traded issue are offered directly to certain types of investors; but for practical purposes, private sales are confined to debt and senior stock issues.

TERM LOANS.   An important form of direct financing is the "term" loan, which usually is a loan repayable in installments over a period of one to twenty years. Insurance companies and commercial banks were willing to extend ten-year loans to qualified borrowers, but more recently most banks are limiting such loans to about five years.

A single insurance company or bank may purchase the entire loan, but frequently a group of institutions co-operate in the purchase. Late in 1947 a group of twenty-seven banks set up a $50-million six-year loan for Joseph E. Seagram & Sons, Inc. Under terms of this borrowing $5 million was payable each year from 1948 through 1951, and the balance, $30 million, was due in 1952. The Western Auto Supply Company borrowed $15 million from the Metropolitan Life Insurance Company early in 1948 with a final loan maturity of 1968. The W. A. Sheaffer Pen Company obtained $4 million in late 1947 from four banks and five insurance companies. The participating banks provided a total of $1,500,000, all payable over the first five years, while the insurance companies advanced $2,500,000 payable between the sixth and fifteenth year. The procedure followed in setting up this type of credit has already been outlined in Chapter 3 and is typical of a majority of private sales.

EQUIPMENT FINANCING. Railroad rolling stock has traditionally been provided through the public sale of special equipment securities. In recent years there has been increasing interest in distributions of these securities to one or to a small group of investors. For example, the Chicago, Burlington & Quincy Railroad Company sold privately an issue of $2,770,000 in late 1947 to the Harris Trust and Savings Bank of Chicago. The proceeds covered 80 per cent of the cost of certain locomotives and passenger cars to the railroad. Three banks bid for the issue. Under this type of plan the lender obtains title to the equipment from the equipment manufacturer and holds it until the security issue has been retired. The railroad itself pays the other 20 per cent of the purchase price. This method has been generally used because of the simplicity of arrangements and certain cost savings. In a few instances, similar methods of equipment financing have been extended to busses, airplanes, and similar items.

The practice of outright purchase of equipment by insurance companies for lease to the railroads is a recent development of a variation in equipment financing. In April, 1950, the Equitable Life Assurance Society announced plans to lease 1,500 cars to the Atlantic Coast Line Railroad on a fifteen-year contract, with the insurance company to pay the manufacturer 80 per cent of the cost of the cars immediately and the remaining 20 per cent over the next five years. From the railroad's point of view, this plan has the advantage of doing away with the necessity for making a down-payment on equipment acquired for use.

Industrial machinery is most likely to be financed through trade creditors or finance companies, but occasionally it is done through investment channels by private placement. There is no single pattern for these sales except that they are dependent on the financial credit of the borrower and usually entail a lien on the equipment.

SALES-LEASES. A relatively new form of private financing is best described by the term "sales-lease" or "sale and lease back." In brief, this financing plan calls for the sale of land and plant by a corporation to an insurance company or other institutional investor. Simultaneously, the corporation enters into a long-term lease whereby it rents these fixed assets from the institution. The monthly or annual rentals are sufficient to amortize the principal investment of the insurance company and return a given rate of interest for, say, a twenty-year period. The corporation is usually given an option to renew the lease at the end of the period at a small rental charge or an option to repurchase the properties. For example, an annual rental of about 7½ per cent of the principal amount, paid monthly, is sufficient to pay interest at the rate of 4½ per cent on the outstanding balance and will completely repay the principal in annual installments in twenty years. Thereafter the annual rental might amount to only 1 or 2 per cent. The corporation continues to pay property taxes and maintenance expenses. An early instance of this form of financing is found in the transaction between the Allied Stores Corporation and Union College. In 1945 the Corporation sold substantially all of its land and buildings for $16,150,000 to the College. Allied then leased these assets for thirty years under a schedule of rentals which would recapture for Union College the entire cost of the purchase, as well as interest. Allied at its option could lease the property for a second thirty-year period at 2 per cent of the land value as then appraised, with a minimum rental of $240,000 annually. The average annual rentals payable over the full sixty-year period would approximate 3.43 per cent of the selling price. The payment of scheduled rentals for the first thirty years is, in effect, guaranteed to Union College by Allied. By this method Allied Stores Corporation released funds which had been invested in real estate for investment in current assets during a period of rapid expansion of sales.

In practice the sales-lease is most attractive where the land value is a relatively high percentage of the total value of fixed assets. As owner of the property, a corporation receives no depreciation allowance on land in computing income taxes. But, by leasing the fixed assets, it can charge total rental expense (which includes an amount for repayment of the investment in land as well as buildings) against income for tax computation. High land value is normally found in commercial areas so that sales-leases have frequently been used by chain stores. This type of fixed asset provides the basis for real tax savings. Industrial plants do not usually offer similar advantages, but many manufacturing concerns can through sales-lease earn a higher rate of return by releasing funds tied up in fixed assets and using them in expansion of inventories. By merely mortgaging the property, a corporation could recapture some of the funds invested in fixed assets. However, a mortgage loan usually is limited to some percentage of the property value, so that less money may be realized through mortgaging than through sales-lease.

The sales-lease method has also been applied to equipment, such as trucks, in a way similar to the equipment-financing plans outlined previously.

SPECIAL AGENCIES

From time to time agencies have been created or designated either to assist in the marketing of long-term securities of business or to supply funds directly on a long-term basis. These agencies have generally been established under emergency conditions on either an industry-wide or nation-wide scale. For example, during the early 1930's, as the depression deepened and bank failures increased in number, commercial banks formed an organization to aid those of their industry facing trouble. Again, during the recent war, the Federal Reserve banks were called on to provide funds for war-plant operation. Few of these special cases have been of sufficient importance to warrant separate discussion, but two agencies which do deserve specific mention are: the Reconstruction Finance Corporation, a federal agency; and the group of promotion or financing companies which have developed in recent decades.

The Reconstruction Finance Corporation

Federal funds were advanced to business during World War I by an agency called the War Finance Corporation. After the war the lending powers of this corporation were used to bolster banks in distress. The Corporation was liquidated in 1929. On January 22, 1932, Congress authorized formation of a corporation as an agency of the federal government and modeled on the lines of the War Finance Corporation to provide financial aid to banks, railroads, and other businesses suffering from the effects of the drastic decline in business then under way. The new agency was hopefully named the Reconstruction Finance Corporation (RFC). The life of this corporation was originally limited to five years. The renewal of the charter has been seriously challenged from time to time, particularly in 1948 and again in 1951. In its lifetime the RFC has assumed and dropped many functions, but it remains an important agency for directing the flow of federal funds to financial and nonfinancial businesses unable to borrow from private sources on reasonable terms. As a creditor, the RFC exercises a degree of supervision over the operations of its debtors much as any creditor might be expected to do.

At the outset the RFC received capital in the amount of $500 million from the government and was authorized to borrow up to $1.5 billion. Subsequently the borrowing authority was increased. In 1947 the limit on borrowing was placed at $14.1 billions for general purposes and $3.0 billions for certain specific purposes, and restricted amounts were named for certain other specific purposes designated by Congress. The government's investment in the Corporation was reduced to $325 million in 1947 and to $100 million in 1948. The huge capacity of this agency to acquire and lend money has had great influence, absolutely and psychologically, on business in this country, and this influence has spread beyond our borders.

The best description of the powers of the RFC is contained in the enabling legislation:

To aid in financing agriculture, commerce, and industry, to help in maintaining the economic stability of the country and to assist in promoting maximum employment and production, . . . the Corporation within the limitations hereinafter provided, is authorized . . . :

1. To buy obligations of or lend to any business
2. To lend to any financial institution
3. To buy securities of or lend to any government or governmental agency to facilitate a project
4. To lend not more than $25 million in event of flood or catastrophe.

No financial assistance shall be extended . . . unless the financial assistance applied for is not otherwise available on reasonable terms. All securities and obligations purchased and all loans made . . . shall be of such sound value and so secured as reasonably to assure retirement or repayment and such loans may be made directly or in cooperation with banks or other lending institutions through agreements to participate or by purchase of participations, or otherwise.[2]

---

[2] Public Law 132, 80th Cong., 1st Sess., approved June 30, 1947. See especially, secs. 4-a, b, c.

Not more than $2 billion in loans are to be outstanding at any one time. The amount disbursed and outstanding, and the nature and variety of loans actually made is suggested by the data of Table 17. The RFC has furnished capital, served as a rediscount agency, and provided a market for debt instruments of many other federal agencies, such as the federal farm and home credit agencies. It has undertaken special projects—e.g., the British War Loan, Smaller Plant Corporation, and subsidy payments associated with price control and rationing during the war. A recent loan which was the subject of much public comment was for financing the Lustron Corporation, an unsuccessful venture in the mass production of prefabricated houses.

Advances to railroads, to other industries, and to financial institutions have been large, although at present they are relatively small. The RFC has supported a number of state and municipal developmental projects—for example, the Queens Midtown Tunnel at New York City. It has been, in fact, the largest single agency for credit extension in the nation.

The losses incurred to March 31, 1947, amounted to $23 million, or 0.2 per cent of the total of funds advanced. Although its operations were intended to fall outside the sphere of private business and introduce no competition between government and private enterprise in the credit markets, its loans obviously have altered the demand for and supply of funds in these markets. The interpretation of "reasonable terms" has undoubtedly been challenged by, and altered the practices of, private lenders.

Criticism of the operations of the RFC led to hearings before a Senate Committee early in 1951. Testimony indicated that political pressure and favoritism influenced lending operations of the agency. Some critics urged the abolition of the RFC; more moderate critics recommended substitution of a one-man administrator in lieu of a board, on the theory that under a single operating head responsibility is more easily placed and favoritism should be minimized. The latter action was taken.

Promotion or Financing Companies

The development and expansion of new industries which have not achieved records that might induce persons with funds either to lend money or to buy stock presents a financial problem for which no satisfactory solution has yet been found. One approach to the solution has been the creation of a few companies—e.g., the American Re-

TABLE 17

RECONSTRUCTION FINANCE CORPORATION NORMAL LENDING AND INVESTMENT FUNCTIONS, MARCH 31, 1947

(In Thousands of Dollars)

	Disbursed since January 22, 1932	Outstanding Balance
Banks and bank receivers	2,198,202	11,742
Building and loan associations and receivers	140,158	.....
Credit unions	600	.....
Insurance companies	90,693	255
Federal land banks	387,236	.....
Federal intermediate credit banks	9,250	.....
Joint-stock land banks	26,195	.....
Livestock credit corporations	12,972	.....
Mortgage loan companies	250,833	9,438
For payment of processing taxes	15	.....
Agricultural credit corporations	178,887	.....
State funds for insuring the repayment of deposits for public moneys	13,065	.....
Railroads	853,035	144,107
Business loans:		
Nonwar	551,216	159,109
War	981,547	114,027
British	390,000	205,327
Smaller War Plants Corporation	41,762	19,100
Republic of the Philippines	25,000	25,000
Mining	9,495	4,982
Self-liquidating and public agency	639,913	43,938
Agricultural improvement districts (drainage districts, etc.)	101,400	17,668
Catastrophe	13,560	874
Sale of agricultural surpluses:		
Foreign markets	47,301	.....
Domestic markets	790,661	55
Public school authorities	23,257	.....
Preferred-stock banks (loans and purchases)	1,170,565	170,214
Preferred-stock insurance companies (loans and purchases)	47,150	1,535
Public Works Administrator securities:		
Railroad	199,283	5,990
Other	453,283	58,005
Export-Import Bank (loans and stock)	201,500	.....
Federal home-loan banks (stock)	124,741	122,672
The RFC Mortgage Company (loans and stock)	300,629	46,072
Federal National Mortgage Association	257,496	11,000
Total	10,530,900	1,171,110
Total:		
Secretary of Agriculture		
Rural rehabilitation	621,113	.....
Farm tenancy	197,235	121,849
Rural Electrification Administration	507,200	423,336
Total loans and investments	11,856,448	1,716,295
Allocations to other agencies	2,802,833	.....
Total	14,659,281	1,716,295

Source: "Government Credit, Part I: The Reconstruction Finance Corporation," *Hearings before the Committee on Banking and Currency, U.S. House of Representatives* (80th Cong., 1st Sess.) (Washington, D.C.: U.S. Government Printing Office, 1947), p. 21.

search and Development Corporation of Boston—which are designed to step into this breach in the financing of business. These companies specialize in supplying funds to expanding business. They may in some instances control the company during its growth period. The investment is made, however, with a view to recovering invested funds after the company has reached a position such that it can obtain needed funds from more usual channels.

These financing companies may obtain their funds from the private estates of a few interested persons or by selling their own securities in turn to investors through investment banking channels. Since, for the most part, they acquire ownership interests in the businesses financed, it is difficult to estimate the cost of their services to these businesses.

SPECIAL PROBLEMS OF SMALL BUSINESS

In recent years much has been written about financial problems of small business. Referring again to Table 13 of this chapter, we may re-emphasize the fact that funds are supplied to both new and going concerns principally by their owners and their friends. Two thirds of new funds of corporate going concerns in the 1946–49 period were obtained from owners by the retention of revenues. Three quarters of the funds of new firms were supplied by owners and persons closely affiliated with either the owners themselves or the new firms. The financial problems of small businesses are related to this fact.

Small businessmen find it necessary to solicit funds initially from relatives, employees, local investors, suppliers, banks, and mortgage creditors. Once started, the firm may supply some or all of additional funds as required by retaining revenues from operations. Few small firms have the opportunity to obtain funds by public distribution of securities.

The lack of a public market for securities is the basis for much comment on small business problems. Such a lack is apparent, but its significance is less apparent. The average initial investment in new firms in the postwar period has been as follows: retail trade, $9,500; manufacturing, $12,000; wholesale trade, $22,000. Public distribution of securities to raise part of these funds would probably cost the businessman from 10 to 50 per cent. It is hard to believe that securities could be marketed to a much broader investing public than is already reached by privately negotiated arrangements now made by small businessmen. And, few small business firms have securities to distribute because they are operated either as sole proprietorships or partnerships.

A more reasonable explanation is that many small firms keep inadequate records of operations. Without good accounting for funds the individual businessman is not in a position to convince potential creditor or ownership investors of the usefulness of investment in his business. The efforts being made through educational programs and by bankers or local investors to raise the standards of record keeping and report preparation are a favorable factor. At the same time, the increased awareness of investors of the usefulness of careful appraisal of small business prospects may increase opportunities for local financing.

A third and possibly most important basis for the suggestion that small businesses have "special" problems lies in an inherent characteristic of such business: unstable revenue. Ability to reinvest earnings to maintain and add to assets is reduced by instability. A firm such as Sears, Roebuck and Company can quite conceivably experience difficulty in selling refrigerators at a time when shoes and farm fencing may be selling rapidly. It might be unable to sell refrigerators in Tuskaloosa but sell them easily in Menominee. A household appliances dealer in Tuskaloosa, however, does not have the advantage of both product and geographic diversification. If business is bad in Tuskaloosa, the small businessman in that city is affected; if competitive selling becomes intense, he is under pressure. Many reasons contribute to the end result that the earnings of small business fluctuate widely. Earnings are higher in good and lower in poor times than those of larger and more diversified concerns. The impact of taxation is probably greater because, when earnings are adequate for financing, taxation hits. Even with recent changes permitting losses to be carried over a short period of time, the present tax structure makes financing out of unstable earnings more difficult than financing out of stable earnings. The source of greatest importance to going concerns is therefore made less available to smaller concerns by instability.

The over-all importance of financial problems to small business may be exaggerated, however. It was noted above that two million firms started operations in the 1945–49 period. Representatives of small businessmen have been quoted as opposed to federal legislation designed to increase availability of funds to small businesses. Men who have closed down their businesses recently place financing low on the list of causes of withdrawal and give higher priority to difficulties in obtaining materials and supplies, employee unreliability, and high labor cost. Some of the harsher critics of small business management point to inadequacy of managerial ability rather than to any particular problem of operation. These things do not sustain arguments for extraordinary treatment of small business financing.

But, proposals for special treatment are frequently made. A program recommended to Congress by the President in early 1950 suggested three lines of attack: (1) government insurance for bank loans of $25,000 or less; (2) creation of regional "capital" banks with funds supplied by commercial banks for investment in ownership equities of small business; and (3) direct lending by federal agencies such as the RFC. Various communities in different states have formed local associations for encouragement and assistance to new and small firms. Two of the more frequently mentioned are the Industrial Corporation of Baltimore and the Louisville Industrial Foundation. A regional association, the New England Industrial Development Corporation, represents a slightly broader approach but supplies counseling service rather than direct financial aid. The probabilities for additional proposals and some action toward facilitating small business financing are high: approximately 3½ million of the nearly 4 million businesses of the United States are small.

CHANGING PATTERNS OF LONG-TERM FINANCING

Owners supply most of the funds for business in the United States. Owner equities are supplemented by advances from large accumulations of investible funds. Tapping thousands of small accumulations of savings by public distribution of securities has been a feature only of the growth of large manufacturing, railroad, and public utility corporations of the United States: it has not been a form of financing used by the hundreds of thousands of firms that make up the small business community. These characteristics of financing seem to have changed very little over the life of this nation.

Nonetheless, changes are occurring. The spread of techniques such as competitive bidding for new issues of securities may have far-reaching effects on public distribution. And the study of small business problems may result in changes in the relative ease of financing new and small going concerns. Three changes which appear to be quite significant for the future of financing of larger businesses are: (1) the extent to which owner equity is being increased by retention of revenues from operations in going businesses; (2) the emphasis on debt financing growing out of the shift of management of the nation's large accumulations of investible funds from individual to institutional hands; and (3) the changing character of public markets for securities resulting from the increased use of private placement in distribution of new securities issues.

Retention of earnings from operations of business where management and ownership are separated functions takes investment decision away from the saver and places it in other hands. The myriad decisions of many individuals are replaced by a few decisions of management. From the point of view of the business firm which benefits by such reinvestment, this transfer of decision to persons most intimately acquainted with operating problems may be wise. From the point of view of a free-enterprise society, the transfer is possibly unwise because it results in reduced freedom of choice for investors.

Institutional management of large accumulations of funds has importance because some institutions, such as insurance companies, are restricted by law or tradition largely to investments in credit instruments. The industrial corporations of the United States show increasing amounts of debt as a source of funds. These two points are probably related: the corporation seeking to supplement funds obtained from present owners can obtain them more readily by offering new instruments adapted to the needs of institutional investors; and the low rates of interest on debt incurred in recent decades have almost certainly been an inducement to borrow. But, a question to be answered in the future is whether individuals and institutional investors, such as investment companies, who can and will invest in ownership equities will increase their investments relative to the creditor class.

Increased use of direct placement in the distribution of new securities issues raises problems too. Many new issues are placed with one or a few larger institutions. Private investors and even smaller institutional investors may find that their opportunities to select investment securities fitted to their investment programs are limited simply because desirable issues are not publicly marketed.

—Loring C. Farwell

QUESTIONS AND PROBLEMS

1. What is "investment banking"? Why are the services of investment banking firms worth their cost to the issuer of new securities? To the buyer of new securities?

2. What is underwriting? How does it differ from selling new securities?
3. What is a "syndicate"? How long would you expect a purchase syndicate to be in existence?
4. Why is investment banking risky? Does the risk carried by the banking firm differ under a "best-effort" contract from that carried under a "firm" contract?
5. What is the principal feature of federal regulation of the public sale of new securities issues?
6. Outline the major advantages and disadvantages of private sale.
7. It appears that the buyer of an issue at a private sale may obtain a higher yield and yet the cost to the issuer may be lower than at a public sale. How can this be true?
8. Describe the major types of private sale.
9. What does the Reconstruction Finance Corporation do?
10. Why do there appear to be "problems" in the financing of small businesses?

BIBLIOGRAPHY

The operations of institutions discussed in this chapter are described more fully in most textbooks on corporation finance and investments. A recent book designed to meet the needs of men entering the investment banking profession is the comprehensive volume by the Investment Bankers Association, *Fundamentals of Investment Banking* (New York: Prentice-Hall, Inc., 1949).

On particular subjects, such as private placement, competitive bidding, and problems of small business financing, articles indexed in the *Reader's Guide to Periodical Literature,* the *Industrial Arts Index,* or the *Public Affairs Information Service* are most helpful. Items of particular interest are: the study made for the Committee for Economic Development by A. D. H. Kaplan of Brookings Institute, *Small Business: Its Place and Problems* (New York: McGraw-Hill Book Co., Inc., 1948); an article by Sidney M. Robbins, "Competitive Bidding in Sale of Securities," *Harvard Business Review,* Vol. XXVII, No. 5 (September, 1949), pp. 646–64; and an article by E. Raymond Carey, "Corporate Financing by Direct Placement," *Harvard Business Review,* Vol. XXVIII, No. 6 (November, 1950), pp. 67–76. Each of these contains references which are of assistance to the reader who desires more information on these subjects.

The best available statistics concerning security distribution are found in the *Statistical Bulletin,* published monthly by the Securities and Exchange Commission, and the *Commercial and Financial Chronicle.* Statistics on other long-term financing are found in articles such as those referred to in the footnote to Table 13 (p. 239) of this chapter. A study which brings together much valuable information is that prepared for the Douglas Subcommittee on Investment (Joint Committee on the Economic Report). It is entitled, "Factors Affecting Volume and Stability of Private Investment: Materials on the Investment Problem," and is published as a *Joint Committee Print* (U.S. Senate, 81st Cong., 1st Sess.).

The bibliography of the next chapter should also be consulted.

Chapter • 9

SECURITIES EXCHANGES, BROKERS, AND DEALERS

IN THE preceding chapter we discussed the origination and marketing of new securities and saw how the savings of the country are funneled into productive use through the services of the investment banker and the securities dealer, and in more recent years to an increasing extent through private or direct placement. If the public is to invest its savings in stocks and bonds, it is important that investors have the means provided for recalling such funds at will without undue loss of principal. In other words, in addition to the origination and the initial distribution of securities to investors there must also be markets in which it is possible for investors to dispose of security holdings and obtain cash. Without such fluidity, savers would be loathe to make their accumulations available for investment. The fluidity is attained through the operations of the nation's securities brokers and dealers and the markets in which they operate.

Brokers and Dealers

In popular usage, anyone in the securities business is considered a "securities dealer." In a broad, loose, sense this is so. But the various kinds of dealers stretch from the large investment banking houses to the one- and two-man offices and the occasional fellow who may keep his office files in the breast pocket of his coat. In the United States nearly 4,000 broker-dealers with 60,000 employees are registered with the Securities and Exchange Commission. An uncounted additional number, who do only a local business, are not registered. To some, the securities business is only a part-time adjunct to selling insurance or real estate; to most, it is their principal, and usually only, work.

Broker-dealers operate in several markets and in different capacities: (1) they may facilitate the distribution of securities either as underwriters or as members of selling groups, as noted in the preceding chapter; (2) they may act as agents for a customer and buy and sell securities on an organized exchange; and (3) they may conduct their securities business in that nebular, indefinite area called the "over-the-counter market."

Broker. A broker is, first of all, an agent for his customer. As such he does what his customer instructs him to do, for which he makes a charge, called a "commission." As an agent he is obligated to do his best for each customer—i.e., to buy at the lowest possible price or to sell at the highest possible price. Failure to do this is a breach of his position of trust as agent. When a broker confirms the fact that he has completed transactions for a customer, he sends him a written statement. A confirmation of a purchase, for example, carries a notation as follows: "As broker, we have this date bought for your account [a given number of shares of a given stock at a given price]." This notation reflects the relationship of the broker to his customer. The confirmation slip will also carry information with respect to brokerage or commission charges and transfer taxes. A confirmation slip adapted for machine bookkeeping is shown in Exhibit 39. The significance of many of the data is clearly indicated by the titles to the columns of the statement. The relation between the securities house and its customer is revealed, however, only by the figure in the column headed "Symbol." A figure 1, 2, 5, 8, or 9 in this column indicates that the security house acted as broker for the customer in the transaction confirmed. Other symbols are defined and certain agreements between the securities house and its customer are stated on the reverse side of the confirmation slip, which is also shown in the exhibit. Nearly all transactions executed for customers on most organized exchanges are on a commission-agent basis.

Securities Dealer. A securities dealer in the technical sense is one who buys and sells on his own account. He meets his customers presumably at arm's length as a principal. He does not receive a commission; his income is the difference in the price paid and the price received for securities passing through his hands. Although he may make some profit (and, of course, experience loss) on the inventories which he may hold, his profit margin frequently is only the difference between bid and ask quotations. For example: a dealer may stand ready to buy a security at 23⅞ and sell it at 24¼. On such

Exhibit 39

Broker's Confirmation of Purchase for Customer
(Machine Bookkeeping Form)

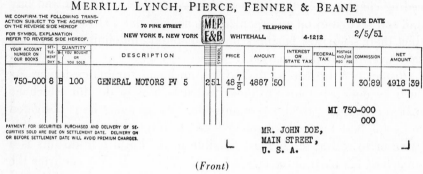

(Front)

(Reverse)

⅜ spread he would expect to cover his expenses and make a profit. It should not be assumed, however, that the dealer realizes a profit equal to the full amount of the spread. With a spread of ⅜ on an actively traded stock selling at about 25, the dealer is more likely to make a profit of ⅛ to ¼ point rather than ⅜ of a point. In maintaining a market for the issue, his cost will probably average higher than the 23⅞ bid and his selling price will probably average lower than his 24¼ offer.

It is generally expected in the securities business that the dealer will make a profit equivalent to about half the spread on an actively traded issue and a profit equivalent to less than half the spread on an inactively traded issue.

In contrast to a broker, the dealer confirms a transaction to a customer as follows: "As principal or as dealer, we have this date sold to you [such and such shares]."

An example of a confirmation of the purchase of stock by a customer in which the securities house itself was the seller is shown in

Exhibit 40

DEALER'S CONFIRMATION OF SALE TO CUSTOMER
(Manual Bookkeeping Form)

OFFICES IN CHICAGO ST PAUL MADISON WAUSAU	THE MILWAUKEE COMPANY EDGAR, RICKER & CO. INVESTMENT SECURITIES 207 E. MICHIGAN ST. MILWAUKEE 2	INVOICE #30 4432 Dec. 21, 1950

Mr. John C. Canter

2148 N. Prospect Avenue

Milwaukee 2, Wisconsin

AS YOUR AGENT WE HAVE { BOUGHT FOR YOU ☐ / SOLD FOR YOU ☐

AS AGENT FOR ANOTHER WE HAVE { SOLD TO YOU ☐ / BOUGHT FROM YOU ☐

AS PRINICIPAL WE CONFIRM SALE TO YOU OF ☒

AS PRINICIPAL WE CONFIRM PURCHASE FROM YOU OF ☐

TRANSACTIONS EXECUTED FOR YOUR ACCOUNT BY US AS AGENTS, ARE SUBJECT TO THE RULES OF THE EXCHANGE ON WHICH SUCH ORDERS ARE EXECUTED. NAME OF THIRD PARTY, DATE, AND HOUR OF EXECUTION WILL BE FURNISHED UPON REQUEST.

SHARES	SECURITY	RATE	MATURITY	PRICE
100 PAR VALUE	R. H. MACY & COMPANY, INC.	Common		32

AMOUNT	BROKERS COMMISSION	TAX	INSURANCE & POSTAGE	SUB TOTAL	ACCRUED INTEREST OR DIVIDEND	TOTAL
$3,200.00						$3,200.00

PAYMENT IS DUE ON   Dec. 27

ADDITIONAL INTEREST OF

WILL BE ADDED FOR EACH DAYS DELAY

Chk. by: *b·v*

Fig. by: VM

DELIVERY INSTRUCTIONS

B-1

Our confirmation of this transaction is subject to the conditions set forth in this statement.
Payment is due on the date shown above. Should payment in full not be received by us on or before the payment date, we reserve the right, at our option, without further notice, to sell out the above described securities and to hold you liable for any loss which may thereby be incurred, or to cancel this transaction. Any descriptive words contained in the title of the securities described above are used for purposes of identification only and are not to be taken as representations of fact.

Exhibit 40. The relationship is indicated on this form, which is used in a manual bookkeeping system, by the "X" in the appropriate square at the upper, right side of the slip. Both the type of confirmation slip shown in Exhibit 39 and that shown in Exhibit 40 may be used to confirm a transaction in which the securities house acted as dealer or one in which the securities house acted as broker.

Under rules of the Securities and Exchange Commission every confirmation must set forth the capacity in which a securities house has acted with respect to a particular transaction. Securities dealers, so far as the public is concerned, operate only in the over-the-counter market. Of course, stock-exchange specialists and odd-lot dealers who are described below are distinctive varieties of securities dealers, but the public has no direct dealings with them as such.

The combined activities of brokers and dealers constitute the securities market. It is the purpose of this chapter to discuss the two principal subdivisions of this broad market through which the transfers of outstanding securities are effected, namely, the organized securities exchanges and the over-the-counter market.

ORGANIZED SECURITIES EXCHANGES

At the present time there are twenty organized exchanges in the United States and Hawaii. Their major service is that of facilitating the sale of preferred and common stocks from one holder to another. Bond trading, which also takes place on some exchanges, is of much less importance. These securities exchanges are referred to as the "organized market" because of their formal organization characteristics.

Security trading in the United States had its inception in Philadelphia, which was the leading city in the colonies. The New York area, however, grew in commercial importance, and securities trading became established there soon after the adoption of the Constitution. Trading was carried on informally among interested parties who would assemble at a public place, such as a coffeehouse. In 1792 the first formal steps toward organizing a brokers association were taken when twenty-four brokers who "met under the shade of a buttonwood tree in Wall Street," where they had been rendering their services for a commission, agreed that "we will not buy or sell from this day for any person whatsoever, any kind of public stock at a less rate than ¼ per cent commission on the specie value and that we will give preference for each other in our negotiations."[1] As would be expected from the character of business at the time, trading took place mainly in shares of shipping companies, banks, and insurance companies and government obligations. At this time the brokers had no established place of business, and much of the trading was carried on out of doors. It was not until after the War of 1812 that a more formal organization was set up in a place of business of its own.

The New York Stock Exchange

With the exception of a few months at the beginning of World War I the New York Stock Exchange, the major organized exchange in the United States, has been in continuous operation providing trading facilities to the financial community, not only in this country but in the world at large. In 1929 the membership was increased from

---

[1] Birl E. Schultz, *The Securities Market and How It Works* (5th ed.; New York: Harper & Bros., 1946), pp. 2–3.

1,100 to the present 1,375. During the 1920's the volume of shares sold ran between two and six million per day, and even reached a one-day high of 16,000,000 shares in October, 1929; in more recent years, one to three million."

ORGANIZATION. The "Big Board," as the New York Stock Exchange is called, is unique with respect to its legal form. It is neither a partnership nor a corporation, but a voluntary unincorporated membership association. It has long been felt by the members that this was the most satisfactory system for permitting the entrance and withdrawal of members and for maintaining the freedom which was considered necessary for proper discipline among them. As a membership association, it was substantially free of governmental regulation until the passage of the federal Securities Exchange Act of 1934, under which the Securities and Exchange Commission is empowered to regulate securities market practices.

After a severe stock-market break in 1937, the governing rules as set forth in the constitution and bylaws of the New York Stock Exchange were revised to streamline organization and trading procedures. The Stock Exchange is no longer looked upon as a private club existing for the benefit of the members but as a public institution with commensurate duties and responsibilities. Its objectives, as set forth in Article I of the revised Constitution, are: ". . . to furnish exchange rooms for the convenient transaction of their business by its members; to furnish other facilities for its members and allied members; to maintain high standards of commercial honor and integrity among its members and allied members; and to promote and inculcate just and equitable principles of trade and business."

CONTROL. The Exchange is managed by a Board of Governors consisting of thirty-three men. Their terms are staggered, and they represent different interests: active brokers and traders, partners of members (officially called "allied members," some of whom come from outside New York City), and prominent men selected to represent the general public. There is an elected, nonsalaried chairman who presides over the board. The president, the chief salaried administrative officer of the Exchange, is selected by the Board and is not otherwise engaged in the securities business.

The functions of the Board of Governors are to draw up, adjudicate, and enforce rules governing the conduct of day-to-day trading business. These rules are designed to maintain fair and orderly markets and adherence to just and equitable principles of trade. Failure to observe them may involve a member in a disciplinary proceeding before the board. Severe sanctions may be invoked, and a member may be subjected to suspension or expulsion.

MEMBERSHIP. Trading on the floor of the Exchange is limited to members of the Association and is not open to the general public. The public is invited to view trading activities from the visitors' gallery. The privilege of membership, the right to participate in trading is termed a "seat," a name carried over from earlier days when the members sat at tables during trading sessions. These seats are valuable business assets commanding a substantial price which tends to vary with the volume of trading and the profits which may be derived therefrom. The price paid for a seat reached a high of $625,000 in 1929, declined to a low of $17,000 in 1942, and is currently (1951) about $70,000.

Membership is limited to individuals over twenty-one years of age, with adequate financial resources, who carry on trading for their own account or for firms (and customers of firms) of which they are a partner. Financial markets tend to emphasize personal relationships. In 1947, and again in 1949, after a lively debate, the membership rejected a proposal to permit the incorporation of member firms doing a general business with the public. Incorporation would reduce the individual liability of the owners of a member house and thus reduce protection afforded customers.

The members of the Exchange may be classified into several groups according to the function they may perform. An individual member may act as (1) commission broker, (2) contract broker, (3) floor trader, (4) specialist, (5) odd-lot dealer, or (6) in any combination of the foregoing five capacities at different times.

Commission Brokers. Commission brokers are members who, as individuals or as partners of commission brokerage houses, execute orders as agents for customers of their firms. These brokers or the firms they represent maintain offices for the convenience of their customers. At these offices there is usually a room which is called the "customers' or board room," where the customer can watch a stock-quotation board on which stock-price quotations are recorded as they come in on the ticker tape. This tape carries a continuous record, reproduced telegraphically throughout the nation, of the transactions taking place on the Exchange. The tape, itself, is usually reproduced on a large screen (Translux) so that anyone in the room can watch it. The Dow-Jones news ticker (broad tape) may be projected on another screen. The board and the two ticker tapes provide valuable information for those who need it and know how to use it. Here, too, so-called "customers' men" or "account executives" greet the public. In many cases these account executives are relied upon by customers for information about companies and their securities and for suggestions as to purchases and sales. A number of the major houses make a practice of issuing suggestions with respect to certain securities in the form of market letters, memoranda, and financial analyses.

In addition to being a member of one or more stock exchanges, the broker or other partners of his firm may also have a seat on some commodity exchanges for the purpose of broadening the type of service available to his customers. For example, the firm of Merrill Lynch, Pierce, Fenner and Beane, a merger of several financial houses, holds nearly seventy-five seats on various stock and commodity exchanges and maintains branch offices in one hundred cities throughout the United States. This firm is the largest of its kind and has about eighty partners.

The schedule of minimum commissions (effective since November 3, 1947) charged by commission brokers for their services on transactions in stocks priced at 50 cents per share or above is as follows:

Money Value of a Round Lot	Commission
Less than $100.00	6%
$100.00 to $999.99	$1\% + \$ 5.00$
$1,000.00 to $3,999.99	$\frac{1}{2}\% + \$10.00$
$4,000.00 and above	$\frac{1}{10}\% + \$26.00$

The commission schedule can be presented in another way—in terms of the cost per share for stocks selling at various prices. Selected commission charges on this basis are as follows:

Price of Stock per Share	Commission per Share
$ 5.00	$0.10
10.00	0.15
20.00	0.20
30.00	0.25
50.00	0.31
75.00	0.335
100.00	0.36

A "round lot" is the unit of trading. It is generally 100 shares; but in the case of high-priced or inactive stocks, the Exchange may designate 10 shares as the unit of trading. In the case of odd lots (amounts less than a round lot), the minimum commission is 10 per cent less than is indicated in the above schedule. In addition to the broker's commission, the seller in any transaction must pay federal and New York State transfer taxes; and odd-lot purchasers also pay a federal tax.

Contract Brokers. Other trading may be carried on by members who assist the commission-house brokers who are not able to execute their entire volume of business themselves. These men are referred to as "two-dollar" brokers because in earlier years they charged a flat two-dollar commission per transaction to fellow stock-exchange members for handling their business on the floor. The contract broker, of course, does not have the overhead of maintaining customers' rooms and branch offices.

Floor Traders. In addition to regular brokers who live on their commissions, the exchange membership includes those who buy and sell for their own account. These members, called "floor traders," may also serve at times as commission or contract brokers; and commission or contract brokers may trade for their own accounts from time to time.

The activities of floor traders have been under study by the Securities and Exchange Commission for some time. There has been agitation for the elimination of their activities on the theory that they contribute to instability of the market in individual securities. Floor traders not only transact business at a reduced rate of commission but they have the additional advantage over the general public that, in an active market, they may be in a position to sense the direction of price changes on the market and promptly take advantage of the small fluctuations. There was much opposition, however, to those who wished to expel the "insiders" in order to turn the exchange into a completely "public market," and such a change has not been adopted. It is argued that, although the floor trader may make a profit from small changes in security prices, he contributes at the same time to the continuity of pricing as prices change. This continuity of pricing, i.e., the absence of abrupt fluctuations as the demand for and supply of securities shift in response to orders from the general public, is an important attribute of an efficient market.

A few individuals own seats on the Exchange primarily to take advantage of the opportunity to buy or sell securities without paying more than member commission rates. For example, for many years the late John D. Rockefeller owned a seat but never appeared on the floor.

Specialists. Security trading is scattered over a wide area in a very large room called the "floor" of the exchange. It is physically impossible for a broker to be everywhere; yet customers' orders must be executed promptly. Brokers, therefore, frequently engage the services of fellow members who specialize in the buying and selling of securities of a limited number of issues at a given post. These brokers are known as "specialists," and they accept the obligation of remaining at the posts where the auction for the issues in which they are specializing is held. It is the responsibility of a specialist to see that orders are executed whenever either buyers or sellers are available or, in the case of orders to buy or sell at specified prices, when prices reach such designated levels. To aid him he keeps what is known as the specialist's "book," a record of buy and sell orders. The data in this book are not available to others because it would give important information not generally known as to market conditions and might stimulate unethical pricing practices.

Odd-Lot Dealers.   Despite the fact that quotations and deliveries are based on round lots, a considerable number of people desire to buy or sell securities in amounts less than the unit of trading because this does not involve such a large commitment of funds. This odd-lot trading, on the part of customers sometimes picturesquely termed "small fry," frequently aggregates 14 to 18 per cent of the total trading volume. In recent years securities dealers generally have sought to encourage securities buying by these investors and to cater to their needs for information and service.

Standard commission houses execute odd-lot orders through odd-lot dealers who specialize in this business. The odd-lot dealer stands ready to buy or sell odd lots at a price usually ⅛th (of $1) away from that of the next round-lot sale on the floor of the Exchange. If, for example, a customer wishes to buy 63 shares of the United States Steel Corporation common stock through his regular commission house, the commission house turns the order over to an odd-lot dealer. If the price on the next sale on the Exchange is, say, 36⅝ ($36.625 a share), the dealer then sells 63 shares at 36¾. If the customer were selling, the sale would be completed at 36½. The odd-lot dealer derives his income from the ⅛th differential plus or minus gains or losses which may be sustained on the relatively small inventory which he may carry.

Requirements for Listing Securities

Not all securities are traded on the Big Board. Shortly after the Civil War the members of the Exchange decided to restrict their trading to a particular list of securities and to require that, in the future, all additions to the list be issues which conformed to certain requirements. As a prerequisite for this privilege an issue must be judged acceptable by the Department on Stock List and admitted to trading by the Board of Governors.

Requirements for listing have gradually become more stringent as the country has developed financially and industrially. The forward-looking administration of the Exchange endeavored early, and with some success, to effect dissemination of vital financial information to the general public by requiring as a condition of listing that each company publish annual financial statements. In addition, applicants are required to file copies of their articles of incorporation and bylaws, copies of the contracts behind securities issues, and information relating to the number of stockholders, the percentage of stock publicly held, and the geographical location and size of individual holdings of their securities. The latter data especially provide information about the character of the distribution of the securities. Stock of a company closely held might have too narrow a market and make it difficult to buy and sell the securities. Furthermore, the securities might become subject to manipulation and artificial price influences. Since 1926, nonvoting common stock, and since 1943, preferred stock without voting power adequate to protect its position, have been refused listing.

As further protection to the public and to facilitate the safe transfer of securities, companies are required to use certificates engraved from steel plates which cannot be easily counterfeited. Provision is made for cross-checking transfers through separate registrars and transfer agents (see Chapter 14) with offices in the financial district on Manhattan Island.

From a public point of view, much of the original function of listing has been superseded by the more rigorous requirements of the Securities and Exchange Commission acting under the Securities Exchange Act of 1934. But companies with a national reputation, and in whose securities there is a nation-wide interest, encounter little difficulty in qualifying their securities for trading. At the present time there are listed on the New York Stock Exchange approximately 1,500 stock issues, common and preferred, of about 1,200 corporations.

Managements of many corporations list their securities because they feel that it enlarges good public relations for the company, that they achieve a better distribution of their stock, that it increases the marketability of outstanding securities, that new financing is facilitated, and that the securities often tend to sell at a higher price by virtue of the larger market growing out of listing.

Securities may be delisted for the following reasons: they do not continue to meet the requirements for listing; public interest in the issue is not sufficient for an active market; the issuing corporation becomes bankrupt or is in process of reorganization; the issue is retired; or at the request of the company (with stockholder approval).

Bond Trading

The New York Stock Exchange also provides a market for bonds. Many bonds, including United States government obligations, are listed for trading; but because of the highly specialized nature of the securities, the institutional character of the market, and relative lack of speculative appeal, most bond trading takes place in the over-the-counter market.

Trading on the Stock Exchange

Security trading on the floor of the New York Stock Exchange is highly organized. Under usual conditions, if, at the same moment, a man in San Francisco should place an order to sell, and a man in New Orleans, an order to buy, 100 shares of an issue, they would each have confirmation of execution of the transaction a few minutes later. Orders are sent by wire and telephone from commission-house offices to open booths on the floor of the Exchange, where clerks make notations and send the orders to the appropriate broker for execution.

Trading in each security is assigned to a definite location at a horseshoe-shaped booth called a "post." Here the brokers, through a series of bids and asks, "make a market."[2] This market has been called a "double-auction market." Both the bidders (buyers) and the askers (sellers) are constantly varying their respective prices either up or down. Sales take place when the highest bidder meets the price of the lowest asker. This is in contrast to the usual auction, in which the bidding is all on the buying side. The actual auction process, of course, is not open directly to the public; but individuals, by watching the ticker tape and getting quotations which in a normal market are only a few seconds old, take a direct and active participation in the determination of price by submitting their orders to buy or to sell to a commission broker.

When a sale has been made, the two brokers (buying and selling) each make a brief memorandum as to the security traded, to whom, the price, and the amount. This information is immediately phoned

---

[2] For another explanation of this term, see p. 292.

back to the commission house, from which the customer obtains a confirmation of the transaction. He may receive the confirmation immediately in person, by telephone, or by telegraph; but, in due course, he will receive a typed confirmation through the mail.

At the time the transaction takes place, a record of the number of shares and price per share is forwarded to the ticker room, where, usually in a matter of seconds, the transaction is recorded on the stock ticker tape, which taps out a continuous record of all round-lot transactions. Occasionally, however, trading becomes so heavy that even modern high-speed tickers fall behind by several minutes or more.

CLEARING CORPORATION.   Under the rules of the New York Stock Exchange, transactions which are executed on the floor must be "settled" in three days. Settlement procedure is similar to that employed by banks clearing checks. The New York Stock Clearing Corporation is specifically set up to expedite this procedure, which may involve several million shares aggregating well over $100 million a day. Settlements are made every day with the exception of Saturday, but, as indicated above, are three days delayed. The three-day delay allows time for necessary bookkeeping, comparisons of records of each transaction at offices of the buying and selling firms, and delivery of certificates and funds. When a broker buys or sells, he merely clears or delivers to the Clearing Corporation the balance of what he "owes" in stock or money. Thus, purchases and sales of stock of the same issue may leave the broker no balance to be received in the form of stock, but there might be a balance of money owing because the transactions were executed at different prices. In contrast to our prompt procedure, European bourses follow the practice of cumulative fortnightly settlements.

The purchasing broker's customer, if he elects to hold in his own possession the stock he has purchased, will receive a certificate by mail after the lapse of several more days, during which the transfer of the stock will be recorded on the books of the corporation. Many customers do not themselves receive their certificates but leave them on deposit with their brokers. Sellers usually deliver certificates to their brokers at or before the time of placing any order to sell unless the broker already has them on deposit.

SECURITY ORDERS.   There are several types of *orders* which may be entered by customers as well as types of security *transactions* which may take place on the floor of the exchange. The most important order is the "market order," which directs the broker either to buy or to sell "at the market" a given number of shares at the best possible price then obtainable.

"Limited" orders are entered by customers specifying that a given number of shares of a given stock be purchased or sold at a specified (limited) price. When the market price reaches the specified level, the limited order must be executed promptly by the commission broker or a specialist at the specified price or a better one (i.e., a lower price on buy orders or a higher price on sell orders). Limited orders may be for a specified time (a day, a week, until a given future date, a month) after which they are canceled unless renewed. Others may be good until canceled (G.T.C.). To protect a profit, one who holds stock but is not able to watch the ticker tape constantly may enter a "stop-loss" order to sell his shares at a specified price below current quotations. Then, if the price of the security should decline to the specified level, the order becomes a market order, the stock is sold, and the investor has limited the extent to which profit may be wiped out by price decline. Stop-loss orders may also be entered in an attempt to limit further losses from adverse price movements.

SECURITY TRANSACTIONS.   The type of security transaction most frequently effected is the outright purchase or sale. The buyer of a stock in this case is said to have assumed a "long" position. His usual aims are to make a profit through market appreciation, receive income through dividends declared, or both. Through such a purchase he becomes a part owner of the corporation and shares in its fortunes.

Margin Buying.   Some security buyers desiring to make as large a commitment as possible with a given sum of money purchase securities on margin. This means, in effect, that they borrow part of the purchase price from the broker in order to meet the daily settlement. The amount deposited or placed with the broker by the customer is called "margin"; and it protects the broker, who has advanced the balance of the purchase price, against loss resulting from price decline.

During the early 1920's a customer's margin frequently might be as low as 10 per cent of the market price. The broker's margin clerk kept a careful check on the prices of issues against which loans were outstanding, and if prices dropped, the customer was required to put up additional collateral (securities) or reduce the loan. If this was not done promptly, enough of the customer's securities would be sold to protect the broker's loan. In declining markets, thin margins frequently contributed to distress and even panic selling, which made for a disorderly market and contributed to further decline of prices.

To remedy the consequences of such action the Congress, in the Securities Exchange Act of 1934, gave to the Board of Governors of the Federal Reserve System the power to fix minimum margins requirements. This power has been exercised to regulate the flow of credit and to prevent an unhealthy speculative boom in the securities market. The Federal Reserve authorities first indicated a minimum initial margin requirement which varied between 25 and 55 per cent, depending on security price. However, in the light of credit conditions, they saw fit, for the twelve-month period beginning January, 1946, to eliminate the purchase of securities on credit by requiring full payment—i.e., 100 per cent margin—for long purchases and short sales. The requirement was lowered to 75 per cent in February, 1947; lowered further to 50 per cent in March, 1949; and raised to 75 per cent in January, 1951. To date no regulations have been made by the Federal Reserve Board with respect to margins which must be subsequently maintained. Nevertheless, the Board of Governors of the New York Stock Exchange has a rule for the guidance of its members that customers must maintain an equity in their account at all times of at least 25 per cent of the current market price. Furthermore, small traders, with an aggregate equity in their account of less than $500, must pay cash.

The securities owner who desires to clear his account merely gives his broker an order to sell. The loan is repaid from the proceeds of the sale.

Short Selling. The essence of a short sale is the sale of stock which is not owned. An individual may feel that the market is about to decline and may wish to take advantage of his "judgment." He therefore gives his broker an order to sell stock at the current price with the hope that he may buy shares at a lower price later and pocket the difference. In order to make delivery to the buyer, who is entitled to receive his certificate at settlement date three days later, the customer's broker borrows the securities from a fellow broker or from a customer and delivers borrowed stock to the buyer.

To protect the lender from whom the stock is borrowed, the lender is given the current market price, and a margin in cash or collateral is deposited with the broker to assure the lender that stock can be purchased if the price rises. The owner (lender), of course, is entitled to dividends on the stock which he owns, but the buyer of the loaned stock also expects the dividends. Therefore, the short seller must pay the lender an amount equivalent to any dividend paid while the shares are borrowed. When money rates are fairly high, the stock lender, rather than the borrower, may pay interest for the use of the money turned over to him as security. If the borrowed stock is scarce, however, this interest charge may be waived, or the borrower may even pay a premium for the privilege of borrowing the stock.

In due course the short seller "covers" his position by buying an equivalent amount of stock and turning it over to the lender, who then returns the money. If the seller buys the stock at a price sufficiently lower than his prior short sale, he will be able to pay brokerage, transfer taxes, and other expenses and make a profit in a period of falling prices.

A short seller may enter with his broker at the time of sale a stop-loss order to buy the stock in order to protect himself against loss should the price rise rather than decline.

There has been considerable controversy over short-selling operations. Some contend that short selling is uneconomic, unethical, or even immoral. That it may at times contribute to a disorderly market seems fairly well established despite the argument that the short sales offset buying by overoptimistic bulls and later impart support buying to depressed markets. Continued short sales, when there is an absence of market support, would accelerate the decline. In 1930 the New York Stock Exchange adopted a rule that short sales could not be made at a price less than the last long transaction. After the market break of 1937 the Securities and Exchange Commission adopted a very stringent rule which limited short selling to prices at least one eighth above the last transaction. A year later the rule was modified so that short sales could be transacted only at the level of the last transaction or higher, if the level of that last transaction represented an advance over the last previous different price.

EX-DIVIDEND PRICING. If a corporation declares a dividend and shares change hands at about the time when the corporation makes up the official list of stockholders to whom dividends are payable, a question may arise as to whether the buyer or the seller should get the dividend. The New York Stock Exchange follows the practice of having a stock traded on an "ex-dividend" basis two full business days before the date of record, i.e., the date on which the official list is prepared. Thus, if the date of record for a dividend is, say, Thursday, August 20, 1950, the share will sell "ex-dividend" beginning with the sale opening the market on August 18. This allows for the three-day settlement delay. The new owner (buyer) does not get the dividend; the seller does. The price of the security may be expected to decline from the last sale on the previous day to the opening sale on the ex-dividend date by approximately the amount of the dividend unless other influences on security prices offset or increase it.

STOCK MARKET AVERAGES. At the turn of the century, Charles H. Dow, a broker–newspaper publisher, was interested in presenting for his readers an indication of the daily fluctuations of securities prices on the Stock Exchange. To give a better picture of the day-to-day movement of the market, he computed an average of the prices of the leading stocks, which at that time were mostly rails. Since then, stock-market averages have undergone considerable change. At the present time, the best-known averages are the Dow-Jones Industrial Average, based on the shares of thirty leading industrial corporations, and the Dow-Jones Rail and Utility Averages, based on twenty rail-road and fifteen utility stocks, respectively. Other stock market indexes—e.g., those of the Standard and Poor's Company—are based on considerably broader lists of stocks. These indexes may be found on the financial pages of most large city newspapers and are followed with great interest by securities buyers.

Other Exchanges

Securities which are not on the trading list of the Big Board may be listed and sold on other exchanges. As mentioned above, there are twenty organized exchanges: sixteen are registered with the SEC, and three have been exempted from registration by the SEC because of the small volume and local nature of business transacted. The fourth exempt exchange is in Hawaii. A list of these exchanges and an indication of the volume of business transacted on them is given in Table 18.

The data in Table 18 show the considerable difference of volume between the Big Board and any of the other exchanges. The New York Curb Exchange, which is second in importance as measured by volume, handles only about one tenth, and the recently formed Midwest Stock Exchange only 2 per cent, as much business as the Big Board.

Nevertheless, the services of these other exchanges have value to the financial community. The securities of many companies which, for one reason or another, are not listed on the Big Board are marketed here. New companies which have not yet established records of operations or companies which are too closely held or which do not have large enough issues outstanding to meet the requirements for listing on the Big Board but which may be accepted under the

TABLE 18

ORGANIZED SECURITIES EXCHANGES IN THE UNITED STATES AND HAWAII

| NAME OF EXCHANGE | VOLUME OF STOCKS SOLD, 1949 | |
	Market Value	Number of Shares
Registered:		
New York Stock Exchange	$ 8,998,825,210	353,374,655
New York Curb Exchange	897,806,777	68,024,468
Midwest Stock Exchange	208,947,161*	8,185,799*
Boston Stock Exchange	152,207,803	3,899,208
San Francisco Stock Exchange	145,233,082	9,795,888
Los Angeles Stock Exchange	122,757,830	8,610,038
Philadelphia-Baltimore Stock Exchange	113,529,216*	4,190,887*
Detroit Stock Exchange	41,697,485	3,077,729
Cincinnati Stock Exchange	13,085,167	395,125
Pittsburgh Stock Exchange	13,637,550	868,941
Washington (D.C.) Stock Exchange	5,598,826	237,825
Salt Lake Stock Exchange	1,423,208	11,041,636
Spokane Stock Exchange	1,326,029	1,873,557
New Orleans Stock Exchange	734,312	32,706
San Francisco Mining Exchange	354,194	4,368,305
Chicago Board of Trade	174,006	21,801
Total	$10,716,337,856	477,998,557
Exempt:		
Honolulu Stock Exchange	$ 3,707,847	310,211
Richmond Stock Exchange	703,277	11,966
Wheeling Stock Exchange	539,217	15,957
Colorado Stock Exchange	174,227	214,030
Total	$ 5,024,568	552,164

* The Midwest and Philadelphia-Baltimore exchanges were formed by mergers during the year. These data include those for the predecessor exchanges.

Source: Securities and Exchange Commission, *Statistical Bulletin*, February, 1950, p. 20.

listing requirements of other exchanges, and companies for which a regional rather than national market is logical, gain the advantages of organized markets which would otherwise be unavailable. Regional investors are more adequately served. A point of technical importance to investors in stocks, say, of Midwestern companies is the fact that the New York State taxes on securities transfers are not applicable to transactions on the Midwest exchange. Nearly half of the securities listed on the Big Board and a quarter of those listed on the Curb are also traded on the other exchanges.

OVER-THE-COUNTER TRADING

Securities houses not only engage in brokerage transactions on the organized stock exchanges and distribute newly issued securities, but they constitute the core of the over-the-counter markets. The majority of securities are neither listed nor traded on the organized exchanges. In fact, of the estimated half-million corporations of the United States, the securities of only 3,000 are traded on organized exchanges. The securities of as many as 50,000 others, however, find their major market in the bid and ask trading through security dealers who "make a market" in particular issues.

Making a Market

A market in the securities of a given corporation is "made" by dealers who stand ready at all times to buy or sell these securities. In doing so, they act as sort of a sponsor. This sponsorship may stem from the fact that they participated in the original distribution or may reflect a personal or professional interest in these securities as trading items.

Trading in the over-the-counter market is not so highly organized as on the exchanges, but nevertheless it is effective for many issues. A customer who desires to purchase "unlisted" securities places an order with his securities dealer. The dealer will then either supply the securities from his own inventory or find the best place to buy them for resale to the customer.

The process of finding the best place to buy is interesting. The dealers throughout the nation who maintain inventories or who can buy securities readily from local investors furnish daily quotations to the National Quotation Bureau. The Bureau, in turn, publishes daily, for distribution to subscribers, quotations on as many as 5,000 issues. The quotation sheets also indicate the amounts of securities available and the dealers' interest in each issue. The quotations are bid and ask prices, the prices at which the dealers stand ready to buy or to sell the particular security quoted. It should be recognized that bid and ask prices are not prices at which actual sales or purchases have been made and are, therefore, not comparable to sales quotations for transactions on organized exchanges. They are, rather, offers; securities may never change hands at the quoted prices; offers are subject to change without notice.

When a firm, which does not itself hold an inventory of a given security issue, seeks to buy securities for a customer, one of the firm's "traders" will probably consult the quotation sheet for information concerning approximate prices and the dealers who are prepared to sell these securities. The trader will then call one or more of the dealers in the issue to obtain current quotations and quantities of shares offered. With these in mind, he will call the customer for confirmation of his interest in buying at a price which it is known he would have to pay to get the securities. If the customer agrees, the firm, acting as broker, will call back the house which offered the securities at the lowest price and arrange for the purchase.

The idea of "maintaining a market," which means buying, selling, and trading in a given issue, must not be confused with that of maintaining a price. Securities prices change frequently with the passage of time. A dealer, of course, is not able to maintain a price in the face of alterations in fundamental conditions. And an attempt to maintain a price in the face of outside influences would undoubtedly be construed as a form of market manipulation.

Types of Securities Traded

Securities may be traded over-the-counter because they do not qualify for listing: the issue may be closely held; or there may be insufficient public interest. On the other hand, the management of the corporation may not wish to comply with listing requirements. Some types of securities, like many preferred stocks and most bonds, because of the small amounts available for trading and lack of general public interest in the issues are traded, if at all, only intermittently in the over-the-counter market. The stocks of insurance companies, banks, and trust companies are usually traded over-the-counter. Although the securities of many of these companies are suitable for listing, it is not the custom for them to be traded on an organized stock exchange. It should be stressed, moreover, that even though a security is listed on an organized exchange it may, nevertheless, be actively traded in the over-the-counter market. This is true of many securities, particularly government bonds, but also of stocks of industrial concerns.

Dealing in Governments

The dealers in federal government and municipal obligations constitute a very specialized over-the-counter market. Many securities dealers handle municipal bonds almost exclusively. Most security dealers will buy and sell United States government bonds, but those who really make the market consist of a small number of the bigger banks and a small group of highly specialized houses operating in New York and Chicago. The big houses may buy and sell in lots of a million dollars or more at a time. Their bid and ask prices are close together and are made in terms of one thirty-second and sometimes even one sixty-fourth of a dollar. The market for United States obligations is extremely sensitive and is probably the most efficient securities market in the world.

The market prices of these securities is determined primarily by the supply of and demand for investable funds; our big savings institutions, life insurance companies, savings banks, and of course the commercial banking system are the leading customers. The buying and selling is influenced strongly by both the controls on credit markets exercised by federal agencies and the changing financial problems of the federal government.

FEDERAL REGULATION OF SECURITIES TRADING

On September 3, 1929, the Dow-Jones Industrial Average, after an almost continuous rise from 65 in 1921, reached the dizzy speculative height of 386. Three years later it had dropped to a depression low of 40. The bankruptcies and hardships which followed in the wake of the depression caused the New Deal candidates in the 1932 campaign to pledge, among other things, a program of financial reform. With respect to securities markets the proposed program was designed to improve trading and the quality of the market by requiring public dissemination of all material information with respect to a security and a company, the elimination of manipulative pools and artificial market influences, and the regulation of credit used for speculative purposes.

The objectives of the regulation of securities markets as set forth in the Securities Exchange Act of 1934 are attained through four different regulatory techniques or approaches: registration of persons, of places, and of things—i.e., brokers, exchanges, and securities; and limitation of the use of credit.

Registration of Securities

In addition to meeting the listing requirements of stock exchanges, all nonexempt securities traded on organized markets must be registered with the Securities and Exchange Commission through its Trading and Exchange Division. Registration requires the filing of much more complete and detailed information than has heretofore been available with respect to the history and current operations of the corporation. Annual audited financial statements must be made promptly available, and interim quarterly reports on sales are now required. The Commission checks these statements as a protection to the public. Furthermore, the proxy solicitations are now more informative; and trading by insiders—i.e., officers, directors, and major stockholders—is subject to report and review.

Registration of Exchanges

The securities exchanges themselves must register with the Commission by filing their constitution, bylaws, and regulations governing the execution of transactions. These rules and regulations must be so designed as to insure a fair and orderly market and adherence by brokers and customers to just and equitable trading principles and practices. The trading rules of the registered exchanges have undergone considerable change. Particularly important have been rules with respect to the handling of customers' securities, execution of orders, and the audit of brokers' financial affairs. Manipulative and deceptive devices are prohibited. Stabilization to aid in the distribution of a special offering or of an additional new block of an already outstanding issue is severely hedged by restrictive rules of the Commission to protect the inexperienced investor whose funds are being solicited.

Registration of Broker-Dealers

As originally passed in 1934, the Securities Exchange Act was designed, primarily, to control trading on the organized stock exchanges. By amendments in 1936, broker-dealers using the instrumentalities of interstate commerce or the mails were required to register with the Commission. In filing a registration statement, they must show that they are men of reputable standing, with a record free of security fraud convictions. In addition, they must conform to certain capital requirements if they make loans to customers.

In this relatively unorganized over-the-counter market the Securities and Exchange Commission has had considerable difficulty in maintaining standards of business conduct at a level deemed essential to the protection of investors and the general public. Price quotations and disclosure of the true character of the market have not always been ideal. Broker-dealers in their semifiduciary capacity and as recipients of the confidence and the money of uninformed investors could and sometimes did take advantage of their inside position to buy and sell at prices materially out of line with the market.

It is fraudulent for a dealer to sell securities to customers at prices bearing no reasonable relation to the prevailing market without disclosing this fact. This was first established in a proceeding as a result of which the registration of a dealer was revoked.[3] The Commission held in this and in other cases involving similar business conduct that the dealer assumes special obligations by virtue of the inherent characteristics of the securities business. The dealer holds himself out as one with specialized knowledge and skill. He cultivates the customer's trust, his reliance upon the dealer's skill, and his confidence in the dealer's integrity. There is an inherent representation in this confidential relationship that the dealer will deal fairly. The duties and obligations are not to be measured by the ordinary standard of arm's-length bargaining.

National Association of Securities Dealers. The technique of regulatory control by registration of persons, i.e., broker-dealers, did not prove entirely satisfactory. Considerable difficulty was encountered by the governing authorities in controlling the detailed, daily, semi-private practices of nearly 4,000 registered broker-dealers and their 60,000 employees, to say nothing of the fringe who did not register and who did an intermittent, part-time, or intrastate business. As a result, the Commission favored the formation of a special trade association for the purpose of policing the activities of its own members. The members of the industry would know better than anyone else what was going on. Therefore, to give more adequate protection to the public and to protect reputable securities dealers from competition with financially irresponsible individuals, the Securities and Exchange Commission joined with members of the industry in sponsoring an amendment to the Securities and Exchange Act:

To provide for the establishment of a mechanism of regulation among the over-the-counter brokers and dealers operating in interstate and foreign commerce or through the mails, to prevent acts and practices inconsistent with just and equitable principles of trade, and for other purposes.

Pursuant to this amendment and under combined industry and government sponsorship, the National Association of Securities Dealers, Inc. (N.A.S.D.), was formed. The Association's objectives are as follows:

To promote through cooperative effort the investment banking and securities business, to standardize its principles and practices, to promote therein high standards of commercial honor, and to encourage and promote among members observance of Federal and State securities laws;

To provide a medium through which its membership may be enabled to confer, consult, and cooperate with governmental and other agencies in the

---

[3] Duker & Duker, 6 SEC 386 (1939).

solution of problems affecting investors, the public and the investment banking and securities business;

To adopt, administer and enforce rules of fair practices and rules to prevent fraudulent and manipulative acts and practices, and in general to promote just and equitable principles of trade for the protection of investors;

To promote self-discipline among members, and to investigate and adjust grievances between public and members and between members.

This code of fair practice is now enforced by the N.A.S.D. through fourteen district committees. Complaints filed by the public, by other members, or by the district committees themselves are heard and penalties are imposed if they appear warranted. Decisions of the district committees may be appealed to the Board of Governors of N.A.S.D., then to the Securities and Exchange Commission, and finally to the federal courts.

Through a staff of examiners the N.A.S.D. is constantly making spot inspections and field investigations at unannounced times to check adherence to the stated objectives.

The principal power of the National Association of Securities Dealers derive from the enabling act which allows the Association to provide that no member may deal with any nonmember broker or dealer except at the same prices, for the same commissions or fees, and on the same terms and conditions as are accorded the general public. Therefore, from a practical business point of view, it is necessary that broker-dealers be members in order to participate actively in securities distribution or over-the-counter trading because preferential trade discounts are important to the net profits of houses dealing in securities.

SECURITY MARKETS AND THE ECONOMY

Both the formally established listed securities market, as found in the organized stock exchanges, and the amorphous and widespread over-the-counter securities market provide an essential service in facilitating the easy transfer of stocks and bonds. They make possible a high degree of liquidity in investment without which funds would much less freely find their way into productive channels. Unless the saver and investor has reasonable assurance that he may sell his holdings and receive cash promptly, he will be less willing to advance his accumulations in the first instance. With a broad and active market it is possible for an investor to shift his investments from one type of security to another, from one industry to another, from one company to another, and from securities to cash, as his judgment may dictate. Such flexibility makes it possible to adapt an individual investment fund to the needs of the moment as fundamental trends may dictate.

In former years, but much less so now, speculative trading rather than investment buying made up a very substantial portion of the trading volume in the securities markets, and such speculative trading by large operators probably accounted for an even larger percentage of the profits of the broker-dealers. Speculative excesses and the resultant "boiling" markets lured many uninformed buyers into the market in search of quick gains. Much of this buying verged close onto gambling, based, as it was, on the sole hope of profit through price change rather than on intelligent buying predicated on fundamental analysis. The uninitiated often not only experienced loss rather than gain for himself; but, even worse, he helped create an unsound market condition that, as a rule, ultimately proved disturbing to the entire economy.

There are many reasons why speculative trading has dwindled, including, among others, the virtual elimination of price manipulation, the elimination of stock pools, the income-tax structure and resulting altered distribution of national income, the search for security, memories of past debacles, and, of course, the economic and political uncertainties both at home and abroad.

To the extent that the securities exchanges provide broad and active markets for securities and thereby give investment in long-term securities high liquidity, they serve an indispensable function in our free-enterprise economy. To the extent that the exchanges might be utilized for speculation of a type that is tantamount to gambling, they contribute to the creation of an unwholesome climate generally detrimental to the country as a whole. Fortunately, the activities of these institutions are today largely of a constructive nature, and every effort is being made by the leaders in the respective markets and by regulatory authorities to minimize deleterious influences.

With a reduced volume of trading in recent years the organized exchanges are seeking to broaden the base of prospective customers in order to build up the volume. They are also finding that, to a considerable extent, even listed securities are being traded over-the-counter rather than through exchanges. Proposals have been made to alter the schedule of commissions in order to make the use of the exchanges more attractive to the over-the-counter houses and thus win additional volume for the exchanges. There is also another interesting development under way—a trend toward the consolidation of organized exchanges in various cities into regional exchanges. In this, the Midwest Stock Exchange, a merger of four smaller exchanges in Midwestern cities (Chicago, Cleveland, St. Louis, and Minneapolis–St. Paul exchanges), is an outstanding example. The purpose is to enlarge the market, reduce costs, improve efficiency, and, of course, increase profitability.

—LORING C. FARWELL

QUESTIONS AND PROBLEMS

1. What are the differences between the operations of brokers and those of dealers?
2. How can you distinguish the organized exchanges from over-the-counter markets?
3. What are the various kinds of members of an organized exchange according to their functions?
4. Name and describe the different types of orders which a customer may give his broker.
5. Describe a transaction for purchase of stock on margin. List advantages and disadvantages of margin trading.
6. Describe a "short sale." List advantages and disadvantages of short selling.
7. What does "listed" mean? Why are some securities "listed" and others "unlisted"? Why are so few "listed"?
8. Describe the process of over-the-counter trading.
9. What securities are normally traded over-the-counter?
10. What are the sources of over-the-counter quotations?
11. What are the major features of federal regulations of securities markets?
12. Compute the commissions which you might expect to pay on the purchase of stock selling at $0.75, $8, $25, and $50 per share.

BIBLIOGRAPHY

The stock exchanges, brokers, and dealers whose operations are described in this chapter are the subject of a voluminous literature. Some description of their activities is to be found in almost any book on corporation finance, investments, or banking. Pamphlets and reprints of articles are published by many commission brokerage houses. Academic journals—e.g., the *Harvard Business Review* or *Journal of Business of the University of Chicago*—may be consulted for articles on almost any phase of the securities business. A book written by Birl E. Shultz, former director of the (New York) Stock Exchange Institute and designed for use by New York Stock Exchange employees, *The Securities Market and How It Works* (5th ed.; New York: Harper & Bros., 1946), provides the reader a detailed picture of the operations of the "Big Board." The over-the-counter market is described by John C. Loeser in a book so titled: *The Over-the-Counter Securities Market: What It Is and How It Operates* (New York: National Quotation Bureau, Inc., 1940). An interesting and informative article, "National Association of Securities Dealers," written by Homer V. Cherrington, appeared in the *Harvard Business Review*, Vol. XXVII, No. 6 (November, 1949), pp. 741–59. Students who wish to extend their knowledge of securities and securities markets usually find it helpful to gain facility in reading and digesting financial news as it is presented in daily newspapers. Two booklets written to assist newspaper readers toward this goal are: *Financial News: How to Read and Interpret It* (New York Times, October, 1947), and C. Norman Stabler's, *How to Read the Financial Section of a Newspaper* (New York Herald Tribune, May, 1948).

Both historical and current information about many companies and their security issues are available in services such as *Moody's Manual of Investments* and *Standard Corporation Records* (Standard and Poor's Corporation). Descriptions of corporate operations, records of prices, dividends and earnings, and summaries of securities contracts are among the data to be found here. Current information about individual companies or securities issues and articles of general interest are found in periodicals such as *Barron's, the National Financial Weekly*, and the *Commercial and Financial Chronicle*. Historical and statistical information concerning the over-the-counter markets is available in Irwin Friend's monograph, *Activity on Over-the-Counter Markets* (Philadelphia: University of Pennsylvania Press, 1951).

The items referred to in the bibliography of the previous chapter will also provide information on the institutions described in this chapter.

Chapter • *10*

THRIFT AND INVESTMENT INSTITUTIONS

CAPITAL formation, the dual process of saving and investing, is a distinguishing characteristic of capitalistic society. More must be produced than is consumed in order to provide for the future growth and development of the nation through maintenance and additions to the stock of producer goods. Mere hoarding of income withholds funds from productive use in industry, just as it reduces effective demand for items of current consumption. To complete the capital formation process so essential to our society, funds must not only be saved; but they must be invested, must be used to provide additional tools of production, to expand plants, to increase inventories, to supply more housing, and in this way enhance the general well-being through a resultant higher standard of living.

Alternative Use of Savings

Who saves and why is considered in the next chapter. We may briefly note here that there are many classes of savers, ranging from the wage earner who puts by a little each payday to the corporations, large and small, who are substantial savers through their sizable retained incomes. For the main part, business savings are used in the operation of a particular business. Individual savers, who constitute the largest single source of savings, may make use of their current savings and their past accumulations in a number of ways, as described below.

HOARDING. Savings may be hoarded and placed in a safe-deposit box or cached in a mattress; but such disposition of savings does not benefit society, and most intelligent savers make more effective use of their funds, except possibly in times of stress, when confidence in the financial order may have waned. There is, of course, another possible exception, the person who seeks absolute privacy in his financial affairs, sometimes reflecting ulterior motives, such as the black marketeer during the war years. Under usual conditions, only a small portion of total savings are sterilized in this way through hoarding.

BUSINESS OPERATION. If the saver wishes to combine ownership and management of his accumulations, he may establish or purchase a business, expand an existing business, or acquire real property. Such use of savings not only involves management responsibilities and requires knowledge and preferably experience in the particular type of enterprise, but it also exposes the savings to a high degree of risk in view of the lack of diversification, because much is ventured in but a single undertaking. More will be said about the factor of risk later in this chapter. In any event, the management of accumulations employed in this way becomes a broad problem of business administration which is not within the direct purview of our study of financial institutions.

DIRECT INVESTMENT. Most savers are not likely to be interested in becoming owners and operators of a business; yet they may wish to have an interest in a business managed by others. They may be willing to lend money or may be willing to purchase stock in a company, which will give them an ownership stake without business management responsibilities. By dealing with one of the agencies or institutions discussed in Chapters 8 and 9—namely, investment bankers, securities dealers, and stock brokers—they may obtain information and counsel as supplementory service to the purchase of bonds and stocks. Usually such securities are bought in the name of the owner, who assumes the responsibility for deciding what to buy in the first place, what to hold and what to sell, and when. He will be a direct investor in American enterprise, either as a lender, if he purchases bonds, or as an owner, if he buys common or preferred stocks.

INDIRECT INVESTMENT. Many savers and investors recognize that the management of accumulated funds is a responsible undertaking, not to be assumed lightly; that there are many hazards to be met; and that adequate training, experience, and knowledge are essential if a program is to culminate successfully. They recognize their own incompetence or disinclination to shoulder the burden, and they deliberately seek to avoid the responsibilities of direct investment.

An examination, later in this chapter, of the risks involved and of the requirements for successful investment management will show why this is so. Yet such savers may nevertheless wish to share, either as lenders or as owners, in the rewards that are expected to flow from a participation in the nation's businesses. But rather than invest directly in stocks and bonds, as mentioned above, these persons may become investors through a number of different types of financial institutions designed to assist the saver and the investor in attaining his goal of relative safety of principal, plus securing an income in the form of interest and dividends commensurate with the risk taken, and perhaps appreciation.

The types of financial institutions available are enumerated in Exhibit 41, "Classification of Investment and Thrift Institutions," and

Exhibit 41

CLASSIFICATION OF INVESTMENT AND THRIFT INSTITUTIONS

Investment Institutions
    Investment companies
        Open-end investment companies (also called "mutual funds")
        Closed-end investment companies
    Investment counsel
    Investment bankers
        Investment counsel services
    Trustees (individual or corporate)
        Individual testamentary or living trusts
        Common trusts (commingled funds)
        Investment counsel services

Thrift Institutions
    Savings banks
        Savings departments of commercial banks
        Mutual savings banks
        Stock savings banks
        Postal savings
    Life insurance companies
    Pension plans
    Credit unions
    Savings and loan associations
    Face-amount installment certificate companies
    United States savings bonds

are discussed in the four chapters that follow. Through such agencies the large and small funds of all manner of savers are channeled for productive employment in business and government. Some of these institutions, those classified as "thrift institutions," are designed to serve primarily, but not exclusively, the saver who is in the process of accumulating a fund of investment proportions; others, those classified as "investment institutions," serve primarily but not exclusively those who already have an investment fund. The distinction is not clearly drawn—there are gradations and overlapping from one extreme to the other. But what both types do, with some exceptions, amounts in essence to pooling the savings of many; and then through the purchase of stocks or bonds or tangible property they make these pooled savings available for the use of industry and government. The agency itself assumes responsibility for investment management.

It is the purpose of this chapter to serve as a prelude to the individual consideration of each of these intermediary investment agencies that channel savings into use by industry and government. We will examine in turn the risks to which all property is exposed; how the businessman endeavors to cope with these risks; and the art of investing—how the professional investment manager seeks to preserve and enhance the capital entrusted to his care. The discussion will tend to show that investing is a specialized undertaking that requires training, experience, and seasoned judgment; that many savers recognize the complexity of the investment problem and are therefore ready to delegate responsibility for the management of their funds, or at least seek assistance; and that, as a result, the investment intermediaries are assuming a position of growing importance in the economy.

Risks in Business

Whichever avenue of investment is adopted—whether combined ownership and management of a business, the direct purchase of stocks or bonds, or indirect investment through thrift and other indirect investment institutions—the savings that are employed will be exposed to varying degrees of risk. Either the owner-manager of a business, the purchaser of stocks or bonds, or the professional investment manager of a thrift or other indirect investment agency must cope with the uncertainties or risks in seeking to preserve principal, earn an income, and, in some instances, preserve purchasing power. Before reviewing the more specific problems of investment management it will be helpful to examine the nature of the risks inherent in all business and in property ownership generally.

Risk is all-pervasive; and while it can be minimized, it cannot be completely avoided. Any property that is acquired subjects the owner immediately to possible loss or damage. In fact, it might be said that the most nearly riskless use of savings is found in the payment of debt. In an obligation is discharged, there is then no risk of losing the money that was paid to wipe out the debt. Risk even affects life itself. From a pecuniary standpoint, the individual cannot know whether he may expect to live the normal life span and provide the anticipated income for his family; whether his life savings are sufficient to maintain himself during the years of retirement; or whether he will live long enough to use up the sum that he has provided for his waning years.

Turning our attention to the purely business risks, we find that writers have classified the uncertainties in various ways, and we can readily recognize at least some of the contingencies without attempting to make anything like a full catalogue:

1. Physical, tangible, property may be lost or damaged through acts of God such as fire, flood, storm, hail, unseasonable weather, too much or too little rainfall, lightning, and similar incidents of nature.

2. Individuals may not live up to the confidence placed in them; and, as a result, property may be lost through stealth, defalcation, or other unanticipated misconduct.

3. Groups of individuals may act with violence and deliberately destroy property; riots, for example.

4. Production and distribution uncertainties may cause loss to a business. Delivery of essential material may be delayed; goods may be partly processed before substandard qualities are detected; a strike may interfere with the prompt sale of physically perishable commodities; and seasonal merchandise may have to be sold at a sacrifice because it did not reach the market in time.

5. Through a change in laws, certain businesses may be outlawed or at least curtailed. Many communities are now forbidding the sale of fireworks; the Volstead Act drastically curtailed the manufacture of liquor and strictly limited its sale; many states have set up barriers to certain types of interstate commerce; and the status of the basing-point method of sale is not clear, and the final outcome may have serious consequences to many business units.

6. The tastes and habits of the public may change, or new industries or processes may replace the old. Today the motion-picture industry is concerned with the effect that television and, more recently, phonevision, may have on the entertainment world; professional football is not certain whether video will swell or curtail stadium attendance; and hard roads and the widespread ownership of automobiles is favoring some market centers and harming others.

7. Every business is constantly exposed to the risks of the market and price changes. Prices tend to fluctuate with the ebb and flow of general business activity, and this risk increases as the time interval between purchase and resale lengthens.

The reader will doubtless be able to supply many other examples (depreciation of the dollar, for instance) and list still other categories of risk, but the enumeration just made will suffice to demonstrate that uncertainty besets the businessman and the property owner. Is it possible to eliminate, or at least minimize, these uncertainties that harass those who are charged with preserving wealth?

Coping with Risks

As already noted, we cannot completely eliminate all risk that confronts us. It is possible, however, to eliminate some risk, to minimize other risks, or to transfer the risk-bearing function in part to those who make spreading of risk a specialty, such as the insurance company, for instance.

Our discussion is still concerned with protecting property generally against the uncertainties and hazards of damage and loss. These risks are fundamental and are pertinent to the investment process, and particularly to the owner-manager of a business. Subsequently we will consider dealing specifically with risk as it affects the individual investor and the professional and institutional investment managers.

Within limits it is possible to minimize risk substantially, if not avoid it completely, by meeting it head on. Distributors of gasoline and other highly inflammable fluids ground their delivery trucks by means of a chain to avoid the danger incident to static electricity. A well-designed fireproof building completely equipped with all possible tested fire-prevention devices and containing appropriate structural features provides reasonably certain assurance against any serious fire loss. The steel and concrete construction of the safe-deposit vault of a metropolitan bank and the precautions exercised by the attending personnel provide reasonably safe protection for the property of patrons. Cashiers' cages of bulletproof glass, equipped with siren alarms and tear-gas bombs, offer considerable assurance against robbery.

If we had all the facts with respect to a given risk, it would be possible to take the necessary precautions; but then there would no longer be a risk. This is another way of saying that lack of understanding—or, more bluntly, ignorance—is the basis for much of uncertainty and consequent loss. Recognizing this fact, many businesses seek through research to find the facts that will permit reduction of risk. Thus, a great deal of attention is being given to studying business fluctuations, and attempts are made to forecast trends of activity. Market surveys are made in a sample area to determine public taste and public acceptance of a certain product before the manufacturer embarks on a nation-wide distribution effort so that necessary adaptations can be made—or, if it seems expedient, the whole idea can be dropped without further cost. Considerable progress is being made by meteorologists in forecasting weather conditions; and their efforts help many businesses avoid heavy losses and even catastrophes—citrus-fruit growers and airline operators, for instance.

An excellent example of the transfer of risk to a specialized agency established for the very purpose of spreading and thereby reducing risk is found in the casualty insurance field. A fire insurance company will, for a fee, insure many individual property holders against complete loss of their particular individual properties as a result of fire. In this way, a possible 100 per cent loss is replaced by a much smaller but certain expense, the annual insurance premium. Sharing of risk in this fashion is possible through a great variety of insurance companies that cover diversified fields of risk, including life. For instance, fire insurance companies also write policies protecting against loss by wind, storm, rain, hail, and water damage as well as against loss by fire. Casualty companies cover a great variety of risks, including automobile fire, theft, and public liability, workmen's compensation, use and occupancy and accident and health, to mention just a few. Marine insurance companies offer protection against loss of ships and cargoes, either inland or on the ocean. Companies writing fidelity and surety contracts insure the employer against loss growing out of the dishonesty and even negligence of the employee. There are many more types of insurance contracts to be had, including, of course, life contracts. A subsequent chapter deals with life insurance companies. (See Chapter 12.)

Securities underwriting provides another illustration of the transfer of risk. If the investment banker underwrites a new offering, he will provide the desired funds at the appointed time, and the issuing company can rely on having the money when needed, whether the new issue has been distributed or not. The flourmiller transfers risk to a speculator when he practices hedging by executing offsetting transactions, one in the actual commodity and the other in the futures market. A loss in the one contract is offset by a profit on the other, and the risk incident to price change is thus reduced approximately to the amount of the brokerage commission that is involved. Any general contractor who has engaged to complete a certain project at a stated price may reduce or spread the risk incident to possible price change by subletting parts of the project to other contractors.

There is still another method for dealing with risk, and that is self-insurance. A large industrial company, such as the International Harvester Company, which has a great number of individual plants scattered throughout the United States and abroad, may in a sense provide its own fire insurance by setting aside each year a calculated sum to cover possible losses. Because the factory units are so widely distributed, there is little possibility of losing any substantial number through fire in any one year. The amounts set aside will gradually build up into a sizable fund that would provide for the replacement of any buildings lost through fire.

The risks we have been discussing confront every businessman, and he has the problem of meeting them. They are of interest to every investor or investment manager because these uncertainties affect the businesses whose stocks and bonds are held.

In the next section we will consider exactly what problems are faced by the person seeking to administer an investment fund, large or small, with the aim of maintaining the principal amount, realizing an income compatible with the risk incurred, and, if possible, garnering a gain in the form of capital appreciation.

The Art of Investing

Many factors are involved, and numerous decisions must be made in the administering of savings and investment funds. This is true whether the fund is under the supervision of a professional adviser who gives full time and attention to investment problems or whether the fund is under the avocational direction of an individual who gives his major time and attention to other pursuits. More than a quarter of a century ago, a recognized writer in the field commented on the business of investment as follows:

. . . the investment of funds is a real business, subject to the rewards of true business foresight and the losses incident to attempts on the part of the poor business manager to invest funds. This is not self-evident. The school teacher, clergyman, lawyer, dry goods merchant, and shoe manufacturer know enough about their own respective businesses to feel assured that the ordinary uninitiated could not succeed without long and specialized training. Yet these same men stand ready to embark on one of the most intricate of businesses—that of investment—requiring perhaps the most extensive specialized knowledge of any profession or business.

To compare intelligently, and with a degree of insight which makes the comparison something more than a guess, the credit obligations of Soa Paulo and the mortgages of the Chicago and Northwestern Railroad, the debentures of the Detroit Edison Company and the common stock of the General Electric Company, requires acumen and a breadth of knowledge compared with which the ordinary professional and business judgments are child's play. And yet it is just such specialized knowledge and acumen which constitutes the business of investment, a business which many, without training or aptitude, feel qualified to embark upon with their own savings and those of their relatives and friends.[1]

Complete development of the topic is hardly appropriate here, and only a few of the more important considerations are presented in order to point out the complexity of the investment management problem.

OBJECTIVE. Every undertaking should have a goal and a plan to reach that goal, and this certainly is true in managing an investment fund. The procedure to be followed with respect to any given fund depends upon two principal considerations: the circumstances of the investor and his temperament.

A widow of forty-five who has just received the relatively modest proceeds of her deceased husband's life insurance policy, representing her all, will doubtless find it advantageous to emphasize safety of principal and to be satisfied with whatever income is consistent with such safety. On the other hand, the scion of a wealthy industrialist, a relatively young man who has a well-paying position, who has already acquired considerable property, and whose prospects appear excellent, can afford the risk of a much less conservative course. He might well buy a moderate, or even a substantial, amount of common stock in a new and speculative enterprise with the hope of realizing a large profit. If the venture is disappointing, he is able to absorb the loss with equanimity. Not so, the widow. Between these extreme positions are many gradations.

With respect to the circumstances of the individual investor, allowance should be made for the following: other property; other income; age; dependents; insurance program; and any other factors that may have a bearing on his financial position and which should be in contemplation in planning the investment program.

No matter what the circumstances of the individual investor may be, attention must also be given to individual temperament. Casper Milquetoast, although his circumstances might justify an aggressive program, might not be so constituted as to withstand the vagaries of the stock market and business trends. Insomnia, perhaps even ulcers, might accompany the sometimes violent fluctuations in the market value of his holdings. A less timid investor might take such ups and

---

[1] Arthur Stone Dewing, "The Role of Economic Profits in the Return on Investments," *Harvard Business Review*, July, 1923, p. 451.

downs in stride and therefore be better able to follow a dynamic program.

Good judgment and patience are other attributes that are essential to successful investing—without them the inexperienced individual, without assistance, is likely to be whipsawed in the changing markets; he tends to buy near the top of the market and to sell near the bottom.

BUSINESS CONDITIONS. Having formulated an investment objective, the next step is an appraisal of the current status of business—the analysis of all the fundamental political and economic factors that have a bearing on interest rates and earnings trends, which in turn determine bond and stock prices. Fundamental factors include labor-management relations, Federal Reserve and government fiscal policy, legislation, foreign developments, the imminence of war or peace, the temper of the business community, changes in the distribution of the national income, and the industrial and agricultural outlook—to name but a few.

Whether to hold cash, to buy, sell, or hold high-grade bonds, or to buy, sell, or hold common stocks, and in what proportions, will depend upon the appraisal of these enumerated fundamental forces as well as upon the investment goal for the fund and the disposition or temperament of the individual investor. In the discussion of business fluctuations in Part III, it will become clear that forecasting the trend of economic events with any degree of accuracy is itself a hazardous task beset by many pitfalls. To cite a few instances of toe stubbing: It was freely predicted that in the early postwar period there would be a large amount of unemployment and business recession, but that never came to pass. In the early months of 1948 a large proportion, if not a preponderance, of economists anticipated the end of the postwar boom and a downtrend in business by midyear or certainly before the end of 1948; but, owing to tax reduction, the European rehabilitation program, and the accelerated defense program, including the draft, the boom continued. Again, early in 1950 a decline in business in the closing months of the year was widely predicted, but Korean developments caused boom conditions.

INDUSTRY ANALYSIS. With the objective charted and the economic outlook evaluated, the next step is the determination of those industries, out of the thirty or forty industries of investment caliber, which are in the most promising position under existing conditions and in the light of the forecast. All industries do not present equally attractive opportunities at the same time; and to select the most promising the investor must be familiar with the fundamentals of each. Or how else could the selection be made intelligently? Under certain conditions, the heavy or producer goods industries may be favored; at other times, it may be the consumer goods industries or the consumer durable-goods industries. A special set of conditions may at a given time single out a particular industry as one that offers striking possibilities, say the oils, for instance, or the rails. Governmental action, legislation, a Federal Trade Commission ruling, or antitrust activity may aid or hinder a given industry. Constant analysis of basic trends and specific-industry trends is essential to sound selection of industry participation.

There is another aspect of industry and company analysis that must not be overlooked. Just as plant and animal life have their cycles of growth, from infancy to maturity and old age, so industries and companies tend to have a life cycle. They develop through successive stages from the formative and promotional phase of experiment, invention, and development, through early growth, established position and expansion, to maturity, and, ultimately, decline. Industries in the early growth stages provide the capital appreciation element for the aggressive investment plan; more mature industries tend to provide certainty of income and relative capital stability for the more conservative investment program. Programs in between will generally have an appropriate blending of the two types.

COMPANY ANALYSIS. Having determined the preferred industries, the next step is the selection of the preferred companies within an industry. In most industries there are outstanding leaders, other companies that tend to follow the leadership of the dominant units, companies that are definitely marginal, and companies that may just be entering the field. In selecting the preferred companies there are many factors in addition to industry position to be considered, a few of which are: caliber of management; financial structure; adequacy of capital; earning power in boom and depression; acceptance of the securities of the company; the essentiality of the company activity; degree of integration; and vulnerability to government regulation. Within a certain industry there may be wide differences in company operation. In the oil industry, for instance, there are companies that are primarily crude producers; others that are primarily distributors of finished products; and many in between that produce and refine crude, buy and refine crude, and buy finished products in varying degrees and distribute the finished products over a wide area. At times one or another type of operation (degree of integration) is favored by conditions and other types of operation are handicapped.

SELECTION OF SECURITIES. The preceding steps in the formulation of an investment program prepare the investor for the final step in the process—the selection of the specific stocks and bonds to constitute the investment portfolio, i.e., the individual bricks that make up the financial structure.

The investment objective that has been formulated and the economic appraisal that has been made guide the investor in setting up an appropriate balance of cash, bonds, and preferred and common stocks. Industry and company appraisal have determined the preferred industries and the favored companies within these industries. In order to select intelligently the items that are to make up the investment fund, the investor should have a sound and comprehensive understanding of both the legal characteristics and the economic or investment function of the great variety of securities that are available to him. Some bonds perform investmentwise much like common stocks; some common stocks act in the market more nearly like bonds. From an investment standpoint, the legal classification is often of little relevance; investment characteristics should usually be the predominant consideration.

It should not be inferred that legal characteristics are not important. In Chapter 7 it was pointed out that there are (to the uninitiated) a bewildering variety of securities and that the simple classification into secured and unsecured bonds and preferred and common stocks is convenient but inadequate.

DIVERSIFICATION. It is usually the aim of the saver and of the investor to maintain the principal value of his accumulations; to obtain a reasonable return consistent with such preservation of capital; and to obtain, without too much chance of loss, a measure of capital appreciation.

Risk cannot be avoided in any investment program, but risk can be minimized. This is accomplished by balancing risks, through diversification—not taking a 100 per cent position at any time. The prudent investor distributes his investments over a variety of holdings: by balancing cash, bonds, preferreds, and common stocks; varying the maturities of bonds; holding securities in a variety of industries and companies; and through geographic diversification.

If diversification is overemphasized, the problem of supervision may be increased to a burdensome point and the performance of the investment fund may be diluted. All companies and all industries are not equally promising, and the more items that are added to the portfolio the lower on the list of preference must the investor reach.

On the other hand, underdiversification, i.e., too high a concentration in too few items, tends to enhance the risk involved. For instance, even if the investor's studies convinced him that a certain industry, and the common stock of a particular company in that industry, presents the outstanding investment at the moment, it would be folly to place all of the fund in that one security. In the world of affairs, nothing is that certain. If the investor's judgment proved to be wrong, the loss might be disastrous. There is the old adage about not putting all one's eggs in one basket—and it applies to the investment process.

KNOWLEDGE OF MARKETS. The investor should have an understanding of the capital and distribution markets discussed in Chapters 8 and 9, the technical procedures, and the terms, fees, and market action.

CONTINUOUS SURVEILLANCE. The admonition to buy sound securities and put them in a strongbox (hold them indefinitely) has long since been discredited. In the economic world the only certainty is the certainty of uncertainty. The level of business rarely remains constant; fundamental trends change; new industries are born, old industries decay; new laws and regulations affect industry and finance; our economy has become increasingly sensitive to domestic politics and to international developments; labor-management relations, social change, and redistribution of the national income are significant factors.

To keep constantly abreast of the myriad of factors that affect investments, either favorably or unfavorably, is at best a difficult undertaking for those who give their full time to the task. In fact, professional investors tend to divide the responsibility, co-ordinate their activities and findings, and act on a group basis.

In addition to decisions with respect to holding, buying, or selling securities, there are other decisions to be made from time to time and clerical details that require attention: bonds mature or are called; coupons must be clipped; dividend checks deposited; rights and warrants should be exercised or sold; companies are reorganized or merged; proxies should be exercised or stockholder meetings should be attended; transaction confirmations should be verified; and at least a simple set of records should be maintained, particularly for the preparation of income-tax returns.

Social and Economic Implications

Investing is a complex business and, as has been indicated, is not an undertaking for the novice unaided, and this is generally recognized by the financial community. Investment bankers, securities dealers, and brokers admonish prospective investors to investigate before investing; they make available the services of securities analysts and investment advisers; and they provide a variety of educational literature on various phases of investing. Seasoned investors take advantage of proffered assistance, and the novice would do well to heed the advice to investigate and accept the help that is offered. To improve public understanding of the saving-investing process, institutions in the securities business are utilizing all media of communication. Dealers and brokers stand ready to furnish full information, but it is generally stressed that decision and action should rest on the individual investor's judgment. It is interesting to note that in a recent advertising campaign of one of the organized securities exchanges the purchase of stock was subordinated to home ownership, life insurance, and a savings bank account.

The individual investor who acknowledges his disinclination or incompetence to assume the responsibility of direct investment, or who does not have a sufficiently large accumulation to make direct purchase of stocks and bonds feasible, may turn his funds over to one of the several thrift or other investment agencies. In this way, he not only may obtain advantage of the experience and specialized knowledge of professional investment managers but may also have the benefit of a wider degree of diversification than might otherwise be possible for a fund of modest proportions. In short, these agencies provide a means for transferring and minimizing risk; knowledge is substituted for lack of knowledge, and diversification for concentration. But the individual investor still has the responsibility for selecting the agency to be employed. The success attained will depend on the ability, astuteness, and integrity of the management of the institution selected.

Thrift and other indirect investment institutions render a valuable service to their customers and to the economy as a whole. The individual saver gets specialized management and diversification of risk and is relieved of the problem of personal supervision and the problem of making decisions of some complexity. This should mean relative safety of principal, relative certainty of income, and, in the case of some of the agencies, possible appreciation in value. Society, on the other hand, obtains the funds that are channeled into business use, and this results in an ultimate increase of producer and consumer goods and therefore in a generally higher standard of living. Waste is minimized.

Individual savers and investors are increasingly patronizing these indirect investment media. This is in part a reflection of high war and postwar earnings and the high rate of saving, but also the result of the altered pattern of income distribution in our country. A larger share of the national income flows to those persons in the middle- and lower-income brackets than in earlier years. They are now able to save more; and in seeking a haven for their savings, they turn in the main to those institutions with which they are familiar. For the most part, these savers are not traditionally buyers of stocks and bonds and therefore know little about investment bankers, securities dealers, brokers, and stock exchanges. As a consequence, there has been a marked expansion in the volume of funds entrusted to savings banks, the savings divisions of commercial banks, insurance companies, and savings and loan associations, some of which agencies have been aggressive in their promotional activities.

There are many who feel that, if this institutionalization of investing continues, it may present a serious problem for the economy. In fact, some hold that the problem already exists. What is this problem? For reasons of law or tradition, savings banks and insurance companies are not substantial investors in equities, particularly not in common stocks. The funds they receive are invested mainly in government and corporate bonds and in mortgages. Little, if any, of these savings become available for the purchase of common stock, equity capital. Yet, a private-enterprise society depends upon an adequate flow of "venture" capital.

The situation is accentuated by the fact that the persons in the higher income brackets, who traditionally did most of the saving and who provided most of the venture capital, apparently find stocks less attractive than formerly. There are many factors that account for this apathy, and one of them undoubtedly is the current income-tax structure. Wealthy persons who might be expected to be in the best position to assume the risk of common-stock ownership find that a tax-free 2 to 2½ per cent income on a municipal bond is more interesting than a common-stock dividend of 6 per cent subject to tax. And besides, there is relatively little risk in the municipal bond, whereas the income and market price of a common stock are both subject to wide fluctuation. It is therefore argued that the institutionalization of the savings of persons in the middle- and low-income brackets, coupled with the effect of taxes on the incomes of persons in the higher-tax brackets, is now drying, or will in the future dry up, or at least retard, the flow of venture capital.

Corporation officials point out that the stock market places such a low value on their outstanding shares that additional stock cannot be sold except at a price that would be unfair to present stockholders, whose equity would thereby be seriously diluted. On the other hand, there are those who contend that there is no shortage of venture capital; that equity capital is being provided by retained earnings; and that common stocks in promising industries would be bought if the prices were attractive. Why common stocks generally have in recent years sold at quotations that have been low in relation to earnings, dividends, and net asset values could lead us into a long discussion. Stated simply, this condition is a reflection of uncertainty and apprehension on the part of investors with respect to the domestic and foreign economic and political outlook, and this is a skein of many threads that we will not seek to unravel here.

It should be noted that if there is not an adequate supply of common stock or equity capital there will not be a base to support additional bonds. For example, if a person wishes to buy a $20,000 home but has no funds to make a downpayment, he is not likely to find a lender that will advance the full $20,000 purchase price. However, if the prospective home buyer has $8,000 of his own, representing his equity, he should have no difficulty in borrowing the other $12,000. By the same token, the extent to which a financial institution will loan money to a corporation, or buy the bonds of the corporation, depends upon the amount of ownership capital of the corporation. Public officials responsible for supervising the financing of public service companies have repeatedly urged that such companies raise a greater proportion of their capital requirements by selling stocks rather than bonds.

The equity-capital controversy is not applicable, or at least not in equal degree, to such agencies as investment companies, investment counsel, including investment banking houses that render a counseling service, and trust institutions. In fact, investment companies as a group hold mostly common stocks, and investment counsel likewise use stocks liberally in the portfolios under their supervision. Savings and loan associations by their very nature emphasize mortgage investments and also buy government bonds. United States savings bonds are, of course, in a class by themselves.

Certain observers point to another possible problem growing out of the indirect investment that is fostered by some of the institutions under consideration. Even though it is admitted that these agencies render a service that is, in the main, praiseworthy from the standpoint of both the saver and the economy as a whole, it is pointed out that savers and investors who do not have direct ownership and responsibility are likely to be unaware, or at least indifferent, to fundamental social trends that might seriously affect the existing private-enterprise system and significantly reshape our social order. It is stressed that a direct stake in American corporations through stock ownership by a greater number of persons would provide the best protection against inroads of collectivism and further socialization. In this connection it is interesting to note the results of a survey conducted by the Survey Research Center, of the University of Michigan, for the Board of Governors of the Federal Reserve System. Findings of this study indicated that, of the spending units (essentially families) with incomes of $2,000 or more, only 5 per cent were favorable to common-stock ownership. And yet, our economy depends on the continuous flow of equity capital, and a larger proportion of the national income is going to the low- and middle-income groups.

There is no easy answer to the foregoing observation. The question might be asked: Would it be desirable and would it advance the interest of the existing order if persons in the lower-income brackets with relatively meager savings, and hardly in a position to risk these savings, were to try direct investment in common stocks without competent guidance? Or, might their experience result in disappointment and breed disaffection? Obviously, a sound solution is required and a challenge is presented to business leaders generally, and particularly to those members of the financial community that are concerned with the provision of long-term capital funds for business.

The problems of investment, whether direct or indirect, represent but one phase of the over-all economic and social scene and are conditioned by fundamental political trends and developments. In this chapter we have considered only one or two social implications rooted in the thrift and indirect-investment institutions. Individual consideration of the several agencies in the chapters that follow will throw additional light on their respective operations and their places in the economy.

—Erwin W. Boehmler

QUESTIONS AND PROBLEMS

1. What disposition may the individual investor make of his savings to contribute to capital formation? What is the effect of hoarding?
2. What is the distinction, if any, that can be made between "thrift institutions" and "investment institutions"? Give examples of both groups— institutions with which you are somewhat familiar.

3. Briefly indicate the various classifications of risk that confront the business enterpriser. Can risk be eliminated?

4. What are the elements or steps in planning a sound investment program?

5. How do you account for the growth of thrift and investment institutions in recent years?

6. State what is meant by the "institutionalization of investment."

7. What are the advantages and the disadvantages of such institutionalization of investment?

8. There is much discussion about "equity capital." What is the controversy?

9. Do you agree that it would be desirable to broaden the ownership interest in American common stocks? If so, to what extent? Might there be any adverse developments? Under what circumstances?

10. Cite examples to show how investment aims or objectives might vary with the individual investors.

11. Do you agree that the safest use of savings might be the retirement of a debt? Discuss.

BIBLIOGRAPHY

For a comprehensive discussion on the risks inherent in business, see one of the earliest treatises on this subject, which, though old, is still considered authoritative: C. O. Hardy, *Risk and Risk Bearing* (Chicago: University of Chicago Press, 1931). And on the risks confronting the investor, consult the standard texts on investments. The topic is well summarized in G. W. Dowrie and D. R. Fuller, *Investments* (2nd ed.; New York: John Wiley & Sons, Inc., 1950), chaps. vii–x. This and other texts on investments such as R. E. Badger and H. G. Guthmann, *Investment Principles and Practices* (3rd ed., New York: Prentice-Hall, Inc., 1941), and J. C. Clendenin, *Introduction to Investments* (New York: McGraw-Hill Book Co., Inc., 1950), discuss the full scope of the problem of investing, including determination of objective; economic, industry, company, and securities analysis; and thrift and investment agencies. A rather short and more popular treatment of investing is found in any one of the following:

Hellberg, Karl (nom de plume). *A Successful Investor's Letters to His Son.* Minneapolis: Carter Press, 1934.

Effinger, R. C. *ABC of Investing.* New York: Harper & Bros., 1947.

Graham, Benjamin. *The Intelligent Investor.* New York: Harper & Bros., 1949.

The latter volume condenses, to a considerable degree, information and guidance taken from a more technical and larger volume, *Security Analysis*, written by the same author in collaboration with D. L. Dodd. Current articles on the equity capital problem and on institutionalization of investment will be found in the periodical literature—particularly the *Harvard Business Review* and the *Journal of Finance*—and in reported addresses in the *Commercial and Financial Chronicle*. Recent articles are:

Anderson, C. J. "Trends in the Supply of Equity Capital," *Harvard Business Review,* Vol. XXVIII, No. 5 (September, 1950), pp. 79–89.

Edmunds, S. "Financing Capital Formation," *Harvard Business Review,* Vol. XXVIII, No. 1 (January, 1950), pp. 33–41.

"1948 Survey of Consumer Finances," *Federal Reserve Bulletin,* Vol. XXXIV, No. 7 (July, 1948), pp. 766–80.

Risk Capital and the American Investor. A pamphlet reproduction by the New York Society of Financial Analysts, of a series of addresses made before the Society (March, 1949).

MILLER, S. L. "The Equity Capital Problem," *Harvard Business Review,* Vol. XXVI, No. 6 (November, 1948), pp. 671–79.

Chapter 11

SAVING AND SAVINGS INSTITUTIONS

THE kind of economy we have in the United States depends on saving. The homes, factory buildings, offices, hospitals, roads, machinery— every produced article that comes to us from the past—had to be saved for by earlier generations. To build newer and better homes, factories, offices, hospitals, roads, and to expand and improve our machinery—to pass on more to our children than we started with— demands continued saving.

Saving, which is so necessary for the good of the economy, is also a prudent plan for the individual. From Benjamin Franklin on, countless homilies have been uttered about why it is good and wise to save, and unwise and foolish to waste. There are many ways in which savers use their savings. Some of the major uses are:

1. To invest in one's own business.
2. To invest in a business owned by more than one person. As shown above, in Chapter 7, this may be a partnership, or it may take the form of buying the stocks or bonds of a corporation.
3. To buy or to increase one's equity in a home; i.e., to pay off a part or all of the mortgage.
4. To provide life insurance and retirement-fund reserves.
5. To provide for the future by placing savings in a specially adapted savings institution or special savings investment.

The first two uses listed above have already been discussed in this text, and we need not dwell on them. The third use of savings—home purchase—will be discussed fully in Chapter 15. The fourth use of savings—life insurance and retirement plans—will be discussed in Chapter 12. It is with the fifth or final form that this chapter is concerned—the specialized savings institution or savings investment.

Reasons for Specialized Thrift Institutions

The preceding chapter supplied the most important reason for specialized savings institutions: an ordinary person has neither the time nor the skill to invest wisely. And most small savers do not have enough money to make investment diversification possible. Some agency is needed to supply this judgment and to create diversification; and to act for the small saver. The savings institutions we discuss here fill that role. They are institutions or agencies that the small, poorly informed savers can "trust" with their precious savings.

Another way of explaining this quality is to stress that most savings institutions undertake a contract to return the same number of dollars that is entrusted to them, with any additions that result from interest or dividends. Some investment companies, discussed in Chapter 13, obtain a higher average return by investing in common stocks, but they do not guarantee the return of a fixed number of dollars. These plans appeal to higher-income groups than do the savings institutions discussed here. When the saver puts a given number of dollars into a savings bank, a savings bond, a share account in a savings and loan association, or a credit union, he expects to have the right to withdraw exactly that number of dollars plus any interest or dividends that have accumulated. If the saver had put this money in stocks or bonds, the amount he might realize by sale fluctuates. He might reap a profit, but he also might suffer a loss. He is not guaranteed a fixed number of dollars. Bond prices may be relatively stable (not all bond prices are, however,); but prices of even the best common stocks move up and down.

Stability of the dollar value of his savings is very important to the small saver. Well-to-do persons can invest their money without the fear of having to liquidate unexpectedly. Small savers use their savings, not just for investment reasons, i.e., to earn an interest or dividend return, but to provide a fund for unexpected needs—the proverbial "rainy day" use of savings. If a saver has to liquidate a variable-value investment unexpectedly, he may incur serious loss. Personal emergencies have a way of coming when prices of stocks and some bonds are at their lowest.

This is not just myth: depressions are one of the commonest reasons why people have to dip into savings. But depression is the very time when variable-value investment forms are likely to sell at their lowest prices. The small saver who uses his savings as a personal emergency fund as well as for investment, therefore, has much to gain by putting his money in the thrift agencies discussed in this chapter and by accepting the relatively low return they yield.

It might be said, therefore, that the kinds of institutions dealt with in this chapter are those that collect the small savings of many persons, generally of moderate means, and use the strategic position of greater size for prudent and profitable investment. Savers thus get some investment income, although possibly not so generous a one as that to be had from variable-value investment forms. But even this point is a disputed one; it is not conceded by many investment students.

A second important reason for the specialized savings institution is that the saver is given a relatively more liquid form of asset. The saver can have access to his savings with little or no delay. Indeed, the type of savings discussed in this chapter have come to be labeled "liquid savings" or "liquid assets."

Deposits or shares in most thrift institutions are not legally convertible into cash immediately. But in practice most of them are converted on request. For example, many banks do not have to pay or "cash" savings deposits until thirty, sixty, or ninety days after notice. The institutions issuing the share type of account frequently are not required to redeem their share obligations for a number of years. The almost universal practice of thrift institutions, however, is to waive this requirement and to pay immediately on request.

One of the modern developments is that most thrift institutions adhere to this principle of immediate cash availability. Many institutions, such as savings and loan associations, were not planned originally to provide such service to their participants, but popular demand has encouraged this practice. And it seems to be agreed that liquidity is important to savers; they shun any thrift institution which does not offer it. The question (admittedly an unanswered and unanswerable one) is: Could all savings institutions maintain this practice in bad times as well as good ones?

SAVING: WHEN, BY WHOM, AND FOR WHAT?

The act of saving—of keeping some income from being used for consumption—seems to be so habitual that saving might be expected to be very steady and regular. But such is not the case. Saving varies a great deal. The factors that make it vary are complex and disputed. Economists and others interested in this subject have not agreed on a satisfactory account of just what controls the level of saving. But a few facts about saving are accepted by almost all observers:

1. Saving moves up and down with income; when income is high, so is saving. When income drops, saving usually drops.
2. The proportion of income saved increases with an increase in total income. For example: if a person had been saving 10 per cent of his $5,000 income, he would probably save more than 10 per cent—possibly as much as 15 or 20 per cent—of any increase in his income.
3. In spite of the short-term swings in saving and the more-than-proportionate change in saving with changes of income, the rate of saving is historically stable. While the year-to-year rate varies, the rate by decades, as near as statisticians can figure out, is more stable—about a net 5 per cent of income.

The parallel movement of income and saving is shown in Exhibit 42. This chart includes the abnormal period of the war when saving was extraordinarily high. But the remaining years tend to demonstrate the first two observations reported above. The chart also shows that in bad times saving dwindles to nothing—may even become negative. During extremely bad times, many people live on their past savings.

Exhibit 42

THE RELATION OF SAVING TO INCOME

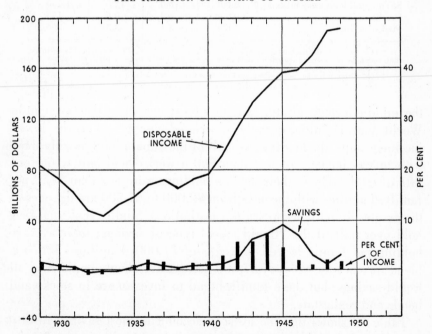

Source: Department of Commerce estimates of national income.

As this chart shows, there was *dis*saving, that is, spending of past savings, during the depression of the 1930's.

Recent Federal Reserve research on saving shows that during all periods, even very prosperous ones, a substantial part of the population is dissaving. These studies show, for example, that during 1948 nearly one third of the population was dissaving, while nearly two thirds were saving. A small number neither saved nor dissaved but just about broke even.

Small Saver Defined

Lest what is said here about the "small saver" be misunderstood, one point should be made very clear: the *very* poor save little; the customers of thrift institutions are those of moderate circumstances,

TABLE 19

AVERAGE BALANCES IN SAVINGS INSTITUTIONS
(For Dates Mostly in 1949)

Institution	Number of Offices	Number of Savers (Millions)*	Savings (Billions of Dollars)	Average Dollars per Account
Commercial banks..........	13,400†	48.0	35.1	731
Mutual saving banks........	531	19.2	19.3	1,005
United States savings bonds..	‡	80.0	56.7	710
Saving and loan associations..	6,000	10.0	12.5	1,250
Credit unions..............	9,000	3.8	0.6	158
Postal savings..............	8,000	4.1	3.3	800

* This figure doubtless contains duplication. The same person will save, not only in more than one type of savings institutions, but often in several institutions of the same type.
† A few commercial banks are almost wholly inactive in savings business.
‡ Sold through banks, post offices, and many other qualified sales agencies.

Source: Compiled from a variety of sources and therefore not precisely comparable in all details.

the middle-income group. Studies of savings show that even after World War II, which greatly stimulated saving among the lower-income groups, the less-favored half of the population (roughly those with family incomes of less than $60 a week) held only about one fifth of total savings; their median holdings were less than $150 per family. Families with incomes from $2,000 to $7,500 are the ones of the greatest importance to savings institutions. Studies show that they hold over half of the "liquid asset" type of savings; their average holding per family is well in excess of $1,000. Families with combined incomes in excess of $7,500 account for about one third of all liquid savings, but these families tend to invest more in stocks and bonds and real estate.

Table 19 shows that the average account in most savings institutions is in the neighborhood of $1,000. It is clear, therefore, that the incomes of customers of thrift institutions are above average. The matter might be put this way: those who have adequate funds for direct investment in stocks and bonds, or who own variable-value types of investment, probably are confined roughly to the upper 5 to 10 per cent; the customers of thrift institutions range from (but also overlap into) this top level on down to the middle level.

The Uses of Savings

Although saving has been studied in detail, our knowledge of the use of savings is surprisingly limited. For example, the amount of total savings has been measured in a number of ways. The various methods lead to different results. Little is known of the amount of savings that is channeled directly into business enterprise. But the limited facts available suggest that savings institutions are receiving a growing proportion of total savings. Higher and more progressive income-tax rates have meant that the proportion of savable income

Exhibit 43
USES OF SAVINGS BY INDIVIDUALS

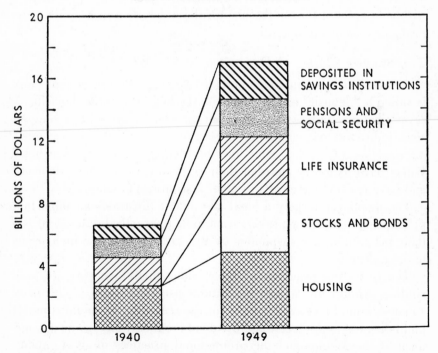

Source: Estimates prepared by author from a variety of sources.

The purchases and sales of stocks and bonds by individuals in 1940 were equal. There was, therefore, no net increase.

available in high-income hands has dwindled. Because of an over-all growth of income the absolute amount and proportion in middle-income groups has increased. And the middle-income groups are the best customers of savings institutions.

The principal uses of saving are shown in Exhibit 43 (p. 325). This shows that savings institutions, broadly interpreted to include the life insurance and pension systems considered in the following chapter, receive and hold a large fraction of total savings.

THE SAVINGS ACCOUNT AND RATES PAID ON IT

The majority of thrift institutions discussed in this chapter were originated and promoted for thrift purposes. Some, however, are tied in with, or were developed from, other lines of business. Savings and loan associations in the beginning were, as their older name (building and loan associations) implies, more concerned with financing home construction than with furnishing an outlet for savings. The savings business of commercial banks is necessarily related to their basic commercial banking businesses. One of the functions of this chapter will be to account for the reasons for these ties, as well as to describe the basic methods of operation.

The Saver's Claim: A Deposit or a Share?

A saver's balance in a commercial bank or a mutual savings bank is called a "deposit" and is subject to the laws governing deposits. A saver's balance in a savings and loan association, a credit union, and some industrial loan companies is generally called a "share account," although recently it has sometimes been called a "savings account." Banks have jealously guarded their right to use the word "deposit" and have resisted the efforts of other institutions to adopt it.

The dispute is largely a legal one, but it illustrates an important principle about savings: savers want to be guaranteed quick access to their money and are suspicious of any savings vehicle which seems to deny them this access.

The operating practices of the various thrift agencies are very similar. Almost all savings institutions use some form of passbook (a small bound book with spaces for the recording of amounts put in and taken out and interest and dividend credits, if any). The appearance of the lobbies and the promotional practices of most savings institutions are very much alike. The greatest differences are primarily in the character of the assets of the various savings institutions. These differences will be explained in detail later, when the several types of institutions are examined separately.

Prevailing Rates of Return

There are fairly sizable differences in the rates of return prevailing at the different types of savings institutions. The major differences represent characteristics of the assets held by the institutions and their resulting earning power. The range of rates and approximate average are shown in Table 20.

TABLE 20

INCOME RATES AT VARIOUS SAVINGS INSTITUTIONS

	Range	Average
Commercial banks................	$\frac{1}{2}$–$2\frac{1}{2}$%	0.9%
Mutual savings banks............	1 –3% (mostly $1\frac{1}{2}$ or 2%)	1.9%
Savings and loan associations......	$1\frac{1}{2}$–3%	$2\frac{1}{4}$% approx.
Credit unions...................	2 –6%	$2\frac{1}{2}$% approx.
Postal savings..................	All same	2%
United States savings bonds, Series E	All same	2.9% (if held to maturity)

Although it would be expected that these rates would be an important matter in the competition prevailing among these institutions, such is not always true in practice. Side by side, operating under nearly identical circumstances, the institutions with the lower rates sometimes outstrip their competitors. Part of the explanation often seems to be in the kind and intensity of promotional campaigns waged.

But while rates are not always important in competition, they may be the decisive factor when all other elements are equal. During recent years the savings and loan associations have done very well; it would be hard to deny the importance of their higher rates in explaining this performance. When the mutual savings banks stepped up their promotion and also raised their dividends in 1948, they took business away from the commercial banks. It would be as wrong to underestimate the importance of rates as to overestimate it.

The differences in return are sometimes thought to reflect the degree of liquidity of the various institutions—i.e., that those with low rates have the highest liquidity. There is some truth in this; but in recent years all types of savings institutions have, in fact, made funds in their savings accounts immediately available. It is not clear that the ordinary user of these institutions understands these remote and subtle differences in ultimate liquidity.

MUTUAL SAVINGS BANKS

Mutual savings banks are the oldest savings institutions in the United States. Two of these institutions were started in the United States in 1816: the Provident Institution for Savings in the Town of Boston, which had the honor of being the first chartered; and the Philadelphia Saving Fund Society, which was the first to be opened to the public for business. The latter is now the third largest mutual savings bank in the United States.

A mutual savings bank is, as its name implies, a "mutual" undertaking. There are no shareholders. The institutions are run not for the profit of shareholders but for the benefit of the depositors. These institutions were initially viewed as philanthropic enterprises. They were patterned after a similar Scottish institution started in 1810 by a clergyman. Reverend Duncan felt that the poverty of the masses would be ameliorated if they were given a place for savings and encouragement to save. He and the other organizers expected these institutions to help relieve the distress of poverty by furnishing a vehicle for savings—a way of helping individuals average out good and bad times. There was a great deal of missionary zeal among the original organizers.

Located Mostly in the East

All but 16 of the 531 mutual savings banks are located in the New England or Middle Atlantic seaboard states. New York and Massachusetts account for more than three fifths of the total number of these savings banks, and these states have almost three fourths of the dollar volume of mutual savings deposits. The location of mutual savings banks by states is given in Table 21.

The height of the boom in establishing these institutions came around the Civil War period. About two thirds of all mutual savings banks were organized between 1850 and 1880. At this time the New England and Middle Atlantic states were not only relatively more important in population than now but were the most prosperous sections of the country and had the largest proportion of income available for saving. By the time savings business developed in any great volume in other parts of the country, the commercial banks and the savings and loan associations had come forward to claim the business. Several times the mutual savings banks have tried to stir up enthusiasm for renewed expansion, but these efforts have failed. Very few new mutual savings banks have been organized in the past two generations.

TABLE 21

LOCATION OF MUTUAL SAVINGS BANKS, DECEMBER 31, 1949

State	Number of Banks	Deposits (Millions of Dollars)
Connecticut.....................	72	1,321
Delaware.......................	2	88
Indiana........................	4	43
Maine..........................	32	236
Maryland.......................	9	398
Massachusetts..................	190	3,249
Minnesota......................	1	158
New Hampshire..................	34	276
New Jersey.....................	23	546
New York.......................	130	11,102
Ohio...........................	3	237
Oregon.........................	1	16
Pennsylvania...................	7	1,062
Rhode Island...................	9	264
Vermont........................	7	85
Washington.....................	3	195
Wisconsin......................	4	12
Total United States...........	531	19,287

Operation and Control

The unique status of mutual savings banks is well demonstrated in the manner of their operation and control. Being without shareholders, there is no ownership interest to elect the board of directors or board of trustees, as would be the case in private corporations. Instead, the governing board of trustees for most mutual savings banks is a self-perpetuating body; the control, very literally, is kept "in trust." The boards of trustees generally serve with little or no remuneration. The trustees are usually business and professional men, and financiers. In selecting their colleagues, boards of trustees try to make the honor of the position adequate to attract people from the very highest level of the business community. As a result, many high-salaried and wealthy men give much time to these institutions with little pecuniary reward. The day-to-day operation of mutual savings banks is carried on by professional bankers.

The Bowery Savings Bank of New York City is the biggest mutual savings bank; its deposits exceed 900 millions of dollars. The Bowery now has its head office on Forty-second Street, across from Grand Central Station in the heart of midtown New York. But once upon a time, it was literally in the Bowery. The humble appeal of the mutual is also illustrated by the name of the second largest mutual: the Emigrant Industrial Savings Bank; and the fourth largest mutual: the Dime Savings Bank of Brooklyn. It is significant that there is only one mutual savings bank in the Wall Street area of New York City: the Seamen's Bank for Savings, at 74 Wall Street. Mutual savings are not institutions of high finance, as "high" finance is popularly understood.

In recent decades mutual savings banks have not grown as rapidly as have other types of savings institutions. Before World War I, mutual savings banks administered a larger volume of assets than either the life insurance companies or the savings departments of commercial banks. Mutuals as a whole have lost ground until they now have only one half or less than half the assets of either of these other two types. This lag may be partially due to the fact that the northeastern part of the United States, where mutuals are concentrated, has not grown so rapidly as have some other sections of the country.

The number of deposit accounts in mutual savings banks is doubtless much larger than the number of individual depositors. Some persons have accounts in two or more institutions and have two or more accounts of different kinds in the same institution. But with allowance for duplication the true number is still large. The average amount due in the so-called "regular" accounts (which exclude savings clubs for Christmas and other special kinds of deposit accounts) is about $1,300.

In most states there is a maximum size for deposit amount in mutuals. In New York State, for example, the maximum is $7,500; in Massachusetts it is $5,000 for a single account.

Mutual savings banks, because they are mutual, do not pay fixed or contractual rates of interest on deposits. Rather, they pay "dividends." But these dividends are maintained at fairly stable rates, and many depositors come to view the dividends as interest. The rates paid by mutuals have usually been higher than those paid by commercial bank savings departments. During 1950, mutual savings banks paid out more than $400 millions of dividends, or about two-thirds of their earnings. This amount included some "extra" dividends. Dividends averaged about 2 per cent on deposits.

Operating Policies

Mutual savings banks earn a return for depositors by investment of the funds they receive. Their investment operations are generally closely hedged about by law. In security investments, for example, the operations are usually confined to the so-called "legal list" of authorized securities. The "legal list" is a device used by some states to regulate the investment operations of life insurance companies, mutual savings banks, and sometimes others. Under this system a state authority publishes and revises, from time to time, a list of securities from which regulated investment institutions must select

TABLE 22

THE BALANCE SHEET OF MUTUAL SAVINGS BANKS,
DECEMBER 31, 1949
(Dollar Amounts in Millions)

Assets

Cash	$ 872
United States Government Securities	11,444
Other Securities	2,368
Mortgage Loans	6,479
Other Loans	106
Other Assets	233
Total	$21,502

Liabilities

Deposits	$19,287
Other Liabilities	94
Surplus, Guaranty, and Unallocated Income Accounts	2,121
Total	$21,502
Number of Depositors (millions of persons)	19.2

their purchases. These listings are usually based on general investment standards or rules contained in the statutes governing these and other financial institutions. This safeguard was imposed because it has been felt that special caution should be observed in dealing with the savings of small savers; it was generally believed that income should be sacrificed to safety. But some have felt that the close legal control has been too strict, that it has destroyed investment initiative.

The consolidated balance sheet of all mutual savings banks is given in Table 22. As this table shows, federal government securities constitute the largest single asset of mutual savings banks. This, of course, is a fairly recent development. For many years prior to World War II, assets of mutual savings banks were about evenly divided between bonds and real estate mortgages. While mutual savings banks never went into mortgage lending to the extent that savings and loan associations have, some individual mutuals carried large mortgage portfolios. The mutual savings banks located in larger cities have followed mortgage practices more like the life insurance companies than have the savings and loan associations: they lend to a considerable extent on apartment buildings, commercial properties, and other large real estate ventures. In contrast, many savings and loan associations lend solely on smaller residential dwellings, and many are limited by law in the amount they can put in bigger types of real estate properties.

Relative Safety

Mutual savings banks have had an exceptional record of safety. Few have failed; and in these few failures, the losses to depositors have been relatively moderate. Because of their investment concentration in railroad securities and real estate, mutuals had investment problems about as great as any other group in the early and mid-1930's. But the depositors of mutuals did not "run" them (few people withdrew deposits in blind panic) as drastically as did the depositors in commercial banks. With less pressure for liquidation, the mutuals were rehabilitated with minimum losses.

More than 190 mutual savings banks of the 531 total are insured by the Federal Deposit Insurance Corporation. The bulk of the insured mutuals—over 150—are located in New York and New Jersey. All of the mutual savings banks in these states are insured (also true of the 7 mutuals in Pennsylvania, the 3 in Ohio, 3 in Washington, and the single mutual in Minnesota and Oregon). Massachusetts and Connecticut have their own state systems of mutual savings deposit insurance. Three mutual savings banks are members of the Federal Reserve System, and 26 are members of the Federal Home Loan Bank System.

A "Central Bank" for the Mutuals

The mutual savings banks of New York State organized and own a commercial bank called the "Savings Bank Trust Company." This bank has acted for them as a kind of central bank. While, as yet, there has not been any period of strain in which to test the facility of this new instrument, it promises to make the mutual savings bank system more liquid. It certainly could help in the mobilization of all available reserves if there were a need. In the meantime, it has acted as a depository for the correspondent balances of mutuals. Because the Savings Bank Trust Company has been a money maker, the mutual savings banks have thereby been able to realize some return from these balances which otherwise would have been left without reward in other money-market commercial banks. The Savings Bank Trust Company has also assisted in the investment planning of individual banks. Its recommendations to the state authorities about "legal-list" changes have been respected and followed.

SAVINGS DEPARTMENTS OF COMMERCIAL BANKS

Commercial banks entered the savings business long after the mutuals were well started. But while the mutuals have remained in the northeastern area of the United States, commercial banks have gone into the savings business throughout the entire country. With the growth of our nation to the west, and, to a lesser extent, to the south, commercial banks have had the advantage of operating in the newer, more rapidly growing areas.

In dollar volume of savings, the commercial banks passed the mutuals about 1910. During the 1920's the commercial banks ran up a

Exhibit 44

RELATIVE GROWTH OF TIME DEPOSITS IN MUTUAL SAVINGS BANKS
AND IN COMMERCIAL BANKS

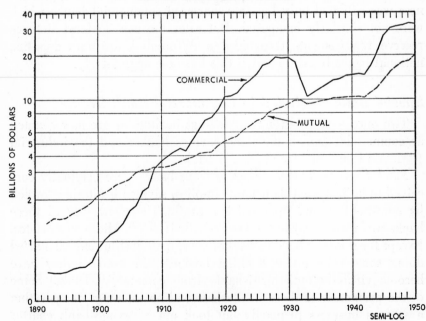

Source: *Banking and Monetary Statistics* and *Federal Reserve Bulletin.*

sizable margin over the mutuals, but a part of this margin was lost during the depression of the early 1930's. The gap widened with World War II until commercial banks now hold practically twice the dollar volume of mutual savings banks. These relative changes may be seen in Exhibit 44 (p. 333).

The commercial banks show several ups and downs in their activity as a savings agency. During the war, commercial banks accounted for one eighth to one fifth of liquid individual savings; mutual savings banks varied between one twentieth and one tenth. But in 1948, mutual savings banks raised dividend rates and initiated vigorous competitive campaigns. In the New York City area they managed to capture a large part of new savings; the gains of savings and loan associations in that area were below national averages, and some commercial banks lost savings accounts. The competitive picture remains fluid.

Effect of Federal Reserve Act

Prior to the establishment of the Federal Reserve System in 1913, national banks had been required to maintain reserves against time and savings deposits as large as those against demand deposits. This chilled national-bank interest in savings; in the main, savings business was solicited only by state-chartered commercial banks which were not similarly hampered. But after the new Federal Reserve reserve requirements recognized a differential for time deposits, national banks began to solicit this business aggressively.

Special Banks Included in Commercial Bank Group

Two once-separate groups of savings institutions are now counted as commercial banks: the stock savings banks; and the industrial ("Morris Plan" or "Hood Plan") banks.

Stock Savings Banks. Stock savings banks were originally conceived to be just what their name implies, savings institutions owned by stockholders and operated for profit. The chartering of these banks was recognized in the laws of a half dozen Midwestern states. Except for a few isolated cases, however, these institutions all started doing some commercial banking business. In practice they have become virtually indistinguishable from commercial banks. Some of the promoters of these institutions had no intention of operating a savings business primarily but took out a savings-bank charter because the capital requirements were often smaller for this form than for an outright commercial bank. There are now only two true stock savings banks of any great significance.

Industrial Banks. The industrial banks are primarily consumer credit institutions and as such are described in Chapter 6. But they have also become important savings institutions. A number of years ago these institutions obtained most of their funds from various kinds of "investment certificates" or share accounts. A few continue to do so, but now many are chartered as commercial banks and have deposit accounts. And during the past decades industrial banks have been becoming more like commercial banks in still other respects. They have become so indistinguishable that they are included in the commercial bank statistics and are regulated as commercial banks in most areas."

Use of Savings Funds

Since commercial banks invest funds that are received from both commercial and savings accounts, there is no clear line of distinction: the assets of a bank represent the investment of both savings and commercial deposits. It would be artificial to speak of certain assets as applying to, or representing the use of savings funds, and other assets as applying to, or representing the use of commercial funds.

There are two evidences of changes in investment policy due to the acceptance of time and savings deposits by commercial banks. When the Federal Reserve Act recognized a differential in reserve requirements for savings deposits, it also provided that national banks could make real estate mortgage loans up to one half (later changed to 60 per cent) of time deposits. It was felt that such real estate mortgages were not liquid enough for the use of commercial funds but that savings funds could be invested in them. The second change was the growth of investment in long-term corporate bonds. Since banks have become extensive investors in such securities, it is sometimes forgotten that this is a fairly recent development. But in the decade following World War I, there was the first emergence of sizable commercial bank investment in such long-term obligations. The usual explanation and justification of this practice was the growth of savings deposits.

Segregation of Savings

In some states, commercial banks which operate savings departments are required to segregate the savings funds and to invest them according to special rules, not unlike those applying to mutual savings banks. Except for such instances, commercial banks are under no greatly different investment restrictions for savings deposits than the general regulations under which they operate. National banks get most of their latitude for investment in real estate mortgages from their savings deposits. But even when not curbed by legal provisions, commercial banks are likely to be strongly influenced in their investment policies by the proportions of savings deposits they have.

During the 1920's, under competitive pressure, the rates paid on savings deposits by commercial banks ran fairly high; but since this period, these rates have generally been rather low. Some justification of the low rates can be found in the somewhat more active (and unstable) nature of savings accounts in commercial banks. There is more "in-and-out" action in commercial bank savings accounts than in almost any other savings form. Also, past experience seems to show that, when depressions set in, commercial banks suffer more pressure for withdrawal or liquidation of savings than do other savings institutions.

UNITED STATES SAVINGS BONDS

United States savings bonds are the newest of the savings vehicles. Because of the great promotional sale of these bonds during World War II, they have come to be used commonly. The $57 billion of these securities outstanding is estimated to be spread among (or at least registered in the name of) more than 80 million persons.

Three classes of savings bonds are currently being sold, distinguished by their series letters, "E," "F," and "G." A person can acquire up to $10,000 maturity value of Series E bonds in any one year; the limit for F's and G's is $100,000 cost value in any one year. The Series E bonds account for about 60 per cent of the United States savings bonds outstanding. The average Series E bondholder has bonds with a cash value of less than $500. A survey of savings made in 1946 indicated that more of the very-low-income persons held Series E bonds than any other savings form. The F's and G's are bought mainly by persons with higher incomes or by trust accounts.

The United States savings bonds are nonmarketable obligations, not usable as collateral for borrowing. They are liquid only because the issuer, the United States government, undertakes to redeem them virtually on demand anytime sixty days after they are sold.

The interest on United States savings bonds depends on the length of time they are held. If E's are held to maturity, they yield 2.9 per cent; the F's and G's yield 2.5 per cent. But for shorter periods (that is, bonds redeemed before maturity), the yield is relatively low.

The low return for the early years was devised in order to discourage early redemption and encourage holding to maturity. This works out in two ways. For example: if a Series E bond is held for 2½ years, the cashing price of $77 for each $75 invested means an interest return of only slightly over 1 per cent (1.06 to be very

TABLE 23

SERIES E UNITED STATES SAVINGS BOND

Illustration based on:
- Maturity value.....................$100
- Issue price.........................$ 75
- Yield if held to maturity........... 2.9%

Period after Issue Date (Years)	Redemption Value	Yield to Indicated Redemption Date (Per Cent)	Yield from Indicated Redemption Date to Maturity (Per Cent)
First ½..........	$ 75.00	0.00	2.90
½–1............	75.00	0.00	3.05
1 –1½..........	75.50	0.67	3.15
1½–2............	76.00	0.88	3.25
2 –2½..........	76.50	0.99	3.38
2½–3............	77.00	1.06	3.52
3 –3½..........	78.00	1.31	3.58
3½–4............	79.00	1.49	3.66
4 –4½..........	80.00	1.62	3.75
4½–5............	81.00	1.72	3.87
5 –5½..........	82.00	1.79	4.01
5½–6............	83.00	1.85	4.18
6 –6½..........	84.00	1.90	4.41
6½–7............	86.00	2.12	4.36
7 –7½..........	88.00	2.30	4.31
7½–8............	90.00	2.45	4.26
8 –8½..........	92.00	2.57	4.21
8½–9............	94.00	2.67	4.17
9 –9½..........	96.00	2.76	4.12
9½–10..........	98.00	2.84	4.08
10..............	100.00	2.90	....

exact!). But if this bond is held to maturity, it will, by repayment of the $100, yield a return of 2.9 per cent. The net yield for the remaining 7½ years (that is, the compounding of the $77 into $100) means an implicit interest return of 3.52 per cent. This holding rate goes over 4 per cent in the later years of the life of a savings bond. Table 23 shows the schedule of both partial rates.

Considering the extreme promotional pressure used in marketing the United States savings bonds during the war, it was widely feared that a large volume of these bonds would be redeemed soon after the war. This fear turned out to be groundless. It has been true, however, that the amount of new money put into savings bonds in recent periods has fallen off materially.

POSTAL SAVINGS SYSTEM

The Postal Savings System was authorized by Congress in 1910. There had been agitation for such a system in prior years, but establishment was opposed as being socialistic and unnecessary. However, the severe panic of 1907 temporarily closed many banks. It was this panic, more than any other single event, which kindled sentiment for the formation of the Federal Reserve System.

At the same time, the proposed Postal Savings System was pulled out of a legislative pigeonhole and enacted into law. It was argued that the banks did not furnish satisfactory savings facilities; therefore, the government should do so. A further factor, already mentioned, was that national banks were (in 1910) still observing the National Banking Act (pre–Federal Reserve) reserve requirements which did not distinguish between demand and savings deposits. As a result, only state-chartered commercial banks had an active interest in soliciting savings deposits. When it is recognized that the mutual savings banks, except for a few scattered ones, were located in the northeastern section of the country the demands for the system can be appreciated.

In order to minimize competition with private savings institutions, the rate of interest prescribed for postal savings was set at 2 per cent, well below the rates then prevailing in private savings institutions.

Competition with Private Savings Institutions

Soon after the Postal Savings System was established, the Federal Reserve Act with its lower reserve requirement for savings deposits was passed. This resulted in a spurt of promotion for savings business by commercial banks. Commercial banks offered 3 and 4 per cent for savings deposits—sometimes more. Low-rate postal savings could not match such vigorous competition. For the first twenty years of existence, postal savings held a relatively unimportant place in the system of savings institutions.

But the banking difficulties of the early 1930's changed the position of postal savings. Within four years almost 10,000 commercial banks disappeared, the majority as the result of failures. People withdrew savings from commercial banks and put them in postal savings. From 1929 to 1933 the Postal Savings System grew almost eight times in size—from $150 million to $1,200 million.

Later in the 1930's, and more particularly during World War II, still another factor stimulated postal-savings growth. During the 1930's interest rates had been declining, and the rates paid by thrift institutions had come down. The 2 per cent postal savings rate, originally a low one, came to be relatively high. During World War II, postal savings had nearly a threefold expansion—from $1,200 millions to $3,300 millions—rather more than most of the major savings institutions. Since the war, postal savings have stopped growing; they have even declined a little.

Extent of System

About 8,000 post offices and branches have postal savings windows. Anyone ten years of age or older may open an account with a $1 deposit. (All deposits must be in multiples of one dollar.) The maximum account for an individual is $2,500.

The Postal Savings System sets aside 5 per cent of deposits for a safety or reserve fund; the remainder is invested mainly in United States government bonds. In the beginning it was expected that most postal savings funds would be redeposited in local banks. At one time this was considered an important provision, since it meant that banks and localities would not be deprived of the use of funds saved in those communities. The rate required of the redepositing banks is 2½ per cent (to cover the 2 per cent paid out plus expenses), and that 2½ rate is now more than banks feel they can afford at prevailing interest rates on their investments. The mechanics for redeposit still exist but are seldom used.

SAVINGS AND LOAN ASSOCIATIONS

Savings and loan associations, and similar organizations, were operating more than a hundred and fifty years ago in England and Scotland. The Oxford Provident Building Association was the first association organized in this country. It was started in 1831 in a suburb of Philadelphia. The most rapid period of development came in the housing boom which followed the War between the States. By 1893, more than 5,800 such associations had been formed.

In the beginning, savings and loan associations were literally cooperative clubs for home building. They usually did not have regular offices, and business might be transacted only one evening a week.

They were operated with the part-time services of members. Each member obligated himself to put a given sum into the association regularly. The members took turns borrowing money with which to build a home. Sometimes the privilege of borrowing was allotted by drawing numbers from a hat. Originally it was intended to disband these associations after every member had built himself a home.

But the associations came to be more formal, to be regulated by law, to keep regular office hours, and to employ full-time officers and clerks. They became more impersonal. Sometimes the moving spirit in the organization of these associations was a real estate promoter or builder who was anxious to have access to some institution that would finance his operations and the buyers of properties he sold. While the connection of builders with these associations was frequently high-minded and principled, this was not always so.

Associations now tend to emphasize less their capacity as financiers of real estate deals and to emphasize more their function as savings institutions. The common title used up until the early 1930's was "building and loan association." Then in the 1930's, there was a general switch to "savings and loan association." Still more recently there has been a move toward calling these concerns "savings associations." The evolution of titles is reflective of the change in emphasis.

There are approximately 6,000 savings and loan associations in the United States. They had total assets of approximately $13 billion as of December 31, 1949. There were 10 million persons with savings accounts in these institutions and 3 million paying for homes with credit from them. Savings and loan associations are found in every state and in the District of Columbia, and there are few communities of over 10,000 population without an active association. In some communities they are known under different names—"building and homestead associations" and "co-operative banks"—but they are all the same type of savings and home-financing institution.

Savings and Loan Association Operations

During recent years, savings and loan associations have attracted from one tenth to one eighth of new liquid savings. Associations now pay dividends of 2 to 3 per cent on their accounts. The exact rate depends upon the practice of the individual institution, which in turn depends in great part upon the earnings on its portfolio of mortgage loans. The mortgage loan investments of associations range from 4 per cent (veterans' guaranteed loans) to 6 per cent. The typical non-FHA, nonveteran loan written in recent years paid interest at the rate of 4½ or 5 per cent.

Dual System of Charter

Savings and loan associations operate under a dual system of charter. There are federally chartered savings and loan associations and associations chartered by the state governments. Of the 6,000 associations in the country, approximately 1,500 operate under federal charters and are known as "federal savings and loan associations." The governmental authority that grants the charter to the institution supervises it. This supervision involves an annual examination of accounts and the security behind the loans and of compliance with the code or charter governing the association.

The policies of a savings and loan association are determined by a board of directors. These boards are drawn from local businessmen and professional men and are elected at an annual meeting of the "shareholders." A professional staff conducts the day-to-day affairs of an association.

Accounts Insured

In a technical legal sense, the account in a savings and loan association is not a liability, as is true of the savings deposit in a commercial bank; it is more nearly an owner's equity. But in practice the associations have tried to give their accounts all the advantages of a bank deposit. Among other attractive features, they have organized an insurance of such accounts which is similar to deposit insurance. Approximately half of the associations, representing over 70 per cent of the assets of all associations, have their savers' accounts insured up to $10,000 by the Federal Savings and Loan Insurance Corporation (FSLIC), a government corporation. The operations of the Federal Savings and Loan Insurance Corporation parallel those of the Federal Deposit Insurance Corporation (FDIC). The holder of an insured share balance in a savings and loan association which becomes insolvent has these options:

1. He may ask for the same share balance in some solvent savings and loan association.
2. He may receive the following: 10 per cent of his share balance in cash; 45 per cent in one-year non-interest-bearing FSLIC debentures; and 45 per cent in three-year non-interest-bearing FSLIC debentures.

The first option is the one more often exercised.

Some 3,700 associations, representing over 90 per cent of the assets of the business, are members of the Federal Home Loan Bank System. This system is similar in some respects to the Federal Reserve

System. It provides a quick source of additional funds if needed to meet the withdrawal of savings.

Current Condition and Activities

As shown in Table 24, savings and loan institutions have invested 5 per cent of assets in cash and bank deposits, about 11 per cent of their assets in government bonds, and most of the balance in monthly-payment or "amortized" real estate loans. Investment in real estate loans is limited, in the case of federal savings and loan associations and most state-chartered institutions, to amortized first mortgage loans on homes and small apartments in the immediate and surrounding communities.

TABLE 24

BALANCE SHEET OF SAVINGS AND LOAN ASSOCIATIONS, DECEMBER 31, 1949

	Amount (In Millions)	Per Cent
Assets		
Cash	$ 658	5.0
United States Government Bonds	1,459	11.2
Mortgage Loans	10,498	80.3
Other Assets	452	3.5
Total Assets	$13,067	100.0
Liabilities		
Share Capital	$11,081	84.8
Borrowed Money	603	4.6
Loans in Process	390	3.0
Other Liabilities	22	0.2
Reserves and Undivided Profits	971	7.4
Total Liabilities	$13,067	100.0

Source: Research Department, United States Savings and Loan League.

Federal savings and loan associations may not lend more than 80 per cent of the appraised value of the mortgaged property except for FHA-insured loans and veterans' guaranteed loans (described in Chapter 15). The legal limit of loan to appraised value at state-chartered institutions varies from 70 to 80 per cent for noninsured loans. Prior to the depression of the 1930's, savings and loan associations in most states were empowered to loan on any real estate (not merely *improved urban residential* real estate, as is the law for most associations today) ; and in Pennsylvania, associations could and did lend on the security of second and third mortgages. Bitter experience with such low-grade credit during the depression of the early 1930's resulted in the legal limitation of loans to the safer and more liquid urban home mortgage loans.

Savings and loan associations in 1949 loaned an estimated $3.6

billion on homes and small apartments. Table 25 shows the purposes of savings and loan credits.

TABLE 25

HOME MORTGAGE LOANS MADE BY SAVINGS AND LOAN
ASSOCIATIONS IN 1949

(*In Millions*)

Purpose of Loan

Purpose of Loan	
Home construction	$1,077
Home purchase	1,541
Refinancing	357
Reconditioning	188
Loans for all other purposes	428
	$3,591

Source: Federal Home Loan Bank Board.

CREDIT UNIONS

Credit unions are primarily consumer credit agencies (they were considered more fully in Chapter 6). But they are becoming more important as savings outlets. Savers' accounts are usually in "share" form, and they are presumably no more liquid than the assets held by these associations. As in the case of savings and loan associations, however, their portfolios have become more liquid with time. Most credit unions follow the practice of repurchasing shares on demand, and their shares are treated as savings accounts by most members. Table 26 shows the leading facts about credit unions in the United States.

TABLE 26

CREDIT UNIONS, 1948
(Dollar Amounts in Millions)

	Total	Federal	State
Number	9,329	4,058	5,271
Members	3.8 million	1.6 million	2.1 million
Loans outstanding	$399	$138	$260
Share accounts	$604	$235	$369
Assets	$702	$258	$443

Source: *Monthly Labor Review*, September, 1949, p. 276.

Since these institutions are "mutual" or co-operative, as is true of mutual savings banks and savings and loan associations, the return on shares is in the form of "dividends." Unlike mutual savings banks, credit unions are operated by officers elected by their members, and the dividend rate is often set by vote of the membership.

The great curb on the growth of credit unions has been the problem of finding a use for the funds placed with them. At first, most credit unions had no problem finding loan outlets for all the funds placed with them. But with the growth of liquidity and the relative decline in the use of consumer credit during the war, these institutions had less demand for their loans. Many of them were forced to limit the amount that a shareholder could put into them. Because of their small average size, these institutions are not too well equipped to provide funds for purposes other than consumer credit.

FACE-AMOUNT INSTALLMENT CERTIFICATES

This particular form of thrift institution is rather rare, there now being only one concern of any size which operates in this field.

A face-amount installment certificate is a sort of contractual savings plan. The buyer contracts to make monthly payments of a fixed amount for a set period—usually ten or fifteen years. If this contract is completed, the seller contracts to repay a lump-sum amount which represents the amounts saved plus interest. If the buyer fails to meet the payments and surrenders his contract in the early years, his refund may be only a part of what he has paid in; if the buyer maintains the contract for a number of years but fails to carry it to maturity, the amount returned to him will usually equal his payments, but with a relatively small interest return.

CONTEMPORARY PROBLEMS OF SAVINGS INSTITUTIONS

The course of events has tended to make the thrift institutions a relatively more important sector of our economy than formerly. These institutions are the savings vehicles of the middle-income group; and what affects the middle-income group, affects these institutions. Several developments of this sort can be mentioned. First, progressive income taxes have reduced the relative inequality of income distribution. Second, World War II seemed to increase the proportion of income which went to middle- and lower-income groups. Third, the increase in productivity during the past several decades has helped all income groups; but it has brought a large part of the lower-income groups beyond the level of bare survival and left them with the opportunity to save without undue curtailment of current consumption.

But the growing importance of these institutions has been paralleled by the emergence of some very knotty problems.

1. During the 1930's it was difficult for savings institutions to find investment outlets for their funds which were safe and adequately

remunerative. Some savings institutions reduced the vigor with which they solicited savings from the public. World War II and post-war capital demands existing at present seem to have solved this problem for the moment. No one knows whether or not it is solved for the future. Some very respectable authorities fear it is not.

2. Low long-term interest rates during the 1930's increase the vulnerability of thrift institutions to interest-rate fluctuations. The long-term yields and prices of investment obligations such as bonds move in opposite directions. When yields go up, prices go down. Thus, if long-term interest rates go up appreciably, the market value of even the highest-quality securities bought during the period of low interest rates would go down. To be specific: During 1943 to 1945, many thrift institutions bought 2½ per cent bonds from the United States government in the war loan drives. These obligations had, when sold, a twenty-five-year maturity. If in 1953, or thereabouts, the market yield for these obligations should go to 3½ per cent (and historically long-term rates have often been at or even above this level), then these bonds would be worth only about $85 for each $100 paid for them originally. This 15 per cent loss in book value could be very serious for many thrift institutions, or, what may be more important, could shake public confidence in these institutions.

3. A third problem is the increased flow of savings through savings institutions. This flow raises the paradoxical problem of an over-supply of savings seeking safe and secure forms of investment while a shortage of risk capital is sometimes claimed to exist. The effort to make savings institutions truly safe is understandable. Concern that the small saver might lose command of his savings is commendable. But if an increased portion of the funds seeking investment go through savings institutions, it is hard to make both the process safe for the saver and the capital available in the form needed by business enter-prise. The great disparities between bond and high-grade common-stock yields during recent years illustrates this problem eloquently.

4. One of the grave problems of thrift institutions is that, while the stability of their dollar liabilities are well assured, the value of the dollars has not been. The subject of money values and price levels is outside this chapter, but it bears in an important way on the public view of thrift forms. Those, for example, who put money in a savings account or buy savings bonds and then find, after a time, that interest accumulation has failed to keep pace with monetary deterioration, are likely to take a jaundiced view of saving. For example, those who put $18.75 into a savings bond ten years ago and now cash the bond for $25.00 discover that the $25.00 will buy

less than the $18.75 did ten years ago. This discovery does not encourage thrift. There is, of course, nothing that either the savers or the savings institutions per se can do about this matter; it is a grave social problem tied with questions of economic instability and the proper management of government fiscal and monetary operations. Wars are generally periods of unstable price levels; postwar periods are also troubled times. And it seems to make little difference whether the war effort is a cold or a hot one! The moral remains clear: savings institutions and national savings habits probably would have a hard time surviving excessive price-level fluctuations.

—ROLAND I. ROBINSON

QUESTIONS AND PROBLEMS

1. Why do so many people trust their precious savings to specialized savings institutions?
2. Why is liquidity more important to the small saver than to the larger investor?
3. At least two or three kinds of savings figures appear in every *Federal Reserve Bulletin*. Study a *Bulletin* and report as many such figures as can be found.
4. From what income levels do savings institutions draw their customers?
5. How do the rates paid by savings institutions influence savers: in the amounts they save, or where they put them?
6. Savings institutions advertise widely in newspapers, on billboards, by direct-mail solicitations, and sometimes by radio programs. Cite at least five such recent advertisements and identify the institution according to the plan of classification used in Chapter 10.
7. If you live in a New England state, list as many mutual savings banks as you know.
8. How do mutual savings banks differ from commercial banks?
9. If you had money which you expected to use as a down-payment on a house sometime within the next two years and you wanted to have it quickly and certainly available for this purpose, what would be a good savings vehicle to use for this purpose?
10. List all (or some number up to ten) of the savings institutions located in the town in which you live, and classify by type.
11. In what respects do savings and loan associations differ from commercial banks? In what respects are they similar?
12. "Savings institutions are as safe as human ingenuity and integrity can make them. But the value of the dollars they hold is far from safe!" What does this mean?

BIBLIOGRAPHY

The most important modern researches into savings are the various surveys of consumer finances made by the Survey Research Center of the University of Michigan for the Board of Governors of the Federal Reserve System. The results of these surveys have been published in annual series of articles in the *Federal Reserve Bulletin,* and later reprinted in separate volumes. The articles in the 1949 survey included:

"Consumer Ownership and Use of Liquid Assets," *Bulletin,* August, 1949.
"Distribution of Consumer Income in 1948," *Bulletin,* July, 1949.
"Distribution of Consumer Savings in 1948," *Bulletin,* January, 1950.
"Durable Goods Expenditures in 1948 and Buying Plans for 1949," *Bulletin,* June, 1949.
"General Financial Position and Economic Outlook of Consumers," *Bulletin,* June, 1950.
"Home Ownership and Expenditures for Housing," *Bulletin,* September, 1949.
"Ownership of Non-Liquid Assets," *Bulletin,* October, 1949.
"Special Data on Automobile Ownership," *Bulletin,* November, 1949.

A somewhat older but still useful account of savings institutions in general appeared in *Banking Studies,* published by the Federal Reserve System in 1941, in the following articles:

Kennedy, David M. "Credit and Savings Institutions Other than Banks," p. 143.
Robinson, Roland I. "Commercial Bank Operations," p. 169.

Two modern articles on the investment problems of savings institutions appeared in the *Journal of Finance:*

Guthmann, Harry G. "The Movement of Debt to Institutions and Its Implications for the Interest Rate," March, 1950.
Jones, Homer. "The Flow of Savings," Part I, October, 1948; Part II, March, 1949.

A book of rather wider application than indicated by its title is:

Welfling, Weldon. *Savings Banking in New York State.* Durham, N.C.: Duke University Press, 1939.

A book of detailed study of the results of mutual savings banking in Massachusetts is:

Lintner, John. *Mutual Savings Banks in the Savings and Mortgage Markets,* Cambridge, Mass.: Harvard University Press, 1948.

Chapter 12

INSURANCE COMPANIES AND RETIREMENT PLANS

No ONE taking the family automobile out for a Sunday afternoon drive can be sure of coming home alive. Indeed, staying home is by no means safe: bathtubs and cellar stairs may be vicious life takers. A pair of roller skates left carelessly on a front walk may injure a visitor badly—and expose the householder to a large damage suit. Fire can cost a family their home; burglars can get their jewelry; a vagrant golf ball can cost one a life's savings.

At any one moment and for any one person these risks are remote; but when they strike, their consequences can be devastating. By co-operating in sharing these risks, however, their severity can be reduced to manageable proportions. Insurance is one of the devices by which people co-operate in sharing risk; and since life insurance is the leading application of the insurance principle, this subject will receive principal attention in this chapter. But several other related applications will also be studied. Annuities are based on the insurance principle and are generally sold by life insurance companies, and so they, too, will be considered. Casualty insurance, such as for fire, marine, and similar risks, will also be covered. And various retirement plans—governmental social security and private pension systems—are of a related nature and will be included.

LIFE INSURANCE

Life insurance is not insurance that one will live but is insurance of some financial protection for those who survive. While life insurance is used to give protection to many sorts of relationships, the commonest relationship requiring such protection is the family. When a man assumes the responsibility of a wife and particularly of chil-

dren, it is partly a financial responsibility: the responsibility to provide support. As long as a man lives and keeps his health, he usually
can discharge this responsibility by working. But some men die pre-
maturely. Unless they have inherited money or saved a lot early in
life—both uncommon occurrences—about the only way of discharg-
ing the responsibility of family support in the event of premature
death is by life insurance.

Exhibit 45

GROWTH OF LIFE INSURANCE "IN FORCE" AND ASSETS

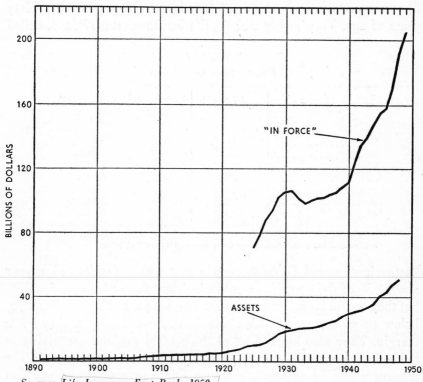

Source: *Life Insurance Fact Book, 1950.*

This fact alone might account for the great importance of insurance, but there is another fact which heightens the importance:
because of the prepayment of insurance premiums through the level-
premium type of policies (to be explained in a few pages), life insurance has become the major traditional private savings institution.
Life insurance companies administer more dollars of savings than
any other private savings institution. The impressive dollar totals of
life insurance may be ascertained from Exhibit 45. *Table 3 found in the
appendix*

The Insurance Principle

Insurance uses the averaging principle. Many events that are separately very uncertain are predictable in large groups. Human life, uncertain for any one person, is fairly predictable for large groups. The likelihood of fire or of an automobile accident is less determinable from large numbers; but the margins of error in prediction, although wider, are such that the insurance principle can be applied to these cases.

The operation of life insurance can be demonstrated by a simple illustration. Pick at random 100,000 healthy Americans all thirty years of age. Very highly trained life insurance statisticians, called

TABLE 27

C.S.O. MORTALITY TABLE

Age (Years)	Alive at Beginning of Year*	Number Dying during Next Year	Ratio of Those Who Die to Those Alive at Beginning of Year
30...................	100,000	356	0.00356
31...................	99,644	372	0.00373
32...................	99,272	389	0.00392
33...................	98,883	407	0.00412
....	......	......	
40...................	95,538	590	0.00618
41...................	94,948	626	0.00659

*The number alive at the beginning of each year is the number alive at the beginning of the year before, minus those who died during that year.

"actuaries," would be quite certain that within the following year about 356 of these persons would die. They do not know which 356, but they would be fairly sure of the number; it might fall somewhat below or go somewhat above this figure, but not by a very great margin. They also know that, of the 99,644 probably surviving to the end of the year, about 372 would die in the following year. The actuary would be able to say with a fair degree of confidence that about 4,462 of these persons would die before they reached the age of forty. And at that age, of the remaining 95,538, about 590 would die before reaching the age of forty-one.

These figures can be shown in a simple table; see Table 27. The figures are taken from the Commissioners 1941 Standard Ordinary Mortality Table, based on 1930–40 experience in this country. This table was adopted by the state authorities in charge of insurance regulation and is used by life insurance companies to compute their premiums, the price paid for insurance protection.

The figures in the third column of the table can be used as the basis of a very simple life insurance plan. Any group of American males large enough to average out the living-dying hazards could join such an insurance plan; those thirty years of age would pay $3.56 for each $1,000 face value of insurance; those thirty-one years of age would pay $3.73; those forty years of age, $6.18; and so on. These amounts are "premiums" and are calculated as follows: 0.00356 of $1,000 is $3.56, etc. The payments to the beneficiaries of those who die would use up the funds "put in" by those insured. In practice, insurance premiums are computed by somewhat more complex means and include other factors; but for illustration, these figures and facts will serve.

Most insurance companies require the insured to pass a medical examination before being accepted; if this were not so, those who found themselves with serious diseases would rush to buy insurance and the insurance companies would suffer what actuaries call "adverse selection."

Types of Life Insurance Contracts

The example just cited, based on Table 27, illustrates the first type of insurance contract—term insurance. Strictly speaking, it was one-year term insurance. In practice, term insurance is more often sold for longer periods, such as five or ten years. The difference in rates is not material; using the same figures as above, a pure five-year term at age thirty would cost about $4.00 per $1,000 each year for five years. When selling and administrative costs (see p. 356) together with an allowance for convertibility and renewability have been added to the "pure" cost of insurance, the gross cost to buyers would be about a half larger.

Term insurance rates creep up year by year. As one grows older, the chances of dying increase. But as people grow older, the cost of insurance increases markedly—and just when they are least able to pay higher costs. In our example above, a man of sixty would have to pay $26.60 per $1,000 for insurance; at sixty-five, $39.65; at seventy, $59.30; at seventy-five, $88.65; and at eighty, $131.85—all exclusive of operational costs. For a person who wants or needs insurance protection for his whole life, the cost of term insurance ultimately would seem unreasonably high. This high cost might tempt such a person to drop his insurance while it is still needed.

Term insurance is often "renewable" and "convertible." Insurance is "renewable" when another contract of the same type (though at a higher price because of advanced age) can be taken out without medical examination. It is "convertible" when it can be exchanged for a contract of some other type without further medical examination. If it were not for the requirement of minimum health standards, renewability and convertibility would mean nothing; for so long as a person's health permits, he can usually buy more insurance.

To overcome the obstacle of an ever-increasing insurance premium, a second type of insurance contract, the so-called "level-premium" insurance, has been developed. This is the most popular of

Exhibit 46

COMPARATIVE PREMIUM COST OF TERM AND WHOLE LIFE INSURANCE

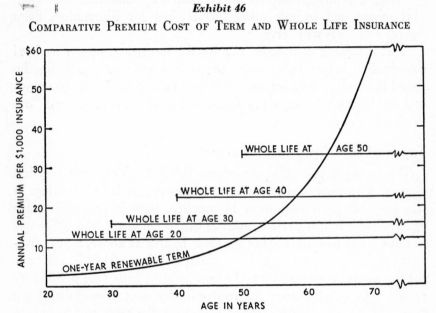

Source: Adapted from *Life Insurance Fact Book.*

all forms. The way in which the premium cost is figured out is too complicated for discussion here; but actuaries have perfected methods for determining the fixed amount, which, paid year after year, will average out to be the same as an advancing term insurance premium. The most popular form of this is the "ordinary" or "whole" life insurance. A comparison of the cost of our first two forms of insurance is presented in Exhibit 46.

The upsweeping curve in Figure 46 is the net rate for one-year renewable term insurance. Any buyer could obtain insurance for the first year at the rate applicable to his age. But as he grew older, he would year by year, pay higher premiums. In contrast, the buyer of whole life insurance always pays a higher rate for his insurance at time of application than he would for term insurance. But the premium remains the same as long as he lives. With allowance for the compounding effects of interest, whole life insurance is a sort of average of term rates. The two forms of insurance tend to "cost" about the same over the whole life of the insured person. The man who outlives the averages does better with whole life insurance; the man who does not live to the average does better with term insurance. But it cannot be fairly said that there is a tendency for one to cost more than the other.

The development of level-premium whole life insurance has had an important bearing on the nature of the insurance business. Because premiums during early years are larger than needed, the accumulation of this excess, called "reserves," means that insurance companies have large sums to invest. It also means that interest is more important in the calculation of insurance cost than if term and other ascending-premium types of insurance predominated.

Two other standard forms of insurance contracts are available. Some insurance buyers want a level-premium insurance. But they also want the premiums to stop after a certain number of years; they want to have "paid-up" insurance. The death benefit is not paid until the insured dies, but his premium payments stop after some specified period. One of the common contracts of this kind is so-called "twenty-payment life." This form of life insurance, called "limited-payment insurance," is available with premiums payable for almost any term the buyer desires.

Sometimes those who classify insurance consider this limited-payment insurance a subgroup of ordinary or whole life insurance.

The fourth type of insurance contract is the "endowment policy." At the end of the policy period the proceeds of an endowment policy are paid to the insured immediately; there is no waiting for death. A man who wanted to make sure his newly born son went to college might have bought a twenty-year endowment policy. If the man died before the twenty years, the sum would be immediately paid to his beneficiary or estate; but even if he lived, the sum would be available at the end of twenty years for his son's college expenses. Later, when we discuss annuities we shall find that some of the more complicated types of so-called "retirement policies" ("How we retired at age fifty-five on $200 a month!") are a combination of endowment policies having annuity settlement features.

The student will note that we have discussed the types of contract in the order of relative cost. The annual premiums for these four types of insurance per $1,000 at age thirty as quoted by a leading insurance company are shown in Table 28.

The several types of policies enumerated here are the basic ones. But many insurance companies sell policies that have other titles: "family-income," "retirement," "educational," and "mortgage-protection" insurance. The number can be as large as the fertile imagination of insurance sales agents. But each of these special types represents some combination or adaptation of the basic types previously examined. "Family-income" insurance is usually a combination of decreasing term and ordinary life insurance with a dash of endowment sometimes added. Retirement insurance frequently is just a dressed-up combination of an endowment and an annuity contract.

TABLE 28

LIFE INSURANCE PREMIUMS

(Age 30)

Five-year term*	$ 6.71
Ordinary life	19.10
Twenty-payment life	30.78
Twenty-year endowment	47.12

* Nonrenewable but convertible. In order to show a net cost, these rates are for "nonparticipating" contracts.

Educational insurance is similar to the endowment policy already discussed. It differs from ordinary endowment insurance in that maturity is the date at which the heir is expected to start college; it does not mature before then, even if the insured man should die. But premiums stop in that event. Mortgage-protection insurance is usually a nonrenewable term insurance, decreasing as the mortgage is paid off.

Dividends on Insurance Policies

Many insurance companies are organized on a mutual basis; they have no stockholders. These companies generally return as dividends any excess they have charged due to conservative calculation of costs and death benefits to the policyholders. These dividends may be used to reduce premiums, may be taken in cash, may be used to purchase added paid-up insurance, or may be left to earn interest.

Some stock insurance companies sell so-called "participating" insurance contracts which involve the payment of dividends and have many of the other features of policies sold by mutual companies.

Insurance Reserves

In discussing the types of insurance contracts above, it was noted that most were "level-premium." For such contracts the insurance company collects more each year in premiums during the early years of a policy than it pays out in death benefits and dividends. Something has to be saved up against that period later on, when the death benefits under the policies will exceed current collections. The amount "saved up" constitutes insurance reserves. Insurance laws usually specify the minimum amount that must be held, but conservative companies often keep more than required by law.

It is the accumulation of reserves, this saving ahead, that makes life insurance companies such important financial institutions from the standpoint of capital formation. If all insurance were of the term type, about as much would be paid out each year as is collected in premiums, and the reserves would be negligible.

The existence of insurance reserves leads to two types of special arrangements: surrender value and loan value. Since the buyer of level-premium insurance is putting something ahead, he is entitled to this amount if he cancels his insurance. This is the "surrender value." The existence of reserves also leads to the possibility of borrowing on insurance; because there is something ahead, the policyholder may borrow the reserve value on his insurance, or a large fraction of it. The insurance company is fully protected because it will not loan more than the surrender value of the policy. The beneficiary under the policy continues to be protected for the face amount of the policy less only the amount of the loan.

Since insurance surrender value and loan value depend on the same fact of "having something ahead," they are usually based on the same figures. Maximum loan value on most life insurance is the same as its surrender value, or a large percentage of it.

Because most insurance contracts require varying amounts of "reserves," most life insurance involves savings. As a result, a portion of the amount paid for insurance, term insurance excepted, can be considered as being "saved," while the remainder is "at risk." The "at-risk" portion simply means that some of the insurance premium must be used to meet current death claims. The division of the four types of insurance contracts between "saved" and amounts "at risk" is shown in Exhibit 47.

This chart is for a person thirty-five years of age. The curve in the twenty-payment life insurance starts rising less rapidly at age fifty-five because premiums are paid up to that age; thereafter the only increase in reserves is due to the compounding of interest on the reserve already accumulated. Both the ordinary life and the endowment policy have upward-slanting straight lines because premiums are paid over the entire life of these policies. The endowment policy chart stops at age fifty-five because the policy would "mature" or be

Exhibit 47

COMPARISON OF PRINCIPAL LIFE INSURANCE CONTRACTS: RELATIVE AMOUNTS SAVED AND "AT RISK"*

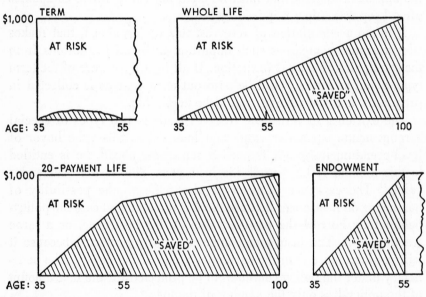

* This chart is simplified and therefore not exactly accurate. Actuarily precise curves would show deviations from straight lines because of changes in death probability due to advancing age and also because of the effect of interest compounding. Because these factors tend to be offsetting, the true "curves" would be nearly straight lines. For all practical purposes, therefore, these charts are a faithful representation of the insurance principle.

completed at that age. The reserve for the twenty-year term insurance is small, because most of the premium, aside from the selling and loading charges explained in the next paragraph, is devoted to death risks.

Loading Charges and Insurance Cost

The rates we quoted above for an actual company were somewhat above those based on the Commissioners Standard Ordinary mortality computations. The chief reason for the higher rates is that it costs money to operate insurance companies, and particularly to sell insurance. These costs are sometimes called a "loading charge"— something added or "loaded" on to cover these costs. In 1949 the expenses of life insurance companies, including selling costs (which are the leading item), were $1.8 billions; in the same year, death benefits paid by insurance companies were $1.5 billions, and "living benefits" (matured endowments, disability payments, annuity payments, surrender values, and policy dividends) were $2.0 billions. Loading charges vary among types of insurance, but in the aggregate they increase the cost of insurance from one third to one half. A fairly large part of this cost is that of selling, the cost of maintaining selling agencies and paying the agents' commissions.

Generally speaking, life insurance agents receive two forms of reimbursement: (1) first year, "sales commissions"; and (2) renewal "service commissions." From the first-year premium, the agent's sales commission may vary from 50 per cent on down, depending on the type of policy sold. Renewal service commissions are 5 per cent or less of premiums paid during the following nine years, again depending on the type of policy. Usually, the longer the premium paying period, the higher the percentage for first-year sales commission and for subsequent service commissions.

Special Types of Insurance

Two special types of life insurance merit separate attention: *group* life insurance and *industrial* life insurance.

Group Insurance. Many employers arrange for group insurance contracts by means of which their employees may be insured. In most group insurance contracts, there is a flat premium rate for all employees, and there is no medical examination. The insurance company, to avoid covering only the older employees and poorer medical risks, usually insists on at least 75 per cent of all employees participating. The typical group life insurance contract ranges from $1,000 to as much as one year's income per individual employee. The average death-benefit group contract in force at the end of 1949 was slightly over $2,000. Cost to the employee is frequently from 50 cents to 75 cents a month per $1,000 death benefit.

In some group insurance contracts, an individual may convert his participation in group life insurance into an individual insurance contract should he leave his employer. When conversion requires medical examination or certification of good health, it is not materially different from buying insurance anew.

The premiums on group insurance are usually paid by a deduction from the employee's pay check. The employer guarantees the life insurance company that writes the group contract against unreasonably or unexpectedly adverse experience. This provision may encourage employers to follow good employee health and safety practices and may influence employment policies.

The group insurance business has grown rapidly: at the end of 1949 there were 60,000 master policies with employers, covering an estimated 24 million employees. The insurance coverage was about $42 billion.

Industrial Life Insurance. Industrial life insurance is the "five-and-ten" part of the life insurance business. It is generally sold to poor people. The typical life policy has a death benefit of less than $300; the premiums are nickels and quarters collected weekly (often on payday) or, more rarely, monthly. Industrial insurance was designed to meet the needs of persons who could not afford the minimum $1,000 death benefit of standard life policies. It is not clear, however, that this reason is always the dominant one. In 1949 almost 106 million industrial life insurance contracts were in force in the United States. Since there are far fewer people than this number who buy such insurance, there is doubtless a great overlapping of contracts; some purchasers are insured under a number of industrial contracts. In many cases the buyers, if they were aware of the advantages of the standard contract, could get more and superior coverage from standard policies with the premiums they are now paying. The total coverage of industrial insurance is nearly $32 billion.

Because of the high cost of operation—the weekly or at least frequent door-to-door premium collection and the costly sales efforts for small policies—this type of insurance is not particularly economical. It is, indeed, in some cases, very costly for the benefits received, even if the cost is spread out and paid in nickels, dimes, and quarters.

While industrial insurance continues to grow, its rate of increase has not been so rapid as that of the other types of insurance. It may be that with prosperity many former buyers of industrial insurance have been able to meet their needs with standard insurance contracts. The rise of group insurance has also given minimum protection for many who might have been the most fertile market for industrial policies. Only a limited number of companies write industrial insurance, and recently there has been no tendency for new companies to join this group. Group insurance, rather than industrial insurance, has received the largest promotional effort.

ANNUITIES

An annuity is a contract purchased by a buyer and sold by an insurance company, in which the company undertakes to pay a fixed sum periodically for a stated period or, more commonly, for the remaining life of the buyer. Although the word "annuity" is derived from "annual" and originally referred to yearly payments, the more common payment interval in modern practice is the month.

The sale of annuities is usually combined with the life insurance business. It is similar in that the insurance company averages out the life expectancy of those who buy annuities just as it does for those who buy life insurance. But the nature of the insurance risk is reversed: life insurance protects against premature death, while an annuity protects one from outliving one's savings for old age. Insurance companies use different tables for life expectancy in computing rates for annuities than they use in calculating life insurance premiums. The life insurance tables tend to understate life expectancy; the annuity tables, to overstate it.

The usual purpose of annuities is to permit a person to use his capital for living expenses after retirement without running short if he lives longer than he had reason to expect. An annuity thus "lives up" capital. For example, assume that a couple both aged sixty-five have saved $25,000 for retirement. The highest completely safe return they could obtain at present would be about 3 per cent. This would net them $750 a year, or $62.50 a month. But the $25,000 would purchase an annuity which would pay about $112 during the life of either or both; that is, as long as either one was alive, he would receive the $112 a month. An annuity on the man's life alone would net about $157 a month. These rates are for so-called "nonrefund life annuities"; under them, there is nothing left for heirs. This illustrates what is meant by an annuity "living up" capital. A "refund" annuity pays less, but heirs receive something if the annuitants die soon after buying their annuity.

Sometimes those with spectacularly large but temporary earnings, such as prize fighters, ball players, or movie actresses, buy annuities which start to pay an income at a relatively early age. This is often to avoid the risk of later becoming impoverished. Such persons, not trusting their financial discretion, often prefer the type of annuity sold by some insurance companies which is noncancellable. The buyer can never change his mind and obtain a lump-sum settlement upon cancellation.

The three important forms of annuity contracts are: immediate life annuities, joint life and survivor annuities, and deferred annuities.

Immediate Life Annuities. A lump sum is paid to the company for which the annuitant receives an income, beginning at once, for life. This type of contract appeals to the individual with no dependents who wishes to use up his capital but also wants to be sure that he will not exhaust his capital before death.

Joint Life and Survivor Annuities. This is a straight life annuity but pays an income to two or more persons, such as husband and wife, while both are alive and then to the survivor for life. Arrangements can be made to have annuity payments at a higher rate while both joint annuitants live, and then at a lower rate during the life of the survivor. The income, for a given sum invested, is lower than in the case of the single annuity.

Deferred Annuities. Regular annual payments, or occasional lump-sum payments, are made during the productive period of the saver to be used to purchase an annuity that begins at a later date, usually at retirement age. At the time of retirement, the type of annuity desired may be chosen.

Special guaranties of a minimum number of annuity payments may be added to the various forms of annuity to meet the needs of those who wish to get back the whole sum they paid in, or to meet some special situation where it is desirable to assure an income for a certain minimum number of years, as where there are children who lack a few years of the age of financial independence. Thus, a minimum number of annuity payments, say for five, ten, fifteen, or twenty years, may be made "certain" if the ordinary beneficiaries should die before that number of years has elapsed. Or a "refund" annuity may be had which provides for the refund to the estate of an annuitant of an amount equal to the excess of his original payment to the company over the amounts he has received, should his death occur before such a sum has been received. The income is lower for annuities with refund than under the ordinary annuity.

Under the federal income-tax law, 3 per cent of the amount paid for the annuity must be treated as income subject to taxation. Annuity income in excess of the 3 per cent of cost is taxable after such accumulated excess equals the amount originally invested. For example, the couple paying $25,000 for an annuity mentioned above would have $750 income subject to tax ($25,000 × 3 per cent). Of course, with deductions that now prevail, they would not have to pay any tax unless they should have other income. Just as is true of life insurance, an annuitant is subject to the risk of reduced purchasing power in the event of price inflation.

The cost of annuities has been increased several times in recent years. In life insurance contracts the unfavorable effects of declining interest rates have been offset by the favorable effects of people living longer. But longer average life *increases* the cost of an annuity. Thus, both lower interest rates and longer life expectancy changes have been working to increase annuity costs. The cost of an annuity which will purchase a life income of $10 a month is shown in Table 29.

TABLE 29

Cost of Annuity Paying $10 a Month until Death

(Immediate Annuity without Refund and without Loan or Surrender Value)

AGE	SIMPLE ANNUITY		JOINT LIFE AND SURVIVOR ANNUITY†
	Male	Female*	
60	$1,873.44	$2,165.52	$2,549.76
65	1,590.72	1,873.44	2,234.64
70	1,323.48	1,590.72	1,921.08

* Note that because of longer life expectancy, female rates for a given age are the same as those for a male five years younger.
† This type of annuity is one taken out by a husband but with the guaranty of continued payments either to himself or to his wife, whichever lives the longer. In the illustration above, it is assumed that both husband and wife are the same age.

Until 1930, annuities were a relatively small part of the business of the insurance companies. But since that time, they have grown rapidly—more rapidly than other insurance company contracts. At present the annual income paid or accrued on annuities exceeds $1.1 billion. More than three million annuity contracts are in force. Some of the annuity contracts are group arrangements under pension plans (discussed later in this chapter), but the bulk of the dollar volume continues to be the classic individual annuity.

LIFE INSURANCE COMPANIES

At present there are about 600 legal-reserve life companies in the United States. About 90 per cent of the business, however, is written by a few dozen companies. Most of these companies sell insurance and annuity contracts in all or almost all of the states, but many smaller companies localize their sales efforts.

About forty years ago the life insurance business was extensively investigated by New York State (the Armstrong Investigation). Charles Evans Hughes, who was later to be governor of New York State, Republican presidential candidate, and Chief Justice of the Supreme Court, conducted the investigation. As a result of this investigation a detailed and comprehensive life insurance regulatory law was adopted. Regulation of life insurance business in other states has been patterned after the New York law to a considerable extent. Recently, however, there have been growing disparities in the form of regulation as the insurance departments of the other states developed independent views. But because of this initial original similarity of regulatory pattern, most companies that can qualify to sell insurance in New York State can meet the requirements of the other states. Because of the large population of New York a national company can hardly afford to neglect this state.

About 70 per cent of the life insurance in the United States is handled by "mutual" companies. These, like mutual savings banks, have no stockholders. The remaining 30 per cent of life insurance is handled by "stock" companies, which are owned by private shareholders. Policies sold by mutual companies "participate" in earnings or in premiums collected in excess of reserve needs; stock companies generally sell nonparticipating insurance. A number of stock companies, however, sell some participating insurance policies. These policies have considerable, but not complete, similarity to the policies of true mutual companies.

Life Insurance Company "Income"[1] and Its Use

Life insurance companies get the major part of their new money from premiums, particularly as long as the amount of insurance outstanding grows. But investment income is of material importance. The relative size of these sources and the use of insurance company "income" are shown in Table 30.

The Investment of Reserves

The investment of reserve funds has become a major financial problem. Insurance companies have had a difficult time finding invest-

---

[1] Life insurance is a special kind of business. The concept of "income" used in private business accounting does not apply to life insurance operations. It is more accurate, therefore, to think of life insurance cash receipts and payments as these are treated in Table 30.

ments that were safe and "legal" (discussed in Chapter 11) and yielded enough income to keep pace with the rates of interest assumed in insurance-premium computations.

Insurance companies have gone chiefly into the long-term investment markets and are the leading buyers of securities in these markets. It has been estimated that in 1947, for example, insurance companies bought 80 per cent of new bonds issued. In an effort to maintain income, insurance companies have also short-circuited the underwriting market and bought capital issues directly (the direct placements mentioned in Chapter 8); have bought store buildings

TABLE 30

LIFE INSURANCE CASH RECEIPTS AND USES OF THE FUNDS, DURING 1949

(Billions of Dollars)

Premium income	7.6	
Investment income	2.7	
Total cash receipts		10.3
Life insurance benefits payments	3.5	
Death benefits	1.5	
Disability payments	0.1	
Matured endowments	0.5	
Annuity payments	0.2	
Surrender values	0.6	
Policy dividends	0.6	
Expenses	1.8	
Other uses of funds	1.0	
Total uses of funds		6.3
Net increase in insurance company assets		4.0

Source: Adapted from *Life Insurance Fact Book, 1950.*

and other commercial real estate on the so-called "buy-lease" basis; and have built large apartment projects for rental income—for example, Parkchester in New York City.

The distribution of insurance company assets at the end of 1948 is shown in Table 31.

The composition of insurance assets has been changed with the emergence of the great national debt. This is shown fully in Exhibit 48. But the holding of United States government securities by insurance companies has never constituted as large a proportion of total assets as in the case of the other major institutional investors, such as commercial banks and savings banks. Since World War II, life insurance companies have reduced their holdings of such securities sharply. At the same time, they have made very large pur-

TABLE 31

LIFE INSURANCE COMPANY ASSETS DECEMBER 31, 1948

(Dollar Amounts in Millions)

		Per Cent
United States government securities	$16,770	30.2
Corporate securities	20,350	36.6
Railroad bonds	$3,005	
Public utilities bonds	8,745	
Industrial and other bonds	7,155	
Stocks	1,445	
Mortgages	10,855	19.5
Policy loans	2,065	3.7
Other assets	5,560	10.0
Total	$55,600	100.0

Exhibit 48

GROWTH AND DISTRIBUTION OF LIFE INSURANCE COMPANY ASSETS

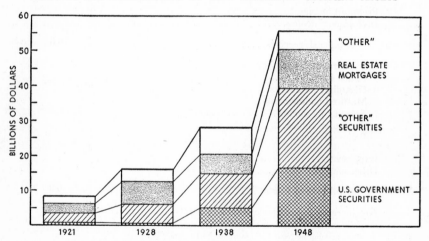

Source: Adapted from statistics in *Life Insurance Fact Book.*

chases of corporate securities. Life insurance companies are now the largest creditors of American industry.

Regulation of the Insurance Industry

The investment of life insurance reserves is subject to the regulations and rules of the state governing authorities, just as other life insurance matters are controlled. But the large volume of life insurance reserves has made regulation difficult.

Perhaps the most common form of investment regulation of life insurance is that which is prescribed by the law of New York State. There is no legal list, as there is for savings banks and trust companies. Rather, the law sets up certain standards as to the type of security, and it is up to the companies themselves to determine whether their purchases meet with the standards of the law. If, at the time of examination, it appears that the New York State Insurance Department does not consider an investment acceptable under the law, that investment becomes classified as a "nonadmitted asset." "Admitted assets" must be equal to reserve liabilities. Because the investment departments of the companies are pretty much acquainted with investment characteristics which qualify purchases as "admitted," there is little danger that companies overinvest in nonadmitted assets.

OTHER FORMS OF INSURANCE

The insurance principle has been applied to an almost endless number of risks. The other forms of insurance provide indemnity in the event of loss due to a wide variety of causes. Some of the more common forms of other insurance are:

1. Insurance against the damage done by fire, water, lightning, windstorm, tornado, earthquake, etc.
2. Insurance of ocean marine transportation (also insurance for inland marine transportation which becomes so very generalized that the so-called "property floaters" on cameras and violins and the like fall into this category).
3. Insurance against accidents and ill health.
4. Insurance of employers against claims of workmen under compensation laws. (This insurance is sometimes compulsory and is sometimes written by state agencies rather than by private agencies.)
5. Insurance against legal liability due to injury of persons or of property. This liability is assumed by the drivers of all automobiles, operators of aircraft, sportsmen, the owners of property (elevators, stairs, icy sidewalks), and parents.
6. Insurance against loss from theft.
7. Insurance of the losses arising from the infidelity of employees: defalcations by those having access to business funds and other valuable property.
8. Surety bonds: a bond that the person will perform as contracted. Contractors and builders are usually expected to guarantee performance by a surety bond. When a person is "bailed" out of jail, the sum posted is a surety bond that the person himself will reappear at the scheduled time to face trial.
9. Title of real property is sometimes not only certified to by the lawyer or title company investigating the title, but sometimes this certification is backed up by insurance.
10. Credit (accounts receivable) is sometimes insured.

This list, long and impressive as it may be, is only a sketchy recital of the full range of insurance forms. There are other forms, such as rain insurance—for example, colleges sometimes insure *against* rain on the days football games are scheduled; and the farmer, by crop insurance, insures *for* rain. The list is too long for full enumeration.

Carriers of Nonlife Insurance

The *agencies* that "carry" nonlife insurance vary even more widely than do the life insurance *companies*. Some of these carriers are large concerns operating different departments to provide a large proportion of the types of insurance just mentioned. These companies are sometimes stock firms; they are also often mutuals. There are a few instances of the *fraternal* or *special* type of carrier for risks that, in the beginning, the standard companies would not assume. For example, both farmer organizations and labor unions have sometimes set up insurance against the risks faced by their members and for which standard insurance companies did not quote adequate rates. In some countries other forms of insurance are sometimes underwritten by financially responsible persons individually or in syndicates. The famous Lloyds of London is simply the modern clublike equivalent of a famous old coffeehouse where financially responsible individuals assembled to participate in syndicates for insuring marine risks. While Lloyds is traditionally an ocean marine agency, there are very few insurable risks on which they will not quote a rate; some of the latter are the risks of war, of political elections, or the birth of triplets.

Costs of Nonlife Insurance

In the insurance of human life, the probabilities of death have been reduced to fairly exact terms. While life probability is constantly changing (and generally lengthening), even the rate and direction of this change have become subject to fairly precise forecast. But in the various other risks listed, many are not subject to any such precise determination. For that reason the insurance rates on these risks contain a fairly wide margin for loss. In many lines the loss claims often run no more than one fourth to one half of the premiums charged. It is this sizable excess which has encouraged the development of the mutual *carrier* of nonlife insurance. Because gross rates need to be high enough to cover unexpected contingencies, the mutual form gives the insured some chance to recover a part of the excess premium paid.

Importance of Nonlife Insurance Carriers

The insurance industry is big. In 1945 it was estimated that the fire, marine, and casualty carriers in the United States had gross assets of $4.5 billion, less than one third of which represented the reserves against unused premiums. This $4.5 billion does not include the assets of the casualty companies that are not fire or marine carriers. It was also estimated that in the year 1943 the annual gross premiums paid for nonlife insurance amounted to more than $3 billion.

Investment Trust Aspects of the Carriers

The stock companies engaged in carrying nonlife insurance have come to have such a margin of assets above their true liabilities for insurance purposes that they are considered to be investment trusts by some investors. Since the investment policies of casualty insurance companies are less restricted than those of life companies, they often invest in common stocks and in other investment media that are not generally open to life companies. In recent years, nonlife insurance stocks have had an investment performance that compared favorably with the very best of the investment trusts. The only disadvantage that these stocks suffer in comparison with mutual investment funds is their lack of tax exemption.

SOCIAL SECURITY

The federal plans for social security cover a wide field: public assistance for the blind, dependent mothers, and orphan children; improvement in the lot of children; unemployment insurance; and old-age and survivors insurance. It is the last, old-age and survivors insurance, which is identified with social security in the public mind and is the subject of particular interest here.

Old-age and survivors insurance benefits were extensively revised in 1950. The system now covers more than two thirds of the total labor force. The proportion that will be eligible for benefits ultimately will probably not be quite this large because of shifts by workers between "covered" occupations and jobs which are not covered.

Security Benefits

The security benefits per person covered are relatively modest. The monthly minimum benefit for a retired person at age sixty-five is now $20; the benefit for a single person under the most favorable circumstances cannot exceed $80, or $150 for a married person. The tax deductions to cover these benefits (the employment tax paid by the employer and wages tax paid by the employee) each are now 1½ per cent of the first $3,600 of the individual's wage or salary, and will remain so until 1954. Payments are scheduled to rise gradually to 3¼ per cent by 1970.

The total fund that had been accumulated for the old-age and survivors insurance by early 1951 amounted to almost $14 billion. Additions to the fund have been accumulating at a rate of almost $2 billion a year.

There is some dispute as to just how adequate the fund is to meet its liabilities. It is called an "insurance fund," but there is more to the liability than just the size of the fund. If outgoing payments should exceed the accumulated reserves in the fund, there would be strong and probably irresistible pressure to provide the margin by direct appropriation. It has been estimated that payroll taxes would have to be several times present levels if social security accounts were to be self-supporting.

The social security principle was thought by some to be socially unwise in that it would weaken saving incentives. So far, there is no evidence to bear out that opinion. The benefits are of such a size as to take the bitter edge off poverty but to do little more than that. The incentive for saving is hard to define in any event; it may be more of a social habit, developed out of the social sanctions, than a wholly rational process.

Unemployment Insurance

Although unemployment insurance is not a savings institution as ordinarily conceived, it has a financial aspect worthy of some attention. The federal program of unemployment insurance operates through state plans for unemployment aid, more so than in the case of old-age and survivors insurance. Unemployment insurance plans, therefore, vary widely and cannot be generalized readily. Unemployment insurance is set up wholly out of a payroll tax falling on the employers (four states are exceptions). The amount of tax varies with the so-called "experience ratings" for individual employers; those who furnish steady jobs pay the least tax; those with variable employment or large turnover pay the most. Unemployment insurance now has a fund of over $7 billion, but its current rate of increase is rather slow. The funds of some states are falling. It would be dangerous to call these funds "savings," but unemployment insurance does take over one of the functions that was previously thought to adhere in private savings.

Unemployment insurance covers over 30 million workers with substantial benefits, and another 4 or 5 million with partial benefits.

RETIREMENT PLANS

Aside from the federal social security plan for old age retirement, there are a number of private pension plans, many of which are of fairly recent origin and some of which are of long standing.

Retirement plans usually operate on the basis of providing an income at retirement age which will supplement social security benefits. Some of the plans were set up long before social security or in industries not covered by social security, and so the schemes are not supplemental, but rather separate, programs of private social security.

The interests of employers in having such plans are many; but two unusually important reasons stand out. The benefits for retirement are cumulative and are usually lost if and when the employee leaves the employment of a company having such a plan (or are lost if a certain minimum period has not passed). This tends to make for stability of employment and low employee turnover. The second advantage is that older, possibly senile, and ineffective workers can be decently retired. Even without any legal obligation, many industries have tried to keep on their "old-timers." Often these oldsters were earning only low incomes and they were of little value to their employers, but to have fired them without provision for a reasonably adequate income would have damaged employee morale. Retirement plans help to solve this problem.

The costs of retirement schemes are material. There are two variations: some plans represent joint contributions by both employer and employee; others depend mainly, and sometimes solely, upon employer contributions. The total cost of these plans runs anywhere from 5 to 20 per cent of payrolls.

Wartime Stimulation

The war period furnished an especially strong incentive to establish pension funds. Excess profits taxation tended to make expense outlays for pensions cheap. When a retirement plan is established, there is usually a large lump-sum obligation that falls on the employer to provide for older employees. If no allowance was made for past service, older employees would be entitled to almost no retirement allowance. Without this allowance, one of the purposes of retirement plans, providing for the dismissal of elderly employees, would be defeated. Consequently, the employer, as a rule, has to make an unusually large lump-sum payment to get the fund off to an actuarially sound start.

The golden opportunity for starting a pension plan occurred when the excess profits tax was in effect. This lump-sum payment could be charged as an expense and most of the amount saved out of taxes. Thus World War II gave the movement a strong impetus. Now it is being pushed by still another factor. The plans are popular, and companies that do not have good pension plans cannot attract superior personnel. Competition is forcing these groups to start such plans, and the competition may become stronger with time. This is particularly true in employment not covered by social security.

Appeal to Corporations

Retirement plans have a special appeal for corporations wishing to add some incentive for executives to stay with them. An upper-bracket executive usually pays rather high income taxes. If an executive's salary were raised, he would be able to keep only a fraction of it. But if the increase were added to a retirement fund, it would not be taxable until paid out as a retirement income. Paid for at lower income rates, and later when all tax rates might be lower, the executive would keep much more of the salary increase. Accordingly, such plans are very useful in recruiting and keeping executive personnel.

One of the oldest and most successful of the plans is that operated by Sears, Roebuck and Company. It has been estimated that there are now 8,000 different pension plans in effect throughout the country. The growth has recently been at a fairly rapid rate. These plans are estimated to cover 14,000,000 persons. Because most of the plans have been adopted by the larger companies, the average number of employees is large. But retirement schemes are spreading to smaller organizations. Small banks, for example, have been particularly active in this field. Banking employment is stable and salaries traditionally low. On-the-job security has been fair, but old-age security needed to be supplemented.

Amounts "Saved" through Pension Plans

There are no reliable estimates as to the dollar volume of funds now resting in these systems or of the annual additions. The recent-ness with which many of the schemes have been established suggests that the dollar volume of funds held is relatively less important than the accretions. Taking an average salary of $3,000 for those 14,000,-000 covered persons and estimating that current contributions average about 10 per cent if both employer and employee contributions are counted, the annual additions from such payments alone would amount to more than $4 billion annually. This seems too large. But investment bankers report that pension funds are important buyers of new securities. Pension plans are a sizable and growing factor in private saving.

Pension Funds in Union Contracts

Most of the early pension plans were voluntarily adopted by companies to solve the problem of superannuated salaried employees. But more recently pensions have come to be bargained for along with wages and working conditions by organized labor groups. The emphasis on this point in the 1949 steel strike and its settlement was the most widely publicized of such pensions. But there had been prior cases, the best known of which is the coal-miners' pension fund. Some of the industrial pension plans have been tied to, or made supplementary to, the social security retirement benefits.

Much of the early dispute about industrial pensions was whether they should be "contributory" or "noncontributory." A "contributory" pension is one in which some deduction for the cost of the pension is made from the employee's pay check. While the morale factor involved in this dispute was important, it made little direct difference to employers. Whether they first added a sum to the pay check and then deducted it, or paid on a wholly noncontributory basis, the employer was bound to treat it as a cost. Pensions under such arrangements amount to a kind of contractual saving.

Establishing pensions for employees nearing the age of retirement involves a special problem. Since there has been no prior accumulation to meet the cost of such pensions, a large lump-sum payment is required. This cost falls entirely on employers. Any company that had many older employees with long years of service would incur larger pension costs than a company with younger employees with fewer years of service. Stability of employment in the past, usually considered a socially desirable accomplishment of an employer, was in a sense penalized.

Company-by-company pensions have the effect of tying employees to the employer with whom they start work. Such plans, therefore, tend to reduce the flexibility and mobility of labor. Many business groups, formerly not friendly to government social security, have changed their views. They now favor organization of pensions on a governmental, rather than a company, basis to restore this flexibility.

CONCLUSION

The popular urge for security has helped to make insurance in all its applications grow more rapidly than any other major private financial institution. The flow of funds in the capital markets leans more on insurance money than on any investor group. Investment bankers now find their best customers among the insurance companies. The pension and retirement plans are increasingly important factors in the capital markets.

The relatively large growth of these insurance-type buyers raises an unresolved conflict. The very essence of insurance is safety. The limitation of insurance investment to safe forms is an understandable requirement. But unless the whole economic structure becomes more stable—something that is still only a hope but not a reality—there will be some residual economic risk. And as insurance grows in importance as an investing institution, the residual investors shrink in importance. Thus the burden of economic risk falls on this shrinking segment. The unresolved conflict, therefore, can be stated as follows: How can safety for the insurance-type investor be provided without making the risk for residual investors intolerably high?

—ROLAND I. ROBINSON

QUESTIONS AND PROBLEMS

1. Does insurance reduce risk?
2. What is the general nature of an insurable risk?
3. What is "adverse selection"?
4. For what purposes is term insurance particularly applicable?
5. For what purposes is whole life insurance particularly applicable?
6. Under what circumstances is limited-payment life insurance preferable to whole life insurance?
7. Illustrate an appropriate use of endowment insurance.
8. In life insurance payments, who gets the dividend? Who gets the premium?
9. Why does level-premium insurance lead to the accumulation of insurance company reserves?
10. How is loan value usually related to surrender value?
11. How is surrender value usually related to the insurance reserves of a life insurance company?

12. What is the difference between group and industrial life insurance?

13. In what kinds of circumstances are annuities used as an alternative to direct investment?

14. What kind of annuity should be sold to a high-earning major-league base-ball star?

15. Do annuity rates discriminate unfairly against females?

16. What has been the principal purpose of life insurance company regulation?

17. Do employers always oppose pension plans?

18. Why has the spread of union-negotiated pension plans led many conservative critics to change their minds about the desirability of social security pensions?

BIBLIOGRAPHY

The large number of texts in the field of life insurance makes any selection of them for this bibliography invidious; the reader may secure access by reference to the catalogue in the library he uses. Texts published since 1948 will reflect the shift of most insurance business from the Old American Experience Table to the newer Commissioners Standard Ordinary Life Table. Aside from texts, the literature of life insurance is rather thin. The proceedings of the Life Officers Investment Seminar (Lake Geneva, Wisconsin) have not been published in full, although some parts are available as articles in the *Journal of Finance.*

Statistics of the life insurance industry may be obtained from the annual *Fact Book* published by the Institute of Life Insurance, 488 Madison Avenue, New York 22, New York. Inquiries to the Institute will often disclose useful material otherwise available only in obscure sources.

There is even less material available on casualty insurance. Most of what is available is in the manuals and texts dealing with general insurance. Again, the card catalogue of the library available to the interested student is the best source.

The literature of social security is also thin. The annual reports of the Federal Security Agency publish the current statistics of social security and some guarded discussion of its more general aspects. One general work on social security, now somewhat out of date, is that by Seymour E. Harris, *Economics of Social Security* (New York: McGraw-Hill Book Co., Inc., 1941). An article of some special interest is one written by Eliot J. Swan, "Economic Aspects of Social Security," in *Housing, Social Security, and Public Works,* Postwar Economic Studies, No. 6 (Federal Reserve System, June, 1946).

Standard literature on pension plans is almost nonexistent; reference to a current periodical index and to the *New York Times Index* would be the best way for the reader to obtain up-to-date comment and material. A fair amount of useful material may be secured from the brochures published by the many trust companies which act as trustees for pension plans.

Chapter 13

INVESTMENT COMPANIES AND INVESTMENT COUNSEL

IN THE three preceding chapters we have examined the problems of investing and also considered how thrift institutions and insurance companies, as indirect investment mediums, assist individual savers in meeting these problems. The institutions discussed in Chapters 11 and 12—the various types of savings banks, credit unions, savings and loan associations, insurance companies, and others—are particularly well adapted for serving the small saver although they serve persons of wealth as well.

It will be recalled that these institutions, reflecting either law or tradition, invest their funds primarily in bonds, mortgages, and preferred stocks. Investments of this kind provide safety of principal and certainty of income to a high degree, but by their very nature they lack the possibilities for increased income and capital appreciation which characterize common stocks. Investors seeking an investment that offers potential income and principal growth must turn elsewhere.

The investor may, of course, decide to conduct his own investment program and buy securities through one of the organized exchanges or in the over-the-counter market. But if he feels the need for help, there are three types of investment institutions ready to assist him in acquiring an interest in common stocks as well as in bonds and preferred stocks: (1) investment companies and (2) investment counsel, both discussed in this chapter; and (3) corporate trustees, discussed in the next chapter.

The investment company serves both small and large investors but is particularly advantageous to the person of small means because he can obtain through the investment company both diversification and specialized management that would not otherwise be available to him. In contrast, investment counsel is feasible only for persons with fairly substantial accumulations, and they obtain highly individualized help through a program specifically designed to meet their particular situations. Increasingly, and particularly through the common trust fund, the corporate trustee is serving the investment requirements of the individual of modest means as well as the more opulent investor.

INVESTMENT COMPANIES

The terms "investment company" and "investment trust"[1] are used loosely and interchangeably to designate a variety of financial institutions through which the accumulated funds of a large number of savers and investors are pooled under centralized management to be invested in securities for the benefit of all the participants. It is the aim of the investment company to provide particularly for the small investor the same opportunity of spreading risk through diversification that is available to the larger investors and to institutional investors—a diversification that the individual small investor is usually not able to accomplish alone. Furthermore, it is the aim of these enterprises to give both small and large investors the benefit of trained, experienced, and specialized management together with continuous supervision, neither of which the individual investor is, as a rule, qualified to supply himself.

Origin of the Investment Company

The investment-company idea had its origin in Belgium (Société Générale de Belgique, 1822), and subsequently similar investment organizations were formed in Switzerland and in France. Still later in the 1860's the investment company movement started in England, expanded steadily for twenty years, and reached the height of its development in the boom period of the eighties. During the formative

---

[1] The British investment companies were originally actual common-law trusts but subsequently changed to the corporate form, becoming limited-liability companies. Notwithstanding the change in legal form, the term "trust" was retained in England and was subsequently popularly accepted in America and applied to various pooled investment funds, whether legally trusts or not. Efforts are being made in the United States by those associated with investment-company sponsorship to encourage the use of the term "investment company," wherever applicable, rather than the misnomer "investment trust"; but it is difficult to change popular usage, and time will be required. Whether investment companies are organized as common-law trusts or as corporations has little effect on their operating policies or procedures. The difference is largely technical and need not concern us here. For a discussion of the common-law or Massachusetts trust form of organization, see Chapter 14.

stage in England there was little regulation of the activities of these investment pools, and unsound and speculative practices were often followed. The Baring Brothers crash and the financial crisis of the early nineties were retarding influences, and there were investment company failures and loss of prestige. Those companies that stood the test thereafter followed more conservative practices, and the British investment companies won public confidence and have, in the main, performed creditably since.

Development of Investment Companies in the United States

The ten years prior to 1925 are generally regarded as constituting the formative period of the investment-company movement in the United States, although the idea took root prior to 1900. With a mild interest manifested in investment companies for a number of years, the development gained force with a rapid expansion in 1927 and 1928, followed by a period of high enthusiasm in 1929 up to the time of the October, 1929, market break. Many of the American companies then only recently formed were at once subject to a market panic of serious proportions, an experience that closely paralleled the early days of the investment company in England, where the Baring crash provided a similar period of difficulty.

Although the idea of pooling investment funds is basically sound, it was abused by many of the newly formed companies in this country. Organized toward the end of a bull market of vast proportions, and influenced by the speculative fervor of the time, many of these companies bought predominantly common stocks and then witnessed a serious depreciation in the value of their portfolios in the ensuing collapse of the market.

Some of the so-called "investment" companies in America were really holding and financing organizations that acquired a major stockholding in companies in which they were interested. The holding companies were designed to effect rather long-term or permanent retention of substantial interests in given situations; the financing companies advanced funds for a relatively shorter time to assist a business during the developmental or perhaps a rehabilitation period, and then sold out and sought other commitments. Other companies engaged in trading operations and emphasized market profits on relatively short-term holdings of securities. Either speculative profits or control were the motivating factors in such companies. They lacked the diversification of a true investment company and, of course, followed more aggressive practices. The American investing public has learned to distinguish between the holding, financing, and trading enterprises, on the one hand, and the investment companies proper on the other.

Following the object lesson of the 1929–32 period, there were many mergers of investment companies, and numerous new affiliations were made. Stated or par values of both preferred and common stocks were written down; investment companies bought in their own senior securities at a discount; and the objectives and operating policies were restated on a much more conservative basis.

The American investor was disappointed by the performance of the investment company and found his glowing hopes dashed. Investment-company management had not provided the expected safety of principal plus appreciation in addition to the expected income from interest and dividends. The pendulum swung in the other direction: investors eschewed management and turned to a co-operative investment device that provided for a minimum of management discretion and which set up a relatively inflexible long-term investment program, operated according to pre-established rules. This device became known as the "fixed trust" because policy was largely prescribed and but little management decision was permitted.

Fixed Trusts

Fixed trusts were established by sponsoring dealers who sold to the public redeemable shares (also called "certificates of beneficial interest"). Each of these fixed-trust shares represented a proportionate interest in a portfolio of securities deposited by the sponsor with a trustee. The securities were generally those of well-known companies, traded on the leading exchanges of the country; and the agreement (trust indenture) set out specifically the securities that might be included. Only limited changes were permitted in this block of underlying securities as indicated in the agreement, the purpose being to minimize management supervision. Some fixed-trust plans required the trustee to sell securities under certain conditions, yet permitted no substitution of new securities. The price of the fixed-trust shares to the investor was determined by dividing the number of shares into the market value of the underlying securities and adding to the quotient an amount to cover the selling charges. Income received on the deposited securities was distributed to the holders of the fixed-trust shares after deducting the trustee's fee and the sponsor's expenses. Fixed trusts were also called "unit trusts," a designation that grew out of the fact that fixed-trust shares were issued against a block or *unit* of underlying securities. When the sponsor had sold all the shares pertinent to one unit, he would set up another block or unit and sell more shares.

Basically the unit-type trust idea—to the extent that it sought to set up a rigid long-term investment program to be operated rather mechanically according to pre-established rules—was not sound. No one planning a program for future years can anticipate all possible developments and make provision for the action to meet such developments. Industries and companies change, and so do the underlying economic fundamentals. This weakness was recognized, and the sponsors subsequently substituted for the fixed-trust plan a modified type of unit trust designed to permit some management discretion and therefore greater flexibility. These newer vehicles were described as "semifixed" or "restricted" management trusts.

Fixed trusts had another inherent disadvantage: possible loss of interest in the project on the part of the sponsor or the possible withdrawal of the trustee if the arrangement did not prove adequately remunerative to the trustee. Any premature dissolution of a unit trust would mean that selling charges would have to be absorbed over a shorter period of time than was originally contemplated (unit trusts were set up for varying periods—ten, fifteen, twenty-five years, etc.).

The first unit trusts were probably created in 1924, but it was not until after 1929 that the unit trusts attained the peak of their popularity. According to the Securities and Exchange Commission (SEC), sales of unit trusts from 1927 to 1936 totaled about $900 million, and about two thirds of these sales occurred in 1930 and 1931. Although more than 150 of these unit trusts were originated, probably a half dozen sponsors distributed most of the shares. In fact, two of the unit trusts together accounted for probably half the total flotations of this type of instrument.

As the SEC estimates indicate, the popularity of the unit trust soon waned after the very early 1930's, and the formation of new unit trusts was discontinued. Likewise, the further distribution of already existing unit trusts ceased. Some of the unit trusts were subsequently converted into open-end investment companies.

Renewed Interest in Investment Companies

Discredited in the years following 1929, the investment company later regained favor, and particularly since the early 1940's there has been a renewed public interest and resultant increase in the use of this type of investment. At the close of 1949 the National Association of

Investment Companies reported that 130 member funds had total assets of $2,768 million, in contrast to slightly over $1 billion at December 31, 1940.

Under authority of the Public Utility Holding Company Act of 1935 the SEC conducted a comprehensive study of the investment companies and holding companies; and on the basis of the findings, Congress passed the Investment Company Act of 1940. This act, discussed more fully later, and the regulation of investment companies for which it made provision served to engender again investor confidence in this form of investment device. The act served to codify many existing practices, modified others, and established some new requirements. According to one writer: "Under the Act as it now exists and under the eyes of the Securities and Exchange Commission as its administrator, the buyer of investment company shares is about as nearly entitled as he ever can be to forget his anxieties about the honest care and administration of his funds."[2]

The act applies to practically all investment companies and, in fact, just about makes registration under the act mandatory because companies that do not register are drastically limited in their scope of activity. They may not use the mails for the purchase or sale of securities and may not engage in interstate commerce. Companies that qualify are called "registered investment companies" and fall into two main classifications: closed-end and open-end.

Closed-End and Open-End Investment Companies

The most obvious and characteristic difference between the closed-end and the open-end investment company is the manner in which the investment company's own securities are bought and sold, but the distinction may also have some significance with respect to capital structure, investment policy, and portfolio constituency.

CLOSED-END. Closed-end investment companies, much like industrial and other business corporations, have a relatively fixed amount of capital stock outstanding. Once distributed, shares are available only in the open market and can be bought either through one of the organized exchanges or through the over-the-counter market, unless the management offers an additional block of shares; but this has happened infrequently and to only a small extent in recent years. There is no provision for issuance or redemption of shares on a day-to-day basis. The market price of shares depends not only upon the mar-

---

[2] A. B. Stevenson, *Investment Company Shares* (New York: Fiduciary Publishers, Inc., 1947), p. 13.

ket value of the underlying securities but also upon the demand and supply of the investment company shares themselves in the open market. For this reason, shares of closed-end companies may often be purchased (or perforce liquidated) at susbtantial discounts below their asset or liquidating value. The discount tends to be wider in weak markets and to narrow, or even to be converted into a premium, in strong markets.

Some closed-end companies have but one class of capital stock outstanding; but most of them have pyramided capital structures, including preferred stock, debentures, and in some cases bank loans, in addition to common stock. Pyramided capital structures provide possible benefits of trading on the equity, also called "leverage." A simple illustration follows: Assume that an individual with $1,000 invested in his business is able to earn a net return of 10 per cent, or $100. Then, if he can maintain that rate of earnings on any capital additions, he should be able to realize a net return of 10 per cent, or $100, on a second $1,000. If that second $1,000 was borrowed at a cost of only 5 per cent, or $50, then there will be $150 net income for the owner of the business. This is equivalent to a 15 per cent return on his $1,000 investment. He will have traded on his equity. The same principle applies to corporations that have senior securities outstanding. Leverage is effective not only with respect to income received from interest and dividends but also with respect to gains realized from appreciation in value of the underlying securities of the investment company. It should be noted, however, that in a declining market, or with declining earnings, a capital pyramid accentuates adversity.

Although most of the investment companies organized in the period of early growth during the 1920's were of the closed-end type, only a few have been established since 1929. Total net assets of closed-end companies have increased but moderately in recent years, and the number of shareholders has decreased. This is in contrast with the growth of the open-end companies, as we shall see.

OPEN-END. Open-end investment companies generally sell their shares continuously on a day-to-day basis, either directly or through licensed securities dealers. The price to the buyer is the asset value of the underlying securities plus a selling charge that ranges from 6 to 9 per cent of the selling price. Shares will be redeemed by the open-end company at the asset value and in some instances less a nominal redemption fee. The asset value of the shares is calculated at regular intervals, sometimes twice daily, and is determined as follows: The market value of the underlying securities is added to the amount of cash and receivables on hand, liabilities are deducted, and the remainder is divided by the number of shares outstanding.

The prices at which shares will be either sold or redeemed are published in leading financial newspapers and on the financial pages of leading general-circulation newspapers. As a rule, there is no over-the-counter trading in open-end shares. An exception is found in the shares of the State Street Investment Corporation, which are traded over-the-counter. State Street discontinued the sale of additional shares in 1944 but continued redemption of the shares at 1 per cent below asset value. However, shares were not presented for redemption; and because of the demand for the shares, they have sold in the over-the-counter market at a premium above asset value. But this is an exceptional case.

Normally, because of the method of selling and redeeming open-end shares, the market price bears a direct relationship to the value of the underlying assets. This contrasts with closed-end shares, which may at one time sell at a substantial discount below asset value and at another time at a premium above asset value. For this reason, and because of the acquisition cost (selling charge), open-end shares do not lend themselves to short-term trading—the fee would tend to absorb the profits, if any.

With relatively minor exceptions the open-end companies have but one class of stock and have no bonds outstanding and no bank debt. The Investment Company Act of 1940 does not permit newly formed open-end companies to have more than one capital issue, and bank borrowing is permitted to but a limited degree. Accordingly, there is little opportunity for capital leverage in the open-end field.

Open-end investment companies are also called "mutual investment funds." The open-end designation obviously can be traced to the fact that there is no fixed amount of capital, the number of shares outstanding varying from day to day with the flow of sales and redemptions. How the term "mutual" originated is not certain, although one sponsor, in testifying before the SEC, said that his open-end company was a mutual fund in equity securities analogous to a mutual savings bank.

GROWTH COMPARISON. Open-end companies have had a very substantial growth in the last eight to ten years. Total net assets of 91 member funds of the National Association of Investment Companies amounted to $1,973,547,000 at December 31, 1949, which compares with $402 million at December 31, 1941. The number of shareholders in the same eight-year period increased from 293,251 to 842,198. The trend in net total assets and number of shareholders for both open-end and closed-end companies is shown in Exhibit 49. Until some time in 1944 the net total assets of closed-end companies exceeded the assets of open-end companies, but since that time the reverse has been true; and open-end assets at the end of 1949 were almost two and one-half times the assets of the closed-end companies.

Exhibit 49

INVESTMENT-COMPANY STATISTICS, 1940–49*
(Total Net Assets and Number of Shareholders)
39 Closed-End Funds

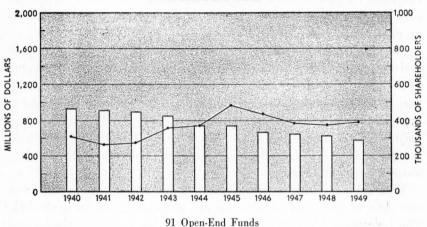

91 Open-End Funds

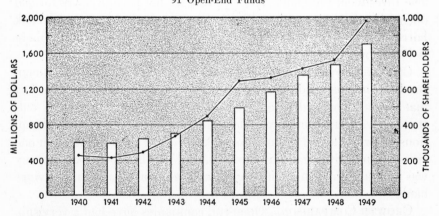

* The number of funds included may vary from year to year. One large closed-end company ceased to be an investment company during 1949 and was not included in the 1949 statistics. Other deletions and additions of new members have been made from time to time. Figures for the number of shareholders are approximate and include both common and preferred shareholders.

Source: National Association of Investment Companies, December 31, 1949.

During 1949, sales of open-end investment company shares amounted to $386 million, repurchases were $108 million, and the net excess of sales over redemptions amounted to $278 million. Closed-end funds obtained new capital, including bank loans, of $1.7 million; repurchases amounted to $19.2 million, so that there was a net decrease in capital of $17.5 million. The number of shareholders of open-end funds increased more than 120,000, whereas preferred and common shareholders in closed-end funds decreased 23,105.

There are a number of explanations for this marked change in relative position. The shares of most closed-end companies have tended to sell fairly consistently at a discount. Not only does this preclude issuing additional shares without diluting the equity of existing shareholders, but many closed-end company managements have bought back their shares below asset value, a practice that serves to reduce total net assets. On the other hand, undoubtedly one of the important reasons for the demonstrated preference of investors for open-end shares is found in the fact that such shares may always be redeemed at approximately the market value of the underlying securities.

Probably the most significant explanation for the growth of open-end companies is found in their distribution method. Usually open-end investment companies arrange to have an individual or a securities house serve as the sponsor (wholesale distributor) of the shares. The sponsor is given the exclusive right to buy shares from the company at the net-asset value for resale to retail dealers who, through their salesmen, sell the shares to the ultimate investor. Sponsors seek to set up a strong selling organization with representatives located throughout the country. Retail outlets include brokerage houses, investment bankers, and securities dealers. Without active sales effort, redemptions might well exceed sales.

The 6 to 9 per cent selling charge does not become a part of the fund but represents compensation to the sponsor or distributor, to the retail dealer, and to the dealers' salesmen. The commission paid the dealer is larger than on securities transactions generally and sufficient to justify active selling campaigns, including person-to-person solicitation. Brokerage commissions and over-the-counter spreads on stocks and bonds generally are not adequate to permit similar selling effort.

With the new pattern of income distribution in our country, there are now many more persons who are able to save enough of their incomes to become potential securities buyers, but many of them know little about stocks and bonds and securities markets. Person-to-person solicitation has served to inform many of these new investors and has undoubtedly been an important factor in the growth of open-end funds. Persons who might not otherwise buy common stocks have been interested in buying these shares on the strength of the diversification and management provided.

That the selling method and educational effort of the open-end companies are a responsible factor in the expansion of mutual funds finds corroboration in the fact that three mutual funds sponsored by investment counselors and established in the early days of the investment company development have not enjoyed a growth comparable to that of many of the open-end companies. The investment counsel funds bear no selling charge; and without sales effort, growth is slow —and this despite the reputation for creditable performance that is generally accorded these three funds. There are at least four investment counseling firms each of which sponsors one or more mutual funds.

INVESTMENT POLICY.   Whether open-end or closed-end, investment companies afford the investor a wide range of choice in investment programs and objectives. From the standpoint of portfolio constituency, investment companies can be classified as follows:

1. Common-stock funds—predominantly or exclusively common stocks
2. Balanced funds—common and preferred stocks and bonds, the proportion varying from time to time
3. Specialty funds:
    a) Exclusively bonds
    b) Exclusively preferred stocks
    c) Speculative common stocks
    d) Single-industry common stocks

For purpose of illustration the portfolio of the Massachusetts Investors Trust is reproduced in the Supplement to this chapter. This investment company is the oldest and the largest open-end fund, and it has a diversified portfolio consisting almost exclusively of common stocks.

The objective and the expected performance of an investment fund are closely related, not only to the nature of the underlying portfolio, but also to the capital structure of the fund itself. Open-end companies, with one or two exceptions, have but one class of shares outstanding and therefore provide no leverage. Closed-end companies may have but one class of stock (nonleverage) or may have a multiple capital structure (leverage), including, in addition to common stock, preferred shares and bonds; and in some cases they may have bank loans as well.

On the basis of the character of the investment portfolio, the nature of the investment company's own capital structure, and management policies, the following types of investment objective are reflected:

1. Primarily capital appreciation
2. Emphasis on income
3. Moderate income and moderate appreciation
4. Maintenance of principal value and stable income
5. Search for unusually promising long-pull opportunities, including perhaps a direct management responsibility

The absolute performance of an investment fund is readily determinable for a given period—by the appreciation in value per share, by the dividends paid from investment income, and by the dividends paid from realized profits on the sale of securities. Figures for a single year are not too significant and may actually be misleading; allowance must be made for the long-range objectives of the fund and the position of securities markets generally at the beginning and end of the period used for calculation.

How well a given investment management has discharged its stewardship on a relative basis presents a more difficult problem and is really a task for a specialist who is familiar with the investment-company field and with securities and investing generally. In selecting other funds for purposes of comparison, he would take into account policy, underlying portfolio, and capital structure of the fund; and he would appropriately appraise the accepted stock and bond averages that might be used as a gauge.

One factor in measuring the effectiveness of a given management is the cost of operating expenses, although there is no relationship between such costs and actual investment performance. According to a Standard and Poor's Corporation report (June 19, 1950), the total expenses of open-end investment companies average about 0.75 per cent of net assets, or about 14 per cent of investment income, each year. About one half of 1 per cent represents the fee for management. Fees and expenses of some of the larger funds are lower than the average. The same source reports that operating expenses of the larger closed-end companies averaged less than 0.7 per cent of net assets, and 13.5 per cent of total cash income, per year; but in some instances the figures were substantially higher.

Some critics of the open-end investment companies hold the view that, because such companies represent continuous marketing operations, their investment policies may be influenced at times by the desire to encourage sales of their shares, and at other times may be conditioned by the need to plan for substantial redemptions. There is probably little validity to the first point; the established companies in the field are undoubtedly governed by more fundamental considerations in portfolio administration. With respect to the second point, in the more than a quarter of century of continuous operation the need to generate cash for redemptions has probably not been an important, or even a mildly important, factor in view of the steady, strong growth trend.

In the case of the closed-end companies, because their shares are all outstanding, there is no continuing merchandising effort and, of course, no need to redeem shares.

It is also pointed out that, although the investment companies are, through their efforts, broadening the ownership interest in American enterprise, they are not materially contributing equity capital for new industry because they tend to emphasize in their portfolios the "blue-chip" stocks, stocks of well-established companies with strong asset and earnings positions. In view of the very nature of the diversified investment company, it would appear logical to expect such a tendency. However, some of the investment companies, open-end and closed-end, are conscious of the equity problem. For instance, a number of investment companies of both types include among their holdings an interest in the American Research and Development Company, which was formed "to encourage research and to aid in the development of small new businesses into companies of stature and importance."

Investment-Company Legislation

The methods and policies of investment companies have been affected by various laws and by stock-exchange regulations. Prior to 1929 there was no special stock-exchange regulation, but the New York Stock Exchange in mid-1929 published requirements with respect to the listing of investment-company shares and about two years later revised these requirements and set up regulations to govern member-firm participation in the fixed-trust movement. The blue-sky laws of the several states, the Securities Act of 1933, and the Securities Exchange Act of 1934 all regulate the investment companies. Revisions in the federal income-tax law, particularly the acts of 1936 and 1942, also affected the industry. Reference has already been made to the Investment Company Act of 1940.

TAX STATUS OF INVESTMENT COMPANIES. Under the Revenue Act of 1936, corporations were taxed on dividends received from other corporations, and full application of this provision would have been harmful to investment companies because it would have meant triple taxation (the business, the investment company, and the individual would all have been taxed). Through conferences, special provision was made to favor with a tax advantage those investment companies that would comply with certain operating procedures. Later the Revenue Act of 1942 (Supplement Q) established a special plan for the taxation of investment companies that agreed to comply with stated conditions. This applied to both open-end and closed-end companies that conformed and which were then called "regulated investment companies," a term that is peculiar to the federal tax law and refers to registered companies that meet the conditions of Supplement Q, which are:

1. The company must elect to be a regulated company (election is irrevocable)
2. At least 90 per cent of gross income must be distributed each year
3. Gross income from the sale of securities held less than three months must be less than 30 per cent of the total gross income
4. At least one half of the company assets must be in the form of cash or diversified securities
5. Not more than 25 per cent of the assets may be invested in the securities of any one issuer

If these requirements are met, the investment company pays no tax on the income distributed but pays a tax of 38 per cent on retained earnings. On retained capital gains the tax to the investment company is 25 per cent. The holder of investment-company shares treats the income received from a regulated investment company as though the income had been received on his own direct investments. The effect of the tax exemption granted to regulated investment companies is to encourage distribution of substantially all income and gains realized during the year.

Companies that do not elect to become regulated investment companies are taxed just as any other corporation.

INVESTMENT COMPANY ACT OF 1940. Every investment company with 100 or more shareholders must register under the Investment Company Act of 1940. As already noted, this act grew out of an investigation authorized under the Public Utility Holding Company Act of 1935. The latter law, in turn, was enacted to regulate the holding companies (themselves something akin to investment companies) which had gained control over vast utility properties in the 1920's.

The Investment Company Act is administered by the SEC and was designed to regulate the practices of investment companies in order to protect the public against certain malpractices and abuses that characterized the operation of some of the investment companies in earlier years. A few of the more important provisions of the act can be briefly summarized as follows:

Management. The law is intended to assure honest and independent management; persons who might be in a biased position (underwriters, etc.) may not constitute more than a minority of the board. Excessive commissions and self-dealing (an insider dealing with the fund as principal for his own gain) are prohibited. The SEC may sue in the event of misconduct. Embezzlement is made a federal offense. And the portfolio is to be maintained in the custody of a bank unless other arrangements are made with the SEC.

Investment Policies. Companies are required to file with the SEC a statement outlining precisely the investment policy that is to be followed, and such policy may be changed only with a majority vote of stockholders.

Shareholder Participation. At least two thirds of the directors must be elected by the shareholders. Management contracts are limited to two-year duration and must have stockholder approval. Shareholders ratify selection of the accountants. All future stock issues must have voting power. And preferred stock must have the right to vote in the event of default in dividends.

Capital. Minimum capital required is $100,000. Closed-end companies are limited as to capital structure: at least 50 per cent of assets must be represented by common-stock equity at the time of issuance of senior securities. Only one class of bonds and one class of preferred may be issued by closed-end companies. Open-end companies may issue only common stock but may borrow from banks if assets are maintained at not less than three times the amount of the loan at all times.

Distribution. All sales of new securities by open-end or closed-end companies must be in compliance with the Securities Act of 1933, and sales practices are voluntarily regulated under the rules of the National Association of Securities Dealers, a self-policing body under the supervision of the SEC.

Summary and Evaluation

There was a time when the terms "investment company" and "investment trust" were themselves confusing and encompassed a bewildering array of organizations. Gradual evolution aided by legislation has brought about a clearer definition and understanding as well as a more precise terminology. The "fixed trust" or "unit trust" was but a passing phase. The intelligent investor is financially literate and distinguishes trading, holding, and financing companies and recognizes that these organizations have particular functions to perform but that such companies are different from the open-end and closed-end investment companies.

All investment companies have the same general objectives: to provide for the small and large investor a diversification of holdings that might otherwise be impossible of achievement; and to provide trained and specialized supervision, a function that the average layman is usually not competent to supply on his own. In short, investment companies provide a means of indirect investment in American industry.

This opportunity is made available in many forms. The indirect investor has many choices beyond that of selecting between open-end and closed-end companies. Some companies provide leverage, others are nonleverage. Some companies have balanced portfolios including common stock, preferreds, and bonds; while others have concentrations in common stock, or in preferreds, or in bonds. One management may seek to take advantage of business fluctuations to a major degree; another tends to be fully invested at all times and attempts little adjustment in portfolio during the course of a business cycle. It is possible to have industry diversification or industry concentration; capital appreciation versus maintenance of principal; and maintenance of long-term purchasing power as against current dollar income. Emphasis on established companies in proved industries is the policy of some investment companies, while others favor pioneering companies in new industries. These enumerated tendencies and policies are blended in varying proportions by different managements.

The investment-company concept of distributing risk and providing continuous surveillance is basically sound. But the test is found in the application of the theory; performance depends, in the last analysis, on management. And that is essentially what the purchaser of investment company securities is buying. It is reasonable to expect that the seasoned professional staff of an investment company should be able to demonstrate a performance superior to that of the average lay investor and sufficiently so to justify the fees entailed. The growth of the investment-company movement tends to support this thesis.

In addition to serving the individual, investment companies serve society generally by providing another conduit for the flow of savings from the saver into industry. Through their sales and promotion efforts the open-end companies particularly endeavor to inform and interest many new potential investors in investing, and they are meeting with obvious success. Because most investment companies emphasize, or at least include, some common stocks in their portfolios, the ownership base of American industry is being broadened.

Apprehension has been expressed that with a continuation of the growth of investment companies these organizations might ultimately come to control American enterprise and thus give a relatively small number of men, the investment-company managers, great power over industry. There would seem to be no early or even remote danger of this sort in view of the fact that total assets under investment-company control are relatively small in comparison with the total income and wealth of the nation. In the nine years from the beginning of the organization to December 31, 1949, the 130 member funds of the National Association of Investment Companies averaged an annual growth in net assets of less than $200 million and even in the last year of the period added only $260 million, to bring the net total assets to $2.8 billion after some twenty to thirty years of operation. Furthermore, the policy of broad diversification that is followed limits the extent of investment in the stock of any one company and thus serves to minimize the threat of control.

It is true, however, that investment-company managements might make their influence felt by bringing pressure to bear on corporate management, particularly if several investment companies collaborated. That this might become a factor of substance was suggested early in 1949. The managements of several investment companies became interested in the internal administrative problems of one of the leading mail-order houses in which the investment companies have sizable holdings. Opinions were publicly expressed by investment-company officials, and shares were in some instances voted to protest the management policy of the mail-order house. As a general rule, however, investment-company managers make no attempt to influence or participate in the management of companies in which they have security holdings.

Closely related to this problem of possible control is the question as to whether an investment company might become so large as to make liquidation of its sizable holdings in any given situation impracticable from a market standpoint. Certainly if the managements of a number of large investment trusts all reached the conclusion simultaneously that it would be wise to sell a given stock, of which they all held large amounts, it is obvious that the market might become seriously depressed if wholesale liquidation were attempted. On the other hand, if many investment-company managements independently concluded to buy a certain stock, their combined action over a period of time might reduce the floating supply of that stock and exert an upward price pressure.

Further growth of the investment-company field is favored by the increasing number of states that are recognizing investment-company shares as suitable for trust-fund (fiduciary) investments.

INVESTMENT COUNSEL

We have already noted that the investor is constantly confronted by a complex situation—a rapidly changing kaleidoscope of politics, business, markets, and international developments; also, that any attempt to reach a successful solution of this problem requires persistent study of the forces at work, continuous supervision, and an understanding of the available tools. One medium to assist the investor, which enables him to delegate responsibility for the management of his accumulations—the investment company—has just been discussed.

Investment counsel, likewise of recent origin, provides another avenue of assistance that makes available to the individual and institutional investor the services of investment specialists. The work of the investment counselor who serves exclusively in this capacity is purely advisory; he handles neither the money nor the securities of his clients; and he receives a fee for his services graduated according to the size of his fund.

Origin of Investment Counsel

Investment counsel developed as an important independent occupation after World War I. Prior to that time, there may have been a few scattered individuals or organizations that furnished investment advice independent of any other activity and on some sort of fee basis. However, most investment advice was supplied as a service supplementary to a principal profession: by lawyers, personal trustees, banks, and trust companies, brokers, security dealers, and, of course, investment bankers.

Up to the time of that war, there were relatively few securities in which there was a wide public interest, and securities buyers were largely of a professional type: banks, insurance companies, and trustees. Except for persons of wealth, individuals had little interest in stocks and bonds and gave preference to such investment media as savings accounts, mortgages, and local, familiar situations. Wartime and postwar developments broadened the interest in stocks and bonds. Such developments included the huge sale of Liberty Bonds for financing the war and the boom in the stock market.

To provide impartial, objective guidance for the growing number of investors, the then newly formed investment banking firm Scudder, Stevens & Clark of Boston decided to become exclusively professional advisers on a fee basis, on the theory that as merchants they could not be completely objective in their relationships with customer-clients. In investment-counsel circles, this organization is generally regarded as the progenitor of investment counsel in essentially the form that it is practiced today.

Discussing the origination of the investment-counsel concept, Theodore T. Scudder has written as follows:

. . . I believe the beginning of investment counsel was more or less the result of my experiences and observations. . . . By 1912 or 1913, public corporate financing and corporate ethics had reached a point where some investors were beginning to recognize that common stocks held a real place in the individual investment program. But, generally speaking, most people still held to the old concept of conservative investment. . . . Recognizing that the average investor had no realization of how he should invest or the knowledge or experience to choose among the increasing number of stocks and bonds available, and, further, that there were no persons who were both experienced and impartial to advise him, I came to the conclusion that there was need for a new profession. . . . Therefore, in 1920 my partner, F. Haven Clark, and I decided to put these ideas into more concrete form. Recognizing that we were sailing uncharted seas, we felt that we would have to start on an experimental basis. Consequently I approached about twenty individuals to explain our ideas of conservative investment and our desire to deal with them on an impartial and increasingly expert basis. . . . We would then diagnose their situation and suggest to them what we believed to be a sound investment program to follow. . . . We suggested that they pay us 1 per cent of the money involved in each transaction. Hypothetically we figured this would pay the cost of serving them over an average period of years. Although many laughed at us in the beginning, we nevertheless found a ready reception of our ideas. The number of clients increased almost as fast as we could take them. In 1921 we invented the term "investment counsel" for the work in our office in Boston. The name was suggested by A. Vere Shaw, who was associated with us at that time.[3]

Within just a few years, and independently, E. P. Farwell in 1924 pioneered in the establishment of investment counsel services in Chicago and later joined with E. E. Sheridan and P. L. Morrison to form Sheridan, Farwell & Morrison, Inc., since absorbed by Scudder, Stevens & Clark. The Scudder organization not only is the pioneer investment counsel organization but is generally regarded as having the largest volume of funds under supervision.

Others followed the lead, and by 1929 there were about 70 investment-counsel firms. The number expanded rapidly during the 1930's and subsequently, so that at the close of 1946 there were almost 900 investment-adviser registrations reported by the SEC. The volume of funds under supervision is regarded as confidential information and is, therefore, not generally available. However, some indication of the magnitude of investment-counsel operations was provided by a 1938 report of the SEC which showed that fifty-odd investment-counsel firms had approximately $4 billion under supervision in 1937.

Operation

SCOPE.   Investment-counsel service is available only for larger funds because most practitioners will not accept for supervision funds under $50,000 and in many cases $100,000. Fees are usually payable quarterly at an annual rate ranging from ½ to 1 per cent on the minimum principal sum and at a gradually declining rate for increments above the minimum. Smaller accounts are not accepted because the minimum work and costs entailed, whatever the size of the fund, would require a fee that the investor would probably consider excessive in relation to the principal and income. To serve the investor who has a smaller fund, some investment counselors sponsor investment companies under their own supervision. Such investment companies have the same management direction as the individual accounts of the counselor, but obviously the portfolio and policies cannot be adapted to the particular requirements of each of the participants.

Investment counsel serves, in addition to the more affluent individuals, a wide variety of institutional investors who do not have adequate funds under control to justify, on a cost basis, setting up a

[3] Quotation from a signed statement supplied to the author.

comprehensive investment organization of their own. Such institutional investors include commercial banks, trust companies, estates, insurance companies, and educational and other endowment funds.

In addition to providing current investment advice, investment counsel often assists in estate planning through co-operation with the lawyer, accountant, and tax specialist of the client.

PROCEDURE.   Usually the investor who has decided to engage investment counsel will sign a one-year contract, renewable quarterly thereafter at the election of either party. Then the procedure will generally be about as follows:

Determination of Objective.   Agreement will be reached with the client on a specific statement of the investment objective, as described in Chapter 10, including the policies to be pursued and any special arrangements to be made or conditions to be observed.

Fund Analysis.   The client will provide a list of all of his investment holdings and the cash that is to be included in the fund. He does not turn over the securities or cash themselves. The fund will be analyzed from the standpoint of suitability for the stated objective. It will be examined with respect to the nature and the quality of holdings. Specific recommendations will be made to sell, hold, or buy given securities, in the light of existing business conditions, in order to bring the fund into conformity with the investment aim. The reasoning that supports each recommendation is presented. The final decision as to what action will be taken rests with the client. However, if the client does not have confidence in the counselor and consistently fails to carry out recommendations, the relationship will probably be terminated at an early date by the counselor, if the client does not previously take the step himself.

Arrangement with the Broker.   Arrangements are usually made by the client with his broker to have confirmations of transactions in duplicate, one copy being sent direct to the counselor, the other to the client. On the basis of these confirmations the counselor maintains an up-to-the-minute record of the client's holdings. If the client wishes to do so, he may give the counselor full discretion in managing the account and instruct the broker to execute the orders that are given by the counselor, rather than having the orders placed by the client himself.

Constant Supervision.   The account of the client is kept under constant and close supervision from day to day, and adjustments are recommended by investment counsel as changing conditions dictate.

Reports on the status of the fund are submitted to the client usually once a month, showing for each item the cost, current market, rate of income, and other pertinent information.

Recommendations are communicated to the client by telephone, letter, telegram, or in person; and clients are usually encouraged to call in person to review the business outlook and discuss the current attitude of counsel on investment policy.

Organization

There are three principal functions in the operation of investment counsel: administration and new business; counseling; and research. Administration is responsible for the over-all business management and the development of new accounts. Counselors are responsible for account supervision; they communicate with the client on recommendations and review his account with him. Research is responsible for appraising fundamental economic and industry trends and for analyzing companies and specific securities. The findings of research are made available to the counselors, who make use of the information conveyed to them in supervising the accounts.

In large investment-counsel firms the research function may be divided among a considerable number of men—some on economic research, others on government and foreign developments; some on heavy industry, others on consumer goods industries; etc. The findings of the research men are co-ordinated into a composite opinion that constitutes the policy of the counseling firm with respect to economic fundamentals, industries, companies, securities, interest rates, earnings prospects, and related factors.

Performance

Client accounts are handled on a confidential basis, and results are not made public. However, it is usually possible for a prospective client to examine a few representative accounts. Satisfied clients may confide in friends and recommend investment counsel just as in the case of other professional relationships. If an investment counsel firm operates a mutual investment fund, the performance of the fund will give an indication of effectiveness of the supervision.

Investment counsel is not infallible and cannot work miracles. However, it should be able to provide a reasonable rate of current income and some appreciation without undue exposure of the fund to risks. That investment counsel is justifying its existence is suggested by the retention of counsel over the years by many individuals and institutional investors and also by the growth in the volume of funds under supervision.

Regulation

Investment counsel is supervised by the SEC under the Investment Advisers Act of 1940, a part of the law regulating investment companies. Subject to certain exceptions, all persons offering investment advice for compensation, either directly or through writings, must register under the act. Those who give advice incidentally and gratuitously are exempt and need not register. Others who need not register are: those who do not advise with respect to securities dealt in on a national exchange; those who are exclusively consultants to insurance companies; and those who do not solicit business publicly and have fewer than fifteen clients.

The use of the term "investment counsel" is limited to those who are registered; fees may not be based on capital gains realized; and registration under the act may not be held out as constituting government approval or sponsorship. The SEC may investigate violations of the act, may obtain information, but may not examine books and records. The SEC may enjoin violators or may refuse or revoke registration.

A measure of control over investment counsel is also effected with respect to the limited number of firms (29) that are members of the Investment Counsel Association of America, an association that has requirements which are more stringent than those of the Investment Advisers Act.

Other Supervisory Agencies

In contrast to the investment counsel firms discussed above, which engage only in investment counsel, there are other advisory and supervisory agencies that provide a similar service. In a census of the Investment Bankers Association of America made in 1940, 34 out of 368 members answered in the affirmative to the question: "Do you engage in the business of giving investment counsel for a fee?" Trust companies and trust departments of commercial banks also render an investment supervisory service, and some sponsor common trust funds (see Chapter 14). Companies such as Moody's Investors Service and the Standard and Poor's Corporation, which publish investment information and financial statistics, also offer investment advice on a fee basis. Some brokerage firms provide gratuitous investment advice through a special staff set up for the purpose.

Ancillary Service

Investors who wish to escape the responsibility for the physical care of their securities as well as the responsibility of making investment decisions may arrange for a discretionary account with investment counsel and for an agency account with a trust company. Under a discretionary arrangement, counsel is authorized by the client to instruct the broker directly to execute transactions for the account. Under an agency account, the trust company holds the securities, receives confirmations from the broker, clips coupons, collects dividends, and provides related services.

—ERWIN W. BOEHMLER

SUPPLEMENT

INVESTMENT PORTFOLIO, MASSACHUSETTS INVESTORS TRUST, DECEMBER 31, 1949[1]

COMMON STOCKS

Shares	Company	Market Per Share	Market Total	Per Cent at Market
AGRICULTURAL MACHINERY				
126,000	International Harvester Co.	$27\frac{3}{4}$	$ 3,496,500	1.3
AUTOMOTIVE				
68,000	Chrysler Corp.	$67\frac{1}{4}$	4,573,000	1.7
55,000	General Motors Corp.	$71\frac{5}{8}$	3,939,375	1.4
	Total		$ 8,512,375	3.1
AVIATION				
50,000	North American Aviation	$11\frac{3}{8}$	568,750	0.2
BANKS				
30,000	Bankers Trust Co., N.Y.	$45\frac{1}{2}$	1,365,000	0.5
14,000	Cont'l Ill. Nat'l Bk. Tr. Chic.	$85\frac{1}{4}$	1,193,500	0.4
10,000	First Nat'l Bank, Boston	$47\frac{3}{8}$	473,750	0.2
5,000	First Nat'l Bank, Chicago	202	1,010,000	0.4
8,000	Guaranty Trust Co., N.Y.	297	2,376,000	0.9
28,500	Manufact'rs Trust Co., N.Y.	$53\frac{1}{4}$	1,517,625	0.5
3,400	Mellon Nat'l Bk. & Tr. Co.	271	921,400	0.3
42,000	Nat'l City Bank of N.Y.	$45\frac{1}{2}$	1,911,000	0.7
12,500	Nat'l Shawmut Bank, Boston	$27\frac{3}{4}$	346,875	0.1
2,500	Security-Fst. Nat'l Bk., Los Ang.	$66\frac{1}{4}$	165,625	0.1
	Total		$ 11,280,775	4.1

[1] From *Twenty-fifth Annual Report of the Massachusetts Investors Trust* (Boston, 1949), pp. 16–20.

COMMON STOCKS (*Continued*)

Shares	Company	Per Share	Market Total	Per Cent at Market
BUILDING				
25,000	Armstrong Cork Co.	$50\frac{1}{2}$	1,262,500	0.5
70,000	Johns-Manville Corp.	$49\frac{3}{4}$	3,482,500	1.3
16,000	Lone Star Cement Corp.	76	1,216,000	0.4
50,000	National Lead Co.	$37\frac{1}{2}$	1,875,000	0.7
70,000	Pittsburgh Plate Glass Co.	$37\frac{3}{8}$	2,616,250	0.9
30,000	Sherwin-Williams Co.	66	1,980,000	0.7
17,000	U.S. Gypsum Co.	$113\frac{1}{2}$	1,929,500	0.7
15,000	Weyerhaeuser Timber Co.	$74\frac{1}{2}$	1,117,500	0.4
	Total		$ 15,479,250	5.6
CHEMICALS				
20,000	Allied Chemical & Dye Corp.	205	4,100,000	1.5
5,400	Dow Chem. Co. (Incl. value 5,000 rts.)	$55\frac{1}{8}$	298,690	0.1
89,000	duPont de Nemours & Co.	$61\frac{5}{8}$	5,484,625	2.0
37,000	Hercules Powder Co.	$52\frac{1}{4}$	1,933,250	0.7
60,000	Monsanto Chemical Co.	$56\frac{3}{8}$	3,382,500	1.2
30,000	Pfizer (Chas.) & Co., Inc.	$55\frac{1}{2}$	1,665,000	0.5
65,000	Union Carb. & Carb. Corp.	$44\frac{5}{8}$	2,900,625	1.1
	Total		$ 19,764,690	7.1
CONTAINERS				
23,000	American Can Co.	$106\frac{1}{2}$	$ 2,449,500	0.9
17,500	Marathon Corporation	25	437,500	0.1
22,926	Metal Box Co., Ltd.	$7\frac{1}{8}$	163,347	0.1
45,000	Owen-Illinois Glass Co.	$64\frac{3}{4}$	2,913,750	1.0
	Total		$ 5,964,097	2.1
ELECTRICAL EQUIPMENT				
90,000	General Electric Co.	$42\frac{1}{8}$	3,791,250	1.4
120,000	Westinghouse Elec. Corp.	$32\frac{5}{8}$	3,915,000	1.4
	Total		$ 7,706,250	2.8
FOODS				
25,000	National Biscuit Co.	$39\frac{1}{2}$	987,500	0.4
22,000	United Fruit Co.	$55\frac{5}{8}$	1,223,750	0.4
40,000	Wilson & Co., Inc.	$12\frac{3}{8}$	495,000	0.2
	Total		$ 2,706,250	1.0
METALS AND MINING				
15,000	Aluminium Ltd.	49	735,000	0.2
10,000	Aluminum Co. of America	$51\frac{1}{2}$	515,000	0.2
36,000	Climax Molybdenum Co.	$12\frac{1}{2}$	450,000	0.1
10,000	Homestake Mining Co.	$46\frac{3}{8}$	463,750	0.2
45,000	Hudson Bay Min. & Smelt.	$41\frac{1}{8}$	1,850,625	0.7
60,000	Int. Nickel Co. of Can. Ltd.	$28\frac{1}{8}$	1,687,500	0.6
75,000	Kennecott Copper Corp.	$50\frac{7}{8}$	3,815,625	1.4
22,000	New Jersey Zinc Co.	$56\frac{1}{4}$	1,237,500	0.4
70,000	Phelps Dodge Corp.	$48\frac{5}{8}$	3,403,750	1.2
20,000	U.S. Smelt. Ref. & Min. Co.	$37\frac{1}{2}$	750,000	0.3
11,000	West Kentucky Coal Co.	$20\frac{1}{2}$	225,500	0.1
	Total		$ 15,134,250	5.4

COMMON STOCKS (*Continued*)

Shares	Company	Per Share	Market Total	Per Cent at Market
MOTION PICTURES				
60,000	Paramount Pictures Inc.	22	1,320,000	0.5
70,000	Twentieth Cent.-Fox Film	24⅝	1,723,750	0.6
	Total		$ 3,043,750	1.1
NATURAL GAS				
35,000	Mississippi River Fuel Corp.	38½	1,347,500	0.5
36,000	Northern Natural Gas Co.	39	1,404,000	0.5
40,000	Panhandle Eastern Pipe Line Co.	37¼	1,490,000	0.5
20,000	Republic Natural Gas Co.	41½	830,000	0.3
55,000	Shamrock Oil & Gas Corp.	27½	1,512,500	0.5
100,000	United Gas Corp.	18⅞	1,887,500	0.7
	Total		$ 8,471,500	3.0
OFFICE EQUIPMENT				
23,000	Internat'l Business Mach. Corp.	227	$ 5,221,000	1.9
47,000	National Cash Register Co.	35¾	1,680,250	0.6
	Total		$ 6,901,250	2.5
OILS				
43,000	Amerada Petroleum Corp.	112¼	4,826,750	1.7
40,000	Cities Service Co.	68¾	2,750,000	1.0
70,000	Continental Oil Co.	60	4,200,000	1.5
72,000	Gulf Oil Corp.	64½	4,644,000	1.7
37,000	Humble Oil & Ref. Co.	85	3,145,000	1.1
18,892	Louisiana Land & Expl. Co.	30	566,760	0.2
43,000	Mid-Continent Petroleum Co.	40¼	1,730,750	0.6
40,000	Mission Corporation	48	1,920,000	0.7
15,500	Mission Development Co.	10	155,000	0.1
25,000	Seaboard Oil Co. of Del.	52¾	1,318,750	0.5
50,000	Shell Oil Company	37¼	1,862,500	0.7
84,000	Standard Oil Co. of Calif.	65	5,460,000	2.0
70,000	Standard Oil Co. (Indiana)	44¾	3,132,500	1.1
60,700	Standard Oil Co. (N.J.)	66¾	4,051,725	1.5
120,000	Standard Oil Co. (Ohio)	25¾	3,090,000	1.1
75,000	Texas Company	60⅜	4,528,125	1.6
	Total		$ 47,381,860	17.1
PAPER				
10,000	Great Northern Paper Co.	40⅝	406,250	0.1
122,000	International Paper Co.	36⅜	4,437,750	1.6
	Total		$ 4,844,000	1.7
RAILROADS				
35,000	Atch. Top. & Santa Fe Ry.	101¼	3,543,750	1.3
25,000	Chic., R.I. & Pac. R.R. Co.	41¼	1,031,250	0.3
30,000*	Illinois Central R.R. Co.	36½	1,095,000	0.4
17,000	Norfolk & Western Ry. Co.	49¾	845,750	0.3
71,500	Southern Pacific Co.	50½	3,610,750	1.3
26,000	Union Pacific Railroad Co.	84	2,184,000	0.8
	Total		$ 12,310,500	4.4

COMMON STOCKS (*Continued*)

Shares	Company	Market Per Share	Total	Per Cent at Market
STEELS				
35,000	Bethlehem Steel Corp.	32	1,120,000	0.4
23,000	Youngstown Sheet & Tube Co.	75½	1,736,500	0.6
	Total		$ 2,856,500	1.0
STORES				
45,000	Associated Dry Goods Corp.	15⅜	$ 691,875	0.2
89,000	Gimbel Brothers, Inc.	15⅜	1,368,375	0.5
15,000*	Hoving Corp.	6	90,000	0.0
30,000	Kroger Company	60½	1,815,000	0.7
60,000	Marshall Field & Co.	24	1,440,000	0.5
95,000	Montgomery Ward & Co.	54⅞	5,213,125	1.9
65,000	Penney (J. C.) Co.	56¼	3,656,250	1.3
40,000	Safeway Stores, Inc.	31½	1,260,000	0.5
125,000	Sears, Roebuck & Co.	44⅛	5,515,625	2.0
	Total		$ 21,050,250	7.6
TELEPHONE				
10,000	American Tel. & Tel. Co.	146½	1,465,000	0.5
TIRE AND RUBBER				
40,000	Firestone Tire & Rubber Co.	56½	2,260,000	0.8
48,000	Goodrich (B. F.) Co.	70	3,360,000	1.2
35,000	Goodyear Tire & Rubber Co.	44¾	1,566,250	0.6
	Total		$ 7,186,250	2.6
TOBACCO				
44,000	American Tobacco Co.	74½	3,278,000	1.2
32,000	Liggett & Myers Tob. Co.	90	2,880,000	1.0
	Total		$ 6,158,000	2.2
UTILITIES				
60,000	American Gas & Electric Co.	50½	3,030,000	1.1
60,000	American Natural Gas Co.	32¼	1,935,000	0.7
33,000	Brooklyn Union Gas Co.	38½	1,270,500	0.5
125,000	Central & South West Corp.	14½	1,812,500	0.7
40,000	Cleveland Electric Ill. Co.	43¼	1,730,000	0.6
30,000	Commonwealth Edison Co.	30½	915,000	0.3
120,000	Cons. Edison Co. of N.Y.	27⅝	3,315,000	1.2
65,000	Consolidated Natural Gas Co.	43½	2,827,500	1.0
23,000	Dayton Power & Light Co.	30⅛	692,875	0.3
67,000	Detroit Edison Co.	21⅞	1,465,625	0.5
135,000	General Public Utilities	16⅜	2,210,625	0.8
25,000	Illinois Power Co.	36½	912,500	0.3
27,500	Kansas Power & Light Co.	16⅜	450,312	0.2
110,000	Middle So. Utilities, Inc.	18	1,980,000	0.7
26,000	N.Y. State Elec. & Gas Co.	53¾	1,397,500	0.5
110,000	North American Co.	19⅛	2,103,750	0.8
37,500	Ohio Edison Company	32⅛	1,204,687	0.4
41,200	Pacific Gas & Electric Co.	33⅛	1,364,750	0.5
83,000	Public Service El. & Gas Co.	25⅝	2,126,875	0.8
23,000	Rochester Gas & Elec. Corp.	32⅜	744,625	0.3
50,000	Southern Calif. Edison Co.	34¾	1,737,500	0.6
125,000	Southern Company	11¾	1,468,750	0.5
65,000*	United Light & Railways Co.	39	2,535,000	0.9
45,000	Wisconsin Electric Power Co.	20¼	911,250	0.3
	Total		$ 40,142,124	14.5

COMMON STOCKS (*Continued*)

Shares	Company	Per Share	Market Total	Per Cent at Market
MISCELLANEOUS				
14,615*	American Research & Develop.†	23¼	$ 339,798	0.1
3,000	American Viscose Corp.	72	216,000	0.1
25,000	Colgate-Palmolive-Peet Co.	42¾	1,068,750	0.4
100,000	Eastman Kodak Co.	46¾	4,675,000	1.7
26,000	Food Mach. & Chemical Corp.	28½	741,000	0.3
30,000	Gillette Safety Razor	34⅝	1,038,750	0.4
15,100	Minnesota Mining & Mfg. Co.	100	1,510,000	0.5
20,000	Newport News S. & D. D. Co.	27⅜	547,500	0.2
181,500	United Merch. & Mfrs., Inc.	12⅝	2,291,437	0.8
	Total		$ 12,428,235	4.5

PREFERRED STOCKS

RAILROADS				
9,500	Southern Railway Co. 5%	54½	517,750	0.2

RAILROAD BONDS

Face Value $1,000				
3,125	Missouri Pacific 1st ref. 5% 1965–81		2,941,215	1.1

CASH AND GOVERNMENTS

	Cash and Receivables—Net		$ 5,680,513	2.0
	U.S. Treasury Bills		3,498,781	1.3
	Total		$ 9,179,294	3.3
Net Assets			$277,490,665	100.0

* No dividend paid in past twelve months.
† Representing 8.25% of the outstanding voting securities.

QUESTIONS AND PROBLEMS

1. In broad terms what is meant by "investment company"?

2. Distinguish between a fixed trust, an open-end investment company, a closed-end investment company, and a holding company.

3. What advantages are claimed for the investment company, particularly with respect to the investor of modest means?

4. What factors account for the rapid rise in net total assets of open-end companies in contrast to the experience of the closed-end companies?

5. Explain through an illustration what is meant by "capital leverage."

6. Are investment companies the answer to the "venture-capital" problem?

7. The experience of American investment companies may be said to have paralleled the experience of the British investment companies. Explain.

8. What is the distinction between a registered investment company and a regulated investment company?

9. Why is it difficult to make a comparative study of the performance of investment companies?

10. What is meant by "investment counsel"? How did the term originate?

11. Outline the general procedure followed by an investment counsel.

12. Who is served by an investment counsel?

13. What should the individual investor expect from an investment counsel?

14. In what respects are investment companies and investment counselors providing a similar service for individual investors? What are the elements of difference?

15. What is the economic justification for an investment counsel and for investment companies?

BIBLIOGRAPHY

In connection with the study of investment trusts and investment companies conducted by the Securities and Exchange Commission prior to the adoption of the Investment Company Act of 1940, the Commission prepared a five-volume report, *Investment Trusts and Investment Companies* (Washington, D.C.: U.S. Government Printing Office, 1939–40), and also published hearings on all phases of the industry and on related activities. A book and also a reprint of a series of articles, both by the same author, A. B. Stevenson, dealing with investment companies and with particular reference to the interests of fiduciaries, are: *Shares in Mutual Investment Funds* (Nashville: Vanderbilt University Press, 1946); and *Investment Company Shares* (New York: Fiduciary Publishers, Inc., 1947), a reprint of articles that appeared originally in *Trusts and Estates* magazine. While appropriate, in the main, for the general reader, both include a discussion on measuring performance. A booklet by E. A. Mennis and R. L. Blair, *Investment Trusts and Funds* (Great Barrington, Mass.: American Institute for Economic Research, 1948), prepared from the investor's point of view, is popularly written and fairly comprehensive; it also sets up requirements for an ideal fund. A discussion of investment policies of investment companies is presented in G. W. Dowrie and D. R. Fuller, *Investments* (2d ed.; New York: John Wiley & Sons, Inc., 1950); and this volume, as well as such other texts on investments as J. C. Clendenin, *Introduction to Investments* (New York: McGraw-Hill Book Co., Inc., 1950), and R. E. Badger and H. G. Guthmann, *Investment Principles and Practices* (3d ed.; New York: Prentice-Hall, Inc., 1941), evaluates the funds as investment media. Comprehensive information on individual investment companies and comparative statistics are available in a volume, published annually, by Arthur Wiesenberger, *Investment Companies* (New York: Arthur Wiensenberger & Company; annually since 1941), which also suggests a method for appraising management results.

The report of the Securities and Exchange Commission on investment companies noted above included a supplementary report on investment counsel; and the hearings that preceded the passage of the Investment Advisers Act of 1940 are also published. One of the most complete statements available on the work of investment counsel is found in Part III, "Investment Counsel— The New Profession," in D. C. Rose, *The Practical Application of Investment Management*, Vol. II (New York: Harper & Bros., 1933). A popular discussion of investment counsel is found in H. G. Carpenter, *The Letters of an*

Investment Counsel to Mr. & Mrs. John Smith (New York: Harper & Bros., 1940). The *Investment Counsel Annual,* published by the Investment Counsel Association of America, New York, includes addresses and papers on various topics pertinent to investment counsel. The "Code of Professional Practice" of the Association appears in each volume.

Chapter 14

TRUSTEE SERVICES

THE observing person will have noted that there is a wide variance in the titles of commercial banks. Some are merely named "Bank"; others may be named "Trust Company"; and still others may combine both concepts and have a corporate title includings the words "Bank and Trust Company." Then, again, there are companies that have very similarly sounding names, but it is found that they are not commercial banks at all but do a purely trust business. There are, in fact, almost sixty different corporate titles represented among those institutions that engage in trust business either exclusively or in combination with some other business activity (usually commercial banking). It is really quite confusing and can only be understood in the light of historical development. But first, what is a "trust"? What is meant by "trust business"? And what are "trust institutions"?

Concept of Trusteeship

The trust is a legal device, and the concept of trusteeship can be traced back to antiquity. The trust has a long and complicated legal history, but for present purposes it is enough to know what a trust is and what it accomplishes. A simple example will serve best to explain this and to prepare the way for a definition of the term "trust."

Assume that a businessman of means wishes to set aside a substantial sum of money for his son, the son to receive part of the income earned on the fund each year and to receive the principal sum when he reaches a certain age. The man then makes arrangements with a third person to have that person accept the money, invest it, pay the income as directed, and ultimately pay the principal sum to the son. A "trust" has then been created.

In this example the businessman is the grantor or creator of the trust. The third person who receives the money (the assets of the trust, or the body, or corpus, of the trust) and who then holds legal title or ownership is the trustee. The trustee holds the title for the benefit of the son, who is the beneficiary and who has a beneficial interest in the trust. The arrangement made by the businessman with the third person is the "trust agreement."

A trust may also be created by means of a deed or by will. If the trust is created by a will, the creator is known as a "testator"; if the trust is created by a living person, the creator is variously known as "trustor," "donor," or "settlor," as well as "grantor."

The relationship between the parties to an arrangement such as has been sketched is one of confidence and trust. The creator of the trust places confidence in the trustee that the trustee will act in good faith in carrying out the agreement as made. This arrangement is also referred to as a "fiduciary relationship," and the trustee is called a fiduciary.

It should be noted, however, that a fiduciary is not necessarily a trustee. There are many other relationships of a fiduciary character: a member of a board of directors is a fiduciary for stockholders; a member of a partnership, for the other partner or partners; an attorney, for his client; and an agent, for his principal. But these persons are not trustees in the strict sense, even though they are in positions of trust and confidence.

What is the distinction? In the trust there is a transfer of ownership to the person that is trusted (the trustee), and he holds the legal title for the benefit of the beneficiary, who has the beneficial interest. In the other instances mentioned, there is no transfer of ownership.

A trust agreement may also be distinguished from a contract. In a contract there must be a *quid pro quo*, a consideration. In enforcing a trust agreement, it is not necessary to show that the trustee received a consideration; to enforce a contract, it must generally be shown that the party who made a promise received something in return. There is another important distinction: a party to a contract need perform only in conformity with the explicit stipulations in the contract; in a trust agreement, the law implies duties on the part of the trustee beyond those specifically stated in the agreement. (The student of law would sum up this significant distinction in this way: the contract is a creature of the common law, and a trust is a creature of equity.[1])

---

[1] It is beyond the scope of this text to consider in further detail the distinction between a contract and a trust agreement and the distinction between the common law and equity. For such a discussion, consult treatises on business or commercial law and

On the basis of this discussion a definition of a trust can be formulated: a trust is an agreement (trust agreement) under which the trustor or creator of the trust, having confidence in another, transfers the ownership of property to that other person (trustee) for the benefit of a third person (beneficiary) who has the beneficial interest in the property.

To expand the definition: the creator may be a beneficiary; the creator may be the trustee; the trustee may be one or more persons or a corporation; and the trust represents a fiduciary relationship that is characterized by the separation of the ownership and the beneficial interest.

Trust Business

To say that trust business is the business of a trustee is not revealing. True, the handling of trusts is trust business, but the term as generally understood today has a much broader meaning and in 1933 was defined by the Trust Division of the American Bankers Association, and approved by the Executive Council of the Association, as follows:

Trust business is the business of settling estates, administering trusts and performing agencies in all appropriate cases for individuals; partnerships; associations; business corporations; public, educational, social, recreational, and charitable institutions; and units of government. It is advisable that a trust institution should limit the functions of its trust department to such services.

This statement will suffice for the present; later the services rendered by trustees for individuals and for corporations will be considered in more detail.

Trust Institutions

Any adult who is duly appointed by a person or court with authority to act may serve as a trustee and may engage in those activities that have been described as constituting trust business. He may be an agent, an executor named in a will, an administrator named by the court to settle an estate, a guardian of the estate of a minor, or a conservator of the estate of an incompetent. Lawyers and accountants give some time to the trust type of business. However, few individuals

---

treatises on trusts. Elementary discussions will be found in H. F. Lusk, *Business Law: Principles and Cases* (4th ed.; Chicago: Richard D. Irwin, Inc., 1951), pp. 2–5 and 6–7, and G. T. Stephenson, *Estates and Trusts* (New York: Appleton-Century-Crofts, Inc., 1949), pp. 10–12.

give their full time to such activity. Particularly in Boston, however, there are individual professional trustees, called "Boston trustees," who are usually lawyers and who devote much of their time to the settling of estates and the administration of trusts but do not engage in a comprehensive trust business.

Trusts services are performed primarily by two types of institutions: trust companies, most of which also engage in commercial banking; and commercial banks that have established trust departments. Other corporations that do trust work include title-guaranty companies, mortgage bankers, and safe-deposit companies. It will now be clear why this chapter is headed "Trustee Services" rather than "Trust Institutions" or "Trust Companies."

History of the Trust Business in the United States

In 1818 the state of Massachusetts chartered the Massachusetts Hospital and Life Insurance Company and gave the company the power, among other provisions, "to make all kinds of contracts, in which the casualties of life and interest of money are principally involved; and to make, execute and perfect such and so many contracts, bargains, agreements, policies, and other instruments, as shall or may be necessary, and as the nature of the case shall or may require." The grant was interpreted by the directors to mean that the company was empowered to accept trusts, and in 1823 the legislature confirmed this interpretation through an appropriate amendment of the charter.

The Farmers' Fire Insurance and Loan Company was incorporated in New York in 1822 to do a fire insurance business and to lend to farmers. A few months after incorporation the company applied for trust powers that were then specifically granted through an amendment of its charter. However, this company (which later became the City Bank Farmers Trust Company of New York City) did not accept its first trust until a number of years later.

In these two corporations are found the beginnings of the corporate fiduciary in the United States. Other states followed the lead of Massachusetts and New York and granted charters that authorized trust business. The Pennsylvania Company for Insurance on Lives and Granting Annuities was organized in 1812 and was expressly authorized to engage in trust business in 1836, but in the preceding year it had already accepted what is believed to have been the first living trust. This company continued doing business under the same name until just a few years ago, when it became the Pennsylvania Company.

Many reasons are assigned for the development of the trust business

in the years 1820–40.[2] The trust business is, in the main, a city rather
than country development; and the twenty-year period witnessed a
change in emphasis from such tangible wealth as farms, cattle, and
related property to intangibles, stocks, and bonds. In the years to
follow, this trend was accentuated by the establishment and growth
of new industries and services, including the railroads, the steamboat,
street railways, gas light, and many others. The populations of cities
were expanding rapidly. Large family fortunes were being accumulated. The corporation was replacing the simple forms of business
organization; and the introduction of various industries served to
change the economy from one consisting primarily of farming and
merchandising. Large accumulations of wealth and intangible property were undoubtedly the significant factors responsible for the
inception and the early, moderate growth of the trust-company movement.

Until after the Civil War the trust business was not of significant
proportions. But thereafter, under the influence of steadily expanding
industrialization, the mounting importance of the corporate form of
enterprise, and, consequently, the growing complexity of business
affairs, there was an increasing need for the type of service rendered
by the corporate trustee. By 1900 there were about 300 trust companies. Trends have since been highly favorable to the rapid growth
of the trust services offered by both trust companies and by banks,
and there are now approximately 2,900 corporate trustees.

Trust Companies versus Trust Departments

As already noted, the trust business was a development incidental
to the insurance business; but soon corporations were chartered by
various states for the express purpose of engaging in trust business,
either by special charters granted by the legislature or under trust
company statutes. These charters were generally so broad that the
trust companies were able to engage in the commercial banking business as well, and did so to the discomfiture of state banks. To meet
this growing competition state banks agitated for, and won, trust
powers and were thus enabled to engage in trust business. At first
national banks were not permitted to do a trust business; and in order
to participate in the expanding volume of trust business, they organized separate affiliated trust institutions under state law. The First

---

[2] G. T. Stephenson, *Trust Business in Common Law Countries* (New York: American
Bankers Association, 1940), pp. 539–40.

Trust and Savings Bank, created in 1903 by the first National Bank of Chicago, was one of the first of such affiliates to be established.

In 1913 the national banks were authorized to serve as fiduciaries, and the Federal Reserve Act was amended in 1918 to extend their trust powers; but the authorization was challenged, and it was not until 1925 that a United States Supreme Court decision unquestionably established the right of national banks to do a trust business. National banks had difficulty in obtaining trust business, however, because their charters ran for only a stated fifty years. To remove this deterrent the McFadden-Pepper Act, passed in 1927, gave the banks indeterminate life. Since that time, the trust business of national banks has grown rapidly.

Today most of the trust business is done either by trust companies that do a commercial banking business or by commercial banks that do a trust business through a department within their corporate structure. There are relatively few true trust companies. It is for this reason that the broad term "trust institutions," rather than "trust companies," is used to designate all of these organizations that are engaged in providing trust services.

Extent of the Trust Business

At the end of 1946 there were 14,818 banks (commercial and savings) in the United States, not including branches, and 2,976 trust institutions, of which less than 100 did no banking business. The banks had total deposits—commercial and savings—of slightly more than $157 billion; the 2,976 trust institutions had personal trust property under supervision amounting to approximately $36 billion. This trust business is concentrated in relatively few large institutions: about 4 per cent, or 114 institutions, account for four fifths of the personal trust property under supervision; and 68 institutions account for almost 72 per cent of the trust business of the country. Two thirds of the trust institutions, each having $1 million or less of personal trust property under supervision, were doing only slightly over 1 per cent of the trust business.[3]

Classification of Services

Trust institutions undoubtedly render a wider range of services than any other financial institutions, and this is certainly true of those metropolitan organizations that do both a commercial banking and a

---

[3] G. T. Stephenson, "Trust Business in the United States, 1947," *The Trust Bulletin*, Vol. XXVII, No. 8 (April, 1948), pp. 19–32.

Exhibit 50

STANDARD TRUST SERVICES OFFERED BY METROPOLITAN BANKS AND
TRUST COMPANIES

Services rendered only to individuals:

Executor under wills

Administrator of intestate estates

Ancillary executor or administrator where principal estate administration
is in another state

Trustee under wills

Guardian of the estates of minors

Conservator of the estates of persons under a legal disability other than
minority

Depositary under court appointment for diminution of surety bonds of
personal executors, administrators, guardians, and conservators

Trustee under agreement:

Securities and other property

Proceeds of life insurance policies

Services rendered only to corporations and similar organizations:

Trustee and depositary under trust indenture under which corporate bonds
and notes are issued

Paying, exchange, and redemption agent

Depositary and exchange agent under corporate reorganization plans

Transfer agent for the transfer of corporate stock and warrant agent for
issuance of subscription rights and acceptance of subscriptions to corporate stock

Registrar for stocks and registered corporate obligations

Dividend-disbursing agent (this service frequently involves mailing of
annual statements, notices of meetings, and similar special services)

Trustee under profit-sharing and pension trusts

*Services rendered both to individuals and corporations and similar organiza-
tions:*

Safekeeping (custody and limited collection service)

Fiscal agency (custody, collection, and maintenance of records)

Supervised agency (custody, collection, maintenance of records, and investment advice)

Escrow agent

Trustee or agent under lease

Title-holding trustee (real estate); commonly referred to as "naked" or
"blind" title-holding trusts

Trustee under agreements for purchase and sale of stock or partnership
interests

Source: Prepared by the Trust Department of the First National Bank of Chicago.

trust business. Corporate trustees are therefore a significant segment
of our financial structure not only from the standpoint of the approximately eighty separate trust services they perform but also in view of
the volume of funds under their supervision. Corporate trustees help

the individual with his personal, financial, and business affairs and provide services that are highly essential, if not indispensable, to corporations and the business life of the nation. It can well be said that corporate trustees are ready to provide almost any service that has to do with the preservation and transfer of property—whether tangible or intangible, personal or real—and, in addition, are ready to assist the individual with personal problems that go beyond the pecuniary.

Exhibit 50 classifies some of the more important standard trust services under three main headings: those rendered only to individuals; those rendered only to corporations; and those rendered to both individuals and corporations and similar organizations. Most of the services listed in this illustration are briefly considered in the following paragraphs, which aim to give the reader some indication of the variety and scope of the work of the trustee.

Services Rendered Only to Individuals

Executor under Wills. A trustee may be named as executor under a will or as co-executor with one or more persons. It is the function of the executor to prove the will and receive court authority to distribute the assets in conformity with the provision of the will, and pay the debts of the estate.

Administrator of Intestate Estates. If the decedent left no will, or if there is a will but no executor has been named, the court will appoint an administrator who is responsible for the settlement of the estate.

Ancillary Executor. If the decedent owned property in a second state, then an ancillary administrator is appointed on court order to administer the assets in that state.

Trustee under Wills. If a person does not wish to have his estate distributed immediately upon his death but prefers to set up a trust for the benefit of his family, or others, he may create a testamentary trust, or trust under will. There may be many reasons for creating such a trust: relieving the beneficiaries of the responsibility for property management; reduction of transfer costs; or the flexibility of the device. The trustee administers the trust in accordance with the provisions of the will, and considerable discretion may be allowed the trustee.

Guardian and Conservator of Estates. Under order of a probate court a trustee may be appointed to administer the estate of a minor, in which instance the trustee serves as guardian, or to administer the estate of an incompetent, in which case the trustee serves as a conservator. In these capacities the trustee functions much like an administrator or executor. When the minor becomes of age, the estate is turned over to him.

Depositary under Court Order. If an individual executor, administrator, guardian, or conservator wishes to transfer the custody of the assets of an estate, he may arrange for a trust institution to become depositary under court order. He is thereby relieved of certain responsibilities and clerical detail, and the fee charged for the service of the trust institution will generally represent a saving, as compared with the cost of an individual surety bond.

Trustee under Agreement. In contrast to a testamentary trust, a competent person may set up a trust during his lifetime. This is done under an agreement of trust which states the intention of the creator and outlines how the trust is to operate to achieve the objectives. There may be any of several motives: to transfer the responsibilities of property management; to make provision for members of the family in this way rather than under a will; to donate to charity, an educational foundation, or religious order; or to minimize transfer costs. There is a wide range of latitude in drawing up such an agreement. The creator may retain varying degrees of investment control or delegate full responsibility; and he may make the trust revocable and subject to amendment, or he may make the trust irrevocable.

Income and principal are paid by the trustee according to the terms of the agreement. The trustee may assume full management control, collect income, review the assets of the trust at intervals, prepare periodic statements, and provide information for income-tax purposes. Such an arrangement is called a "living" or "voluntary" trust. If the trust is not revocable, the assets of the trust are essentially gifts.

Trustee under Agreement—Insurance Trust. Another form of living trust that has some of the color of a testamentary trust is the life insurance trust. The creator deposits his life insurance policies with a corporate trustee under an agreement that provides for the distribution of the proceeds of policies which may be paid into the trust during the life of the donor or at his death. The trust is said to be inactive during the life of the creator; but upon his death, it becomes active. Such a trust may be set up to provide liquid assets to meet the tax problem upon death of the creator, particularly in the event that there are nonliquid assets in the form of a closely held business or substantial real estate. Much as in the case of a testamentary trust, provision may be made to have the trustee hold the assets of the trust for a considerable period after the death of the donor and to pay out income or principal periodically. The donor may, of course, reserve the right to control the deposited policies during his lifetime.

A life insurance trust may be: funded (premiums are paid out of the income received on securities deposited with the trustee); partially funded (the premiums are paid in part from income on deposited securities and the balance is paid by the creator); or unfunded (all premiums are paid by the creator).

Services Rendered to Corporations

Trustee and Depositary under Trust Indenture. Corporations in need of additional capital often provide it through borrowing by means of a bond issue. If the bond is secured, the corporation executes a deed of trust under which the ownership of the pledged property is conveyed to the trustee for the benefit of the bondholders. The duties of the trustee are outlined in the mortgage indenture and may be many and varied. It is the responsibility of the trustee to make certain that the agreement is carried out. If there is a default in interest or principal payments, the trustee forecloses on the pledged property. Whatever action is needed to protect the individual bondholders and to enforce the provisions of the indenture is taken by the trustee. The advantage of using a trustee is obvious: thousands of bondholders located in many parts of the country, if not the world, would find it difficult, if not impossible, to follow the affairs of the debtor corporation, to determine if indenture provisions are being met, and, if not, to take appropriate action in unison.

Paying, Exchange, and Redemption Agent. A corporation may arrange to have a trustee serve as agent in making interest payments and principal payments on maturing obligations and assist in connection with the issuance and exercise of subscription rights. Salary payments to executives may be made through a trustee in order to keep amounts in confidence.

Depositary and Exchange Agent. In the event of a corporation reorganization, merger, or recapitalization, the holders of old securities exchange them for new securities. To assist in this process a trust institution may be employed to receive the deposit of old securities, issue a receipt, and then deliver the new securities upon surrender of the receipt. Sometimes cash payments are involved as well.

Transfer Agent. A trust institution may be employed to maintain the record of present stockholders and make all necessary transfers from sellers to the buyers. Because the transfer agent holds the stock record book, the transfer agent is often appointed the dividend-paying agent. Trust institutions are also used in connection with the transfer of bonds.

Registrar. Stock exchanges in the United States usually require that listed shares be registered with an agent other than the issuer. Such a registrar provides a check on the transfer agent (which is often the issuing corporation), maintains an orderly record, and prevents overissuance. Obviously, a given trust institution cannot logically serve as both registrar and transfer agent with respect to a particular security. A trustee, however, may also serve as bond registrar for a registered bond issue.

Dividend-Disbursing Agent. The transfer agent is often appointed the dividend-disbursing agent and, in addition to paying the dividend, may mail out the annual financial report of the corporation and notices of meetings and perform related services.

Trustee under Pension and Profit-Sharing Trusts. An increasing number of employers are setting up retirement programs for their employees in the form of either profit-sharing or pension plans, or a combination of the two. Usually a trustee is appointed to serve as depositary. If the trust is self-funded, the trustee invests the assets and maintains a complete and accurate record of contributions by employer and by employee and of the specific participation of each beneficiary. If the trust is operated on an insured basis, the trustee purchases individual annuity contracts for each employee covered by the plan out of sums deposited with the trustee by the employer.

Services Rendered to Individuals and Corporations

Safekeeping. Trust institutions usually maintain safe-deposit vaults for the safekeeping of securities, jewelry, and other valuable property. In addition, trust institutions take custody of securities and other valuable papers and provide a limited amount of service in that connection, such as the collection of sums due and providing notices of maturing bonds, stock dividends, warrants and subscription rights. Sales and purchases are made as directed.

Supervised Agency. Services in addition to simple safekeeping are also provided, including: complete agency service plus investment advice, a complete record of all transactions and monthly statements showing the status of holdings, periodic review of the portfolio, and the requisite information needed for income-tax returns. Such service may be rather comprehensive and may roughly parallel that provided by investment counselors, discussed in Chapter 13, but it includes the added feature of custodianship.

Escrow Agent. Trust institutions serve as stake holders (escrow agents). Property may be placed with the trustee under certain conditions stipulating that the property is to be turned over to a third person in the event that certain conditions are met. If the conditions are not met, the property is to be returned to the original party that placed it with the escrow agent. Thus the deed to a piece of property may be placed in escrow along with the purchase price, pending the examination of the title. If the title is clear, the deal is consummated; if not clear, the parties are returned to their original positions. The seller receives the deed; the buyer has the deposited money returned to him.

Trustee or Agent under Lease. In financing the acquisition of rolling stock a railroad may use equipment trust certificates. An arrangement is made by the railroad with a manufacturer to pay part cash upon delivery of an order of equipment, the balance to be paid in notes. These notes or equipment trust certificates are then sold to the public. Title to the rolling stock is placed in a trustee, who leases the equipment to the railroad for a rental that is sufficient to pay principal and interest on the notes. The trustee agrees to protect the interests of the investors who hold the certificates. Airline companies and other industries use this financing device.

Other Trust Services

The numerous trust-institution services described in the preceding pages are by no means all-inclusive, and no attempt was made to discuss the many purposes for which trusteeship may be used. Some writers distinguish retirement trusts, spendthrift trusts, discretionary trusts, protective trusts, trusts for emergencies, sheltering trusts, rewarding trusts, common trust funds, and community trust funds.

Common Trust Fund

A common trust fund represents a single trust made up of many smaller fiduciary funds each one of which has a proportionate share in the income and assets of the common trust. It makes available to persons of small means the advantages of trust administration, which would otherwise be too costly in view of the size of the individual fund. In effect, the common trust is much like an open-end investment company. It makes specialized management and diversification feasible for modest accumulations of capital from the standpoint both of the trustee and the beneficiary.

Common trust funds, also called "commingled" or "composite" trust funds are, then, a means of collective investment. They were originated about 1930, when a number of banks, including particularly the City Farmers Trust Company, of New York City, the Brooklyn Trust Company, of Brooklyn, and the Equitable Trust Company, of Wilmington, Delaware, experimented with the idea. Double taxation under the Revenue Act was a handicap, however, because the income of the fund itself was taxed and then the income received from the fund by beneficiaries was taxed. The Revenue Act was amended in 1936 to exclude from taxation common trust funds organized by a bank or a trust company in states permitting commingled funds, if the funds are operated in compliance with Federal Reserve requirements.

Various states passed the necessary enabling legislation in 1937 and succeeding years; and the Federal Reserve authorities, on December 31, 1937, prescribed regulations permitting three classifications of common trust funds: funds limited to not over $1,200 from a single account; funds limited to not over $25,000 from a single account, which limit was later increased to $50,000; and mortgage investment funds. The two last-named funds are subject to strict regulation. There are now thirty-four states that have authorized the formation of common trust funds; and by early 1950, 74 trust institutions had established 89 commingled funds in twenty-one states and the District of Columbia. In 1949, when there were 69 commingled funds in operation through 57 institutions, the Committee on Common Trust Funds of the American Bankers Association reported that 43 of these trust institutions had about $320,000,000 under supervision for 18,690 participating trust accounts, or about $17,000 per account.

Trustmen see great possibilities for the growth of trust business through the commingled fund. They point out that more than half of the property owners in the United States die without a will; that trust institutions settle only about 5 per cent in number, and 10 per cent in volume, of the estates that pass through probate; and that one half of the estates passing through probate are under $5,000 and four fifths are under $10,000. Furthermore, over 44 per cent of trusts administered by trust institutions have an income of not over $750, indicating a principal amount of $25,000 or less.[4] On the other hand,

---

[4] G. T. Stephenson, "Trust Business in Prospect, 1950–1980," *The Trust Bulletin,* Vol. XXIX, No. 10 (June, 1950), pp. 19–36.

Exhibit 51
TREND OF ESTATE TAX RETURNS FILED

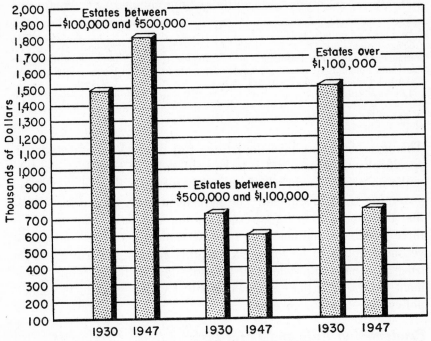

Source: Adapted from *Burroughs Clearing House*, July, 1950.

it is also recognized that estates of $500,000 or more, and certainly estates of $1,000,000 or more, will be fewer in number under the new pattern of income distribution in this country (see Exhibit 51).

Community Trust Funds

It is interesting to note the role of trusts in philanthropy. At the end of 1949, 76 philanthropic trusts had assets of slightly more than $100,000,000, representing 829 separate funds; and their aggregate disbursements in 1949 amounted to almost $3,900,000. The assets of these community foundations practically doubled since 1939 and more than tripled in the last twenty years. The resources of the five largest community trusts at December 31, 1949, were as shown in Table 32. The deferred amounts represent principal being withheld subject to prior nonphilanthropic uses.

Trust Provisions

The trust agreement generally states the policies and outlines the activities of the trustee in the administration of the assets of the trust.

TABLE 32

RESOURCES OF LARGE COMMUNITY TRUST FUNDS

	Available	Deferred	Total
New York Community Trust.........	$19,258,489.31	....	$19,258,489.31
Chicago Community Trust...........	10,653,977.00	$3,880,000.00	14,533,977.00
Permanent Charity Fund, Boston.....	8,703,925.12	....	8,703,925.12
Cleveland Foundation...............	7,755,512.06	3,538,499.38	11,294,011.44
California Community Foundation, Los Angeles (10/31)..............	4,327,186.66	3,161,075.24	7,488,261.90

Source: *The Trust Bulletin*, Vol. XXIX, No. 9 (May, 1950), p. 26

The agreement may give the trustee full discretion; may designate specifically what property is to be held, sold, or purchased; or may make no provision, in which case the trustee is limited by the law governing trust investment. The agreement may, of course, specify that the trustee is to be governed by the state law. Thus there are three possible situations: The trust agreement may spell out the investment policy to be followed, and this governs the trustee. If the trust agreement stipulates that the state law shall determine investment policy, or if the agreement is silent with respect to investment policy, the state law governs.

Prudent-Man Rule and Legal Lists

Trustees derive their investment powers and are governed by common law and state statutes, by the instructions in the agreement of trust, and by court decisions. Some states follow the "prudent-man rule," which permits the trustee (unless restricted by the trust agreement) to make such investments as a prudent man would make, having due regard for the preservation of principal and the regularity of income. This principle was first enunciated by the Supreme Judicial Court of Massachusetts in 1830 and is, therefore, often referred to as the "Massachusetts rule." A few states adopted this rule by statute before 1942, in which year a model prudent-man statute was proposed; and since then, many other states have adopted the rule. New York became the twentieth state, when it adopted a modified prudent-man statute effective July 1, 1950. Under the New York law the trustee is given discretion with respect to the investment of 35 per cent of the value of a trust fund, and the remaining 65 per cent must be invested in fixed-income securities as prescribed by the statute. The practical effect of this statute is that the trustee in New York may now invest up to 35 per cent of a trust fund in other securities, including common stocks. When allowance is made for the fact that New York trust institutions have about one third of the personal trust property of the nation under their supervision, this change in the law may have an important long-run influence on equity prices, and particularly in view of the expected growth in industrial pension funds.

States that do not follow the prudent-man rule set out specifically the kinds of investments that may be purchased by a trustee, and the securities that meet the requirements under the law constitute what is called the "legal list" of the state. Under the prudent-man rule, if not modified as in New York, there is no legal list.

In a legal-list state, if there are losses to the trust fund because the trustee did not conform to the requirements of the law, or because the trustee did not exercise good care or judgment, the trustee must make good the loss. Under the prudent-man rule, if there is a loss as a result of a transaction that a prudent man would have completed, the trustee is not liable.

Corporate versus the Individual Trustee

The corporate trustee, as opposed to the individual trustee, has a number of attributes, some of which are undoubtedly to a large extent responsible for the fact that the corporate trustee dominates the field.[5] The more important features for comparison are given in the following paragraphs:

Continuous Existence. The term of a trust agreement may run for many years, and the individual trustee may not live to carry out the responsibility he assumed. Or, he might become incompetent or otherwise be unable to serve. Administration of the trust might then be interrupted, pending the appointment of a successor trustee, or an accounting might become necessary, and there might even be legal proceedings—all involving a charge against the principal of the trust. The corporate trustee, on the other hand, has perpetual existence.

Continuous Capacity. Even a trust institution cannot give assurance that a given trust officer placed in charge of a particular trust will be continuously able to serve, but the trust institution is in a position to make an immediate replacement with a qualified substitute.

Financial Responsibility. The resources of the trust institution give assurance of financial responsibility, and this is recognized in

---

[5] Thomas H. Beacom, "Functions and Services of a Trust Department," in Sec. 7, Part II, of *Fundamentals of Investment Banking* (Chicago: Investment Bankers Association of America, 1947).

most states, in that a surety bond is not required of a trust institution.

Responsiveness to Obligations. Because the administration of trusts and related activities constitute the principal business of a trust institution, the institution is almost certain to discharge its duties with dispatch and to the letter. There is not quite the same degree of assurance that an individual trustee will do so.

Specialization. The large trust company offering a comprehensive and wide range of services will usually have a well-diversified staff of specialists competent to handle in a co-ordinated way the various problems that are likely to arise in the administration of a trust or other fiduciary responsibility.

Group Judgment. Not only does the corporate trustee have the advantage of the co-ordinated findings of staff specialists, but the action to be taken is generally subject to the review of administrative groups or of committees of officers. Regulation F of the Federal Reserve Board of Governors requires bank-board or committee action with respect to the acceptance or relinquishment of a trust account and requires periodic review of the account, as well as a review of day-to-day action with respect to purchase, sale, or retention of trust holdings.

Impartiality. The corporate trustee is able to act objectively and impersonally with respect to the parties in interest.

Adaptability. Metropolitan trust institutions generally have a staff that is equal to providing whatever experience, skill, or service may be necessary, no matter how diversified the requirements.

Obviously, the individual trustee can lay claim to certain of these attributes, too. He may well have an advantage in the personal administration of property, particularly with respect to relatively small estates. His close acquaintance with the decedent and his familiarity with the affairs and the family of the decedent may be advantageous. He may be able to keep down costs of administration, and his personal interest and attention may be definitely helpful in accomplishing the aims of the testator. The individual trustee may be more enterprising in exercising discretion and less restricted by rules and policies.

Oftentimes an individual is named as co-executor or co-trustee to act with a corporated fiduciary. Such an arrangement combines the facilities of the corporate trustee with the advantage of having an individual trustee participating. The individual is relieved of much detailed responsibility, which is assumed by the corporate fiduciary, but he is able to supply the desired personal element.

Compensation of the Trustee

At one time, persons accepted responsibility as executors, guardians, and similar fiduciary relationships as a matter of honor and did not expect to be paid, but it is otherwise in our country today. Fiduciaries have a right to receive reasonable fees for services performed, whether or not compensation is mentioned in the trust instrument. The fees may be based on principal or income, or both, and may be payable out of either income or principal, or both. The rate of compensation is not uniform throughout the country, and it is not even feasible to indicate a range of fees because there are too many variables—for example, section of the country, law of the state, size of city, basis of calculation, precise nature of service rendered, etc. Compensation may be stated in the will or trust agreement, defined by statute, or determined by a court, or may for certain services depend on custom in the area. Each trust institution has a detailed list of fees for all the various services offered, and this information may be had on request.

Only a few examples of compensation rates are cited for illustration:

In New York the compensation of an administrator is established by statute and is based on the value of the total estate, real and personal: first $2,000, 5 per cent; next $20,000, 2½ per cent; next $28,000, 1½ per cent; and 2 per cent on the balance. In Washington the compensation, established by court on the value of the entire estate, real and personal, would be about as follows: first $5,000, 5 per cent; next $45,000, 3 per cent; next $200,000, 1½ per cent; and 1 per cent on the balance. In both instances an executor, in the event the will did not mention compensation, would receive the same compensation as the administrator.

Compensation of a guardian in Maine would be established by the court at about 5 per cent of the income annually and 5 per cent of the principal upon termination. In Pennsylvania the court would base the guardian's compensation entirely on principal.

In Georgia a trustee under a will would receive, under the statute, 2½ per cent on all sums received and on all sums paid out; whereas in Kentucky he would receive 5 per cent of income and one fifth of 1 per cent of principal, annually, and extra allowance for unusual services.

Trust-institution charges for a full-management agency for a securities investment, including custody, continuous analysis, and con-

stant surveillance, come nearer being standardized and would probably be about as follows: if the principal is under $100,000, an
annual charge of $5 per $1,000; if the principal is between $100,000
and $200,000, a fee of $250 and $2.50 per $1,000; if over $200,000,
a fee of $550 plus $1 per $1,000.

The above samplings afford some indication of the rate or amount
of trustee compensation and the variability and complexity of the fee
structure which makes generalization and comparison difficult.[6]

Business Trust

A special form of trust organization is sometimes used for operating a business, and it bears some resemblance to the corporate
form of enterprise. Instead of having a charter, the business trust is
conducted under a trust agreement. Participants in the business turn
over the assets of the enterprise to a board of trustees, who serve in
much the same way as the board of directors of a corporation. The
creators of the trust receive transferable trust shares, more technically
called "certificates of beneficial interest," which are much like shares
of corporate stock. In contrast to the general responsibility of a
trustee in the usual common-law trust to observe the prudent-man
rule, the trustees of a business trust may, under the trust agreement,
be made liable only for serious negligence of actual fraud. This is
in recognition of the fact that trustees, as managers of a business,
must necessarily take business risks. The trust agreement usually
also provides for the limited liability of the owners of trust shares.
Furthermore, if the trust agreement so provides and creditors are
given notice, creditors may look only to the property of the trust for
payment. However, if the owners of the trust shares are to have but
limited liability, they must surrender control of the business to the
trustees or the business trust may be construed a partnership by the
courts.

The business trust found its first application in Massachusetts and
so it is frequently called the "Massachusetts trust," but it is also
known as a "voluntary association under a declaration of trust" and
as a "common-law trust." The business trust as here described should
be distinguished from "trust" used in the sense of monopoly. For
instance, certain attempts to gain control of an industry utilized the

---

[6] The foregoing illustrations and discussion of compensation are based on the much
more comprehensive exhibits of charges covering a great variety of trust services, as
reported in G. T. Stephenson, *Estates and Trusts* (New York: Appleton-Century-Crofts,
Inc., 1949), Chap. XV.

trust device and therefore became known as "the tobacco trust," "the oil trust," etc., although the terms "tobacco monopoly" and "oil monopoly would have been more appropriate.

The business trust owes its origin to the fact that corporations were, at one time, limited to the ownership of a single piece of real estate held for investment purposes, whereas the business trust was not similarly restricted. The business trust had certain tax advantages over the corporation; but now that it is taxed much like the corporation, the remaining advantages on this score are probably nominal. While the business trust may have some of the advantages of a corporation, such as limited liability, transferability, and ease and flexibility in raising capital, it has the disadvantage of not being known or understood by many persons, and the law pertaining to business trusts is not so uniformly or clearly developed as in the case of the corporation.[7]

Treatment of the business trust might appropriately have been included in Chapter 7, along with the discussion of other legal forms of business organization; but consideration was deliberately deferred pending the development of the trusteeship concept in this chapter. The board of trustees of a business trust should not be confused with the professional trustee, individual or corporate, to whom most of this chapter has been devoted. The trustees of a business trust are responsible for the continuing operation of a going business. The professional trustee is responsible for the operation of an industrial or commercial business usually only for a short time, such as the interim period pending transfer from an estate to the heirs. Oftentimes the trustees of a business trust may be, not only trustees, but the creators and the beneficiaries as well; they emphasize creation and production and the taking of risks. The professional trustee, on the other hand, as a matter of tradition and practice, tends to emphasize preservation of what others have created and produced, and seeks to minimize risk.

Voting Trust

There is still another application of the trustee concept. For the purpose of continuing management and perpetuating policies, the

---

[7] For an extended nontechnical discussion of the business trust, its origin, uses, advantages, and disadvantages, see H. G. Guthmann and H. E. Dougall, *Corporate Financial Policy* (2d ed.; New York: Prentice-Hall, Inc., 1948), pp. 30–37, or H. V. Cherrington, *Business Organization and Finance* (New York: Ronald Press Co., 1948), pp. 35–46.

stockholders of a company may agree to transfer their shares of stock in the company to trustees, receiving in return voting trust certificates that are transferable. These certificates have no voting power but do have the right to dividends. The trustees vote the stock and thus control the operation of the business but may not sell the stock. Such an arrangement is generally maintained for a relatively short period of time, and at the expiration of the voting trust the shares of stock are returned to the owners, who surrender the voting trust certificates.

Summary

Trust institutions perform a great variety of useful services of economic and social importance, and on the basis of the foregoing discussion it should be apparent why the trust institution has been called an "omnibus of finance." Conservation of wealth, in the sense of safekeeping and directing capital into productive employment, is undoubtedly the outstanding characteristic of trust operations. In fact, to the extent that the trust institution gives direction to the sound and constructive use of funds, and thus avoids the wasteful use of assets, trust institutions might even be considered creative, despite what has been said in the immediately preceding section. Actually there is an increasing tendency among trustmen toward the acceptance of responsibility not only for the traditional role of conservation but also for growth of the funds under their administration. To this end, common stocks are increasingly being recognized as appropriate for trust investment to a greater degree than in earlier years. The spreading adoption of the prudent-man rule is indicative of this trend. The trust institution in its capacity as administrator, executor, guardian, and conservator aids in conserving and distributing property as it passes from one generation to another; and in the process, it protects the interests of minors and incompetents.

Trust institutions perform many functions that are essential to the smooth functioning of the industrial and commercial corporate structure of the nation. They serve as fiscal and transfer agents, registrars, and trustees in connection with debt-financing, profit-sharing, and pension funds. The spreading adoption of pension plans by businesses, on either a contributory or noncontributory basis, may add substantially to trust business in coming years.

Trust institutions, as guardians and trustees, also serve individuals in a more personal and intimate way that transcends the purely financial. They look after the physical welfare of minors and incompetents and provide guidance in meeting many of life's problems.

—ERWIN W. BOEHMLER

QUESTIONS AND PROBLEMS

1. What is a trust? Define and give an illustration.
2. Are a trustee and a fiduciary identical? Explain.
3. Is there any difference between a "contract" and a "trust agreement"?
4. What does the term "trust business" encompass?
5. How do you account for the origin and the growing importance of the corporate trustee as a financial institution?
6. It is said that corporate trustees perform some eighty different services. Without listing any specific services, indicate in general terms what functions corporate trustees perform.
7. What specific services do corporate trustees provide that are highly important to corporate business organization in this country?
8. In what ways does the corporate trustee serve the individual?
9. In what way does the trust company offer a service that might be considered competitive to the investment counselor? The open-end investment company?
10. Why do many trustmen feel that the common trust fund offers real possibilities for expanded trust operation?
11. Distinguish between "prudent-man-rule states" and "legal-list states." The trend is in which direction—giving trustees more or less discretion?
12. Can it be said that the services of the trustee transcend the financial?
13. What advantages, if any, are afforded by the corporate trustee as against the individual professional trustee? May a nonprofessional individual trustee provide any special advantage? How might the two sets of benefits be combined?
14. To what extent are trustee fees standardized? Obtain a schedule of charges from a local trust institution and compare the rates with the few examples given in the text.
15. Explain what is meant by a "voluntary association under deed of trust."
16. Why might a trust institution be called an "indirect" or "intermediary" investment agency?
17. Are trust institutions likely to become a more important factor in the equity capital market? In the venture capital market? If so, name some supporting instances.
18. What is the nature of a community trust? Do you have one in your community? Total Assets? How much was disbursed in a recent year?

BIBLIOGRAPHY

A comprehensive coverage of trust services for the individual is found in G. T. Stephenson's *Estates and Trusts* (New York: Appleton-Century-Crofts

Inc., 1949), which is written for senior and graduate college students, not as a manual or text for professionals, but rather to provide the individual with the information that an informed person should have about fiduciary services offered by the professional trustee. A detailed history of trust institutions in this country is provided by J. G. Smith's *The Development of Trust Companies in the United States* (New York: Henry Holt & Co., 1928); and a review of trust institution business and practices in the United States is included in G. T. Stephenson's *Trust Business in Common Law Countries* (New York: Research Council, American Bankers Association, 1940), which emphasizes foreign trust business. The American Bankers Association, Trust Division, periodically publishes a *Bibliography on Trust Business*, compiled by Genieve N. Gildersleeve.

There are two monthly publications, devoted to estates and trusts and published primarily for trustmen, that frequently contain articles and analyses of a general nature of interest to nonprofessionals: the *Trust Bulletin*, published monthly, September to June, Trust Division, American Bankers Association, New York, and *Trusts and Estates*, published monthly, Fiduciary Publishers, Inc., New York.

Chapter • 15

URBAN REAL ESTATE FINANCE

ALTHOUGH the financing of urban real estate transactions has much in common with the other fields of financing discussed thus far, it also has characteristic differences that distinguish it from business or consumer financing. The social and political implications of housing, for example, are so broad that they cannot be discussed in detail in this chapter, and yet public interest in housing is one of the factors which distinguishes this field of financing from others.

The size of investment in real property—i.e., land and property permanently affixed to land—also affects financing in this field. About one half of the wealth of the United States is invested in real property.[1] Roughly 10 per cent of national income originates in construction of real property, rentals and interest on real estate indebtedness, and payments for the services of brokers, lawyers, insurance companies, and others who serve buyers and sellers in the real estate market. The "average" house bought with a government-insured loan in 1949 had an appraisal value of $8,502; and the purchase was financed with a mortgage of $7,154, to be paid off over twenty-three years. The value of the house was slightly more than twice the purchaser's annual income. Approximately 15 per cent of the income of the "average" individual in the United States is spent on housing and household operation. The cost of new construction of all types of buildings and other real estate in the United States for the one year, 1949, exceeded $19 billion.

The problems which, however, most directly influence the methods of financing in this field stem from two important characteristics of the financing: approximately 75 per cent of all single-family homes and 50 per cent of all commercial and industrial properties are

---

[1] David L. Wickens, *Residential Real Estate* (New York: National Bureau of Economic Research, Inc., 1941), p. 1.

purchased on long-term credit; and the price of real estate is subject to rapid fluctuation. The long-term nature of real estate credit transactions emphasizes the necessity for security behind loans. The type of security usually taken is the right to repayment from the proceeds obtained by the sale of property owned by the debtor. The security is, however, no better than the opportunity afforded the creditor to recover amounts due by this sale of property. Sharp swings of real estate prices become of considerable importance to a creditor in attempting to determine how secure his position actually is.

In this chapter we shall discuss the credit principles and practices now in use, the extent to which credit is used in real estate transactions, the types of institutions which supply funds to the real estate market, and the agencies of the federal government which are active in the financing of real estate.

CREDIT PRINCIPLES AND PRACTICES

In making secured loans, creditors must place emphasis on both the nature of the assets securing the loan and the characteristics of the borrower to whom the loan is made. Generally, the longer the term of a loan, the greater the emphasis which must be placed on the analysis of the security behind the loan.

Appraisal

Analysis of security begins with an appraisal of the property, i.e., a determination of its value. Real estate loans represent a large proportion of the value of the property against which they are made. Loans equaling from 80 to 95 per cent of the value of the property are quite common in residential financing, and loans up to 60 per cent are common for commercial or industrial financing. When the margin between value and amount of loan is as narrow as these data indicate, the creditor must soundly appraise the property before he can safely advance funds.

The appraisal of real estate values is not easily accomplished. Each unit has individual characteristics. The appraiser does not have the guide offered by comparison with exactly similar units currently sold as might be the case in, say, the market for automobiles. It is possible to make an estimate of the cost which would be incurred to construct a similar building on the same land—that is, to estimate reproduction cost—and then estimate the extent to which existing real property has depreciated from "new." This approach, however, is obviously more easily applied to property recently constructed than to property of considerable age, and it does not provide a useful guide to the measurement of the value of land on which other property is constructed. Another approach to appraisal is the estimate of all of the future benefits—for example, rentals—which the owner will get and the present price which such a stream of future benefits should command. In other words, the appraiser can look at past, present, and future. He can estimate past costs, adjusted to present conditions; he can estimate present selling price, based on current market prices for other real estate; and he can estimate the present worth of the future stream of benefits which an owner would receive. But, at best, an appraisal value is the summation of informed opinions. Valuation is a field which encourages the utilization of specialists.

Legal Documents

A second phase of analysis of the security behind a loan is the determination of the legal position of the debtor. If the creditor, in case of default, is to depend for protection on obtaining possession of property, it is important to establish the debtor's ability to provide the security. This involves knowledge of the instruments of real estate finance and inspections to see that all legal steps have been properly taken.

The instruments of real estate finance are more detailed in character than for most other credit transactions because of the nature of real estate itself. Real estate is immobile: each parcel is unique. Possession does not indicate ownership. Ownership of real estate is transferred not by change of possession but by the passing of a legal document called a "deed." Because relatively large sums of money are involved in the ownership of real estate, parties to a transaction take precautions not typically found in other dealings.

EVIDENCE OF TITLE. Before anyone may safely loan money on the security of real estate, he must make certain that full ownership of the property is actually in the name of the borrower, and he must further make certain that no other claims to the property are outstanding.

There are a number of systems followed to assure the validity of a person's title, the most common of which is to have a lawyer examine an "abstract" or make a search of the records filed in the county recorder's office. In many cities there are title companies which insure the owner of real estate against the risk that title to the property may not be in his name, and which promise to compensate him against loss if some other person later proves to have title to the property. In a few areas, the county government issues a certificate of title known as a "Torrens certificate," which is a guaranty of the validity of title to property.

THE MORTGAGE INSTRUMENT. A real estate loan is, in almost every case, accompanied by a mortgage (or by a trust deed, which is used in some states as a substitute for the ordinary mortgage). A "mortgage," briefly defined, is a transfer of title to property, given by a debtor to a creditor as security for the payment of a debt—with the provision that the transfer is void if the debt is paid by the day named and if interest payments are made as promised. The debt itself is always evidenced by a note similar in its essential parts to any promissory note except that it includes a reference to an accompanying mortgage.

In the very early days of the use of mortgages in England and early in history of this country, the lender could immediately take possession under the transfer of title given in the mortgage if the borrower failed to make his interest and principal payments on the exact due date. Frequently the lender might even take possession of the property at the time the loan was made, and might retain it until the loan had been paid. Such stringent interpretations of the transfer of title have been greatly modified by statutes and by court decisions. The law now takes the view that it is unreasonable for the lender to retain the full value of the property when it was merely transferred as security for a debt. The creditor has a right only to the proceeds from the sale of the property up to amounts owing to him.

Present-day law in most states provides that borrowers have a right to "redeem" pledged property within a reasonable time after the debt has been defaulted and the property has been forfeited to the lender. This right is known as the "equity of redemption."

The typical real estate mortgage instrument used in a home loan transaction includes the date, names of the borrower and lender, exact "legal" description of the property, brief statement of the amount of the debt and terms for repayment, and a number of promises which the borrower makes in addition to the promise to repay the debt according to the agreed schedule and to make interest payments on agreed upon dates.

For a typical home loan these promises or "covenants" include provisions as follows: (1) to pay all taxes, special assessments, and other charges levied by the local government upon the property; (2)

to keep the property in good repair and not to permit any "waste" of the property; (3) to keep the property fully insured against fire, windstorm, and other hazards as the lender may require; (4) not to permit the property to be used for any unlawful purpose; and (5) to allow no substantial changes, alterations, or additions to the property without the creditor's permission. Finally, the mortgage is signed by the borrower, witnessed, and notarized.

LAND CONTRACT. Sometimes people buy property without paying the full purchase price in cash but by signing a long-term "land contract." This is a form of installment sales contract whereby the purchaser agrees to pay for the property in installments, frequently running for as much as twenty years with interest paid on the unpaid portion of the contract price. In essence, the land contract performs the same function as the combination of mortgage and mortgage note just described above.

COSTS. Because of the detailed nature of title verification and the necessity of either a title insurance policy or careful examination of an abstract by an attorney, together with the charge for "recording" a mortgage in the county recorder's office, it may cost from $50 to $250 to cover legal, title, and recording fees alone. Typically, these costs are paid by the borrower.

The complexities of mortgage loan laws and protection granted borrowers under state laws give rise to substantial expenses on the part of the lender if the borrower defaults on his loan and it becomes necessary to foreclose on the mortgaged property and acquire title by purchase at the foreclosure sale. In some states—for example, Illinois and Kansas—it may take from fourteen to twenty months to acquire possession and a marketable title to property through a fore-closure sale. In Illinois, the state with the highest foreclosure costs, the expense of acquiring property through payment of attorney's fees, sheriff's fees, court costs, costs of title search, etc., may run as high as $400 to $500 on a home foreclosure. In only about half of the states may a lender acquire a marketable title to property through foreclosure in less than one year and at a cost less than $100.

Adaptation of Loan to Borrower's Capacity

If the creditor is assured that the security is good, then he must also assure himself that the terms of the loan agreement are adapted to the borrower's capacity to meet future payments.

LOAN TERMS IN THE 1920's. During the 1920's the emphasis placed on the borrower's ability to meet the payments stipulated in a loan contract was not so great as it is today. Most real estate loans were "straight" loans; that is, the note and mortgage provided that the entire principal amount would be due on one final maturity date. Interest payments were usually made at six-month intervals. The final interest payment and the maturity date were commonly five years from the loan date. During the interim, no payments on principal were required. The borrower was expected to make provision for the accumulation of a sum sufficient to meet the payments when due. In practice, loans were frequently renewed because, at the maturity date, the borrower could pay some, but not all, of the principal of the loan and negotiate a new loan for the balance. As a result, loans on a creditor's books were seldom shown to be in default, but there was no information as to the borrower's ability to meet the final payment when it fell due.

The relation between amounts loaned and the value of property securing loans in the 1920's appears conservative at first glance. Because of the law and the custom under which they operated, few lenders made first mortgage loans for more than 50 to 60 per cent of appraised value. On the other hand, few borrowers were in the position to make down-payments amounting to 40 or 50 per cent of the purchase price of property. Therefore, in the 1920's a substantial business of making second and third mortgage loans developed. A person buying a house at a purchase price of $12,000 would borrow $6,000 on a first mortgage, $3,000 on a second mortgage, and pay the remaining $3,000 from his own savings. If he did not have as much as 25 per cent of the purchase price saved, he might even borrow the remaining $3,000 on a third mortgage. The interest rate on the first mortgage would probably have been 6 per cent, and the second and third mortgage loans would bear interest at rates within the range of 10 to 20 per cent a year. Unlike first mortgages, second and third mortgages would probably require payments of both interest and principal at monthly or quarterly intervals. The principal of these junior claims would be repaid before the maturity date on the senior mortgage.

DEPRESSION EXPERIENCE. In the general depression of the early 1930's, weaknesses in real estate credit practice became apparent. Borrower's did not accumulate sufficient funds with which to meet the final payment on mortgage debt within the five-year periods for which loan agreements ran. They depended upon renewal. Even those who had saved a considerable portion toward repayment of mortgage indebtedness found that their savings dwindled as depression continued. Creditors could not collect amounts as they fell due, and yet the creditors themselves were under pressures to meet their own expenses. The rate of foreclosure increased rapidly as creditors attempted to enforce their rights. The ensuing debacle aroused public attention and caused a number of states to pass laws by which debtors were relieved of the immediate necessity to pay off the principal of loans, although, as a rule, they were expected to continue paying interest. This type of remedial action weakened the position of creditors, who then had no way in which to withdraw funds invested in real estate loans. Congress took steps in 1933 to bring relief to both debtor and creditor by establishing an agency to buy and hold mortgages. One important change in private financing which emerged from the depression was the improvement in the adaptation of loan terms to borrower capacity to pay.

CURRENT PRACTICE. The lessons of depression are reflected in the now almost universal acceptance of the so-called "amortized" loan not only for financing residential real estate transactions but also for commercial and industrial credits. Amortization means, in effect, "killing off." By the terms of an amortized loan, the borrower agrees to make regular, usually monthly, payments on principal as well as of interest. The loan is gradually reduced and finally paid off within the agreed period of years. At the same time, the loan period is lengthened so that the borrower may be expected to make the necessary payments and retire the loan without seeking renewal and without borrowing on junior mortgages. Under current practice, the first mortgage loan may amount to as much, in proportion to the value of the property, as the combined first and second (and, perhaps, third) mortgages did in the 1920's—that is, 80 to 90 per cent.

Residential Loans

Interest rates on home mortgage loans in the period since 1937 have ranged from 4 to 6 per cent. In the 1930's, the usual maturity date was between 10 and 20 years; but in the postwar period, 1945–49, maturity dates as much as thirty years removed from the loan date have become frequent. With most loans on a level monthly-payment basis, part of each payment is a return of money borrowed; part is interest. The portion of the fixed monthly payment representing interest becomes smaller with each payment. Terms on an amortized mortgage loan are illustrated in Table 33.

Some idea as to the monthly payment required on loans of various maturities and various interest rates is given in Table 34. This table shows the monthly payments required to amortize a loan of $1,000 during the indicated term. It shows, for example, that a person can pay off completely a $10,000 loan at 5 per cent, extending over twenty years, with payments of $66 per month. This is less, in most instances, than the amount for which a person can rent equivalent property, although, of course, the amount of the monthly payment on the loan is not the only out-of-pocket expense involved in owning a home.

To the monthly payment required to pay interest and amortize the

TABLE 33

TERMS ON AN AMORTIZED MORTGAGE LOAN

Amount borrowed............$1,000
Interest rate.................   5%
Time outstanding.............10 years

TIME		MONTHLY PAYMENT			BALANCE DUE ON LOAN
Years	Months	Total	Interest Portion	Principal Repayment	
0	1	$10.61	$4.17	$ 6.44	$993.56
0	2	10.61	4.14	6.47	987.09
0	3	10.61	4.11	6.50	980.59
3	1	10.61	3.13	7.48	742.83
3	2	10.61	3.10	7.51	735.32
3	3	10.61	3.06	7.55	727.77
8	1	10.61	1.01	9.60	231.79
8	2	10.61	0.97	9.64	222.15
9	10	10.61	0.13	10.48	20.60
9	11	10.61	0.09	10.52	10.08
Final payment		10.12	0.04	10.08	0.00

principal, many lending institutions will require that the borrower add an amount equal to one twelfth of the annual fire insurance premium and annual property tax bill. Depending, of course, on the type of property and the city, the additional payment for taxes and insurance will range from $10 to $20 per month on a house valued at $10,000 to $15,000.

The down-payment required for conventional loans—that is, loans neither insured nor guaranteed by federal agencies—on homes and small apartments varies greatly depending upon the policy of the lending institution and upon business and real estate conditions. In periods of a housing surplus and when homes sell for an amount approximating the cost of reproduction less depreciation, creditors will make loans with 20 to 30 per cent down payment. In periods of great housing shortage and inflationary prices, such as experienced in the postwar years, 1945–49, practically all lending institutions required at least a 35 to 40 per cent down-payment, with a 50 per cent down-payment being quite common. On loans insured or guaranteed by federal agencies, the down-payment tends to be smaller (in fact, under the present law, the down-payment on a $7,000 house may be smaller than that usually asked on a $1,500 car), since the lender is protected by the government against substantial loss on the loan.

The procedure followed by a person seeking a loan on a home will vary a great deal, depending on the individual case and the custom of the community in which he lives. If an individual is buying a

TABLE 34

MONTHLY PAYMENT REQUIRED TO REPAY AN AMORTIZED MORTGAGE
LOAN OF $1,000

Maturity	4%	4½%	5%	5¼%
10..............	$10.12	$10.36	$10.61	$10.85
12..............	8.76	9.00	9.25	9.50
15..............	7.40	7.65	7.91	8.17
18..............	6.50	6.76	7.03	7.30
20..............	6.06	6.33	6.60	6.88

house, he will most frequently purchase the house through a real estate broker. Since most purchasers of homes are unfamiliar with real estate and real estate financing, they will rely on the real estate broker to assist them in obtaining the necessary loan. As a result, the broker is in a position to direct the individual purchaser-borrower to a lending institution of the broker's choice, and the broker frequently arranges the details with the institution lending the money on behalf of the purchaser-borrower. In other cases, the individual will contact a lending institution of his choice directly.

Where a house is to be constructed or is under construction for sale, the contractor gets a loan from a lending institution which disburses funds to him periodically as the house is being built. At the time the house is sold to an individual, the purchaser takes over or "assumes" the loan, and the lending institution releases the contractor from any further obligation on it.

The procedure followed in the case of a home purchase or in refinancing a loan is outlined in the following steps:

1. Borrower signs loan application, which includes:
    Data about borrower

Location of house

Some details of house

2. Lender investigates the borrower's credit
3. An appraisal of the value of property is made (the borrower must usually supply or pay for a survey of the property)
4. Loan is approved by the loan committee, and the borrower is notified
5. Title investigation is made
6. Mortgage is recorded
7. Loan is "closed":

Note signed

Money disbursed to borrower or to some other person designated by him

Lending institutions in some areas, depending upon the competitive situation, give 24- to 48-hour service in approving loans and notifying borrowers that the loan will be made as requested or subject to some modification. The subsequent steps in making the loan may take from one week to many weeks, depending upon the complexity of the title and the speed of service given by the local title insurance companies, abstract companies, or attorneys employed to investigate titles.

Commercial Loans

Most loans on retail store locations, office buildings, large apartment buildings, and other commercial properties are made by life insurance companies and commercial banks; and in the East, by the mutual savings banks. Sometimes small commercial properties are financed by savings and loan associations. There is no arrangement for government guaranty or insurance of loans on commercial properties, as in the case of residential properties, except that large apartment buildings can be financed with a government-insured loan if the apartment meets certain qualifications.

The making of loans on commercial properties is a highly specialized business requiring a thorough knowledge of commercial real estate values, trends in business districts, the nature of the use to which the building is to be put, and the credit of the borrower. The most important phase of commercial real estate lending is the valuation of the property. This essentially involves an estimate of the rental income, operating expenses, the net income of the property, and, finally, the value of property which can earn this estimated amount of net income.

Life insurance companies and banks are limited by law to loans from 50 to 66⅔ per cent of the value of the property. Thus, substantial down-payments are required in loans on commercial real estate. Practically all commercial loans are amortized. The amortization rate frequently is greater during the early years of the loan. But the amortization schedule does not always provide for complete repayment of the principal during the life of the loan. Maturities run from five to thirty years, depending upon the nature, use, and location of the property and the credit of the borrower. If the property is rented under a long-term lease to a tenant of unquestioned credit, such as a large drug or grocery chain, larger loans will be granted than if the property is rented to a local firm whose business reputation and credit may not be so firmly established. In making these loans a great deal of care is taken by the lender to assure that the required payments on the loan bear a logical relationship to the gross and net income of the property.

Industrial Loans

More and more small industrial concerns and in some cases large, nationally known manufacturing companies are financing the purchase or construction of a factory building, warehouse, or office with an ordinary real estate mortgage loan instead of through the traditional device of a bond issue or the sale of preferred stock. The field of industrial financing is a particularly complicated and specialized business, and the same is true of appraisal of industrial property. Most of this type of mortgage lending is done by life insurance companies. Large mortgage firms which represent the life insurance companies have men on their staffs who specialize exclusively in making industrial loans. And the loan departments of life insurance companies themselves include men who are specialists in these loans.

The rates and terms on industrial real estate loans vary greatly. Interest rates are somewhat lower than on home loans because of the large amount involved in a typical transaction. There is less cost per dollar invested in making and following up on loans of large principal amount than in smaller home loans, averaging only $5,000 to $6,000. During the postwar period the interest rate on most industrial loans has ranged from 3½ to 5 per cent, with an average rate in the neighborhood of 4½ per cent. There is no insurance or government guaranty available on industrial loans, such as that provided for home loans. Most industrial loans are written to be amortized in ten years, with 50 per cent and sometimes 60 per cent amortization required in the first five years of the loan. Payments of principal and interest are required quarterly or monthly.

EXTENT OF URBAN REAL ESTATE FINANCING

As already indicated, approximately 75 per cent of residential and 50 per cent of commercial and industrial real estate transactions are completed through credit arrangements. The relative importance of real estate financing in the United States is indicated in Table 35, which shows a classification of the amounts of indebtedness outstand-

TABLE 35

ESTIMATES OF PRIVATE DEBT IN THE UNITED STATES
Amounts Outstanding at Year-End, 1949 and 1939
(Billions of Dollars)

	1949	1939
Corporate, nonmortgage	$104.7	$ 69.5
Urban mortgage	58.4	30.3
Noncorporate, nonmortgage	36.9	19.0
Farm mortgage	5.4	6.6
Total private debt	$205.5	$125.5

Source: Based on *Survey of Current Business*, October, 1950, Table 1, p. 10, and Table 6, p. 15. Subtotals do not add to totals because of rounding.

ing at the ends of the two years, 1939 and 1949. Figures for "corporate" debt exclude mortgage loans,[2] so that the comparison between urban mortgage debt outstanding and the total gives a reasonable picture of the relationship of urban real estate loan credit to all credit. It is impressive to observe that 24 per cent of all credits to private borrowers outstanding at December 31, 1939, and 28 per cent of those outstanding at December 31, 1949, were based on urban mortgages.

A second indication of the extent of real estate financing is provided by a comparison of the new financing for different types of users. For the year 1949, for example, a total of $11.8 billion was advanced on home loans; $5.1 billion was the total amount of new issues of corporate securities; and the total amount of funds obtained by corporations from all sources was $14.2 billion. States, counties, cities, towns, villages, and districts of the United States borrowed $2.9 billion, part of which amount was used to pay off existing debt.

---

[2] Corporate debt figures include amounts of outstanding bonds, which may be secured by real estate.

Although not strictly comparable, these figures serve to show, in an approximate way, the relative importance of real estate financing.

In Table 35 the totals for urban real estate mortgage debt for the years 1939 and 1949 were, respectively, \$30.3 and \$58.4 billion. In order to compare the relative amounts of residential and business real estate financing, these figures have been broken down into subclasses in Table 36. Of course, "multi-family residential" properties represent housing. The proportion of financing of individual housing to the total for urban real estate is greater, therefore, than is evident

TABLE 36

URBAN REAL ESTATE MORTGAGE DEBT
Amounts Outstanding at Year-End, 1949 and 1939
(Billions of Dollars)

	1949	1939
One- to four-family residential	\$37.3	\$17.6
Multi-family residential and commercial	21.1	12.7
Total urban mortgage debt	\$58.4	\$30.3

Source: *Survey of Current Business*, October, 1950, Table 6, p. 15.

from the data for "one- to four-family residential" alone. Yet, this class accounted for more than one sixth of the total of all private indebtedness, as is shown in Table 35 for 1949.

PRIVATE SOURCES OF REAL ESTATE CREDIT

The principal sources of real estate credit are private investment agencies: savings and loan associations, commercial banks, insurance companies, mutual savings banks, individual investors and firms making occasional investments in real estate although not principally engaged in real estate financing. Only a small amount of actual financing is handled by federal agencies—but federal agencies play an important role in this field, as the next section will show. The amounts invested by different lenders in the credits outstanding at the ends of 1939 and 1949 are shown in Table 37. The changes in the relative importance of savings and loan associations, commercial banks, and insurance companies as creditors between 1939 and 1949 reflect growth of these loan agencies. These agencies now supply 58 per cent of the total funds, whereas in 1939 they supplied 40 per cent. The amounts of debt held by individuals and others indicates the extent to which this remains a field in which individual investment is important. Many properties are sold on the basis of a down-payment with the seller himself taking a mortgage and note to cover the balance of the purchase price. A fact which Table 37 does not reveal is the dominance of the savings and loan associations in residential financing, and of insurance companies in commercial and industrial financing. Savings and loan associations accounted for about 31 per cent of the loans on residential properties, and insur-

TABLE 37

SOURCES OF URBAN REAL ESTATE CREDIT
Amounts of Debt Held at Year-End, 1949 and 1939
(Billions of Dollars)

	1949	1939
Savings and loan associations	$11.6	$ 3.8
Life insurance carriers	11.8	4.8
Commercial banks	10.7	3.6
Mutual savings banks	6.7	4.8
Home Owners' Loan Corporation	0.2	2.0
Individuals and others	17.4	11.3
Total urban mortgage debt	$58.4	$30.3

Source: *Survey of Current Business*, October, 1950, Table 6, p. 15.

ance companies for 27 per cent of commercial and industrial financing, in 1949.

Savings and Loan Associations

Savings and loan associations have already been discussed in Chapter 11 as savings institutions. In 1949 these associations advanced $3,646 million on urban real estate, about one third of the total of such loans from all sources.

Commercial Banks

Most commercial banks today make real estate loans through their trust departments and as a part of their regular lending activities. Banks usually have a department which handles real estate loans. They have specialized personnel familiar with the legal and technical aspects of real estate finance. Commercial banks make all types of real estate loans, including loans on homes, on apartments, both large and small, on retail store properties, on office buildings, and on small factory buildings. Loans are generally limited by law to 60 to 66⅔ per cent of the value of the property and to a maturity of ten years (except for loans insured or guaranteed by federal agencies). Today most loans made by banks are amortized loans. In the case of loans on homes, most banks prefer to make loans insured by federal agencies because they can make loans up to 90 per cent of the value of the property with amortization to be completed within twenty to thirty years.

Currently, commercial banks and trust companies originate approximately 20 per cent of all urban real estate loans. In 1949 they loaned $2,445 million, and at the close of the year they held approximately $11 billion of such loans in their portfolios. Most of these loans are on property in the banks' own or neighboring communities. Some banks, however, purchase government-insured loans made on homes in distant cities.

Mutual Savings Banks

Mutual savings banks (described in Chapter 11) are found mainly in Massachusetts, New York, and Connecticut. Their real estate lending activities are largely confined to those areas, although recently some banks have begun to make loans on properties in other states. At the end of 1949, mutual savings banks had $5 billion, or 25 per cent of their assets, invested in real estate mortgage loans. In 1949 they advanced $750 million on urban real estate.

Insurance Companies

At the end of 1948, insurance companies had invested $9,865 million in urban real estate mortgages, approximately $3.5 billion of which was in mortgages on residential properties. About 18 per cent of all insurance company investments at that time were in urban real estate mortgages. The participation of these companies in the urban real estate field has increased. In 1949 they advanced $1,046 million on mortgages in amounts of $20,000 or less.

A definite preference is shown by life insurance companies for larger loans. Some companies actually exclude loans below a certain size—say $8,000. Their loans are made on the whole range of urban land improvements from large office buildings to single-family homes. They are generally limited by law as to the percentage that the loan may bear to the value of the property, and the actual percentage loaned is generally much lower than is the case for other lenders. For about one half of the companies the maximum ratio permitted is 60 per cent. Only a small number of the companies can make a loan as high as 70 per cent of the value of property if there is no government guaranty or insurance of the loan.

The loans made by life insurance companies on real estate security are frequently among the lowest interest-rate loans made by any type of lender. The rate at which these companies can afford to make real estate loans depends largely upon the interest rates on their alternative forms of investment, mainly corporate, municipal and government bonds. Four per cent loans on office buildings, retail store properties, and small factory buildings are profitable when yields on high-grade corporate bonds are as high as 3 per cent. When yields on high-grade bonds are as low as 2½ to 2.75 per cent, insurance companies can afford to make loans on individual homes at rates as low as 4 per cent, with even lower rates on larger loans on commercial property or large apartment developments.

A number of the larger eastern life insurance companies have financed the building of large apartment developments, such as Parkchester and Stuyvesant Village in New York City. In these cases they own the apartment buildings and the land outright, as permitted by special laws. The ownership of real estate by lending institutions is a quite recent departure from the traditional methods of real estate finance and more will probably be done along this line in the next several decades. At the end of 1948, life insurance companies owned $1 billion of urban real estate.

Early in 1951 the Prudential Life Insurance Company announced an interesting development. The company had acquired the air rights over a portion of the railroad tracks (about the area of a city block) of the Illinois Central Railroad in Chicago, together with the title to enough small parcels of land to permit the sinking of caissons for a large office building to house the Middle Western operations of Prudential and to provide additional office space as well.

The Mortgage Correspondent System

Life insurance companies active in the mortgage field lend over a wide area—that is, several states. This program necessitates special methods of obtaining and keeping in touch with their mortgage loan investments, including direct purchase of loans, use of salaried local agents, or appointment of exclusive loan correspondents, known generally as "mortgage brokers" or "mortgage bankers."

The last-named method is most commonly used by the larger insurance companies and works somewhat as follows: A local real estate broker or mortgage banker in a community is selected by the mortgage lending officer of an insurance company to solicit loans and take applications in his community. The applications are checked by the loan correspondent and then submitted to the home office for final selection and approval. When an application is approved, the funds are disbursed by the insurance company and the correspondent is charged with "servicing" the loan, that is, looking after the loan until it is fully discharged. He must see that interest and principal payments are made when due, that the property is kept in good repair, and that taxes and insurance payments are kept up to date. If the loan has to be foreclosed, then that, too, must be handled by the loan correspondent, who will frequently rent the property or manage it for the life insurance company and later arrange its sale to some new buyer.

The correspondent is compensated for his services by sale of the loan instrument to the life insurance company at one or more "points" above par. For example, a $10,000 loan might be sold at a price of 102, where par is 100. This would mean that the insurance company would pay the correspondent $10,200, the additional $200 covering the costs of making the loan and possibly some profit on the transaction. In addition, the life insurance company would typically pay its correspondent one half of 1 per cent of the loan balance annually. For example, if the loan were written at an interest rate of 5 per cent, the correspondent would collect this interest charge from the borrower, and remit 4½ per cent (or 90 per cent of the total interest collected) to the life insurance company and keep the remainder as his fee.

Individuals

In contrast to most other major fields of credit, individuals as well as institutional investors engage in lending funds on real estate. In 1949, loans from individuals amounted to $2,039 million, approximately one sixth of the total from all sources.

FEDERAL AGENCIES

When the depression emphasized a number of fundamental weaknesses in the mortgage field, particularly in the financing of homes and apartments, the federal government, in the closing days of the Hoover administration, initiated a broad program for strengthening and improving the facilities for mortgage finance and for improving housing conditions. Implementation of this program is reflected in the activities of the federal agencies created to do the job." [26]

Home Owners' Loan Corporation

The primary vehicle for aid to lending institutions and to homeowner borrowers in the depression was the Home Owners' Loan Corporation (HOLC), established by act of Congress in 1933. Its purpose was to make loans to home owners in danger of losing their properties through foreclosure and to prevent continued liquidation of real estate credits by lending institutions. At the time the Home Owners' Loan Act was passed, the foreclosure rate was more than 1,000 per day on nonfarm home properties. Many family incomes had been reduced or stopped entirely, making it impossible for payments on mortgage loans to be met. Property values were declining, equities behind the loans were being wiped out, and the whole mortgage credit structure was weakened.

The HOLC relieved this situation by refinancing defaulted home loans on a long-term amortized basis at an interest rate of 5 per cent, which was later lowered to 4½ per cent. Lenders received bonds of the Corporation in exchange for the unpaid principal amount of the mortgages of individuals. As a result of this transfer, the borrowers became debtors of an agency of the federal government. The lender received government-guaranteed bonds which could be sold to obtain cash needed to meet the lender's own contractual obligations.

The HOLC was established on the theory that many families hard hit by the severe depression and temporarily unemployed would be able to keep possession of their homes if their mortgage loans, particularly the ones which were on a short-time basis and coming due for renewal, were rewritten on easier and amortized terms. By stretching out the period of repayment and lowering the interest rate, borrowers' monthly payments were reduced to $7.91 per $1,000 of loan, which in most cases was small enough to be carried. As an additional relief to HOLC borrowers, a moratorium on principal payments in some cases of extreme distress was granted for the first three years after passage of the act. The borrower temporarily had only interest plus taxes to pay.

A flood of applications were received by the HOLC as soon as its operations commenced. During the three years from June 13, 1933, to June 13, 1936, when it ceased making loans, it received 1,885,000 applications and granted 1,017,821 loans, totaling $3.1 billion. Of the total amount loaned by the HOLC, some $2.7 billion went to former creditors in payment of the indebtedness due them, and 70 per cent of this was disbursed to financial institutions. At the end of 1949, total loans on the books of the Corporation amounted to less than $50 million.

The HOLC was probably one of the most popular of the New Deal creations and, as a whole, rendered a distinct and valuable service to financial institutions as well as to home owners. It gave banks and savings and loan associations a source of cash with which to pay withdrawals, and it helped to expedite the liquidation of closed banks. Many marginal loans were reorganized and placed on a basis which the borrower was able to meet, and many potential foreclosures were avoided.

Agencies to Assist Mortgagees

Three agencies were established to assist lenders by providing a means of converting outstanding loans to cash. The Federal Home Loan Banks and the Federal Savings and Loan Insurance Corporation have been mentioned in Chapter 11. Establishment of a third agency, the Federal National Mortgage Association (FNMA) of Washington, was authorized under the National Housing Act of 1934. Although the act provided for formation of a number of associations, only the FNMA has been established. It may engage in the business of buying or selling first mortgages. The FNMA was of small effect in the mortgage market until 1949, when, for a time, the low rates on some mortgages encouraged lenders to offer them for sale at par.

Housing and Home Finance Agency

Operations of three major federal housing agencies are co-ordinated through the Housing and Home Finance Agency (HHFA), which was established by Congress in 1947. The main subdivisions of this agency are: the Home Loan Bank Board (HLBB), the Public Housing Administration (PHA), and the Federal Housing Administration (FHA). The activities of two agencies (the home loan banks and FSLTC) operated by the Home Loan Bank Board were commented on in Chapter 11, and reference has already been made in this present chapter to the HOLC, another agency operated by the Board. Public Housing Administration activities are principally directed toward the development of low-rent housing facilities for lower-income groups. A brief comment on the concept of public housing will be included in the final section of this chapter.

Federal Housing Administration

The government agency which has received most publicity in home mortgage operations is the Federal Housing Administration (FHA), which was created by the National Housing Act of 1934. Contrary to popular conception, the FHA does not make loans of any sort. It insures payment on loans made by private lending institutions on homes and rental apartments. In effect, the FHA is an agency for placing the credit of the federal government behind the credit of individuals who borrow to buy or build residential property.

The agency was created by Congress at a time when the residential construction industry was lagging, and the new legislation was designed to stimulate it to greater activity. It was the theory that, by providing government insurance against loss on home mortgage loans, more credit would be made available for the financing of homes with lower down-payments and longer maturities and thus make it possible for more people to buy or build homes.

Other purposes of the act included: the accomplishment of certain reforms in mortgage lending practice, the encouragement of improvement in housing standards and conditions, the provisions of a system of mutual mortgage insurance, the development of a national market for mortgages, and an increase in the liquidity of mortgages. These changes and reforms did bring more capital into the mortgage market, particularly from commercial banks, and did effect substantial improvement in small-house design and construction.

The FHA carries on several rather distinct activities created under different titles of the National Housing Act.

Insurance of loans made for the repair and modernization of homes was provided under Title I of the act. Under the terms of this title, lending institutions are insured against loss on loans made for the repair, improvement, or modernization of property, such as repairing the roof, installing a modern heating and plumbing system, building a garage, painting and redecorating the house, etc. These loans are generally limited to $2,500 in amount and are not secured by a mortgage. The maximum term is thirty-six months. They are discount loans and carry an effective interest rate as high as 9.72 per cent. From the beginning of the program in 1934 to December, 1949, $3,946 million of these loans have been made, chiefly by commercial banks and finance companies.

The FHA insurance of home mortgage loans for the construction or purchase of a home or the refinancing of an existing mortgage debt under a system of mutual mortgage insurance was created under Title II of the act. A mutual mortgage insurance fund was created with the initial capital subscribed by the RFC and the fund built up by premiums paid to the FHA by borrowers on FHA-insured loans. Any loss from defaulted loans is met out of this fund, with the lender in effect trading the defaulted loan for a debenture of the FHA, which is guaranteed as to principal and interest by the federal government.

Briefly, the insured mortgage plan works somewhat as follows: An individual borrower applies for a mortgage loan at a savings and loan association, bank, or other approved FHA lending institution. The necessary application papers are sent to the local FHA office for approval. The loan is an amortized direct-reduction loan: the borrower makes monthly payments of principal and interest on the loan plus one half of the annual insurance premium, which the lender in turn pays to the mutual mortgage insurance fund. This premium is one half of 1 per cent of the unpaid balance of the loan. Whenever an insured mortgage is in default, the lender must notify the FHA and start foreclosure proceedings according to FHA regulations or otherwise acquire title and possession of the property. Having foreclosed a defaulted loan and taken title to the property, the lender may transfer title and possession of the property to the FHA and obtain, in exchange, debentures of the mortgage insurance fund bearing not more than 3 per cent interest and with a maturity the same as that of the mortgage in exchange for which they were issued. The debentures are issued for an amount covering the unpaid principal amount of the loan plus the payments made by the mortgagee for taxes, special assessments, insurance premium, and also foreclosure costs to a maximum of $75.

To be eligible for insurance under Title II of the act, the loan must meet certain detailed requirements. The security must be a first mortgage on a property designed principally for residential use for not more than four families; the note may bear interest at a rate not greater than 4¼ per cent (originally 5 per cent, later 4½ per cent); and the property must be located in an approved section of a city in a neighborhood that meets certain standards. A loan must not, in most cases, exceed $16,000, or 80 per cent of the appraised value of the property, or have a maturity longer than thirty years. The loan on houses priced at less than $10,000, however, may be as much as 95 per cent of the value.

Most of the loans insured under Title II are on small residences. Under a special section of this title, provision is made in addition for insuring, under certain conditions, amortized mortgage loans up to $5 million on rental and co-operative housing projects; such insured loans are limited to a maximum of 90 per cent of the value of the property and may have a term as long as thirty years. From the time of the passage of the National Housing Act in 1934 to the end of 1949, a total of 1,622,687 loans on one- to four-family residences had been insured under Title II. These loans totaled $8,652 million, and about 50 per cent of them were on newly built homes. During this same period, 381 rental housing projects, with a total of 43,388 apartment units, were built with Title II insured mortgages totaling $168 million.

The impressive size of these data does not mean that all real estate loans are backed by federal guarantees, however. As Table 38 below indicates, most residential real estate loans are conventional loans,

TABLE 38

TOTAL HOME MORTGAGE LOANS OF $20,000 OR LESS
By Type of Loan
(Millions of Dollars)

Year	Total	"Conventional"*	FHA Insured	VA Guaranteed or Insured
1939	$ 3,507	$2,811	$ 696	....
1940	4,031	3,269	762	....
1941	4,732	3,821	911	....
1942	3,943	2,970	973	....
1943	3,861	3,098	763	....
1944	4,606	3,899	707	....
1945	5,650	4,984	474	$ 192
1946	10,589	7,865	422	2,302
1947	11,729	7,548	895	3,286
1948	11,882	7,883	2,118	1,881
1949	11,828	8,191	2,213	1,424

* Difference between total and sum of data on insured and guaranteed mortgages.
Source: Housing and Home Finance Agency, *Housing Statistics*, March, 1950, p. 22.

and less than half are insured or guaranteed by either the FHA or the Veterans' Administration (VA), as described in the next subsection.

The Veterans' Emergency Housing Act passed in May, 1946, reactivated the Title VI program of the FHA and a new title (VIII) was added by the Housing Act of 1948. Under these titles the FHA is empowered specifically to aid in the development of housing for veterans and for military personnel. Title VI permits insurance of loans up to 90 per cent of the "current necessary costs" of constructing homes for veterans. Title VIII permits insurance of loans to builders of rental housing for military personnel on or near military posts.

Initiated as a purely temporary agency to stimulate the home building industry, the FHA is now well established as a permanent mortgage insurance agency of the federal government. It was partly the effect of the FHA to broaden the scope of real estate markets, which had been local in operation. Through the use of the indirect government guaranty, generally lower interest rates on home mortgage loans have been achieved and a measure of unity in both interest rates and requirements for acceptable mortgages has been brought into the home mortgage market. A much higher degree of standardization of mortgage loan terms, lending plans, and borrower requirements exists now than previously.

As a result of these changes, the liquidity of home mortgage loans has been increased considerably and the vast resources of the commercial banking system have been brought into the mortgage market. The commercial banks and life insurance companies which were in need of an outlet for their idle assets leaped at the opportunity presented by the FHA insurance program and now hold in their portfolios approximately 80 per cent of all FHA loans outstanding.

Veterans' Administration Guaranteed Loans

The most significant measure enacted to provide home mortgage loans to veterans of World War II is Title III of the Servicemen's Readjustment Act of 1944, commonly known as the "GI Bill of Rights." This act with subsequent amendments provided that the Veterans' Administration, backed by the United States Treasury, would guarantee or insure loans to veterans made by private financial institutions, savings and loan associations, banks, and insurance companies. It is a program of staggering proportions. Within the first three years of operations, up to December 31, 1947, over $6,107 million of home loans to 1,056,000 veterans had been made under its provisions. This compares with loans of $1,100 million insured in the first three years of the FHA program and with the $3,093 million in loans made by the HOLC in the three years it was actively lending. At the end of five years, $9,073 million of loans had been made under the provisions of this act.

The law offers a guaranty for real estate loans to qualified veterans up to $7,500, or 60 per cent of the total loan, whichever is less. This guaranty is unusual in that, through it, the Veterans' Administration takes the "first risk" on the loan. The guaranty is designed to take the place, up to the amount of the guaranty, of the usual cash downpayment ordinarily associated with mortgage lending.

The nature of the VA guaranty can be most easily understood by reference to what might happen in a case involving a default and subsequent foreclosure, as outlined in Table 39. As can be seen by studying this table, lenders can make larger loans to veterans than they could to nonveteran borrowers on the same house. The Veterans' Administration loans no money. It merely endorses the veteran's credit up to the amount of the guaranty in such a manner that the veteran can substitute this guaranty for cash, and the lending institution may make a loan to a veteran equal to the amount it would loan

TABLE 39

RELATIONSHIPS OF CONVENTIONAL AND GUARANTEED LOANS

	Ordinary Loan	GI Loan
Purchase price of home..............	$12,500	$12,500
Amount lending institution would be willing to lend *at its own risk*........	$7,500	$7,500
Amount actually loaned..............	$7,500	$12,500*
Amount of down-payment...........	$4,500 in cash	None*
Assuming loan defaulted immediately after being made and property was sold for........................	$8,000	$8,000
Loss to lending institution...........	None, since only $7,500 was loaned	$4,500, but lender is reimbursed to the extent of the VA guaranty
Loss on down-payment or guaranty....	$4,500 loss to borrower	$4,500 loss: VA loses to the extent of its guaranty unless it can later collect this amount from veteran
Actual loss to lender.................	None	None

* Subject to modification under terms of Regulation X, described on p. 451.

on that house to a nonveteran plus an amount equal to the VA guarantee.

The *insurance* of loans (as distinguished from *guaranty* of loans just described) provided by the Veterans' Administration under a different section of the act offers a type of insurance in which lending institutions are reimbursed for all losses on loans to qualified veterans up to 15 per cent of the aggregate of principal amount of such veterans' loans made. This means that, if a lending institution made $15 million in insured veterans' loans, it would have to its credit an insurance reserve of $2,250,000. If the losses of this lending institution on the total of these $15 million loans amounted to only $2 million, the lender would be reimbursed by the Veterans' Administration in full for its losses on these loans. Lenders make either insured

or guaranteed loans. The guaranty privileges are used more frequently. The Veterans' Administration also has the authority to make
direct loans of $10,000 or less in areas where veterans are unable
to borrow at the 4 per cent rate. Table 40 indicates the relative
participation of various financial institutions in the veterans' home
loan program.

Toward the end of 1947 and in subsequent months following a
rise in yields on government and corporate bonds and an increase
in the operating expense of lending institutions, many lenders became

TABLE 40

PERCENTAGE OF TOTAL VETERANS' GUARANTEED AND
INSURED HOME LOANS BY TYPE OF LENDER
Loans Made July, 1948, through June, 1949

Commercial banks.............................	33
Mortgage companies.........................	24
Savings and loan associations......................	23
Mutual savings banks...........................	11
Life insurance companies........................	9
Total.......................................	100

Source: Veterans' Administration, *Annual Report, 1949*, p. 83.

somewhat reluctant to make GI loans because the interest rate is
limited to 4 per cent, but the amount of lending at this rate increased
in 1949 and 1950.

Federal Reserve Board's Regulation X

Under the terms of the Defense Production Act of 1950, the President of the United States was empowered to regulate certain aspects
of real estate financing until June 30, 1951. The President, in turn,
by an executive order, delegated this authority to the Federal Reserve
Board, an agency responsible for regulating many of the money and
credit relationships in this country. The administrator of the Housing
and Home Finance Agency must concur in decisions relating to residential real estate financing.

The Federal Reserve Board's Regulation X became effective on
October 12, 1950. The regulation as issued requires minimum down-
payments ranging from 10 per cent on properties valued at $5,000
or less to 50 per cent on properties valued at $25,000 or more. For
veterans, the regulation establishes minimum down-payments ranging from 5 per cent on property valued at $5,000 or less to 45 per
cent on property valued at $24,250 or more. The regulation as issued
applies only to one- and two-family houses. The powers delegated to

the Board permit not only considerable change in regulation of down-payment proportions for residential housing but also regulation of payments on credit agreements in any area of real estate finance.

PRESENT PROBLEMS AND OUTLOOK

In recent years the question has been frequently raised with respect to real estate financing: "What will happen if we have a serious depression?" Federal action through guaranty and insurance of home mortgage payments has undoubtedly encouraged assumption of debt by individuals and, at the same time, has encouraged lenders to accept credit based on real property. During the past few years, the proportion of homes owned by occupants has passed the 50 per cent mark. Although second and third mortgage financing have declined in importance, the initial proportion of debt to value of property has not declined and probably has risen in the 1940's relative to the 1920's.

The general shift from straight to amortized loans has added an element of strength. Creditors learn more promptly whether debtors are able to pay up mortgage debt because that ability is reaffirmed monthly. The budgeting of consumer incomes resulting from the regular payments of principal and interest probably has had a salutary effect on debtor recognition of their responsibilities as debtors. On the other hand, a schedule of regular payments has the disadvantage of making more difficult the problem of the debtor in bridging even a short, sharp break in the flow of his income; and the rate of building-up of owner equity in real estate is probably slower under the present type of amortized debt plan than it was under the accelerated amortization enforced by the types of second and third mortgage terms which prevailed in earlier years.

A substantial element of strength is added also by the mere existence of agencies such as the FHA and the Federal National Mortgage Association, which can take mortgages over from lenders and in this way relieve the lending agencies of some of the dangers of a credit "freeze." The success with which the federal agencies can perform this function has not, of course, been tested in any pronounced fashion, but the results of HOLC financing seem encouraging. The existence of an agreement such as that with the FHA, however, does not relieve creditors of the disagreeable and locally unpopular task of foreclosing defaulted mortgage notes.

It is probably reasonable to conclude that short periods of unsettled economic conditions will be bridged more easily on the whole and without upheavals in the real estate markets. But there is little basis on which to judge whether the present condition of high proportionate indebtedness on high-priced real estate slowly amortized over long periods will prove sound financing if a severe decline of either real estate prices or personal incomes, or both, should occur.

A second question, which has hardly begun to be debated, is: "What part should public housing play in the construction of residential housing for the country as a whole?" Public construction is a large segment of all construction: in 1949, 27 per cent of the $19.3 billion total was publicly financed. But, the largest amount of public activity is in the construction of recognizably public properties: roads, schools, military installations, parks, sewers, public buildings. Although the government is empowered to grant funds to states and municipalities for public residential construction, less than one quarter of a billion dollars was spent for this purpose in 1949.

Large housing projects can be and have been carried out with private financing. The question as to the advisability of governmental financing arises when the cost of housing to occupants is considered. The debate is fundamentally one of what minimum standards of housing are acceptable in a society such as that of the United States at the present time and whether privately financed projects can supply minimum housing requirements at prices which occupants can afford to pay. In effect, the suggestion that public financing is required is a suggestion that the nation must subsidize the families at low income levels if they are to be suitably housed. It now appears that many years will pass before this debate is satisfactorily resolved. It is quite possible that it may simply lose importance as changes in taxation or in stability of business—to name only two important factors—alter income distributions and economic problems generally.

—LORING C. FARWELL

QUESTIONS AND PROBLEMS

1. Why is the financing process of great importance to the market for real estate?

2. What does "amortization" mean?

3. What are the leading legal formalities of the real estate finance deal? Why do these tend to be of greater importance in real estate than in other personal transactions?

4. What are the differences in practice in financing commercial and residential properties?

5. What factors may be considered by a lender in judging a real estate loan application?
6. Outline the functions of the Federal Housing Administration.
7. Distinguish between the insurance and the guaranty features of Veterans' Administration operations.
8. Why do banks and insurance companies hold a large proportion of the federally insured loans? Why do savings and loan associations and individuals refrain from insuring the loans they make?

BIBLIOGRAPHY

The wide range of differences in various phases of real estate ownership and financing increases the difficulty of suggesting materials for further reading. Many readers would probably find useful suggestions in an old but still pertinent publication of the United States government, *How to Judge a House* (Washington, D.C.: U.S. Government Printing Office, 1931). It may also be helpful to read a discussion of real estate as one phase of a general discussion of personal finance, such as chapter xvi, "Owning a Home," in the book by David F. Jordon (revised by E. F. Willett), *Managing Personal Finances* (New York: Prentice-Hall, Inc., 1945). A suggested general text on real estate is that by William H. Husband and Frank Ray Anderson, *Real Estate Analysis* (Chicago: Richard D. Irwin, Inc., 1948). Detailed treatments of specialized aspects are found in books such as S. L. McMichael, *Appraising Manual* (New York: Prentice-Hall, Inc., 1944), and Robert Kratovil, *Real Estate Law* (New York: Prentice-Hall, Inc., 1946). The annual reports of the Housing and Home Finance Agency are sources of information about federal activity in the real estate field and statistics on real estate markets. These reports also include lists of publications by the Agency. The most useful source of current statistics on real estate is *Housing Statistics,* a monthly publication of the Housing and Home Finance Agency.

Chapter • 16

FARM CREDIT INSTITUTIONS

THE financing of agriculture is a problem that has come to the attention of the general public only in the last several decades. Prior to World War I the credit needs of farmers were not especially great: land had been available at low prices, application of expensive power machinery to agricultural production was in its infancy, and the general type of farming in vogue did not require the credit advances now necessary to "carry" specialized commercial farmers over the period between harvests. As a consequence, the credit demands of farmers were reasonably well handled by such private agencies as local banks, merchants, and dealers.

The advent of World War I resulted in an enlarged demand for agricultural products, an increase in land values, and an expansion in the acreage under cultivation. These conditions brought with them a marked rise in the volume of farm mortgage financing. The postwar slump in farm-product prices introduced a series of misfortunes that continued to beset farm operators until the middle 1930's. The inadequacies of the farm credit system to meet conditions generated by war and aggravated by depression attracted general attention and produced the many specialized institutions and arrangements which now exist.

CHARACTERISTICS OF AGRICULTURAL FINANCE .

Two outstanding features in the field of farm financing are: (1) the long term for which funds must be advanced, and (2) the use of the mortgage note as the principal credit instrument. Although the mortgage may seem to provide adequate security for the lender in years of relatively stable prices, the fact that mortgage notes not uncommonly run for two decades or more permits time for the entrance of substantial swings in the prices of farm products, which may seriously affect the ability of the borrower to meet his obligation. This risk has the effects of restricting the amount of credit available for long-term financing and of increasing the rate of interest the borrower is required to pay.

Other factors combine with those mentioned above to impair the farmers' ability to obtain credit on terms comparable to those received by his industrial or commercial cousins in urban centers. Among the limiting factors, many of which will doubtless continue to prevail, are these: the average size of the producing unit is small; farms are scattered over the entire nation; and a great majority are widely separated from the surplus investment funds concentrated in the capital markets. Moreover, the small size of farms and the hazards of operation limit their ability to obtain funds by the use of the corporate form of organization. It should not be inferred that farmers are legally barred from incorporation. The practical limitation is that securities issued by relatively small and risky units would probably not find a ready market.

Business and Social Factors Intermingled

Another significant factor is the close connection between family and business affairs. Farming is normally carried on as a family venture; and in view of the lack of adequate accounting, it becomes almost impossible to distinguish the costs of operating the farm from the living expenses of the farm family—business and social considerations are closely intermingled. The credit position of the farm borrower is, therefore, often dependent upon the size of his family, its standard of living, its health, plans for the education of children, and other matters difficult to analyze. It is not easy to separate processes of production and consumption or to determine whether an extension of credit is for productive or consumptive purposes.

The high degree of risk associated with agricultural production has not only limited the farmer's ability to obtain credit by restricting his use of the corporate form of organization but has reduced the availability of funds from all possible sources. Risk is not due alone to the hazards of weather, insect pests, or other natural forces. The demand for many agricultural products is inelastic; i.e., a slight increase of supply is accompanied by a sharp decrease in price, with the result that an increase in volume of product is often accompanied by such a decline in farm prices that credit bases are undermined. Furthermore, the slow recovery of funds invested in the farm and farm equipment makes it difficult for the farmer quickly to recoup the losses of bad years.

Thus, as a small-scale producer in a very risky enterprise, the farmer has been forced to depend mainly upon his own savings and the credit which he could command in the local lending market, where funds were scarce and rates high.

Types or Classes of Credit

In view of the increased recognition of these hazards, privately owned financial institutions at the turn of the century and especially at the time of World War I found it difficult, if not impossible, to provide funds under the terms applicable to other borrowers. Other sources were needed.

Farmers have long been conscious of their political power and in recent years have used it to their advantage in the field of agricultural finance. They have had powerful lobbies furthering their interests in Washington and, because of the geographical composition of the Senate, have obtained important concessions in recent years. In fact, the most significant classification used in a discussion of agricultural credit is *public* versus *private*, an indication of the position achieved by publicly sponsored lending agencies that were established as a result of pressure placed upon the Congress by farm organizations.

A second very common basis of credit classification in this field is *time*, or the term for which the advance is obtained, namely: short term, represented by loans running for six months or less; intermediate term, represented by loans with a maturity date of from six months to three years; and long term or investment credit, represented by loans of from three to forty years.

General Methods of Lending

As our discussion develops, it will be noted that four general methods of lending prevail. First there is the direct method in which no middleman intervenes between borrower and lender. Ordinarily, this method can be used only when debtor and creditor are residents of the same community and when the creditor has complete confidence that the borrower will repay. Typical of such loans are those made within a family, as from father to son, or uncle to nephew.

Second, in an agency loan involving a middleman, the lender takes the note (and probably a mortgage) of the farmer, but the agency negotiating the loan either has acted as an agent of the investor or has sold the note to him as principal. The middleman may not be a financial institution. It is not uncommon for a rural dealer in implements or in dairy supplies (such as cream separators, milking machines, and similar equipment) to accept promissory notes in partial payment on equipment. The notes may then be sold or discounted with an investor, who retains the paper until it matures. A variation of this method, involving a financial institution, has been adopted by private mortgage companies that issue long-term certificates, in various denominations, representing fractional shares of a single mortgage.

A third general method is termed the "bond system." An agency making either long- or short-term loans forms a pool of the notes received from borrowers. Against the security thus provided, the agency issues bonds and sells them in conveniently sized denominations to investors. A part of the success of publicly sponsored lending agencies, soon to be discussed, is doubtless due to the use of this method. The investor does not purchase the note of an individual borrower. Instead he holds an obligation of the lending institution resting upon its diversified portfolio of assets.

Fourth, several kinds of institutions make loans that are completely indirect. They obtain funds from one group and lend to another with no direct connection between the persons at opposite ends of the transaction. This is typical of the operations of an insurance company, which collects premiums from policyholders in widely separated areas and invests a portion in farm mortgage notes. Loans made by savings or commercial banks from funds left by depositors are also in the class of indirect loans.[1]

PRIVATE SOURCES OF FARM CREDIT

Long-Term Mortgage Loans

Before the federal land banks became active in the field of mortgage lending in 1917, agriculturists depended entirely upon private sources of credit—e.g., life insurance companies, commercial banks, local mortgage companies, and others. In fact, these institutions still retain a prominent place in the business. Table 41 indicates the relative importance of the several lending groups.

Although Table 41 does not reflect their operations, private mortgage companies are an important immediate source of long-term

---

[1] William G. Murray, *Agricultural Finance* (2d rev. ed.; Ames: Iowa State College Press, 1947), chap. xiii.

farm credit. The few private institutions now in operation cover extensive areas by using local branches or agents. The latter accept the application, investigate the prospective borrower, appraise the property, and forward the application and a report to the central office for action. Mortgage companies then commonly sell the notes they acquire to institutions or private investors or deposit them with a trustee as security for an issue of bonds. Proceeds from the sale of securities are then advanced to borrowers and result in the acquisition of more mortgage notes by the lending institution.

TABLE 41

FARM MORTGAGE DEBT

Total Outstanding and Amounts Held by Principal Lender Groups, United States, Selected Years, 1910–49

BEGINNING OF YEAR	TOTAL FARM MORTGAGE DEBT	AMOUNTS HELD BY PRINCIPAL LENDER GROUPS (THOUSANDS OF DOLLARS)				
		Federal Land Banks	Federal Farm Mortgage Corporation	Life Insurance Companies	Insured Commercial Banks	Individuals and Others
1910	3,207,863	....	......	386,961	406,248	2,414,654
1920	8,448,772	....	......	974,826	1,204,383	5,975,968
1930	9,630,768	....	......	2,118,439	997,468	5,313,129
1935	7,584,459	1,947,442	616,737	1,301,562	498,842	3,219,876
1940	6,586,399	2,009,820	713,290	984,290	534,170	2,344,829
1945	4,932,942	1,209,676	347,307	933,723	449,582	1,992,654
1949	5,108,183	868,156	77,920	1,035,719	847,841	2,089,192

Source: U.S. Department of Agriculture, as reproduced in *Agricultural Finance Review*, Vol. XII (November, 1949), Table 1, p. 87.

Although commercial and savings banks and trust companies, especially when located in rural areas, have retained their interest in farm loans, Table 41 indicates that their volume since 1930 has been only about half as large as the loans of insurance companies. Long-term loans by commercial banks have been made in the face of the traditional policy of such banks to engage primarily in short-term self-liquidating loans. This is not true of savings and trust institutions, whose list of "eligible" investments has always included first mortgages on improved real estate.

Insurance companies have also been continuous lenders on farm mortgages. The amount of their holdings has been characterized by variations closely related to fluctuations in the value of farm real estate. Some of this variation may be observed in Table 41 but would be more noticeable if annual data were exhibited. In acquiring their mortgages, insurance companies often work through local farm mortgage companies, brokers, and rural banks. Large companies have made use of extensive field organizations patterned after those of mortgage companies.

The large amount of mortgage loans held by individuals, as shown in Table 41, is chiefly in the hands of two classes: a large group of well-to-do people investing in real estate loans because of an unshakable faith in the fundamental quality of mortgages as an investment; and former landowners, retired and active, who have sold acreage on terms calling for a down-payment with reduction of the balance by installment payments. They are able and willing to hold the paper until maturity as a form of investment. Others in this field include endowed schools, fraternal organizations, and churches.

An examination of the over-all mortgage debt of farmers as represented in Table 41 and Exhibit 52, discloses that loans trebled between 1910 and 1930 but fell sharply thereafter to less than $5 billion in 1945. In 1946 a reversal set in that continued into 1950. The Bureau of Agricultural Economics has estimated that the farm mortgage debt stood at $5.4 billion on January 1, 1950. Although this is an increase of approximately one sixth since the low point of 1946, the debt is generally considered moderate, in view of the excessive heights reached following World War I (1923). Moreover, the current high level of farm income enables debtors to make payments on their current obligation with less burden than was formerly the case.

Short-Term Credit

Short-term credit is available to the farmer from the same private sources that supply urban businessmen and consumers. Chief among these is the commercial banking system. Local loans to farmers are made on both unsecured and secured notes. Seldom do banks require real estate mortgages as security for short or intermediate term advances; but they often accept liens on livestock, growing crops, farm implements, etc. Consumer-type loans—usually excluded from consideration of agricultural credit—are secured by the item purchased just as they are in urban centers, i.e., by claims on automobiles, major electrical appliances, farm equipment, and household furnishings.

Private sources of noncash credit include merchants and dealers who advance trade or "store"-type credit on open-book accounts or promissory notes. Dealers in feed, seed, fertilizer, implements, groceries, and other production and consumption items "carry" their rural customers for large amounts.

The volume of outstanding short-term loans made by commercial

Exhibit 52

TOTAL FARM MORTGAGE DEBT AND NON–REAL ESTATE FARM DEBT
OWED PRINCIPLE LENDERS, UNITED STATES, JANUARY 1, 1911–50*

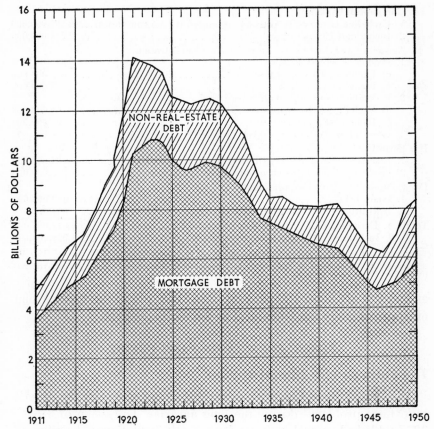

* Excludes nonrecourse commodity loans, held or guaranteed by the Commodity Credit
Corporation.

Source: U.S. Department of Agriculture, Bureau of Agricultural Economics.

banks, and supplemented by advances of merchants and dealers, has
tended to decline as federally sponsored agencies have grown. Data
as of July 1, 1949, in Table 42 show, however, the significant position
still maintained by privately owned and operated commercial banks.

Although fluctuations in the total volume of non–real estate farm
loans tend to follow the pattern of growth and decline of mortgage
debts, as shown in Exhibit 53, the upturn has been much sharper
than that of the long-term debt in the years following World War II.
The Bureau of Agricultural Economics has estimated the non–real
estate debt to be $5.3 billion as of January 1, 1950. The expansion,

TABLE 42

NON–REAL ESTATE LOANS TO FARMERS BY PRINCIPAL CREDIT INSTITUTIONS
Amount Outstanding, July, 1949

I. Commercial banks:
  1. Excluding Commodity Credit Corporation (CCC) guaranties....$2,267,000,000
  2. Including CCC guaranties................................. 2,819,000,000
II. Agencies supervised by the Farm Credit Administration:
  1. Production credit associations:
    a) Excluding CCC guaranties............................. 523,000,000
    b) Including CCC guaranties............................. 523,000,000
  2. Federal intermediate credit banks:
    a) Excluding CCC guaranties............................. 61,000,000
    b) Including CCC guaranties............................. 61,000,000
  3. Regional agricultural credit corporations*.................... 1,000,000
III. Farm Home Administration:
  1. Emergency Crop and Feed Loan Office...................... 82,000,000
  2. Production and subsistence loans........................... 278,000,000
IV. Commodity Credit Corporation:
  1. Loans held... 333,000,000
  2. Institutional loans guaranteed............................. 551,000,000
Total: 1. Excluding CCC loans held or guaranteed................$3,211,000,000
    2. Including CCC loans held or guaranteed................. 4,094,000,000

    * Transferred from Farm Credit Administration, April 15, 1949, for liquidation.

    Source: U.S. Department of Agriculture, as reproduced in *Agricultural Finance Review*, Vol. XII (November, 1949), Table 13, p. 96.

an increase of almost 100 per cent since 1946, places this type of loan on approximately the same level as the mortgage debt.

PUBLIC SOURCES OF FARM CREDIT

The Farm Credit Administration

The United States Congress, in various attempts to solve the American "farm problem" during the long agrarian depression of 1920–33, established several separate farm credit institutions. The purpose of the Farm Credit Administration (FCA), created in May, 1933, was to unify and co-ordinate the operations of these federally sponsored agencies by bringing them together into one administrative organization. Although originally established as an independent agency, the FCA was subsequently made a division of the Treasury, and in July, 1939, was transferred to the Department of Agriculture. Today it does not include the governmental agencies making all types of loans—e.g., commodity loans, rehabilitation loans, and electrification loans—but it is by far the largest and most important of the federal agricultural credit organizations. The permanent institutions operating within the FCA include federal land banks and national farm loan associations, production credit corporations and associations, federal intermediate credit banks, and banks for co-operatives.

Exhibit 53

NON–REAL ESTATE LOANS TO FARMERS HELD BY PRINCIPAL LENDERS,
UNITED STATES, JANUARY 1 AND JULY 1, 1910–50*

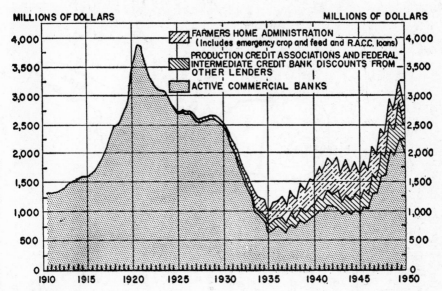

* Excludes nonrecourse commodity loans held or guaranteed by the Commodity Credit Corporation.

Source: U.S. Department of Agriculture, Bureau of Agricultural Economics.

ADMINISTRATIVE ORGANIZATION OF THE FCA. For purposes of handling mortgage loans (and other types of advances of the FCA) the nation was divided into twelve districts somewhat similar to the regional setup of the Federal Reserve Bank System. Boundaries of the farm credit districts follow state lines, and an attempt has been made to include diversified crop areas within each district. (See Exhibit 54.) The cities in which district offices are located are Springfield, Massachusetts; Baltimore, Maryland; Columbia, South Carolina; Louisville, Kentucky; New Orleans, Louisiana; St. Louis, Missouri; St. Paul, Minnesota; Omaha, Nebraska; Wichita, Kansas; Houston, Texas; Berkeley, California; and Spokane, Washington. Areas contiguous to these cities are serviced by the district banks.

Governor. The administrator in charge of the FCA is called the "governor." He is appointed by the President of the United States for a term of six years, maintains an office in Washington, and is directly responsible to the Secretary of Agriculture. He has several assistants, called "deputy governors." Four commissioners are the chief executives under the governor, and they have charge of the federal land

Exhibit 54

FARM CREDIT ADMINISTRATION DISTRICT BOUNDARIES AND
LOCATION OF DISTRICT UNITS

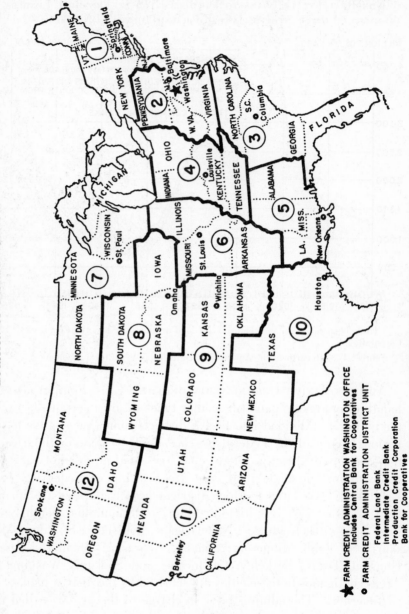

★ FARM CREDIT ADMINISTRATION WASHINGTON OFFICE
   Includes Central Bank for Cooperatives

⊙ FARM CREDIT ADMINISTRATION DISTRICT UNIT

   Federal Land Bank
   Intermediate Credit Bank
   Production Credit Corporation
   Bank for Cooperatives

Location of National Farm Loan Associations and Production Credit Associations Not Shown banks, intermediate credit banks, production credit associations, and banks for co-operatives, respectively. These officers are also appointees of the President, have offices in Washington, and serve for an indefinite term. Their duties are supervisory only; credit advances and other operations are handled by personnel within the separate agencies. Exhibit 55 indicates the credit divisions and service divi-

Exhibit 55

FARM CREDIT ADMINISTRATION ORGANIZATION CHART

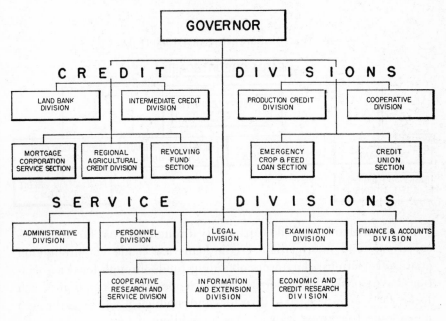

sions of the FCA. Each credit division is supervised by a commissioner.

In each of the twelve districts of the FCA, all activities are under the direction of a farm credit board and an advisory committee. (See Exhibit 56.)

District Boards. Each district board has a personnel of seven; four are appointees of the governor and three are elected by the borrower-members of local credit associations. Members serve for three years, meet at regular intervals (at least once a month), and determine policies of the lending agencies under their jurisdiction. The advisory group includes the general agent and the presidents of the four districts units making up the FCA. The general agent and his staff work closely with the Washington office to achieve a district program that is co-ordinated with the policy of the headquarters unit.

Although the four credit units comprising the district organization operate under the same board of directors, they have no other corporate connection with one another. They have separate presidents and staff, who are responsible only to the corresponding commissioner in the Washington office.

Local associations through which funds are channeled to individual farmers and cattlemen are characteristic of two of the lending units.

Exhibit 56

ORGANIZATION OF TWELVE FARM CREDIT DISTRICTS

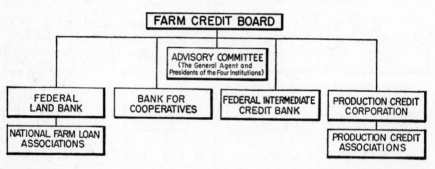

Federal land bank funds flow primarily through national farm loan associations, and intermediate credit loans are made via production credit associations. Borrowers obtaining funds through local associations have stock and membership in the co-operative associations. Each local elects its own board of directors and conducts its business through a secretary-treasurer, who acts as a middleman between borrowers and the district bank.

Long-Term Farm Mortgage Lending

FEDERAL LAND BANKS. The principal units in the Federal Farm Loan System are the twelve federal land banks which make long-term farm mortgage loans through national farm loan associations. The main objective of the land banks, as created by the Federal Farm Loan Act of 1916, was to obtain funds in the investment centers of the country for lending to farmers on a long-term, low-interest-rate basis. Prior to this time, mortgage loans were usually made through small local loan agencies and, in some areas, by life insurance companies. No agency attempted to service more than a small area, and so no uniformity of practice or of rates existed. Competition was intense for making good loans, but few lenders were interested in granting advances where risks were large.

The general plan of operation provided by the act is simple. Mortgage notes of individual farmers are pooled and held as security behind the issue of tax-exempt federal land bank bonds. The sale of these bonds provides the chief source of loan funds of the banks.

The administrative organization of the system orginally was the Federal Farm Loan Board, a bureau within the Treasury Department. The Board functioned independently from 1916 until the FCA became the administrative unit in 1933.

NATIONAL FARM LOAN ASSOCIATIONS. Within each district, local co-operatives, known as "national farm loan associations," were chartered by the Farm Loan Board (in recent years by the FCA) as the agencies through which farmers obtain their loans. Ten agriculturists, who together wish to borrow a total of no less than $20,000, are the minimum number able to form a local association. Each member subscribes to stock in the local organization to an amount equal to 5 per cent of his loan. The local association subscribes in equal amount to stock of the district land bank. It endorses and becomes liable for the individual loan paper, which is then held by the district bank. When loans are paid, the face value of the stock is repaid and the farmer ceases to be a member of the association.

Loans: Restrictions and Regulations. Mortgage loans of federal land banks are made only to active operators or farm managers in amounts ranging from $100 to $50,000. The early limit on advances to one person was $10,000; loans above $25,000 must receive special approval of the Land Bank Commissioner in Washington, D.C. All loans are secured by first mortgages on farm real estate or permanent improvements. No loan may be made in excess of 65 per cent of the appraised value of land and 20 per cent of the value of insured improvements. With approval of the Land Bank Commissioner, land banks are authorized to make direct advances to individual borrowers in communities not served by local farm loan associations. Loans made by federal land banks have maturities from five to thirty-six years, with the typical term falling between twenty and thirty years. All are repayable in regular annual level payments. Interest rates charged the farmer borrowing through local loan associations are not more than 1 per cent above the interest rate paid by the district land bank on its most recent issue of bonds. In no case, may the rate exceed 6 per cent, and in recent years has been 4 per cent. On direct loans (those made where local farm loan associations are not involved), the rate may be one half of 1 per cent above that charged on association-made loans.

Purposes of Loans. The purposes for which loans may be made are:

Purchase of land for agricultural uses
Purchase of farm equipment, fertilizer, and livestock
Erection of buildings, fences, or other improvements
Payment of debts incurred in farming operations
General agricultural uses of the borrower

Lending Experience. Data on the actual use of funds in past years indicate that about 10 per cent were applied to the purchase of land, 4 per cent for the erection of buildings and improvement, 70 per cent for retiring mortgage debt, 10 per cent for the payment of other debts, and the balance for the purchase of livestock, fertilizer, and farm equipment.

The lending history of federal land banks has exhibited a great variation in the number and amount of loans made annually. The range has been from a low of $28 million in loans to 7,000 borrowers in 1932 to a high of $730 million to 190,000 farmers in 1934. The improved position of farm-product prices after 1937 enabled farmers to reduce their mortgage indebtedness substantially and curtailed the activity of the land banks. In fact, only $64 million was advanced in 1940 to 17,000 borrowers. As noted above, mortgage lending expanded again in 1946 and continued at an increasing rate into the first half of 1950. In 1949 over 35,000 loans, aggregating over $164 million, were made. A notable feature of recent lending is an increase in the average size of mortgage loans—from $2,270 in the years 1937–40 to $4,430 in 1949.[2]

Source of Loan Funds. The original source of operating funds for federal land banks was subscription to stock by the United States Treasury—$750,000 for each of the twelve banks, divided into shares having a par value of $5. The principal volume of loan funds has been received, however, from the sale of land bank bonds through regular investment channels. These bonds are now the joint and several obligations of the twelve banks. The total issue is limited to twenty times the amount of combined capital and surplus of the banks. Although they have fluctuated widely in value in the past, the bonds are now well regarded by investors and are included in most of the legal lists of investment securities eligible for purchase by sav-

---

[2] *Agricultural Financial Review,* Vol. XII (November, 1949), Table 1, p. 51.

ings banks and trust institutions. As funds were received by the banks from the sale of their bonds, from earnings and repayments, and from other sources, the Treasury-held stock was retired by the banks. Return of Treasury stock was completed in November, 1940, although some funds earmarked as paid-in surplus belonging to the government were retained by the system until June, 1947.

LAND BANK COMMISSIONER LOANS. As a result of the severe decline in farm-product prices and the large increase in mortgage foreclosures in the depression of the early 1930's, Congress passed the Emergency Farm Mortgage Act (1933) authorizing land bank commissioner loans. These are direct advances from the Land Bank Commissioner in Washington, D.C., to farmers unable to obtain adequate credit from federal land banks. The Commissioner, acting as an agent of the Federal Farm Mortgage Corporation (FFMC), loaned primarily for the purpose of refinancing mortgages already in or on the verge of default. Emergency loans of this nature are limited to $7,500 per borrower, may be on second mortgages, have a maturity not to exceed forty years, and carry a rate of 5 per cent or less.

Funds for making these loans were made available through the sale of bonds by the FFMC. The issue is limited to $2 billion. Each bond is fully guaranteed by the United States and is fully backed by the mortgages received from borrowers when the loans are granted. A modification of the Farm Mortgage Act in 1947 withdrew the power of this agency to make further loans.

Intermediate-Term Agricultural Credits

In the primary postwar depression beginning in 1920, short-term loans made by local commercial banks became "frozen" as farm prices dropped. Many ranchers and farmers became unable to pay their obligations and engaged in a mad scramble to obtain renewals. When commercial banks were forced to charge off uncollectible loans as depression losses, the situation became desperate. Failure of more than 400 banks in six agricultural states in 1921–22 provided the stimulus for remedial action by Congress.

FEDERAL INTERMEDIATE CREDIT BANK SYSTEM. By an amendment to the Federal Farm Loan Act (March, 1923), Congress created an Intermediate-Term Credit System designed to make credit available to farmers on terms longer than the usual short-term grants supplied by commercial banks.

The act provided for the establishment of twelve federal intermediate credit banks, one to be located in each of the cities serving as headquarters for the federal land banks. Each bank was to operate under the supervision of the district farm credit board.

Although located and administered in conjunction with the land banks, the intermediate credit banks are quite distinct. They are entirely government owned. Their primary operation consists of rediscounting negotiable agricultural loan paper, with a maturity of less than three years, presented by commercial banks, livestock loan companies, agricultural credit corporations, and productive credit associations.[3] They may not make advances directly to individual farmers or stockmen but are permitted to deal directly with cooperative marketing associations.

Source of Funds. The banks were originally capitalized at $5 million each, all supplied by the government. Now they obtain funds primarily by the monthly sale of consolidated debentures varying in length from three to twelve months. The law permits sale of five-year issues, but none have yet been used. Security for debentures, which are joint and several obligations of the twelve banks, is held in the form of notes of agriculturalists which have been endorsed over to the banks by the lending institutions; the federal government assumes no responsibility for the debentures. The participation of each bank in an issue is limited to ten times the amount of its capital and paid-in surplus. Other sources of capital (rarely used) include rediscounts with Federal Reserve banks and loans from other banking institutions and from the Reconstruction Finance Corporation.

Lending operations of intermediate credit banks were relatively insignificant during the first ten years of operation. At first, much of the paper they were expected to purchase, especially from commercial banks, was not acceptable to the intermediate credit banks, and the commercial banks had no trouble obtaining funds from established sources on high-quality paper. A small but profitable and useful business developed in the cattle- and sheep-raising districts of the West, but an aggregate of less than $100 million was advanced in 1929. Even when the depression was deepest in the farming and ranching areas in 1931 and 1932, the volume of loans made by the banks did not reach the expectations of the designers of the act. Loans were about $152 million in 1932, and $143 million in 1935.

---

[3] Rediscounting in the field of agricultural finance is not quite the same as in commercial lending. Here it does not mean purchase of an instrument at below face value. When granting an advance, the intermediate credit bank usually advances the face value of the note and charges the local agency an interest rate on the funds extended.

Significance of the System. The early failure of the intermediate credit banks to supply funds on a wholesale scale was due to the fact that they were unable to deal directly with farmers. Thus, if an area contained no solvent agencies from which the individual could borrow, there was no opportunity for the banks to pump funds into that area via the rediscount process. It will be noted later in this chapter how creation of the Production Credit System in 1933 permitted rediscounting of notes of farmer-borrowers with intermediate credit banks. Although loan funds thus became more available, the volume of extensions has never been very great. The true significance of the system rests in the fact that it stands ready and able at all times to dispense credit.

Short-Term Agricultural Credits

To provide a corrective of the chief weakness of the Intermediate Credit Bank System, Congress authorized (June, 1933) the creation of twelve production credit corporations. These, in turn, were to foster the organization of local associations to make short-term loans to farmers and other agriculturalists. Borrowers' notes received by local associations were to be rediscounted at intermediate credit banks. It was expected that operation of the new agencies would expand the volume of business of the Intermediate Credit Bank System by generating a flow of funds into a community having inadequate local lending agencies.

FEDERAL PRODUCTION CREDIT CORPORATIONS. Production credit corporations are located in the twelve federal land bank cities. They are chartered and wholly owned by the federal government. At their inception in 1933 the government provided each with $7 million of capital. The governor of the FCA now has authority to adjust the amount of capital to meet current requirements. The funds are used primarily to capitalize local production credit associations by purchase of the Class A stock of the latter. Any residue may be invested in approved securities—usually federal government obligations.

PRODUCTION CREDIT ASSOCIATIONS. The local production credit associations correspond to the national farm loan associations of the Federal Land Bank System. They may be formed by a minimum of ten farmer-borrowers, although initiative for creation of the local association rests with the central corporation of the district. Charters are granted by the district corporation after being approved by the governor of the FCA.

Borrower-members of the association must purchase Class B stock equal to 5 per cent of their loans. Class A stock of the local may be sold only to inactive or nonborrowing members, production credit corporations, and investors. Only Class B stockholders have the right to a voice in management. Thus, control of the local organizations rests with active borrowers. In recent years approximately 500 local associations, with about 450,000 members, have been in operation. On July 1, 1949, 252,458 loans outstanding totaled $528 million.[4]

Lending Practice. Production credit associations make secured loans to assist their members in the planting, cultivating, harvesting, and marketing of farm crops of all kinds; to aid in the production of livestock, and in the acquisition of feed, seed, and machinery; and to provide funds for repairs of farm buildings and for the refunding of outstanding debts incurred for agricultural purposes. Loans as small as $50 are permitted. The maximum unsecured loan is limited to one fifth of an association's capital and surplus except that special permission may be granted by the district corporation with approval by the Production Credit Commissioner for advances in excess of 50 per cent of capital and surplus. Acceptable security consists of a chattel mortgage on growing crops, livestock, or personal property. When a loan is made, the maturity is limited to one year; but renewals may extend its term to three years. Actually, loans are seldom made for as long as a year because they tend to liquidate themselves when a crop is marketed. Interest rates are limited to three percentage points above the discount rate charged at the district intermediate credit bank. The latter rate remained unchanged at 1½ per cent in the years 1939–48; hence the rate to local borrowers was 4½ per cent. Rediscount rates gradually increased to 2 or 2¼ per cent in 1949, and rates to borrowers climbed to over 5 per cent.

Interest is charged only upon funds for the time they are used. Borrowers generally repay on the installment plan, the interest being paid only on the unpaid balance.

Sources of Loanable Funds. It might be assumed that the largest source of loanable funds of the local associations would be the sale of Class A and Class B stock. This is not the case, however. Funds received from the sale of stock must be invested in approved securities, mainly obligations of the federal government. Such bonds may be used as security or collateral for a loan from the intermediate credit bank, thereby permitting stock sales to become a source of funds indirectly. But the major portion of funds made available to

---

[4] *Sixteenth Annual Report of the Farm Credit Administration, 1948/49* (Washington, D.C.: U.S. Government Printing Office), Tables 4 and 5, pp. 110–13.

borrowers comes from discounting borrower paper at the intermediate credit banks. The law permits local associations to rediscount with other financial institutions, with the approval of the governor of the FCA. Up to the present time the intermediate credit banks have been able to meet all demands for funds from local associations.

Competition with Commercial Banks. There is evidence that commercial banks in many rural areas have been antagonized by the lending activities of production credit associations. There is little likelihood that these associations will replace commercial banks, because they offer no checking-account facilities; nor do they provide many of the other features of general banking service. But their ability to lend to farmers at 4½ or 5 per cent is a competitive weapon of great significance. During the dark days of 1933, when first established, the associations supplemented the inadequate volume of short-term credit available at commercial banks. Now, however, rural banks have sufficient funds to care for local needs. Many resent what they feel is unfair competition from associations able to offer low rates on funds made available through government borrowing.

BANKS FOR CO-OPERATIVES. In the Farm Credit Act (June, 1933), Congress created an agency, the Central Bank for Cooperatives, whose sole objective was the financing of farm co-operatives. For years the solution to America's "farm problem" had seemed to depend upon the co-operation of agriculturalists in reducing the overhead expenses of planting, harvesting, and marketing. With that in mind, Congress had authorized the intermediate credit banks (1923) and the Federal Farm Board (1929) to lend directly to co-operatives on products handled by these associations.

Loans made by intermediate credit banks were often "participation" agreements in which local commercial banks made advances up to six months and the government bank took maturities in excess of six months. The credit institutions supplemented the activities of each other to obtain an orderly marketing program covering the entire year. Loans were not numerous, however; and in 1929, when commercial banks were able to supply adequate credit on favorable terms, co-operative borrowings were as low as they had been in 1923. The co-operative movement was not fostered especially by the act of 1923.

Federal Farm Board loans to co-operatives could be made for a variety of purposes from a $500 million revolving fund voted by Congress. Loans were numerous, especially on cotton. Large advances were made also to price-stabilization corporations dealing in wheat and cotton. When these attempts to stabilize prices of major agricultural crops proved fruitless, the Farm Board was discontinued and the FCA was set up in its place. The development of co-operatives had not been aided particularly by the Farm Board.

Banks for co-operatives were established in each of the headquarter cities of the twelve farm credit districts, and a Central Bank for Cooperatives was located at Washington, D.C. The former were to handle direct loans to co-operatives within their districts, while the latter would make loans too large for a district bank and loans to co-operatives whose activities extended into more than one district.

Source of Funds. Loan funds have been acquired by banks for co-operatives primarily from paid-in capital and surplus that was diverted to their use from balances remaining in the revolving fund of the Farm Board. The amount of government ownership interest is changed from time to time and approximated $175 million in 1949. A second source of funds is the federal intermediate credit banks, which agree to rediscount all commodity loans made by co-operatives for amounts in excess of $100,000. The law permits the Central Bank to raise funds by sale of debentures and permits district banks to borrow from the Central Bank in Washington.

Types of Loans. Banks for co-operatives make three types of loans: commodity loans, operating capital loans, and facility loans. The first type are short term. The proceeds are used in the handling, sorting, grading, and packing of farm products. The loans are usually secured by first liens on the commodity that is being prepared for market. Operating-capital loans are designed to supplement funds advanced by members of the co-operative society and are used to defray miscellaneous costs of operation. They may be secured by liens on real estate, commodities, equipment, inventories, accounts receivable, etc. Operating-capital loans are usually retired when income is received from marketing the product. The third class, or facility loan, may have a maturity up to twenty years. Such loans seldom run for more than ten years, however, and usually are repaid by annual installments. Co-operatives use the proceeds of such loans in constructing or purchasing warehouses, receiving and sorting stations, and other fixed or relatively permanent property. These loans are secured by first liens upon the facility acquired. On June 30, 1949, interest rates were 2 to 2¼ per cent on commodity loans, 3 per cent on operating capital loans, and 4 per cent on advances for construction or purchase of facilities. During the year ended June 30, 1949, 1,164 co-operatives borrowed $357 million. These loans represented the financing of local co-operatives, with an estimated membership of 2½ million farmers.[5]

The co-operative movement has been greatly aided by this system, perhaps not as much through grants of credit at low rates of interest as by the variety of other services provided. The Commissioner's office makes suggestions on management and farm practices, provides legal and accounting services, makes commodity studies and in other ways is attempting to fill long-felt needs of agricultural communities.

Aggregate Loans of the Farm Credit Administration

The volume of loans made annually by agencies supervised by the FCA and the total outstanding vary considerably from one year to another. The significance of public advances to farmers and ranchmen can be fully appreciated only if some statistics are examined. The data of Table 43 show that over 5 million loans, with a total net value of almost $17 billion, were made between May 1, 1933, and June 30, 1949. Outstanding on the latter date were loans of approximately $1.8 billion to 634,000 agriculturalists.

Other Government Lending Agencies

The Commodity Credit Corporation (CCC) is an important farm credit agency operating within the jurisdiction of the Department of Agriculture but not as a part of the FCA. Created in 1933, under the authority of the National Recovery Act, the CCC was authorized to engage in crop buying, selling, lending, and otherwise assisting in removing depression from agriculture. Its primary function has been to "peg" or support prices of farm products and to permit orderly marketing of crops when excessive production has tended to undermine farm income. In recent years this activity has had little to justify its continuance. The general well-being of farmers could be maintained without benefit of governmental aid, because farm product prices have risen to near their all-time high.

In order to support the price of basic commodities such as corn, cotton, rice, wheat, tobacco, etc., the CCC places a loan value on the product. This is often an amount in excess of the current market price. The CCC may lend directly to farmers, but the advances are usually made in co-operation with local banks or lending agencies. The CCC agrees to purchase the loan paper or notes of the borrower

---

[5] *Ibid.*, pp. 15–20.

FINANCIAL INSTITUTIONS

TABLE 43

LOANS MADE BY INSTITUTIONS UNDER THE SUPERVISION OF THE FARM CREDIT ADMINIS-
TRATION FROM MAY 1, 1933, THROUGH JUNE 30, 1949, AND LOANS OUTSTANDING,
JUNE 30, 1949 *

INSTITUTION	LOANS MADE MAY 1, 1933, THROUGH JUNE 30, 1949		LOANS OUTSTANDING JUNE 30, 1949	
	Number	Amount	Number	Amount
Farm mortgage loans:				
Federal land banks.........	572,286	$ 2,316,261,717	303,567	$ 880,138,999
Land Bank Commissioner...	679,675	1,217,804,683	73,380	65,496,576
Joint-stock land banks......	529	2,479,723	1	3,250
Total................	1,252,490	$ 3,536,546,123	376,948	$ 945,637,825
Loans to co-operatives:				
Federal intermediate credit banks......................	....	218,642,942	......	646,077
Banks for co-operatives.....	18,665	3,693,738,635	1,666	248,008,203
Agricultural Marketing Act revolving fund..........	254	106,993,997	10	915,303
Total................	18,819	$ 4,019,375,556	1,676	$ 249,596,588
Other loans and discounts:				
Production credit associa- tions..................	3,616,183	7,007,096,482	252,458	528,026,386
Federal intermediate credit banks (excluding loans to co-operatives)...........	......	11,885,782,212	......	642,956,359
Regional agricultural credit corporations............	232,729	550,631,029	3,032	1,487,363
Total................	3,848,912	$19,443,509,723	255,490	$1,172,470,108
Subtotal..............	5,120,321	$26,999,431,402	634,114	$2,367,677,521
Less: Federal intermediate credit loans to and discounts for other FCA institutions...	....	10,173,174,886	......	579,974,681
Net..................	5,120,321	$16,826,256,516	634,114	$1,787,702,840
Joint-stock land bank liquida- tion fund................	20	2,082,679	......	....
Net total..........	5,120,341	$16,828,339,195	634,114	$1,787,702,840

* Figures may not total, owing to rounding.
Source: *Sixteenth Annual Report of the Farm Credit Administration, 1948/49,* (Washington, D.C.:
U.S. Government Printing Office), Table 1, p. 107.

from the local lender under certain conditions. If the price of the
commodity falls below the loan value, the farmer allows the CCC
to take the product (which has been inspected and sealed into storage
at the time it was pledged) as payment for the loan. The CCC absorbs
the loss. If the market price rises above the loan value, the farmer is
permitted to sell the crop, repay the loan, and keep the residue. A

modification of this plan was adopted in 1948. Farmers are not now required actually to take a loan and pay interest to the government. They may obtain an option to deliver a stated maximum amount of produce to the government between the date of harvest and the beginning of the next crop season. When, and if, the commodity is delivered, the government turns the loan value over to the farmer. The farmer may, however, not exercise his option to deliver but may sell his product if the market price rises above the loan value. This assures the farmer of a minimum price but permits him to get a better price, and it eliminates the trouble of making loan applications and placing his product in storage elevators or warehouses whose receipts are acceptable as security for commodity loans." (29)

The CCC was originally authorized for only two years. But its life was prolonged by repeated renewals, and it was granted a permanent charter in 1948.

Its capital in 1933 of $3 million (all held by the federal government) was increased to $100 million in 1936 and must be maintained at that figure—by subscription of the United States Treasury if necessary. The CCC was initially permitted to borrow a maximum of $4,750 million; its obligations are guaranteed by the federal government. As a result of two successive years of large crop production in 1948 and 1949 and a declining demand for agricultural products, the financial requirements of the CCC increased rapidly and were expected to continue rising. In anticipation of this enlarged need of funds, Congress increased the borrowing power of the agency by $2 billion in June, 1950.

Realized losses on price-support operations during the period from October, 1933, through January, 1950, were only $483 millions; but over-all losses resulting from related activities of the supply and export program, by subsidy and other payments, had mounted to over $2.3 billion. Despite these losses and the continuing dissatisfaction on the part of the nonfarm population, it would seem that the CCC is here to stay—a view that finds substantiation in the granting of the permanent charter and enlarged borrowing power.

The Rural Electrification Administration (REA) was created in May, 1935, by executive order and given statutory recognition by Congress in 1936. It is an agency of the Department of Agriculture with authority to lend to co-operatives, municipalities, and other public organizations, as well as to power companies and individuals, to finance construction and operation of electric facilities in rural areas not served by existing utility companies.

At the end of 1949, borrowers of the REA included 975 rural

electric co-operatives, 41 public power districts, 24 other public bodies, and 25 commercial power companies. Loans made during the calendar year 1949 amounted to about $420 million, bringing the cumulative total to almost $2 billion. Borrowers have repaid $223 million—about 10 per cent of it prior to maturity dates.

Legislation for financing rural telephone loans became effective in October, 1949. The program will also be administered by the REA.

The Farmers Home Administration was established in 1946 by the merger of the Farm Security Administration and the Emergency Crop and Feed Loan Division of the FCA. The Farm Security Administration had been established ten years earlier to aid in financing "garden-city" communities such as the "Greenbelt" towns near metropolitan centers.

As now established, the Farmers Home Administration makes cash loans to farmers unable to obtain funds elsewhere on fair and reasonable terms. These grants are: (1) operating loans having maturities up to five years, designed to increase production and elevate the standards of farm practice; or (2) ownership loans with maturities as long as forty years, used in the original acquisition of a farm home or its enlargement or betterment. The Administration may also insure farm-ownership loans made to the farmer by private loan agencies. In that part of the Housing Act of 1949 which relates to rural housing, Congress authorized this agency of the Department of Agriculture to grant housing loans, at 4 per cent interest, for periods up to thirty-three years. Other financial aid, consisting of small remedial loans or temporary grants, was provided to aid farm families until something more fundamental may be done to provide safe and sanitary housing facilities. Twenty-seven million dollars was appropriated in October, 1949, to cover grants and loans made in the fiscal year ending June 30, 1950.

During the first ten months of 1949 the Farmers Home Administration advanced more than $78 million in operating credit and approximately $12 million in loans for use in purchasing, enlarging, or developing farms. It also insured or guaranteed the payment of $9.5 million in farm real estate loans made by private individuals and financial institutions.

Summary and Conclusions

The scarcity of funds for investment in agriculture was only one facet of the "farm problem" of the United States in the early years of this century. The serious nature of this shortage was recognized by Congress, however, and the federal land banks were established in 1916 to make long-term mortgage funds available at "fair" rates of interest. As other financial difficulties arose, other legislative acts were passed and lending institutions were created to deal with the specific problem under consideration. Piecemeal action of this sort, however, was not very effective. The credit agencies were unable, either separately or collectively, to prevent deterioration in the financial position of agriculture from 1920 to 1933.

The United States was confronted with a very grave emergency in 1933, and from both the political and the humanitarian points of view it seemed necessary for those in authority in Washington to do something to relieve the economic pressure on our agrarian population. One significant result was the co-ordination of four federally sponsored financial institutions into the FCA. The separate agencies of the FCA have functioned successfully and are seldom the objects of severe criticism. They were established from time to time in the attempt to deal with recognized defects or inadequacies in the rural credit system and, when established, provided supplementary funds rather than credit that placed them in direct competition with existing private lending agencies. Although it is true that some institutions within the FCA were capitalized with federal funds appropriated by Congress, most of that capital has been returned. In the main, then, the agencies of the FCA today provide a channel through which surplus funds of private investors and institutional lenders are made available to individuals or co-operatives producing agricultural products. They are not dispensing charity to improvident borrowers having no ability to repay. Rather, they are making sound loans to responsible producers, and their loss ratios compare favorably with those of private financial institutions.

The portion of the farm program that is being criticized, and more severely so as time goes on, is the effort of the CCC to improve the well-being of an entire class of producers through policies that interfere with the free play of competitive markets. The weight of economic principle is against permanent adherence to a program that embraces the payment of millions of dollars in subsidies, grants excessive loans on crops that exist in oversupply, and undermines the export market because prices are maintained at artificially high prices. These tactics may, in large measure, account for the increased well-being of the farm population and the success that the federally sponsored credit agencies have had in collecting their loans. But the program, if long continued, may bring a serious misallocation of resources and exert a crippling effect upon our economy.

—FRANK H. GANE

QUESTIONS AND PROBLEMS

1. Would you, as an investor, be as willing to purchase securities of incorporated farms as of incorporated industrials? Why or why not?

2. Which important agencies of the Farm Credit Administration make use of the "bond" system described on page 458? State the essence of this method.

3. Obtain recent data on the total farm mortgage debt, and comment on possible reasons for the current movement. Are private agencies holding as large a proportion as they did in 1940 and 1945?

4. What is the difference between a first and a second mortgage loan?

5. Why was the Federal Farm Mortgage Corporation organized? What is its relation to Land Bank Commissioner loans?

6. What is the primary source of funds used by the intermediate credit banks in their rediscounting operations? What is the rate being paid currently for such funds?

7. What factor retarded active participation by the intermediate credit banks in reviving an area that had been desolated by financial ruin?

8. Why have rural bankers made more complaints about competition from lending activities of production credit associations than from federal land banks?

9. Do rural banks now have unused lending power? Explain. How may the ability of a bank to make loans be measured?

10. Explain the price-support program of the Commodity Credit Corporation. Why is there growing discontent with this form of activity among the general population?

11. Expand the following sentence into a paragraph: "The long-run effects of subsidizing agriculture will produce a misallocation of economic resources."

BIBLIOGRAPHY

In keeping abreast of the operation and current position of the governmental credit agencies, the annual reports of the Farm Credit Administration and the annual issues of the *Agricultural Finance Review* are essential. In addition to occasional articles of a general nature on agriculture, the monthly *Federal Reserve Bulletin* contains data on agricultural production, farm prices and support levels, farm trade, non-real estate loans to farmers by commercial banks, loans of federal farm agencies, and other material.

The following are recommended for readers who wish to appreciate the economic implications of farm finance:

Horton, D. C.; Larsen, H. C.; and Wall, N. J. *Farm Mortgage Credit Facilities in the United States.* Misc. Pub. No. 478, Bureau of Agricultural Economics, U.S.D.A., Washington, D.C., 1941.

Murray, W. G. *Agricultural Finance*. Rev. ed. Ames: Iowa State College Press, 1947.

Sparks, E. S. *History and Theory of Agricultural Credit in the United States*. New York: Crowell, 1932.

Among college textbooks in the field of money, banking, and credit, the following contain one or more chapters on agricultural finance:

James, F. Cyril. *The Economics of Money, Credit and Banking*, chap. xxiv. 3d ed. New York: Ronald Press, 1940.

Prather, Charles L. *Money and Banking*, chap. xxix. 4th ed. Chicago: Richard D. Irwin, Inc., 1949.

Westerfield, Ray B. *Money, Credit and Banking*, chap. xxxv. Rev. ed. New York: Ronald Press Co., 1947.

PART III

•

MONETARY FINANCIAL INSTITUTIONS

Chapter • 17

MONEY

THE prevailing organization of production is based upon the principle of specialization—a specialization not only of geographical areas and individuals but of businesses and financial agencies as well. The efficiency of production in modern economic society depends upon a minute division of labor, but the latter in turn is dependent upon an effective system of exchange. No person will confine his efforts to the creation of a single commodity unless he is fairly certain that a reasonably steady market exists for his product, on one hand, and an adequate supply of both the goods he needs for consumption and the materials required in his production operations, on the other. Thus the degree of specialization and the volume of production are closely related to the ease with which producers are able to exchange their wares for the goods and services brought to market by others.

MONEY AND ITS FUNCTIONS

Although some exchange could be made by barter, the shortcomings of this method are so great that present-day markets would utterly collapse if dependent upon it. A long process of evolution has culminated in a complicated monetary and credit system in which institutions of finance, transportation, and insurance co-operate to provide markets where the output of specialized producers is exchanged. These markets require the development and use of money for the mediation of trade. In this system of roundabout or capitalistic production, personal income is received in money, and practically all payments involve the use of money. Unspent balances are saved in money through the large number and variety of financial institutions considered in previous chapters. These institutions in

485

turn invest the savings in securities of private companies or governmental units, which then spend money in the purchase of a variety of goods and services and in the payment of debts. Governments assess taxes that are paid in money and issue obligations whose value is measured in money and which are ultimately repaid in money.

But the significance of money is not limited to our markets and the distribution of our savings. Many political problems of national and world-wide interest have a large monetary ingredient. For these reasons, it is often asserted, not only that we live in a money and credit economy, but that our economic prosperity and health are tied closely to the manner in which our monetary system is administered. For example, if anything occurs to divert the normal flow of money from its continuous circuit from consumers to producers and back again to consumers, the entire economy is affected. The volume of goods produced, the number of workers employed, the size of wage payments, and the rate of savings may all be changed and an inflation or deflation be generated. It is our purpose in this chapter to examine briefly the role played by money in the contemporary economic scene.

Functions of Money

As noted in Chapter 1, a significant function of money is its use as a medium of exchange. This may historically have been its first use; but as barter began to give way to the use of money, the price of each article of trade was stated in terms of money, and money was recognized to function both as a medium of exchange and as a standard or measure of value. Moreover, as the world developed into an exchange economy, man found it no longer necessary to retain the product of his labors until he wished to barter it for a specific commodity. He could sell his product at any time, store the money received, and use it as a medium of exchange at a later date. Thus, money came to function as a store of value. As time passed, business expanded, specialization increased, and an ever-expanding variety of commodities appeared in the markets. Transactions arose in which payment, for one reason or another, had to be made at a later date. Contracts covering transfers of this nature specified the medium to be used in making payment and how much of it and of what quality. Money thus became a standard of deferred payment.

Money may function in other ways; but, without doubt, the uses mentioned above are basic to the economy of today. Any businessman in a money economy may quickly ascertain the value of his product in terms of all other products. He can store purchasing power as savings in a form easily convertible into any or all kinds of goods, services, or securities; and he can arrange to make or receive payments at dates extending far into the future.

Characteristics of Good Money

If money is to perform its varied functions in a satisfactory manner, it must meet some very definite tests. It must possess certain qualities.

When used as a medium of trade, money should be light in weight and small in bulk; i.e., it should be portable. Also, money should be sufficiently durable to stand the wear and tear of constant handling. It must be easily recognized but difficult to counterfeit; and it must be issued in denominations that permit easy consummation of small, as well as large, transactions. It is important also that money should be homogeneous; that is, each unit of the same denomination should be as good as another if prices in all sections of a nation are to be precise and comparable.

If money is to act as a satisfactory store of value, or standard of deferred payment over a period of time, it must have relative stability of value. Nothing is satisfactory as a unit for measuring value if it changes substantially in purchasing power from one year to another or from one decade to another.

Monetary Evolution

Chapter 1 contains a list of commodities that have been used as money at various times in the history of the world. It is possible to classify these articles as consumers goods, capital instruments, ornaments, and tokens or paper certificates representing wealth of some form.

No written history traces the evolution of these money forms, but it is well known that gold and silver coins have been the favored commodity media of recent times. These metals possess the characteristics most nearly satisfying the demands of trade for good money. Both exist in limited quantity and therefore have relatively high value in small bulk. They are durable, especially when hardened by mixture with small amounts of base metal. Annual additions to the existing supply are insignificant in comparison with the present stock and thus exert little influence on value within short periods of time. Thus, these metals have been more stable in purchasing power than most of the articles that were formerly used as money. Because the luster of gold and silver endeared them to all peoples, these metals have been used not only for local or national money but on an international basis as well.

The processes of monetary evolution are still in motion. Probably few of our readers have observed the use of gold as a medium of exchange, at least in domestic trade. The place of gold has largely been taken by a variety of credit instruments in the form of government paper money, bank notes, personal checks, and "token" coins. The increased use of credit instruments, among the inhabitants of all countries of the world, has been due to several factors, including the need for nations to economize in the use of expensive commodity money, the desire to provide flexibility in the money supply, and the desire to broaden the opportunities for managing the national economy. As we shall note later, these "debt" forms constitute by far the largest portion of the money supply in the United States today.

Definition of Money

A precise definition of money has been deferred pending a consideration of its uses and characteristics because it is difficult to define money without relating the definition to the work that money performs. If viewed from this angle, it may be said that money is anything that is generally accepted and passes freely from hand to hand as a medium of exchange. If it is a successful medium, an object may also serve as a standard of value and perform the other functions noted above.

At times, arguments develop over the question of whether to include personal checks drawn against bank deposits in the definition of money. Throughout this text, bank deposits payable on demand are considered to be money. An individual check is not legal tender, and ordinarily it passes by endorsement in a restricted area in which each person acquiring the instrument knows the one who drew it or the one who has endorsed it. Thus, it is logical to contend that the check has limited circulation, that it is not a "generally acceptable" medium of exchange and is, therefore, not money. But, because the individual instrument is a means of transferring title or ownership of a bank deposit from one person to another in an endless process involving thousands of checks, the deposit credit that passes from person to person and bank to bank may truly be classed as money. It is our belief that demand deposits must be included as an integral part of our money supply.

MONETARY SYSTEM OF THE UNITED STATES

The monetary system of a nation consists of all the forms of money, created and regulated by law, that are necessary to achieve the functions that money is designed to perform. A system usually contains four elements, viz.: a standard of value, paper currency issued by the federal government or a central bank, coins of small denominations, and demand deposits of commercial banks.

Table 44 shows money in general circulation and the amounts held in the Treasury and in Federal Reserve banks. At present, gold is impounded by the federal government, and gold certificates are used only between the Treasury and the Federal Reserve banks. By far the most important type of money shown here and used as a medium of exchange is the Federal Reserve notes. The volume outstanding on May 31, 1950, was over $22 billion, an amount approximately five times as great as all other forms of paper and coins together. The relative volume of Federal Reserve notes and the $4.2 billion of combined Treasury currency is indicative of the important role being played currently by our Federal Reserve institutions. Two decades ago (1930) total paper money and coins in circulation was only $4.2 billion; and of this, Federal Reserve notes were $1.4 billion, or only 33 per cent. On May 31, 1950, Treasury currency, as shown in Table 44, was only about one sixth of the total circulation, and Federal Reserve notes made up the remainder.

The volume of demand deposits is not shown in Table 44 but amounted to about $85 billion at the end of May, 1950. Thus, the total effective supply of money of the United States was approximately $112 billion.

The monetary system of the United States is unnecessarily cluttered by most of the paper issues shown as Treasury currency. Many of the items included in this category are relics of former days and, it is hoped, will gradually be reduced in volume or completely wiped out by the action of some future Congress. We could hardly dispense with subsidiary silver coins and minor coins, but all other forms listed under Treasury currency are unnecessary. If Federal Reserve notes of one $1 denomination were issued, there would be no need for silver certificates or standard silver dollars.

Treasury currency includes some items of historical interest. For

TABLE 44

UNITED STATES MONEY, OUTSTANDING AND IN CIRCULATION, BY KINDS
On Basis of Circulation Statement of United States Money
(Millions of Dollars)

Kinds	Total Outstanding, May 31, 1950	Money Held in the Treasury — As Security against Gold and Silver Certificates	Money Held in the Treasury — Treasury Cash	Money Held in the Treasury — For Federal Reserve Banks and Agents	Money Held by Federal Reserve Banks and Agents	Money in Circulation* — May 31, 1950	Money in Circulation* — April 30, 1950	Money in Circulation* — May 31, 1949
Gold..........................	24,231	23,039	1,192 †	....	2,816	....	....	....
Gold certificates.............	23,039	....	....	20,183	779	41	41	43
Federal Reserve notes........	23,521	....	48	....	182	22,694	22,723	23,205
Treasury currency—total......	4,606	2,299 ‡	69	....	....	4,355	4,285	4,259
Standard silver dollars........	493	280	40	....	3	169	168	163
Silver bullion................	2,019	2,019	....	....	....	....	....	....
Silver certificates and Treasury notes of 1890..........	2,299 ‡	....	....	....	120	2,180	2,122	2,079
Subsidiary silver coin.........	1,001	....	15	....	26	961	951	938
Minor coin...................	379	....	9	....	10	360	358	355
United States notes...........	347	....	4	....	21	322	319	318
Federal Reserve bank notes....	280	....	1	....	3	276	279	312
National-bank notes...........	88	....	‖	....	1	87	87	93
Total—May 31, 1950.........	§	25,338	1,309	20,183	3,777	27,090	....	....
April 30, 1950..............	§	25,349	1,308	20,220	3,814	....	27,048	....
May 31, 1949...............	§	25,416	1,315	20,301	3,819	....	....	27,507

* Outside Treasury and Federal Reserve banks. Includes any paper currency held outside the continental limits of the United States; totals for other end-of-month dates shown in table above.

† Includes $156,039,431 held as reserve against United States notes and Treasury notes of 1890.

‡ To avoid duplication, amount of silver dollars and bullion held as security against silver certificates and Treasury notes of 1890 outstanding is not included in total Treasury currency outstanding.

§ Because some of the types of money shown are held as collateral or reserves against other types, a grand total 1 of all types has no special significance and is not shown.

‖ Less than $500,000.

Source: *Federal Reserve Bulletin*, July, 1950, p. 858.

example, United States notes were first issued in 1863 when the government was very hard pressed for money with which to carry on its military activities. President Lincoln signed the bill creating these "greenbacks." Silver certificates and Treasury notes of 1890 were issued as part of the program of "doing something for silver" in the period of unsettled monetary affairs prior to 1900. National-bank notes were issued by commercial banks operating under Federal charter after 1863 and were an important part of our circulation until 1935. They may no longer be issued. Federal Reserve bank notes were initially issued early in the history of the Federal Reserve System to aid in the retirement of national-bank notes. They failed to achieve that goal, were reissued once or twice for use as emergency currency, but now are of no practical significance. National-bank notes and Federal Reserve bank notes are classed as Treasury currency because they are now obligations of the United States Treasury rather than of the original issuing banks.

How Good Is Our Monetary System?

We have noted the functions that money performs, and we have examined the various kinds of money provided for our use by the banks and by the government. The question naturally arises: How well does our monetary system function?

To the extent that we are considering money as a medium of exchange, the answer to our question is simple and direct. Our monetary system functions smoothly and provides media adequate to our needs. But when we consider money as a store of value and a standard of deferred payment, the answer is not so positively in the affirmative or so simply stated. In the remainder of the chapter attention is directed to changes in the value of money and the problems arising therefrom.

CHANGES IN THE VALUE OF MONEY

Literally millions of individuals in the United States maintain savings accounts and hold debt obligations repayable sometime in the future in fixed sums of money. It is equally true that millions of contracts involving lending operations, sales of goods on credit, purchase of life insurance, leasing of land, and other kinds of transactions stipulate or imply an obligation to pay money at a future date. All recipients of future income are deeply interested in receiving a dollar the value of which when it is received is at least equal to its value at the time when the contract was drawn. If a decline in value should occur, the economic status of recipients of fixed dollar income would be impaired. Unfortunately, although money is relatively stable in value when compared to many things, wide fluctuations in purchasing power do occur and bring serious consequences to certain economic groups. On the other hand, unjustified gains are reaped by the debtor group when the value of money rises.

Money and Prices

When a commodity is chosen to act as a standard of value, the unit of account (the dollar in the United States) is defined as a specified quantity of the selected article. If we assume, for the moment, that gold is to be used, the definition has the effect of placing a fixed price on gold at the mint and in the bullion market. This fixed and unchanging price of gold (in terms of money) should not, however, be interpreted as giving a fixed and unchanging purchasing power to gold. Ordinarily a fixed price of a commodity or service does mean fixity of value, for value almost universally is expressed in the market in terms of money or price. But it would be absurd to state the value of money in terms of its price. Rather, the measure of the value of gold, when it is used as money, must be stated in terms of the things for which it can be exchanged.

Attempts to measure the value of money by comparing its ability to command one or a few commodities in exchange for itself may be highly artificial and inconclusive. For example, on one date a dollar may purchase two dozen eggs, and a year or two later may purchase only one dozen. It would then appear that in the interim the dollar had lost one half its ability to command eggs; that is, its value would appear to have been reduced by 50 per cent. In the same period, however, the dollar may have doubled its ability to command sirloin steak, and its value would then appear to have increased 100 per cent. If only these two comparisons were used to indicate fluctuations in the value of money, no satisfactory conclusion would be obtained.

Money is spent not only for eggs and meat but is, in fact, spent for an innumerable variety of goods and services; it has "generalized" purchasing power. Attempts to indicate the direction and degree of its fluctuations in value must, therefore, be based upon its ability to command a composite unit made up of representative portions of all the things for which money is generally spent—that is, not the price, of eggs alone, nor of meat, nor of any other particular thing, but a composite price of things in general, often called the "general price level."

Index Numbers

For the purpose of measuring changes in the general level of prices, a statistical device, known as an "index number," has been developed. Essentially, the method used is to obtain the average price of each commodity to be included for a given year or over a longer period of time, known as the "base period." Thenceforth, as changes occur, the new prices are expressed as percentages above or below the price prevailing in the base period.

Because the average annual price of such dissimilar items as a ton of coal, a drum of oil, and a bushel of wheat cannot in them-

TABLE 45

COMMODITY PRICE CHANGES
(Wholesale)

COMMODITY	AVERAGE ANNUAL PRICE		RATIO OF PRICE IN CURRENT YEAR TO PRICE IN BASE YEAR
	Base Year	Current Year	
Wheat (per bushel)...................	$ 1.06	$ 1.80	170.00
Pig iron (per gross ton)...............	22.18	24.39	110.00
Rubber—crude (per pound)...........	0.75	0.467	62.3
Beef (per pound)....................	0.17	0.252	148.3
Average price relative................	....	....	122.65

selves be averaged to obtain the "average general level of prices," the average price of each commodity during the base period is set up as 100 per cent. Changes of individual prices in subsequent periods are stated as percentages of the base period price and are called "price relatives." These price relations are averaged and compared with the average of the base period. Deviations of the average of price relatives in subsequent periods then show as percentage changes above or below the 100 per cent taken as the base. A purely hypothetical case (see Table 45) will serve to clarify this description.

The right-hand column of Table 45 contains the price relatives which show the current price as a percentage of the price of the base year. Thus, if wheat is being considered, the 170 indicates a rise of 70 per cent in the price of wheat in the period from the base year to the current year. These price relatives are averaged to obtain the index number 122.65, which indicates that the general level of prices has increased 22.65 per cent since the base year. It is evident that, if prices have risen, the amount of money required to purchase a given bill of goods has also increased; the value of each unit of money has, therefore, declined.

If we wish to compute the degree to which the value of money fell as the general price level increased to 122.65, we may say that the value of money has fallen reciprocally, and use the formula:

$$\frac{\text{Base-year price level}}{\text{Price level of current year}} = \frac{\text{Value of money in current year}}{\text{Value of money in base year}}.$$

The base year price level is always 100; the value of money in the base year is also 100. Our index (122.65) has provided the price level of the current year. By substitution, we obtain the purchasing power for the current year:

$$\frac{100}{122.65} = \frac{x}{100},$$
$$122.65x = 10,000,$$
$$x = 81.53.$$

Thus the value of money fell 19.47 per cent (100 − 81.53), while the price level rose 22.65 per cent. It must be recognized that there is no comprehensive measure of the price level. Therefore, no more than rough significance can be attached to these computations. They are shown here only to illustrate a crude device for measuring the changing value of money.

It is not the function of this text to consider the problems of selecting the type of average to be used in an index, or the method of weighting the commodities included, i.e., determining the economic significance of each item and the other technical aspects related to the construction of index numbers. It must be noted, however, that there are several different types of indexes and that each has definite merits and also certain shortcomings. Some indexes deal exclusively with prices at wholesale, others at retail; some include only raw material prices, others the prices of raw material, semifinished goods, and finished products. Cost-of-living index numbers that include the costs of services and rents as well as commodity prices are usually considered more satisfactory than commodity index numbers for showing changes in the value of the consumer's dollar.

Although index numbers may be presented in the form of tables, variations in the general price level can be more fully appreciated when the data are plotted in chart form. Exhibit 57 illustrates the monthly average of wholesale prices in the United States from 1911

Exhibit 57

WHOLESALE PRICES IN THE UNITED STATES

(Bureau of Labor Statistics Indexes, 1926 = 100)

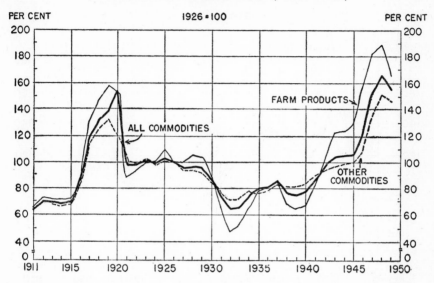

Source: *Historical Statistics of the United States, 1789–1945*, Series L 15–25, p. 233, for years 1911–45; *Federal Reserve Bulletin*, June, 1950, p. 733, for 1945–49; Publication No. 493, U.S. Department of Labor, Bureau of Labor Statistics, *Wholesale Prices, 1913–1928*, p. 31, for data on other commodities, 1913–28.

to 1949. The chart is based on the index of the United States Bureau of Labor Statistics, commonly referred to as the "BLS Wholesale Commodity Price Index." Exhibit 58 is a chart of consumers' prices, 1913 to December 31, 1949.

Effects of Changing Purchasing Power

The significance of price changes, or changes in the value of money, is due primarily to two factors. One is that the prices of different items do not all change at the same time, or in the same direction, or to the same degree. The second factor, and it is closely related to the first, is that individual, business, and industrial incomes do not automatically and quickly adjust themselves to changed expense requirements, and vice versa. The result may be serious hardship for certain groups as the general price level fluctuates.

If we assume that all prices, including commodities, interest, wages, and rent, stood at 100 in 1940 but moved upward to 200 in 1950, it is apparent that the real position (purchasing power) of those people who depend entirely on current income unaffected by long-term con-

Exhibit 58

CONSUMER PRICES IN THE UNITED STATES

(Bureau of Labor Statistics Indexes, 1936–39 = 100)

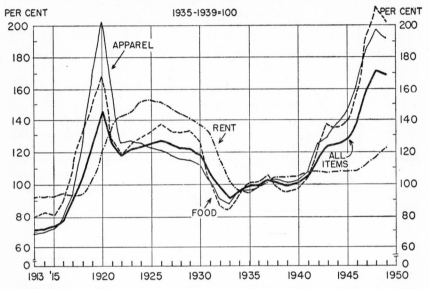

Source: *Historical Statistics of the United States, 1789–1945*, Series L 40–47, p. 236, for years 1913–45; *Federal Reserve Bulletin*, June, 1950, p. 732, for 1945–49.

tract would be but slightly affected. Incomes would double, but costs would keep pace and the net effect would be nil.

Actually, however, the relationships existing within the price structure in 1940 would be very likely to change in the ten years under consideration. Normally, the price paid for labor (wages) does not advance as rapidly as wholesale prices. Nor do wages usually advance as soon as retail prices. (These statements are less generally true now than before 1940.) Further, those people receiving an income in the form of rent or interest have the amount of income stated in long-term contracts which usually permit no adjustment in the rate. Insurance companies receive premium payments and pay benefit claims based on expenditures and income of past years. The current premium income and benefit liabilities are on a contract basis not subject to adjustment to present conditions. Users of public utility services pay a rate per unit of product which is adjusted as the expenses of operating utilities fluctuate, but only after considerable delay. The return on common stocks of utility companies would therefore be likely to fall as expenses rise and find reflection in lower prices of the securities.

Business profits in general, however, would be likely to react in just the opposite way, although the amount of dividends paid to shareholders seldom keeps pace with expanding profits. There would be no change in interest payments to holders of bonds or long-term notes. In short, the welfare of different groups in society would be affected differently by a rise in the general price level because the increased "income" and increased expenses are not immediately distributed equitably to wage earners, to owners of land and capital, and to the management of industry.

For a specific illustration of the effect of changes in the purchasing power of money, let us assume that in 1938, when the consumers' price index shown in Exhibit 58 was at 100, a businessman retired on a pension paying him $100 a month. As time passed, note that his living expenses in the form of food, rent, and apparel (as represented in the index) rose until, in 1948, he was spending almost $170 for items that cost only $100 ten years earlier. If his pension were his only source of income, the standard of living of the pensioner would be seriously undermined by the decreased purchasing power of his monthly income.

A decline in the price level may work an equally unjust fate upon an agriculturist who goes heavily into debt at the top of a price cycle for the purchase of capital improvements or more land. The expenditure is justified only if the price of products available for sale remains high. If prices decline, the resulting income may be too small to permit the buyer to meet principal payments on his debt or even to make interest payments on the obligation. This type of situation was faced by farmers who borrowed money to purchase land and equipment when prices were at their high in 1918–20. In the ensuing collapse of agricultural prices in 1921 (see Exhibit 57) and the resumption of their downward movement from 1928 to 1932, thousands of farmers were forced into bankruptcy.

The possibility that sudden or long-continued reductions in the value of money may wipe out accumulated savings, business profits, and even the very business venture itself is a positive deterrent to the expansion of a private-enterprise economy.

It is sometimes contended that merit is attached to a relatively high, rather than to a low, price level. Actually, no price level is sacred in itself. If it is high, other factors will tend slowly to adjust themselves upward to it; if it is low, adjustment will be downward to it. The significant aspect of any price level is its stability. Regardless of its position, the price level is the basis for a multitude of contracts involving payment and receipt of money in the future. Any marked departure from an existing level results in a disturbance to the entire economic structure and in a "violation" of the contracts made at the former level. It now should be evident that a "good" monetary standard is one which contributes to the stability of the general price level.

Causes of Change in the Value of Money

It is easy to demonstrate that the value of money is the reciprocal of the general price level or that the purchasing power of a unit of money rises as the price level declines. Determining the causes of such variation, however, is not easy. In fact, this aspect of economic theory is one of great complexity and controversy. Its importance is so generally recognized, however, that despite its complexity it has commanded widespread attention as political administrations have attempted to discover and correct the forces that have introduced sudden great shifts in values.

If the prices of only a few commodities change, economists usually attribute the fluctuations to variations in demand or supply of the items in question. If there is a change in a general price index composed of hundreds of individual items, economists look elsewhere for the causes. An explanation is likely to be found in one or more of several factors, including variations in the demand for and the supply of money and bank credit and in changes in the attitudes of individuals and businessmen that result in a changing tempo of spending or saving and investing. Other possible causes may be found in the actions of our own and foreign governments; also, changes in public policy often appear to change rates of saving and spending, to modify interest rates, and even to redirect productive effort into new and unexplored fields. These and other factors considered in the chapter on business fluctuations exert important, although sometimes undeterminable, influences upon the general price level and, by the same token, upon the purchasing power of money.

Undoubtedly, many citizens of the United States are convinced that the most important cause of a decline in the value of the dollar is an increase in the supply of dollars available. For generations a school of economic theorists has so popularized the *quantity theory* of money that many people consider a change in the supply of money to be almost the sole cause of a change in its value. We must admit that there is logic in the thought that, if the supply of purchasing power were doubled, an adjustment would take place, so that, in the long run, the general price level would be approximately doubled also. But economists are unwilling to accept the idea that changes in the value of money during normal periods of peacetime activity are due solely or even mainly to changes in the volume of money.

On the other hand, there is general agreement among economists and the general public that a great expansion of the supply of paper money is a basic cause of severe price inflation in which the value of the monetary unit depreciates almost to zero. In many such instances the central government, either through weakness or by design, contributes to instability and deterioration in the value of money. These cases are often called "hyperinflation," to distinguish them from cases of "simple" inflation, in which money loses some but not most of its value. Hyperinflation is usually associated with costly wars and the expenses of reconstruction. After World War I and World War II, the United States experienced inflation in which the wholesale commodity price level rose 75 to 100 per cent. These changes, clearly shown in Exhibit 57 (p. 495), were relatively mild when compared to the hyperinflation generated by excessive issues of the "continental" currency of our post-Revolutionary period or by the drastic inflation in Germany after World War I. During and after World War II there were again instances of hyperinflation in Greece, China, and Hungary. In several other countries the loss of monetary value was nearly as serious.

Most cases of hyperinflation reflect some or all of the following characteristics: (1) government expenditures "get out of control" and go far beyond the economic capacity of the country; (2) government revenues become inadequate or dry up altogether; taxes and tax collection become demoralized and wholly inadequate; (3) confidence in the fiscal operations of the government fall to the point where financing by interest-bearing debt obligations is not practicable; and (4) the government uses its legal-tender powers (or those of its central bank) to "print" or create money to cover its own expenditures.

The case of hyperinflation in Hungary during and after World War II is fairly typical of all such cases and illustrates the basic points made above. The essential facts are roughly as follows: before the war the Hungarian pengö was worth about 17½ cents; in other words, it took about 5.7 pengös to equal a dollar; by July, 1946, it took about 6.3 quintrillion (63 followed by 29 ciphers). But the change to this astronomical figure is not the truly impressive point. The big loss of value took place between May, 1945, and July, 1946. During this period the pengö depreciated to 400 to the dollar. The figure of 400 pengös to the dollar means that one pengö was worth one quarter of one cent. The fall from 17½ cents to ¼ cent is serious. The decline from ¼ cent to nothing or virtually nothing is just a big paper flurry that came after the financial structure was in ruins.

Now to apply the four points about hyperinflation presented above to the Hungarian situation:

1. Hungary was first occupied and dominated by the Germans; then occupied and dominated by the Russians. Both "liberators" made crushing demands for reparations and occupation costs; the Hungarian government could meet these demands only by an inflation of the central-bank currency, since it could not raise enough by taxes.
2. The tax authorities of the Hungarian government became almost powerless to collect revenues. The tax system, already antiquated, broke down almost completely.
3. Genuine borrowing by the government became impossible. At no period was the money market such that borrowings at reasonable levels of interest cost would have been possible. Normal savings almost disappeared. At one period, short-term interest rates hit the fantastic level of *100 per cent per day.*
4. It has already been mentioned that the government had to resort to central-bank currency to meet reparation and occupation costs. The notes of the central bank were legal tender.

It should be noted that, as the people of a nation become aware of a rapid expansion of printing-press money, they anticipate further increases in prices and add fuel to the fires of inflation by rushing out to purchase goods as soon as they acquire any money. The increase in velocity of turnover has exactly the same effect as an increase in the supply of money and exerts a cumulative effect to push prices higher. Almost without exception, financial and industrial chaos and economic breakdown follow in the wake of excessive inflation.

Many believe that a primary role of governments is to fight inflation and ensuing depression by every available means. Obviously, the initial step to be taken by a government is the establishment of the best possible monetary standard.

Other aspects of government action and the control of economic instability will be discussed in Chapter 21. We turn now to a brief consideration of the monetary standard.

THE MONETARY STANDARD

Unit of Account

Irrespective of physical composition, all the different kinds of money in use within one nation are issued in fractions or multiples of a basic unit called the "unit of account" or standard monetary unit. The basic unit of each nation is always given a distinctive name. In the United States it is the "dollar"; in Great Britain it is the "pound sterling"; in France, the "franc"; etc. In our system the unit is defined by the Congress as being equivalent in value to a specified quantity of gold.

It should be emphasized that when a commodity standard is adopted, such as the gold standard, the basic unit of value is applied to a given weight of metal rather than merely to a coin. General acceptability of a coin may be enhanced by a government stamp, but nothing is thereby added to the value of the metal. In fact, when gold is used in large quantities for settling international balances, preference is usually expressed by debtors for sizable bars with weight and purity attested by government certification.

Functions of Standard Money

Not only does the standard unit of value serve as the measuring rod for determining the value of all goods and services exchanged in the market place, but it also establishes a basis for determining the value of each type of circulating medium. This is ordinarily done by providing for complete interchangeability of all forms of money. If the standard is a commodity, such as gold, parity may be obtained by making some of the circulating money or coins out of the metal itself. If coinage is either not feasible or not desirable, all forms of other metal and paper currency may be made redeemable in standard bullion (the uncoined but standard metal). Similarly, the parity of bank-deposit credit may be maintained by forcing banks to keep reserves of gold, or lawful money redeemable in gold, in order to provide for the direct or indirect convertibility of their demand liabilities (customer deposits) into standard money. Thus, in spite of the fact that very few transactions may be settled in gold, a nation is assured that its currency structure and its price level are closely coupled to the value of the chosen unit of account. If the value of the unit remains fairly stable, it tends to create confidence among businessmen and increases their willingness to enter long-term contracts in which money is used as a standard of deferred payment.

If the monetary standard is a commodity having universal appeal, other nations will make it the basis of their financial systems. The standard then will function as an international medium of exchange, may aid in stabilizing foreign exchange rates (as will be explained in Chapter 22), and may thus contribute to an expansion of international trade.

But all units of account and monetary standards are not defined in terms of a commodity such as gold or silver. Since World War I, many countries have been unable or unwilling to tie their systems rigidly to gold and therefore have adopted some form of administered paper standard. Under such a plan the word "standard" has lost its traditional meaning because circulating forms of currency are not related to, or convertible into, a valuable and generally acceptable commodity. If a small gold reserve is held, a link between paper forms of money and gold may remain and extend a stabilizing influence upon the volume of currency and the general level of prices. On the other hand, if no metallic base is present, the system exists only on the basis of governmental decree or fiat, and the value of money is regulated by monetary authorities. Regulated paper issues are usually made legal tender for all government and private obligations, and legislative restrictions are placed upon the amount that may be issued. Because other forms of money (of a commodity type) are not available, fiat issues are generally acceptable and function satisfactorily as media of exchange as long as the volume of currency issued bears a wholesome relationship to the volume of trade to be financed.

Ordinarily, paper standards have been adopted only by nations facing financial emergencies. There is then a possibility that previously established limits on volume will be removed and the value of the unit will fall.

Standard Money in the United States

In our monetary system the unit of account was at first defined by Congress (1791) as a specified amount of gold or a specified quantity of silver. This bimetallic standard encountered many difficulties, and the nineteenth century in America presented a complex picture of monetary legislation.

THE GOLD COIN STANDARD (1900–1933). In 1900, however, an unequivocal gold standard was adopted. It defined the dollar as 23.22 grains of pure gold. This meant that the mint price of gold was fixed at $20.67 an ounce and that the United States Treasury would purchase, or sell, unlimited amounts of the metal at that price. Gold coins were made legal tender for all government and private debts; paper money and subsidiary coins were convertible into gold; and no restrictions were placed upon the use and movement of gold coin or bullion.

With the exception of a few months during World War I, when an embargo was placed on gold shipments, the United States maintained this standard until 1933.

GOLD STANDARD ABANDONED, 1933.   Financial trouble that developed in widely scattered areas of the world after 1929 brought collapse to the international gold standard abroad and produced fears among depositors of American banks that our banking system would be unable to meet gold drains. Runs upon banks, withdrawal of money for hoarding, and wholesale bank failures finally led to state, and ultimately (1933) to federal, closing of all banks. The United States Treasury ceased all gold payments and the redemption of gold certificates. Congress authorized the President to prohibit hoarding of gold and silver by individuals and to require all persons to surrender gold coin and bullion and gold certificates in exchange for other kinds of money.

These actions meant abandonment of the gold-coin standard in the United States, but steps were soon taken in an attempt to restore confidence and to provide a satisfactory new basis for our monetary system.

GOLD RESERVE ACT.   The Gold Reserve Act of January 30, 1934, and the presidential proclamation the following day, established the monetary standard now in effect in the United States. These measures provide that there shall be no gold coin or gold certificates in general use, no free redemption of currency in gold, and no hoarding or transporting of gold except under Treasury license. The Treasury is empowered to deal in gold and to provide for conversion of currency to the extent necessary to maintain all forms of United States money at par with gold.

Gold bullion for use in settling foreign balances and for use domestically in the industrial arts may be obtained under license from the Treasury. Reserves maintained against gold certificates are held in bullion form. Title to all gold coin and bullion formerly held by the Federal Reserve System is transferred to the Treasury in return for gold credits or gold certificates. The latter are used as substitutes for gold in all the reserve and collateral requirements of Federal Reserve banks. Gold certificates may "circulate" only between Federal Reserve banks and the Treasury.

"PROVISIONAL" GOLD STANDARD, 1934.   On the day following

the passage of the act, President Franklin Roosevelt established the content of the dollar at $15\frac{5}{21}$ grains of gold 0.9 fine, or 13.71 grains of pure gold.

It will be recalled that the dollar formerly in use had consisted of 23.22 grains of fine gold and that this established a mint price of $20.67 an ounce. During the autumn and winter of 1933–34, in a series of steps, the Treasury Department had increased the price of gold to $34.45 an ounce by January 16, 1934. The proclamation of 1934 reducing the metallic content of the dollar to 13.71 grains had the effect of raising the mint price of gold to $35 an ounce. The weight of the dollar became 59.06 per cent of its former weight, and this accounts for the popular statement that we now have a 59-cent dollar. The power of the President to change the weight of metal in the gold dollar was continued for several years but was finally allowed to expire (June 30, 1943) without further modification of the gold content.

In spite of the expiration of the specific power of the President to change the gold content of the dollar, it should not be assumed that the value of the unit is free from the possibility of administrative change. The Gold Reserve Act states that the Secretary of the Treasury, with the approval of the President, may buy and sell gold at home or abroad "at such rates and upon such terms and conditions as he may deem advantageous to the public interest." This provision is sometimes interpreted to mean that no upper limit is placed upon the price of gold and that a devaluation of the dollar would result from any action by the Secretary of the Treasury to raise the price. It appears unlikely that any such move will be made; and even if it should occur, it is not likely to have any substantial effect upon our domestic price level.

The monetary standard, sometimes called a "provisional" gold standard, established by the Gold Reserve Act of 1934 and the proclamations and regulations issued thereafter, may be described as an "international gold-bullion reserve standard." It differs, not only from the old-fashioned gold-coin standard almost universally in use before World War I, but also from the gold-bullion and the gold-exchange standards established by various nations after that war.

Nature of the Present Monetary System

As already stated, in its domestic aspects the system provides for a gold dollar, defined as 13.71 grains of pure gold, to serve as the standard of value; but no gold coins are issued. Money in circulation, as illustrated in Table 44 (p. 490), consists of silver dollars, subsidiary silver, minor coin, and government and bank notes. All these money forms are full legal tender; none is redeemable in gold, except under Treasury regulation designed to "maintain equal purchasing power of every kind of currency of the United States."

A gold market continues to exist but is not "free," as formerly. Gold will be released for use in domestic industry and the arts only under license obtained from the Treasury.

Despite the restrictions on gold and the fact that paper money may not be redeemed in gold for domestic monetary uses, the monetary system is not a fiat standard in the usual sense of the term. The huge gold stock—which has not been less than $10 billion since 1935 and has averaged in excess of $20 billion since 1939—acts as a reserve for Federal Reserve notes and deposits and may be employed by the Treasury whenever necessary to equalize the purchasing power of all forms of credit money with the standard. Gold may also be used by the Treasury in preserving the value of the dollar in foreign exchange markets, as will be noted in Chapter 22.

The descriptive title of the new standard contains the word "international" because it is the policy of the government to redeem in gold the currency of an individual for use in settling foreign trade balances and to release gold to the Federal Reserve banks to be "earmarked" for such use in the future. Gold has been willingly used by our government in helping to establish the International Monetary Fund and the International Bank for Recovery and Reconstruction. The Treasury will buy unlimited quantities of gold from foreign and domestic producers at $35 an ounce less handling charges.

CONCLUSION

Perhaps attention should be redirected to the question which caused us to embark on the long discussion on value, prices, and monetary standards. That is the query: How good is our monetary system in achieving its functions? As noted earlier, the money we use daily as media of exchange is quite satisfactory. But as long as fluctuations in prices continue to exist in the United States, as they have existed for 150 years, there is something to be desired in our monetary machine.

In subsequent chapters further consideration will be directed to control devices which may increase the stability of our economy and reduce fluctuations in the value of our money. Of especial significance to us will be those controls which operate within or through our financial institutions.

—FRANK H. GANE

QUESTIONS AND PROBLEMS

1. Why is a distinction often made between the primary and secondary functions of money? How can it be demonstrated that secondary functions exist only because of the existence of primary functions?
2. What qualities of gold and silver have resulted in their use as coined money? In what respects are gold and silver superior to cattle, diamonds, and tobacco as media of exchange and standards of value?
3. Why does the dispersion of prices within the general price structure create so many economic problems?
4. If prices fall in one phase of the business cycle and rise in another phase, do the economic results of the fluctuations not balance off?
5. Is the United States in danger of experiencing a "hyperinflation"? What factors are operating to increase prices? What tends to retard an increase? Does the existence of a large idle labor force increase or decrease the likelihood of inflation? Explain.
6. Demonstrate that an increase in the velocity of the use of money has the same effect upon the price level as an expanded money supply.
7. In a country with a managed paper monetary standard, what guides may be used in determining the "proper" volume of money that should be issued?
8. What factors determine the amount of currency outside the Treasury and the banks in the United States? What specific forces have operated to increase the money supply since 1940? Were other factors at work to increase the supply in the 1930's?
9. If the rest of the world, other than the United States, decides never to return to gold-based currency systems, what will happen to the gold hoard of the United States?

BIBLIOGRAPHY

Stimulating works in nontechnical terms of value to beginning students of the subject of money include:

Angell, Norman. *The Story of Money.* New York: F. A. Stokes Co., 1929.

Crowther, Geoffrey. *An Outline of Money.* Rev. ed. London: Thos. Nelson & Sons, Ltd., 1948.

Robertson, D. H. *Money.* New ed., rev. New York: Harcourt, Brace & Co., Inc., 1929.

Woodward, D. B., and Rose, Marc A. *A Primer of Money.* New York: McGraw-Hill Book Co., Inc., 1932.

A scholarly defense of the quantity theory of money in its strict form is presented in the work by I. Fisher, *The Purchasing Power of Money* (rev. ed.;

New York: Macmillan Co., 1920). A notable contribution to the literature appears in R. G. Hawtrey, *Currency and Credit* (3d ed.; New York: Longmans, Green & Co., 1928). Outstanding in the field of monetary theory is the work by John Maynard Keynes, *The General Theory of Employment, Interest and Money* (New York: Harcourt, Brace & Co., Inc., 1936).

The following textbooks, to be found in the libraries of most colleges and universities, may be used with great benefit:

Chandler, L. V. *The Economics of Money and Banking.* New York: Harper & Bros., 1948.

Hart, Albert Gaylord. *Money, Debt and Economic Activity.* New York: Prentice-Hall, Inc., 1948.

Peterson, J. M., and Cawthorne, D. R. *Money and Banking.* New York: Macmillan Co., 1949.

Prather, Charles A. *Money and Banking.* 4th ed. Chicago: Richard D. Irwin, 1949.

Thomas, R. G. *Our Modern Banking and Monetary System.* 2d ed. New York: Prentice-Hall, Inc., 1950.

Woodworth, G. W. *The Monetary and Banking System.* New York: McGraw-Hill Book Co., Inc., 1950.

Chapter 18

CREDIT CREATION BY THE BANKING SYSTEM

THE total volume of money in the United States in the spring of 1950 was approximately $113 billion. A relatively small portion of this ($4.3 billion) was Treasury currency in the form of coins and government paper money; over $23.2 billion was in Federal Reserve notes; and the remainder in demand deposits of commercial banks. Thus, more than $85 billion, or about 75 per cent of the effective money supply, was in the form of "checkbook money." An explanation of how the latter type of money is created and how its volume varies as the demand for it ebbs and flows is our objective at this point. A discussion of the elasticity of Federal Reserve notes, our second most important kind of money, will appear in Chapter 20.

Types of Deposits

In the description of commercial banking (Chapter 3) demand deposits were classified as "primary" and "derived." The former arise from lodgment of cash, or from receipt of a collection item and make a net addition to the liquid assets of the bank. Derivative deposits are "created" or derived through loans and investments made by the bank. They add nothing to the bank's liquid assets; on the contrary, they force the bank to tie up a larger amount of its assets as reserves and render the bank somewhat less liquid. Because borrowers normally have the proceeds of a loan added to their deposit accounts, the creation of a net addition to the purchasing power of the economy in this way may properly be termed a "monetary" function of commercial banks.

RESERVES AGAINST DEPOSITS. Regardless of the origin of a deposit, whether derived or primary, the bank is forced by law to maintain a liquid reserve against its obligation. The present legal requirement in the United States is merely a crystallization of experience. Goldsmith bankers of seventeenth-century England realized the necessity of keeping a reserve on hand to meet withdrawals of cash by depositors. The size of the reserve maintained was not a matter of law but was determined by the experience and judgment of the goldsmith. In some nations today, including England, there is no legal compulsion upon banks to hold cash reserves, but reserves are maintained, nevertheless.

LEGAL RESERVES. In the United States, legal minimum reserve requirements against deposits of commercial banks have been enforced for over a century. One of the notable features of the "model" banking law enacted in Louisiana (1842), and one of its most widely copied provisions, was the requirement of a specie or cash reserve equal to one third of all the banks' obligations to the public. Many states incorporated a similar reserve provision into their banking statutes prior to the Civil War, and in 1863 the principle was written into the National Banking Act. Minimum reserve requirements were included in the Federal Reserve Act of 1913, although details of the provision were modified.

As the law is now administered, legal reserves of commercial bank members of the Federal Reserve System consist only of a deposit of specified size in the Federal Reserve bank of the district. Under the National Banking Act, reserves were permitted to be partially in the form of vault cash and till money, partially as deposits with correspondent banks, and partially as items in the process of collection. Now member bank reserves for the nation must be concentrated in the twelve Federal Reserve banks. As we shall see in Chapter 20, legal minimum reserves were formerly a fixed proportion of time and demand deposits. Today the proportions are subject to alteration, within limits, by the Board of Governors of the Federal Reserve System.

Functions of Reserves

Originally, it was thought, the purpose of bank reserves was to assure noteholders and depositors of the ability of the bank to redeem its demand obligations in cash. It gradually became apparent, however, that legal minimum reserves had to remain in the vault or on deposit with a Federal Reserve bank. They could not be used, and they gave little assurance to depositors that obligations payable on demand would be honored by the bank. Thus, legal reserves seemed to be a form of "frozen-liquid" asset. To be able to pay cash to depositors, the bank is forced to maintain some liquid reserves over and above that required by law.[1]

The primary function of legal minimum-reserve requirements today is to provide a restraining influence upon the freedom of banks to expand credit by lending and creating checkbook money. As we shall see later, altering the reserves of commercial banks is regarded as a means by which central banks influence the ability of their members to create deposit credit.

Loan Expansion of a Single Bank

Since the subject of loan expansion and deposit creation is a complicated one and at the same time an important one, we shall attempt to develop the fundamental principles with the aid of simplified hypothetical cases or illustrations. This may make the presentation seem somewhat unreal but is justifiable if the principle can be clearly established.

Suppose that we are first dealing with *one* bank that belongs to a system in which the required reserve against deposits is 10 per cent. If this bank receives new reserves that originate outside the banking structure, i.e., from receipt of newly mined gold or from an import of gold received from a foreign country, the balance-sheet entry recording the increase in reserve money would be as follows:

Assets	(1)	*Liabilities*
+ Reserves..............$10,000		+ Deposits..............$10,000

Note that other items on the statement are ignored; the assumption is that existing deposits are adequately supported by a legal reserve in the Federal Reserve bank and that working reserves are maintained as vault cash and balances with correspondent banks. We are now able to center attention on the lending operation relating solely to the receipt of the new reserve money.

For the transaction illustrated above, the actual reserve ratio is 100 per cent. That result is obtained by dividing $10,000 deposits into $10,000 reserves. But the law permits a bank to operate, in our assumed case, with as little as a 10 per cent ratio. Knowing this, you ask: Would it not be logical for the banker to increase his earnings by making loans and investments to the full extent permitted by his

---

[1] Member-bank funds on deposit in Federal Reserve banks in excess of legal minimum requirements are called "excess reserves." Excess reserves plus the funds kept in cash in the vaults of the bank or on deposit in other commercial banks are termed "working reserves."

new reserve? In other words, would the bank not lend, at once, to one or more borrowers, enough to create deposits that would bring the new ratio down from 100 per cent to 10 per cent?

If this were done, the maximum loans granted and the derived deposits added to the bank's liabilities would be $90,000:

(2)

Reserves..................$10,000	Deposits................$100,000
Loans and discounts........ 90,000	

It must be remembered that borrowers request loans because they have payments to make. Loans are seldom made either earlier than needed or larger than needed. Hence, on the very day the advance is made by the bank, checks will be written against the borrower's derived deposit account. If some of these checks are paid to local citizens who take them to the bank on which they are drawn for deposit, then to this extent the bank will not lose either reserves or deposits. Title to that portion of the borrower's deposit account returned to the bank will be shifted to the account of the payee of the check. This bookkeeping transaction will cause the bank no problem; no reserve will be lost and deposits will be maintained.

It is likely, however, that a much larger portion of the borrower's new deposit will get into the hands of businessmen who do not patronize the bank on which the check is drawn. Some checks may be deposited in other local banks; many may go to a distant area from which the borrower purchases inventory or supplies. Checks drawn by borrowers and sent to creditors in other communities will be cashed or deposited with other banks for collection. They will ultimately be presented to the drawee bank for payment. If we assume an extreme situation, it may happen that checks are written for the entire amount of deposits created for the borrowers of our bank and that not a single dollar is redeposited in our bank. This means only one thing. The lending bank would be faced with a claim for $90,000 and have only $9,000 in reserve that could be applied to settlement of the debt.

Our next consideration is: How much may the banker lend on the basis of the original deposit of $10,000? Obviously, against the new deposit, the bank must maintain a 10 per cent reserve. The $10,000 may be thought of as being composed of two parts: one is the $1,000 (10 per cent) necessary to act as reserve for the deposit; the other $9,000 is "excess reserves." If it is assumed that the owner of the original deposit does not check against his account, the bank may consider that it has $9,000 in free funds available for lending.

If the borrower retained the proceeds of the loan in his deposit account, the bank statement would show:

(3)

Reserves.................$10,000	Deposits.................$19,000
Loans and discounts....... 9,000	

The reserve ratio at this point is more than 50 per cent ($10,000 divided by $19,000); yet it may be as low as the individual banker feels is safe. Or, from his point of view as a lending officer, the banker's loans are as large as he can grant without incurring the risks of technical insolvency (inability to meet claims immediately).

The keen-minded reader may wish to take issue with our statement that one bank will limit its loans to the amount of its excess reserves. He realizes, in the first place, that in each lending operation a partial balance will probably be unused, leaving some reserve with the lending institution. Moreover, he will assert that some checks drawn on the lending bank will be redeposited in it, thus allowing some reserves to remain as a basis for an additional expansion.

With these contentions we are in partial agreement. Banks not uncommonly do request lenders to observe the "20 per cent rule" of keeping an average deposit balance (compensating balance) during the term of the advance. Maintenance of an *average* balance does not mean, however, that the borrower refrains from checking out *all* his loan and having no balance at all during a portion of the loan period. With respect to the second objection advanced, it may be said that, while some checks are almost sure to be deposited in the drawee bank, no banker can accurately anticipate how many will return. In the absence of an accurate forecast he will not create excessive deposits, for he dares not run the risk of being caught short of reserves.[2]

Loan Expansion in a System of Banks

Oddly enough, the fractional reserve ratio required by law limits the ability of an individual bank to expand its loans but permits

---

[2] Two attempts to determine the volume of checks that are redeposited in the drawee bank have been given wide publicity. Professor C. A. Phillips reached the conclusion that a large part of checks drawn by the borrower, perhaps as much as 99 per cent, would be deposited in other banks. He estimated also that about 20 per cent of the deposit is retained as an unspent margin. If both estimates are accurate, the bank could lend $1,220 on the basis of $1,000 excess reserve. J. S. Lawrence estimated that one third of the checks drawn are redeposited in the lending bank. He calculated that the individual bank may lend almost $1,800 on the basis of $1,000 surplus reserve while maintaining a primary ratio of 10 per cent. In view of the disparity of these estimates, each lending institution is inclined to "bank on" the most conservative figure, i.e., the amount of excess reserves. For detailed discussion, see J. S. Lawrence, *Stabilization of Prices* (New York: Macmillan Co., 1928), chap. xxiii.

multiple expansion of the reserve for the system as a whole. This apparent anomaly, sometimes called the "riddle" of commercial banking, may be stated in this fashion: Why is it possible for the system of banks to expand credit to a multiple of excess reserves while an individual bank is restricted to lending only the amount of its excess?

To explain this seeming paradox, we return to the commercial bank having new reserves and continue with the hypothetical illustration. Receipt of the deposit is shown as before, as it appeared in transaction (1):

(4)

Reserves................$10,000   Deposits................$10,000

Granting a loan to the full extent of its excess reserves creates the following change when the borrower's deposit balance is credited. This is identical with (3) above:

(5)

Reserves................$10,000   Deposits................$19,000
Loans and discounts........ 9,000

At this point it is necessary to introduce another bank of the system, a bank in which checks drawn against the lending bank are deposited. This we may designate as Bank 2.

If we now assume that all the derivative deposits of the lender bank are checked out and flow into Bank 2, the statement of the lending bank becomes:

(6)

BANK 1

Reserves..................$1,000   Deposits................$10,000
Loans and discounts......... 9,000

Bank 2 has acquired $9,000 of deposits and reserve from the original bank. Its statement shows the following changes:

(7)

BANK 2

+ Reserves...............$9,000   + Deposits...............$9,000

The receipt of new deposits forces this bank to set up a minimum legal reserve of $900 (10 per cent of the $9,000 deposits). But since the reserve is only a fraction of the new reserve received, an excess reserve is created. This is $8,100, the amount of total receipts minus the $900 in required reserve.

On the basis of the excess reserve so acquired, Bank 2 may grant loans to approximately the same extent. Assuming borrowers deposit the proceeds of their loans, the position of the bank then becomes:

(8)

BANK 2

| Reserves.................\$9,000 | Deposits.................\$17,100 |
| Loans and discounts........ 8,100 | |

If the process continues, another bank, which we shall call "Bank 3," will acquire new reserves from Bank 2. For example, checks aggregating \$8,100, or the entire sum loaned by the second bank, may be deposited in Bank 3. As the checks are collected through the clearinghouse, the reserves and deposits of the third bank would expand by \$8,100, as shown in (9).

(9)

BANK 3

| Reserves.................\$8,100 | Deposits.................\$8,100 |

This bank is now in a position to lend its newly acquired excess reserves. As loans of \$7,290 are made the new relationship of reserves, loans and deposits will appear as in (10).

(10)

BANK 3

| Reserves.................\$8,100 | Deposits.................\$15,390 |
| Loans and discounts........ 7,290 | |

As deposits of Bank 3 are checked upon and paid out, the final status of this bank will show it also to have a reserve ratio of 10 per cent. Thus:

(11)

BANK 3

| Reserves.................\$ 810 | Deposits.................\$8,100 |
| Loans and discounts........ 7,290 | |

As all banks in the system become participants in the diffusion, an ever-diminishing portion of the original deposit is passed from bank to bank until the amount involved finally becomes negligible. It is unnecessary to include added detail of computation to show expansion in successive banks. The upper portion of Table 46 indicates the changes resulting when five banks participate.

The process does not come to an end with the five banks shown in Table 46. As the filtration continues and embraces a larger and larger number of commercial banks, expansion approaches its limit. At that point, the aggregate volume of deposits supported by the $10,000 new reserve is $100,000, and new loans aggregate $90,000. The limit of expansion in the system is the new reserve multiplied by the reciprocal of the reserve ratio—in this case 10/1, or 10. It is possible for the system to expand purchasing power in the form of deposits by a multiple of its excess reserves, whereas an individual bank is limited to a sum that closely approximates its excess. Thus, the "riddle" is explained.

The individual banker sometimes is resentful of those who contend that he can "create" money by granting loans. He always lends or

TABLE 46

MULTIPLE EXPANSION OF BANK CREDIT

Bank	Additional Deposits Received	Additional Loans Made	Additional Reserves Retained
1	$ 10,000	$ 9,000	$ 1,000
2	9,000	8,100	900
3	8,100	7,290	810
4	7,290	6,561	729
5	6,561	5,905	656
Subsequent banks	59,049	53,144	5,905
Ultimate total	$100,000	$90,000	$10,000

invests only funds held in excess of legal requirements. To him this is not the "creation" of anything. It is merely a diversion from one form to another. Nevertheless, it is true that, because reserves are required to be only a fraction of deposits, the excess reserve of an individual bank may be expanded throughout the system, as explained above, to several times its own size.

Expansion through Bank Investment Account

Although our illustration of bank credit expansion has been developed solely by considering loans, it may work with equal facility through an increase in other types of advances. A bank with excess reserves may experience no local demand for loan funds and may have to take the initial step in acquiring earning assets. It is of little moment whether the bank makes a loan or purchases commercial paper, bankers' acceptances, or securities in the open market. In any case, the recipient of the funds deposits them in a bank, thereby increasing its reserves and giving it a basis for lending or investing. The extent of ultimate expansion is nowise different from that in the case of the loans developed above.

Limitations upon Full Expansion

It must be admitted—in fact, we hasten to admit—that there may be limitations at work which will cause expansion to fall short of its theoretical maximum. One of the assumptions implicit in the process is that of a continued demand for loan funds. If this is not the case, a bank may take steps and continue expansion through its investment program. Thus the mere lack of demand for loans is only a temporary obstacle. A second assumption is that banks throughout the system are granting loans in about the same volume. When this is the case, depositors are likely to be drawing checks in favor of each other for about the same volume, and no bank will be distressed by persistent adverse balances at the clearinghouse. Another implicit assumption is that an increase in loan volume does not influence the volume of currency in circulation. It is usually true, however, that an expansion in loans and derivative deposits is accompanied by an increase in the amount of coin and paper money held outside banks. When this occurs, bank credit expansion tends to be more limited because bankers will have a smaller reserve foundation for the support of created deposits. A more significant limitation is a policy of bank management that prefers the preservation of a liquid position at the expense of full expansion. It is normally true that banks desire to maximize the income obtainable from loans and investments. During uncertain times, however, they do depart from this position, preferring to remain highly liquid by keeping large amounts of excess reserves. When this happens, as it did during the middle and late 1930's, the realized expansion on the basis of increased reserves is much less than the possible maximum.

One further limitation may be mentioned. If, for example, Bank 2, in our illustration, happens to be in debt to the central bank when it receives surplus reserves from the original lending bank, it may retard all further expansion by applying the newly acquired funds against its debt at the central bank rather than expanding loans.

Contraction of Bank Credit

If momentarily we overlook the qualifications just mentioned and go back to our original thesis, we can say that, under the conditions assumed, an increase in reserves may be followed by a tenfold increase in checkbook money. By the same token, if full expansion existed, a loss of $1 of reserve would force a reduction of $10 of deposit credit. Loss of reserves may be due to export of the standard monetary metal to settle foreign trade debts, to hoarding by individuals, to a flight of capital abroad to insure protection of basic value, to the retirement of money designated as "lawful reserve" for deposit credit, or to other factors. Regardless of the cause of contraction of basic reserves, it is almost certain to be followed by a multiple reduction of bank loans and investments and demand deposits.

An individual bank whose reserve falls below the legal minimum will draw money from other banks by sale of investments, will call loans payable on demand, and will allow earning assets of near maturities to "run off," i.e., be paid in cash with no further reinvestment in similar assets. Contraction may not progress so fast as expansion because banks, hesitating to "put the squeeze" on borrowers by forcing them to pay loans at once, may borrow reserves from the central bank of the system. Later, as an orderly liquidation of the commercial bank's assets generates a flow of cash into the bank, the debt to the central bank is repaid and contraction of credit occurs.

Recent Changes in Reserve Requirements

The 10 per cent legal minimum reserve assumed in the illustrations in this chapter is hypothetical. Actually, required reserves today (March, 1951) approximate 20 per cent or double the amount assumed. The effect of increasing required reserves is to reduce the potential limit of expansion. If, under our 10 per cent assumption, $1 of reserve could support $10 in deposits, the $1 can under a 20 per cent requirement act as a base for only one half as much, or $5. And if commercial banks avail themselves of aid from the Federal Reserve banks by borrowing to build up reserve balances, the maximum limit of expansion per dollar of reserves is now only one half as much as before 1936, when minimum reserve percentages were increased.

Reference has been made several times in this discussion to the credit-granting activities of the Federal Reserve System. Further treatment of the possibilities of credit expansion and the creation of checkbook money is postponed until the nature of central banking and its place in the processes of expansion and contraction has been presented.   —Frank H. Gane

QUESTIONS AND PROBLEMS

1. What are two functions of the reserves of commercial banks?
2. Why are time or savings deposits not discussed in an explanation of bank credit expansion?

3. Explain and illustrate the process by which the system of commercial banks may achieve a multiple expansion of credit in spite of the fact that any individual bank in the system may lend or invest an amount approximately equal to its excess reserve.

4. If it is assumed that the legal minimum reserve against demand deposits of commercial banks is 15 per cent, how much could be loaned if the following composite balance sheet data were given?

Reserves held by Federal Reserve bank. . $120,000   Deposits outstanding. . $675,000

5. What factors may limit credit expansion of commercial banks?

6. From sources of banking data, such as the *Federal Reserve Bulletin,* find figures showing the volume of commercial bank credit and the size of reserve funds. If expansion to the theoretical limit took place, how much would bank deposits increase?

BIBLIOGRAPHY

One of the best early treatments of the relation of deposits, reserves, and loans is found in Chester A. Phillips, *Bank Credit* (New York: Macmillan Co., 1921), Part I. An excellent analysis is found also in R. G. Rodkey, *The Banking Process* (New York: Macmillan Co., 1928), chap. xv. See also chapter xxiii of J. S. Lawrence, *Stabilization of Prices* (New York: Macmillan Co., 1928).

Of the many books on money and banking containing chapters devoted to bank credit expansion, the following are typical:

Bradford, F. A. *Money and Banking,* chap. x. 4th ed. New York: Longmans, Green & Co., 1937.

Peterson, J. Marvin, and Cowthorne, D. R. *Money and Banking,* chaps. xii and xiv. Rev. ed. New York: Macmillan Co., 1949.

Westerfield, Ray B. *Money, Credit and Banking,* chap. x. New York: Ronald Press Co., 1947.

Chapter • 19

BUSINESS FLUCTUATIONS

OUR economy is far from stable. Sometimes business is good; sometimes it is poor. During some periods it is easy for anyone to find work; there seem to be more jobs than persons to fill them. Then again, job openings seem to disappear; even good, experienced, and diligent men cannot find gainful employment. During some periods, business profits are high and most businesses get along very well; at other times, almost all businesses suffer difficulties and profits dwindle or even disappear. The prices of commodities and securities go up and then down.

Although all these kinds of ups and downs by no means coincide exactly, there is a great deal of similarity among them: the favorable events which characterize a period of "prosperity" come at about the same time, and the events associated with depressions seem to bunch. "Booms and busts" are general economic events reflected in employment, prices, profits, and many other economic factors.

The Problem of Economic Instability

The fact that there are fluctuations is confirmed abundantly by a study of the business records of the past. The volume of economic goods produced has varied widely. Price levels and therefore the value of money have moved up and down. High levels of employment have been followed by periods of considerable unemployment. The income for the nation as a whole fluctuates widely, and for some persons the range of swing is wider than for others.

It is because these fluctuations are roughly simultaneous—that is, the various economic factors rise and fall at about the same time— that the problem is a social one and not just one of isolated or special interest. Exhibit 59 displays some of the leading economic series which reflect business fluctuations. This chart shows how closely

519

these series move up and down together. It also shows that some series move rather more violently than others. Later in this chapter we shall have quite a bit to say about the range of fluctuation of various segments of the economy.

Popular interest in business fluctuations has been particularly keen in recent years. During almost all of the 1930's this country, and the

Exhibit 59

SELECTED ECONOMIC SERIES

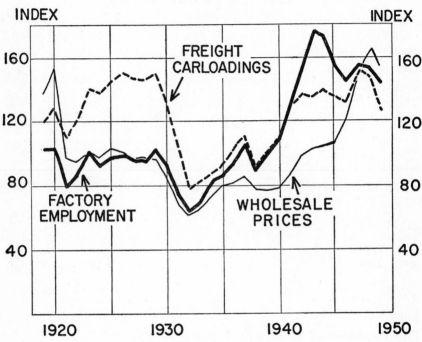

Sources: The index of factory employment (1939 = 100) and the index of wholesale prices (1926 = 100) are compiled by the Bureau of Labor Statistics. Freight carloadings are based on figures collected by the Interstate Commerce Commission with the index (1935–39 = 100) prepared by the Federal Reserve. All figures are currently reported among the business indexes of the Federal Reserve.

rest of the world as well, suffered a prolonged depression. During a large part of this period many were unemployed. From the fall of 1930 to the spring of 1941 there were only six months in which unemployment in the United States was less than 5 million (five of the six months being in the latter part of 1937), and there were forty-three months in which unemployment exceeded 10 million. Then in the frantic preparation for World War II and during the war itself there was the opposite circumstance—a great shortage of labor. In the period following the war, inflationary developments emerged more openly, and again the economy was in a boom stage with a shortage of manpower.

To some it seems that we almost never enjoy a "normal" economic period. The word "normal" is, indeed, a dubious one. A cynic might almost conclude that the normal state of affairs is either boom or "bust" with short breathing spells in between.

Even though the United States has enjoyed an almost unbroken period of prosperity since World War II, the fear of depressions has never quite vanished. Whenever there was a slight relapse of prices or employment, talk of depression revived. The fear of depression itself probably helped to sustain the prosperity for a while; business concerns did not permit inventories to rise unchecked, and consumers bought with more restraint than might have been expected in light of their large liquid savings. In most foreign countries the fear of inflation is more common than the fear of depression—because they have experienced inflations. But in the United States, the fear of depressions seems to be more common and stronger.[1]

Financial Institutions and Instability

Financial institutions are sensitive to the influences of business conditions. They suffer when the rest of the economy is having difficulties, and they prosper when the rest of the economy is enjoying good times. Indeed, financial institutions are particularly sensitive, both for reasons of profit and for financial conservatism, to the state of business health. Furthermore, there are some who believe that our financial system plays a special, and not always beneficent, role in causing economic instability. For this reason, financial institutions have an added interest in business fluctuations: many of the efforts to cure or avoid depressions bear mainly on the financial system. Some diagnoses of economic fluctuations have stressed financial factors; others look elsewhere. But the prescriptions for cure have almost always involved finance. The Federal Reserve System was one of the first great efforts to rid the economy of panics and depressions. More recent proposals for cure usually involve management of government finances—"fiscal policy"—toward this end. Both of these are financial cures. And so, before attention is turned to Federal

---

[1] This assertion now may appear hard to support when inflationary forces seem to be dominant. There is currently more concern about the shrinking value of money than about unemployment. Nevertheless, one not infrequently hears ominous talk about a "big crash," as if the chief danger of an inflationary period was that it would inevitably be followed by a depression.

Reserve monetary management and the fiscal management of the federal government, as will be done in the following two chapters, the general subject of economic instability, the popularly called "business cycle," will be considered.

The first part of this chapter will consider various theories which claim to explain variations in business activity. It can be fairly said that at present there is no explanation which seems universally valid or widely accepted. But at the same time, there are elements of truth in many of the explanations. Some of the explanations that appear most nonsensical have, nevertheless, some relevance. These various explanations will serve to stimulate thought even if they cannot be accepted in their entirety. The next section of this chapter will winnow out a few widely, if not universally, accepted postulates about business fluctuations. Finally, the effect of business fluctuations on financial institutions will be considered.

EXPLANATIONS OF BUSINESS FLUCTUATIONS

Business fluctuations are a grave social problem; they have attracted the attention and thought of many. The attempts to explain their cause cover a wide range of theory and fact. While knowledge about business fluctuations has grown, the explanations have not come into much closer agreement. Thus, with scholars and specialists still arguing, it is difficult to summarize fairly the whole range of views. The following sections, therefore, should be treated more as a sketchy recital than as a scientific summary. The reading list at the end of the chapter will help those anxious to learn more of business-cycle theory.

Some of the variations among explanations of business fluctuations are more a matter of emphasis than absolute differences of opinion. But even when the variations are rather moderate, they sometimes lead to important differences in the policy recommendations of the analysts. For example, the most popular current explanation of business fluctuations has to do with the rate of capital investment. But, starting with the agreed importance of this element, some analysts come out with the conclusion that more governmental intervention in the economic system is needed; other analysts use it to argue for less governmental intervention. Thus we are faced with the need for being careful; for small differences in diagnosis seem to lead to rather larger differences in prescription.

Some of the explanations of business fluctuation belong in the realm of "crank" literature. But in this uncertain world, who is to judge what is fantastic and what is profound? The idea of "relativity" served as a vaudeville jest for years—but from it came the atom bomb. By the same token, it is dangerous to be dogmatic about what are and what are not fanciful explanations of business fluctuations.

Monetary Explanations

The oldest and commonest explanation of business fluctuation relates to *monetary* factors. Although the current tendency is to rate these factors rather less important than formerly, they still attract a large following. According to these theories, money systems are at fault. Some feel that money systems do not supply an amount of money or "purchasing power" which is in keeping with the volume of real economic activity. It is maintained that there is not enough money in some periods, and too much in others. The effect of an excess or of a deficiency of money is said to be twofold: prices move up or down, and economic activity responds in sympathy. And since the diagnosis of economic ills relates to purported monetary deficiencies, it is natural that the more popular prescriptions have been to tamper with the money system. Monetary tinkering not only has a long history; it still claims many adherents.

There have been many subvariations in the monetary explanation of economic instability: some hold that our laws relating to money, and to the banking system which supply money in the form of bank deposits, are too inflexible; others hold that the laws are far too flexible, and they tend to overdo the matter of accommodating demands for money.

Still other explanations point to the interest rate as a causal factor. It is thought that, when interest rates are too low, they encourage overborrowing and thus overspending; when rates are too high, they have the opposite effect.

Still another and very crude monetary explanation of business fluctuations asserts that there is a damaging alternation of money hoarding and spending. The records clearly show that in some years our total money stock is active, each dollar being spent many times, but that in other years the supply of money is much less active. It has been thought that at times people put a much higher premium on holding money (hoarding) than at other times, and that it was this alternating tendency to hold or spend money that created either booms or "busts." As with all simple theories, this one has been spun out to great length with all sorts of variations.

Other Explanations

Other explanations place major emphasis on *overbuilding* or *over-investment* during boom times. In simple terms this means that, when times are good and profit prospects are favorable, more homes, stores, apartments, and machines are produced than are really needed. For example, it is pointed out that, when hotel profits were good in the 1920's, so many hotels were built that all of them could not possibly be operated profitably. Then for ten years almost no hotels were built. The hotels were finally used to capacity only with the high volume of travel and the billeting of soldiers during World War II and the subsequent housing shortage. The same was true of electric-power generating capacity. So much capacity was provided during the 1920's that a decade passed before there was enough secular growth in power consumption to use this generating capacity fully.

Still other explanations are based on the uneven rate at which *inventions* and *innovations* are developed. It is argued that during some periods the rate of technological advance has been very rapid and that this induced new construction to take advantage of the new methods. Then these waves of innovation slowed down and business was retarded.

It has been observed that *inventories* increase in some periods and decline in others. The usual reason is that buyers anticipate requirements to take advantage of an expected rise in prices, and permit inventories to shrink in the face of expected lower prices. In the scientific writing on business cycles it is common to explain many of the shorter-term swings as "inventory cycles." The inventory cycle is thought to be shorter than other kinds of cycles because the period in which the glut is accumulated and then dissipated is shorter than is true of an oversupply of machinery and buildings.

The list of explanations could be extended indefinitely. Some explanations are deduced from the fact that *agricultural crops and livestock production* vary because of natural factors. Good weather may prevail almost everywhere, and crops are good. Or bad weather may cause widespread crop failure. Thus agricultural income may go up or down. Like the rest of us, farmers are good buyers only when they have income. There is even a theory that business fluctuations are based on sunspot variations. This is often linked with agricultural production.

Some view the problem of business fluctuations as one of *mass psychology*. They point out that, when a sizable group of business leaders and others in positions of influence become optimistic, their conviction comes to be shared by the majority of the population. Soon everybody is hopeful and happy. Under this pervasive influence, business may actually turn out to be very good, in response to free and easy spending. A wave of pessimism can have a cumulatively opposite effect.

Business-fluctuation theories have even been based on the length of women's skirts: short in good times; long in periods of adversity. While this seems like utter nonsense, it may have some validity. Fashion, as all sophisticated persons know, is not a self-generating whim, but a tool of the garment trades for stimulating business. When consumer demand seems to slacken, the garment industry marshals the women-opinion media to change styles, to make wardrobes obsolete, so as to require complete replenishment. The style change is usually of a sort that precludes making old garments fashionable through alteration. When is the garment industry most likely to need such stimulation? Obviously, when business prosperity is starting to run a little thin.

Theories of Cycle Periodicity

Another aspect of business-cycle speculation deals with the length of the period between peaks and the regularity of the swings. At one time it was widely held that a major cycle tended to run its complete course in about seven years. But the records do not fit this scheme very well. One of the facts that upset this theory is that during the 1930's we had ten consecutive years during which we had very large unemployment. There were variations within this period, but a new idea of perpetual depression gained some currency. Some thought that without the war this era of bad times would have lasted even longer.

In business-cycle theory more than one cycle period is recognized: a six- to thirty-six-month basic-inventory cycle; a business machinery and equipment cycle of about six to ten years; a construction cycle of perhaps fifteen to twenty years; and some accept the idea of a fifty-year cycle superimposed on top of all these others—a sort of cycle related to changes in the social structure and to waves of economic innovation. For example: the railroad cycle from 1860 to 1910; the automobile and electric-utility cycle from 1910 to the present.

GENERALLY ACCEPTED FACTS ABOUT BUSINESS FLUCTUATIONS

Even though disagreement as to what *causes* business fluctuations is general, there is agreement on the fact of fluctuations and certain of the characteristics. These characteristics have great significance in understanding and in interpreting the way in which financial institutions operate. As we shall see, many of the evolutionary changes in financial institutions have been due almost directly to the fact that they have had to adapt themselves to the characteristics of business fluctuations—i.e., guard against their impact.

Durable versus Nondurable Goods Industries

One of the most widely accepted views of business fluctuations is that the production and sale of durable goods have a unique role in explaining economic instability. Durable goods are just what their name implies—things which last a long time in use: houses, buildings, machinery, automobiles, railroad tracks and equipment, and the like. Some are more durable than others, but they all have several years' service implicit in their physical nature. Nondurable goods and services are those which are used up at once or fairly quickly: food, personal services, and the like. Some twilight-zone goods, like clothing, are somewhat durable but not long-term durable, as is true of houses.

History indicates clearly that the production of durable goods fluctuates much more widely than that of nondurable goods. This is shown in Exhibit 60. The reason for this fact is evident. Since durable goods are "durable," there is an option as to the length of time they may be used. People can continue to enjoy the use of automobiles even if none are currently made; that was done during the war. When times get bad and income falls, or profits disappear, people can make the old durable goods last a little longer, use the same old machines. But this cannot be done with nondurable goods, particularly the very perishable ones. The current production of ice cream, for example, will be almost exactly equal to the current consumption.

This does not mean that there is no fluctuation in the production of nondurable goods; rather, there is less fluctuation. Although the rule does not hold exactly, one can almost say that the degree of fluctuation in the production of any commodity or product is directly related to its normal service life. Production of gasoline and food, for example, are both likely to fluctuate very little (except as weather conditions may affect food crops). The production of clothing fluctuates rather more, automobiles still more; and items, like housing, which last for very long periods have an enormously wide range of fluctuation. Residential construction in 1933 was less than one

Exhibit 60

DURABLE AND NONDURABLE INDUSTRIAL PRODUCTION
(1935–39 = 100)

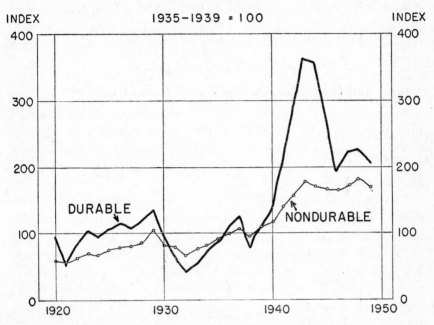

Source: Compiled and published by the Federal Reserve Board.

twenty-fifth the value reported in 1950. With allowance for changes in prices, the physical volume of construction was at least ten times as great in 1950 as it was in 1933.

Variability in durable-good production affects financial institutions in an intimate and important way. One of the major functions of certain financial institutions is to invest money. Investment is largely, even if indirectly, related to expenditures for durable goods. Therefore, the operations of a large number of important financial institutions are directly conditioned to one of the more variable factors responsible for business fluctuations.

Some Prices Fluctuate More than Others

Not only do certain classes of economic production fluctuate more than others, but some prices fluctuate more than others. However, the articles on which prices fluctuate the most are *not* the same ones for which production fluctuation is the greatest. If anything, the relationship may well be the opposite. Production of food and gasoline, already noted, has been relatively stable. But the prices of farm products and of crude oil are among the most wildly fluctuating. On the other hand, the price of machinery and automobiles and other durables may not fluctuate widely and are slower to show the influence of poor times. Interest rates are one of the most important of the more volatile price groups and are of great importance to financial institutions.

Booms and Busts Tend to Build on Themselves

In the course of a business cycle, there appears to be a tendency toward a definitely cumulative effect which causes a boom, once started, to grow even larger; or a "bust," once started, to deepen. In the long run, both extreme swings must end; but for a while, they feed on themselves.

The usual explanation for this is as follows: When prices start moving up, buyers buy more than currently needed because they anticipate still higher prices. When prices start falling, buying is curtailed in anticipation of even lower prices. Also, when prices go up, profits are likely to increase even more rapidly, so that business managers take an optimistic view and are disposed to expand. Rising income tends to generate even bigger demands; falling income, smaller demands. Thus the cumulative effect.

Sometimes there is an even more specific cumulative effect which is due to the relative durability of producer goods. Assume that certain industrial machines have an average useful life of ten years. If the demand for the product of these machines is just equal to their capacity, the orders for these machines will be just equal to replacement needs, which, under the assumption, should be 10 per cent of those in use. If demand for the product of these machines increases 10 per cent, the number of machines must be increased 10 per cent; but the orders for *machines* are thereby doubled. In other words, a 10 per cent increase in the demand for the product of the machines results in a 100 per cent increase in the demand for the machines. And a fall of 10 per cent in the demand for the product may result in a drop in the demand for the machines to nothing.

The cumulative tendency can be illustrated in the changes in investment policy of *financial institutions*. It has been averred that the alternating waves of pessimism and optimism are reflected in changing credit judgments. Financial institutions tend to exaggerate the swings in business fluctuations by being, in turn, bullish and then bearish. When they are bullish, they invest freely and hopefully in business ventures; when they become frightened, they stop investing money so freely. Thus, business enterprisers vary their own capital expenditures, depending on how freely they can get money. The extension of many of the governmental lending agencies (to be outlined in Chapter 21) can undoubtedly be attributed to the belief that privately owned financial institutions, suffering from fright or caution induced by bad times, were not granting credit to meritorious borrowers.

War and Business Fluctuations

Unquestionably, war is one of the major factors that affects the timing and magnitude of business fluctuations. War causes vast demands for military goods, which, superimposed upon the usual civilian demands, tend toward inflation. And war finance, because it almost invariably expands the money supply, is inflationary. The unavoidable wartime postponement of certain civilian demands tends to concentrate large demands right after the war. These swollen demands are usually followed by a substantial drop in postwar demand, once the pent-up needs are met. Then, too, the devastation of productive facilities throughout war-torn areas and the political instability of countries that are or were in the center of actual conflict are factors that tend to generate excessive boom and "bust."

War-boom influences affect financial institutions in a variety of ways. War has always changed the nature of financial institutions, but World War II is still too recent and its effects too pervasive to be fully appreciated or analyzed at this time.

Great Variability in Duration and Range of Business Fluctuations

The earlier, fairly rigid notions about typical duration of the full swing in business fluctuations have largely disappeared. Most observers now feel that no such regularity exists; for that reason, the word "cycle" has lost some of its appeal. Some explain that the variation in the duration and in the severity of business fluctuations is due to many types of cycles, long and short. Others see in this circumstance evidence that there is nothing regular or recurring about business fluctuations; that fluctuations can be caused by a great enough variety of factors which are themselves variable. Timing cannot be expected to be regular. Whatever the line of explanation, there is general agreement that the intensity and duration of swings is highly variable.

For this reason, there is less confidence in the possibility of achieving even reasonably reliable business forecasts. A few decades ago, business forecasting was popular; many books were written on the subject. But such hopes were not too well founded. Without a regularly recurring pattern, forecasting the future is uncertain and often wrong.

This affects the managerial policies of financial institutions. At one time it was widely believed that the management policies of financial institutions could be varied and adapted to the expected level of business activity. But with this hope blasted, the managements of financial institutions must cope, often blindly, with an unknown and uncertain future. Some kinds of risk taking which were tolerated in the 1920's are now frowned upon. Eternal vigilance and continuing adaptation to the changing scene are essential to successful financial management. To this end the nature and scope of protective managerial policies for financial institutions, particularly commercial banks, have become more conservative in recent years.

Business Fluctuations Are International in Range

It is now generally recognized that business fluctuations do not trace independent courses in the various countries of the world; instead, the courses tend to move in rough unison. Through international trade and capital transactions, the effects of either good or poor times in leading countries tend to be transmitted to other smaller countries. A fuller account of how this happens will appear in Chapter 22, which will deal with international financial relationships. The leading countries seem to follow parallel courses of prosperity and depression. It is believed in some countries that the natural advantages of free trade cost too much because free trade makes a country more vulnerable and exposes it to the poor times in those countries with which it does business. Following World War II, the British financial papers were constantly expressing more concern about the possibility of a great depression in the United States than at home. There was fear of the effect it would have on the market for what Britain sells to the United States—whiskey and woolens, for example.

It has even been claimed that international depressions are one of the prime breeders of war. Many attribute World War II to the international depression of the 1930's—and there is much logic to this contention. And as a corollary, business fluctuations then become a political issue as well as an economic one. (Governmental policy in relation to depressions will be treated in Chapter 21.)

SPECIFIC WAYS IN WHICH BUSINESS FLUCTUATIONS AFFECT FINANCIAL INSTITUTIONS

It has been shown that certain acknowledged characteristics of business fluctuations affect the operations of financial institutions. In addition to the broad general influences, there are more direct influences that merit careful attention. It can be said, without exaggeration, that financial institutions are very vulnerable to the effects of fluctuations in business activity.

The Demand for Credit Is Highly Variable

Credit is the main stock-in-trade of financial institutions. Because the demand for credit accommodation by business concerns is more likely to arise out of the production of durable rather than nondurable goods, such demand for credit fluctuates widely. It will fluctuate to an even greater extent than the demand for durable goods. There are two reasons for this:

First, part of the demand for machines is for replacing those worn out. Provision for such replacement is generally made through depreciation allowances accumulated as the machines wore out. Thus, if the accounting is properly managed, there is no need to finance replacement of worn-out equipment.

Second, many concerns can finance a part of their needs out of earnings. Credit demands, therefore, are dependent on earnings and likely to vary widely. The records show that they do.

The Safety of Financial Obligations Varies Widely

One of the prime prerequisites for an efficient financial system is the reasonable assurance that most debtors will meet their obligations promptly in the ordinary course of business. In good times, this expectation is generally realized. But in poor times, particularly if prolonged, this confidence erodes and may even vanish. In 1932, credit grantors were shocked when honored and well-known companies were not able to pay their debts. Creditors hesitated to trust persons and companies about whom there would normally have been no doubt at all. When fear prevails, the financial system becomes partly paralyzed.

Saving Varies Widely

Saving is the real foundation for investment. In economic terms, saving is the source of "supply" for investment credit. But saving varies widely, depending on various factors, including the level of business activity. Saving varies much more violently than income. In a sense, this is fortunate for the economy as a whole; if one fluctuates, it is better that both should. The demand for investment credit, as well as the supply, varies in the same direction and roughly at the same time! For financial institutions it means a large volume of new business at intervals; at other times almost none, which is not so fortunate for them.

Interest Rates Vary Widely

That interest rates vary widely with fluctuations in business volume is not so widely recognized as some of the other factors we have mentioned, but is nevertheless unquestionably true. And not only are interest rates widely variable, the short-term rates vary more than long-term rates. This fact is immediately evident in Exhibit 61.

There are two ways in which the variability of interest rates is of concern to financial institutions. The first has to do with their income. The main source of income for many financial institutions, notably commercial banks, is interest. Variations in interest affect the rate of their current income.

The second influence grows out of the fact that the yield and price on a fixed-payment obligation, such as a bond, move in opposite directions. For example, assume a twenty-year bond with a 3 per cent coupon:

> If its price goes *up* from 100 to 110, its yield goes *down* from 3 per cent to 2.37 per cent.

> If its price goes *down* from 100 to 90, its yield goes *up* from 3 per cent to 3.71 per cent.

These yields are calculated by the somewhat involved mathematics of finance but may be read from the tables of bond yields and prices used by bond traders. This means that the market value of securities, which are held in large amounts by many financial institutions and which are the stock-in-trade of financial concerns, may fluctuate widely. If the financial enterprises do not have to sell the obligations but can hold them to maturity, they can, perhaps, avoid capital losses from this cause. But if they find it necessary to sell any of their holdings, they may suffer losses.

Exhibit 61

INTEREST RATES

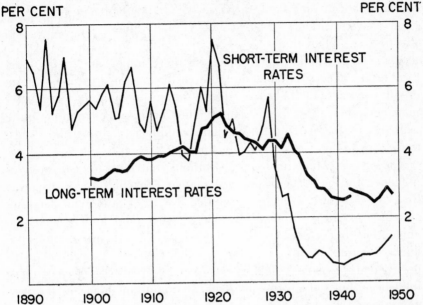

Sources: The commercial paper rates are those reported by the leading dealers and have been compiled from a variety of sources by the Federal Reserve (see *Banking and Monetary Statistics*, sec. 12). The long-term bond yield from 1900 to 1942 is the hypothetical figure of yield for a 20-year high-grade corporate bond compiled by David Durant in the National Bureau of Economic Research study of corporate bond yields. The long-term yield shown for 1942–48 is that of taxable United States Treasury long-term bonds as complied by the Treasury Department.

For a variety of reasons, financial institutions—particularly commercial banks—usually have relatively thinner capital equities than ordinary business corporations. Stated another way, the proportion of the owners' capital investment is small in relation to deposits. But in any business, the owners' equity bears the burden of capital gains and losses. So, with a thin capital equity, such gains or losses have a magnified effect on the ownership interest. Therefore, financial institutions tend to be exceptionally sensitive to fluctuations in interest rates.

Summary of How Business Fluctuations Affect Financial Institutions

One might conclude that financial institutions are both affected by business fluctuations and are themselves sometimes a contributing cause—sometimes they are cause, sometimes they are affected. The three primary ways financial institutions are affected by business fluctuations are: first, in the rates of interest they both receive and pay out; second, in the capital gains they receive or the losses they suffer due to changes in interest rates and the market valuation of investment securities; and, third, in the volume of business done. In good times with lots of investment activity, these institutions are prosperous. When times turn bad, the volume of business they do drops. The fluctuations in volume are more important for the long-term financial institutions than those more concerned with short-term credit. Commercial banks have depression problems; but if prudently managed, these institutions can weather business fluctuations quite well. On the other hand, investment banking is a proverbial "rags-to-riches-and-then-back-again" business.

The ways in which financial institutions contribute to or themselves influence business conditions are many. The chief ways are two: first, the volume of money supplied by the commercial banking system probably influences the level of spending; and, second, the amount of investment credit extended by financial institutions influences capital outlays and, through this channel, the general prosperity of the economy. The experts dispute the exact degree of these influences, but nobody denies them an important place in the economic scene.

CONCLUSION

The foregoing account has made evident the complexity of business fluctuations. But even though they are not fully understood, we cannot put off attempting a cure of them. Doctors often have to treat disorders they do not understand fully; medical treatment has to be in advance of medical science. The popular demands for "doing something about" business instability account for many of the monetary and governmental activities that will be considered in the next two chapters. But one injunction is worth bearing in mind: until the problem has been solved, the search for a better understanding of it should proceed.

Some feel that economic instability is our greatest economic problem. It may even be more than that. In the conflict between totalitarian systems and our system of economic freedom, the factor upon which the totalitarians depend more than any military weapon is our inability to avoid depressions. *Pravda* watches business conditions in the United States almost as closely as our own financial press. At any sign of weakness, its publishers chortle editorially. They hope we will collapse of internal weakness. Our problem is to avoid a serious depression. But we cannot solve the problem by exhortation; if a depression comes, it cannot be cured by optimistic statements from business leaders. "Prosperity is just around the corner," a mistake in overoptimism during the early 1930's, came to be the butt of cynics' jokes later on. But, as our review of proposed cures will indicate, an overuse of governmental powers to counter depressions also presents grave difficulties.

—ROLAND I. ROBINSON

QUESTIONS AND PROBLEMS

1. What are the economic characteristics of periods of prosperity? Of periods of depression?

2. Classify the period since 1925 into intervals of prosperity and intervals of depression. Omit such intervals as are not properly classifiable into either category.

3. List, with short explanations, the major purported causes of business instability.

4. Why should the production of durable goods fluctuate more than the production of nondurable goods?

5. It has been said that "inflations do not cure themselves; they grow cumulatively worse until they are intolerable." Explain.

6. The phrases "postwar inflation" and "postwar depression" are frequently heard, sometimes in the same discussion. How can war be charged with producing both of these evil effects?

7. Is the business cycle a true "cycle"?

8. The London Economist publishes a weekly review of business conditions in the United States. Is this flattering attention to our problems caused by idle curiosity, friendly interest, or something else? Why should English readers care one way or the other?

9. What is the relationship of interest rates to business conditions? Have there been any important exceptions to this usual relationship?

10. What are the two ways—one favorable and one unfavorable—in which financial institutions are affected by a rise in interest rates?

11. Why has concern about business instability led many, including some rather conservative persons, to accept larger governmental intervention into economic affairs?

12. Can faith cure depressions? Defend either a "yes" or a "no" answer.

BIBLIOGRAPHY

The literature of economic instability is large. For the serious reader, the selected bibliography appearing in the appendix to Readings in Business Cycle Theory, sponsored by the American Economic Association (Philadelphia: Blakiston, 1944), is perhaps the most comprehensive guide available. A simple and well-organized textbook of the subject is Business Cycles: Their Nature, Cause, and Control, by James A. Esty (New York: Prentice-Hall,

Inc., 1941). A somewhat more rigorous but penetrating review of business cycle theory is *Prosperity and Depression*, by Gottfried von Haberler (3d. ed.; Geneva: League of Nations, 1941). The third edition of this work is the most comprehensive, but it is not always available. Copies of earlier editions, particularly the second, can be used with profit. In a general survey of this subject, one of the very best simple accounts of the problem is chapter viii of *Money* by D. H. Robertson. This work, originally published in the Cambridge (England) Economic Handbook Series, is now available in an American edition published by Pitman, New York. Still another useful treatment in fairly short compass is the work by A. G. Hart, *Money, Debt, and Economic Activity* (New York: Prentice-Hall, Inc., 1948), Part III. The following are useful treatments of economic instability marked by objectivity and a high order of intellectual content:

Clark, J. M. *Strategic Factors in Business Cycles.* National Bureau of Economic Research in co-operation with the Committee on Recent Economic Changes, 1935.

Economic Staff of the Committee for Economic Development. *Jobs and Markets.* New York: McGraw-Hill Book Co., Inc., 1946. (Not a systematic treatment of business cycles but simply written and addressed to the problems of economic instability which prevailed in early postwar days.)

Wright, David McCord. *The Economics of Disturbance.* New York: Macmillan Co., 1947. (This is an excellent, rigorous, and original analysis.)

Chapter • 20

THE FEDERAL RESERVE SYSTEM

THE power of commercial banks to expand credit is a monetary power —the power to change the amount of money in the economy. The irresponsible exercise of this power could be very damaging to the economy. Generally the power is so important that sovereign governments reserve it for their own use or undertake to regulate its use closely. This has been done in the United States by our Constitution. The exercise of the power to regulate money is usually delegated to the central bank of a country, although in practice treasuries are often dominant forces in monetary policy. In the United States the Federal Reserve System acts as the country's central banking system. This chapter will be devoted to the Federal Reserve System and therefore to monetary regulation.

Although monetary regulation is the function of the Federal Reserve System, the System originated with the intention, rather, of curing weaknesses in the banking system which had been exposed by earlier events. From time to time, there had been financial panics: 1873, 1884, 1893, and 1907.

IMPERFECTIONS OF THE NATIONAL BANKING SYSTEM

A panic could take any one of several courses, but almost all of them involved these two features: (1) suspension of "specie payment" by *all* banks—that is, banks stopped paying out legal-tender cash; and (2) the closing of the doors of many banks for good. Panics were usually the signal for the beginning of what we now call a "depression"; earlier, such periods were often simply labeled "hard times." The only event at all like a panic in more recent years was the banking holiday in 1933, when all banks were closed briefly. Although panics were attributed to a wide variety of factors, they

537

were generally considered the result of banking weakness. When the public grew impatient with the distress entailed by panics, there arose a widespread demand for banking and monetary reform. Congress was prodded into passing the Aldrich-Vreeland Bill in 1908 by the panic of the preceding year. The last section of this bill, somewhat as a sop to critics, created a National Monetary Commission. This commission was instructed to study the financial and monetary system and to recommend changes. It labored for four years and employed the most eminent monetary scholars of the day. The experts published a long bookshelf of reports, which are still recognized as monumental documents in banking literature.

But the most important result of the labors of the Commission was that it led, indirectly, to the formation of the Federal Reserve System. The Federal Reserve Act, which was expected to cure the shortcomings of the banking system, was passed December 23, 1913. During the following year the various parts of the Federal Reserve System—the Federal Reserve Board and the Reserve banks—were organized and opened for business, and by the end of 1914 the System was an operating reality.

Inelastic Note Issue

The National Monetary Commission had concluded that panics were due to imperfections of the national banking system: the note issues of national banks were inelastic, and their reserves were scattered. The framers of the original Federal Reserve Act had modest intentions based on this rather simple diagnosis of the monetary problem. They intended to make the currency system flexible and to centralize bank reserves.

National-bank notes had been backed by a 100 per cent reserve of government bonds. This was intended to make them safe, and it did. But this requirement made the total volume inflexible. Since the supply of bonds was limited and since most of them were already used as note security, there was no margin with which to meet excess demands. Added supplies of notes to aid in seasonal expansion in the volume of business and to care for the long-run needs of a growing economy were not forthcoming. And restrictions on the supply of money retarded the volume of trade and tended to depress prices and profits.

The growth of deposit banking during the nineteenth century reduced the significance of note issue. The fixed limit on national-bank notes might have seemed no handicap. But as the volume of deposits and prices and retail trade increased, there was a greater demand for hand-to-hand money. National-bank notes failed to supply this need.

Decentralized Reserves

The other weakness, immobile bank reserves, was similar in nature. The decentralization or scattering of gold or lawful money reserves through the requirement that each national bank hold a portion of its reserve in its own vault introduced another form of inelasticity into the system. Some banks tended to hold only the minimum required cash reserves in their vaults and to deposit the remainder of required reserves, together with any excess reserves, with their city correspondents. When seasonal demands in an outlaying community led to increased need for currency, the local banker drew against his correspondent bank balance. When seasonal pressures were bunched at one time of the year, this put city banks under extra pressure. They often had to reduce their outstanding loans at this season to meet the demands for cash.

The ability of banks to lend was limited by the extent to which they could attract reserves to their institutions. Widespread withdrawal of specie by country banks led to reduction of funds in the banks of redeposit, with consequent reduction in their capacity to extend loans and create deposit credit. In periods of large seasonal demands in agricultural areas, and especially in periods of financial difficulty, the reserves of the system were drawn rapidly from financial centers. This movement precipitated more than one collapse of New York City banks and produced widespread distress.

A CENTRAL BANK CREATED

The framers of the Federal Reserve Act set out to cure these defects, but they did something more than they had intended: they created a central bank. That had been quite contrary to their intention; they had been at pains to organize a regional system with reserve banks in various areas. But they reckoned without the influence of money-market economics: the system they created was a central bank.

A central bank or a central banking system is primarily "central" to the operation of commercial banks. It uses this central position to influence the extent to which operating commercial banks extend credit and expand deposit liabilities. This influence is made effective in a variety of ways. In the first place, member banks are required to keep their reserves in the form of deposit balances in a Federal Reserve bank. The ratio of reserves to deposits influences the amount of credit that can be extended. As was shown in Chapter 18, a 20 per cent reserve requirement means that $1 of reserves in a bank will support $5 of deposit liabilities. But, if the requirement is increased to 25 per cent, then the $1 of reserves will support only $4 of deposit liabilities. In the beginning, the reserve percentages were established by law and could be changed only by new legislation. Since 1935, however, the required reserve percentages have been determined within specified statutory margins by the Federal Reserve Board.

But the Federal Reserve has a further channel of influence. It can manage the volume of its own deposit liabilities by expanding and contracting the amount of Federal Reserve bank credit. And the major use of reserve bank deposits is as the cash-asset reserve of member banks. The expansion and contraction of Federal Reserve bank credit is accomplished in two major ways: by direct lending to member banks and by the purchase or sale of United States government securities in the open market. The first method is usually called "rediscounting," and the second is called "open-market operations."

Federal Reserve credit operations have a "leverage" effect because they have a multiplied effect on the volume of member-bank deposits. Decreasing member-bank reserve requirements by $1 or adding $1 of reserve deposits by rediscounting or by open-market operations makes possible the expansion of member-bank deposits by $4 or $5. This is true because of the multiple expansion of deposits in banks.

This leverage effect made it possible for the Federal Reserve to cure the defects of the national banking system. The currency system was made flexible because the Federal Reserve banks could issue several dollars of Federal Reserve notes for each dollar of reserves held whenever there was a demand for added currency. And member-bank reserves were "mobilized" because the total could be increased by exactly the same method.

Every modern commercial banking system has at its core a central bank. And most of these central banks are concerned with the control of monetary expansion or contraction. Some central banks were established very early in the banking history of their respective countries. For example: the Swedish central bank, the Riksbank, was opened in 1656;[1] the Bank of England was organized in 1694; the

---

[1] It did not exercise full central banking powers until 1897.

Bank of France more than a century later, in 1800. Other central banks have been more recently organized: for example, the Bank of Canada, in 1935. Some central banks did not start business as central banks; they came to do a central banking business only by accident or slow evolution. In almost every case, the functions of central banks have changed greatly with the times. The degree of change has been particularly striking in recent decades.

Modern central banks perform many services for commercial banks in addition to their monetary responsibilities. For example, central banks use member-bank reserve balances as the basis for check-collection services; act as currency depots; examine and supervise member banks; collect, interpret, and dispense economic information relating to credit problems; and act as fiscal agents, custodians, and depositories for their treasuries and other governmental agencies. But monetary regulation continues to be their biggest job.

STRUCTURAL ORGANIZATION

The Federal Reserve was superimposed upon an operating banking system: its structure was, therefore, "built around" the banking system then in existence. But as time has passed, the Federal Reserve System has been modified to meet new needs. The System is ordinarily thought of as consisting of the Board of Governors, located in Washington, D.C., the twelve Reserve banks, and their branches. But the System may be thought of as including, in addition, those commercial banks which are members. Other bodies may also be considered parts of the System: the Open Market Committee, the Federal Advisory Council, the President's Conference, and other informal System groups. The structural parts of the Federal Reserve System are described in the following sections.

Membership

Each national bank located in the continental United States is required to be a member of the Federal Reserve bank of the district in which it is located. State banks are free to joint or not, as they wish; and most large state banks have joined. Smaller state banks, however, have generally not joined, and only about 1,900 of the 9,200 state banks in the United States belong to the Federal Reserve System. Thus, although only about one fifth of the total number, the state member banks have about two thirds of the deposits of all state banks. Since there are about 5,000 national banks, total member-

ship in the System of 6,900 banks is slightly less than half of the
commercial banks in the United States. The dollar resources of member banks are nearly seven eighths of all commercial banking resources in the country. Some state banks are not members of the
Federal Reserve System because they prefer to continue making non-
par "exchange" charges. Other banks are not members because they
do not have adequate capital. Still others do not want to meet the
higher reserve requirements of membership.

Board of Governors

The major policy-forming section of the Federal Reserve System
is the Board of Governors, formerly known as the Federal Reserve
Board. The Board consists of seven members, known as "governors,"
who serve fourteen-year terms so arranged that a vacancy occurs
every two years. The Board members are appointed by the President
of the United States with the advice and consent of the Senate. The
executive head of the Board is the member designated as "Chairman"
by the President. In practice, the Chairman serves "at the pleasure"
of the President. The Board is primarily a policy-forming agency.
It is located in Washington, D.C., and employs a staff of about five
hundred persons.

Federal Reserve Banks

The operating functions of the Federal Reserve System are pre-
formed by the Federal Reserve banks (often called the "Feds" by
bankers). There are twelve Federal Reserve banks located in the
leading cities of the country, as shown in Exhibit 62, along with the
twenty-four branches operated by Federal Reserve banks. These
branches are rather more frequent in those areas of the country
where distances are great and mailing time is long. The Boston Reserve Bank has no branches, and the great New York Reserve Bank
has only one. On the other hand, the Dallas, Atlanta, Kansas City,
and St. Louis Reserve banks each operate three branches; the San
Francisco Reserve Bank operates four. A clearly defined territory
is marked out for each Federal Reserve bank and branch. These
boundaries are shown in Exhibit 62.

Each Reserve bank has a board of nine directors: three Class A,
three Class B, and three Class C. Both Class A and Class B directors
are elected by the member banks of the district. Class A directors
must be bankers; Class B must be businessmen. In these elections

Exhibit 62

BOUNDARIES OF FEDERAL RESERVE DISTRICTS AND THEIR BRANCH TERRITORIES

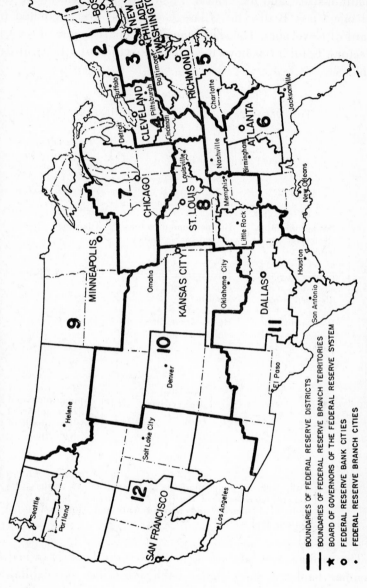

BOUNDARIES OF FEDERAL RESERVE DISTRICTS
BOUNDARIES OF FEDERAL RESERVE BRANCH TERRITORIES
BOARD OF GOVERNORS OF THE FEDERAL RESERVE SYSTEM
FEDERAL RESERVE BANK CITIES
FEDERAL RESERVE BRANCH CITIES

Source: Board of Governors of the Federal Reserve System.

the member banks are divided into three groups: the "large," the "medium-size," and the "small"; and each group elects one Class A and one Class B director. Class C directors are appointed by the Board of Governors. The chairman of the board is one of the Class C directors. Exhibit 63 shows the top organization of a Federal Reserve Bank.

Exhibit 63

TOP ORGANIZATION OF A FEDERAL RESERVE BANK

Six Directors Elected by member banks		Three Directors Appointed by Board of Governors
Class A (must be a banker)	Class B (must be a businessman)	Class C
Banker director: elected by big banks	Businessman director: elected by big banks	Chairman
Banker director: elected by middle-sized banks	Businessman director: elected by middle-sized banks	Deputy Chairman
Banker director: elected by small banks	Businessman director: elected by small banks	Director

President of Reserve bank

First Vice-President

} Appointment and salary approved by the Board of Governors

Other officers and employees of Reserve banks (under general supervision of the Board of Governors, but the individual salaries and appointments not subject to formal approval)

The capital stock of each Federal Reserve bank is owned by the member banks. Each member bank subscribes for capital in the Federal Reserve bank equal to 6 per cent of its own capital and surplus. So far, only half of this subscription (3 per cent of member-bank capital and surplus) has been called. Each member bank receives a cumulative dividend of 6 per cent on its Federal Reserve bank stock. Although profit is not a primary goal of the Federal Reserve System, sometimes large profits have been made. At one time, excess earnings were paid to the United States Treasury as a franchise tax, but that has been discontinued. Federal Reserve earnings during World War II were large, and a part of these earnings were paid to the Treasury by voluntarily putting a tax on Federal Reserve note issues.

The Federal Reserve banks are, to a very considerable extent, service agencies: they clear and collect checks, count and ship currency, effect the wire transfer of funds, issue and retire government securities, and act as agents for the Treasury and other governmental offices in a variety of ways. These service functions, although less well known to the public than the monetary operations, account for a large portion of the time and energy of the almost 20,000 employees and officers of the Federal Reserve banks and are described later in greater detail.

Open Market Committee

Decisions about the purchase and sale of United States government securities and related policies are made by the Open Market Committee, which represents both the Board of Governors and the Federal Reserve banks. The Committee consists of twelve members: the seven governors and five Reserve bank representatives that are selected by the twelve Reserve banks. Open-market purchases and sales are conducted by a manager, who in practice is an officer of the Federal Reserve Bank of New York. This bank, because of the importance of New York as a money market, is the leading Federal Reserve bank.

The Federal Advisory Council

The Federal Advisory Council consists of twelve members. One is appointed by each Federal Reserve bank. It advises the Board of Governors on economic conditions and banking problems throughout the country. It meets four times a year in Washington and recommends action both through private conferences and conferences with the Federal Reserve governors and through public statements. It is a purely advisory body.

Informal Parts of the System

The actual influence on public policy of any agency, such as the Federal Reserve System, cannot be measured purely by legal or formal organization. Other informal segments are often very important—sometimes more important than the legal advisory bodies.

The twelve presidents of the Federal Reserve banks have formed a Conference of Reserve Bank Presidents, a body which is not required or contemplated by law. This group has, nevertheless, considerable influence in forming Federal Reserve and general governmental financial policy. The chairmen of the boards of the twelve Reserve banks likewise have periodic conferences.

Interrelationships within the System

The maze of relationships already described provide an indication of the complexity of the Federal Reserve System. Later in this chapter, after the functional operation of the System has been described, the reasons for some of these structural arrangements will become more evident. Exhibit 64 shows in some detail the structural and the functional organization of the Federal Reserve.

As this diagram shows, the complexity of the Federal Reserve organization is partly accounted for by the number of things the System has to do in combining various credit controls and other more direct financial regulations. But some of the complexity also grows out of the efforts to divide the power of the System among its various parts. Centralized power makes for simpler organization diagrams, but many fear centralization of monetary and financial power. The price of decentralization is organizational complexity.

The Public-Private Blend in Organization

The Federal Reserve System is probably more a public than a private agency, but it has aspects of both. Ownership of the capital stock of individual Federal Reserve banks is vested in the private commercial banks of the country, who elect two thirds of the directors of the Federal Reserve banks.

The Board of Governors is clearly a public agency; the way in which its membership is determined shows this to be true. Furthermore, the major lines of monetary and credit authority stem from the Board of Governors. The Board of Governors constitutes a majority of the Open Market Committee. The Board establishes reserve requirements; and, although the individual Reserve banks conduct discount operations, their discount rates are reviewed, and in effect determined, by the Board of Governors. The general rules under which member banks conduct discount operations are established by regulations issued by the Board. The regulation of security loans, consumer credit, and interest rates on time deposits is vested in the Board of Governors. It might be said that the monetary authority of

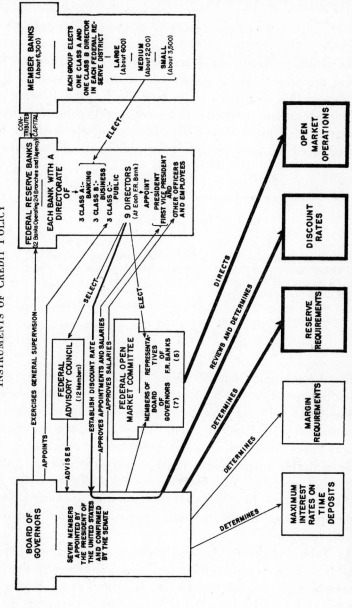

Source: *Banking Studies* (Washington: Federal Reserve Board, 1941), p. 376.

the System is centralized and that the policies for the conduct of service functions are more nearly private and decentralized.

PRINCIPLES OF FEDERAL RESERVE BANKING

The monetary functions and responsibilities of the Federal Reserve System are what make it a true central banking system. It is the purpose of this section to show how the Federal Reserve System banking operations are used both to serve and to control the monetary system in the United States. The framers of the Federal Reserve System cured the inelastic note issue and immobile reserves of the

TABLE 47

COMBINED STATEMENT OF TWELVE FEDERAL RESERVE BANKS,
APRIL 12, 1950
(Billions of Dollars)

Assets		Liabilities	
Gold certificates	23.0	Federal Reserve notes	22.9
Other cash	0.2	Member-bank reserve accounts	16.0
Discounts and advances	0.2	Other liabilities	4.3
United States government securities	17.6	Capital accounts	0.9
Other assets	3.1		
Totals	44.1		44.1

National Banking System by giving the Federal Reserve System the power to expand central-bank credit. Chapters 3 and 18 showed that commercial banks are able to increase the volume of deposits by extending credit. The "fractional"-reserve principle operates for central banks as well as for commercial banks. The Federal Reserve banks are able to provide a flexible currency and to regulate the volume of reserves available to member banks by virtue of their credit operations. In subsequent discussion of open-market and discount operations, it should constantly be recollected that these are "credit operations."

As Table 47 shows, Federal Reserve bank balance sheets are roughly similar to commercial bank statements except that Federal Reserve notes are a large part of the liabilities of the Reserve banks. Commercial banks in this country no longer have note liabilities. Other less important differences will emerge as we proceed.

The four elements which dominate the statement shown are: the gold-certificate reserves and "open-market" (United States government) securities on the asset side of the balance sheet, and Federal

Reserve notes and member bank reserve deposits on the liability side. This can be seen even more clearly in Exhibit 65.

The Significance of Reserves in Modern Banking

The role of banking reserves has already been discussed in Chapter 18. A prudent banker tries to keep ample cash reserves. And when the prudence of the banker is not strong enough, laws requiring

Exhibit 65

THE FEDERAL RESERVE BALANCE SHEET, APRIL 12, 1950

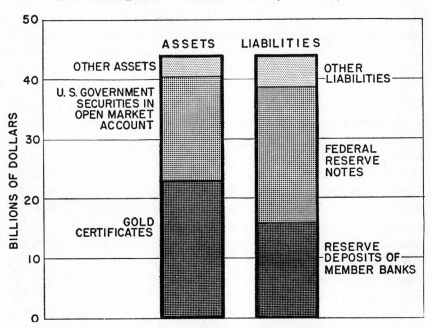

banks to keep minimum reserves have the same effect. But any banker who keeps excess reserves fails to earn as much as he could safely earn. Thus, banking reserves tend to fall between two limits: (1) they must be as high as prudence and the law require; and (2) they should not be higher, else profits will be missed.

Therefore, the amount of reserves available to banks is a direct limit on the amount of credit they can extend. The effectiveness of the Federal Reserve System depends on the operation of this principle. Since the System can control the amount of reserves available to banks, it can control, indirectly, the amount of credit extended by banks. And this controls the volume of bank deposits. But since deposits are, as shown before, money, Federal Reserve controls are monetary controls. It is sometimes said that the Federal Reserve is the regulator of money and of the money market.

The Federal Reserve System and the Money Market

If reserve controls, influencing the expansion and contraction of bank credit are "money-market" controls, what is the "money market"? A market is a place or an arrangement for buying and selling of goods or services. It is a place for, and a method of, getting buyer and seller together. Some markets can be dramatized by virtue of their physical characteristics. The New York Stock Exchange is a fine example; the Chicago Board of Trade, another. But other important, even though informal, markets exist. The "market" for farm land is just as much a market and perhaps just as important as the market for corporate securities.

Similarly, "money market" does not refer to a physical place, a building or group of buildings, but rather to all those agencies, in a given business and financial center, that bring borrowers and lenders together. It is through such agencies that the use of money is bought and sold. The term "money market" is generally restricted to dealings in short-term credit: in that market the commercial banks are the primary lenders; its customers, the primary borrowers. But there are other sectors of the money market in practice. The underwriters and dealers in securities use commercial bank credit; on the other hand, commercial banks, at least in recent years, are often buyers of long-term securities; and as a result the money market really includes almost all financial institutions—certainly a large portion of those considered in this book. In physical terms we think of Wall Street in New York City and of La Salle Street in Chicago as money markets; but two banks across the street from each other in a farming village also form a local "money market."

The price in the money market is interest. This interest price is usually quoted as a percentage rate. For example, if money is said to be worth 3 per cent, that means that for each $100 borrowed the price to the borrower is $3 a year. Money commands a high price when it is scarce; a low one when it is plentiful. In that respect, money is like anything else. And this quality of being plentiful or scarce best explains the relation of the Federal Reserve to the money market. When the Federal Reserve lowers the rate at which it will lend to member banks (rediscount rate), buys government bonds or acceptances in the open market, or lowers reserve requirements, it either makes more reserves available or makes them available to banks at a cheaper price. This makes banks more willing to lend, which is

the same thing as saying that "money" is more plentiful. The opposite
Federal Reserve action makes money scarcer.

Reserve Requirements of the Federal Reserve Banks

Federal Reserve banks must themselves maintain reserves. This
requirement is the method by which Congress keeps a general check
on Federal Reserve banks to make certain that they do not use their
discretionary powers irresponsibly. In this respect, the significance
of this reserve requirement is very much like the significance of
reserve requirements for operating commercial banks—reserve requirements are a form of public regulation. Until World War II,
Federal Reserve banks were required to maintain a 40 per cent gold
certificate reserve against Federal Reserve notes and a 35 per cent
reserve against deposits. In 1945 these two requirements were reduced
to a uniform 25 per cent gold-certificate reserve.

Since the Federal Reserve banks, as well as member banks, are
subject to a fractional reserve requirement, this means that ultimate
deposit expansion can be a double multiple of basic monetary reserves. The illustration of this is as follows: The first stage of the
double multiple expansion takes place at the Federal Reserve bank
level. The reserve bank 25 per cent reserve requirement means that
$1 of gold certificate reserves will support $4 of deposits, which are
mostly held by member banks as reserve balances. The extension
of $3 of reserve bank credit will accomplish this expansion. The
resulting Federal Reserve bank balance sheet elements would be:

Assets	Liabilities
$1 gold certificates + $3 reserve-bank credit }	= $4 deposits of member banks (reserve balances)

Member banks account for the second stage of this double multiple
expansion. If member-bank reserve requirements average roughly
20 per cent, $4 of reserve deposits at the reserve bank will support
$20 of member-bank deposits. The extension of $16 of member-bank
credit in the form of loans or investments will accomplish this expansion. The member-bank balance-sheet elements would be:

Assets	Liabilities
$4 reserve deposits at reserve bank + $16 member-bank credit }	= $20 member-bank deposits

The $4 member-bank reserve balance at the reserve bank is the
same $4 which is the asset of the member bank. Thus these two trans-

actions could be consolidated according to ordinary accounting rules, and the result would be:

Assets	*Liabilities*
$1 gold certificates $+$ $19 reserve-bank and member-bank credit	= $20 member-bank deposits

This illustration assumes, rather unrealistically, that both the reserve banks and the member banks extend credit to the full limit permitted by existing reserve requirements.

The Federal Reserve seldom has operated close to the legal limit. On the rare occasions that it has, there was not much doubt about the fact that the law would be changed if necessary. The requirements are long-term "out-of-bounds" stakes put up by Congress, not day-to-day, month-to-month, even year-to-year guides to credit policy.

Federal Reserve Notes

The close relationship between member-banks reserve balances and Federal Reserve note issues is not accidental; it is this feature which makes the currency system responsive to the needs of the country. Most persons provide themselves with currency by cashing checks at commercial banks. Banks, in turn, obtain currency, directly or indirectly, from the Federal Reserve banks. Neither the government nor a Federal Reserve bank ever "puts money into circulation" in the sense of taking the initiative in issuing money. Deposits are convertible into currency to the extent the public demands—and the agency for making this conversion possible is the Federal Reserve System. But the amount of currency in circulation is determined by public demand, not by governmental manipulation.

When a commercial bank orders currency from a Federal Reserve bank, its reserve balance deposited with the Reserve bank is decreased by the amount of the currency ordered. Thus, currency demands have a close and intimate effect on the amount of reserves available to banks. In recent years the policy of the Federal Reserve System has been to manage its credit so that these currency demands are met without pinching the reserve accounts of member banks.

FEDERAL RESERVE MONETARY CONTROLS

The framers of the original Federal Reserve Act might have flinched had they been accused of creating "monetary controls." They were trying to cure the defects of the past; they thought the Federal Reserve should service the banking system with adequate reserves, but not control the banking system. But the margin between "accommodating" the banking system with such added reserves it might need and "controlling" the banking system is a narrow one. The very act of judging just how great the need for bank reserves may be, is itself an act of control.

The simple principles of Federal Reserve control of member-bank credit expansion were outlined briefly in the opening of this chapter. Now that we have had an opportunity to learn more about central-banking principles and organization, it is time to look at the operation of the credit controls in a rather more discerning way.

Federal Reserve Rediscounting Operations

The principal method for extending Federal Reserve credit was originally expected to be by rediscounting. Member banks were expected to borrow at the Federal Reserve when in need of funds. These borrowings were rediscounts, because loans of a commercial nature which had already been discounted once by member banks were the basis for rediscounting at the Federal Reserve banks. The rate of interest charged by the Federal Reserve is the rediscount rate.

In the early days of the Federal Reserve, rediscounting operations were of central importance. The rediscount rate was the most vital single factor in the money market. Near the end of 1920, Federal Reserve rediscounts reached a peak of about $2¾ billions. This was more than one eighth of member-bank demand deposits.

The rediscounting channel for making Federal Reserve credit available has dwindled as the importance of open-market operations has grown. When the Federal Reserve System was originated, loans were the chief earning asset of commercial banks. It was only natural that banks should depend on rediscounting loans to secure added liquidity. But banks came to hold larger amounts of marketable securities, particularly governmental securities. Selling such securities was a much easier and more convenient way of getting added liquidity than rediscounting. And selling by commercial banks is, of course, the counterpart of open-market buying by the Federal Reserve System. Some banks still rediscount, but the practice is far less common now. Many banks pride themselves on never borrowing. While it would be wrong to dismiss or belittle rediscounting as a monetary service, and the rediscount rate as a monetary control, the importance of these factors is not great.

The way in which rediscounts are recorded is as follows: Assume that the member banks rediscount commercial paper with the Federal Reserve to obtain $1,000 added reserves: the skeleton bookkeeping entries are as follows:

Assets	Liabilities
Federal Reserve bank statement:	
(1) + Rediscounts......... $1,000	+ Reserve balances due member banks........ $1,000
Member-bank statement:	
(2) + Due from Federal Reserve bank........ $1,000	+ Borrowings from Federal Reserve bank......... $1,000

and with augmented reserve balances the bank can then proceed with credit expansion, as will be illustrated in connection with open-market operations. Pressure by the Federal Reserve to reduce discounts causes multiple contraction in a like fashion.

The effect of changing discount rates cannot be illustrated directly by skeleton entries similar to those used above, but can be observed indirectly. Low rediscount rates naturally encourage banks to borrow; a low rate is an implied invitation by the Federal Reserve authorities to borrow, and the funds can then be reloaned at a profit. High rates, on the other hand, are an implied discouragement; furthermore, there is less profit in relending high-cost funds. Most banks have long-standing arrangements with many of their borrowing customers. They do not like to change rates charged these customers with every shift in the credit winds. But if the banks can lend or renew loans only by rediscounting, and at a rate which makes loans unprofitable, the banks will naturally be more reluctant to make loans and more likely to reject the marginal applicants.

Federal Reserve Open-Market Operations

The original Federal Reserve Act permitted Federal Reserve banks to buy and sell United States government securities. The public debt was then small, and the importance of this power was overlooked. But, as already shown in the analysis of commercial-bank operations, the purchase of securities by a bank extends credit just as effectively as making a loan. The same is true of the Federal Reserve.

The first important use of open-market operation came in the early 1920's. By the time of the great depression in the early 1930's, open-market operations were the chief credit power of the Federal Reserve System. As will be shown in a later section, the effectiveness of open-market controls has been shackled by the public-debt responsibilities of the Federal Reserve. But whether used as a monetary control or as a public-debt management device, open-market operations continue to be of dominant importance.

When Federal Reserve banks purchase United States government securities from a bank or an individual investor, they pay for them with a check drawn on themselves—a kind of cashier's check. When these checks are returned to the Reserve banks, they are added to "member-bank reserve balances." The skeleton entries for a Federal Reserve bank purchase of $1,000 of United States government securities on the books of the Reserve bank are:

Assets	*Liabilities*

(3) + United States govern-
      ment securities..... $1,000
	+ Member-bank deposits
	   (reserve balances)..... $1,000

If the securities were sold to the Reserve bank by a commercial bank, the commercial bank statement would be changed as follows:

(4) − United States govern-
      ment securities..... $1,000
   + Due from Federal Re-
      serve bank......... $1,000

If the securities were sold to the Reserve bank by an individual who deposited the check he receives for them in his bank, the skeleton entries on the books of the commercial bank would be:

| (5) + Due from Federal Re-
      serve bank......... $1,000 | + Deposits.............. $1,000 |

Federal Reserve Control of Member-Bank Reserves

When the Federal Reserve System was inaugurated, the classification of commercial banks into central reserve city, reserve city, and country banks under the National Bank Act was retained. But a distinction was made between time and demand deposits. Reserves required against each type of deposit differ in size, and the minimum or "legal" requirement must be held as a balance in the regional Federal Reserve bank. Cash in the vault of a member bank and balances on deposits in other commercial banks were no longer counted as legal reserves. In short, reserves were all "deposited" in the central bank.

As noted above, the Federal Reserve can control member-bank credit by varying the percentage rates of reserve requirements as well as by controlling the amount of reserves available. The circumstances that led to the statutory introduction of this device were rather special. Excess reserves in commercial banks have usually been considered abnormal. But in the early and mid-1930's, a combination of very low short-term interest rates and a gold inflow created a large volume of such excess reserves. It was feared that these excess reserves would ultimately lead to inflation. Increasing the cost of rediscounting by higher rediscount rates could not mop up these excess reserves because banks were not in debt to the Federal Reserve; neither could open-market sales absorb the excess because the amount of securities owned by the Federal Reserve was less than the amount of excess reserves. But increasing reserve requirements could do the job. And so the power to double reserve requirements was added by the Banking Act of 1935. Table 48 shows the permissible range of member-bank reserve requirements under that act.

TABLE 48

MEMBER-BANK RESERVE REQUIREMENTS (IN PER CENT)

	Statutory Minimum	Maximum (Double)
Net Demand Deposits		
Central reserve city banks (New York and Chicago)....................................	13	26
Reserve city banks (about 60 other cities)...	10	20
"Country" banks (all other locations)......	7	14
Time deposits (all banks)...................	3	6

Changes in reserve requirements have been made more frequently as time has passed, often in conjunction with open-market operations. The chronology of Federal Reserve changes in reserve requirements is shown in Table 49.

When the Federal Reserve Board makes a change in reserve requirements, that change by itself does not produce any discernible changes in banking statements. But the action may force material changes to be made. If reserve requirements were to be lowered when there is little demand for loans and few opportunities for investments by banks, the only change would be that banks would have more "excess" reserves.

Likewise, an increase in reserve requirements, when all banks have "excess" reserves, ample to cover the new and larger requirements, might have no visible effect. But an increase in requirements that caught some banks short, i.e., found them with reserve deficiencies, would necessitate credit contraction. For example, if an increase in reserve requirements were made which created a deficiency of $5,000, the member bank would be forced to liquidate assets of some form and build up its balance in the reserve bank—or effect a reduction in its deposits. Under present conditions, the normal action

TABLE 49

Member-Bank Reserve Requirements
(Percentage of Deposits)

Effective Date of Change	Net Demand Deposits*			Time Deposits (All Member Banks)
	Central Reserve City Banks	Reserve City Banks	Country Banks	
1917—June 21............	13	10	7	3
1936—Aug. 16............	19½	15	10½	4½
1937—Mar. 1............	22¾	17½	12¼	5¼
May 1............	26	20	14	6
1938—Apr. 16..........	22¾	17½	12	5
1941—Nov. 1..........	26	20	14	6
1942—Aug. 20..........	24	....	....	....
Sept. 14..........	22	....	....	....
Oct. 3..........	20	....	....	....
1948—Feb. 27..........	22	....	....	....
June 11..........	24	....	....	....
Sept. 16..........	....	....	16	7½†
Sept. 24..........	26	22	....	7½‡
1949—May 1..........	....	....	15	7†
May 5..........	24	21	....	7‡
June 30..........	....	20	....	6‡
July 1..........	....	....	14	6†
Aug. 1..........	....	....	13	....
Aug. 11..........	23½	19½	....	5‡
Aug. 16..........	....	....	12	5†
Aug. 18..........	23	19	....	....
Aug. 25..........	22½	18½	....	....
Sept. 1..........	22	18	....	....
In effect May 1, 1950.....	22	18	12	5

* Demand deposits subject to reserve requirements, which, beginning August 23, 1935, have been total demand deposits minus cash items in process of collection and demand balances due from domestic banks (also minus war loan and Series E bond accounts during the period April 13, 1943—June 30, 1947).
† Requirement became effective at country banks.
‡ Requirement became effective at central reserve and reserve city banks.
Source: *Federal Reserve Bulletin*, May, 1950, p. 533.

is for the member to sell [2] government securities to the reserve bank and have the sale price credited to its reserve balance.

Assets

(6) − United States government securities..... $5,000
+ Due from Federal Re-
serve bank......... 5,000

[2] Strictly speaking, the Federal Reserve only buys from and sells to "recognized" dealers in government securities, and these dealers in turn buy from and sell to member banks and others. The direct form of statement used here, however, is accurate for all analytical purposes—and it is simpler!

Application of Credit Controls

The credit controls may be used by the Federal Reserve in several ways, the leading ones being:

1. To change the volume of reserves available to banks
2. To offset other factors which affect bank reserves, such as gold inflows or currency demands, so as to keep bank reserves from being changed
3. For "outside" purposes, such as supporting the prices of federal government securities

The first of these methods was illustrated a number of times during the 1920's when Federal Reserve action was taken primarily for this purpose. Indeed, commodity prices were so stable during that decade that many came to believe that the riddle of "boom and bust" had been solved. During the early 1930's the Federal Reserve also used the credit controls to increase the reserves available to banks, but also in part to offset the currency drain produced by the runs on banks and the currency hoarding. Thus, that period illustrated both uses. But during the middle and later 1930's, much Federal Reserve action was for the purpose of offsetting the gold inflows—to keep them from increasing bank reserves dangerously. The increases in reserve requirements were for this end. And during World War II, contrary to popular impression, the major credit action of the Federal Reserve was to offset the increased demand for currency. It was after the war that the third of the purposes enumerated was best illustrated. In late 1947 and during most of 1948, the Federal Reserve supported the prices of long-term Treasury bonds.

These several episodes in Federal Reserve policy can be read from Exhibit 66. A careful reading of this chart demonstrates several points. It shows, for example, that increases in gold stock and Federal Reserve credit tend to *increase* member-bank reserves. Increases in currency in circulation tend to *decrease* member-bank reserves. This chart also shows that changes in gold holdings have been a leading influence on the reserves available to banks.

FEDERAL RESERVE DIRECT CREDIT CONTROLS

In addition to the general monetary controls exercised by the Federal Reserve System, the System has been made responsible for the operation of a number of direct credit controls. The philosophy underlying each of these regulatory systems varies. Rather than generalize, it is safer to explain each one in turn.

Exhibit 66

MEMBER-BANK RESERVES AND RELATED ITEMS

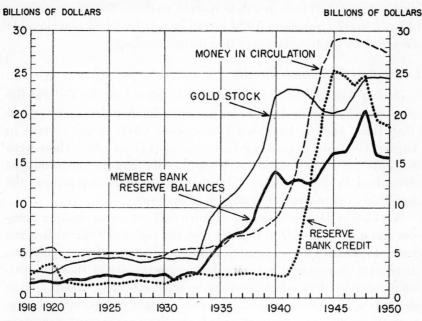

Source: *Federal Reserve Bulletin* and annual reports.

Stock-Market Margin Control

The Federal Reserve is empowered to control margin requirements on security loans. The control may be used to cut down the borrowing power of persons seeking credit toward purchasing or carrying securities (stocks or bonds). As explained in the discussion of the organized stock exchanges, purchasers of stock may pay the broker only a portion of the purchase price of a stock and ask the broker to advance the balance. The broker may obtain the funds needed by borrowing from a commercial bank. This loan is secured by the purchased stock. In the 1920's a stock could sometimes be acquired with a cash margin as low as 10 to 20 per cent.

The Securities and Exchange Act of 1934 gave Federal Reserve bank authorities the power to determine the maximum loan value (stated as a percentage of market price) at the time the loan is granted. As the margin requirement rises, the loan value decreases and the amount of credit flowing into the exchanges tends to be reduced or stablized. This regulation applies to the loans of banks to customers as well as to direct broker loans.

The philosophy of stock-market regulation goes back to the belief that violent fluctuations in the stock market disturb business conditions. Margin trading made for violent fluctuations in credit and stock prices; therefore, regulate margin trading. The great collapse of stock-market prices in 1929 certainly was hastened and possibly deepened by the liquidation of thin margin trading.

Control of Consumer Credit

During World War II and for a while thereafter, the Federal Reserve exercised control over consumer credit. Regulation W was in effect from August, 1941, until November, 1947. It was revived in August, 1948, and expired again at the end of June, 1949. There were demands for its re-enactment as soon as the Korean situation was recognized in mid-1950, as more than mere police action; and the regulation was re-enacted in the fall of the year.

World War II Regulation W required all consumer lending agencies and credit vendors to register with the regional Federal Reserve banks, to obtain a license, and to conform to details of the regulation. In general, it required a larger down-payment and a shorter maximum maturity than was customary on such contracts. Retail charge accounts were also regulated. The result was a reduction in the aggregate amount of credit extended for the purchase of consumer goods. But a more fundamental economic result was the reduction of the demand for goods at a time when they could not be produced in volume, when prices were tending to rise, and when citizens needed to refrain from competing with the military services for essential manpower and materials.

The philosophy of consumer credit regulation has already been considered in Chapter 6.

Control of Interest Paid on Time Deposits

Since 1933 the payment of interest on demand deposits has been forbidden by law, and the interest paid on time deposits has been subject to the administrative control of the Federal Reserve. This regulation is a relatively inactive one; there has been no change in it since January 1, 1936. The 2½ per cent maximum rate of savings deposits, for example, is higher than almost any commercial bank pays. The regulation, therefore, is relatively ineffective at the present time.

The philosophy underlying this regulation is this: If member banks, competing among themselves for the acquisition of deposits, paid a high rate for them, they would be forced to seek a high investment return. High yields and speculative risks go hand in hand; and so, by making it unnecessary to pay high rates, the pressure for risky investment is relieved.

FEDERAL RESERVE FINANCIAL SERVICES

Although the Federal Reserve System is better known to the public for its monetary and regulatory functions, a large part of the System's personnel and energies are devoted to providing the various financial services previously mentioned.

Clearing and Collecting Checks

When a check from some faraway place is cashed or deposited in a bank, the collection of the amount called for in the check requires rather more trouble than the casual customer might think. The direct collection of each out-of-town check would be tedious and costly. Traditionally this was done by few city banks who specialized in this business. They were compensated by the balances that their country correspondents kept with them. When the Federal Reserve System was initiated, it required member banks to keep their legal reserves with the Federal Reserve banks. These balances could be used to settle the flow of clearings and collections and, as a result, the Federal Reserve was well situated to assume this function. Thus, Federal Reserve banks offer collection services to their members and even to nonmember banks under limited circumstances.

While the Federal Reserve has not completely displaced the city correspondent in the collection of out-of-town checks, it has assumed a leading role. The major portion of such collections are now routed through Federal Reserve channels. To perform this service, the Reserve banks maintain large staffs of specialists and operate these transit departments day and night. They use air mail extensively and have developed other devices for the most expeditious handling of checks. A large proportion of bank checks now have on their face a routing symbol which is an instant indication of the location of the drawee bank and how items on it should be collected. For an example of such a routine symbol, see Exhibit 67, which explains the meaning of the symbol $\frac{70-113}{710}$, which appears on the face of the checks of an Evanston, Illinois, bank.

Because the Federal Reserve banks use each other for the collection of checks that must be sent from one district to another, they have amounts "due to" and "due from" each other to be settled. This is done by an interdistrict settlement fund, which operates according to the clearinghouse principle described in Chapter 4. In the interdistrict settlement fund, telegrams take the place of messengers and face-to-face calculation.

Once upon a time, a great many banks made an "exchange" deduction for checks drawn on them and collected by mail. When these deductions were charged back to the persons cashing or depositing

Exhibit 67

CHECK-ROUTING SYMBOLS

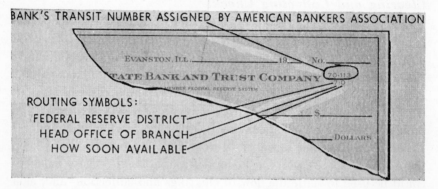

such checks, these check payments were worth less than "par." During those days, mail-order catalogues sometimes asked: "Please remit with postal money orders or drafts on a Chicago bank. If you pay with your own check, please add 15 cents to cover exchange charges." This practice has almost disappeared. Most banks now pay at "par," and checks may be freely sent almost any place. The only limitation to Federal Reserve collection services is that they cannot handle items drawn on the few remaining nonpar remitting banks.

Currency Supply and Redemption

The notes of Federal Reserve banks now furnish about 85 per cent of the currency in circulation. Thus, Federal Reserve banks are directly the most important currency source. But since the Reserve banks are also the agent of the Treasury in the issue and redemption of all other forms of currency, such as silver certificates, greenbacks, and coins, virtually all of the currency business of the country is handled through the Reserve banks.

The Reserve banks maintain elaborate equipment for this service. They have complicated coin-counting machinery and experts to count bills and examine for counterfeits. A visitor to a Reserve bank may see pennies, nickles, dimes, and quarters being handled by scoop shovels and deft-fingered clerks counting thousand dollar bills. Banks located near a Reserve bank can order and obtain shipments of currency in a matter of an hour or two; banks located farther away may have to wait for a day or two. But in times gone by, currency has been flown in chartered planes or delivered by speeding armored trucks to meet emergency needs—often in a matter of hours.

When a member bank orders currency shipped to it, payment is made by a deduction from the reserve balance of the bank; when the bank returns or redeems currency, the proceeds are added to the bank's reserve account. This illustrates mechanically what was explained in an earlier section: the Federal Reserve note and the reserve-deposit liabilities of Reserve banks are interchangeable.

Issuing and Retiring Federal Government Securities

The Federal Reserve banks are the agents of the United States Treasury in virtually all public-debt transactions. When the Treasury sells securities, the purchasers send their orders to the nearest Federal Reserve bank. The securities are issued by the Reserve banks. When the coupons on outstanding Treasury obligations are presented to a bank for payment, the coupons are sent by the bank to the nearest Reserve bank. When the holder of a large denomination Treasury bond wants it replaced by several smaller denomination bonds, the nearest Federal Reserve bank will do this quickly. Savings-bond sales and redemptions channel through the Reserve banks. The great size of the public debt has made this function a mechanically large one. Reserve banks keep marketable federal government bonds in their vaults for member banks, and they will keep savings bonds in their vaults for individuals.

Fiscal Agency for Other Government Bureaus

The Federal Reserve banks act as fiscal agents, depositories, and custodians for the Reconstruction Finance Corporation, the Commodity Credit Corporation, and other government agencies. They pay out the proceeds of loans made by these agencies; hold the notes, mortgages, or other documents that are pledged as collateral with them; and collect debts owed them.

In many ways these services performed by the Reserve banks for governmental agencies are similar to the services performed by the trust departments of commercial banks for their corporate customers.

Wire Transfers of Funds

Sometimes legal or other reasons call for prompt payment of funds at remote points. A businessman in New York may need to make a payment in San Francisco even faster than is possible by air mail. Through a wire transfer, the banker of the New York businessman can arrange to make this prompt payment. The Federal Reserve bank only charges the actual cost of sending the coded telegram. A reduction of the New York bank's reserve balance, an increase in the reserve balance of the San Francisco payee's bank, and a transfer of funds in the Federal Reserve interdistrict settlement fund are all that is needed to complete this transaction.

Bank Examination and Supervision

The Federal Reserve System exercises regulatory authority over bank holding companies and grants trust powers to national banks. State member banks are examined by Federal Reserve examiners. The application of the Clayton Act to banks—an effort to avoid monopoly due to interlocking directorates—is in the hands of the Federal Reserve System.

THE EFFECTIVENESS OF MONETARY CONTROL

Many of the original goals for the Federal Reserve have been achieved. The currency system is now both flexible and responsive to public needs. Check collection and clearing is rapid and economical. The financial structure is, on the whole, safe and liquid. Many of these goals were not easy to attain, but they have been so well achieved that their importance is sometimes forgotten.

However, many of the goals which were in the minds of the originators of the Federal Reserve have not yet been reached. Economic instability, for example, is still an unsolved problem. The creation of the Federal Reserve may have failed to cure economic instability because it is due to nonmonetary factors. But some of the failure may have been due to the fact that the monetary controls have been timidly used or have been used for purposes not envisaged by those who organized the System.

Instruments of Credit Regulation Are Drastic

The instruments of credit regulation are very drastic. They are, if used with vigor, exceptionally effective on the side of curbing credit expansion. But the Federal Reserve System has not always applied the instruments during periods when credit contraction would seem to have been indicated. Why has there been this conflict between logic and practice?

The instruments of credit regulation exercised by the Federal Reserve System are so powerful that there is often hesitancy to use them. Contraction of credit may be induced, but the secondary effects of it might be very damaging. Credit contraction may mean that legitimate bank borrowers can no longer get the loans from the banking system that they had been expecting. The effects of credit regulation on interest rates may be considerable; the resulting fluctuations in prices of securities may be very unsettling to the financial market as a whole.

In other words, the problem confronting credit authorities is often not the lack of powers in any absolute sense but rather the inability to use existing powers with sufficient delicacy and precision.

A Large Public Debt Inhibits Credit Regulation

Commercial banks "monetize" either public or private debts—that is, expand deposits by making loans or buying securities. There are, however, definite limits as to how far commercial banks are disposed to go in monetizing private debts. In the first place, all such obligations have some degree of credit risk (the debtor may not repay as he contracts to do), and so the amount a bank can afford to assume of this risk is limited. In the second place, even if the commercial banks do not themselves show adequate restraint in the monetizing of private debts, the Federal Reserve can use its credit influences to limit bank reserves and thereby slow down the process of monetization.

But Federal Reserve action is not anywhere near as effective in dealing with public-debt obligations. These obligations involve no credit risk, and so the normal restraints on private purchase are not so strong. And, furthermore, the Federal Reserve is not in a strong political position to thwart Treasury borrowing from the banks. The universal opinion, based on experience, is that the Treasury is closer to the governmental administration than the Federal Reserve is,[3] and

---

[3] In the period since the foregoing paragraphs were written, a sharp difference of opinion between the Treasury and the Federal Reserve has broken into the open. It was evident in several episodes of Treasury financing. Finally the President of the United States intervened in this dispute. The President took the Treasury side, as expected. The present somewhat uneasy settlement involving a new nonmarketable Treasury 2¾ bond (March 9, 1951) and a somewhat freer bond market may be only a temporizing compromise in a long-continued period of friction.

that central bankers who try to challenge the leading role of the Treasury usually end up out of office. And, quite apart from the matter of conflict, a large public debt puts special obstacles in the path of the Federal Reserve System. The Treasury Department has the direct responsibility for public-debt management. This is a difficult task, and the Treasury Department naturally would not welcome a policy which makes this task even harder. If the Federal Reserve System follows a "hard-money" policy—that is, tightens reserves— then interest rates are bound to rise. But high interest rates can increase the cost of carrying the public debt considerably. They also make refunding or maturing obligations more difficult. At the present time, interest on the public debt is over $5 billion a year, and an increase of interest rate of 1 per cent would increase this cost by $2.5 billion. The Federal Reserve obviously cannot help but be cautious in the use of its credit authority when it considers the direct effect that its monetary policy will have on the cost to the Treasury of carrying the public debt. This dilemma may be the most serious unsolved problem now facing the Federal Reserve System.

—Roland I. Robinson

QUESTIONS AND PROBLEMS

1. What was the "simple diagnosis" of monetary problems upon which the original Federal Reserve System was based?
2. What were the defects of the national banking system which the Federal Reserve System was expected to cure (and did cure)?
3. There are twelve Federal Reserve banks; yet they are called a "central banking system." What characteristics justify treating them as "central" banks?
4. Draw a rough organization chart of the Federal Reserve System.
5. Enumerate the factors in Federal Reserve organization which tend to make it a private agency and those which make it a public agency.
6. By what process does the Federal Reserve provide a flexible currency? How does it make bank reserves flexible?
7. Show how the limitation of bank reserves limits the amount that credit banks can extend.
8. Why are bank-reserve controls often called "money-market" controls?
9. What is the leading price in the money market? What makes this price high or low?
10. Do "Federal Reserve" reserve requirements have the same significance as "member-bank" reserve requirements? Explain.
11. What are the two leading ways in which Federal Reserve banks extend credit? Why is one of these ways more "passive" than the other?

12. Show the skeleton entries for the sale of $1,000 of United States government securities by the Federal Reserve to a commercial bank for both the Federal Reserve System and the commercial bank.
13. "The Federal Reserve monetary controls are all related in one way or another to the fact that our banking system operates with fractional reserves." Explain.
14. The nonmonetary controls are sometimes labeled "direct" controls. Why? (Clue: Price control is a direct control.)

BIBLIOGRAPHY

By far the best simple account of the Federal Reserve System is the one published by the System itself: *The Federal Reserve System: Its Purposes and Functions*. This was completely revised in 1947 by E. A. Goldenweiser, the distinguished head of Federal Reserve research work for many years. Goldenweiser's study of *Monetary Management* for the Committee for Economic Development (New York: McGraw-Hill Book Company, Inc., 1949) is a somewhat more advanced but excellent critical treatment of the policy problems of the recent past. Kemmerer's *The ABC of the Federal Reserve System* is a standard treatment of the subject. The current, or twelfth edition (New York: Harper & Bros., 1950), was revised by his son Donald L. Kemmerer. Written from the outside, it takes a somewhat more critical view of the System and its performance. For a view more reflective of the money-market attitude toward the Federal Reserve System, E. Sherman Adams' *Monetary Management* (New York: Ronald Press Co., 1950) is both readable and authoritative. Mr. Adams was an officer of a New York money-market bank for several years. G. L. Bach's *Study of Federal Reserve Policy-Making*, an outgrowth of the Hoover Commission study of the federal government (New York: Knopf, 1950), is of rather more interest to the political scientist than to the economist; it is, nevertheless, a very readable account of the problems of framing public monetary policy. Study No. 8 in the Postwar Economic Studies published by the Federal Reserve System, *Federal Reserve Policy*, contains a number of useful essays by leading economists within the System.

For current discussion of monetary policy, the *Federal Reserve Bulletin*, published by the Board of Governors, and the monthly reviews of business and credit published by the various Federal Reserve banks are good sources. The National City Bank Letter on *Economic Conditions and Government Finance* frequently publishes excellent critical reviews of Federal Reserve policy. The hearings before, and the reports of the so-called Douglas Committee of, the Eighty-first Congress furnish a large, if undigested, body of opinion and data with respect to the current Federal Reserve dilemma. This committee also circulated a questionnaire among bankers and economists and published a summary of the replies. Although diffuse, these replies are valuable source material with respect to the state of prevailing "expert" opinion.

Chapter 21

FINANCIAL ASPECTS OF GOVERNMENT

GOVERNMENT has been mentioned frequently throughout this book—a reflection of the fact that government is an element of steadily growing significance in our economic and financial life. There are dozens of ways in which this may be observed. Even in peacetime, government—whether federal, state, or local—is one of the most important buyers of goods and employers of persons; government expenditures are to be observed at almost every turn. Government collects taxes from almost every pay check. Government is a vast debtor; it owes money to millions of its citizens and to almost all financial institutions. But, at the same time, government is an important lender and banker. Government intervenes as a kind of guardian or policeman in the financial markets. But, most notable of all, government now plays a central role in determining the level of economic activity and the size of the national income.

These subjects are too diverse to lend themselves readily to orderly treatment. This chapter, therefore, will follow a pattern slightly different from that which has prevailed in earlier chapters. The purpose of this chapter will be twofold: (1) While several governmental aspects of finance have already been discussed, the list is not yet complete; and so the presentation of a more systematic account of governmental financial influences is the first aim. (2) Because the incidental comments on governmental finance made so far have not been adequate to reveal a general pattern of governmental financial policy, such policy will now be reviewed in a more concentrated way to show its influence on over-all economic conditions.

One great area of government financial activity, the operation and regulation of our money system, has already been amply treated, and no further comment is necessary. The following additional government financial aspects are considered in this chapter:

Government expenditures
Government revenues
Government debt and borrowing
Government as a lender
Government as a financial policeman
Government as a fighter of inflations and depressions

These subjects are, to a large extent, interrelated; for example, government expenditures (first category) may be used to fight a depression (sixth classification listed). The six-fold division, therefore, is only to help organize our analysis; it is not a perfect compartmentalization of the subject.

One note of explanation: At many stages in this chapter it may appear as if the importance of the federal government is overemphasized, and state and local government may seem neglected. Such emphasis is partly intentional. Federal government financial policy is not only more important but also more complex than local government financial policy.

GOVERNMENT EXPENDITURES

Expenditures of government represent the outlay decided on through the processes of a political democracy. Appropriations are made by the legislative branch of the government; the actual spending is done by the executive branch. The purposes of expenditures are often explainable only in terms of the way in which the legislative process works—or the way in which executive departments of the government operate. The formal titles used in the budgets and appropriation bills are not fully meaningful. The proposed budgetary outlays of the federal government for the fiscal year 1951 are shown in Table 50.

It must be recognized that there is a certain amount of inaccuracy in any sort of classification of governmental expenditures. For example: the national defense expenditures include amounts for dredging rivers and harbors—projects that may be related to national defense in a general sort of way but which are often "porkbarrel" projects. It should be recognized that "welfare" expenditures include some outlays which are hardly for welfare purposes, as the word is commonly understood—items such as the administrative expenses of some government bureaus, which are to a large extent, but not wholly, devoted to welfare activities. Governmental accounting is, therefore, often less precise than private accounting.

War: Its Direct Costs and Its Aftercosts

By all odds, war causes the greatest volume of government expenditures. In peacetime, we maintain costly departments of national defense—war, navy, and air. In wartime, government expenditures grow vastly, not only for the military services but in many ways—for a merchant marine, for raw materials, for public health, and the like. The great peaks in governmental expenditures are always easily identifiable as the result of war.

TABLE 50

FEDERAL CASH PAYMENTS TO THE PUBLIC

From Proposed Federal Budget for Fiscal Year 1951
(Millions of Dollars)

National defense...............................	$13,798
International affairs............................	4,934
Veterans' benefits.............................	7,051
Social welfare................................	5,061
Housing and education.........................	1,668
Agriculture...................................	2,193
National resources............................	2,223
Transportation................................	1,684
Finance, commerce, and industry................	97
Labor..	1,810
General government costs......................	1,098
Interest on public debt........................	4,057*
Other..	110
Total....................................	$45,784

* This does not include accrued interest on savings bonds. With allowance for this, the interest on public debt would be nearer $5 billion.

Not only is war the direct cause of a large share of federal government outlays, but the aftermath of war is expensive. Pensions, bonuses, and benefits for the veterans of wars are important costs. The aftermath of war is felt in government expenditures in still other ways. Aid to our allies in war did not end with hostilities in either World War I or World War II. The cost of the later aid may be charged to war, however. International outlays are often justified as helping to reduce or minimize the chances of future wars or to increase our chances of winning those we must fight.

Welfare Expenditures

Welfare expenditures include many kinds of outlays. One expenditure of very long tradition, and also of considerable recent importance, is that for pensions and assistance to veterans of our armed forces. Some of these expenditures are found in national defense outlays, but others are considered "welfare." But the greater portion of welfare expenditures is accounted for by three special kinds of outlays: (1) expenditures of the federal government to ameliorate the effects of depression (WPA type of outlay) or to prevent depression (the public-works type); (2) social security outlays; and (3) special agricultural aid.

Depressions have proved to be costly to government. During depressions, government revenues decline because income drops. Government costs, however, may not decline. There is a growing public belief that government should purposely increase its outlays greatly during periods of depression to compensate for the shrinkage in private spending. Government expenditures for minimum relief and welfare are not so controversial; it is the advisability of purposely larger government outlays of a "compensatory" nature that arouses so much difference of opinion. It is widely believed, for example, that "public works" should be undertaken during periods of depression. Public works include construction projects such as school buildings, roads, dams, and other capital-type outlays which are within the sphere of governmental activity. Depression means that people are idle and unemployed. It is argued that some of the social waste of depression can be recovered by concentrating public works in periods of idleness and unemployment. Even projects of dubious economic merit are better than doing nothing if they create something of value—psychologically and aesthetically, if not economically. They help to keep depressions from becoming progressively worse, and tend to preserve morale. More will be said about this subject later in this chapter.

In recent years the *social security* functions of both the federal and state governments have become one of their largest and most expensive activities. We now have a system of unemployment insurance, programs of old-age assistance, and aid for the dependent. Many of the economic hazards which were formerly the burden of the individual—unemployment, old age, and extreme poverty—have been "insured away" through governmental plans. Various programs of public health are similar in nature.

Social security finance is related to the fight of government on depression. While the purpose and effect of social security is not limited to depressions, these social security accounts tend to pay out more than they receive during depressions, and to collect more than they pay out during good times. Thus, this is one kind of compensatory spending.

The background of governmental *"welfare" expenditures for agri-*

culture is an involved one. The federal government went to the economic rescue of agriculture in the otherwise properous 1920's when
programs for agricultural aid were started. At that time, money was
appropriated for purchasing agricultural surpluses. The kind of policies pursued by the federal government to aid agriculture has changed,
but the purpose remains constant—keeping the farmer happy and
prosperous.

The conflicting characteristics of alternative proposals for supporting agricultural income illustrate one of the subtle problems of measuring the "cost" of governmental operations. Some of the proposed
devices would raise the price (or support the price) of agricultural
products on the open market. The cost to the public would not be fully
reflected in the direct government costs; it would also include the
higher grocery-store prices. Other proposals for support of agricultural income have involved letting agricultural prices find their market level and then paying direct subsidies to those farmers who
co-operated with the government by appropriate programs of crop
limitation. This sort of scheme might cost the government more in
direct outlays than the first plan. But it might cost the public less in
total than the first plan. How is "cost" to be measured?

Interest on the Public Debt

In a later section we shall deal with public debt. It will be pointed
out there that, mainly because of war, we now have a huge public
debt. The interest on it accrues at the rate of about $5 billion a year.
At present budgetary levels, this represents about 15 per cent of the
total expenditures of the federal government. As a dollar figure, this
is a new high; as a percentage of the federal budget, it is not far out
of line with past experience. The cost of public debt service (interest)
exceeded this 15 per cent level after the War of 1812; after the Civil
War; and after World War I. But interest rates were then much
higher.

Regular Government Departments

Aside from the "special-purpose" functions of government already
considered, there is the regular recurring cost of governmental administration. These figures encompass expenditures for the activities
of the State Department; the administration of Treasury Department,
including the promotion and sale of savings bonds; the national re-
source conservation work of the Interior Department; and the many
activities of the Department of Commerce, such as taking the census.

How Extensive Should Government Services and Functions Be?

Many public services have come to be performed primarily by government: government builds roads and allows them to be used freely; government operates the postal services; government provides educational facilities at no cost to the user or for tuition fees far below full operating costs; government provides parks and other recreational facilities. These services, to the extent that the charges for them do not cover costs, represent community or socialized consumption.

In some cases, these expenditures are supported because it is felt that they are socially desirable. Education is a prime example of such an outlay. The philosophy of free public education is that society as a whole benefits if its members are educated.

But some other cases are by no means so clearly evident. While a toll-road system might be very inconvenient, one can ask with fairness: Why should roads be built at public expense? Why should railroads, for example, pay taxes in part to build roads on which their competitors, the trucks and busses, may operate? Why should a nondriver pay for the roads that automobile owners use? Sometimes there are efforts to make special revenues, such as gasoline taxes, apply primarily to road building; but still a large part of the expenditures for highways, used primarily by automobiles, come out of general revenues.

Or, to cite another example: Why should zoos be free, publicly supported, institutions? If there are enough persons who like to stare at and smell curious beasts to support private, admission-fee, zoos or circuses, let private enterprise supply the need. Or is this right? What is the principle involved?

It is hard to find a clear logical explanation to account for all these cases, but often it is simply that a certain type of expenditure appeals to enough citizens who are willing to roll the political logs to get it adopted. Other people may not understand clearly that they are paying for something for which they do not have much taste.

Because government is often remote, there is the very common tendency to ask government to do this and that; to build more school buildings, increase social security benefits, or do something about pet projects. The cost seems remote. But "having government do something about it" does not per se make it cost less. The social policies of what we do and what we do not want government to do have many pros and cons, but there is in government no magic that does away with cost.

On the other hand, the fact that a project would not be privately profitable does not mean that it has no social virtue: it may be infinitely "profitable" in a social sense. For example, if government can, through spending freely, reduce the severity of depressions, the net gain in social good would be worth vast sums. If, through projects such as the Tennessee Valley Authority, government can turn eroded, underproductive areas into productive areas, the net gain may be very high. If public health measures can improve the national well-being, the benefits would exceed anything that money can measure.

GOVERNMENT REVENUES

When government needs money, it generally gets it by taxing or borrowing. Borrowing will be dealt with later; taxes here.

There are a few revenue sources aside from taxes and borrowing. Some government revenues come from postal fees or partial-cost-covering fees, such as tuition at state universities. The federal government obtains some revenues from the sale of public power, and such incidental income receipts as from the sale of war-surplus goods. But these cases are exceptional; the important revenues of government are from taxes.

The Types of Taxes

There are many different types of taxes. In modern times, governments collect the following types of taxes:

Income taxes
    Personal income taxes
    Corporate income taxes
        Regular
        Excess profits
Death and estate taxes
Property taxes
    Real estate
    Personal property
Sales taxes
    General sales taxes
    Excise taxes
Import duties (also sometimes called "excises," but they do not depend on
            the transfer of property by sale)
    Payroll taxes

Why are there so many taxes? One of the reasons, probably the leading one, is that to rely on any one type of tax too much would be "unfair" or would have undesirable economic effects. Sometimes the matter has been determined simply by expediency. For example, the general sales tax did not have widespread usage until the depression of the early 1930's. Although the sales tax has many unfavorable features, and particularly during a depression, it has one shining merit—it is collectible.

Part of this classification of taxes has been a matter of constitutional law and expediency. The federal government is limited as to the type of taxes it may use; the income tax, for example, could not be applied until authorized by a special constitutional amendment. Property taxes of the ordinary sort may not be used by the federal government. Some states have constitutional prohibitions or limits on the taxes they may levy.

Because our tax system represents, to a very great extent, a kind of "off-the-cuff" improvisation, there are many elements in it that cannot be explained logically but only in terms of the history and circumstances of the moment when the taxes were adopted.

Who Pays the Taxes?

The question "Who pays the taxes?" is much harder to answer than would be expected. It is not hard to find out who is billed for the taxes in the first place. But are the real economic costs of taxes borne by the person who pays them in the first place? No!

For example, corporation taxes are an important source of tax revenue. But who bears the burden of a tax paid by a corporation? A few moments' reflection shows that the corporation itself, as an inanimate being, cannot absorb the ultimate burden of the taxes it pays.

Are they borne by the shareholders of the corporation, or are they passed along in the prices for products charged by corporations?

If corporate taxes are passed along in product prices, as many think that they are, then the ultimate bearer of these taxes becomes the group which buys the products of the corporation. Another alternative is that corporate shareholders may get smaller dividends as a result of taxes. In their final effect, corporate taxes may be far less equitable than they first appear to be. They may be as objectionable, on grounds of social equity, as is the sales tax.

Who Should Pay the Taxes?

The commonest answer to the question "Who should pay taxes?" is: "Those able to pay." It is usual to assume that those able to bear the burdens should do so. The physically able expose themselves to the risks of battle, while the physically weak are sheltered.

Rules, however, have relevance only if they serve some purpose. Is the ability-to-pay rule, for example, a good tax rule? Taxes affect the economy in many ways. Owning a home, buying a security, taking a job—all these are influenced by the taxes that bear on each transaction. And some taxes, while apparently fair, may have an adverse economic effect.

For example: it might be assumed by most people that a rich man is able to pay more taxes than a poor man—and should. But suppose that the rich man is rich by virtue of organizing productive businesses. Suppose that a high tax burden may induce the rich man to figure "Why bother?" and to place his money in tax-exempt municipal bonds and go fishing. It is conceivable that a higher relative tax on the poor man, if it induced business expansion by the rich man, might benefit the poor man; his income after taxes might be higher by virtue of the better wage opportunities offered by the rich man.

The illustration has still another bearing. The existence of tax-exempt municipals shows the pervasive influence of government finance.[1] At first glance, it seems like a fine thing to promote economy in government expenditures, as seems to be done when municipalities issue tax-exempt securities. But if the existence of these securities offers a tax-exemption haven for the rich investor, they may cost the community much more than they save.

What about the Total Tax Bill?

Government is a fighter of inflations and depressions, as we will find out. One of the weapons for this fight prominently advocated by many is fiscal policy. This is an adjustment of government expenditures and revenues according to economic conditions. (More will be said of this subject later.) Economic policy, therefore, deals not only with the proper kind of taxes, and who should pay them, but how big the total tax bill should be, and when it should be changed.

It is obvious that, when individuals or businesses are taxed more, they can spend less for other things; when they are taxed less, they can spend more. Consequently, it is averred that the total tax bill should go down during depressions so as to encourage more spending, and that it should go up during inflations so as to discourage spending.

This principle would seem easy to follow, but it is far from that.

---

[1] The interest income from securities issued by state and local governmental units is exempt from federal and sometimes from state income taxation.

We have further questions, such as: Whose taxes should go up in inflation and down in depressions? Should the authority to vary taxes be delegated to some administrative agency which could change them promptly when economic conditions warranted change; or should tax authority continue to be reserved to legislative bodies? How can the principles of fiscal policy and fairness be reconciled? For example: a sales tax is a fine way of curbing inflation, but it is opposed by many as a regressive tax, since it takes a larger percentage of the income of the poor than of the rich.

GOVERNMENT DEBT AND BORROWING

The level of the public debt depends on the balance of receipts and expenditures: when the expenditures exceed the receipts, the public debt grows; an excess of revenues over expenditures reduces public debt. This may be illustrated by a governmental budget.

The Budget in Government Finance

The budget of the federal government is presented to Congress each January. It includes audited returns for the fiscal year ended on the previous June thirtieth, estimates for the current fiscal year, and a proposed budget for the following fiscal year. Congress then decides, by its tax legislation and appropriations, whether to undertake the proposed or a modified plan of operation for the government. Usually in August the President presents a revised budget for the fiscal year just started, which allows for changes in plans resulting from congressional action.

Public budgets are extraordinarily complex documents in appearance—the annual federal budget is as big as a Manhattan telephone directory. In essence, however, budgets consist of just three parts: estimates of revenues, of expenditures, and of the resulting "surplus" (if revenues exceed expenditures) or "deficit" (if expenditures exceed revenues). A surplus is usually applied to the retirement of the public debt; a deficit is met by increasing the public debt. The budget usually covers general plans for these debt operations. The proposed budget of the federal government for the fiscal year ending June 30, 1951, presented in January, 1950, reduced to the very simple terms we have been considering, is summarized in Table 51. Here it is shown as a simple cash statement.

Taxes are deflationary; expenditures inflationary. Movements of the public debt are, therefore, an index of the net inflationary or deflationary influence of the federal government. An increasing debt (indicative of an excess of expenditures over revenues) is inflationary in its impact; a declining debt, the opposite.

TABLE 51

UNITED STATES CASH RECEIPTS AND EXPENDITURES
Fiscal Year
(Billions of Dollars)

	1948	1949	1950 (Est.)	1951 (Projected)
Net cash receipts.........	45.4	41.6	41.7	43.1
Net cash expenditures.....	36.5	40.6	46.5	45.8
Surplus (+) or deficit (−).	+ 8.9	+ 1.1	− 4.8	− 2.7

The Enormous Growth of Public Debt

Largely as the result of the two great world wars, but also of depression expenditures during the 1930's, the United States has a huge public debt. Most of the public debt is owed by the federal government. State and local debt, now only about one tenth of the total public debt, was formerly a much larger proportion of the total. Before World War I, state and local debt was several times greater than federal debt.

It is hard to realize just how large this debt is—what the dollar figures mean. Some try to demonstrate it by reducing its amounts per individual. For example: our net public debt is now equal to about $1,700 for each man, woman, and child in this country (that is, $250 billion divided by our population of approximately 150 million persons). Or, another demonstration of size: the public debt is about one half of the total debt obligation of the nation (promissory notes, mortgages, bonds, etc.). Government is as big a debtor as all other debtors put together!

The form of public debt most familiar to everyone is the savings bond. This is an important, but far from dominant, form of public debt, as is shown in Exhibit 68, which sets forth the chief segments of the federal debt.

One characteristic of the federal debt not shown by this chart is its average maturity—that is, how "fast it falls due." The public debt is not necessarily reduced whenever a portion of it matures; the more likely event is that a new security issue is sold to "refund" the maturing one (provide funds for payment of the maturing issue). Much of our public debt is relatively short-term. One of the unsettled questions of public policy is how much of the debt should be converted ("refunded") into longer-term forms. During a war, public borrowing may have to be in relatively short-term forms. But it has been traditional that, as soon after the war as possible, the debt should be "refunded" into long-term form. So far, this has not been done to any material extent following World War II. It seems unlikely that it will be done in the near future.

Exhibit 68

THE DEBT OF THE FEDERAL GOVERNMENT, DECEMBER 31, 1949

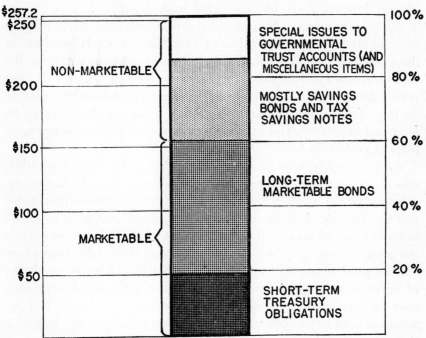

The economic aspects of this problem will be considered under two headings: (1) the economic burden of the public-debt interest charge, and (2) the special monetary significance of public debt.

In the preceding section it was pointed out that the payment of interest on the outstanding public debt is a large part of our federal budget and an appreciable portion of national income. It is argued by some that this burden is more imaginary than real. They point out that service on the public debt does not use real economic resources. It simply means that taxes are collected from one group and then redistributed to others as interest on the public debt. This view is true, but it minimizes the burden of public debt. While no real economic resources are used, the redistribution of income which results from servicing the public debt may have important economic consequences. The distribution of income influences persons in the amount they save and spend and in their willingness to enterprise.

In Chapter 18 it was explained how some forms of private debt (the debts of business concerns or individuals) are the basis for the expansion of bank deposits. Since bank deposits are money, this process may be called "monetizing debt." Public debt may likewise be monetized. In other words, there is no absolute difference between the monetary influence of public and private debt. Both public and private debt are bases for increasing bank deposits.

But there is an important practical difference: public debt is much more likely to be monetized than private debt. As was pointed out in the preceding chapter, the Federal Reserve System can limit the monetization of private debt. Theoretically, it could just as well limit public-debt monetization. In practice, however, it is not so easy to do this. The Federal Reserve can either assist the Treasury in its financing or can "control" the market; but, under inflationary conditions, it cannot do both.

As has already been pointed out, the big additions to the public debt have been the result of war, with World War II having accounted for the major part of our present indebtedness. During this war the Treasury had an extraordinarily difficult financing problem. It made every effort to sell as large a part of the public debt outside the banking system as was possible. Savings bonds, the kind of securities sold to average citizens, were distributed by every device of persuasion known to modern salesmanship. It would have been easy to finance the war by selling the securities to banks, but the results would have been even more inflationary than the financing that was undertaken.

However, all of the securities could not be sold outside the banking system; some financing had to be done within it. This created a larger volume of bank deposits, which had the effect of creating more money.

The problem of managing the public debt does not end with a consideration of the period in which public debt is rising. During the decade following World War I much of the public debt, which was held outside the banking system, tended to drift into banks. In other words, to avoid monetizing public debt it is necessary to refund the public debt in such a way that excessive amounts do not drift to banks.

How Big a Debt Is "Too Big"?

A large public debt has the two dangers we have already discussed: the burden of the interest charge on it, and the monetary danger it presents. But the point at which these become material dangers is far from evident. In the mid-1930's when the public debt in the United States was about one tenth its present level ($25 billion as against $250 billions), there was much solemn talk about how much public debt we could tolerate. At least one respected economist gravely concluded that we could afford a $50 billion debt, but he clearly implied that any level beyond that would be dangerous.

Experience seems to indicate that the problem is not so much the size of the debt as the way in which it is managed. And, since we now have a tremendous public debt, the policies of management become extremely important.

There is, therefore, no strict answer to the question of what is a "too big" public debt. The public debt at the present levels of national income is tolerable, and some increase could be borne. But the dominant position of this debt in the financial structure of the country means that private financial institutions and practices will live in the shadow of public financial policy in a way that was never true in the past. Financial leadership is now almost literally in the hands of government.

GOVERNMENT AS A LENDER

In the preceding chapters we have already encountered a number of cases of government as a lender:

1. The federal government dominates the field of agricultural credit and is represented in it by a great number of agencies.
2. Urban real estate credit has been mightily influenced by the operation of a variety of federal agencies. The influence is not so much by direct lending as by insuring loan payments.
3. Business credit has been available through the Reconstruction Finance Corporation and the Federal Reserve banks. During World War II the armed forces guaranteed certain loans needed for procurement purposes, the so-called "V" loans. A government corporation, the Smaller War Plants Corporation, made business credit available in certain cases.

There is one very great obstacle in trying to summarize the characteristics of government as a lender: the great variety of purposes and policies in the various lending operations of government. Some government loan operations are intended to make credit available where private agencies are not providing what is believed to be adequate service. But very often, lending operations have come to be guided by other goals: stimulation of certain types of economic activity, such as residential construction, or war production. Often there has been an element of subsidy in these credit operations.

TABLE 52

LOANS BY GOVERNMENT CORPORATIONS AND CREDIT AGENCIES, MARCH 31, 1949

Corporation or Agency	Millions of Dollars
Department of Agriculture:	
Farm Credit Administration:	
Banks for co-operatives	$ 261
Federal intermediate credit banks	489
Federal Farm Mortgage Corporation	61
Rural Electrification Administration	1,066
Commodity Credit Corporation	1,764
Farmers' Home Administration	256
Housing and Home Finance Agency:	
Home Loan Bank Board:	
Federal home loan banks	362
Home Owners' Loan Corporation	344
Public Housing Administration	295
Federal Housing Administration	21
Federal National Mortgage Association	309
Reconstruction Finance Corporation	960
Export-Import Bank	2,144
Federal Works Agency	89
All other	3,806
Total	$12,228

CLASSIFICATION OF LOANS BY PURPOSE

Purpose of Loan	
To aid agriculture	$ 4,209
To aid home owners	851
To aid industry:	
Railroads	141
Other	337
To aid financial institutions:	
Banks	5
Other	367
Foreign loans	6,098
Other	589
Less: Reserve for losses	*370*
Total loans receivable (net)	$12,228

The very great complexity of government as a lender may be gleaned from an examination of Table 52. This table is not exact, in that it includes some government corporations which are not primarily credit agencies. But at the same time, the table falls short of showing the full significance of government in lending, in that credit insurance operations are not included. One of the most important forms of government influence on the credit system is through its credit insurance.

The Origin of Various Governmental Loan Programs

The federal government has usually started lending operations in response to some particular demand. Some unusual circumstances would arise, and easy credit would often be one of the proposals for cure of the circumstance. One of the commonest cases would be that a special group, such as war veterans or farmers, would feel that they merited more consideration than existing private lending agencies were giving them. The governmental program would be for the purpose of *improving service or lowering interest rates or relaxing credit standards*. For example, farmers have felt for several generations that they did not get credit on as good terms as their city cousins. The federal land banks were established as far back as 1917 in response to such a widespread feeling. It was partly a matter of interest rates, but also a matter of the terms of the credit—the amount that would be loaned on land of a given value. A decade and a half later, production credit associations were established when the commercial banking system, shaken and decimated by the depression of the early 1930's, was not lending very freely. Farmers felt that they could not get enough credit on reasonable terms. When the Federal Reserve banks were granted the authority to make industrial advances in 1934, it was asserted that business needed longer-term credit than banks were willing to extend.

The justification of these attitudes is debatable. Sometimes government lending activities have been established at times when private credit grantors were temporarily incapacitated or shell-shocked by panic conditions. But government lending activities have usually continued beyond the period of critical need and often have seemed to be competitive with quite adequate private facilities. On the other hand, it is sometimes contended that the existence of the public credit agencies, whether active or not, has a therapeutic effect on the competitive viability of the private lending agencies.

Still another kind of governmental lending to be illustrated is that of *distress credits*, a kind of salvage operation when private credit operations founder. This is a little like the preceding case, but it is different because the circumstances at the time of establishment are more urgent. For example, the Home Owners' Loan Corporation, as indicated in an earlier chapter, was hastily established in 1933 to provide a haven for distressed home mortgages. It was for the purpose of giving relief to home owners who were being threatened by their mortgage creditors with foreclosure.

Still another illustration of distress credits is found in the loans made by the RFC to banks and railroads in the early 1930's. There were only about three years in which credit was extended to these groups; since then these credits have been in liquidation.

There is no principle to be drawn from these illustrations except that, whenever a new and special difficulty arises, it is likely that government will create a new agency or adapt an old one to "do something about it."

Another kind of government lending and credit operation might be labeled: *"Lending to influence economic activity."* The operations of the Federal Housing Administration have already been mentioned in Chapter 15. Other illustrations would be the Rural Electrification Administration, the double purpose of which was to make electricity available to farmers who had not before enjoyed it and also, in some cases, to create consumers for public power generation projects. But the Rural Electrification Administration was first promoted to help cure unemployment. Still another illustration is the Export-Import Bank. This bank serves a complex system of political and economic aims. It was originally intended to do just what its name indicates: stimulate exports and imports, and to finance them when other sources of credit were not available. Its present purposes, however, extend far beyond this simple goal.

In most of the cases mentioned, provision of credit facilities has been part of a somewhat broader program of economic and social stimulation. If government wants to stimulate the consumption of electricity by farmers, the total program must include: facilities, provisions for financing, and a plan of promotion to obtain acceptance. This is in the nature of a "package deal."

A specific illustration of this type of credit is the case of a manufacturer of prefabricated housing. The Reconstruction Finance Corporation loaned sizable amounts to this manufacturer; the project later failed and the loan was foreclosed.[2]

Another kind of government lending is often simply: *"Loans as a subsidy vehicle."* Commodity Credit Corporation loans are primarily

---

[2] Disclosures of a congressional investigating committee, headed by Senator Fulbright, subsequent to the drafting of this section have shown that this loan and others were seriously tainted with improper political influence, if not with outright fraud. These disclosures only illustrate the point already made above, that continued lending by government agencies in periods of prosperity involves dubious assumptions about the real need for credit not met by private agencies.

a part of the policy of supporting agricultural prices. Many loans of the Farm Security Administration, for example, were made on such bases that the chances of repayment were not good and furnished, in effect, a kind of subsidy. It was originally expected that many Home Owners' Loan Corporation credits would fall in this group; but, as already noted, this did not turn out to be the case. During World War II, the armed services, through the administration of the Federal Reserve, guaranteed a number of loans made by commercial banks to war producers. Credits to the extent of $10.3 billion were approved, and only $335 million of applications (3 per cent of applications received) were rejected. The smallest credit was $400; the largest was $1 billion. Since the sole criteria was the "ability to produce," it was expected that these loans would inevitably result in material losses. It was hoped that the stimulation of war production would be adequate compensation. As it turned out, these credits resulted in very small losses.

GOVERNMENT AS A FINANCIAL POLICEMAN

Government acts as financial policemen in many ways, and earlier sections of this book have already given adequate attention to some of the leading policing activities:

1. The Federal Reserve System often acts as a regulator of the money markets.
2. The markets for long-term capital raising and trading are extensively regulated by state blue-sky laws and by the Securities and Exchange Commission.
3. The Interstate Commerce Commission supervises and regulates railroad financing.
4. Commercial banks are examined and regulated in a number of ways and by a number of agencies.
5. Public utility financing is often supervised by state utility commissions and more recently by various branches of the federal government.
6. Consumer credit agencies, particularly the small-loan companies, are under special statutes and are regulated by established state agencies.

The remaining aspects of governmental regulation of finance are of smaller importance. They represent incidental aspects of broader problems of public policy and public regulation.

Holding Company Regulation

Until the later part of the nineteenth century, corporations were forbidden to own the stock of other corporations. But then New Jersey, largely for reasons of revenue, changed the law so that a corporation could own the stock of another corporation. Since that time, many other states have followed suit. In the field of public utilities this device has often been used in a way that has tended to evade state regulation and also sometimes to defraud investors. Because some public utility holding companies were guilty of malpractices, all of them came under suspicion. These concerns are now mostly being, or have been, liquidated under the provisions of the federal Public Utility Holding Company Act. Some states also limit the operation and financing of holding companies for other purposes.

Monopoly and Finance

Except in the case of public utilities, competition is expected to keep prices and other business policies reasonable. Competition was considered the great regulator by classical economists from the day of Adam Smith to the present.

But business concerns have a natural distaste for competition. "Price chiseler" is an epithet used to deride a competitor for doing just what Adam Smith praised him for doing. So we have had developed a certain amount of public regulation to enforce competition and fair practice: the Sherman Anti-trust Law; the Clayton Act forbidding interlocking directorates; the Federal Trade Commission Act; and others.

The use of financial devices to assist monopoly was very common in the period near the turn of the century. The elder J. P. Morgan appears to have been a man of great personal restraint in the use of monopoly power, but he was "midwife" to a great number of business combinations that clearly reduced competition. And since that day, the field of finance has often been suspected of monopoly in the public mind. "Wall Street" is still used as an opprobrious epithet.

GOVERNMENT AS A FIGHTER OF INFLATIONS AND DEPRESSIONS

Of the many roles of government in our complex economy, that of government as a fighter of inflations and depressions, is coming to occupy a very large place in the minds of many.

Extreme business fluctuations are a source of great social waste. At times some cannot get jobs and, being without income, go hungry. At the same time, farmers cannot sell what they raise at prices that pay for taking the produce to market. Food rots while men starve. It is not only wasteful to have unemployment, but there are even more serious consequences. Doles and handouts demoralize individuals and families and undermine the working habits of those who receive them. The fear of job loss haunts even those who keep a job. Insecurity, so the psychologists tell us, is a very eroding fear. And even in times when business is good, the fear that business may subsequently deteriorate has damaging consequences. Businessmen cannot plan as boldly as they might like; they are beset by the fear that times will not remain good; if they erect additional plants, these plants may be unprofitable.

The evils of inflation are not so immediately evident. A prosperity which improves income and increases prices seems pleasant and stimulating to almost everyone except a few fixed-income recipients. But when price rises become material, there comes to be a hectic race in which everyone tries to keep even—and nobody seems to win. When inflation is allowed to get out of hand, as it has sometimes in other countries, the results are devastating. War is the most frequent cause of inflation.

Monetary Policy and Business Fluctuations

For a long time, business fluctuations were believed to be the result of monetary factors. This belief led to efforts to remedy these fluctuations through monetary means, and there was hope that the Federal Reserve System could provide such a cure. It was felt that, by restraining the money and credit system in boom times and encouraging it in periods of depression, the range of fluctuation could be moderated. As late as in the 1920's many thought that this experiment had been successful. But events proved otherwise. In spite of the monetary influence of the Federal Reserve System, economic conditions continued to fluctuate.

Although there is less confidence in monetary management than formerly, monetary policy continues to be a significant factor. Whatever may initiate a swing in business activity, there is no doubt that an extreme of rigid and inflexible money factors, or an extreme of uncontrolled flexibility, serves to aggravate the fluctuations once they have started. And so, even if not a primary factor, money management is now widely accepted as an ameliorating device.

For some classes of financial institutions—commercial banks particularly—the operation of governmental policy in the field of money is of very great importance. Commercial banks, as we have learned, feel the immediate impact of Federal Reserve policy in their credit operations. But the influence extends to an even wider range. All investment and credit institutions are influenced by the levels of interest rates; and, to a considerable extent, interest rates are influenced by the monetary policy of the Federal Reserve System.

Public Works and Public Spending

All levels of government—federal, state, and local—spend money for roads, hospitals, school buildings, public buildings, parks, flood-control dams, military installations, and the like. These are public works. It has been contended that government should time its expenditures for public works so as to provide an offset for shrinkage in private capital expenditures. If times are good and private business concerns are erecting buildings and making capital expenditures, then government should refrain. But if times get poor and private business concerns stop such capital outlays, then government should step in, construct roads, school and other public buildings, flood-control dams, and similar projects.

There is hardly any dispute about the wisdom of such a policy, so far as the policy is feasible. Conservatives and liberals, alike, accept its logic. But the difficulty is summarized in the phrase ending the first sentence of this paragraph: "so far as the policy is feasible." Should school children be forced to attend school in decrepit buildings, possibly fire hazards, while waiting for a depression? Should sick persons be forced to go to inadequate hospitals until unemployment emerges? Should floods be allowed to rip until the stock market falls? Can military defense programs be held back waiting for the price indexes to slide?

In other words, should society be forced to forego its public works any more than its private works? In very graphic terms, should people, when they have good jobs and a satisfactory income and are buying many new automobiles, be forced to drive their cars on inadequate roads? Must they wait until times are bad to drive their then not-so-new "jalopies" over wide, new, well-engineered roads?

There is still another facet to the problem: What is a necessary public work? Is it considered just as essential in good times as in bad? During the depression of the 1930's, unemployed youths were inducted into the Civilian Conservation Corps. The Corps did many things: planted trees, improved public parks, and built benches at scenic observation points. In boom times, society can forego such projects. But in poor times, there is a public advantage in getting some work done, particularly if the only alternative for the unemployed is to loaf. But how confident can we be that the marginal ventures into public works will be demobilized when the excuse for them has passed?

Governmental Fiscal Policy

In recent years there has emerged a somewhat more sophisticated view of public expenditures. It is related to the public-works policy just discussed, but it covers a much wider scope. It is fairly evident that, when governments collect taxes, this process reduces the money that is available for private persons to save or spend. When governments spend, this process returns funds to the economy. When governments collect more taxes than they spend, this process tends to curb private expenditures. The government program for taxing, spending, and borrowing constitutes fiscal policy. It has been argued that government should try to influence the level of activity in the private economy through stimulation (spending more than is taxed) in poor times and through restraint (taxing more than is spent) in boom times.

The social wastes of depression have been so impressive that many believe government should guarantee everyone a job. And the means most often proposed to implement this goal is fiscal policy. This proposal will subsequently be discussed more fully. But first some thought must be given to the problems of public finance.

Public versus Private Finance

In a free enterprise economy, the goal of business is profit, and business financial arrangements are all directed to that end. The problem of individual finance is to manage income so as to secure the maximum of pleasure and security from it. But the problem of governmental finance is different: it grows out of providing social services such as public education, and out of fighting wars, and even, as we have seen, out of dealing with depressions.

It is sometimes said that the financial operations of government have a strategic position. What is meant by the "strategic position" of government in the field of finance? Because of its monetary and tax powers, government does not have to limit its operation to "profitable" or "income-producing" operations in the narrow sense of "profit" and "income." To make profits, businesses must produce what is wanted so they can sell what they produce for enough to cover expenses, with a little left over. The individual, if he wants to eat, sleep, and live in reasonable comfort and still have something left over as security for sickness and old age, must manage his income prudently. He must "economize."

There are many expenditures which may be wise socially but would seldom be profitable. War is the most obvious example. If attacked by a foreign power, could we depend on private expenditure to fight a successful defense? Without public education, would as many go to school as now do? In a complex civilization, broad and general education is of vast importance, and it can be obtained only by public expenditure. Flood control for rivers, and conservation of game, natural resources, and soil, probably would be possible only with public outlays.

Where is the margin which separates desirable from doubtful public expenditure? In the mid-1930's the Tennessee Valley Authority (TVA) was established to build dams and finance improvement projects in the valley of the Tennessee River. This river, a proverbial flooder, was surrounded by bad eroded soil and a population becoming steadily more impoverished. The project cost almost three quarters of a billion dollars. But at the same time, it created undeniable improvements. This area came to be the home site for part of the atomic bomb project. Some have lauded TVA achievements; some have mistrusted its socialistic aspects. Obviously, such a project could not have been undertaken for private profit. Did its social gain justify its great cost?

But the management of public finances also has dangers. The tax and monetary powers of government can be abused and made to serve ends of waste and of fraud. Taxes cannot be considered a price in the same way as prices on goods and services in a private economy. It is true that a citizen with children in public schools may consider the taxes he pays as a "price" for this service. It is not a true price in the economic sense, however, because it is paid by all citizens, whether or not they have children to take advantage of this service.

There is still another danger implicit in government finance. One of the tenets of democratic freedom is that the individual may use his income as he desires, short of creating a public nuisance. Government taxation and expenditure tend, however, to enforce a prescribed pattern of consumption. For illustration, consider the case of two men who have the same income and spend the same amount for bare necessities. One prefers to dissipate; the other prefers to collect eighteenth-century pottery. If government taxes the extra income of both individuals and builds public parks with the proceeds, what have we gained and what have we lost? Free choice in consumption has been taken away from both men. Neither cares much for the public parks; one seeks revelry, the other closets himself with his pottery. Even if we do not agree with these tastes, there is no doubt that freedom has been encroached upon. Each has been forced to forego the tastes he enjoys for a less pleasurable one.

A somewhat technical difference between government and private finance is in the accounting concepts used. Most private accounting is on an accrual basis; this means that the costs of capital expenditures are charged against the period in which the capital goods are used rather than against the period when cash was paid for them. Governmental accounting is on an almost purely cash basis. Expenditures are counted when made, no matter for what purpose. A TVA system of dams built to last a century or more is just as current as a tank of gasoline in an army jeep. As a result, "deficit" does not mean the same thing in government finance as it means in private finance. The following example gives a striking illustration of this difference: In almost all businesses, large capital expenditures are made in years of large profits and when the future prospects for profits are bright. If a public utility company should make a large outlay to improve its plant and equipment in a given year, this outlay, being charged to capital account, does not impair the profits of the concern for that year. But if this utility kept its books on the same basis as government does, it would show a huge "deficit" in the year in which this outlay was made, rather than comfortable profits. Indeed, if business did not accrue capital costs, many American businesses would have been running "deficits" in the prosperous periods of 1924–29 and 1947–50.

Government Finance in Depressions

The Employment Act of 1946 provides that the maintenance of adequate employment opportunities shall be one of the goals of public finance. Since the dangers of inept fiscal policy have been outlined, its potential advantages will now be sympathetically considered.

In a free private-enterprise economy, every individual and every business must limit their outlays to what they have saved, plus current income. An individual or a business can sometimes spend more than this amount by going into debt, but such action is obviously often very imprudent. When "times start looking bad," the prudent individual or business starts to cut expenditures. But that may be the very process for turning a small recession into a major depression. Business concerns dislike to lay off men; indeed, they frequently keep employees on the payroll even though not needed. But if business is to survive, expenditures must be kept in line with expected income. If all businesses do this, the result may be a continued downward spiral of reduced expenditures, reduced employment, reduced income, reduced expenditures—around the circle, down and down.

The only agency with the resources and strategic position to attempt to halt this process before it has run its natural course is government. The federal government, because of its monetary powers, does not need to be concerned about debt in the same sense as other debtors must be. Government debt and the service (interest paid) on it can always be covered by creating and issuing additional money, if need be. Governments, so long as they have sovereign powers to tax and issue money, never become technically insolvent.

Governments undoubtedly can do a great deal to influence the level of employment, but one may reasonably ask just how much they *should* do. Should government guarantee employment opportunities? Will government expenditures waste economic resources; destroy, or compete unfairly with, private enterprise? Will the public debt, its monetary consequences, and the incident taxes destroy economic incentives? These questions lie at the core of what is, and for some time doubtless will be, one of the greatest issues of difference among citizens of good will.

Political crystallization of the popular feeling that government ought to "do something about depressions" is deep-seated. During World War II, it was widely feared that there might be a serious relapse after the war into the dismal depths of depression from which this country had suffered for more than a decade before the war. It turned out to be a groundless fear, but it was a widespread one. This fear prevailed not just in the United States; in England, the relatively conservative coalition government adopted a full-employment policy in 1944. The victory of the Labour Party in 1945 was taken as evidence that the earlier employment policy was rather milder in sentiment than popularly desired. In Canada, there has been governmental declaration of a full-employment policy; likewise in Australia and Sweden. Many other governments, while not adopting an explicit full-employment policy, have given the idea commendatory blessings.

In the United States the idea of governmental support of full employment was endorsed by both major parties. There were differences, presumably, in the ways in which they thought it should be achieved or the vigor with which they might have pursued such policies, but the endorsements have put the issue beyond political dispute.

Even though the issue is accepted as settled in general terms, there nevertheless remain great differences of opinion about the extent and character of governmental acts to support such policies. It is to be noted, for example, that the word "full" was deleted from the title of the Employment Act. But it was, nevertheless, implicitly dedicated to creating and encouraging such "full" employment through governmental policy. The language of the policy section of the act was debated and revised many times, and its final form shows the marks of compromise:

SECTION 2. The Congress hereby declares that it is the continuing policy and responsibility of the Federal Government to use all practicable means consistent with its needs and obligations and other essential considerations of national policy, with the assistance and cooperation of industry, agriculture, labor, and state and local governments, to coordinate and utilize all its plans, functions, and resources for the purpose of creating and maintaining, in a manner calculated to foster and promote free competitive enterprise and the general welfare, conditions under which there will be afforded useful employment opportunities, including self-employment, for those able, willing, and seeking to work and to promote maximum employment, production, and purchasing power.

It is not to be presumed that the act was expected to be just a depression cure and without interest in inflation. But implicitly and unavoidably the emphasis of the Employment Act and its tools of policy are more significant on the side of a cure. That assumption grew out of the belief that depressions are more probable and damaging than inflations. Events seem to indicate this was a mistaken belief.

CONCLUSION

All over the world, not just in the United States or just in the big countries, the role of government is becoming more important. This is as true of the most staunchly democratic nations as of the totalitarian states. A larger role in finance is just one of the aspects of this development. Although this development is viewed apprehensively by a minority, it has neither been widely feared nor resisted.

A debate about the wisdom of this development would be outside the proper role of this text; however, one clear conclusion may be drawn from it: The level of moral responsibility and economic wisdom required if government is to play this new role well calls for a better-informed citizenry. The problems that have been surveyed in this chapter are admittedly difficult. But they are the prob· lems that lie near the core of public policy. The way in which they are solved may well turn out to be the most important financial development of the forthcoming decade.

—ROLAND I. ROBINSON

QUESTIONS AND PROBLEMS

1. Demonstrate with figures from Table 50 (on page 570) the importance of war in federal expenditures.
2. Why is it that these figures do not permit a precise measurement of war influences?
3. Should the federal government economize in its expenditures during a depression, or should it spend freely?
4. Outline what you think the proper extent of governmental services should be. What principle do you use to include or exclude marginal functions?
5. What guiding principles may be used in selecting taxes to be levied?
6. Does tax exemption for the interest on municipal bonds result in governmental economy? (Assume government to include federal, state, and local forms.)
7. Why do taxes tend to be deflationary?
8. Why do governmental expenditures tend to be inflationary?
9. Compare the economic significance of paying interest on the public debt with that of spending public money for the dredging of unnavigated rivers and unused harbors.
10. Does public debt have the same significance as private debt; is it more dangerous, or less dangerous? Or not dangerous at all?
11. When does a big public debt become too big? (If ever!)
12. Pick some example of governmental lending recently reported in the newspapers, and classify it according to the principles enumerated in the section on "Government as a Lender."
13. What are the advantages to a compensatory fiscal policy? What are the dangers?
14. What fiscal policy do you think appropriate for the present?
15. Should accrual accounting principles be applied to the financial budgets and accounts of the federal government?
16. The Employment Act of 1946 has been called a "weak act with a strong precedent." Explain.

BIBLIOGRAPHY

The sources cited in the bibliographies of the two preceding chapters also bear on the subject of government and finance. This is particularly true of the more modern accounts of Federal Reserve policy, which all reflect the difficulty of separating fiscal and monetary policy. For a treatment of the strictly fiscal aspects of government, Taylor's *The Economics of Public Finance* (New York: Macmillan Co., 1949) is a readable and comprehensive source. *Fiscal Policies and the American Economy*, edited by Kenyon Poole (New York: Prentice-Hall, Inc., 1950), contains several relevant chapters— particularly chapter ii by Roland I. Robinson, which treats the relationship of monetary and fiscal problems at a somewhat more sophisticated level than attempted in this text. The task-force reports on *Lending Agencies* prepared by the Hoover Commission and published by the U.S. Government Printing Office are the most modern critical reviews of these activities. Appendix R of this series is one of the better short reviews of governmental lending operations and policies.

The four essays in Part IV of *Postwar Economic Problems*, edited by Seymour Harris (New York: McGraw-Hill Book Co., Inc., 1943), contains a number of views sympathetic to the use of fiscal measures to combat economic instability. The December, 1949, issue of the National City Bank Letter on *Economic Conditions and Government Finance* contains a strongly critical review of present fiscal policy. A somewhat more moderate review of the problems of fiscal policy is contained in chapter v, "Federal Budgeting and Fiscal Policy," by Arthur Smithies in *A Survey of Contemporary Economics*, edited by Howard Ellis (Philadelphia: Blakiston, 1949) under the sponsorship of the American Economic Association. *Financing American Prosperity*, a symposium of the views of six leading economists published by the Twentieth Century Fund in 1945, contains a diversity of views about the relationship of government to the financial process. The summary and analysis chapter is particularly useful for one who is short of time.

PART IV

•

INTERNATIONAL FINANCIAL INSTITUTIONS

Chapter • 22

INTERNATIONAL FINANCIAL RELATIONSHIPS

THE fundamental foundation of trade and exchange, whether considered within the bounds of one country or across international frontiers, is the same. Trade is based on the facts that production costs are not everywhere the same and that geographic and climatic conditions make it impossible to produce certain products in all regions. When physical impediments to production are not present, a region or a country tends to export the things whose costs and prices are comparatively low within its borders, and to import items whose costs of production are comparatively high domestically but low in the exporting country.[1] We may ignore the finespun theories of economists who explain which nation gains most from foreign trade. Our primary concern is to point out the financial relationships arising from trade and the international movement of money and credit.

Although the fundamentals of domestic and international commerce are similar in many respects, trade across national frontiers often introduces differences. Trade laws and customs may not be the same, language barriers may exist, credit on open account is seldom granted, and transactions are usually on a wholesale basis. The principal difference, however, arises from the fact that international payments usually involve two kinds of money. For example, an American exporting machinery to Brazil expects to be paid for his shipment in dollars, while the Brazilian purchaser expects to pay in cruzeiros, the monetary unit of his country.

---

[1] Absolute costs of production may be less significant than comparative or relative costs. If costs for all items of trade are higher in one nation than in another, the high-cost nation will tend to specialize in the production of goods in which its cost disadvantage is the least.

INTERNATIONAL PAYMENTS

The difference in monetary units, and the consequent necessity of converting the money of one country into that of another, introduces a "transfer" problem and an "exchange" market. The latter is a market in which the moneys of all important nations may be exchanged for one another. Actually, the items bought and sold are seldom coin or paper currency issued by foreign governments or central banks, but rather are bills of exchange or telegraphic orders stated in terms of foreign monetary units.

These claims are similar to the negotiable instruments described in Chapter 2. They are drafts or checks drawn on traders or checks drawn on a bank, and are commonly called "exchange." To be more specific, "sterling exchange" consists of claims stated in terms of British pounds sterling, the monetary unit of account of Great Britain; and "dollar exchange" means claims for dollars on businessmen or financial institutions in the United States.

The Foreign Exchange Market

The foreign exchange market has no formal organization such as characterizes the stock exchange or a board of trade. It consists primarily of the foreign departments of large commercial banks but includes also a few small houses and individuals who deal with each other directly or through middlemen. Very few tradesmen enter this market personally in order to acquire or dispose of the instruments used in financing their own operations.

Metropolitan banks with foreign departments facilitate the international movement of goods, securities, and credit through foreign branches or correspondents with whom they maintain deposit balances. If a demand for foreign funds arises in the United States, these banks are able to draw checks or drafts against their foreign balances to meet the demand. If deposits abroad are depleted, thus limiting the supply of exchange available in America, banks in this country may replenish them in several ways. Formerly it was possible to ship gold direct from a commercial bank in the United States to a branch or correspondent abroad. This practice is now either impossible or so enmeshed in governmental restrictions here and abroad that it is used infrequently. A more usual practice is for the American bank to purchase drafts, drawn by local exporters and payable in foreign funds, and forward them to the branch or correspondent for collection; the proceeds are credited to the deposit account of the American bank. It may be possible also for unused funds to be transferred from other foreign centers to the market where reserves are low. Finally, if other means of replenishing the deposit are not available, the American bank may borrow from foreign banking institutions and deposit the proceeds to its foreign account. Thus, a large commercial bank with a foreign department is always in a position to meet the demands of its domestic customers who are making foreign payments or investments. Similarly, the American bank provides a ready market in which drafts drawn by American exporters on their foreign customers or foreign banks may be sold for cash or deposit credit.

Relatively few American commercial banks maintain balances in foreign institutions, although large city banks have accounts, numbering in the hundreds, located in banks scattered over the entire world. For example, the Continental Illinois National Bank and Trust Company of Chicago carried balances in 379 foreign banks, and the First National Bank of Chicago owned deposits in approximately 300 overseas banks in June, 1950. As a result of the system of domestic correspondent relations described in Chapter 4, foreign exchange drawn on banks of any nation may be purchased and sold at almost any commercial bank in any part of the United States.

Balance of Payments

A continuous flow of transactions, of varying types and size, makes up the supply and demand factors in the exchange market. The balance of payments published in most countries annually is a summary form of computation or estimate of these factors for the year. The balance contains aggregates of merchandise and service transactions, of credit operations, and of cash payments. All claims by foreigners upon individuals or institutions in the United States appear in our balance as debits, whereas claims of Americans upon foreigners appear as credits.

Because the balance of payments summarizes aggregate data of all transactions taking place within a given year, the statement must balance. If goods are imported, something must be exported to pay for the merchandise purchased. The export may be in the form of other goods (including gold) or services, or securities, or promises to pay; but the aggregate value of the credit items is equal to the aggregate value of the debt for the year.

At any particular time, however, receipts from abroad and payments to be made abroad do not generally cancel out. There remains a balance to be settled, i.e., paid or received. Such temporary lack of balance is reflected in the exchange market by variations in the demand for, or supply of, bills of exchange and by short-run variations in the rates of exchange as adjustments are made.

Debits (Claims on the United States by Foreigners)

Among the international transactions that result in payments by Americans to foreigners, thereby increasing the domestic *demand* for exchange, are: commodity imports, including gold and silver; employment of the services of foreigners in shipping, insurance, etc.; tourist expenditures by Americans traveling abroad; lending to foreigners by purchasing short-term credit instruments and long-term securities or by making direct foreign investments; repayment by Americans of loans previously made to us; paying interest and dividends on American securities owned abroad; and remittances by Americans to friends, relatives, charitable organizations, or others in foreign countries. Obviously, the reverse of each of the above transactions is a credit in the American balance of payments—i.e., a claim on foreigners by Americans—and generates a supply of foreign exchange in the domestic market.

The accompanying illustration (see Table 53) of the United States balance of payments for the year 1939 is typical of the form in which such summaries are published.[2] The statement is divided into three major parts, consisting of current transactions, gold movements, and capital transactions. It is evident that current transactions are confined to shipments of merchandise, often called "visible" items, and to a large group of service items often called "invisible." A net credit of $859 million on merchandise trade indicates that the value of goods exported has exceeded the value of merchandise imports. This is often referred to as a "favorable balance of trade"; the concept should always be restricted to merchandise transactions only. The total debits and credits of "other current transactions" show a net debit of $127 million, which indicates that other nations were paid that much more by Americans than was received in the United States for the services included in that category.

Although it has been said that the total debits and credits for the year must balance, it should not be assumed that a balance exists

---

[2] Although the balance sheet of 1939 was drawn up after the world had abandoned the gold standard, and followed closely upon the heels of deep depression, it is considered more useful for purposes of illustration than a wartime or postwar exhibit.

TABLE 53

UNITED STATES BALANCE OF INTERNATIONAL PAYMENTS, 1939
(Millions of Dollars)

Type of Transaction	Payments or Debits (−)	Receipts or Credits (+)	Net Debit or Credit Balance
I. CURRENT TRANSACTIONS:			
A. Merchandise trade...................	2,318	3,177	+ 859
B. Other current transactions:			
Shipping and freight.................	367	303	− 64
Travel expenditures..................	290	135	− 155
Personal remittances.................	144	36	− 108
Institutional contributions, net.........	43		− 43
Interest and dividends...............	230	541	+ 311
Government aid and settlements.......	18	2	− 16
Other government items..............	81	42	− 39
Silver...........................	91	14	− 77
Miscellaneous adjustments and services, net...............................	....	64	+ 64
Total of other current transactions..	1,264	1,137	− 127
Total of all current transactions........	3,582	4,314	+ 732
II. GOLD MOVEMENTS:			
Net gold imports or exports..............	3,574	....	
Net change in earmarked gold............	....	556	
Net gold movement...................	....	....	−3,018
III. CAPITAL TRANSACTIONS:			
A. Long-term capital movements:			
Net flow through change in United States assets abroad...................	....	113	
Net flow through change in foreign assets in United States.................	86	....	
Balance on long-term capital movements........................	....	....	+ 27
B. Short-term capital movements:			
Net flow through change in United States assets abroad.....................	....	211	
Net flow through change in foreign assets in United States...................	....	1,259	
Balance on short-term capital movements........................	....	....	+1,470
Balance on all capital transactions......	....	....	+1,497
Unexplained items.....................	....	789	+ 789
Grand total........................	7,242	7,242	± 0

Source: Adapted from *The United States in the World Economy* (Washington, D.C.: Department of Commerce, 1943), facing p. 216, No. 1. Items may not total, owing to rounding of figures.

within the three separate divisions shown. In fact, a balance within the divisions would be a practical impossibility. This is due to the fact that some nations have highly developed industrial and agricultural economies, while others have made much less progress in that direction. If all nations tried to maintain a balance of each of the separate divisions, there could be no regular stream of loans or investments flowing from the highly developed to the less well-developed nations. Adoption of a national policy to attain equilibrium of this sort would present an obstacle to the free movement of capital that would harm both lender and borrower nations.

Further examination of the exhibit shows the largest single item of the 1939 balance to be a debit of $3,574 million, representing net gold imports into the United States. This figure is of exceptional size. It resulted from receipt of vast stores of "refugee" gold shipped here for safekeeping by foreign owners in areas beset by political unrest and on the verge of open warfare.

In Table 53, Division III, or "Capital Transactions," is divided into short- and long-term movements and represents either the creation of new capital claims or the cancellation of previously existing claims. The short-term capital account is made up of changes in foreign bank balances and temporary investments in the money markets of foreign nations. The long-term capital account is the investment section of the balance of payments. Transfers of funds intended for purposes of permanent or relatively long-term commitment abroad are included. All give rise to a long-term capital claim. The large debit total in the third section of the balance of payments indicates an excess of short- and long-term capital investment by foreigners in the United States in 1939.

A short-term lack of balance in the flow of international payments and receipts coupled with long-term equilibrium is not paradoxical. Just as an individual businessman or company has a variable flow of products and cash through the business over the period of a year, so is there seasonal or short-run variation in the over-all flow of goods, services, securities, and currency for the country as a whole. The active factors used in restoring equilibrium are primarily short-term capital movements or loans and gold shipments. It is possible that a change on long-term capital account will be used to achieve a current balance, but obviously a nation would resort to the sale of some of its long-term capital to meet a current deficit only in an emergency.

Under conditions prevailing before World War I and during a

portion of the interwar period, gold shipments and short-term capital movements satisfactorily performed their function of adjusting short-run imbalance in international exchange. A drastic change occurred in the decade from 1930 to 1940, however. Collapse of the gold standard in the early 1930's, the spread of industrial depression and low prices over the United States, and the heavy investment of foreign funds in long-term securities in the United States brought vast quantities of gold to this country. Widespread political unrest abroad and the fear that gold would be nationalized or impounded by various foreign countries would have resulted in heavy gold movements into the United States. But when the American dollar was devalued (1933–34) and the price of gold increased from $20.67 to $35 an ounce, the United States became a veritable haven for gold. The balance of payments of the United States was so favorable in terms of trade, and the imports of gold and credit so excessive, that it became increasingly difficult for foreigners to acquire dollars abroad. Thus a serious and continuing dollar shortage was created. Even before World War II, many nations found it necessary to curtail imports from the United States and to ration the small amounts of dollar exchange that were available.

The Dollar Shortage

The problem faced by foreigners in acquiring dollar exchange and gold for use in settling exchange obligations was further accentuated by World War II. This was due not only to the continued concentration of gold in America but also to the inability of foreign producers to compete successfully against the United States for world markets. Unfortunately, the problem of dollar scarcity abroad remains today as a major obstacle to the restoration of multilateral trade. America still retains a large percentage of the world supply of gold. Her technical superiority as a producer on a low-cost, mass-production basis is not seriously challenged by any other nation. Moreover, many American producers are protected against competition by high tariffs. The mass of American consumers maintains a preference for articles of domestic production. Additional factors contributing to the shortage of dollars abroad are the restrictive trade policies of some nations and the attempts of others to maintain an artificially high value on their currencies.[3] By a devaluation of the pound sterling in the autumn of 1949, England initiated a rather

[3] Alvin H. Hansen, *Monetary Theory and Fiscal Policy* (New York: McGraw-Hill Book Co., Inc., 1949), pp. 212–13.

general movement among world currencies for some alleviation of the dollar shortage. But the problem continues to exist.

As a consequence of the dollar shortage abroad in recent years, the burden of financing American exports has fallen heavily upon the government of the United States. Some credit advances have been offset by similar items from abroad; but the net value of American governmental loans, gifts, and other unilateral transfers has amounted to billions of dollars. Typical of these, which were omitted from consideration in our discussion of credits and debits in the balance of payments, are Lend-Lease as practiced during World War II and the European Recovery Program since then. Total grants by the United States government rose to an all-time high of $5 billion in 1949. If credit advances from the United States should be severely curtailed before Europe and Asia have rebuilt and restored their productive capacities, American exports will be drastically cut; and, without doubt, the dollar shortage will become catastrophic for some nations. Fortunately, considerable progress in the readjustment of agricultural and industrial production is presently being made (1951) in many regions, and the situation will improve if open warfare (World War III) can be averted. The problem is, however, less a matter of international finance than one of politics or military expediency. We shall refer in later paragraphs to the governmental controls resulting from the conditions of imbalance that have plagued the world since 1930.

Rates of Exchange

The term "rate of exchange" as used above is merely a statement of the cost or price of a unit of money of one country expressed in terms of the money of a second country. Thus, a rate of 2.80 on London in New York means that the value of one British pound is $2.80 in United States currency. The rates indicate that the relative values of the money units of the two countries, or, regarded collectively, the rates quoted in the United States on all foreign currencies, is a form of index of the external purchasing power of the dollar.

Although we speak of the "rate" of exchange as if there were only one price in a market at one time, this is not true. A classification of rates reveals the following:

Buying rates and *selling:*　Rates maintained by the same operator or institution in the foreign exchange market. The difference is called "spread" and represents the gross profit margin for the operator

Over-the-counter rates:	Charged persons applying to an institution for a small amount of exchange
Market rate:	Lower than over-the-counter rate and used when a broker or bank sells a large volume to another
Sight rate:	Applies to sale or purchase of instruments payable by the drawee at sight
Time rate:	The price of a draft payable a designated number of days after acceptance by the drawee
Spot rates:	Paid for drafts available for immediate delivery
Forward rates:	Quoted on instruments that are not yet drawn but that will be created and delivered in the future

Seldom does the published table of foreign exchange rates appearing in the daily press contain all these rates. The common form of quotation includes banker's sight drafts and cables, at the top of the rate structure, i.e., having the highest prices; following that will appear commercial sight drafts and commercial bills of varying lengths of time. Bills maturing several weeks or months in the future are quoted at lower rates than cables or sight drafts, which provide funds abroad immediately or in a very short time. The differential between long and short bills is accounted for primarily by the going rate of interest and the time span separating maturities of the two instruments. Difference in risks is a second cause of rate differentials.

MARKET DETERMINATION OF EXCHANGE RATES

In a "free" market, one in which governmental controls are absent, exchange rates tend to move upward in response to an increase in net demand, and vice versa. As noted above, a demand exists whenever it becomes necessary for an individual or an institution to make a payment to a foreigner. Debits in the balance of payments generate a demand for foreign exchange.

In Gold Standard Countries

If two countries are on the same metallic monetary standard, such as gold, they define their monetary unit as a specific quantity of pure gold, maintain a government market for the purchase and sale of gold at fixed prices, and place no restrictions upon imports or exports of gold coin or bullion. Under such circumstances the rate of exchange between the two countries considered will fluctuate closely about the *mint par* of exchange.

MINT PAR OF EXCHANGE. "Mint par" is the ratio of the pure gold content of the two currency units. For example, in the years before World War I and again in the period 1925–31, when both England and the United States were "on gold," the British pound sterling contained 113 grains of gold and the dollar of the United States contained 23.22 grains. The ratio of 113 to 23.22 is 4.8665. Thus the New York price on London pounds centered about $4.8665.

SPECIE POINTS. However, an increase in the demand for sterling (growing out of an excess of British exports to the United States or the necessity by Americans to make payments in England) would tend to force the rate above $4.8665. The upper extreme to which the price might be driven, under these circumstances, was approximately $4.8865. This specie export point could not be passed because, if the rate went above it, the debt or payment in England could be settled more cheaply by an export of gold from the United States. In other words, as long as the cost of shipping 113 grains of gold was two cents, the rate of exchange per pound would not go more than two cents above mint par. At the upper gold point, the demand for bills of exchange decreased and a demand for gold took its place.

Conversely, the lower limit on the pound-sterling rate was about two cents below mint par, or about $4.8465. American exporters drawing bills on British banks to finance shipment of goods would refuse to sell them to domestic dealers in exchange for less than $4.8465 per pound. Rather than sacrifice on the rate of exchange, exporters would agree to pay for the cost of importing gold that could be sold in the United States at the rate of $4.8665 for 113 grains.

Under the conditions assumed, gold shipments would be made by banks rather than by traders. If sterling bills could be sold at prices above the gold export point, banks would use the funds received in buying gold and shipping it abroad and then would sell bills against the resultant balances in London at the high price. But if all banks attempted to take advantage of the opportunity, competition among them would soon bring the price of exchange down to $4.8865. Also, if sterling drafts arising out of the export trade could be purchased at less than $4.8465, banks in America would buy them and send them to England for conversion into gold at the rate of 113 grains for each £1 draft. The rate in New York would then rise to $4.8465 or higher.

What has been said above with respect to the rate of exchange between America and England would apply equally well to any two nations on the gold standard. Under the assumed conditions, relative stability of exchange rates would exist. This leads to the inference that the purchasing power of gold is everywhere the same and that any disequilibrium of prices between gold-standard countries would be adjusted by an automatic flow of gold.

If the demand for gold is substituted for a demand for bills of exchange, the gold flow operates to correct short-run disequilibrium in the balance of payments. The more fundamental correction that is said to follow a gold movement takes place slowly and is in the nature of a long-term adjustment. Supporters of the gold standard note that, for example, a loss of gold by a nation will reduce metallic reserves behind currency and bank deposits, may cause a constriction of total income and purchasing power, may tend to increase short-term interest rates, and may find reflection still later in a decrease of the volume of business and the general price level. The opposite will tend to be true in the country or countries receiving the gold. As prices abroad rise relative to those of the domestic market, the movement of foreign trade tends to reverse itself and to restore the former equilibrium.

The relative stability of foreign exchange rates achieved through fluctuations in the quantity of currency reserves, incomes, and prices is considered by many economists and political scientists to be worth less than it costs. The pressure exerted upon an economy by a heavy and long-continued gold drain may result in almost complete business stagnation, with widespread unemployment and impoverishment of many citizens, particularly the working group. Moreover, the deflation in the country losing gold may finally be transmitted through the fixity of exchange relationships to other gold-standard nations. This may occur, first, because the people of the depressed nation would be unwilling or unable to import from the gold-receiving nation whose prices were rising and whose exchange rates were fixed at former levels and, second, because individuals in the gold-receiving country would take advantage of the depressed prices of the other nation by importing its products. Thus, in the nation receiving gold, a reduction in its exports would doubtless be accompanied by a partial reduction of sales in the domestic market. If the velocity of turnover of the expanded money supply also decreased, the decline in volume of both domestic and foreign trade could induce a business depression.

Inconvertible Paper Currencies

Mint parity ceases to exist when a nation abandons the gold standard and no longer maintains a market for gold at a fixed price or places restrictions upon the free movement of the metal across its boundaries. Fixity of exchange rates is abandoned along with the abandonment of the gold standard. Under these conditions, foreign exchange rates reflect the relative purchasing power of the two currencies, not in terms of gold, but for other goods, services, and securities.

PURCHASING POWER PARITY. "Purchasing power parity" may be explained as that rate of exchange which tends to equalize prices in the two countries being considered. A simple illustration will clarify this point: Assume that both England and the United States are on a fiat monetary base. Also assume that a ton of a certain kind of steel made in the United States is shipped to London at a total cost of $90 and competes in the British market with an identical product whose cost is £30. It is evident that, if the purchasing power of the two currencies is measured by their command over steel, then £1 is equal to $3.

The simplicity of the illustration suggests a refinement. Money has generalized purchasing power that is best represented by an index of wholesale commodity prices. Hence, if comparable indexes exist in the two countries and include primarily commodities traded in world markets, the purchasing power parity may be computed by use of the following formula:

$$\frac{\text{Index number of country A}}{\text{Index number of country B}} \times \text{Former mint par of exchange}$$

A specific illustration of the method of calculation is available in the period following World War I, when England was on a fiat standard. The United States had maintained its gold standard with the exception of a temporary embargo on gold shipments in 1917–18. Late in 1921 the British price index stood at 200 (1913 = 100) and that of the United States at 150 (1913 = 100). By calculation, a parity of 3.6498 is obtained in the following manner:

$$\frac{150}{200} \times 4.8665 = 3.6498$$

Thus the pound had purchasing power equivalent to $3.6498, and the actual rate on pounds in New York was near enough at the time to lend validity to the theoretical calculation.

Deviations of daily rates from the calculated parity may be due to the activities of speculators, imposition of tariffs, changing estimates of the future position of the rate, statistical inaccuracies of the index numbers, and governmental interference in the exchange market. In spite of its inaccuracies or other shortcomings, the purchasing-power-parity theory continues to be useful as a guide in determining exchange rate policy by nations on inconvertible-paper monetary standards.

However, when used as an aid in determining monetary policy, there is the implicit assumption that gold imported into a nation will be used as a basis for an expansion of currency or bank deposits and will thus contribute to an increase in the general price level. The opposite effect will, supposedly, apply if gold is exported. The purchasing-power-parity theory is thus seen to contain the strength and weaknesses of the quantity theory of the value of money.

GOVERNMENTAL REGULATION OF FOREIGN EXCHANGE MARKETS

In the years immediately prior to World War I, fluctuations in foreign exchange rates were limited to small deviations around mint par of exchange. Such stability not only facilitated the operations of international trade but made more obvious the fact that international movements of long-term capital would be impossible unless the lender was given the protection of long-term rate stability or a clause in the contract assuring return of a specified amount of gold.

World War I and its aftermath brought growing recognition that a gold-standard nation is not insulated from financial panic and the repercussions of economic instability elsewhere. It was manifest also that the economic structure of the world was vastly different in the 1920's from what it had been before 1914. This was due in part to the destruction of productive facilities by the conflict itself, to the creation of new nations which were jealous of their economic and political status, to the maldistribution of gold and other liquid assets, to the loss of prestige suffered by the Bank of England, and to the development of intense nationalism that placed roadblocks across former routes of trade. The semi-automatic operation of the prewar gold standard was recognized to have been due to the relative freedom of goods, capital, and men to move across international boundaries. After the war and as a complement to the rising spirit of nationalism, demands arose in many nations for the management of foreign exchange rates for benefit of the internal economy.

Central Bank Activities

During the late 1920's, when most of the nations of the world returned to the gold standard, central banks exercised limited control over exchange rates by varying their rediscount rates and by sterilizing gold imports. For example, when a central bank increased its rediscount rate, it tended to encourage an influx of funds which would be profitably invested in the short-term capital market. A continued reduction of the discount rate would have the opposite effect. An import of gold could be sterilized by the sale of securities —of equal amount—by the central bank. Thus, monetary reserves that had been increased by gold imports would be reduced when used as payment for securities sold by the central bank.

However, as financial troubles spread over the world in the late 1920's and early 1930's, the power of the central banks to influence exchange rates diminished. Short-term balances were not always attracted to the market with the highest interest rates. Sometimes, as in the Central European crisis of 1931, they fled from such centers because investors doubted the soundness of monetary and financial conditions within the high-rate nation. Moreover, the size of these "fugitive" or "hot-money" balances became so large that sales of securities by central banks were too small to neutralize their movements. The problem of exchange-rate stabilization during such flights of "fear" capital was made more difficult as the demands for exchange tended to drive rates above their normal level. Because most of the leading countries abandoned the gold standard and adopted inconvertible currencies within two years after the Central European crisis in the spring of 1931, central banks did not have time to perfect any technique for modifying exchange rates.

In a fiat monetary system, fluctuations in foreign exchange rates have no direct effect upon the size of monetary reserves. In fact, there may be nothing worthy of the name "reserves." It might be presumed, therefore, that dropping from a gold base would also result in abandoning plans for the regulation of exchange rates. This has not been true. On the contrary, control of foreign exchange and rate regulation became almost universal instruments of governmental policy in the expansion of economic nationalism in the 1930's. Regulatory schemes adopted included several devices which we will examine: depreciation of currencies, stabilization funds, and complete exchange controls.

CURRENCY DEPRECIATION. Currency depreciation has been called a "weapon of economic warfare" adopted in an effort to expand exports or perhaps to generate a domestic price inflation in the country under consideration. Its method is to depress artificially the foreign values of the currency below its purchasing power parity, thus making the country a "cheap" market in which to buy. The objective is to obtain a favorable balance of payments that will produce gold imports. For example, devaluation of the British pound in the autumn of 1949 reduced its value in America from $4.02 to $2.80. As long as prices in England remained unchanged, the American dollar acquired about 30 per cent more purchasing power in England, thus tending to reduce the flow of goods from the United States to Britain and to increase American imports from England.

STABILIZATION. To prevent wide and rapid swings in exchange rates, nations on an inconvertible-paper basis often appropriate a large sum and make it available to the national treasury or central bank for use in buying and selling exchange or gold at prices which can be maintained. The objective is to provide only short-term or day-to-day stability of rates and not to "peg" long-run values at arbitrary or predetermined levels. This type of regulation can usually be used only by wealthy and powerful nations whose exchange plight or whose "adverse" balance of payments is not serious. In emergencies, however, the fund may become exhausted; and stabilization then degenerates into exchange control.

England established an "exchange equalization account" soon after leaving the gold standard in 1931; the United States followed suit by using $2 billion captured in the currency devaluation of January, 1934; and France did likewise in 1936. For a time these three nations undertook to co-operate in maintaining relative stability between the dollar, the franc, and the pound. It was hoped that concerted action of this sort would be followed by other nations; and, in fact, the union was joined by several smaller countries of northwestern Europe. The agreement was adopted partially to counteract the system of German exchange controls that was then evolving. Outbreak of military hostilities in 1939 checked this form of international financial co-operation until the Bretton Woods monetary conference in July, 1944.

EXCHANGE CONTROL. In a third type of regulation, typified by the German practice, all exchange rates, markets, and foreign trade become enmeshed in a complex of rigorous controls that practically destroy the exchange market itself. The objectives of full control extend far beyond a desire merely to maintain rate parity. Rather, the objectives are to obtain a discriminatory bilateralism in trade, i.e., a "favorable" balance, and to generate a high degree of self-sufficiency for military purposes. Germany, Japan, and many nations of southeastern Europe and South American countries that made use of full exchange controls felt unable to bear either the risk of currency depreciation (in the form of a domestic inflation) or the expense of setting up huge stabilization funds. In short, the balance of payments was so "unfavorable," the gold reserves so inadequate, and the possibility of restoring equilibrium so slight that the only remedy appeared to be complete domination of foreign-trade and exchange relationships.

Specific aspects of the technique of exchange control include many things. Among them is the establishment of official rates which must be paid to obtain foreign exchange. This assumes an "official" market in which purchasers are discriminated against if the uses to which the funds are applied do not receive governmental approval or sanction. Also, fixation of the rates at which domestic currency may be acquired by foreigners is determined on a discriminatory basis. Residents of the country are required to surrender foreign currency to the local government, and requests to obtain foreign currencies are handled on a priority basis. Favorable treatment is accorded importers of strategic materials by placing vast quantities of exchange at their disposal; exporters of goods whose sales the country desired to promote are rewarded by high rates on the exchange received, and somewhat lower prices are paid for bills arising from other exports.

INTERNATIONAL FINANCIAL CO-OPERATION

Prior to World War I, international banking relationships were confined largely to private arrangements between the parent bank and its foreign branches or between correspondent banks in different countries. There was some co-operation between the central banks of important nations; but because the United States had no Federal Reserve System until 1914, the banking system of America had limited contacts with foreign banks.

Several factors operated to reduce the financial isolation of American banks in the second and third decades of the century. The comparative stability of the currency of the United States during and after World War I and the large volume of foreign lending elevated the domestic banking system to a position of international importance. The process was assisted by the newly established Federal Reserve System, by the choatic condition of national currencies of European countries, and by the maze of indebtedness which covered the world as a result of the war and the Treaty of Versailles.

The gold standard had been abandoned during the war years or immediately thereafter by most important nations. Gold movements and transfers of foreign balances from one nation to another soon became greatly restricted despite the fact that payment of war debts and reparations required a vast volume of transfers. The old "semi-automatic" economic forces of international trade and settlement were unable to achieve satisfactory results. Thus, a distinct need for international financial co-operation developed.

As noted above, central banks worked together to foster the movement of gold into certain areas, adjusted discount rates for the purpose of sterilizing gold imports, and advanced credits to central banks in other countries. These steps were taken primarily to aid nations in a return to the gold standard and to reduce the strains arising from the transfer problem. The actions of central banks in these matters were purely voluntary and, therefore, often sporadic and uncertain. Their actions were frequently undertaken at a time when national affairs required a sudden withdrawal from a program of co-operation or a complete reversal of their former policy. Not until the Bank for International Settlements was established in 1930 did a means of achieving some measure of continuous co-operation become available.

Bank for International Settlements

The Bank for International Settlements (B.I.S.) was established in 1930 as a nonpolitical financial institution for handling the transfer of reparations payments remaining unpaid from World War I. But the Bank was given power also to (a) buy and sell gold coin or bullion for its own account or for central banks, (b) hold gold in central banks, (c) accept custody of gold for central banks, (d) make loans to or from central banks, and to (e) buy or sell foreign-exchange instruments and marketable short-term government securities. In short, it appeared to function as a central bank for central banks. But it was not limited to dealing with central banks. It could exercise the same powers for the accounts of commercial banks, individuals, or corporations. The B.I.S. was not permitted to issue notes (currency), "accept" bills of exchange, lend to governments, hold current deposits for government, or purchase a controlling interest in any business venture.

Unfortunately, the B.I.S. came into existence as the postwar decade of prosperity was drawing to a close. Some of its funds were immobilized by the European crises in the spring and summer of 1931, and it was forced to drop its function of transferring reparations.

It then became essentially an advisory agency and an investment trust handling large loans for distressed central banks. As more and more nations left the gold standard, the difficulties of the Bank increased, for it had been set up to deal with gold and gold-exchange standard countries. In the remaining years of the 1930's, resources of the Bank decreased to such a low point that the institution was unable to play any significant part in the conferences by which the countries of the world readjusted their currencies. Even its staunch supporters now agree that the B.I.S. did little or nothing in providing additional facilities designed to supplement the existing financial mechanism and to induce financial equilibrium among countries of differing degrees of development.

The Tripartite Agreement

The creation of a stabilization fund such as the one established in the United States in 1934 was not in itself an instrumentality of international co-operation. Its primary purpose was to protect the American dollar from sudden wide fluctuations in value. Formal co-operation with other nations was not required to protect the fund against losses resulting from adverse movements in the value of foreign currencies so long as the important nations of western Europe adhered to the gold standard. Losses could be averted because the fund was able to convert, at a moment's notice, foreign balances held in Europe into gold having a fixed price.

But in the autumn of 1936, when France, Switzerland, the Netherlands, and Belgium dropped from the gold standard and ended their policies of selling gold, co-operation became necessary to prevent losses. England, France, and the United States then made a mutual agreement pledging themselves not to engage in competitive currency depreciation and to avoid excessive rate fluctuation. Managers of the funds arranged to communicate with each other daily by cable or telephone and state the price in their own currency at which they would buy gold for the next business day. There was no agreement, however, to maintain the rate for more than twenty-four hours at a time. If the trade or currency position of a country seemed to call for an adjustment, it would be made—either upward or downward, as conditions demanded.

The American fund was used primarily in support of the currencies of the nations in the pact. It did this by entering the market to purchase exchange and by facilitating the shipment of gold to the United States. The apparent objective of this action was to forestall development of a depression in this country that might have accompanied excessive depreciation of foreign currencies. Although the European phases of the stabilization plan had to be abandoned upon the outbreak of hostilities and the adoption of more formal systems of exchange control in 1939, the American fund continued to offer some support to currencies of nonbelligerent South American nations thereafter.

Bretton Woods Agreements

Representatives of forty-four nations at the United Nations Monetary and Financial Conference meeting at Bretton Woods, New Hampshire, in 1944 adopted agreements to establish an International Monetary Fund and an International Bank for Reconstruction and Development. After ratification by most of the nations participating, the agreements became effective January 1, 1946.

THE MONETARY FUND. The purpose of the International Monetary Fund is to restore a sound framework for postwar currencies by restoring international trade based on the gold values of each member-nation's currency. If it is necessary to restore equilibrium in international balances of payment, the gold values of currencies will be modified. A pool of different currencies will be maintained for use by nations requiring funds for the settlement of international obligations. This pool will be available to a nation only upon the exhaustion of its own private resources. These provisions show that the fund is designed to provide the advantages of the stable rates of a gold standard and, at the same time, provide a means of attaining the flexibility of rates that may prevail under an inconvertible-paper standard. To date, however, rather than achieving stability by the means provided in the plan, nations whose currencies have faltered have withdrawn from participation in the Fund.

The formal statement of the purpose of the Fund, as contained in the Articles of Agreement, follow:

(i) To promote international monetary cooperation through a permanent institution which provides the machinery for consultation and collaboration on international monetary problems.

(ii) To facilitate the expansion and balanced growth of international trade, and to contribute thereby to the promotion and maintenance of high levels of employment and real income and to the development of the productive resources of all members as primary objectives of economic policy.

(iii) To promote exchange stability, to maintain orderly exchange arrange-

ments among members, and to avoid competitive exchange depreciation.

(iv) To assist in the establishment of a multilateral system of payments
in respect of current transactions between members and in the elimination of foreign exchange restrictions which hamper the growth of
world trade.

(v) To give confidence to members by making the Fund's resources
available to them under adequate safeguards, thus providing them
with opportunity to correct maladjustments in their balance of payments without resorting to measures destructive of national or international prosperity.

(vi) In accordance with the above, to shorten the duration and lessen the
degree of disequilibrium in the international balances of payments
of members.

The Bretton Woods agreement established a quota of capital
contribution for each member nation for both the Fund and the International Bank for Reconstruction and Development. Each member
contributes some gold and some domestic currency. The amount
turned over to the Fund was based upon the prewar national income
and the world-trade positions of each signatory nation. The gold
portion of the contribution was 25 per cent of the quota or 10 per
cent of each nation's net holdings of gold and United States dollars,
whichever was the smaller. The total initial fund subscribed was
$8.0 billions, of which $2,750 millions was made by the United
States. Congress authorized the use of gold held in the United States
stabilization fund for payment of the gold portion of this contribution. The gold value of these assets is to be maintained, each member
nation being obligated to compensate the Fund if there is a decline in
the value of its domestic currency held by the Fund.

METHOD OF OPERATION. A great portion of the volume of financial transactions between member nations continues to be settled
through well-established channels. In fact, as long as a nation's balance of payments remains in equilibrium, nothing will pass through
the Fund. If, however, a scarcity of foreign currency develops, the
private market will come to the fund through central banking channels or through some other authorized fiscal agency of the member
nation. When a country applies to the Fund for a certain foreign
currency, it is a borrowing transaction. The country whose currency is depleted by the transaction is said to be "lending." The
borrower nation pays by leaving its own currency with the Fund.
The amounts paid in are retained by the Fund, and those loaned are
used immediately in purchasing or making payments in the lending
nation.

Limits are placed upon the amount any nation may borrow. If the amount borrowed proves inadequate to effect equilibrium in normal times, the limits may be suspended or the borrowing nation may obtain permission from the Fund to revalue its currency. Under certain conditions the Fund may require a borrower nation to reduce its debt by repurchasing its currency from the Fund. This procedure will limit a member's use of the Fund when it has adequate other means of paying its foreign obligations or when additions are being made to its currency reserve. If a member persistently has a deficit (or a surplus) in its currency transactions with the Fund, the latter may recommend changes in the currency value of the member that would restore a balance. If a member nation devalues its currency without consent of the Fund, a market for its currency will not be maintained, nor may it borrow from the Fund. During a period when a nation is struggling to re-establish its currency on a stable peacetime basis, exchange controls of the type described earlier may be retained. These may not be permanent, however, or the member will be dropped from participation in the Fund.

Advantages expected to flow from continued operation of the Fund in the postwar reconstruction period include the following: If some degree of equilibrium in trade is fostered, gold movements will be reduced, and accompanying disturbances to currency reserves will also be reduced. Internal monetary policies may be pursued by member nations without fear of a disastrous loss of gold. Domestic currency reserves may be buttressed by loans from the Fund. A persistent adverse balance of payments may be altered by a change in the par value of the currency unit.

THE "WORLD BANK." Although the forty-four signatory powers of the Bretton Woods agreements were confident that the Fund might achieve the *temporary* objectives of international monetary co-operation, they believed that *persistent* causes of economic disequilibrium could be corrected, or alleviated, only by an organization that would promote international movements of long-term investment capital. For this purpose they created the International Bank for Reconstruction and Development, frequently called the "World Bank."

All member nations of the Bank must also be members of the Fund; in February, 1950, forty-eight nations were participants. The initial plan of organization authorized 100,000 shares of capital stock of $100,000 par value, making a total of $10 billion. Ninety-one per cent of this was allotted to the original forty-four members. The $900 million, or 9 per cent, remaining was reserved for nations that were expected to subscribe in subsequent years. The allotment of the United States, the largest subscriber, was $3,175 million; that of the United Kingdom, second largest, $1,300 million; and that of Panama, the smallest subscriber, $200,000. Only 20 per cent of the par value of each share was paid in, the remainder being subject to call only as needed to make good on defaulted loans guaranteed by the Bank. Two per cent of each subscription was paid in gold and 18 per cent in currency of the member nation.

In addition to the payments received from subscription to its capital stock, the Bank has obtained over $260 million from the sale of bonds. The balance sheet of June 30, 1950, lists a $100-million issue of 2 per cent serial bonds, issued in the spring of 1950, due 1953–62, and a $150-million issue of twenty-five-year 3 per cent bonds due in 1972. These obligations are payable in American dollars. Two other issues, aggregating $10.5 million, are payable in Swiss francs in 1954 and 1956.

World Bank bonds are offered to the general investing public and financial institutions through investment banking channels. They have been declared "eligible" for investment by savings banks and trust funds.

Responsibility for policy formation and general oversight of the Bank management rests in the hands of a large Board of Governors. Each member nation is represented on this Board by one governor. Voting power is distributed, as in the Fund, with member nations having 250 votes on the basis of membership, plus one additional vote for each share of stock held. On this basis the United States at one extreme has 32,000 votes and Panama, at the other, has but 252.

Actual direction and management of the Bank is entrusted to an executive directorate of twelve paid members chosen by the Board of Governors. This smaller board selects its own president, who functions as chairman. He has a vote only when it is necessary to break a tie. Headquarters of the Bank are in Washington, D.C.

Scope of Activities. The title of the Bank indicates its primary function, i.e., the promotion of long-term loans to member nations needing funds for reconstruction or development. Advances may be made directly from the Bank's own capital or from funds borrowed by the institution through the sale of its bonds to the general public. In addition, the Bank may guarantee, in whole or in part, loans made by producers in the usual private investment channels. Total loans of the Bank are limited to its unimpaired capital, reserves, and surplus. Loans must be made only on projects which appear, to the Loan Committee, within the power of the borrower to service currently and to repay ultimately. Loans may be made to private agencies (if guaranteed by the home government) and to governments themselves.

Purposes and Policy. The purposes of the Bank, as described in Article I of the Articles of Agreement, are:

  (i) To assist in the reconstruction and development of territories of members by facilitating the investment of capital for productive purposes, including the restoration of economies destroyed or disrupted by war, the reconversion of productive facilities to peacetime needs and the encouragement of the development of productive facilities and resources in less developed countries.

 (ii) To promote private foreign investment by means of guarantees or participations in loans and other investments made by private investors; and when private capital is not available on reasonable terms, to supplement private investment by providing, on suitable conditions, finance for productive purposes out of its own capital, funds raised by it and its other resources.

(iii) To promote the long-range balanced growth of international trade and the maintenance of equilibrium in balances of payments by encouraging international investment for the development of the productive resources of members, thereby assisting in raising productivity, the standard of living, and conditions of labor in their territories.

 (iv) To arrange the loans made or guaranteed by it in relation to international loans through other channels so that the more useful and urgent projects, large and small alike, will be dealt with first.

  (v) To conduct its operations with due regard to the effect of international investment on business conditions in the territories of members and, in the immediate post-war years, to assist in bringing about a smooth transition from a wartime to a peacetime economy.

Accomplishments to date. In the first four years of its lending activities (June, 1946—June, 1950) the Bank had made twenty-four loans for projects in thirteen countries, aggregating about $757 million. Of the total disbursements of $567 million made by December 31, 1949, about $5 million was spent in Africa and Asia, $27 million in Canada, $51 million in Latin America, and $63 million in Europe. Approximately $420 million was spent in the United States.[4]

No loan had been made, up to June 30, 1950, with a maturity later than 1977, and about one half of the advances will mature prior to 1972. The largest loans made up to this time were $250 million to Credit National, guaranteed by the Republic of France, and $191

---

[4] Press Release No. 199 (August 2, 1950) and Press Release No. 172 (February 16, 1950). Statement of Mr. Eugene R. Black, president of the International Bank for Reconstruction and Development, before the Economic and Social Council at Lake Success, New York.

million to the Kingdom of the Netherlands. Both loans carried an interest rate of 4¼ per cent.

Early loans, granted in 1947, were made primarily for European reconstruction; but since the beginning of 1948, principal advances have been for development purposes. These consist of loans for the development of electric power in Chile, Mexico, Brazil, Belgium, Finland, and El Salvador; for agricultural machinery in Chile, Colombia, and India; for timber production in Yugoslavia and Finland; for railway reconstruction in India; and for shipping in the Netherlands.

A significant consideration of the Bank in making a loan is protection of the lender's capital, i.e., the borrowers' ability to pay. What may be more important, however, is its attempt to make the most effective possible utilization of the member-nation's resources. This may at times require nothing more than a short-run grant to aid in restoring the temporary balance of an international account. A more fundamental long-term objective is to remove the basic cause of disequilibrium and to create a sound and lasting basis for productive international investment.

Potential Usefulness of the Bank. An evaluation of the long-run effects of the Bank can hardly be made on the basis of only four years of operation, but the Bank seems at this time to be doing a highly creditable job. Its loans have been limited not by a lack of money so much as by lack of information about the borrower nation and by the lack of well-planned projects ready for immediate execution. However, the scope of the Bank is being widened; and through its economic missions and the reports of its technical experts it is making data available that has thus far been unknown to private investors in the international field. The cumulative effects of these studies and reports will doubtless find reflection in larger advances in the near future than in the immediate past.

Directors of the World Bank deny that the Bank can, or should, provide the answer to all, or even a major part of, the world's ills. It is, for example, beyond both the power and the purpose of the Bank to cure the present "dollar shortage" or to assure the maintenance of full employment throughout the world. But the hope is expressed that by providing technical advice and stimulating foreign long-term investments the production levels and living standards in many of our neighbor nations will be raised. The contributions already made by the Bank and by the Fund are substantial beginnings;

they will undoubtedly become increasingly significant as the institutions mature.

Concluding Statement

The existence of an international gold standard and relatively stable exchange rates prior to World War I made the financing of foreign trade and the movement of investment funds from one nation to another a comparatively simple process.

The war of 1914–18 and its repercussions drove the world, except the United States, from the gold standard, destroyed stability of exchange rates, and seriously disrupted trade and financial relationships. Before the traditional methods could be restored or acceptable substitutes provided, the depression of the early 1930's prostrated world currencies again. The breakdown in international trade was followed by growth of bilateralism, adopted first by Germany and later by several other nations as one phase of the economic mobilization for war. World War II virtually closed the remaining channels of private international trade and concentrated control of commerce and finance in the hands of governments.

Although the government of the United States is a leading champion of nondescriminating, multilateral trade conducted by private individuals and firms, during all the years since 1930 private enterprise in this nation, and more especially in other foreign nations, has been severely handicapped by governmental exchange regulations and control.

Reconstruction of world trade and finance after World War II was a much greater problem than after World War I. The increased difficulty came about partly as a result of the greater magnitude of destruction of World War II but also partly as a result of governmental intervention in trade and finance. Even today (1951) foreign trade is still regarded as part of international power politics and as an instrument to be used by any nation seeking military predominance.

It is to be hoped, although perhaps not to be expected, that the World Bank created at Bretton Woods may aid greatly in restoring international trade to its former position and in returning it to the field of private enterprise. If the credit of the Bank becomes thoroughly established—and admittedly a fine start has been made—the new institution may do much to re-establish the international flow of private capital. However, because the Bank is a multi-currency institution operating in the currencies of all its members, its success rests upon stability of international monetary relations. This may prove to be its greatest handicap. Only time can tell!

—FRANK H. GANE

QUESTIONS AND PROBLEMS

1. Why is an absolute advantage in production not essential to a profitable export trade?

2. What are the principal divisions in the international balance of payments of the United States? Which individual items have accounted in recent years for the largest credits and the largest debits?

3. Does an excess of exports over imports tend to create a supply of foreign exchange or a demand for exchange? Explain.

4. Explain, or give an example of, financing an import of merchandise from England to the United States.

5. What makes money "hot"? Explain how a flight of capital from country A to country B affects the rate of exchange in both countries.

6. Explain how exchange rates are determined between two gold-standard nations.

7. Why do exchange rates usually exhibit greater instability between paper-standard countries than between nations on gold? What forces may limit the range of fluctuation when paper standards are in use?

8. What is meant by the "structure" of foreign exchange rates?

9. What action might be taken by a central bank in attempting to "sterilize" a large import of gold? Would it ever be possible for commercial banks to prevent a gold import from enlarging the volume of bank credit? Explain.

10. For what reasons was the Exchange Stabilization Fund of the United States established? Why was the Tripartite Agreement adopted? Why did the latter cease to function effectively in Europe after the late 1930's?

11. Explain how currency devaluation affects foreign exchange rates. Does it exert any influence on the domestic price structure? Explain.

12. Summarize the main features of the International Monetary Fund. From current reports of the Fund, summarize its recent activities.

13. Outline the purposes of the International Bank for Reconstruction and Development. How is the Bank organized to achieve its objectives?

14. From annual reports and press releases of the Bank, bring data on its loans up to date.

BIBLIOGRAPHY

The elements of foreign exchange and the methods used in financing transactions are explained in college texts such as:

Chandler, L. V. *Economics of Money and Banking.* New York: Harper & Bros., 1948.

Thomas, R. G. *Our Modern Banking and Monetary System.* 2d ed. New York: Prentice-Hall, Inc., 1950.

Westerfield, Ray B. *Money, Credit and Banking.* Rev. ed. New York: Ronald Press Co., 1947.

Whittlesey, Charles R. *International Monetary Issues.* New York: McGraw-Hill Book Co., Inc., 1937.

Whittlesey, Charles R. *Principles and Practices of Money and Banking,* Part H. New York: Macmillan Co., 1948.

Woodworth, G. W. *The Monetary and Banking System.* New York: McGraw-Hill Book Co., Inc., 1950.

More detailed treatment of a general nature, now in need of revision, is found in

Southard, F. A. *Foreign Exchange Practice and Policy.* New York: McGraw-Hill Book Co., Inc., 1940.

Special aspects of the subject that may be studied with great benefit to more advanced readers are contained in the following:

Ellis, Howard S. *Exchange Control in Central Europe.* Cambridge, Mass.: Harvard University Press, 1941.

Enke, Stephen, and Salera, Virgil. *International Economics.* New York: Prentice-Hall, Inc., 1947.

Heilperin, M. A. *International Monetary Economics.* London: Longmans, Green & Co., 1939.

Holm, George W. *International Monetary Cooperation.* Chapel Hill: University of North Carolina Press, 1945.

International Bank for Reconstruction and Development. *Annual Reports.* 1946 to date. Washington, D.C.

International Finance Section, Princeton University. *Survey of United States International Finance.* Princeton, N.J.: Princeton University Press, 1950.

International Monetary Fund. *Annual Reports.* 1946 to date. Washington, D.C.

Lary, H. B., and Others. *The United States in the World Economy.* Washington, D.C.: U.S. Department of Commerce, 1943.

League of Nations. *International Currency Experience.* Geneva, 1944.

U.S. Department of Commerce. *International Transactions of the United States during the War, 1940–1945.* Washington, D.C.

INDEX

INDEX

This volume has been set on the Linotype in 12 and 10 point Bodoni Book, leaded 1 point. The size of the type page is 27 × 46½ picas.